FTM

James Green

FTM

Female-to-Male

Transsexuals in Society

Holly Devor

Indiana University Press

Bloomington and Indianapolis

The paper used in this publication meets the minimum
requirements of American National Standard for Information
Sciences—Permanence of Paper for Printed Library Materials,
ANSI Z39.48-1984.

Manufactured in the United States of America

Library of Congress Cataloging-in-Publication Data

Devor, Holly.
    FTM: female-to-male transsexuals in society / Holly Devor.
        p.   cm.
    Includes bibliographical references and index.
    ISBN 0-253-33631-7 (cl : alk. paper)
        1. Transsexuals—Case studies.   2. Transsexualism.
    3. Gender identity.   I. Title.
    HQ77.9.D49   1997
    306.77-dc21   97-18640

1   2   3   4   5   02   01   00   99   98   97

Contents

Foreword
by Jamison "James" Green

MY FIRST ACQUAINTANCE with any literature on female-to-male (FTM) transsexuals occurred in 1984 when I was trying to determine what options were available to me as a male-perceived, masculine-identified, female-bodied individual. What I found then and for the most part since has consisted mainly of critiques of highly dysfunctional families; accounts of "gender dysphoric" children presented to clinicians by their homophobic parents; dismissive, tut-tut attitudes toward girls who "refused" to give up their "tomboy" ways; a great deal of misogyny and sexism; studies that generalize about FTM experience based on one or two interviews; the assumption that the FTM process is the mirror image of the male-to-female (MTF) process; and the constant refrain that "not enough study has been done." At last, here is a book that opens a window on FTM lives without condescending, either to the reader or to the population it describes.

This book deserves a wide readership among people interested in female-to-male transsexuals as well as among transsexual men themselves. Psychotherapists and medical practitioners who work with transgendered clients primarily see male-to-female people and as a result often base their theories and judgments about all transsexuals on the MTF population. FTM candidates are therefore forced to break down stereotypes even as they are supposedly working on their issues in therapy or simply trying to obtain basic medical care. And transsexual men do not always have contact with others like themselves. It is highly beneficial to be able to compare experiences and ideas. For too long, most of what we have been able to find out about ourselves (from nontranssexuals) has been dismissive, depressing, or downright frightening. No wonder so many of us report we thought we could not be transsexual because we had never seen ourselves reflected in the literature.

Holly Devor gives readers access to the experience of transsexual men as no clinical treatment–oriented survey could ever do. She examines her subjects' social relationships, and instead of postulating curative ideologies she accepts the reality of their lives, reporting to you and me about the depth and breadth of their experience, allowing us to see how they have come to accept themselves, how they have worked to manage their transitions, how they perceive the world through transformed eyes.

Writing with an intelligent and accessible style, Devor balances exposition, analysis, and excerpts from her subjects' interviews to present a coherent picture of what social life is like for FTMs as they find their identity and learn about themselves. Readers may even follow the responses and voices of particular subjects, since Devor has noted subject pseudonyms, by response type, for each analyzed research question. Overall, the text is logical, clear, and almost as engaging as a dramatic narrative. All that's missing are clear descriptions of the characters so we can visualize these men on our mental television screens; but since their identities are confidential we cannot see their faces.

Like Devor, who indirectly notes in her introduction that participants in her study were more forthcoming about themselves than they ever were with psychotherapists, I have been privileged to have conversations with hundreds of FTM transsexual men. In my capacity as president of FTM International, Inc., the world's largest and longest-running educational organization for and about FTM transgendered people and transsexual men, I have personally provided peer support and professional referrals to many of the 750 subscribers to our quarterly newsletter. I have visited with transsexual men in the United States, Canada, Great Britain, Western Europe, and Japan, and I have corresponded with men in these and other countries. And while clearly every transsexual man will not find all his thoughts or feelings or history precisely reflected in this text, I feel that Devor has managed to capture much of the essence of FTM experience and perspective. Some of it is not pretty to look at, and I must admit to feeling some concern that readers would project the experience of some men as related through this text onto all transsexual men. Of course, Devor cautions against that, but I expect some readers will be unable to resist the easy assumptions, just as some transsexual men may be offended by any representation that casts negative light on our situation. In the long run, however, I think we must acknowledge the difficult truth that we are not all perfect beings, though perfection is something we have all been striving for in our own ways, on our own terms.

Devor's feminist perspective, combined with her sociological analysis (as opposed to the therapeutic or academic analysis of earlier texts, many of which she reviews in chapter 2), serves in my mind to lend a new and much-needed perspective on the experience of transsexual men. We do not exist in theory; we exist in fact, in relationship to our families, our friends, our lovers. Men and women, trans and nontrans, we are not all just like the men presented here, but I suspect we can each find something in common with them. This book should find a place as the first realistic text about female-to-male transsexual people. It should open eyes and doors; eyes that have not seen us, doors that have been closed to us, and doors that have been closed to the nontranssexual world. I expect this book will generate considerable discussion in the FTM community, in Gender Studies classrooms and journals, and among all men and women who think seriously about self-actualization, gender, sexuality, even spirituality. I hope this book heralds a period of dialogue between transsexual men and the nontranssexual world. I hope it heralds the end of the objectification and marginalization of transsexual men. I hope it makes readers hungry to know more of us. There are *many* more of us.

Acknowledgments

Many people contributed to the creation of this book in ways both large and small. First and foremost, I wish to express my deep gratitude to the many transsexual people who generously volunteered to patiently answer my many questions and to educate me about their lives. In particular, I thank the forty-five individuals who agreed to let their stories become the basis for this book and those additional individuals who allowed their images to serve as illustrations for this book. I also want to take this opportunity to say thank you to the many transsexual and transgendered people who shared other bits of their lives with me at the many meetings, conventions, and social occasions at which our paths crossed. They, too, taught me much. Several transsexual and transgendered individuals have also become my friends in the course of this research. The times which we have shared have included many thoughtful hours of discussion about this book and this topic so close to all of our hearts and minds. Among others who shall remain anonymous, I thank Johnny A., Jason Cromwell, James (Jamison) Green, Jake Hale, Mike Hernandez, and Rupert Raj-Gauthier for the pleasure and stimulation of their friendship.

A number of other people who have also helped me to do the work of putting together this book deserve my heartfelt thanks. Number one among them is Lynn Greenhough, my life partner. She has patiently endured my frequent absences from home for research and writing and has lovingly done whatever she could to ease the process for me. Throughout the seemingly endless years which it has taken to produce this book she has always cheerfully chewed over one more idea with me, one more time, every time that I have asked it of her. Her insights and critiques have always been both finely honed and gently delivered. I couldn't have done it without her.

I thank my research assistants, Noreen Begoray, Beverly Copes, Robin Conover, Sheila Pederson, and Sandra Winfield, for all of their hard work which contributed greatly to bringing this book to fruition. My thanks also go to Pam Duncan, Lin Fraser, and an anonymous reviewer for their careful reading of the first draft of this book and for their useful suggestions for improvement. My thanks, too, to my editor at Indiana University Press, Joan Catapano, for her ongoing support of my work. I further express my gratitude to the Social Sciences and Humanities Research Council of Canada and to the University of Victoria for their generous financial contributions to this work as it progressed.

Introduction

Ever since I began working on this project, people have been asking me what made me interested in female-to-male transsexualism in the first place. Not everyone has had the nerve to come right out and ask if I, too, am transsexual, but I'm sure that it has passed through the minds of more than the few people who have been so bold as to put the question. No, I am not, one (although doing this work has certainly caused me to interrogate myself as to possible transsexual leanings). I've also been asked if any of my friends, lovers, or family have been transsexual. Again, I have to say no. So how did I find my way into the world of female-to-male transsexuals?

My earlier work includes my first book, *Gender Blending: Confronting the Limits of Duality*.[1] My interest in the phenomenon of gender blending grew out of some of my own experiences and those of some of the people whom I knew. In that book, I looked at the lives of females who, although they thought of themselves as women, didn't always successfully communicate that fact to others. Often to their dismay, such people ended up being treated as if they were men in situations where they had not intended for that to happen. Furthermore, I found that gender blending females frequently were women whose lack of obvious femininity was apparently motivated by their desire to resist sexist stereotyping. They felt very woman-identified, and they were perplexed when their feelings led them to be mistaken for men. *Gender Blending* was my attempt to make sense of the phenomenon.

Having finished that project to my satisfaction, I was ready to move on to new questions. At the time, it seemed a simple and logical step from there for me to ask about what is going on when females intentionally want to be seen and to live fully as men. At that point, I was quite naive about the phenomenon. I didn't know a single female-to-male transsexual person or any intentionally passing women, and to my knowledge I had never met any such people (although I had casually known several male-to-female transsexuals over the years). I was even so ignorant of what female-to-male transsexualism was all about that before I began this project I actually thought that I would be working mostly with women. I got over that misconception pretty quickly!

In the beginning, I tried to contact both female-to-male transsexuals and women who purposefully passed as men but did not see themselves as transsexual. As it turned out, I found it almost impossible to contact women who passed as men, so I abandoned, for the time being, that portion of the project. The project and this book therefore became entirely focused on people who identified themselves to me as female-to-male transsexuals.

What I Actually Did

How I Contacted People

Not knowing a single female-to-male transsexual person meant that I had to cast my net out into the waters and see what happened. After getting approval from the ethical standards committees of the universities with which I was associated, I drew up an advertisement describing myself and my project and started to distribute it. I sent it out to English-speaking North American publications which I knew to have a transsexual readership. I also sent it out to publications which I knew to have a lesbian readership on the assumption that some passing women and perhaps also some transsexual people might read such publications. I also approached several medical clinics which I knew to have transsexual clients and asked them to post copies of my advertisement. I also spoke about my project with friends and acquaintances and asked for their assistance in making my work known.

I discovered through this technique of soliciting participants that there were a number of loosely knit local communities of female-to-male transsexuals in various locations in North America. In each place there seemed to be at least one individual who was generally acknowledged as a spokesperson for the local community. A few people also had national or international reputations. Those people who were more accustomed to being transsexual advocates were generally the first ones in an area to respond to my requests for participants for my research project.

Of my study sample of forty-five, ten persons (23 percent) wrote or phoned me after seeing advertisements in various publications.[2] To the best of my knowledge, postings through clinics provided only two participants (5 percent). We began by discussing my philosophy and my intentions over the telephone. If I seemed acceptable, we then arranged for an interview. After the successful completion of an interview, these key informants were tremendously helpful in recommending me to their peers.

One person even mailed out a substantial number of my advertisements to transsexual people on his personal mailing list. Thirty participants (68 percent) in this study, some of whom had also seen my advertisements, volunteered after personal referrals from people who had already become participants. Six persons (14 percent) volunteered to participate after having heard of the project from me or from a mutual acquaintance.

I first met a transsexual man early in 1987. Over approximately the next four years I conducted interviews with forty-six female-to-male transsexuals and five passing women. The stories told to me by forty-five self-identified female-to-male transsexuals form the basis of this book.

Interviews

I was not able to travel to all of the locations where willing participants lived, therefore I could not interview personally all who volunteered to be interviewed. I met personally with twenty-three participants (51 percent) and interviewed them face-to-face at times and places which were convenient for them.[3] In eighteen cases (40 percent), I mailed a list of the questions I used to guide face-to-face interviews to participants who had agreed to do self-interviews.[4] I asked them either to write out their answers or to speak them into a tape recorder and send them to me. Self-interviews completed in this manner tended to be less detailed than those done face-to-face. When transcribed, they were on average about half the length of the interviews which I conducted in person. In four cases (9 percent), participants answered some questions in a face-to-face interview with me and replied to some questions in a self-interview.[5]

Interviews were designed to be completed in two sessions lasting approximately two hours each when done in person. As it turned out, many interview sessions lasted between two and three hours each and self-interviews often took many hours longer to complete. However, sixteen participants (35.5 percent) did not complete a second interview. In all but one such case, I had lost contact with the persons in question between the time when I conducted the first interview and the time at which I attempted to gain a second interview. One person declined a second interview saying "my contribution to science is complete." Another participant withdrew all of his contributions after one interview because he objected to having his words analyzed and included in a work written from a feminist perspective.

Part one of the interviews consisted of questions about demographic information, gender issues in relationships with family members, gender issues in relationships with peers, gender issues in school experiences, childhood abuse experiences, and sexual and romantic experiences. Part two covered the following areas: physical health, gender identity development, body image development, transsexual identity development, transition experiences, and philosophical questions about the meanings of sex, gender, and sexuality. (See appendix for the interview questions.) In-person interviews were loosely structured so as to allow participants more freedom to follow their own thoughts to their own conclusions. As a result, in those interviews, topics were not always covered in exactly the same way, and unique information sometimes arose.

In hindsight I can see a number of shortcomings in the interview questions. The biggest problem was that more than one-third of the participants did not complete a second interview. One problem with the format of several questions was that I asked people to discuss various issues in terms of their first and last, best and worst, rather than their most typical experiences. As a result, some examples given by participants were more extreme than usual and any number of important incidents may have been ignored. Other biases may have been introduced when I asked more questions about relationships with women than about relationships with men or when I focused more on intimate and family relationships than I did on relationships with peers.

This research, of course, was also subject to all of the usual benefits and problems associated with interview research. It is my hope that I was able to establish good rapport with most of the participants and thereby to receive full and honest answers to my many questions. It was also surely true that in innumerable ways, large and small, my attitudes, beliefs, and characteristics influenced the responses which participants offered to my questions.

Furthermore, as is true in any research of this type, I have no way to verify any of the answers which participants gave to me on any subject. As with any self-report data, these data are subject to problems arising from distortions due to my own leading of participants, due to participants' desires to present favourable images of themselves, or due to inaccurate recall of events long past or intensely emotionally charged. In particular, I noted that there were a number of instances wherein participants recalled single events as having taken place at two different times in their lives when I inquired about them on two different occasions. I have simply taken my best guess, based on clues in context, as to which answers given by participants reflected their most accurate recall. In any event, the differences were not major ones.

Finally, on top of all of these difficulties, there were also technical problems with several interviews. Tapes jammed in the recorder; batteries ran low without my knowledge. Some people spoke too softly to be recorded, or their words were muffled when their clothing rubbed against the lapel microphone which we used. Thus some information was lost and there were gaps in what I recorded despite the fact that participants were generous enough to answer my questions.

Observations

In addition to the interviews which form the heart of this book, I have also learned a great deal from many other transgendered and transsexual persons whom I have met over the years since I began this work. Although their words do not appear directly on these pages, they have helped me to broaden and deepen my understanding of gender in many important ways. In the course of working on this book, I met and shared time at meetings, conferences, and social events with several hundred female-to-male transsexual individuals in seven major North American cities. I also became personal friends with three participants and their families, sharing holiday times together and staying in each other's homes when traveling. In addition, I served for three years, 1991–1994, on the board of directors of a transgendered persons' advocacy organization, the International Foundation for Gender Education (IFGE), attempting to facilitate female-to-male participation within the IFGE.[6] I am happy to say that when I completed my term on the board of directors of the IFGE, transsexual men had been elected as directors and the IFGE had initiated active programs for female-to-male transsexuals.

Handling and Analysis of Data

All original interview audiotapes, disks, or hard copy replies to self-interview questions were identified only by a code number. All identifying information has been kept in a locked storage cabinet. Completed interviews were transcribed to computer disks. All names of participants and their associates which appear in this book are pseudonyms.

I and my research assistants read through the transcribed interview materials and, with the assistance of a text-analysis computer program, marked segments of the interviews with codes identifying the nature of their content. We were then able to compile files containing all of what was said by the entire group of participants on any particular subject. I read and annotated these compilations in search of themes which indicated commonalities among the participants' experiences, perceptions, and opinions. I then made up a series of tables which summarized the nature of the sentiments expressed in the coded segments. Each table was organized along themes which usually ended up as chapter sections. Within each table, information was subdivided and positioned in such a way as to readily allow important comparisons to be made. These tables were supplemented by information from my field notes and organized in such a way as to facilitate ready reference to original transcripts where my notes, tables, or coded segments were unclear or insufficient to particular purposes.

Who Participated

Thirty-six participants (80 percent) were born and raised in eighteen states or territories of the United States.[7] Six participants (13 percent) were born and raised in four provinces of Canada.[8] Two (5 percent) were born and grew up in central Europe; one of them later moved to the United States, the other to Canada. One participant (2 percent) had lived the bulk of his life in New Zealand. Thus at the time of their interviews, thirty-seven participants (82 percent) lived in the United States, seven (16 percent) in Canada, and one (2 percent) in New Zealand.

Thirty-seven participants (82 percent) were Caucasians of European heritage. Six (13 percent) were of mixed heritage, including two Eurasians, three of Amerindian and European heritage, and one of Polynesian and European heritage. One participant (2 percent) was African American and one (2 percent) was Hispanic American.

Participants ranged in age from twenty-two to fifty-three years, with a mean age of thirty-seven years at the time of their first interviews. All participants had at least a high school education, with the average being four years of post-secondary education. Participants' incomes ranged from a low of "meager" to a high of U.S. $75,000 per year. Median income for the thirty-nine participants who provided information was approximately U.S. $18,500 per year.[9]

Most participants (85 percent) had been raised in Christian homes. Among the thirty-nine participants who supplied information about their religious backgrounds,[10] ten (26 percent) were raised as Catholics[11] and twenty-three (59 percent) were raised in Protestant homes (Anglican, Baptist, Christian Science, Episcopalian, "fundamentalist," Lutheran, and Mormon).[12] Three participants (8 percent) grew up in Jewish homes,[13] and three (8 percent) were exposed to no religious training as children.[14] Only thirty participants offered information about their religious beliefs as adults.[15] Most of those who did mention the topic explained that they had done some religious searching. Sixteen participants (53 percent) explored less common religious philosophies, including Wicca, the teachings of Rajneesh, Islam, unformalized Eastern or nature-based spiritual philosophies, and "fundamentalist" Christian "cults."[16] Three participants (10 percent) had eventually become atheist or agnostic,[17] and twelve (40 percent) more or less retained their original form of faith.[18]

Participants were at a variety of stages of transition when I met and interviewed them. I have detailed their statuses in chapter 19, "Making the

Changes," and provide here only a brief overview. At the time of their last interviews, all participants identified themselves to me as transsexual; however, not all of them had taken steps toward beginning their lives as men. Seven participants (16 percent) were living as women at the time of their last interviews,[19] one of whom had previously lived as a man for a number of years and temporarily had returned to living as a woman.[20] All participants who were living as men at the times of their last interviews had received hormone therapy. As a group, they averaged 7.9 years of living as men and 6.5 years of hormone therapy. Thirty-four participants (76 percent) had undergone breast reductions, mastectomies, or both.[21] Twenty-three participants (51 percent) had had hysterectomies,[22] two of which had been done for medical reasons other than sex reassignment.[23] Only two participants (4 percent) had "genital free-up" operations.[24] Four participants (9 percent) had phalloplastic surgeries.[25]

It is also noteworthy that six participants (13 percent) had been openly political in aid of the interests of transsexual persons.[26] It would seem logical to assume that considerably fewer than one in ten transsexual persons has been politically active in his own interests. Therefore, although this group of participants probably includes a greater diversity of female-to-male transsexuals than have participated in most previous research, articulate transsexual advocates obviously were overrepresented in this group.

What Participants Said about This Research

At the times of their interviews, I asked several people about their experience of being participants in this research project. Most of their comments were positive ones which focused on the beneficial effects of having the opportunity to consider once again some of the formative aspects of their lives. Keith, who did a self-interview, expressed such sentiments when he said:

> It was helpful to me to clarify my own viewpoints. . . . some of the questions that were asked in these interviews are things that gave me pause to stop and think exactly about that particular aspect, and that helps me clarify myself and my own viewpoints.

Dennis thought that the interview process was better than therapy.

> I've bared my soul more to you than to anyone about this, and the way you listen and respond is something that I haven't experienced before. And I just would never talk about these things with anyone. And it's not the same as talking to a therapist.

Some participants also noted that although they found the interview process to be generally either benign or helpful, there were moments when my questions caused them to unearth and relive painful parts of their pasts. Several people said that they had thought again, as one put it, about "part[s] of my life I would like to forget as much as possible." For example, Ken remarked:

> It was kind of fun remembering some things . . . affirming some of the goals that I had as a kid. What was least useful to me were some of the memories. The first paper asked a lot of personal questions, and . . . some of them hurt.

A few of the participants who completed written rather than verbal self-interviews were less than pleased at the length of time involved in writing out their responses. They noted that some of the questions were repetitious. Bill complained about the length of the list of interview questions. Nonetheless, he, like Ken, enjoyed "the opportunity to pick my own brain" and appreciated that "painful memories . . . give texture to my life . . . so this study has helped me to get some perspective."

In addition to my direct questions, several participants spontaneously made comments which reflected some of their experience of participating in this work. In particular, several participants remarked that they had told me things that they had rarely if ever disclosed to anyone else. Ken said that, for him, the anonymity and distance of his self-interview allowed him to speak more freely about childhood sexual abuse, of which he would have been too "ashamed" and "guilty" to speak in a face-to-face interview. Similarly, Bruce, in his face-to-face interview, interspersed certain of his comments with "I'd never say that in my support group. . . . I've told you more than I've told anybody [laughs]. You have my life down." Eli also complimented me by writing, "I've spilt a lot of beans in my day . . . but never such a mess of beans all at once as I did to you upon the occasion of your research interview. Uncanny. Refreshing. Thank you."

Furthermore, while writing this book I have also produced a few articles based on this research and presented several papers at scholarly conferences. I have shared written copies of that work with participants who expressed an interest, and I have received verbal feedback from some participants and other female-to-male transsexuals who have been in attendance at conferences where I have presented my papers on this topic. I am pleased to report that with only one exception, all female-to-male transsexuals who have communicated their opinions to me have enthusiastically told me that I have represented their reality well. I proudly consider their endorsements to be the highest of praise. I have endeavored to do as well in the writing of this book.

Conventions Used in Writing This Book

Name and Pronoun Usage

I have tried both to remain respectful of the preferred genders of the persons involved in this research project and to accurately reflect the gender statuses of persons being discussed. To that end, I have used pseudonymous men's names throughout the text. Furthermore, I have referred to persons who were living as men at the time of their interviews using masculine pronouns regardless of their hormonal or surgical statuses. I have referred to those participants who were living as women at the times of their interviews using feminine pronouns. In those cases where persons were living as men at the time of their interviews but were talking about events lived as girls or as women, I have used mixed gender pronouns in the same sentences. In parts of sentences referring to the persons doing the talking, I have used masculine pronouns, whereas in parts of sentences which refer to times when persons who were the subjects of stories were living as girls or women, I have used feminine pronouns. For example, "He remembered that as a girl, she had been a tomboy." This may seem confusing at first, but I think readers will become accustomed to it and will find that once they have made the necessary mental adjustments, these pronoun conventions tell such stories most clearly.

Key Terms

I have used a number of common terms in specific ways throughout this book. Not everyone uses them exactly the same way I do. I have therefore defined my usages here so as to eliminate some confusion and misperceptions which might have otherwise arisen. Please bear these meanings in mind when reading the remainder of this book.[27]

When I use the term *identity* I refer to persons' acceptance of sex, gender, or sexual categorizations as descriptive of themselves. When I use the term *attribution* I refer to the categorizations made by others as descriptive of persons' sexes, genders, or sexualities. These terms become especially important when considering questions of transition and assimilation for female-to-male transsexuals, during which time there may be dramatic differences between their own identities and the attributions made about them by others.

When I use the word *sex*, I refer only to the physiological status of persons as female, male, or intersexed. All of the following criteria have been used by various people to define biological sex status: chromosomal configuration, gonads, internal reproductive structures, external genitalia, hormonal secretions, sex assigned at birth, and psychological sex identity.[28] One or another of the participants has used each of these criteria at some time. In this discussion, I will generally confine my discussions to anatomical sex. Thus, although female-to-male transsexual persons always remain female on the basis of their genetic makeups, their bodies can change from female to hermaphroditic to male.[29] The state of mind which underlies the desire to undergo sex reassignment is extreme *sex dysphoria*.[30] However, because of the incompleteness of most female-to-male sex reassignments, I prefer to focus more on issues of gender.

When I use the word *gender*, I refer only to the social statuses of persons as women (girls), men (boys), or variously transgendered, regardless of their sex statuses. This distinction is especially important for transsexually identified individuals whose social statuses or identities may be quite different from that which their genetic sexes or body morphologies would typically suggest. The state of mind which characterizes transsexual and transgendered persons' desires for gender reassignment is *gender dysphoria*. Gender identities and attributions can be based upon either of two main criteria: *gender styles* or *sexes*.

I use the term *gender styles* to refer to those culturally defined and social prescribed behaviours and beliefs which characterize people as varying degrees or combinations of *feminine* or *masculine*. Whatever gender styles dominate in persons' interactions with others serve as major indicators of their gender statuses in social situations. In other words, when people's gender styles are predominantly masculine, other people will assume that they are men; when people's gender styles are predominantly feminine, other people will assume that they are women. When persons' gender styles are such a blend of masculinity and femininity as to render them indeterminate as men or women, they may be attributed with some form of transgenderism. However, if it is known that persons' sexes and genders do not match in the usual fashion, then persons' known sex statuses will usually override any gender style cues in the attribution or identification of gender statuses. Thus most non-transsexual persons identify their own genders and those of other people on the basis of sex statuses when they are known to them. However, transsexual persons often use their gender identities as the basis of their sex identities.

When I use the term *transgendered*,[31] I refer to persons who have bodies of one sex and who think of themselves either partially or fully as members of the atypical gender but who do not experience profound sex dysphoria.

When I use the terms *female-to-male* or *male-to-female transsexuals*, I refer to persons who have begun to identify themselves as transsexual or are in the process of transforming their genders and sexes. When I use the terms *transsexual men* and *transsexual women*, I refer to persons who identify themselves as transsexual and who have begun to live full-time in their preferred gender statuses. However, when I refer collectively to groups of persons who include both types of transsexual persons, I use the terms *female-to-male* or *male-to-female transsexuals* to describe those persons. I make these distinctions to highlight several points. I wish to emphasize that those persons who have begun their lives in their preferred genders are men (or women) and to de-emphasize their female (or male) origins. However, I retain the designation of transsexual as an adjective describing what kind of men (or women) persons are in order to recognize the important differences between themselves and men (or women) who have lived their whole lives in their preferred genders. I use the term female-to-male transsexuals (or male-to-female transsexuals) as the more generic term to recognize a minimum commonality in groups which include persons at a variety of stages of transition and where a less sex-specific term such as *transsexual persons* would be inappropriate.

Actually I prefer, and have elsewhere used, the term *transsexed* rather than the term *transsexual* because I consider the latter to be misleading. *Transsexed* emphasizes that such persons cross from one sex status to another sex status, whereas *transsexual* suggests that sexuality is central to gender and sex dysphorias. Questions of sexuality, although often related, can be incidental to desires for gender and sex reassignment. In this book I have used the more widely used term, *transsexual*, so as to maximize effective communication until such time as a change in terminology can be established.

When I use the word *sexuality*, I refer to the patterns of sexual *fantasies*, *desires*, and *practices* of persons. I recognize that *fantasies* with no desires for actual sexual practice, *desires* for actual practice, and actual sexual *practice* often are not congruent or consistent either across persons' lifetimes of experience or within particular temporal periods of individuals' lives. That is to say that, in the real world of everyday people, there may or may not be considerable overlap between sexual practices and desires or fantasies. For instance, masturbation typically involves fantasy or desire of sexual contact with others accompanied by solitary practice. By the same token, many sexual practices engaged in with others are accompanied by sexual fantasies or desires for practices or partners different from those actually transpiring or present at any given moment.

When I discuss the sexuality of participants, I make use of the concepts of *gendered sexuality* which refer to interactions of sex and gender, with sexuality. In view of the fact that I believe that all sexualities are gendered, I reserve the terms *heterosexual, homosexual,* and *bisexual* to refer to the *sexes* of persons involved in particular sexual patterns of fantasy, desire, or practice. Bearing in mind that I conceptually separate sex and gender, I reserve the terms *straight, lesbian, gay,* and *bi* to refer to the *genders* of persons involved in similar sexual patterns of fantasy, desire, or practice. Thus I use the terms *heterosexual, homosexual,* or *bisexual* when considering persons' bodies, whereas I use the terms *straight, lesbian, gay,* or *bi* when considering their genders. In this way it becomes possible to speak with accuracy and without contradiction about a cross-living transsexual man who is sexually attracted to female women as both homosexual and straight.

Keeping Track of Participants

In many places throughout this book I have provided both counts and percentages of total numbers of participants who said or did particular things. In the majority of instances where I have done this, not all participants provided information which was usable on the subject under consideration. In most cases, the gap in information was due to the kind of limitations in my research techniques which I have already outlined. In a few instances, participants simply did not want to discuss a topic or gave answers which may have seemed clear to me at the time but which I found unintelligible when later analyzing the data. Percentage calculations are therefore based on the number of usable responses to particular questions. I have used a note to explain the new terms of reference each time they changed.

I also have endeavored throughout this book to provide enough information so that readers may follow the development of particular participants if they so wish. To this end, I have supplied the names of all individuals to whom I referred whenever I made aggregate statements about subsets of participants. Thus whenever I made a statement as to the number of persons who said or did something I listed the names of all relevant participants in a note attached to that statement.

What I Left Out, What I Have Put In, and Why

I have made no attempt to detail medical options. Hormone therapy modalities and surgical techniques vary between localities and change rapidly over time. Whatever I might say at the time of this writing would most assuredly apply to only a few times and places, and only temporarily to those. For similar reasons, I have avoided discussions of legal options. Each jurisdiction varies as to its treatment of transsexual persons. Laws, policies, and procedures change almost daily. I have therefore chosen to describe some of what participants actually experienced in these areas and leave it to interested readers to contact local or national support organizations for timely advice in these matters.

Although I have noted in this introduction selected demographic information about the participants, I have not analyzed participants' responses on the basis of such variables as race, class, education, ethnicity, religion, or geographic location. Because of the small numbers of persons who were represented in some demographic categories, or because of the variations in persons' memberships in other categories over the lengthy periods of time covered by this study, I chose instead to limit analysis to issues of gender, sex, and sexuality. I have attempted, however, to allow these aspects of participants' lives to be evident in some of the direct quotes which I have taken from participants' own words. By so doing, I hope to offer at least some hints as to how these elements might have impinged on participants' transsexual identities.

What I have focused on, in detail, is describing and theorizing the processes whereby persons first come to identify themselves as members of an initially seemingly incongruous social category and then remake their lives so that they function as credible and apparently native-born members of that social grouping. In order to do so I have looked closely at both micro- and macrosocial aspects of the intra- and interpersonal organization of gender, sex, and sexuality in the lives of forty-five diverse individuals. Although these forty-five participants are a statistically representative sample of neither transsexual persons nor the population at large, they are a diverse group. I have used their stories to ground and give life to my theoretical conjectures about the development, manipulation, maintenance, and support of identity in social context. I believe that what can be learned from their biographies can be instructive for the understanding of many more commonly undertaken identity processes. Thus, by implication, I assert that most of the issues confronted by transsexual persons are neither theoretically nor practically distinct from those of other members of society and that gender and sex dysphorias and gender fluidity are a part of all of our lives.

Lastly, what I have done in this book is to attempt to give voice to the transsexual persons who allowed me to have access to the stories of their lives. Ultimately, the editorial decisions were all mine. I chose whom to quote, when to quote them, and how to edit their words. I made the theoretical and descriptive comments in which their words were embedded and took on meaning. However, I have tried to make my choices with compassion and respect. I have tried to give each participant a chance to be speak on these pages, and I have done my best to let their words guide mine. My goal was to tell their stories, not to trumpet my own.

Some Personal Notes

I have learned a lot in writing this book, so much that I can barely envision the person I was when I began this project. As I move through my life now I see people and social relations as infinitely more variegated than I did before. It is as if every colour which once seemed solid and opaque has become a shimmering and ephemeral dance of light and colour, always moving, always changing, looking different from every angle. I welcome the complication that these new insights have brought to my life.

I also feel enriched by the new friends whom I have made. I have found that among transsexual and transgendered people my own gender, sex, and sexuality uncertainties seem more manageable. This seems to be the case not only by comparison with the magnitude of their issues but, more importantly, because of the unflinching honesty of self-examination with which so many transsexual and transgendered people confront their own fears. I have been inspired by their examples to proceed through my own personal development with a bravery modeled after theirs.

What I take away with me now is a much deeper appreciation for diversity and an enhanced tolerance for change in myself and in others. I eagerly anticipate and actively encourage the infinite multiplication and nuancing of gender, sex, and sexuality which transsexual, transgendered, gay, bisexual, lesbian, and queer people are increasingly unearthing for all of us to see, to enjoy, and to enjoin.

PART I

First Questions

C. Jacob Hale

1 | Have Female-to-Male Transsexuals Always Existed?

Have transsexual people always existed? This is an impossible question to answer because the concept of a transsexual as a distinct type of person has had currency only since the latter half of the 20th century. Perhaps there have always been people who, if they lived today, would call themselves transsexual and would request sex reassignment. Perhaps there have been people in other times and places who would have said that they felt "trapped" in a body of the wrong sex. We can only speculate on the basis of the very incomplete historical record available to us today.

The issue becomes especially difficult when the question is narrowed to focus specifically on female-to-male (FTM) transsexuals. The lives of women throughout history have been less well recorded than those of men. The reasons for this are myriad and have been well argued by historians of women. Sexism must be attributed with the lion's share of responsibility for this silence, but a long tradition of a lack of regard for the social history of everyday life must also be held accountable.[1] The few stories which survive from antiquity have largely been in the form of myth, some of which may have been embellished from fact. The surviving accounts of females who lived some parts of their lives as men in the centuries between the time of the ancients and now have been recorded largely because those females were somehow publicly chastised for living as men. For each person who was found out, there were no doubt many more whose gender transformations were never discovered.

I have searched for predecessors of today's female-to-male transsexuals in historical records of females who lived their lives as men. Some of them left behind indications of their motivations. Others were discovered to be female on the occasions of their deaths, and so we may only guess as to their reasons for recasting themselves so successfully as men. Even so, those who went on record explaining their reasons for passing as men usually were doing so as part of some sort of legal defense. The price of answers unacceptable to the authorities of their day was often high; sometimes the accused paid with their lives. Hence even what we know from those persons who were able to voice reasons for their transformations may tell us more about what they thought would be acceptable to the authorities of their day than about their own actual motivations.

It is therefore crucial to have some understanding of what gender meant to players in their particular time periods. The bifurcated concept of gender that the Western world holds dear today and upon which the definition of transsexualism is based has not always been ascribed to by the peoples whom the West claims as cultural ancestors. This means that although we may be tempted to retrospectively name behaviours by today's standards, if we wish to begin to understand their meanings for those who lived them, we must peer at them through the lenses of their times as best we are able.

I have chosen to cite, as the precursors of today's female-to-male transsexuals, those female-bodied persons of other times and places who lived at least several years of their lives as men. I have included in this catchment those who would today be called heterosexual, lesbian, gay, bisexual, or transgendered crossdressers. I have also included those who, by the standards of their day, might have been attributed with "slight" hermaphroditism but who would probably not be so designated today. I have therefore included female crossdressers of other cultures who took on many of the characteristics of the men of their society but who may or may not have felt the need, as do transsexuals of today, to be considered to have become males as well as men. By modern definitions, probably only some would be classified as transsexual, while in their own worlds they may well have been afforded the full social status of men.

I have, for the most part, restricted my investigations to people of Western European extraction and those whom they claim as ancestors. I have therefore included discussion of the female cross-gender practices of Greeks and Romans of the classical period, ancient Hebrews, and early Christians. This discussion is followed with tales of early Christian crossdressing saints who lived during the classical period. The next section looks at the medieval period in Western Europe. The sixteenth and seventeenth, eighteenth, nineteenth, and early twentieth centuries are then reviewed. I have closed my investigation in the 1950s, when the case of Christine Jorgensen was splashed across the headlines of newspapers in Europe and North America and brought transsexualism to the attention of the general public. I have also noted some of the female cross-gender practices of the Native peoples of North America and briefly mentioned those of some African and Asian cultural groups which have either influenced or been influenced by Western European culture.

Ancient Greeks and Romans

The ancients believed that the world had been created and was guided by a multiplicity of gods and goddesses. Richard Hoffman has argued that gender was a fluid concept in polytheistic societies such as those of the ancient Greeks and Romans (or in the polytheistic societies of many contemporary indigenous people).[2] The basis of his contention lies in the religious beliefs of such peoples. Polytheistic pantheons are made up of many different visions of godliness. Societies based on polytheistic cosmologies tend to see the world as having come into being through sexual interactions between gods, or between divine personages and humans, or between deities and animals. It is not uncommon in such creation myths to encounter supernatural beings who change sex or gender, who incorporate aspects of both male and female in one being, and who change themselves or others from humanlike creatures into beasts and back again. In such societies, the gods are taken as divine examples after whom earthly mortals might model themselves. If there are no clear demarcations between the sexes or genders in the heavens, Hoffman argues, the dividing lines on earth will be likewise blurred and permeable.

Thomas Laqueur has presented a somewhat different but not altogether conflicting perspective.[3] He argued that from antiquity until the eighteenth century there was really only one sex but that the number of genders varied through the centuries. That one sex, of course, was male. Females were seen as essentially males who lacked sufficient "vital heat" to cause their reproductive organs to become external to their bodies. As Laqueur argued, it was believed that what we now know as vaginas were (not analogous to, but *were*) inverted penises, that labia were the female foreskin, that uteri were scrotum, and that ovaries were testicles.[4] Further, it was believed that bodies could change from female to male as a result of raising the body temperature through vigorous exercise or that if females spread their legs too widely their internal organs might fall out of their bodies and they would thus become males. Sex changes could also be wrought by miracles performed by saints. Note, however, that all such transformations always proceeded from female to male, or, in the parlance of the time, from less to more perfectly developed. Due to the fact that all people were seen as essentially male, it was not possible for males to turn into females, although there was always the dreaded danger that they might become womanish.[5] Thus there was only one sex—male—which manifested itself in the variations of gender called women and men.

Theoretical distinctions notwithstanding, practical social distinctions were made between women and men in the ancient world. Each had clearly defined appropriate social roles in the world of everyday life. Flesh-and-blood women (as opposed to goddesses) in classical Greece and Rome were considered to be profoundly inferior to men. Aristotle, for instance, wrote in the fourth century B.C.E. that it is a permanent and unchangeable state of affairs that "the male is by nature superior, and the female inferior; and the one rules and the other is ruled."[6] Women were protected and cared for within the family, but they had no formal power in the larger society. Women were ruled first by their fathers, later by their husbands or older brothers, and eventually by their sons. Their socially prescribed reason for existence was the production of children and keeping of the household for the paterfamilias. Few women were ever allowed to run their own lives.[7]

Commoner women who were dissatisfied with their approved social roles had few choices outside of the relative safety of the family. They could only become fallen women. They could survive through prostitution or as concubines; there were no other options. Slave women also served their masters in these sexual capacities. Some aristocratic women fared better. If there were no male heirs in their families, they were allowed to inherit wealth in their own right. If a family had produced scholars for generations and a daughter showed an aptitude for study, she too might be allowed to become a scholar and have some independent life of the mind. But the only route out of their restricted roles imaginable to most women was simply to become men through the interventions of goddesses who had many and great powers.[8]

Surgically created transsexuals clearly did not exist in classical times, but stories of female-to-male sex changes and of women whose lives mimicked those of men have survived. One Greek tale which has survived to this day involved the birth of a girl child to the woman Galatea, whose husband, Leucippus, had threatened to kill any female children she bore. In order to save the life of her daughter, Galatea dressed her as a boy until she began to reach puberty. Galatea then appealed to the goddess Leto to change her daughter into a son. Leto obliged, thus saving the life of the doomed female child.[9]

Several Roman authors also recounted tales of female-to-male sex changes. Martial, for instance, told of a woman who ate, drank, played sports, and was sexually active with women in a way that outdid most of her male contemporaries. Lucian described the woman Megilla as having shaved her head in the fashion of men and then boasted that she was "a man in every way."[10] Pliny reported on several instances of female-to-male sex changes, one of which he claimed to have witnessed with his own eyes. He flatly stated that "transformation of females into males is not an idle story," an opinion which seemed to be shared by many of his compatriots.[11] These gendered values and belief systems of the Greeks and Romans stood as the basis for Western European cultural values throughout the dark ages and for several hundred years beyond.

Jewish Thought and the Early Christian World

The creation myths of monotheistic Judaism and hence also of early Christianity were in conflict with those of the Greeks and Romans. The Hebrew God was not born of any kind of sexual union; nor did the God of the Hebrews create the world by sexual intercourse. Furthermore, there were no sexual liaisons of any kind between gods, nor between deities and humans. Hebrew monotheism demanded clearly delineated and permanent differences between both the sexes and the genders. Humans who worshiped a monotheistic God and wished to act "in God's image" therefore created a society in which there were strict divisions between all things: between heaven and earth, between holy and profane, between the divine and humans. In such a world view, the sexes and the genders were kept as cleanly demarcated as possible at all times, with men holding the highest spiritual ground.[12]

The early Christians built much of their theology on a mixture of Greek and Roman philosophy and Jewish law. For the early Christians, like the Greeks and Romans among whom they flourished, sexes reflected the social character of persons' actions and beliefs rather than immutable biological facts. The early Christians also elaborated on the Jewish concept of *spiritual* gender crossing, which held that females' acquisition of certain masculine traits improved them spiritually.[13] The Christian Saint Jerome expressed a philosophical truism and a social reality of his time when he proclaimed in the fourth century C.E. that as "long as woman is for birth and children, she is different from man as body is from soul. But when she wishes to serve Christ more than the world, then she will cease to be a woman and be called a man."[14] Thus women could elevate themselves spiritually by renouncing their flesh and devoting themselves entirely to their religion. It was believed that those women who did so with the greatest fervor could thereby transform themselves into men.

Although the early Christians believed female-to-male sex changes to have been possible, the stories which have been told and retold over the ages have been of gender rather than sex changes. Quite a few pious early Christian females, it would seem, took Saint Jerome literally and made themselves over as men: Anastasia Patricia, Athanasia, Dorotheus, Eugenia, Euphrosyne, Marina, Pelagia, Perpetua, and Theodora, to name a few.[15] Even though such religiously zealous women were officially prohibited from disguising themselves as men for the purposes of joining male religious communities, many of those who did so were later revered as saints.[16]

The story of Pelagia is illustrative of this phenomenon. In one version, Pelagia started out as a dancing girl and prostitute in Antioch. Upon her conversion to Christianity she became ashamed of her past and departed Antioch to start a new life disguised as a man. In his new identity as Pelaius, he lived out the remainder of his life in Jerusalem as a dedicated Christian.[17] It was only after his death that the sex of Pelagius was discovered to have been female. In another version, Pelagia was a marriage resister who fled her fate before her marriage could transpire.[18] She dressed herself as a man and took up residence in a monastery; later, as Pelagius, he was elected to the position of prior of a convent. Unfortunately, the portess of the convent got pregnant and condemned Pelagius as the perpetrator. Pelagius, who offered no credible defense, was expelled from the convent and died in disgrace. Pelagius's femaleness was discovered only after death.

The story of Marina contains similar themes. Marina's story started out when her father entered a monastery. As long as she was a daughter he could not bring her with him, but by disguising her as a son he was able to continue to care for his offspring. The "son" Marinus lived on at the monastery after the father's death. As in Pelagius's story, Marinus was accused of seducing a woman and making her pregnant. Marinus and the infant were thrown out of the monastery, whereupon they lived as beggars until finally readmitted some years later. It was only after the death of Marinus that the body was found to be female.[19]

The values of the ancient Greeks, Romans, and early Christians dominated the societies of the medieval European period. For hundreds of years, few intellectual advances were made by Christian thinkers beyond the state of knowledge and philosophy reached by the ancients.

The Middle Ages

The early Middle Ages were a time of social disintegration in the Western world. The trade, commerce, and cities of the Roman Empire fell into disrepair, and the overarching state institutions established by the empire devolved into decentralized idiosyncratic rule by local small-scale despots. The Christian Church grew in importance as a governing body because it retained a centralized but widely arrayed, more orderly communications network and a hierarchical system of agents strategically deployed in every village and town.

Over the course of the thousand years following the fall of the Roman Empire, Christian Europe initially languished in a shambles, then gradually began to rebuild. Agricultural methods improved production sufficiently to support a larger population base, a ruling class, and the growth of feudalism. Larger towns, trade and commerce, and governments were once again established. But as civilization grew in Europe, millions of people lost their lives to wars, the crusades, and the Black Death. Throughout most of this highly unstable period, the Christian Church and Jewish religious institutions provided the only learned intelligentsia. It wasn't until the fifteenth century and the Renaissance that the new humanism began to flourish.

The lives of most women in medieval Europe were dominated by the cycles of reproduction and agricultural production. Survival for peasant women usually meant marriage. Marriage meant an entire adult life spent either pregnant or nursing a baby while working at all labours of agricultural production except the sowing of fields. Sometimes, when not enough was produced on the land to support a woman's family, peasant women would also hire themselves out to work for others at half, or less, of the wages which a man might make. Those women so unlucky as not to become married or so unfortunate as to become widowed found themselves in dire straits. Honest work for single peasant women paid too poorly to support life. Their only options were prostitution or thievery. Some women, knowing their limited choices as women, chose instead to become men. Then, at least, they might be able to remain independent, alive, and ostensibly honest.

Medieval Christian women of the upper classes who wished to bypass an adult life entirely consumed with the production of male heirs might become nuns. Life as a nun offered certain advantages over that of a married woman of the time. Nuns were generally educated, and there were more possibilities for a measure of power and authority for well-born women within the Christian Church hierarchy than were available to them in secular life. However, within the Church, as within the society at large, women were ever and always subordinate to men. Very few women ever reached positions of power and authority within Church structures. For this reason, one way for Christian females to fully realize their religious callings or their desires for power was to disguise themselves as men.[20]

Many stories tell of females who lived as men throughout the medieval period. One of the most famous is the story of Joan, who is reputed to have reigned as Pope John VIII Angelicus in the 850s. Many versions of her life history exist today, although none is believed to be entirely factual. According to one account, Joan, who was born in England, was taken by her father to Mainz, where she learned to read and write. While she was studying there she fell in love with a monk named Ulfilias. To be close to her beloved, she dressed herself as a man, John, and went to live in Ulfilias's monastery. According to this version of the tale, their love was never consummated. From Mainz they traveled together to Athens, where they continued their scholarly pursuits until the untimely death of Ulfilias.

A disconsolate Joan/John set out to return to their monastery in Mainz but was waylaid in Rome by ex-students who persuaded John to give some lectures. One impressive success led to another, culminating in John's ascension to the office of pope. While reigning as pope, John met a young monk who reminded Joan of Ulfilias. The two became sexually involved. Joan became pregnant by the young monk, but, as she was believed to be a man, her increasing girth was not recognized for what it was. The story climaxes with Joan/John giving birth to a son while in the midst of a papal procession through the streets of Rome. She was deposed in disgrace, and she and her infant died shortly thereafter.[21]

Whereas the story of Joan/John is now commonly believed to be no more than a fable, the twelfth-century tale of Saint Hildegund is widely believed to be based in fact. Hildegund was the daughter of a German knight widower who wished to make a pilgrimage to Jerusalem. He had no one with whom to leave his daughter, so he dressed her as a boy, Joseph, and took her along on his journey. Knowing that he was near death, the father entrusted his son to another knight, who turned out to be a thief. The boy was stripped of his valuables and left to his own devices. The youthful Joseph then went on to barely survive a series of misadventures wherein he was first condemned to death as a thief and later almost hung to death by a band of thieves. Somehow Joseph made it home to Germany intact and lived out his days peacefully in a monastery. After his death, Joseph was discovered to have been female.[22]

Joan of Arc, perhaps the most famous gender rebel of the Middle Ages, was later sainted for her exploits. She started out life as a fifteenth-century French peasant girl. She never hid her femaleness but did, in every other way, attempt to live her life as a great and noble man. She claimed to have had a vision in which she was directed to remain virginous and to use her energies to save the kingdom of France in the Hundred Years War against England. She convinced the leaders of France to allow her to dress in soldier's armor and direct their armies into battle. She participated in seven successful military campaigns as a maiden soldier among men and was credited with having inspired the troops to victory. Eventually her fortunes turned, and she was captured by her English enemies.

The English did all that they could to discredit the Maid of Orléans as a liar and heretic. But Joan held fast to her visions until finally she was confronted with a death sentence and her own funeral pyre. She then renounced her claim to divine guidance and signed a confession, only to recant a few days later. Throughout her trial and again after rescinding her confession, she always presented herself in the clothing of a man, and as

a soldier. Only during the few days when she stood confessed and convicted did she permit herself to be dressed as a woman. When she returned
to her original claim to divine inspiration, it was more than the English
could allow. They once again dressed her in women's clothing and burned
her at the stake. Today she is known as Saint Joan, the peasant girl who
renounced her sexuality and followed her visions, dressed as a man, to
inspire armies of men to victory in the service of their king.[23]

The Sixteenth and Seventeenth Centuries

The sixteenth and seventeenth centuries were dangerous times to be a
woman who was in any way exceptional. These were the "burning times"
during which hundreds of thousands (some say millions) of women were
killed as witches. Europe was reeling from monumental changes, and
someone had to bear the brunt of the uncertainty of the times. During
these years, the Protestant Reformation and the rise of lay clergy shook the
European continent and plunged it into a ferment of struggles for religious
hegemony. A commercial revolution was changing the class structure,
causing unprecedented inflation, and the devaluing of money at the same
time as the age of exploration was opening up vast new sources of wealth.
Literacy was increasing, and the invention of the printing press made possible the dissemination of information at an unprecedented rate. The authority of the Roman Catholic Church was in decline in the face of the
new humanist intellectual currents of thought of the Renaissance, and its
power was under attack in the increasingly well organized drive for political dominance by the monarchies of Western Europe. Of course, through
it all, there were wars.

Women's bodies became one of the battlegrounds on which these
many forces competed for supremacy. In these centuries between the Middle Ages and the beginning of modern times, women, who were thought
to be more ruled by uncontrollable sexual energies than were their more
highly evolved brothers, came to be seen as the embodiments of evil passions. Both warring religious factions cast blame on women for leading
men into temptations of the flesh and for doing the work of the devil.
Women, unschooled keepers of the older oral wisdom and ways of healing,
were vulnerable and easy targets both for displays of power by all stripes
of religious reformers and for the disdain of the humanist modernizers.
Women died in unprecedented numbers in the wake of these sweeping
changes, largely for the crime of doing what they had been doing for centuries.

During the sixteenth century, evidence first started to surface of females who lived their lives as men for reasons apparently unconnected to

their religious aspirations. Very little information is available as to their reasons for passing as men, but the way in which the stories were recounted in public records makes it seem that their reasons had to do with their sexual orientations. It may be that their motivations for their deviations were in fact sexual, but it is also entirely possible that the times were such that transgressing women were likely to have been seen as sexually motivated. In these centuries, women were increasingly seen as sexually capable of acting independently. The words *tribade, hermaphrodite,* and *Sapphic* first appeared in the French and English languages around this time.[24] They were words which could be used to describe and contain forms of sexuality which previously had been subsumed under other rhetorics. During this period, crossdressing females who were sexually active with other females were often presumed to be hermaphrodites, a third gender, capable of sexually penetrating their partners.[25] If they were unfortunate enough to come to the attention of the authorities, they were usually examined for evidence of enlarged clitorises. If medical personnel found what they considered to be an oversized *female* penis, the woman could, in some jurisdictions, be charged with sodomy, which, unlike crossdressing, was a capital offense.

Henri Estienne reported the story of one such mid-sixteenth century French female who was burned alive for socially and sexually impersonating a male. Her crime was that she had successfully lived as a man for many years, during which time he had learned a trade and had taken a wife. She was executed specifically for the crime of marrying a woman and consummating their nuptials by performing intercourse using a dildo. Her crime was against her God and her Church: defiling the sacrament of marriage by falsely declaring herself to be male and performing nonprocreative sex, or sodomy, with his wife.[26]

A report by Montaigne concerns another French female who was hanged for impersonating a man in marriage. The person in question also transformed herself into a man, learned a trade, then married a woman. Soon after, he was exposed as a female by someone from her hometown who recognized her. He was offered the possibility of saving his life by returning to living as a woman, to which he replied that he would prefer death. In this case, crossdressing was considered a crime but was not punishable by death. The crime for which she was hanged was the defilement of the marriage sacrament by using a dildo to sexually penetrate a woman, i.e., sodomy. The wife of this male impersonator was not considered to have committed a crime. She was assumed to have been the unwitting victim of the husband's masculine sexual aggressions.[27] In this case, the crossdressing female's steadfast refusal, at the cost of her life, to return to being a woman would seem to point strongly to the kind of profoundly felt cross-sex identity characteristic of twentieth century female-to-male transsexualism.

The seventeenth century produced a proliferation of reports of females living as men for some portion of their lives. Most of the females involved were young and facing destitution when they took up their lives as men. Many of them temporarily became men in order to travel to distant lands, to fight for their countries in wars, to have legitimized love relationships with women, and/or to make enough money to survive a few years longer. Some of the females who took up living as men for these reasons found that their lives as men suited them well. They never returned to their lives as women and were discovered to be female only after their deaths. Some were unmasked and forced to return to being women. Still others flagrantly lived as men even though it was well known to their contemporaries that they were females.[28]

One of the most infamous crossdressing females of the time was the Englishwoman Mary Frith, who was popularly known as Moll Cutpurse. Although Frith did live briefly as a man, her pattern is more reminiscent of twentieth century transgendered females than of female-to-male transsexuals. I have included her here because of her repute. Several other females, in the records from their trials, justified their own lives as men by referring to those renowned female crossdressers who preceded them and inspired them to think that such conversions might be possible for them, too. Moll Cutpurse was probably one such role model.

Frith was born in London at the end of the sixteenth century. At a very young age she began to exhibit signs that she would be happier as a man. She disliked women's clothing and enjoyed engaging in the strenuous physicality expected of young men. As an adult, Frith donned men's clothing and worked as a shoemaker for a while, but she soon tired of honest labour and decided to live by her wits. She earned herself the nickname Moll Cutpurse for her skill as a pickpocket. Frith claimed to be a hermaphrodite and went about dressed sometimes as a man, sometimes as a woman, and sometimes as both.[29] The story of her life was celebrated by her contemporaries in several forms of popular literature.[30]

Another renowned character of this period was Queen Christina of Sweden. Christina's dedication to living her life as a man was impressive. She abdicated her throne and her country in order to be able to live as the gender she preferred. Because of her regal birth she was unable simply to disappear into the throng as a man. She made the best compromise available to her. She lived as a female man.

Christina, born in 1626, was reported to have been a disappointment to her parents for not having been born a male. Her father, King Gustavus Adolphus, had her educated as if she were male and so she grew to be a young woman who preferred men's ways. At the age of eighteen, she was crowned Queen of Sweden, and she spent the next ten years, until her abdication in 1654, scandalizing her subjects by in every way living her life as if she were a man.

Christina decided to step down from the throne because of her people's demands that she produce an heir.[31] On the subject of marriage she said, "I am a mortal enemy of its yoke, and would not submit to it for the empire of the whole world. God having willed that I should be born free, I will never consent to give myself a master."[32] She was, though, more than willing to have many love affairs with both men and women.

After her abdication, she went to Denmark, where she took up a new life, living as a Count Dohna but known to be female. Her subsequent travels took her through many countries. Eventually she became a Catholic and settled permanently in Rome, where she became a generous patron of the arts. She was able to live the rest of her life comfortably there because the Pope had given her special permission to wear men's clothing whenever she wished.[33]

Catalina de Erauso was a Spaniard whose exploits were publicized in two autobiographies and a number of biographical accounts written by others whose imaginations were piqued by her fascinating career. She, too, did everything in her power to live her life as a man. Born in 1592, she was placed in a convent by her family while still a child. When in her teens, she deserted the convent dressed in men's clothing, which she had fashioned from her nun's habit. Successful in her disguise, de Erauso supposedly passed time with several family members without being recognized. But the nuns at her convent were not so easily fooled, and de Erauso was forced to flee the area in order to avoid being exposed as a female.

De Erauso sailed from Spain to Latin America under the name of Alonso Diaz Ramérez de Guzman, and enlisted in the armed forces. De Guzman served in Mexico, Panama, Peru, and Chile. He distinguished himself in battle and rose to the rank of ensign but was repeatedly involved in murderous fights when off duty. When he feared that he might be put to death for one such incident, he saved his life by disclosing to a bishop that he was female. De Erauso was allowed to return to Spain, where, known to be female, he continued to wear male attire and capitalized on a reputation as the "nun ensign." De Erauso continued to dress as a man, dying a soldier's death back in South America in 1645.[34]

In the Dutch Republic, long-term female crossdressing appears to have gone virtually unrecorded both before the seventeenth and after the eighteenth centuries. In an extensive study of archival records for the period 1550–1839, Rudolf Dekker and Lotte van de Pol documented fifty-four cases of noncasual crossdressing among Dutch females during the seventeenth century and another fifty-six cases during the eighteenth century.[35] The story of David Jans, christened Martigen Jens, is in many ways typical of the Dutch female crossdressers of the seventeenth century.

After both of Martigen's parents died while she was a young child, she was sent to live with a married sister. She was betrothed to be married while she was still very young, but, unwilling to proceed with the union, she fled from her commitment when she was fifteen. Initially she tried to support herself as a woman making silk thread, but the amount of money she could earn that way was inadequate to her subsistence. In desperation she took up life as a man, both to hide from her family and better to provide for herself.

As David Jans, Jens attempted to join the army, but because David looked even younger than Martigen's sixteen years, he was refused. Rejected, he returned to working at making silk thread, this time as a young man. Instantly David earned considerably more than Martigen had and rapidly rose to the position of foreman.

Later, when David appeared old enough, he successfully enlisted in the army. As a soldier, he was unable to handle some of the heavier tasks but was able to trade them off to other men who were happy for his assistance with some of the things at which they were less skilled. In this way, David became close friends with another soldier. Eventually David's comrade became suspicious concerning his sex and forced a confession from him. The man tried to blackmail David, first for money, then for sexual favours. David handed over the money but resisted the sexual demands. This crisis passed and the two became fast friends once again. David's secret was secure for a while longer.

David was finally discovered to be female after becoming so seriously ill in Africa that he was unable to prevent his clothing from being removed, whereby his female anatomy was revealed. The colonial governor was dismayed to have a single white female in his jurisdiction and demanded that she either return home or marry. Feminine clothing and a suitable husband were procured and a marriage took place. The husband soon became ill and died, after which Jens was sent home and little more is known of Jens's life.[36]

When considering the possibility that some female crossdressers of previous eras might have qualified as what we today call transsexuals, it is important to remember that even now many female-to-male transsexuals move in and out of marriages as women, in and out of lesbian relationships as women, and in and out of living as men before they finally make a commitment to a permanent transsexual transition. The fact that Catalina de Erauso publicly exploited her notoriety as the "nun ensign" says more about economic opportunities for women than it does about de

Erauso's gender. Once exposed, she made the best of her situation until her star faded and she returned to living as a man.

Similarly, Martigen (David Jans) Jens should not be dismissed as a dilettante for returning to women's garb and marrying a man after having been exposed as female. Jens knew well that the economic opportunities for women at home were minimal compared to those in the colonies. There was no possibility of an independent and honest life outside of marriage for a woman of that time and social station. We can only guess why Jens made the particular choices that she did. Perhaps gender issues were paramount, perhaps economic; perhaps it was more an issue of independence of spirit or quest for adventure that led Jens and others like her to live as men. Perhaps it was all of the above, perhaps none.

The Eighteenth Century

The Enlightenment brought tremendous and far-reaching change to the nations of Western Europe and their colonies. The scientific revolution was well under way; the Industrial Revolution was gearing up. Unprecedented wealth was accumulating in Western Europe from increased efficiency at home and from exploitation of the colonies. The new liberal philosophies of democracy and equality and the social and political revolutions which they encouraged transformed forever the face of power. While all of this brought improvements in the standards of living of the middle and upper classes, in the rapidly growing cities the poor became more desperate; the gap between the educated, culturally sophisticated elites and the common people only widened. In the midst of such intense ferment, new ways of understanding the world were imperative. The intelligentsia searched for ways to justify the new social order within the context of their new liberal and scientific principles. It came to be assumed that the application of skepticism and reason to any question would result in the uncovering of the correct way to proceed. Progress was the watchword of the times. The eighteenth century saw the dawn of what we now call the modern world.

The structure and function of the family also began to shift during the eighteenth century. As cities grew and the urban middle class became larger and more powerful, there came to be more opportunities for middle-class women to earn income in the world of trade, commerce, and cottage industry. As the prosperity of the middle classes increased, they employed more servants in their homes, thus providing more economic opportunities for poor women. The combination of these forces also influenced the ways in which people organized their home lives. Marriages began to be made for love, motherhood came to be seen as an occupation, and the home began to be a place where family members socialized and found comfort rather than simply a work place or an economic partnership.[37]

Thomas Laqueur has argued that during the eighteenth century the relationship between what we now call sex and gender profoundly shifted.[38] Science replaced religion as the final arbiter of reality, and anatomy replaced spiritual heat as the basis for gender. It was Laqueur's contention that by the dawning of the nineteenth century, the two genders which had previously been seen as variations of the one sex, male, had come to be defined by science as based on two distinct biological sexes. Women and men were as they were because their biologies made them so. But this transition proceeded unevenly as the old and the new philosophies battled for hegemony—just as, in some ways, they continue to do so today.

The relative hierarchy of power between the genders was not substantially changed for the majority of the common people. Women's lives still mostly revolved around the demands of reproduction and the rearing of children. However, the changes which began in the eighteenth century and intensified in the nineteenth forced those who defended patriarchal power to find new rationales for keeping better educated and more economically independent middle-class women subordinated. They depended more on scientific reason rather than on the word of God, but the outcome was the same. A proper woman's place was still in the home. The pre-modern view had been that women were spiritually inferior; from the modern perspective, women were seen as biologically defective.[39]

What this might have meant for female crossdressers and those who sat in judgment of them was that it became much more difficult to imagine females becoming males due to some stepping up of intangible spiritual constitutive factors. During the eighteenth and into the nineteenth century, the old model was challenged by an increasingly widespread belief in a two-sex, four-gender model wherein homosexual females (known in England as *sapphists* or *tommies*) and homosexual males (known as *mollies* or *sodomites*) were thought to be third and fourth genders. The legitimate genders (women and men) were believed to be based on physiological sex (female and male), whereas the illegitimate genders (tommies and mollies) were believed to be the result of improper upbringing.[40]

During this eighteenth century period of gender confusion, as today, the societies of Western Europe and the American colonies were fascinated with gender ambiguity. Gender was in the process of becoming physically rather than psychically grounded. Certainly in many countries females continued to crossdress as a way of life, but they became increasingly seen as acting against nature and social order rather than in concert with their inner souls. Many records survive of these female crossdressers. Some of them from court transcripts, as in previous centuries; some of them from newspaper accounts of the lives of men discovered after their deaths to have been female; and some of them from fictionalized songs, limericks, rhymes, plays, and novels written by fascinated members of the public.

Maria van Antwerpen was one of more than fifty eighteenth century Dutch female crossdressers who left behind records of their lives.[41] She was born in Breda in 1719. When she became an orphan at age twelve, she was taken in by an aunt, who treated her badly. Feeling that she would do better on her own, she first found work as a maidservant and later joined the military. She enlisted in the army as a young man, Jan van Ant.

Two years later, the young soldier married a woman who seems not to have known him as other than a man. Four years subsequently, when the army was stationed in Breda, her hometown, someone recognized and exposed Maria to the authorities. She became a celebrity as a result of her arrest. Songs were written about her and a ghost-written autobiography was soon published.

Maria was exiled, and after some wanderings dressed in women's attire, she settled in Gouda. A pregnant woman there convinced her to take up living as a man again and to marry her to save her honour. He again enlisted in the army, left it once more, took up other work, and reenlisted for a third time. At age fifty, van Antwerpen was once again exposed as a female and brought to court. The punishment was again banishment. Nothing further is known about the remainder of her life other than the date and place of her death in Breda in 1781.

In her autobiography and in the records from her trials, van Antwerpen cited a number of reasons for her change of gender, some of which sound like those given by today's female-to-male transsexuals. As do many transsexual people, van Antwerpen said that she was a female in appearance only and was by her nature a man. She also claimed that she was different from other females in her social predilections and should have been a man. She apparently felt so much like a man that she wore men's undergarments even when she was dressed as a woman. For a while, she also insisted to the courts that she had sired the second wife's children.

Like other female crossdressers of her day, she defended her choices in life by pointing out that she had been poverty stricken and that the only way for a female in her predicament to make money was through prostitution. It was more morally correct, she righteously opined, that she should fight in the nation's army than be forced by poverty to prostitute herself. She said that she married because once she had become a man it was necessary to marry in order not to raise suspicion; but later, when faced with severe criminal consequences, van Antwerpen denied ever having had sexual contact with the wives.[42]

Similar tales of crossdressing females abound. In Europe and the

Americas females transformed themselves into men in order to gain access to freedoms and fortunes otherwise denied to them: Catherine Vizzani of Italy,[43] Ann Granjean of Spain and France (who may have been a hermaphrodite),[44] Catherine Margaretha Linck of Germany,[45] and Deborah Sampson of the American colonies,[46] to name just a few among many. Clearly there were many more who never left behind any record of their transformations.

Most of the more than fifty British female crossdressers whose stories are on record seem to have crossdressed either in search of adventure and economic opportunity or in pursuit of military men whom they loved.[47] Hannah Snell was one of a number of poor English women of the eighteenth century who made the military her way of earning an honest living. In 1745, when she was twenty-three years old and six months pregnant, her husband abandoned her. When her baby died shortly after birth she set out to find her wayward spouse. Having no legal way to support herself as a woman, she made herself over into one James Gray and joined the army. James soon became aware of a plot by another soldier to harm a local girl and exposed it. In revenge for having been thwarted, the schemer denounced James for dereliction of duty. Surprisingly, James survived five hundred lashes for this infraction without being discovered to be female. But when a woman from his hometown appeared on the scene, James decided that desertion was preferable to being unmasked.

Soon after, James joined the marines and was shipped off to India, where he proved to be a valiant comrade in arms. Upon returning to England, James learned that the long-gone husband had been convicted and executed for murder. Perhaps in a moment of nostalgia for her previous life, James disclosed the secret of his sex to a fellow marine. The man proposed marriage, and when he was rebuffed he spread Hannah's secret. Hannah became something of a local celebrity and took up acting, specializing in playing "breeches" roles in the theater, i.e., impersonating men on stage.[48] Eventually Hannah desired a more stable life. She petitioned for and was awarded a military pension, which she used to open a pub. She continued to trade on her fame by dressing as a man and emblazoning her establishment with a sign which read, "The Widow in Masquerade or the Female Warrior."[49]

Charlotte Charke was less adamantly committed to fully becoming a man than some of the other crossdressers of her day but was very public about her determination to live as if she were a man. Her story illustrates some of the ways in which broader economic and social opportunities for women in the eighteenth century may have made room for more gender variance, within certain limits.

Charke made her living and found fame by playing breeches roles in the theater. She claimed in her autobiography to have come by her talents naturally, having begun crossdressing at age four. Unlike many of the actresses who regularly performed such roles in the eighteenth century, Charke also dressed as a man in her everyday life, openly courted women, and visited female prostitutes. For a period of time, while secretly married to a man, she even adopted the persona of "Mr. Brown" and lived as if married with a "Mrs. Brown." The fact that she came from a well-known family and was a popular stage personality seems to have protected her from some of the more pernicious reactions which such behaviour inspired when taken up by less well placed females. She was also careful never to step too far over social boundaries. She never attempted to legally marry a woman and always publicly denied having any carnal knowledge of women.[50] As was the case with so many others, Charke carved a niche for herself from which she could express her gender without sacrificing the few comforts and privileges which she had managed to accrue.

The trial records of the German Catharina Margaretha Linck show that there were still definite limits to how far the impersonation of a man could be taken in certain parts of Europe. Disguised as a man, Linck enlisted in the army. He later deserted but was apprehended and escaped death only by disclosing her femaleness. Linck joined the army again, but she was exposed by the doctor who had physically verified her femaleness at her original desertion trial and was sent back to being a woman. She remained there only briefly. After a third expulsion from the army, Linck continued to live as a man. As the civilian Anastasius Lagrantinus Resenstengel, he courted and wed a woman who eventually discovered that her husband was a female. In the course of their married life, the couple had sexual relations during which Resenstengel sexually penetrated his wife using a leather dildo. Later, when Resenstengel proved to be a less than ideal provider, the wife's mother, with the help of a friend, managed to disrobe Resenstengel and remove the dildo. Resenstengel's mother-in-law submitted the tool as evidence in Linck's sodomy trial.

Linck was tried and beheaded for the crime of defiling the sacrament of heterosexual marriage. She was considered to have been guilty of sodomy for having used a dildo to sexually penetrate another woman. Her wife was also convicted of sexual misconduct for continuing to participate in sexual acts even after becoming aware of the sex of her husband. The wife's punishment was second-degree torture.[51] Linck/Resenstengel's dogged return again and again to life as a man and persistence in behaviours which she presumably knew could lead to a painful and public death penalty might be taken as persuasive arguments for what we would today call transsexuality.

On first blush, it would seem that the females of the eighteenth century were bolder than their predecessors about embarking on lives as men. But perhaps the fact that there exist records of so many of their lives speaks more to the preoccupation of eighteenth century Europeans with issues of crossdressing and the boundaries of sex and gender[52]—a preoccupation which was only to become more pronounced in the centuries to follow.

The Nineteenth Century

Many of the patterns of everyday life continued to change dramatically during the nineteenth century. Almost all remaining vestiges of feudalism had been wiped out by the early years of the century, and the power of the Christian Church had been sorely curtailed. Rapid population growth, intensive industrialization, and massive urbanization in Western Europe and North America restructured the lives of women and men. A working class was built from among people whose ancestors had worked the land for generations. Trade unions began to form, and the first rumblings of Marxism and socialism began to stir in response to the phenomenal expansion of capitalist industrialism.

The middle-class grew rapidly and became increasingly influential as its men became captains of industry. Women of the middle class demanded and gained greater educational and professional opportunities at the same time as the norms of their day told them that their proper places were as asexual "angels of the hearth." These women may have been able to gain some measure of education and opportunity for participation in public life, but they continued to be almost totally barred from any real power. By the middle of the century, these "new women" began to talk about suffrage and feminism and to demand more influential roles in society, but they did so at the risk of being labeled as sexual deviants. Any female who was not passive, asexual, and subservient was subject to the charge of acting contrary to nature.[53]

By the nineteenth century, science had delved deeply into the anatomies and physiologies of women and men and had pronounced their reproductive capacities essentially different. These biological differences came to be used as justifications for fundamental social hierarchies of gender.[54] Extensive propaganda was produced extolling the virtues of full-time wives and mothers. Women, whose literacy rates were high enough to warrant a literature directed at them, were exhorted to remain true to their evolutionary destinies and devote themselves to reproduction and the care of their homes.

The political character of the shift to the modern model of sex and gender is underscored by the fact that much of the scientific evidence used in such arguments was either available prior to this shift and ignored or, though new, could just as easily have been used to fortify the old model as the new one. The world was changing. Social relations were changing. New resources needed to be called into play to combat the rising demands of women, racial minorities, the poor. Biologically based social Darwinian arguments of congenital difference were employed by both sides.[55] Those defending white, middle-class, patriarchal power cast difference as inferiority, while those demanding the rights of women claimed that their femaleness carried with it an innate moral superiority.[56]

At the same time, the rapid development of cities meant that large numbers of people from diverse geographical areas poured into overcrowded working-class districts or set out for the New World in hopes of economic improvement. In the early years of the industrialization process, whole families worked together in the new factories that had sprung up in the rapidly expanding cities. Later, women and children were regulated out of factories: married women were sent home, children were sent to schools. Few working-class women were able, through legal means, to earn enough to survive outside of marriage.[57] Working-class women's struggles were with survival in the overcrowded slums of the big industrial cities.

Whereas the most common employment for single women was as domestic servants, factory work paid better, but still far less than what men made for doing the same jobs. Female factory workers were often unable to survive without resorting to granting sexual favours to men in return for economic favors.[58] Under these conditions, prostitution remained the one occupation most open to single poor women in which they could independently support themselves. Not surprisingly, some females of the nineteenth century preferred to live honestly and independently as men. As before, most came from among the poor. The social displacement, the anonymity of urbanization, and the unskilled nature of most factory work facilitated gender change for those females who were so inclined. They could change their attire, relocate to a city where no one knew them, and sell their labour along with thousands of other young men.

Once again, many of those female crossdressers about whom we have records were in the military fighting the wars which were instrumental in the building of modern nation-states in Europe and North America; many were in trouble with the law; while others managed to escape detection for their entire lives only to be discovered to be female after their deaths. As always, we can only guess at their true motivations. The penalty for females caught living as men were no longer as severe as they had been in earlier times, but public humiliation was still a powerful deterrent. Those who were unmasked during their lifetimes most often gave economic need or a desire for freedom of movement as motivation for their gender change. Others simply said that it suited their natures.

Although most female crossdressers of this period whose lives became a part of the public record came from the workingclass, female members of the aristocracy were also known to have crossed gender lines. Krafft-Ebing gave a detailed account of the case of a Hungarian count, Sandor V. (Countess Sarolta Vay), who exhibited some of the characteristics which are now associated with female-to-male transsexualism.[59] The count came to Krafft-Ebing's attention because of a legal entanglement related to his marriage to a young woman.

The child, born Sarlota, was named Sandor by her father and raised as a boy until age twelve, whereupon the child's mother attempted to turn Sandor back into Sarlota. That proved more than the combined efforts of the mother and a boarding school could manage, and so Sandor was granted a reprieve. In an interview with Krafft-Ebing, Sandor declared that he "had an indescribable aversion for female attire, indeed for every-thing feminine, but only in as far as it concerned me; for, on the other hand, I was all enthusiasm for the beautiful sex."[60] Count Sandor acted on these attractions by having many affairs with beautiful young women and eventually marrying a woman whose family did not, for some time, know of the count's femaleness. When they did discover that Sandor was a fe-male, they initiated legal action against him. Sandor was acquitted by the courts of all responsibility for his actions on account of what Krafft-Ebing called "congenitally abnormal inversion of the sexual instinct."[61]

The wife's family's original innocence of Sandor's femaleness was un-derstandable. The count was decidedly masculine in all social aspects, and Sandor also presented a credible masculine physique, being narrow hipped, broad shouldered, and hirsute. To augment what nature had given him, Sandor also fashioned an approximation of what nature had denied him; he wore an apparatus simulating a scrotum and penis inside of his pants. Sandor's story is similar to those of many contemporary female-to-male transsexuals who often speak of the same kind of aversion for feminin-ity for themselves but abiding attraction to it in others. Similarly, many female-to-male transsexuals are very adept at passing as men without the assistance of any aids other than what they can fashion for themselves.

Dr. James Barry also seems a likely candidate for inclusion in the ranks of predecessors to today's female-to-male transsexuals. Barry began to pass as a young man at age ten, when he entered medical school, and continued to live as a man until his death. Born in 1795, Barry graduated from Edinborough Medical College in 1812 and a year later took up a post as a medical doctor in the British army. Recognized as an innovative and highly skilled physician, he was credited with having performed the first successful Cesarean section where both mother and child survived and with introducing a number of important dietary and sanitary measures. In Barry's long and successful medical career he worked as a medical inspector in South Africa and as a medical officer in Jamaica, Saint Helena, Barbados, Antigua, Malta, Corfu, the Crimea, and Montreal. Barry, who was also known for being hard to get along with, was promoted many times for his excellent medical skills and demoted again almost as many times for his argumentative disposition.[62]

Barry also had a reputation as a fop and a flirt. He was reputed to have made advances to the best-looking women with whom he came into contact, but there is only a suggestion of even a single sexual relationship ever having developed. Although Barry was known as an odd-looking little man with strong opinions, his femaleness was never suspected. His transformation had been so complete that the revelation after his death that he was female came as a great shock to those who had known him and was either denied or covered up by most of his medical colleagues.[63]

As in previous eras, the military was also a favourite avenue of escape from womanhood for many young females with otherwise dismal economic prospects. In the United States alone, literally hundreds of working-class young men who fought on both sides of the Civil War were actually females who were moved by patriotism or economic necessity.[64] Most have disappeared into the invisibility of the history of the poor, but a few have left their marks, including Franklin Thompson (Sarah Emma Edmonds Seelye), who fought for the North,[65] and Harry T. Buford (Loreta Janeta Veasquez), who fought for the South.[66]

Other females in the United States simply took advantage of the opportunities offered to young men in the anonymity of the larger urban centres. They unobtrusively went about their business until some misfortune caused their lives to become a part of the public record; some were discovered to be female only after running afoul of the law. Frank Blunt's femaleness came to light as the result of an arrest for theft.[67] Johann Burger was found to be a female after having been arrested for "abducting" his wife.[68] Milton Matson was exposed as a female, after twenty-six years as a man, when he was arrested for passing bad cheques.[69]

Others lived unquestioned as men for many years only to have their femaleness discovered when illness put them, incapacitated, into the hands of doctors. Harry Gorman, a railroad employee, passed undetected for over twenty years, only to be found to be female after being admitted to hospital for a broken limb. Gorman claimed to know at least ten other females who lived in the same fashion.[70] Charles Winslow Hall was a female artist who found that life was easier as a man. Only two years after changing over to being a man, he fell mortally ill while crossing the Atlantic with Mrs. Hall. Shortly before his death, his female anatomy was discovered by the attending physician.[71] Katherine Vosbaugh, known as "Frenchy" and later as "Grandpa" during sixty years of living as a man, was identified as a female after being hospitalized for pneumonia two years before his death.[72]

Still others, like the early Christian crossdressing saints, managed to pass undetected until after their deaths, only to have their femaleness revealed by those who attended to their bodies before burial. Hiram Calder worked as a baker and lived as a man for thirty-five years.[73] Little Jo Monoghan, an expert bronco buster, was discovered by an undertaker to have been female.[74] Charles Durkee Parkhurst drove a stagecoach for almost thirty years, including throughout the California Gold Rush. He was renowned for being tough and on time. When his friends came to lay him out in his best suit for his funeral they discovered that Charley had been a female all along.[75] Nicholai de Raylan was married twice, fought as a U.S. soldier in the Spanish-American War, and worked as a secretary to the Russian consul. To avoid detection he carefully specified how his body was to be dealt with after death, but he died in hospital and was there discovered to have been female.[76]

Several U.S. female crossdressers achieved considerable notoriety as men in their lifetimes. Murray Hall was one such person who, had he lived today, might well have called himself transsexual. Hall was well known in New York as a politician influential with Tammany Hall. He drank, smoked, and chased the ladies in a way that made his manhood appear to be beyond reproach among those who knew him well. He married twice, adopting a daughter in the second marriage. In his sixties he suffered from breast cancer. For fear of exposure of his secret, Hall refused treatment for many years, until days before death finally overtook him. It was only on his deathbed that he allowed a medical examination, which served as the source for the sensational obituaries about the tough little man from Tammany Hall which subsequently appeared in the *New York Times* and other prominent newspapers.[77] Hall, said to be seventy years old at his death in 1901, had lived undetected as a man for over thirty years.

Any or all of these people may have secretly wished that there was a way to transform their bodies into male ones. If so, they would truly be the predecessors of those who are today known as female-to-male transsexuals. They lived in societies which had no place for them. There was no gender called "female who is a man." Perhaps, had they known of the customs of some of the Native peoples of their own and other lands, they might have found a name or a place for themselves there.

Native Cultures

Western Europeans first began to have sustained contact with North American Native peoples early in the seventeenth century, but most of the more extensive ethnographic accounts of their lives were not written until a century or more later, well after indigenous peoples had begun to suffer the effects of colonization. Reports about cross- or mixed-gendered practices among North American Native peoples were first written by highly moralistic Christian missionaries and by ethnocentric anthropologists. More recently, some of the most extreme forms of Eurocentric biases in such ethnographies have begun to be countered by less prejudiced accounts, which indicate that many present-day Native cultures continue to retain some of their earlier flexibility with regard to gender.[78]

More than thirty-three Native North American tribes have been identified in which there was an established role whereby females could live their lives partially or fully as men.[79] A similar role has also been reported among the Tupinamba of Brazil.[80] Only two tribes are known to have had such roles for females and not for males: the Kaska and the Carrier in what is now Alaska. It seems that females who became established in a cross-gendered role were usually held in high regard. Some authors have discounted reports to the contrary as examples of the retrograde influence of an imposed Christian morality.[81]

These roles were more mixed-gender roles than they were complete cross-gender roles. The individuals involved retained their female status and often some of their womanly roles at the same time as they were afforded the social rights and privileges of men. As such, these mixed-gender roles differed from the modern transsexual role in that a complete transformation of both gender and sex was not attempted. This may simply be an artifact of the level of technological skill available, although it seems more likely that it is a reflection of a more flexible gender system based on polytheistic spiritual beliefs. I have included them in this discussion because some non-Native North American female-to-male transsexuals have expressed a desire to live in a similar fashion but feel that, social norms being what they are, they must alter their bodies to fit their gender.

Female mixed-gender roles were more likely to be found in less complex, less agriculturally based, traditional societies. These peoples were distributed along the Pacific coast of North America, ranging from what is now southern California north into subarctic regions, and in the Plateau, Great Basin, Southwest, and Plains regions.[82]

Female mixed-gender roles could take a variety of forms. One might become recognized as a mixed-gendered female as a result of a vision experience or simply as a result of showing a marked interest in the life style of men. In most Native cultures, the role involved crossdressing and taking on the vocational activities usually done by men, most notably hunting. Some females emulated some of the sexual practices of the men of their tribes as a part of their mixed-gender role, and some took wives as part of their roles as men. Others remained single or were bisexual or heterosexual in their practices, and some married men.

One of the better-known females of this type came from among the Kutenai people, whose lands included what is now western Montana, northern Idaho, and southeastern British Columbia. This person's story is perhaps somewhat unusual in the way in which he began to live as a man, but it is particularly apt for a discussion of predecessors to today's female-to-male transsexuals: he claimed to have undergone sex reassignment surgery. He told his kin that the white man to whom she had been married had performed sex change surgery on her before he had returned to live among his own people. His announcement was understandably greeted with some skepticism by his peers.

He claimed that her sex change gave him great spiritual powers, and he called himself Gone to the Spirits. He wore men's clothing, went on raids, and otherwise participated in warfare; took up shamanism (usually practiced only by men); and married a succession of women. Gone to the Spirits's brother, one of the biggest skeptics regarding the supposed sex change, spied on Gone to the Spirits when she was naked and a few years later announced to the entire community that Gone to the Spirits was in fact still female. That resulted in an embarrassing situation but did not prevent Gone to the Spirits from continuing to live as a man until his death almost thirty years after adopting the life style of men.[83]

Similar female mixed-gender statuses have been reported among nineteenth and twentieth century polytheistic peoples contacted by Western European colonialists in other parts of the world. Certain Hindu females have been reported to take on the role of men.[84] Several African tribal groups have female mixed-gender roles. The Nandi of Kenya,[85] the Nuer of Sudan,[86] the Lovedu of Transvaal, the Babamba and the Mindossi of the Congo, the Lovale of Zimbabwe, the Mende of Sierra Leone, and the Ibo of Nigeria all have institutionalized female husband or male daughter roles which are related to kinship structural needs. In each of these societies, as in North American Native cultures, when females take on such roles they are traditionally reclassified as female men.[87]

The incursion of colonialism and its attendant Christian morality weakened these institutions by introducing more rigid conceptualizations of gender into traditional societies. A European observer of the Ibo people noted that under the influence of colonialism, the queen of one region ceased to wear the traditional crown and instead took up a man's hat as a symbol of her power. Furthermore, traditionally flexible Ibo gender roles were so corrupted by Western European influences that some women of high social stature began to wear European men's clothing and to bind their breasts so as to more closely approximate the look of power imported by Christian colonialists.[88] It was not until the late twentieth century that Europeans and non-Native North Americans started to realize that they might benefit from an infusion of traditional values from the many Native peoples whom they had so zealously colonized.

The Twentieth Century

In the early years of the twentieth century, before the First World War, industrialization and urbanization continued with vigour. More and more young, unmarried women moved into the labour force, only to leave paid employment again after they had married and begun to have children. As the century unfolded, working-class women increasingly eschewed domestic service and agricultural production in favour of factory work, while middle-class women strove for greater education and worked mostly in low-level white-collar jobs in offices or as teachers and nurses.[89]

The war years enhanced women's opportunities for economic independence. Women moved into the jobs vacated by the men who went to war, and although women still earned considerably less than men doing the same work, their absolute and relative wages did rise during the years of the war.[90] However, the depression of the 1930s signaled a loss of independence for working women. Those women who had jobs when the downturn hit were pushed out of them by government and business economic initiatives, as well as by pressures brought to bear by social norms, which dictated that men needed jobs more than did women. The social and economic dynamics of the Second World War again sucked women back up into the labour force for basically the same reasons as applied during the First World War. After the war years, in the 1950s, women were again forced out of paid employment so that returning soldiers could regain their positions as family breadwinners.

Throughout the first half of the twentieth century, the ideal of the family home as a refuge from the harsh and competitive public world of industry and commerce continued to grow in prominence as work in impersonal industrialized cities came to dominate the lives of the largest segments of the population of Western Europe and North America. People married for love, and the family became idealized as a place of conviviality and companionship. The role of women in all of this was to provide succor to their husbands and children and to be anchors for their emotional and social lives.

It was also during the early years of the twentieth century that science finally and most decisively usurped the power of the Christian Church to explain the functioning of the universe and its human players. The forces underlying the natural world and human social behaviour were no longer assumed to be driven by inscrutable divine decree but rather to be understandable through the deducible laws of science. These were the years during which the ideas of Einstein and Freud gained ascendancy, during which physicians and the new science of psychology came to be regarded as the ultimate authorities on the human condition.

These were also times of tremendous fascination with issues of gender and sexuality. Sexology emerged as a new and burgeoning field of study, concerned with cataloguing the vast variety of human sexual and gender persuasions. By the beginning of the twentieth century, gender and sexuality largely had become conflated and both were widely believed to be driven by biological causes which were manifested in the newly discovered psychologies of members of society.

In the new parlance, female partial crossdressers, who had previously been known as "inverts" for their abandonment of their socially appropriate gender roles, came to be commonly thought of as "lesbians."[91] For most of the twentieth century, the term *lesbian* was closely associated with "mannish women" of the type made famous by Radclyffe Hall's characterization of the fictional Stephen Gordon in *The Well of Loneliness*.[92] As the century matured, the category "lesbian" also came to include feminine women whose passions were aroused by other women.

One outgrowth of the increased public awareness of lesbianism as a possible way of life was that females who might once have thought that the only way for them to love women was for them to become men could identify themselves as mannish lesbians. Although this was clearly a stigmatized social position, it remained nonetheless a female status even when the occupant, for all intents and purposes, lived as a man.[93] Many of these women no doubt thought of themselves much as did masculinely attired Stephen Gordon in the *The Well of Loneliness*: "I can't feel that I am a woman. All my life I've never felt like a woman. . . . I don't know what I am; no one's ever told me that I am different and yet I know that I am different."[94]

The Stephen Gordons of the world still walked the earth as women— unhappily, perhaps, but as women. There also continued to be females who left behind their lives as women and lived as men. They too were classified by the new sexologists: Krafft-Ebing described them as suffering from "gynandry"; Edward Carpenter called them an "intermediate sex";[95] Havelock Ellis said that they were "congenital inverts" who should be pitied but tolerated.[96]

The German sexologist and homosexual rights advocate Magnus Hirschfeld preferred to think of crossdressing as a phenomenon separate from homosexuality.[97] He popularized the word *transvestite* to describe persons who live out gender identities discordant with their physiognomies.[98] Hirschfeld also perspicaciously pointed out that transvestism could be found in the lives of persons of any sex or sexual orientation. This attitude was quite progressive for his day and indeed continues to appear as such even today. By way of illustration, when Hirschfeld was called upon to examine a young female who petitioned the police for permission to go by a masculine name and appearance in public, he rendered the following expert opinion:

> Sexually abnormal persons who are forced into a lifestyle that stands opposed to their nature often thereby fall into depressed mental states that at times even lead to suicide. . . . Considering her sexual abnormality and psychological characteristics, wearing men's clothing is quite natural for the patient. The granting of permission is a question of existence for her. Forcing her to live as a woman can have an adverse effect on her disposition. In men's clothing she causes no public outrage, while in her women's clothing she caused a disturbance. The very difficult existence of the petitioner would be greatly reduced by the police tolerating a masculine first name on the part of the petitioner. . . . From a medical standpoint, we have to state that Miss T. has valid grounds for her petition.[99]

Females such as Miss T. would seem to fit the description used today for female-to-male transsexuals. Hirschfeld's farsighted sentiments foreshadowed those of Harry Benjamin and others who charted the parameters of the transsexual condition half a century later.[100] In 1952, when newspaper headlines loudly proclaimed to the world that George Jorgensen had been surgically and hormonally transformed into Christine, the idea that a man could change not only his gender but also his sex became a reality in the minds of the public. But because Jorgensen had gone from male to female it was still many years before most females like Miss T. believed that such transformations might be possible for themselves.

Cora Anderson, also known as Ralph Kerwinieo, lived as a man during the early years of the twentieth century. Kerwinieo was exposed as a female in Milwaukee in 1914 by his second wife, Dorothy Kelnowski, six months after their marriage. Kerwinieo had lived successfully as a man for thirteen years, including the period of his first marriage to Marie White. Subjected to a legal hearing, Kerwinieo was ordered to revert to wearing women's clothing. Lurid newspaper reports followed.

Anderson published a defense of her actions, taking a decidedly feminist tack. Anderson had been a nurse and had found that "two-thirds of the physicians . . . made a nurse's virtue the price of their influence in getting her steady work." "Is it any wonder," she asked, "that I determined to become a member of this privileged sex, if possible?"[101] She further justified her actions by arguing that women's rights and economic opportunities were so severely curtailed that her choice was logical in the face of such discrimination:

> In the future centuries it is possible that woman will be the owner of her own body and the custodian of her own soul. . . . [Now] the well cared for woman is a parasite, and the woman who must work is a slave. . . . it is still a man-made world—made by men for men. . . . Do you blame me for wanting to be a man—free to live as a man in a man-made world? Do you blame me for hating to again resume a woman's clothes and just belong?[102]

Jack Bee Garland, also known as Babe Bean, lived part of his life as a known female crossdresser and part of it completely as a man. His path resembled that followed by many transsexuals. Garland was born in 1869, a descendant of a Louisiana Supreme Court judge and the founder of the Mexican consulate in San Francisco. She was a tomboy as a youngster, and her parents decided that the only thing that would cure her of it was a stint in a convent. As a way out of her cloistered existence, she married her brother's best friend, but within a few months she divorced and took up a new life as a man.

When Babe Bean was arrested in Stockton, California, for impersonating a man, she claimed to have lost her speech in an accident and wrote out her answers to the questions of the police. She made no attempt to hide the fact that she was female and was granted permission to continue in masculine attire as long as there were no fraudulent activities associated with it. Bean became a local celebrity and newspaper columnist for the next year. She then disguised herself as a boy, Jack Garland, and wrangled her way onto a series of ships headed for the Philippines and the Spanish-American War. After arriving in Manila, she was arrested by military police for impersonating a man. She again was allowed to go about her business, this time as a war reporter, after convincing a judge that there was no law against her crossdressing.

Three years later Garland arrived in San Francisco, where he passed the remainder of his life as a man. Jack devoted his life to unofficial social work among the homeless men of the city. Jack was never known to take up any intimate relationships with women, but his biographer, Lou Sullivan, himself a gay transsexual man, suggested that Garland may have felt homoerotic attractions to the men in whose company he passed the second half of his life. Jack Garland died in 1936. After his death he was discovered to have been the female Babe Bean, born Elvira Virginia Mugarrieta.[103]

Dr. Alan Hart, born as Alberta Lucille Hart in 1890, would almost certainly qualify as a female-to-male transsexual by today's standards. Hart's story came to light as a result of the publication of his case history by a psychiatrist whom he consulted about a fear of loud noises. In 1917, at age twenty-seven, Hart procured a hysterectomy, the closest thing to a sex change then available, and began living full-time as a man. Hart married a woman whom his psychiatrist reported was "fully cognizant of all the facts"[104] and went on to have a successful career as an x-ray technician and an author of both fiction and nonfiction books on medical themes.

Another famous crossdresser was Colonel Victor Barker, born in Jersey in 1895. Barker spent the first twenty-eight years of her life living as a woman. She married one man, becoming Valerie Arkell-Smith, and lived with him for five years, during which time she bore two children. Shortly after leaving the marriage, she assumed a new identity as Victor Barker.

Barker married a woman named Elfrida Haward, who later denied any knowledge of Barker's femaleness. Over the next six years Barker became well known in England for his anti-Semitic and anti-communist activities on behalf of the British Fascist party. In 1929, he was arrested in connection with a bankruptcy charge and was discovered, while in custody, to be a female. Barker was then charged with perjury in connection with the marriage to Haward and sentenced to nine months in a prison for women. The details of the case were splashed all over the newspapers, and Arkell-Smith/Barker became something of a celebrity. After release from prison, Arkell-Smith returned to being Victor Barker and remained as such for the next thirty years until his death in 1960. Barker's dogged persistence in living as a man despite being publicly humiliated by the courts and the press would seem to suggest that Barker's commitment to changing genders might have been as profound as those who are now called female-to-male transsexuals.[105]

The successful English artist Gluck, a stereotypically mannish woman, was born as Hannah Glukstein to a wealthy and close-knit Jewish family. Throughout her life she devoted herself fully to her career as an artist and made every effort to establish a reputation for herself as a painter independently of her family's extensive circle of influence (which could reach as far as the Queen of England). She eschewed her given name entirely and her family name in part, demanding that she be referred to only as "Gluck, no prefix, suffix, or quotes."[106] She always wore men's clothing and conducted herself in a masculine manner in all ways. During the 1920s,

1930s, and 1940s she carried on affairs with women of the highest strata of English society and yearned to be able to marry them as a man.

In the 1930s, she met the love of her life, Nesta Obermer. On one occasion, Gluck wrote to Nesta as "my darling wife" and referred to herself as her "boy." On another, she said, "Love, you are such an inspiration to me, and that you should be my darling wife too is all any man can expect out of life, don't you agree? . . . My darling heart, we are not an 'affair' are we—We are husband and wife."[107] It seems clear from both her actions and her words that she felt that on some level she was a man.

Gluck lived until 1978, long enough to see word of female-to-male transsexuals begin to appear in the news. By that time, she was in her eighties and well past the time of life during which one considers such options. She died in a nursing home, still impeccably dressed, as always, in menswear. It seems likely that Gluck would have identified with the female-to-male transsexuals of today.

Although there probably have been females who desired to change their sex throughout history, such a transformation was never actually completed until 1949, three years before the famous Christine Jorgensen case. Michael Laurence Dillon's transformation probably constituted the world's first successful sex reassignment. Laura Maud Dillon was born in 1915 to an aristocratic English line; the infant's mother died shortly after giving birth. The young child was raised by two spinster aunts in aristocratic seclusion from common people.

Dillon showed the classic symptoms of female-to-male transsexualism from an early age. She disliked feminine playthings and pastimes and preferred masculine attire and activities as often as she was allowed to indulge in them. When Dillon reached adolescence she displayed no romantic interest in boys and experienced a great deal of anxiety about the physical changes which puberty wrought. In particular she was distressed by her budding breasts, which she bound for a time with a belt to diminish their prominence as much as possible.

At age eighteen, Laura started to have an inkling of what her problem was. She realized that other people thought that she was a woman, whereas she did not feel at all like one. But she had no idea what to call herself. In 1933, five years after the obscenity trial of Radclyffe Hall's *The Well of Loneliness*, she did not even know that mannish women like herself might be lesbian. When a friend suggested that her penchant for men's clothing might be because she was lesbian, Dillon was surprised but not appeased. That was not to be her way.

During college, Dillon started to crossdress occasionally and go out to men-only events with sympathetic male friends. The rest of the time, she looked to be a mannish lesbian. Although she suffered a great deal of unpleasant and unwanted attention for her appearance, it was still more comfortable for her than the alternative of making a more feminine presentation. Eventually, after graduating from Oxford, Dillon understood that what she needed was to change completely into a man. She sought out a doctor who was an expert on sex problems and presented her case to him. He shied away from surgical intervention but did supply her with potent testosterone tablets for self-administration.

Dillon immediately began to take the pills and soon noticed dramatic bodily changes beginning, changes which rapidly made it impossible for Laura to continue to exist. Dillon's voice became lower, menstruation ceased, and facial hair commenced to grow. Unable to make use of the Oxford degree issued to Laura Dillon when looking so much the man, Dillon took on the name Michael and worked for four years at unskilled labour while the hormone-induced changes proceeded.

During this time, Dillon was admitted to hospital in connection with other problems and while there was treated entirely as a male. A sympathetic doctor suggested that surgery and a name change might be in order. Dillon was thrilled with the double mastectomy he had in 1942. In 1944, at age twenty-nine, Dillon officially had his birth certificate changed to read Michael Laurence Dillon, male. That same year he contacted Sir Harold Gillies, who was a world-renowned specialist in reconstructive plastic surgery. Gillies had some experience reconstructing male genital organs damaged in wartime, and he agreed to work on Dillon. Four years and countless operations later, Dillon had a crude and badly scarred penis and scrotum which he would never have occasion to use in sexual intercourse of any kind.

Dillon became a medical doctor and enjoyed fifteen years of a relatively peaceful existence as a man. In 1958 a keen-eyed reporter noticed a discrepancy between the family's listing in Burke's Peerage, which listed Dillon as Laura Maude, and in Debrett's peerage, which listed him as Michael Laurence. Soon the story was in newspapers across the English-speaking world. Dillon, crushed by the exposure, reacted by cutting short his medical career and "disappearing" to India, where he lived out his remaining four years of life as a Buddhist monk, writing books and articles under his ordained name, Lobzang Jivaka. Dillon died at age forty-seven in 1962.[108]

When Christine Jorgensen's sex reassignment was loudly announced to the world in 1952, her surgeon, Christian Hamburger, was deluged with requests from people who wanted to undergo the procedures. Over 100, or 23 percent, of those requests were from females who wished to become males.[109] The existence of the transsexual phenomenon had become public knowledge.

Female-to-male transsexualism takes many forms. Not all people who identify themselves as men in women's bodies are able to effect hormonal and surgical transformations. Not everyone who feels "trapped in a body of the wrong sex" even knows the term *female-to-male transsexual.* Not everyone has access to sex reassignment technologies. Stories continue to surface regularly in the press about female men.[110] As in earlier times, without access to their innermost thoughts and feelings, we can only guess whether they too are transsexual. Michael Dillon was the world's first surgically sex reassigned transsexual man. Thousands more have followed, and still thousands more have continued to do what such females have done throughout the ages—recreate themselves as men and go about their business.

Conclusions

Have there always been female-to-male transsexuals? Probably. Certainly only recently has there been a specific diagnostic category and an extensive treatment for the condition, but at least half of the complaint which epitomizes female-to-male transsexualism seems to be as old as the human condition. The evidence seems clear that there have always been females who felt the need to live their lives as men. However, the current definition of female-to-male transsexualism also includes a stipulation that transsexual persons must feel repugnance for their primary sex characteristics and desire to have them refashioned to approximate male ones. There is no way to know how extensively female crossdressers of other eras felt such desires. That will have to remain a mystery, for the very postulates on which such a question lies simply did not have meaning until quite recently.

Throughout most of the history of the formative cultures of Western European societies, gender was as much a sign of sex as sex was of gender. The true sex of an individual was as likely to be argued in a court of law or a medical examining room on the basis of a person's religious devotion or propensity for needlework as on the basis of anatomy.[111] Yet *the* insignia of sex was the penis, i.e., males had one and females did not. A person's anatomy was something which *could* be changed, but only in accordance with divine will, not at the hands of humans.

Under the reign of such ideologies and technologies of gender, the expectation that persons would feel the need to change their primary and secondary sex characteristics had little meaning. Of course persons who felt themselves to be men would want to have penises. Of course there was no way less than a miracle that one not so endowed could have a penis. Until recently, the only way for female-bodied persons to have penises was to handcraft them for themselves. To express a genuine wish for an actual sex change, during most of the history of Western European societies, was to be so immodest as to claim access to divinity or to court the charge of contracting with the devil. Heresy, blasphemy, witchcraft, and devil worship were all far more serious crimes than was mere crossdressing. A few persons flirted with the death penalty and usurped the divine right to manufacture the male member. Most satisfied themselves with less thoroughgoing imitations of manhood.

Although the end of the nineteenth century saw the consolidation of the two sex medical model wherein females and males came to be seen as essentially biologically different from one another, the acceptance of biological difference as the source of social difference is far from complete even now. In the everyday world, people still give credence to social behaviours as indicators of the rightness of their own sexes and those of others. Many female-to-male transsexuals, along with their doctors, still use their behavioural aptitudes as pieces of the puzzle in coming to terms with unconventional genders. Today, medical sciences dominate most discussions of sex and gender, and so most explanations of transsexualism lean heavily on theories of an as yet undiscovered biological cause for the transsexual phenomenon. While physiological underpinnings for female-to-male transsexualism may one day be proven, there seems to be little doubt that, whatever the causes, there have always been and probably always will be females who are willing to risk their lives for the privilege of living in the world as men.

2 | Theories about Transsexualism

THEORIES ARE ATTEMPTS to explain something. When that something is transsexualism, what people are usually most interested in trying to explain are the causes of transsexualism. Less often, theorists apply their attention to proposing explanations for how it is that transsexuals occupy a particular social space and how by so doing their presence in society may change what sex and gender mean for all of us. In this book, I will be interested in better understanding both questions, but in a reversed order of priority to what has been the more usual approach of most researchers. I am interested in the etiology of transsexualism, but I am interested in it mostly for what such knowledge can tell us about how society organizes and perpetuates gender and for what we can learn about how our concepts of gender mutate in response to the challenges presented by gender variance.

Although most theoretical attention to questions of etiologies has been on the level of the individual, I will start my discussion by looking at transsexualism as a social phenomenon. Only after I have outlined some ideas about how transsexualism and transsexuals are situated within contemporary European and North American cultural contexts will I take on the job of describing more psychological and biological approaches to explaining transsexualism.

There are a few issues which the reader should keep in mind while absorbing this material. Firstly, these proposals are only theories. They are based on observations made by reputable scholars, but there is no consensus among their various proponents that any of them represent the actual circumstances of real people's lives. At best they represent averages and approximations; at worst they function as rigid delineations which have been forced onto the rich diversity that is human life.

Secondly, although I have discussed these theories one at a time, the world doesn't work that way. What I've tried to do in my overview of these theories is to nest the various levels of theory more or less in the way in which I think we experience them. In other words, I've started with the larger social environment. From there I've moved on to psychological theories about the more specific realities of people's experiences with their families and friends. Next I've discussed some ideas about how the particulars of individuals' biological makeups might play significant roles in explaining their transsexualism. I've finished off with my own critique and synthesis of these various theoretical approaches.

Another thing to keep in mind while reading through these theories is that, with one major exception (the work of Leslie Lothstein), researchers have directed the vast majority of their attention to male-to-female transsexuals. As a result, most theories are about the meanings and causes of male-to-female transsexualism. I have included some of these theories because that's almost all there is and because they provide an interesting jumping-off point for asking questions about how things might be similar or different concerning female-to-male transsexualism.

Finally, when thinking about the causes of transsexualism, remember that transsexualism is a very complex phenomenon. Influences from many different directions have to come into play to result in persons calling themselves transsexual. Also keep in mind that transsexualism actually refers to the condition of desiring certain outcomes—*gender and sex reassignment*—which people want for various reasons. The problems that these reassignments are meant to address are called *gender and sex dysphorias*, or extreme dissatisfaction with one's assigned gender and sex. However, people can come to their gender and sex dysphorias from a lot of different directions. Sometimes these theories may make it seem as if there were only one road to Rome. History, simple logic, and the facts tell us otherwise.

Transsexualism as a Social Phenomenon

The idea that a person could be transsexual is a relatively new one. As discussed in the previous chapter, persons who felt that they wanted to change their social gender and physical sex seem to have been around for a long time. However, the idea that it might be possible to satisfy such desires is a recent social product. I call it a social product because the idea of transsexualism makes sense only in the context of a number of historically specific ways of understanding gender and sex: people using the concept must agree (1) that there is something called sex that distinguishes different types of gendered people from one another on the basis of physical characteristics, (2) that there are only two legitimate sexes and that everyone naturally belongs to one or the other, and (3) that it is possible to make use of various medical and social procedures to transform persons from one sex into another one.

Thomas Laqueur has made the case that our current bifurcated concept of sex is a sociopolitical development of the nineteenth century. Prior to that time, he argued, there was only one sex, but there were two genders.[1] Today we are accustomed to thinking of human beings as two distinct sexes (females and males), two distinct types of gendered persons (women and men). We do this as a result of our interpretations of the meanings of particular physical insignia. Other cultures are considerably less dogmatic in this regard.[2] The cultural acceptance of the idea that these two categories of human beings are essentially different, nonoverlapping, and normally neither negotiable nor transferrable are necessary preconditions for the creation of the contemporary type of person known as transsexual.

Bernice Hausman has traced some of the developments during the later half of the twentieth century which she has argued were essential underpinnings to the acceptance in the public mind of the concept of transsexualism. Although I have already argued that there probably have been people throughout the ages who would today claim the title transsexual for themselves, I concur with Hausman's proposition that it has been only since the 1950s that people could be meaningfully known as transsexuals.

The axes of her arguments, and the basis of such demands, revolve around questions of the possibilities of transforming individuals' sexes. As Hausman has pointed out, the diagnoses of transsexualism and gender dysphoria both rely on demands for gender and sex reassignment as defining characteristics of the condition. Such demands are usually couched in language which assumes that persons' gender identities may take precedence over the evidence of their bodies as the bases for sex reasssignments. That is to say that, for both transsexual persons and their attending physicians, intractable gender identities at odds with seemingly normal bodies can act as sufficient causes for transsexual identities, transsexual diagnoses, and the application of sex reassignment technologies.[3] Thus Hausman's observations in part support Laqueur's contentions that although the two-sex model has achieved primacy over its older competitor, the victory is not complete. Gender can take primacy as a more essential feature than sex and justify the transformation of sex in its service. Paradoxically, however, sex reassignment also serves to bolster the seemingly socially necessary normative alignment of sexes and genders.

Furthermore, there could be little or no demand for such surgeries if the medical technologies required to perform them were not in existence. The medical specialties which form the foundation of sex reassignment surgeries are endocrinology and plastic surgery, both of which began to be widely available only in the later half of the twentieth century. Endocrinology, Hausman argued, provided "medicine with the tools to enforce sexual dimorphism."[4] Those individuals who had previously been left to live their lives with statistically uncommon hormonal mixtures in their bloodstreams could, as a result of new medical abilities, be made to hormonally conform to medically/socially agreed upon norms. Thus endocrinology made it possible to systemically boost the rate of hormonal dimorphism beyond that which occurs as the result of less dichotomized natural processes.

The increasing prevalence of plastic surgery through the later half of the century also contributed to the creation of transsexualism as a diagnostic category and as an identity. Elective cosmetic surgery developed as a medical specialty to treat conditions which caused their bearers psychological discomfort but which did not interfere with physical health or functionality. It is this facet of plastic surgery which came to be important in facilitating societal acceptance of sex reassignment surgery. Radical surgical and hormonal procedures came to be seen as justified if they could alleviate severe psychological distress, even in the absence of physiological dangers or abnormalities.

As these medical developments became available, they became identified as possible solutions for feelings of being "trapped in the wrong body." As more and more members of the public came to know that sex reassignment surgery was available, persons who felt the need of these services learned what to call themselves (transsexual) and how to describe their psychological state (gender dysphoric) in order to gain access to desired transformative medical procedures.[5] As Virginia Prince has quipped, transsexualism became a "communicable disease" in the sense that the more publicity it received, the greater the number of people who claimed it as their own.[6]

Janice Raymond has objected to the prevalence of transsexualism and has argued that transsexualism has been eagerly adopted by a patriarchal society as an efficient way of quelling challenges to the sex/gender system which controls and confines women's access to power. She has taken a position that transsexualism should be seen as a moral and ethical, and hence, a social rather than a medical problem.[7] Her stance was that "patriarchal society and its social currents of masculinity and femininity is the *First Cause* of transsexualism" (emphasis is Raymond's).[8]

Her position stands on some of the same propositions as does Hausman's. Raymond contended that transsexualism has become an intelligible concept only because society has not been prepared to seriously entertain challenges to the idea that there are two and only two genders and sexes or that all members of society must conform to one and only one set of them, from their births until their deaths. Raymond, like Hausman, also contended that transsexuals' bodies are products of modern medical expertise. However, Raymond's approach to this issue was in opposition to most widely accepted professional positions. She clearly stated that she believed it morally unethical to use advanced medical technologies to allow individuals to escape the dilemma of finding themselves unable to bear living within the confines of their originally assigned sexes and genders.

Raymond was therefore interested in "morally mandating [transsexualism] out of existence"[9] because in her opinion "transsexualism is a 'social tranquilizer' "[10] *"that is undercutting the movement to eradicate sex-role stereotyping and oppression in this culture"* (emphasis is Raymond's).[11] Raymond, speaking mostly about male-to-female transsexualism, built her argument around two points. One was her outrage at what she saw as the presumption by patriarchy that men could create women according to their own sexist images. Raymond contended that persons who once lived as men could never "be real women" and that to think otherwise is "to collude in the falsification of reality."[12] She suggested that a male-controlled medical establishment was only too happy to cooperate with the wishes of males who wanted to become women because it gave them an opportunity to usurp the generative powers of women and to do so using men as the raw materials of their endeavors. They could thus avoid interference from women who might demand liberalization of gender roles.

Raymond's other basis for opposition to the continued practice of sex reassignment was that she saw female-to-male transsexuals as women who were being surgically removed from the front lines in the fight against sexism. Her perspective was that female-to-male transsexuals are women with powerful potentials as rebels against the restrictions of patriarchal gender roles. Patriarchy can "assimilate" and thereby "eliminate"[13] the disruptive potential of these nonconforming females by turning them into men. Thus, she argued, the apparent purity of patriarchal gender dichotomies can remain unmuddied by the confusing presence of extremely masculine women (or similarly feminine men).

In the end, Raymond's proposed solution to the dilemma of transsexuals was that they should remain in their original genders and sexes and participate in consciousness raising. She seemed to think that transsexuals would come to share her opinion that patriarchy had brainwashed them into thinking that they could not remain as nonconforming women and men. Her analysis remained entirely on the level of the social and political and never delved below the surface into the psychological realities of living and breathing human beings.

Although Raymond claroned some important warning cries concerning the symbolic meanings of transsexualism within the theoretical framework of patriarchal society, she failed to adequately and compassionately confront the humanity of transsexual people themselves. It is certainly within Raymond's rights to demand of herself that she dedicate every moment of her life to putting herself on the front line in the fight against sexism. It is also within her prerogatives to suggest how this might best be done by others who might care to join her. But she moved into the realm of insults and condescension when she implied that transsexual people lack political sophistication and moral fiber.

Sandy Stone, a male-to-female transsexual who worked for years as an engineer at the feminist recording company Olivia Records, took up Raymond's challenge.[14] Stone, whom Raymond criticized for her active involvement with feminism, called upon other transsexuals to actualize the radical political potential of transsexualism.[15]

Stone agreed with Raymond's contention that transsexuals who go through their transition and then disappear into the normative fabric of everyday life, passing as genetically born males and females, do little to challenge the gendered structure of society. Instead, Stone pointed out that transsexualism carries with it a radical potential to destabilize gender dichotomies. However, that potential can be realized only if transsexuals are willing to publicly declare themselves as transsexuals. Only those who choose to mark themselves as transsexuals can begin to explode the convenient and pervasive patriarchal mythology that the only way to become a woman or man is to be born that way. Stone called upon transsexuals to choose to politically exploit their status, to use their very particularly gendered positions to highlight the social constructedness of gender categories, and to point the way to new, less oppressive methods of constructing and multiplying gender categories. This radical work has in fact been undertaken by both female-to-male and male-to-female transsexuals.[16]

Finding a Role Which Fits

Some would argue that people are born transsexual, that it is not something which is learned, but rather something which persons come to recognize about themselves. However, even the most biologically oriented of theorists generally agree that there is always a social component to the development of transsexual identities. Persons may be born with biological predispositions, but they still have to find their way to knowing that transsexualism is what such feelings are called and that gender and sex reassignment are what can be done about them.

We all grow up in societies which have rules about gender and sex. As we become socialized to understand these rules and customs of everyday social interaction we learn how to tell what constitutes membership in particular gender and sex statuses. We learn where our positions are supposed to be in the gender and sex hierarchies of our societies and how we are supposed to behave if we are interested in gaining and sustaining socially approved positions. We also learn to recognize others' social roles and statuses and how to act appropriately in relation to the people who occupy them. Some people also learn the rules of other statuses because they imagine that one day they too may occupy those positions in society.

Not all roles in society are equally valued. Class, race, ethnicity, physical ability, religiosity, and other qualifiers modify the broad hierarchies which place men above women in social status and power. Some positions, such as homosexual, lesbian, crossdresser, transgendered, and transsexual, are clearly seen as stigmatized by most segments of society. Many people also see being female as a stigmatized position in society.[17]

As children, and later as adults, each of us must find our way to identify those roles which we find best suited to our temperaments. For some of the luckier members of society this process is largely unself-conscious. They simply grow up into the roles which their families and social positions have deemed best for them to occupy. Many are not so lucky as to find gender to be an unconflicted process. Most people start out by trying to conform to what they feel is expected of them by the people who play significant parts in their lives. As we grow older and more independent in our thinking, we start to search for ways of being which we feel are more accurately expressive of our more personal inner selves. This can be a tortuous process for those who feel that none of the readily available roles in society are suitable for them.

A number of theorists have made useful comments on the processes involved in acquiring, managing, and changing roles in society. Vivienne Cass described the process of developing homosexual identities.[18] Frank Lewins proposed a six-step model of transsexual identity development and assimilation.[19] Brian Tully described a sequence of explorations which he observed being employed by many transsexual people.[20] Jeremy Baumback and Louisa Turner also discussed a step-by-step process of transsexual identity formation.[21] Helen Rose Fuchs Ebaugh included transsexuals in her description of the experiences which she described as "becoming an Ex."[22] Anne Bolin took an anthropological approach to the exit and entry of roles which transsexual people undergo and described gender and sex reassignment as a ritualized rite of passage.[23] All of these authors, with the exception of Lewins, acknowledged their debt to Erving Goffman's work on the management of social stigma.[24]

Cass, in her model of homosexual identity formation, proposed that individuals who are in the process of coming to accept new identities go through six stages of evaluation and reevaluation. Cass's model clearly is applicable to transsexual identity formation and consolidation and can be applied to many other circumstances.

In the initial stage, *identity confusion*, people start to question whether their current identities properly encompass their internal dispositions. If a new identity which is being considered is seen as potentially discrediting or otherwise disruptive to an established sense of self, persons may attempt to ward off growing suspicions that a change of identity might be needed. A transsexual identity, at least initially, certainly qualifies as such an identity.

People who have begun to have feelings which they can identify as having the potential to tag them as members of a new identity group may wish to divert the growth of such an identity by employing a number of different tactics. They may suppress the kinds of actions and feelings which prompted such suspicions to arise in the first place; they may avoid dwelling upon the meanings of those behaviours and inclinations; they may attempt to fit their activities and emotions to a more palatable explanation; or they might simply avoid thinking about a change in identity at all.

When such diversionary tactics are unsuccessful, the persons involved will be forced to entertain the notion that they might belong in a different identity group. At this point, they enter what Cass called the *identity comparison* stage wherein they compare their original identities with their newly emerging ones to see which do better jobs of explaining their senses of themselves. At this stage, the prevailing feeling is "I may be __." This stage is characterized by a feeling of no longer fully belonging in the prior identity but not yet having moved wholeheartedly into an intermediary one.

People at this stage typically feel displaced from their familiar locus of identity. Some people may feel frightened by the possibility that they may be members of a new identity group and will do what they can, both behaviourally and emotionally, to discount mounting evidence to that effect. They may increase behaviour conforming to their old identity in an attempt to bolster security in their original identity. However, persons also may welcome the possibility of a new identity because it starts to give them ways to explain their long-standing feelings of discomfort. But even if the prospect of a new identity does provide some relief, persons may still choose to conceal this incipient identity while they take more time to assimilate the idea that they may be other than they had always thought themselves to be.

The identity comparison stage can result in a retrenchment of the original identity, a suicidal escape from the dilemma, or movement into the next stage, *identity tolerance*. At this stage, the overriding concern is "I probably am __." People at this point of the process have not yet accepted the new identity as their own, but they have come close enough to that point that they are willing to tolerate thinking that it may be true. Such an admission usually propels people into searching out more information. If contacts with the members of the new identity group have negative affect, the whole process may be abandoned or deferred to a later date. When information and contacts with people in the new identity group prove rewarding, persons undergoing this process may also begin to shift their reference group so that opinions of people in the new identity group start to have greater weight in their own identity formation processes.

Cass called the next stage *identity acceptance*. At this stage, people on the road to new identities accept those identities and actively shift their attention to fostering a stronger sense of what that means. They may look for ways to validate that people like them are healthy and normal members of society. Some people at this stage will want to publicly acknowledge that they have come to a new identity; others may want to carefully manage who has access to that information until such time that it is no longer possible to do so.

Theoretically, the next stage is that of *identity pride*. This stage consists of taking steps to minimize the importance of the opinions of people who are not members of the new identity group and to maximize the value of in-group perspectives. The validation provided by support groups, therapists, gender identity clinics, or loved ones can promote such identity pride. Prioritizing of transsexual others can be a valuable aid in successfully negotiating the rigors of the gender transition process and developing identity pride.

The final stage described by Cass is that of *identity synthesis*. In this stage, persons have become sufficiently complacent in their new identity that they are able to move their new identities to a less than central place in their lives. Those who are able to reach this phase can live their lives in their new identities neither glorifying nor reviling themselves for their new social positions as members of a stigmatized minority group.

Lewins also proposed a six-stage theoretical model of identity transformation. His model was specifically based upon and intended to explain the experiences of male-to-female transsexuals as they change their lives from those of men to those of women.

Lewins's first stage, *abiding anxiety*, covers feelings prior to Cass's identity confusion stage but may overlap with it to some degree. Lewins describes this stage as comprising "uncomfortable, and at first inexplicable feelings about sexual [*sic*] identity and gender."[25]

The second and third stages which Lewins described are *discovery* and *purging and delay*, which roughly correspond to the kinds of activities descibed by Cass's identity comparison stage. By naming a stage as discovery, Lewins pinpointed the fact that transsexualism is often a concept which is not readily available to persons. Thus he emphasized that before an identity can be deliberated over, persons must be aware of its possibility. Furthermore, Lewins noted that many transsexual persons have many reasons to want to avoid accepting transsexual identities if other options are viable for them. Many male-to-female transsexuals attempt to deny their incipient feelings of transsexualism by episodes of purging their lives of all things feminine. However, although female-to-male transsexuals often delay their acceptance of transsexual identities while they engage in identity explorations and comparisons, they only rarely go through purges wherein they attempt to expunge masculinity from their lives and masquerade as ideally feminine people.

Lewins's fourth and fifth stages, *acceptance* and *sex reassignment*, are self-explanatory. However, Lewins misses the fact that gender reassignment usually precedes sex reassignment by one or more years. Cass's identity tolerance and acceptance stages would cover much the same territory. Lewins's sixth stage, *invisibility*, has no counterpart in Cass's model, whereas Cass's pride and synthesis stages do not appear in Lewins's formulation. It seems to me that all three stages might apply to the lives of transsexual men. Some transsexual men live their lives visibly as transsexual and with great pride. Some transsexual men prefer to keep their gender histories to themselves and move through their social worlds simply as men rather than as transsexual men. Other transsexual men prefer neither to hide nor to purposefully present their transsexualism in their everyday lives.

Tully's model of how people come to see themselves as transsexual shares some features with Cass's and Lewins's models. He started by theorizing that gender socialization is a lifelong process. Like Cass and Lewins, he assumed that persons' gender identities are not necessarily fixed in childhood but that they may be influenced and altered throughout the life span. He contended that when people find that they are unable to live up to their own gender role expectations or those of the people around them, they may begin to question the idea that gender and sex are permanent, unalterable attributes. They may begin to think that perhaps the reason they can't be the way they feel that they ought to be is because they should be someone else. Such feelings fly in the face of everyday logic. How can a person become someone else?

Tully pointed out that the discovery of transsexualism as an identity option can offer a way out of a seeming conundrum for people suffering from extreme gender and sex dysphorias. People who cannot find a way to live satisfactorily in their original gender and sex can cogently explain to themselves and to others why it is that what seems to be an impossibly fractured life story (first woman and female, then man and male) is, in fact, consistent and understandable. What might otherwise appear to be illogical, impossible, stubbornly antisocial, or psychotic becomes a diagnosable and treatable medical condition when seen through the rubric of transsexualism. As such, rent gender and sex identities can become healed. A person who seemed a failure at one gender and sex can, through a transsexual transformation, become a success at another. Transsexualism thus offers a medically legitimized route out of what otherwise would be an imprisoning set of ascribed statuses.

To make such a project work, transsexuals-to-be must first convince themselves and then others that they are transsexual. Tully theorized that they do this by rethinking the meaning of gender and sex related events in their lives and rejecting alternate explanations for them. The processes involved could be described in terms similar to those proposed by Cass and Lewins. Tully, like Hausman, concluded that because transsexualism is cast as a problem which comes entirely from internal sources, which will not respond to any treatment other than gender and sex reassignment, and which pervades all aspects of one's life, only a global and permanent change can ever offer an adequate solution. Tully theorized that in this process "alternative pathways and less dramatic adjustments do not match sex reassignment surgery for its capacity to be symbolically commensurate in its promise of salvation to the depth of despair and confusion which severe gender dysphoria involves."[26]

Baumbach and Turner neatly argued that the process by which persons come to identify themselves as female-to-male transsexual is threefold. Furthermore, it was their contention that to analytically simplify it any further would be a mistake. As did Lewins, they argued that persons who would become transsexual start with a sense of gender dysphoria. They point out that many girls and women entertain such feelings without ever becoming transsexually identified. In their second stage, girls and women who experience gender dysphoria conclude that they would be more comfortable with their gender were they to become boys or men. Once again, they note that numerous girls and women also feel that way without ever thinking of themselves as transsexual. It is only those females who take one final step who qualify as female-to-male transsexuals. Baumbach and Turner proposed that in order to qualify as transsexual, females must experience gender and sex dysphorias, conclude that their condition would be improved by gender and sex reassignment, and pursue both. Thus Baumbach and Turner offered a streamlined and succinct model of how female abiding anxieties about gender and sex can become translated into transsexual identities. Their three stages therefore roughly approximate Lewins's and Cass's first four stages.

Ebaugh also proposed a theoretical framework for understanding the stages involved in exiting one master status, such as a gender status, and entering into another one.[27] In particular, she directed her attention to "the process of disengagement from a role that is central to one's self-identity and the reestablishment of an identity in a new role that takes into account one's ex-role," a process which she called *role exit*.[28]

Ebaugh characterized ex roles as unique because "the new identity incorporates vestiges and residuals of the previous role. To be a nonmember is essentially different from being an ex-member in that nonmembers have never been part of the group."[29] This distinction describes an essential difference between those who were born with full social rights to their gender and those who have had to acquire their membership in their gender status. Those who come to their final gender status later in life will have an insider's appreciation of the other gender in a way that those who have not lived it can never have. They forever have a privileged and more poignant understanding of the minutiae of the "opposite" gender which often makes them seem especially sensitive or insightful men or women.

Although Ebaugh applied her theory of role exit to the situation of transsexuals, her material on transsexuals, in my opinion, did not fit her model as well as it might have because she misnamed what it is which transsexuals exit. She spoke of them as leaving behind the role of transsexual to become women or men. I think her model explains more if transsexual people are considered to leave behind one gender and sex and enter into the other gender and sex, with a transsexual identity overarching the process.[30]

It seems to me that the transsexual role never gets entirely exited. Male-to-female transsexuals, in some cases, may have the option of obfuscating their pasts as males, thereby apparently abandoning their transsexual histories. Female-to-male sex reassignment surgery has not yet reached sufficient sophistication that female-to-male transsexuals have the option of even attempting to put their transsexualism entirely behind them. Female-to-male transsexuals and their intimates are continually confronted with visages of their less than perfectly male bodies. However, for all transsexual persons, their transsexualism always remains a piece of potentially stigmatizing information which needs to be managed indefinitely.

The process of becoming an ex generally begins with persons entertaining doubts about the correctness of an original role or status. This stage of *first doubts* is similar to Cass's identity confusion stage and to Lewins's abiding anxiety phase. These first doubts, for many transsexual people, co-exist with their first conscious thoughts about gender. For others, they start to appear later in life in the form of a generalized but unspecified discomfort which eventually crystallizes as a particular complaint about gender and sex.

How transsexuals-to-be move on from the stage of first doubts can be a function of their level of knowledge about gender and sex reassignment.

Persons who are not aware of the availability of gender and sex reassignment may feel stymied by profound unhappiness in their original gender and sex. Once persons become cognizant that it is possible to do something to change their gender and sex, they will often begin *seeking out and weighing alternatives* in an attempt to decide on a course of action. It is during this period that attachments to others, and the responses of others to proposed changes, can take on tremendous importance. If the responses of significant others in the lives of persons considering a role change are supportive, accepting, or even neutral, that may be taken as confirmation of the correctness of those moves. This, Ebaugh's *testing stage*, is similar to what Cass called the identity comparison stage and what Lewins considered to be the discovery stage.

According to Ebaugh, when a person considering a role exit takes a decision to proceed, the next step usually involves *anticipatory rehearsal* in the new role. The characteristics of this phase are similar to what Cass called the identity tolerance stage and to what Lewins called the acceptance stage. These practices enable role exiters to begin to train significant others to relate to them in the new role at the same time as the exiters themselves are becoming more adept at the behaviors, group values, and norms associated with the new role. Such *role rehearsals* serve to increase role exiters' attachments to, and identification with, the new role as well as making it easier for them to slip smoothly into it when the final transformation is undertaken.

Shifting values and behaviours in this way may also serve to further alienate role exiters from the groups from whom they are exiting and thereby move them to further acceptance of their new identities. This may happen in two ways. On the one hand, role exiters may find that their new roles suit them better and so they feel less attachment to their old roles and their associated norms. Simultaneously, as role exiters conform less and less to the values of their previous groups, the members of their old groups may feel the exiters' new behaviours as assaults on their social cohesion and so may begin to reject role exiters. The combined effect may well be that role exiters find themselves feeling expelled from their old roles while slipping with ease into their new roles.

For transsexual persons, such anticipatory role rehearsal may start at an extremely young age and form part of their growing awareness of "being trapped in the wrong body." For others it may only be consciously and deliberately begun as part of the transition process after transsexual identities have been accepted. Those who fall into the latter group may *redefine earlier events* which seemed insignificant at the time, recasting them as early, previously unnoticed, indicators of the validity of their transsexual identities.

Most role exiters also pass through an uncomfortable stage wherein they feel that they have not entirely passed out of the old role nor yet become full members of the new role. Ebaugh called this stage *the vacuum*, which she described as "a period of feeling anxious, scared, at loose ends, that they didn't belong. . . . 'in midair,' 'ungrounded,' 'neither here nor there,' 'nowhere.' "[31] Most transsexual people report such feelings during the initial phases of their transitions. For some female-to-male transsexuals, this period may be interminable if they feel that they cannot become completely integrated into their new roles until their naked bodies can pass without explanation as male.

One of the major features which distinguishes the ex role from other roles is that role exiters always retain some vestiges of their previous roles as part of their new ones. Role exiters never forget their origins, even if they prefer to manage very carefully who has access to that information. When others will not let role exiters forget their pasts, the effects can be extremely disquieting.

For many people, the roles that exiters have rejected are more salient than the ones which they have chosen to enter. This factor is a major stumbling block for transsexual persons. Most non-transsexual persons believe that birth sex and assigned gender continue to define people regardless of the extent of changes wrought on social, hormonal, or surgical levels. It is in this sense that transsexuals may exit their original genders or sexes but never completely exit the role of transsexual. Few people, once they know that a person has changed gender and sex, can ever simply forget that information. Thus the adjective *transsexual* describes a socially understood type of role exiter, much the same way as do the terms divorcee, retiree, and widow. For some non-transsexual people, the previous genders and sexes of transsexual people retain their defining power, while for others, the new genders and sexes take on that function. In either event, the label *transsexual* describes the fact that a person has exited one gender and sex and entered another.

Bolin studied this role-exiting process using anthropological observation of members of a male-to-female transsexuals' support group. She proposed that the stages through which male-to-female transsexuals pass fit the model of a *rite of passage*. A rite of passage can be characterized by three stages. The first stage, *separation*, involves a ritualized renunciation of the original role or status. When people accept the transsexual label as descriptive of themselves and begin to search for ways to change their genders and sexes, they have begun their rite of passage. In the second stage, *transition*, an individual is neither one status nor another. Transsexual persons are in the transition stage after they have undertaken gender reassignment but before they have completed sex reassignment. A rite of passage is completed in the *incorporation* stage when a person becomes fully enmeshed in the new status. Bolin cited the completion of sex reassignment surgery as the point where male-to-female transsexuals become incorporated into their new statuses as women and as females.

Bolin's model seems to fit the situation of male-to-female transsexuals more precisely than it does that of female-to-male transsexuals. While both pass through separation and transition phases, male-to-female transsexuals are, in two ways, more able to become fully incorporated into their new statuses upon the completion of sex reassignment surgery. Firstly, male-to-female sex reassignment surgery can be completed (barring complications) in a single surgical session, whereas female-to-male sex reassignment surgery is always done in several operations, which, for both financial and medical reasons, may be spread over the course of years. Secondly, many female-to-male transsexuals choose to defer phalloplastic surgeries until such time as surgical techniques become sufficiently perfected that the results would require no explanations in physically intimate circumstances. This longer and more open-ended transition phase for female-to-male transsexuals makes it difficult to clearly demarcate a point where they can be said to have become fully incorporated into the male role. With these caveats in mind, female-to-male transsexuals' transitions may also be seen as examples of a rite of passage.

Summary and Commentary

We live in a changing and growing social world. What seems true today may well be subverted by new developments tomorrow. This is as true of the world of scientific discoveries as it is of the art world or the world of families. Things make sense to us because we have arrived at a common symbolic language which enables us to communicate effectively across the barriers presented by our individual sacs of skin. Each of us is restricted in our abilities to fully express our own individuality by the limitations which our cultures impose upon our imaginations. We cannot choose to be that for which our time and place has no concepts.

It has been only since the middle of the twentieth century that the idea that one might be transsexual has had any currency. Before transsexualism could make any sense as a concept, a number of historical developments had to have transpired. A first step was the idea that people can be divided into two incommensurate classes, called woman/female and man/male, on the basis of physiological characteristics. Then there had to be both the technological ability and the social will to allow persons to alter those characteristics which denote sex. Advances in the fields of endocrinology and plastic surgery brought about the necessary preconditions for transsexualism to become both technologically and socially possible.

As transsexualism was thus becoming possible, it was also entering into the public consciousness as a transitional gender and sex status. Those people who had previously been unable to find any socially intelligible way to conceptualize their feelings of being misplaced in their gender and sex came to have transsexualism available to them as a diagnosis of their condition and to have gender and sex reassignment as possible solutions. Transsexualism thus began to serve as a kind of safety valve for releasing some of the pressures brought to bear on the boundaries between rigid patriarchal gender distinctions. Those who could not fit themselves to either of the two available genders and sexes, rather than being forced to become agents of change, were able to find relief by jumping from one side of the gender and sex divide to the other.

Persons who are in search of ways to describe accurately who they feel themselves to be often experience discomfort in their identities and feel a need for new and more accurate ones. In searching for more suitable identities, they can only choose from among those which their society has to offer. When people happen to become aware of possible roles that they think might be descriptive of how they see themselves, they will often go through a process of "trying it on" to see how well it fits. If they like the fit and others respond well to them in it, they may choose to leave behind their commitments to their prior social roles and take on identities in new ones.

When persons come to identify themselves as transsexual, they take up the project of exiting their previous gender and sex statuses. As they take themselves through a rite of passage, they engage in the project of adopting new gender and sex statuses as completely as social behaviour, endocrinology, and plastic surgery allow. At some point, most people who have undergone a transsexual transformation come to feel that they have indeed left behind their originally assigned genders and sexes.

Current social meanings for the concept of transsexualism, however, do not allow for a complete abandonment of persons' prior gendered and sexed histories. Transsexualism is understood as a kind of ex role wherein persons' past genders and sexes remain as a kind of residual which forever colours newly acquired statuses. This causes most transsexual people some distress, as they would prefer to be unremarkable as men or women. They therefore commonly opt to treat information about their transsexualism as potentially stigmatizing and manage access to it very carefully. Ironically, those who choose this route reinforce, by their social invisibility, the apparent impermeability of the gender divide. On the other hand, those politicized transsexual persons who have sufficient identity pride to publicly claim their transsexuality act to further erode the dichotomizations of gender and sex.

Psychological Theories about the Etiology of Transsexualism

Psychological theorists who concern themselves with transsexualism are most interested in how family dynamics work to produce gender and sex dysphorias severe enough to cause people to find gender and sex reassignments to be attractive solutions to their psychic anguish. The theorists who work from this perspective generally make only brief comments about the part that the social milieu plays in the lives of persons who feel profoundly gender dysphoric. Their attention is on the level of the individual.

Psychological explanations for the etiology of transsexualism often start out by giving a cursory nod to the possibility of biological underpinnings to transsexualism. These are usually dismissed as accounting for only a very minor proportion of all persons requesting gender and sex reassignment and as predisposing factors which will require the appropriate psychodynamics for them to come to fruition as full-blown transsexualism. Some theorists begin their examinations of family dynamics with theoretical pictures of the psychological profiles of the grandparents (most often the grandmothers) of transsexual persons. They hypothesize that grandparents of transsexuals instigate a chain of psychological events which culminate in the creation, by their children, of a transsexual grandchild. Other theorists instead focus more exclusively on parent-child relations. Most of the widely accepted recipes for the psychological creation of transsexual persons are completed with a light dusting of social interaction. Factors such as religious intolerance of homosexuality[32] and cultural inflexibility of gender roles[33] might be brought under consideration. Finally, psychologically oriented theorists note that transsexuals-to-be must become exposed both to the idea of transsexualism and to an environment in which it might be possible to pursue gender and sex reassignment before they can fully develop transsexual identities.[34]

The work of Robert Stoller, who produced some of the earliest attempts at psychological explanations of the etiology of female-to-male transsexualism, forms the basis for much of this school of thought.[35] Stoller believed that female-to-male transsexualism was different from male-to-female transsexualism in that females become transsexual as the result of psychological trauma whereas males might or might not come to their transsexualism that way. He contended that although male-to-female transsexuals could be divided into primary and secondary transsexuals on the basis of such factors as the age of onset of symptoms and whether or not they went through an adequate Oedipal stage, female-to-male transsexuals should not be classified in this way. Nevertheless, Stoller contended that the etiology of female-to-male transsexualism was almost a mirror image of the etiology of male-to-female transsexualism.

Stoller suggested that the transsexual process begins with grandparents who instill in the mothers of female-to-male transsexuals-to-be a sense that being female is of little value. These mothers, when they were children, wanted to be males like their fathers. As adults, they abandoned these dreams, married, and converted their desires to be males into desires to have male children. Their daughters, who later became transsexual, did not get enough attention from their mothers. This might have happened for a number of reasons: because the infants were not the boy children for whom their mothers had wished, because the mothers were ill and unable to attend to their daughters, because the children turned out to be infants who did not want to be cuddled, or because they otherwise struck their parents as masculine and therefore were treated with the greater distance which parents typically reserve for boy children.

Stoller further theorized that girl children who do not receive sufficient warmth and closeness from their mothers naturally turn to their fathers in search of that attention. Once so directed they may learn any number of things from their fathers. They may learn that their mothers are sources of frustration or that they are persons who take up a lot of emotional space in their families without providing much succor. Furthermore, their fathers may present femaleness as a less-than-desirable condition and subtly seduce their daughters away from modeling themselves after their female parents. They may learn that their fathers expect them to take on a masculine role of caring for their "weak" mothers. In short, their fathers may teach them that they should be little men. By this point in Stoller's picture of the etiology of female-to-male transsexualism, the seed has been sown.

As these girl children grow into adults, their masculine demeanors may prompt others to treat them as if they were boys. Thus the patterns which Stoller suggested started in early childhood are further shaped by socialization experiences among peers. Other more feminine girls may turn away from transsexuals-to-be at the same time as those girls who will grow up to be transsexuals are increasingly turning toward boys and their pastimes. Most of them will likely also find that they are becoming romantically attracted to other girls during adolescence and that some girls, but few boys, are attracted to them for their masculinity. As a result, an extended period of sexual relations with women becomes highly likely. Stoller contended that butch lesbian women follow a similar developmental pathway. He maintained that female-to-male transsexuals differ from female homosexuals only in a matter of the degree of intensity of the causative family dynamics.[36]

Richard Green, a close associate of Stoller's, developed a theoretical model describing the etiology of extreme boyhood femininity in males.[37] Green made no attempt to generalize his theory to lesbian women, but he did comment on the etiology of female-to-male transsexualism. Green's formula was "Give a female child a male-derivative name, provide a stable warm father, make mother an unpleasant or emotionally unavailable woman, and reinforce rough-and-tumble play."[38] His prescription for the creation of female-to-male transsexuals, a gender-reversed version of his "sissy boy" theories, was remarkably similar to Stoller's. If Green's theories prove to be generalizable to the foundations of extreme masculinity in females, they would seem to add weight to Stoller's contention that masculine lesbianism and female-to-male transsexualism are closely aligned.

Unlike other theorists, Leslie Lothstein has written extensively about the etiology of female-to-male transsexualism. Lothstein, taking a psychoanalytic approach and citing Stoller as "my personal mentor,"[39] came to the conclusion that female-to-male transsexuals were not being properly served by gender clinics. He felt that sexism and "a pervasive anti-psychotherapy tradition among transsexual clinicians"[40] combined to result in female-to-male transsexuals being only superficially psychologically examined by persons authorizing gender and sex reassignments. In Lothstein's opinion, far too many females were being allowed to accomplish gender and sex reassignment. He argued that they would be far better served by extensive psychotherapy.

Lothstein believed that female-to-male transsexuals were being poorly served by gender clinics because the clinics were failing to uncover female-to-male transsexuals' underlying pathologies. If these pathologies were to be recognized for what they were, according to Lothstein, they could be addressed through psychotherapy; gender and sex reassignments then would be not only unnecessary but also unethical.

It was Lothstein's opinion that "most female transsexuals . . . have serious personality disorders and while not psychotic, they have subtle thought disorders which affect their sense of reality and their ability to relate to others."[41] He thought that the reason others had so consistently missed this point was that gender clinicians accepted the myth that female-to-male transsexuals were "stable." According to Lothstein, clinicians were often fooled because female-to-male transsexuals who conformed well to social expectations concerning appropriate dress and demeanor and were generally well-behaved and cooperative patients were also assumed to be psychologically stable and therefore good candidates for gender and sex reassignment. He argued that this apparently greater emotional stability was an artifact of the different social responses to gender nonconformity in females and males. His point was that youthful female masculinity is fairly well tolerated in society and that masculine females generally reach puberty before they begin to have to pay a high price for their gender nonconformity. Hence gender and sex dysphoric females have time to develop relatively effective repertoires of social skills before they begin to suffer as social outcasts.

Lothstein's analysis of the etiology of female-to-male transsexualism began from the assumption that it does not have a single set of causes but rather is "a number of diverse gender disorders involving profound psychological impairment, and a final common pathway—a request for sex reassignment surgery."[42] Nonetheless, there were some commonalties in the backgrounds of the females who came to Lothstein's clinic requesting such surgery.

Lothstein characterized the families of the female-to-male transsexuals whom he studied as being rife with "disorganization, chaos, and overstimulation. . . . outright violence . . . child abuse and incest. . . . abandonment, loss, separation, and death."[43] Not surprisingly, after having grown up in such families, few such females were close with their parents and many were depressed or otherwise suffering from psychological distress. Also not surprisingly, those females who grew up in families where they watched their mothers being regularly beaten and abused, or where they themselves were physically, emotionally, or sexually abused by older male family members, came to see femaleness as a position of weakness and to see maleness as a position of strength.

Lothstein argued that the female-to-male transsexuals whom he studied were unable to identify with femaleness because of the vulnerability and defenselessness they saw as women's lot. According to Lothstein, they saw femaleness as both "despised" and "dangerous."[44] They also identified maleness as a condition which rendered its occupiers invulnerable to abuse and as a position of strength from which males could aggressively control those around them. Curiously, Lothstein seemed to think that it was a sign of pathology for females to come to such conclusions under these circumstances. Charitably, he does grant that adopting a transsexual identity may be the best way to cope with such family dynamics.

Lothstein put primary blame on the parents of female-to-male transsexuals for causing their daughters to become so identified. He held their mothers responsible for "defective mothering and impaired empathy"[45] while castigating their fathers for playing "the final and decisive role"[46] as they "seduce . . . manipulate, and control"[47] their daughters, convincing them to turn away from their mothers and entirely identify with men and masculinity. Secondarily he criticized friends and acquaintances of female-to-male transsexuals, along with gender professionals, for complicity in encouraging the blossoming and fruition of female-to-male transsexuals' male identities. In Lothstein's opinion, such support is a mistake; female-to-male transsexualism is a gender pathology and female-to-male transsexuals should be discouraged from pursuing sex reassignment. They should instead participate in long-term psychotherapy aimed at enabling them to live satisfactory lives as females.

Other theorists have observed similar patterns in their female-to-male transsexual clients. Susan Bradley, for example, offered an etiological formula which started out with female children born with a possible biological predisposition to being "sensitive individuals with poor anxiety tolerance" who were difficult as infants.[48] Owing to an elevated incidence of alcoholism and male violence in their families and to maternal unavailability, mothers in particular and femaleness in general were seen by such children as epitomizing weakness, vulnerability, and victimization. Fathers and maleness, by contrast, were seen as characterized by violence and intimidation. Kenneth J. Zucker and Bradley suggested that daughters in these families react to such situations by identifying with maleness as found in their aggressive and dominant fathers and thus begin their route into transsexualism.[49]

Another variety of psychological theories about female-to-male transsexualism attempts to explain its origins in terms of a kind of dissociation, or splitting off, of parts of one's personality in response to emotional trauma. According to theorists who hold such views, children who are to become transsexual feel too much aggression toward their mothers because they feel rejected by them.[50] They split off a part of their personality, which they then use to embody and safely isolate the aggression. One part of their personality thus becomes associated only with imagined good outcomes and one portion becomes associated only with imagined bad outcomes. Among transsexuals-to-be, the good part is also associated with the gender and sex to which they were not assigned at birth. Object relations theorists maintain that it is this kind of dissociation which, if untreated through psychotherapy, develops into transsexualism.

Summary and Commentary

Psychological theorists often begin their speculations about the etiology of female-to-male transsexualism with the idea that there may be some biological predisposition toward transsexualism in some females. But they do not attribute this factor with much explanatory weight. Instead they turn to theories about family dynamics. They may note that female-to-male transsexualism appears similar to lesbianism in its genesis in mother-loss trauma. Some start their analysis with family dynamics in the grandparental generation; others focus only on the interactions between parents and their transsexuals-to-be children.

These psychological theories generally paint mothers of female-to-male transsexuals as providing inadequate motivation for their daughters to identify with them and with femaleness. They may have been unable to provide adequate role models because of psychological or physical illness or alcoholism or because they were too thoroughly abused by their husbands. The daughters who later become transsexual may be unable to identify with femaleness because of the trauma of feeling emotionally rejected or abandoned by their mothers, because of the trauma of watching their mothers be victimized by their husbands, or because they themselves have been physically or sexually abused by older males.

In psychological theories, fathers are generally held responsible for both discouraging femininity and encouraging masculinity in their daughters. Fathers may speak and act abusively toward their wives, thus communicating to their daughters that they hold women and femininity in very low regard. In response to such examples of misogyny, their daughters may choose to identify with their fathers, who seem to embody strength and dominance, rather than their mothers, who appear vulnerable and debased. Fathers may desire a son and so endorse masculinity in their daughters. If their wives are withdrawn or unavailable, fathers may attempt to fill the gap by spending large amounts of time with their daughters, who accompany them in their daily routines. In the process they may impart to their daughters a vital appreciation of all things masculine.

It has also been proposed that children may respond to traumatic events by splitting off parts of their personalities according to gendered dividing lines. They may, as a result of feelings of having been rejected by their parent(s), begin to see one gender as the source of their rejection and the other as the basis of their salvation. Over time, these feelings may coalesce into a transsexual identity.

Finally, family and friends may be either indifferent to or appreciative of a growing masculinity in those young girls who later become female-to-male transsexuals. More masculine peers may accept these girls as their comrades, whereas more feminine peers may reject them for their nonconformity to gender norms. In any event, there will be only minor social stigma attached to their masculinity until they reach their teens. At that point, social stigma for masculinity may increase dramatically. In their teens, they may find that their romantic leanings are toward girls at the same time as boys show little sexual interest in them. Their masculinity may further mark them as probable lesbians, and so they may find themselves rapidly propelled or seduced in that direction.

At some point, such females become aware of the possibilities of gender and sex reassignment and begin to identify themselves as transsexual. Some friends, family, and gender specialists may further reinforce the adoption of this identity by validating the apparent appropriateness of it. The final step is the pursuit of gender and sex reassignment.

Biological Theories about the Etiology of Transsexualism

Few theorists ascribe to purely biological theories about the etiology of transsexualism. Those who lean toward biological explanations tend to espouse hybrid theories, which presume that biological predispositions must be planted in fertile soil to grow to fruition. John Money's theories of gender transpositions[51] or gender cross-codings[52] form the basis of many of these approaches. Money argued that the interpretation which best explains the development of gender identity and sexuality is one of *"nature/critical period/nurture."* He maintained that nature sets up beginning biological parameters within which developing humans grow. Parts of those parameters are critical periods during which people are biologically primed to respond to a variety of stimuli from both internal and external sources. If particular stimuli from the environment impinge upon a person during critical periods, they will instigate permanent changes. The same stimuli at other times will have little or no effect. Money hastened to point out that according to a principle he called *developmental determinism*, whatever factors are critical and whenever they exert their influence, the results are immutable. His position was that biological, psychological, and social learning influences all leave lasting imprints on the brains of those who experience them. Therefore, in one sense, all are biological influences which cannot be undone by well directed and determined mental efforts.

Little research has focused directly on the question of possible biological bases or critical periods for the development of transsexualism. However, quite a lot of attention has been directed at questions of the origins of differences in gendered and sexual behaviours of the sexes. These bodies of knowledge are of possible use in understanding transsexualism.

The most basic question to be asked is whether there is a genetic basis for transsexualism. This question has not yet been systematically investigated, although there have been some reports of transsexualism among siblings and identical twins.[53] As most female-to-male transsexuals spend a goodly portion of their lives living as lesbians, the results of research into the heritability of sexual orientation may also offer some hints as to the origins of female-to-male transsexualism. The evidence so far seems to indicate that male homosexuality is more likely to be partially due to genetic factors than is female homosexuality.[54]

Bailey, Pillard, Neale and Agyei studied the incidence of lesbianism among identical twin, non-identical twin, and early adopted sisters of 147 lesbian women.[55] Identical twin sisters were assumed to share all genetic information, whereas non-identical twin sisters were assumed to share some genetic information and adopted sisters were assumed to share none. The researchers further made the questionable assumption that all sisters from the same family would have grown up under similar social, psychological, and environmental conditions. They found that there was a significantly greater proportion of lesbian pairs among the identical twin sisters (in approximately 50 percent of the sets, both were lesbian) than there were in either of the other two groups (approximately 16 percent of non-identical twin sisters and about 6 percent of adopted sisters were both lesbian) and that there were no statistically significant differences between the incidence of lesbianism in non-identical twin and adopted sisters of lesbian women. They concluded that some undefined genetic information may be correlated with lesbianism. The authors also cautiously suggested, however, that the 50 percent of identical twin sets where one sister was lesbian and one heterosexual might be a valuable source of information about the effects of environment on sexual orientation.

Dean Hamer and his colleagues followed a similar line of research. They studied the family trees of seventy-six gay men and found that 13.6 percent of these men's brothers were also gay. This rate was considerably higher than the 2 percent of men whom Hamer's group found to be gay in the general population.[56] They also found that the gay men who were genetically related to their research participants tended to be either uncles or cousins through their mothers' sides of their families. They therefore theorized that if homosexuality is heritable then the gene(s) in question must appear on the X chromosome because in their sample homosexuality tended to be passed to males through their mothers. They then went on to recruit forty sets of homosexual brothers to study their genetic make-ups. They located a section on the long arm of the X chromosome (Xq28) which was shared by thirty-three of the forty sets of homosexual brothers. They concluded that it was highly likely that in many cases male homosexuality is a heritable trait. They cautioned, however, that in some families the trait appeared to be passed through the fathers' lineage and that there were others in which no genetic basis could be found. Hamer and his associates failed to find a similar Xq28 linkage between lesbian sisters.

A possible genetic basis for transsexualism has been sought in studies of the histocompatibiblity-Y (H-Y) antigen status of transsexuals. The H-Y antigen is normally involved in the formation of testicular tissues and generally can be found in the bodies of males but not females. Wolfe Eicher and his coworkers found that the majority of the female-to-male transsexuals whom they tested had H-Y antigen present in their bodies. Later attempts to replicate these results have failed, and so the data remain inconclusive.[57]

Another approach has been to study brain structures in relation to differences in sex and sexual orientation. It is important to keep in mind, however, that it remains unclear whether transsexualism causes, or is caused by, the differences which have been discovered.[58] Three areas of the brain have received the most study: the hypothalamus, the anterior commissure, and the corpus callosum. The hypothalamus is a dense collection of neurons located in the centre of the brain. In response to neurological, physical, and chemical stimuli, it synthesizes and secretes hormones which in turn cause certain endocrine gland reactions.[59] Both the anterior commissure and the corpus callosum serve as conduits within the brain which allow information to be passed between the left and right hemispheres. The anterior commissure is involved in the transfer of information related to sight, sound, and smell, but the specific nature of the information transmitted through the corpus callosum is unknown. Electroencephalograms (EEGs) have also detected abnormal brain functioning in a sizable minority of transsexual people, especially among female-to-male transsexuals, the significance of which remains elusive.[60]

The general theoretical explanation for presumed or demonstrated differences in the brains of persons of different sexes, genders, or sexual orientations centres on the prenatal effects of androgen baths of the brain at critically sensitive periods of fetal development. It is hypothesized that such well-timed doses of androgens cause permanent reorganization of brain structures in a masculine direction. Theoretically, the brains of females can be masculinized without having any obvious effects on the internal or external genitalia. Such changes may not become manifest until considerably later in life, when they may become activated by environmental or hormonal stimuli.

Two small collections of nuclei within the hypothalamus have been studied extensively in lower animals and found to be implicated in sexual differences. The medial preoptic area and the anterior hypothalamus appear to be controlling regions in male-typical sexual behaviour and the ventrolateral portion of the ventromedial nucleus appears to regulate female-typical sexual behavior in lower animals. Simon LeVay looked at the relative sizes of interstitial nuclei 1, 2, 3, and 4 of the anterior hypothalami in human brains taken from cadavers. Interstitial nucleus 3 was found to be more than twice as large in presumed heterosexual men than in presumed heterosexual women and in men known to be homosexual.

LeVay concluded that the size of this area of the brain differed on the basis of sexual orientation rather than on the basis of sex.[61]

Researchers in the Netherlands similarly compared the sizes of the central subdivision of the bed nuclei of the stria terminalis region of hypothalami taken from the brains of deceased heterosexual men and women, homosexual men, and transsexual women of several sexual orientations. They found that transsexual women and heterosexual women had nuclei of similar sizes, whereas heterosexual and homosexual men's nuclei were significantly larger.[62] Brains from lesbian women and transsexual men were not tested, and so the implications for the study of sexual orientation, sex, or gender identity among persons born as females remain unclear.

Laura Allen and Roger Gorski studied the sizes of the anterior commissures from postmortem brains of homosexual men and presumed heterosexual men and women.[63] They were interested in the anterior commissure because it is not known to be directly related to the regulation of any sexual activity yet has been shown to differ in men and women. They found a size difference related to both sex and sexual orientation. The anterior commissures from male homosexuals were the largest. Those from presumed heterosexual men were the smallest. They found no statistically significant difference between the sizes of the anterior commissures of homosexual males and heterosexual females, but when heterosexual males and females were compared, the sizes of their anterior commissures were found to differ significantly. Allen and Gorski extrapolated from these results to suggest that whatever early biological developmental events might cause homosexuality probably affect the whole brain, not just areas specifically involved in sexual activities. Brains from lesbian women were not tested, and so the generalizability of these results to gender identity and sexual orientation in females remains an open question.

In another piece of research, a group of researchers looked at the sizes and shapes of the corpora callosa of living transsexual and non-transsexual females and males using magnetic resonance imaging (MRI). They concluded that there were no size differences among the four groups. They did, however, find that non-transsexual males and females differed slightly in the shape of their corpora callosa, with females having a more bulbous splenium area toward the rear of the brain. They also noted that previous research results which found sex differences in corpora callosa had not controlled for right- or left-handedness. They pointed out that left-handed people consistently have larger corpora callosa. This may account for previous findings of sex differences.[64]

Hormonal differences have long been sought as an explanation for both sexual orientation and transsexuality. The earliest such investigations simply looked for gross abnormalities in testosterone or estrogen levels between homosexuals and heterosexuals or between transsexuals and non-transsexuals. Although often sought, such differences have not been reliably found to exist. There has been evidence, however, to suggest that female-to-male transsexuals have a higher-than-average incidence of menstrual difficulties and polycystic ovarian disease, both of which suggest hormonal abnormalities.[65]

Other research has pinpointed the estrogen positive feedback effect (EPFE) on luteinizing hormone (LH), also known as the LH surge. Luteinizing hormone is secreted by both males and females from the anterior pituitary under stimuli from the hypothalamus. In males, it stimulates the interstitial cells of the testes to produce testosterone. In women with normal menstrual cycles, LH surges under the influence of estrogen during the follicular stage of the menstrual cycle. It stimulates ovulation and growth of the corpus luteum, as well as prompting the ovaries to release progesterone and further estrogen. When extraneous estrogen is administered to heterosexual females at any point in their menstrual cycles, a similar LH surge can be elicited. Under certain circumstances, an LH surge can also be elicited in men.

Gunter Dörner, who has been at the forefront of this kind of research, has concluded that homosexual men are more likely than heterosexual men to respond to injections of estrogen with LH surges similar to, but not as dramatic as, those of heterosexual women. He also reported a similar contrast between male-to-female transsexuals who were sexually attracted to men and those who were sexually attracted to women. He further reported that female-to-male transsexuals with normal menstrual function exhibited the expected LH surge in response to estrogens.[66] By contrast, Seyler et al. reported that LH surge responses of nine female-to-male transsexuals whom they studied were intermediate between those of heterosexual women and men.[67]

Dörner, taking a purely biological approach, hypothesized that differing LH responses of homosexual and heterosexual and of transsexual and non-transsexual people were the result of pre-natal hormonal abnormalities which affected the structural organization of their hypothalami, causing them to become insufficiently masculinized in homosexual males or excessively masculinized in homosexual females. He presumed that this resulted when varying quantities of androgens washed over immature hypothalamic structures at critical prenatal developmental periods.[68]

Dörner's work has been criticized on several accounts. A number of Dorner's German colleagues went so far as to publish a public statement in a major sexological journal criticizing his work for its homophobia.[69] On less political and more methodological grounds, his work has not been independently replicated and therefore should be treated as highly speculative.[70] Furthermore, evidence suggests that the LH surge effect in male-to-female transsexuals is male-typical before sex reassignment surgery and female-typical afterward. Thus the LH surge effect in males may be regulated by some as-yet-unidentified testicular product rather than the result of some mechanism preset in utero.[71]

Richard Pillard and James Weinrich attempted to incorporate much of this range of biological research into a comprehensive theory of gender transpositions.[72] Their theory was largely a biological one in which they shared many of Money's assumptions about developmental determinism functioning within a framework of nature/critical period/nurture. Pillard and Weinrich's model of gender transpositions is appealing in its comprehensiveness. It has been both highly praised[73] and sorely criticized for overgeneralizing from the data on which it was built and excessively stretching to reach conclusions from inconclusive evidence.[74]

These theorists built their model on two biological processes which they argued were formative of gender, sex, and sexuality. They started by pointing out that all human development begins by proceeding in a female direction. The authors then argued that in order for human embryos to develop into males they must both be *defeminized* and *masculinized*. These were conceived of as separate processes which normally happen in several stages at different points in the developmental process and at different times for different parts of the body. Thus, they argued, a malfunction or mistiming in either or both of these processes would result in either an intersexed condition of the body or a gender transposition of the mind/brain. Although they credited both hormonal and socialization influences for defeminization and masculinization, their arguments focused most closely on pre- or perinatal hormonal controls on gender and sexual development. They further argued that it was only after puberty that gendered behaviours become two-dimensional wherein one might be either/or, neither/nor, or both masculine and feminine.

Pillard and Weinrich proposed that the best way to understand the full range of human gendered and sexual behaviours and identities is to visualize a four-part grid with degrees of masculinization forming one axis and degrees of defeminization forming the other axis. Thus normative heterosexual women and most male-to-female transsexuals would inhabit the corner of the grid representing both the least masculinized and the least defeminized people, whereas normative heterosexual men and most female-to-male transsexuals would occupy the corner of the array representing both the most masculinized and the most defeminized people.

In the portion of their grid denoting defeminized but unmasculinized persons, they placed some male-to-female transsexuals; certain males who because of insensitivity to androgens look, feel, and act like women; and some lesbian women. They did so because, Pillard and Weinrich argued,

all of these people exhibit low levels of the characteristics of both masculinity and femininity. In the corner representing people who had been masculinized but undefeminized, they placed most gay men and many lesbian
women who, they argued, exhibit some combination of both fairly well
developed masculinity and femininity.

Pillard and Weinrich concluded that "sexual orientation is the result
of a complex developmental process . . . with antecedents and not rigid determinants in . . . biobehavioral masculinization and defeminization"[75]
and that "in humans (and perhaps most primates as well), masculinization has become, through heterochrony, somewhat or greatly decoupled
from defeminization. This decoupling provides evolution the opportunity to produce human beings with novel combinations of masculinization
and defeminization."[76] It is through these mechanisms, they argued, that
female-to-male transsexuals are made.

Summary and Commentary

Little biological research has been directly focused on transsexualism
as such, and so those who would theorize about the etiology of transsexualism must extrapolate from data which have been gleaned from studies
searching for the origins of gender, sex, or sexual orientation differences.
A few twin and family pedigree studies have pointed to a possible genetic
basis for sexual orientation, and a great many studies have looked into the
influence of hormones on the brain and endocrine system. The bulk of this
research has been driven by hypotheses about organizational effects of prenatal and perinatal hormones on structures of the brain and the activational effects of pubertal and adult hormones. The hypothalamus of the
brain has been particularly singled out as a major centre implicated in the
control of gendered and sexual behaviors.

Few strictly biological theories have surfaced about the etiology of
transsexualism or sexual orientation. Most theorists subscribe to a na-
ture/critical period/nurture model, with an emphasis on the nature/criti-
cal period parts of the template. It still remains unclear, however, what
influences produce the many permutations which we call gender, sex, and
sexual orientation. There may be a genetic coding for gender identity or
sexual orientation. There may be centres in the brain which differentiate
between women and men and between homosexual and heterosexual persons. Little is known with any certainty.

Summing Up Theories about Transsexualism

Theories are a way of simplifying the immense diversity of life so that
we can feel that we comprehend at least some portion of the complexity

with which we are daily confronted. It is unlikely that any one theory or theoretical approach will ever be adequate to explain the origins of gender and sex dysphorias in all people who identify as transsexual. It is more likely that the circumstances of most people who identify themselves as transsexual can be best understood as a blending of causes, some of them biological, some psychological, all of them within the context of the meanings given to the events and "facts" of their lives. In some cases, certain influences might seem stronger than others, but it seems to me most likely that all have a part to play.

Firstly, the social context must have within it a set of shared meanings for sex and gender which direct people in interpreting the circumstances of their lives. It is my best guess that the idea of transsexualism exists because we live in a patriarchal world which requires us to see genders and sexes as dichotomized and normally permanent; which privileges men more than women, males more than females; and which stigmatizes homosexuality. Sexism and homophobia thus combine to foster many of the family dynamics which have been implicated in the etiology of transsexualism: child abuse; wife abuse; downtrodden, depressed, ineffectual, and sometimes violent or alcoholic women; enraged, overbearing, abusive, and sometimes violent or alcoholic men; and the ravages exerted by compulsory heterosexuality[77] imposed on those for whom it does not fit. These circumstances are beyond the control of individual transsexual persons, yet they are often formative in their lives.

Secondly, social circumstances must exist which provide both a rationale and means for accomplishing gender and sex reassignments. Otherwise, people who are profoundly unhappy in their sexes or genders may have the desire to be members of another gender and sex but will have no way to reach that state. Cultures in many parts of the world now have some version of the concept of transsexualism. The concept is available. But what makes particular people accept it as descriptive of themselves and go through the arduous process of pursuing and obtaining gender and sex reassignment?

It would seem that there may be a biological basis for transsexualism in at least some people. My own feeling is that biological causes are not present in all cases, that in a few people they may be deterministic, while in most others they may play only a minor role. Where they are a factor, it seems to me that future research might uncover either, or both, a genetic or hormonal mechanism. While it is too soon to say, as a matter of policy I place my bet on diversity. I assume that anything which nature has managed to create and sustain as long as the impetus toward transsexualism seems to have existed could have survived so long only if there were multiple ways of ensuring its continued existence. I therefore expect that there are many ways to become transsexual.

It is also my best guess that transsexualism exists because the natural world thrives on diversity. We allow ourselves to think in a finite number of categorical concepts because it is simpler for our limited intellects that way. Nature is far more complicated. I believe that genders and sexes naturally occur in far more than the two types which patriarchal gender schemas prescribe. Transsexualism is too enduring and widespread a phenomenon to dismiss as an "error of nature." Nevertheless, because we all must find ways to live within the confines of our cultural understandings, multitudes of people daily force themselves to conform to their societies' gender norms. Although gender and sex reassignment is satisfying for most transsexual people, many would be happier with a more intermediate gender or sex status than any that are now available to them—could such be negotiated.

It also seems likely that in most cases family dynamics play a large part in the establishment of gender and sex dysphorias. This is not to deny that some transsexual people may be biologically predisposed to their transsexualism but to say that family dynamics can amplify or dampen biological propensities to gender and sex dysphorias or can create gender and sex dysphorias in persons not otherwise so disposed.[78]

The kinds of patterns described by psychologically oriented theorists make a great deal of sense, up to a point. Certainly it seems possible that female children who are unable to identify with their mothers or other women as good role models and who see men as both powerful and terrifying might, on some less-than-conscious level, decide that they want to be among those who wield power. Just as certainly, the social organization of patriarchy will make it difficult for females so inclined to find an abundance of strong and contrary evidence.

I say "up to a point" because I take exception to the implication in many theories that female-to-male transsexuals, by virtue of their being transsexual, are pathologically ill. It seems to me that to grant that transsexual persons may have been psychologically formed in reaction to unhealthy family dynamics is not equivalent to saying that they themselves are necessarily unhealthy. Nor does it necessarily follow that the best way for them to deal with their unhappiness is to find its source, unravel it, and rebuild. Although I doubt that there is much that can be done to the human psyche that cannot be undone, I wonder about the human cost and consequences of some tasks. It seems to me like a waste of talent to send Hercules to do the task of Sisyphus. Some people adapt to adversity by becoming strong and escaping. For them, that may be the optimal solution.

PART II

Childhood Years

David

3 | Finding Out about Gender
Theories of Childhood Gender Acquisition

ALL MEMBERS OF society must learn about gender. For most people, however, their growth into the genders chosen for them at their births is a largely unself-conscious process. People who become transsexual clearly do not follow the same unquestioned path from sex to gender that is used by most members of society. Before looking into the gender acquisition processes of the female-to-male transsexual participants in this study, it is important to understand how gender is usually acquired in the lives of more average people.

What Is Gender?

Each society has an overarching gender schema which provides broad outlines of gender identities, roles, and power relations within which individuals and groups must negotiate their own genders. Subcultural groups and individuals will vary in their local interpretations of genders, but the dominant gender schema supplies the norms against which members of society are measured.

In North America, the dominant gender schema is a patriarchal ideology in which males and all things which have become culturally associated with maleness are attributed with more value than corresponding characteristics associated with females and femaleness. It is also a biologically deterministic construct in which genders are assumed to follow slavishly from the two recognized sexes.

The main propositions of what I call the dominant gender schema in North American society are social constructs. Not everyone agrees that they are all true, least of all me, but they generally carry the full weight and moral authority of descriptions of "reality." As such, they form the basis of social relations concerning gender, sex, and sexuality.[1] These propositions include the following:

1. *Sex* is an intrinsic biological characteristic. Normally, there are two and only two sexes: male and female. Sexes are usually determined

from visual inspection of genitalia. Sometimes sexes are determined on the basis of genetics.

2. Normally, all persons are either one sex or the other. No person can be neither. Normally, no person can be both. No person can change sex without major medical intervention.

3. *Genders* are the social manifestation of sexes. Normally, there are two and only two genders: men (boys) and women (girls). All males are first boys and then men. All females are first girls and then women.

4. All persons are either one gender or the other. No person can be neither. No person can be both. No person can change gender without changing sex.

5. *Gender styles* are culturally defined expressions of gender and sex. There are two main gender styles: masculinity and femininity. Males are naturally inclined to display masculinity. Females are naturally inclined to display femininity. Most males are masculine men. Most females are feminine women.

6. Many persons do not exactly fit their expected gender styles. This is due to imperfect socialization or to pathological conditions.

7. Those persons who are males, boys, men, or masculine deserve greater social status, authority, and power than those who are females, girls, women, or feminine.

Sexes are presumed, according to this schema, to be biologically determined properties which members of society simply recognize on the basis of scientific evidence. Genders are presumed to be naturally occurring social manifestations of sexes. The distinctions between genders and sexes are, in everyday life, therefore usually treated as insignificant. Genders and sexes are assumed to be innate human features, whereas the behaviors appropriate to those genders and sexes, gender styles, are what the ideology of the dominant gender schema presumes people must learn to express properly. Furthermore, because of the biologically deterministic underpinnings of this system, it is assumed that the basic attitudes and actions of gender and sex will "come naturally" to most people but that learning is required in order to improve the grace with which people execute their socially predetermined gender styles.

One of the many reasons that members of society attempt to conform to social roles, including genders, is that they provide a convenient shorthand useful for communicating membership in groups or categories within society. Gender styles thus enable social actors and audiences to recognize and classify genders on the basis of nonspecific commonalties which persons may have with others of a similar type. At the same time, people may want to present themselves using socially approved gender styles as a way of obscuring their individuality or camouflaging their variation from an ideal or normative type. Thus gender styles may serve the dual purposes of facilitating social group identification and masking individual characteristics which could otherwise discredit individuals' presentations of themselves.

However, no one actually conforms perfectly to gender style ideals, and most members of society are somewhat aware of the performance aspects of genders. Shakespeare proclaimed, "All the world's a stage, and all the men and women merely players."[2] Erving Goffman spoke of the "dramaturgy" of everyday life.[3] Most members of society remain concerned that they don't "do" their gender quite as well as they might, and many people put a great deal of effort into trying to do a better job of it.

Gender styles are not uniquely defined but rather have multiple interpretations possible within different contexts. Therefore the effectiveness of the gender styles employed by social actors in given situations depends upon the context in which the negotiation of meaning takes place. Actions which would seem masculine in one context may seem quite feminine in another by contrast to the still more masculine conduct of others. It is therefore impossible to simply say that certain behaviours, objects, or opinions are reliable indicators of femininity or masculinity. Rather, each behaviour must be recognizable in a vast array of circumstances under which every conceivable combination of gender styles, age, sex, race, class, ethnicity, level of mental or physical ability, and type of sexuality can function to confuse the meanings of actions. Therefore it is my contention that rather than defining gender styles through specific actions, opinions, or objects, the best approach is to look at femininity and masculinity as meanings made recognizable on the basis of *relational styles* of self-presentation. In this way, gender is read within a context of cultural meanings and against a backdrop of specific personal relations and past experiences.

When people recognize others as men and women, gender styles, clothing, and other gender props are taken as indicators of the genders of those who use them to identify themselves. When clothing and other cues do not correspond well with persons' gendered styles of relating to others, relational style cues take precedence as indicators of genders. Sexes are assumed to correspond with genders as prescribed by the dominant gender schema, so that persons who dress like women but act like men will be thought of as men and as males. When sex is known to be inconsistent with either gender or gender style, the biologism of the dominant gender schema will dictate that sex is taken as the final arbiter of gender. For instance, most people will think of a perfectly presentable man as a woman if the sex of the person is known to be female. Thus gender styles are used in everyday life as primary indicators of genders and, by implication, of sexes, unless sexes are known to differ from genders.

Popular conceptions of the gender styles of femininity and masculinity reflect the hierarchical relationship of females to males under patriarchy. Although members of both genders are conceived of as sharing many of the same human attributes and propensities, albeit in different relative proportions, most activities are divided into suitable and unsuitable categories for each gender. Persons who take part in the activities considered appropriate for another gender will be expected to do so poorly. In some cases, such behaviours are ignored by observers and therefore do not compromise the integrity of persons' gender displays. In other cases, they are labelled as inappropriate, and those who adequately perform such activities may be rewarded with ridicule or scorn for blurring the gender dividing line. On the other hand, those who can provide a relatively unblemished presentation of a particular gender style will be attributed with the gender and sex associated with that style.

The gender styles of femininity and masculinity share a common relational dilemma, and each style can be practiced to varying degrees by persons of any gender or sex status. Each is a simplification of, or a retreat away from, the complexity inherent in the immense diversity of human nature. Each represents a way to claim membership in a particular gender. Each also provides a socially accessible and acceptable way to protect one's self from the dangers inherent in public exposure of imperfect conformity to the demands of the dominant gender schema. Many social roles can be seen in a similar light.

The central relational theme of masculinity is to maintain separateness[4] and to provide protection and enrichment to the lives of certain selected others who are accepted as in-group members. Masculinity can be recognized in aggressiveness, emotional distance, and toughness. These stances can be translated into actions which provide either safety for one's own or danger to others.[5] Contacts with those parts of themselves which masculine people perceive as their "private" selves, as opposed to their more publicly acceptable masculine presentations, are strictly controlled by masculine persons and only parsimoniously granted.

Masculine persons' gender styles thus hinge on providing safety and aggressively pursuing advantages for themselves and for others under their protection. Masculinity can lead to effectively coordinated hierarchies functioning for the common good or to similar alliances turned to destructive violence. Either end can be masculinely pursued by means of masculine persons' expansion of their sphere of action in manners which are intended to either accrue more advantages or to repel threats. When such masculine actions are met by masculine counter-expansion, masculine actors are faced with the possibility of either diminished accomplishment and a tarnished masculinity or the danger of the continuation of the original threat. Thus, because gender styles can be asserted only through relational contrasts, masculinity carries with it the dangers of limitless escalation of acquisition, or attack and counterattack, until a clear dominance hierarchy can be established through victory or defeat.

The most common avenues of avoidance of such inflation of hostilities lie in controlling competition through institutionalized hierarchies or through withdrawal of contact. Clearly defined hierarchies prevent unbridled escalation of rivalries by exerting socially legitimated channels and limits for competition and by providing methods of establishing who may reasonably expect to remain aloof from whom. Hierarchies therefore allow room, in many circumstances, for masculine people to save face and maintain safe social distances from others while faultlessly withdrawing from threatening situations.

Femininity is characterized by a set of behaviours, opinions, and props which likewise serve to claim membership in a social status and to provide persons' intimates and themselves with safety and succor. Feminine people tend to focus their energies on the establishment of communion through the submersion of the self to the needs of others. The characteristically feminine drive for communion can also be a strongly creative or destructive force. Feminine selflessness can provide the basis for the development of strong community and family ties or can lead to violence or self-destructiveness.

The relational style of femininity is enacted through a fostering of expanded in-group identification wherein others are seen and see themselves as in-group members whose interests are served by mutual cooperation. When feminine people are unable to incorporate others into their own in-groups through their own attempts at inclusiveness, their next step may be to attempt to induce others to take such actions toward them. In such scenarios, feminine actors may contract their use of social space in such ways as to invite others to feel protective of them. If successful, the net result would be the same: others expand their social spheres to include feminine actors in their definitions of their self-interests and commonality is established. Thus feminine actors prefer voluntarily inclusive relational conditions and cooperation. Feminine persons attempt to foster situations wherein similarities rather than differences with others are prominent.[6]

Feminine people tend to deal with dangers by attempting to neutralize them by establishing a sense of in-group solidarity. Where this method fails, feminine actors may resort to whatever means are necessary to effectively eliminate perceived dangers to themselves or to others in their care. Feminine actors can be forced to extreme measures because when they believe the establishment of communion to be impossible, they are left in extremely vulnerable positions. They have already attempted to establish common ground by demonstrating that they themselves are nonthreatening, and in so doing they have effectively forgone the option of repelling threat through counterthreat. Thus feminine actors are left with only the most drastic of fallback positions. Having excluded themselves from the possibility of meaningful competition, they can achieve safety for themselves and those in their care only through the aggressive elimination of threat by whatever definitive means are available.

Patriarchal gender schemas both reserve highly valued attributes for males and actively support the high evaluation of any characteristics which might inadvertently become associated with maleness. Thus, whereas active expressions of power are designated as masculine, femininity must be expressed through modes of dress, movement, speech, and action which communicate receptivity and sensitivity to the needs of others. Femininity therefore serves a contrapuntal function to delineate and magnify the hierarchically dominant social status of masculinity.

Consequently, feminine demeanors indicate subordinate status. They minimize spacial use and communicate a message of "no threat." People appear feminine when they hold their arms close to their bodies, their legs close together, and their torsos and heads at oblique angles. People also look feminine when they point their toes inward and use their hands in small or uncertain gestures. Other people also tend to stand more closely to feminine people, often invading their personal space. People who make frequent appeasement gestures, such as smiling, are also recognized as feminine. Perhaps as an outgrowth of their practiced efforts at fostering communion, feminine people tend to excel over masculine ones at the ability to interpret correctly and to effectively display nonverbal communication cues.[7]

Speech which is characterized by inflections, intonations, and phrases which convey subordinate status is also heard as more feminine. Subordinate speakers use more polite expressions and ask more questions in conversation. Speech in higher pitches is also often interpreted by listeners as feminine or as childlike and ineffectual.[8] Feminine styles of dress tend to greater restriction of movement of the body or an emphasis on sexual characteristics. The more distinctly gendered the dress, the more this is the case.[9]

Masculinity, like femininity, can be demonstrated in many ways. Pleck has argued that it is commonly expressed in North American society through the attainment of some level of proficiency at some or all of four main attitudes of masculinity: persons who display success and high status in their social group; "a manly air of toughness, confidence, and self-reliance"; "the aura of aggression, violence, and daring"; and a conscientious avoidance of anything associated with femininity.[10] In patriarchally organized societies, where masculine values become the basis of the rules of the society as a whole, such values lead those who subscribe to them to view feminine females as "born losers."

Masculinity is conveyed through body postures, speech patterns, and styles of dress which give the impression of dominance and authority. People who maximize the amount of space that they physically occupy appear most masculine. Masculine-looking persons hold their arms and hands in positions away from their bodies and stand, sit, or lie with their legs apart. They stand erect and move forcefully. Their movements tend to be more abrupt and stiff, communicating force rather than flexibility and cooperation. Masculinity can also be conveyed by stern or serious facial expressions which suggest minimal receptivity to the influence of others, all characteristics which are important elements in the attainment and maintenance of dominance.[11]

Speech and dress which likewise demonstrate or claim superior status are also seen as characteristically masculine. People who tend to make more attempts to control the direction of conversations seem more masculine.[12] People who speak more loudly and assertively, use less polite forms, and interrupt the conversations of others more often also seem more masculine. Masculine clothing tends to emphasize the size of the upper body and allow freedom of movement in order to encourage an illusion of physical power and a look of easy physicality. Such appearances create an aura of aggressiveness central to an appearance of masculinity. Expansive postures and gestures combine with these qualities to insinuate dominance.[13]

Although in the minds and experiences of most people masculine behaviors are the domain of men and feminine ones are the province of women, research shows that dominant persons of any gender tend to use influence tactics and verbal styles usually associated with men and masculinity while subordinate persons of any gender tend to use those considered to be the province of women.[14] Several studies have also indicated that masculinity tends to be associated with social adaptability, dominance, or high self-esteem in both men and women.[15] Feminine attributes qualify one for secondary expressive and cooperative social roles, while masculine characteristics train one for primary instrumental and dominant social roles within patriarchal social structures. Femininity, then, can become a stumbling block to emotional well-being and material success in a patriarchal society. Masculinity, by contrast, can function as a minimum basic requirement for success in mainstream society, regardless of one's gender or sex.

Theories of Childhood Gender Acquisition

The family is a crucible in which we learn our first and, some would say, most enduring lessons about how the social world works. Among the most important of those lessons are those about gender. It is within family settings that we first learn what gender is, who has it, and where we are supposed to fit into the scheme of things.

In a society which classifies people on the basis of a simple binary system, thereby denying the infinite diversity of nature, many people, both male and female, do not easily fit within stereotypical notions of femininity and masculinity. Nonetheless, society demands that parents and other adults attempt to teach children to conform to their society's norms of masculinity and femininity. When parents transfer not only their beliefs but also psychological and physiological reproductions of those beliefs to the children in their care, the "universality" of gender as the primary organizing principle of all human endeavor is continuously reinforced and reconstituted within and between each succeeding generation.

There are many theories about how it is that parents and other family members transfer their notions of gender to children. Some theories grow out of psychoanalytic traditions which place a major emphasis on intra-psychic patterns learned by infants in the first years of life. Some theorists step back a bit from the hothouse of the family to propose that gender is a cultural artifact learned from many sources along with other socially appropriate behaviours in the process of growing up. Some see this process as one which acts upon more or less passive recipients, while others argue that children take more active roles in the learning of gender.

Psychoanalytic theorists propose that the experiences of the first two to three years in a person's life are the bedrock upon which all other experiences stand and the weave through which all other experience must be filtered in order to be understood. They hypothesize that the major psychological events of these first years of life are indelibly etched into persons' psyches and that, although the effects of those experiences can be modified, they can never be entirely erased. Psychoanalytic theorists further suggest that young children normally come to identify with the gender styles of their same sex parents and therefore use them as models in building their own gender repertoires. They propose that over time this imitation process leads to an identity and a personality easily understood by any member of society as either masculine or feminine. They also claim that although this process of gender identity and gender style acquisition is a naturally occurring one, it is nonetheless one which can easily go wrong.[16] Chodorow, in a discussion of the preverbal period of infancy, speculated that:

> when there is some major discrepancy in the early phases between needs and material and psychological care, including attention and affection, the person develops a "basic fault," an all pervasive sense, sustained by enormous anxiety, that something is not right, is lacking in her or him. This sense, which may be covered over by later developments and defenses, informs the person's fundamental nature, and may be partly irreversible.[17]

According to this school of thought, femininity is thought to be more highly developed in children who are allowed and encouraged to maintain their attachment to their mothers longer and to let go of their mothers in a slower and more gradual release. Masculinity is fostered in children who are encouraged to separate from their mothers more quickly and radically and thereby develop a stronger sense of being "not female."[18] In dichotomized gender systems, the only alternative to female is male.

Social learning theorists approach the question of gender identity and gender style development from a somewhat different perspective. They start from the recognition that societies exert pressures on their members to conform to established social patterns by selectively rewarding some behaviors and discouraging others. They propose that gender is a cultural artifact learned along with other socially appropriate behaviours in the process of growing from infancy to maturity. They further argue that infants are born into the world basically as blank slates capable of being inscribed with any type of social behavior which their cultures might demand. According to such theorists, already socialized persons are also capable of becoming resocialized into new and possibly widely disparate cultural enactments of gender if they are given the opportunity to re-experience social learning processes in new social settings.[19]

Cognitive developmental theorists also agree that children are socially trained to their genders. They additionally maintain that there are age-graded limitations on what people are capable of understanding. They assert that in order to absorb and make sense of the complexity of the social world which they experience every day, children and adults alike must somehow engage in mental processes which organize and therefore simplify experience. These theorists suggest that very young children begin to understand gender by recognizing that the people of the world can be divided into two large groups on the basis of gender styles. They further suggest that once children begin to identify with a gender group, they actively attempt to learn how others in that group perform their gender styles and imitate them to the best of their understanding and abilities. As children mature into adults, their conceptual abilities become more sophisticated and their gender styles acquire more subtle nuances and phrasing.[20]

Other theorists have expanded on these concepts to argue that within patriarchal societies, people have little choice but to learn to function within the sexism of the dominant gender schema. Therefore members of society come to use gender preferentially to explain social phenomena which could also be cogently explained using other terms of reference. These theorists further argued that those people who have learned to be the most accepting of social expectations of gender are most likely to use gender as a way to understand their interchanges with other people. What this can mean in everyday life is that they may do this to the exclusion of any other plausible explanations for their own actions and feelings or those of others.[21]

As discussed in the last chapter, biologically oriented theorists have argued that many aspects of gender are controlled by male and female physiology. They argue that gender identity and aspects of gender styles such as aggressiveness or patterns of sexual responsiveness are prepro-gramed into the brain before birth. Other theorists have pointed out that the gender lessons which people learn throughout their lifetimes should not be thought of as abstract and disembodied thoughts. They argue that whatever people learn with their minds is also encoded in the very physical structures of their brains.[22] In fact, the period of most intense early child-hood gender identity and personality formation, the first years after birth, correspond to the period during which the brain is undergoing its most intense postnatal period of growth.[23] As infants and young children learn to identify with and enact particular genders, they build a repertoire of gendered activities and attitudes. It is theorized that these patterns are em-bodied in neural growth in various parts of the brain. Once such synaptic formations are established, they facilitate the occurrence of later responses of a similar nature. In this way, experience becomes facility, and the expe-riences of the first years of life may thus become the original source of many of the patterns which will follow throughout one's life.[24]

Parental Contributions to Gender Acquisition

The bulk of children's experiences during the first few years of life occur in interactions with family members. In most families the major caregivers during those years are mothers. Fathers for the most part play supplemental roles in child rearing, especially during the very earliest years of upbringing. But, although they may spend fewer hours with their children, the role of fathers in the gender development of their children is far from inconsequential. Men have been consistently found to be more intensely concerned than women with their children's conformity to socially acceptable gender styles. They tend to be stricter with their sons and less lenient than mothers are with either their sons or their daughters. Fathers, although they spend less time with their offspring, devote more of their child care energy to gender style training than do mothers and are more intent that their boy children be masculine.[25] Women, on the other hand, although still active gender educators, tend to be more evenhanded in the gender training which they transmit to the children around them.

Parental attitudes and beliefs about gender come into play even before their children are born. Although most adults state that they would like to have an even number of sons and daughters, they report a strong preference for a first or only child to be a boy. Fathers show an especially pronounced preference for sons. When mothers report a preference for sons over daughters, it is most often in deference to the wishes of their husbands or other family members. Mothers report only a slight preference for the birth of sons over daughters, while fathers' preferences for the birth of sons can be as much as three times greater than their preferences for daughters. These preferences have been found to be consistent among a diversity of ethnic groups in North America and over a period of several decades of research.[26]

When parents are dissatisfied with the sex of a child their dissatisfaction can lead to greater conflicts between parents and children, especially between parents and the daughters whom they had hoped would have been sons. Fathers who had wanted sons spent less time with their daughters, exerted stricter discipline, and demanded more obedience of them than did fathers who had wanted daughters. The most intense difficulties between daughters and fathers who had wanted sons occurred while the girls were between the ages of seven and fifteen years.[27]

Regardless of their original preferences, parents begin to socialize their children according to gender stereotypes immediately upon the birth of a child, if not before. Parents of newborns who are only a few days old have been found to perceive their infants as conforming to the common stereotypes that females are "soft, fine-featured, little, inattentive, weak, and delicate" and that boys are not. Fathers more than mothers tend to perceive their infants as acting in these ways even though female infants at birth are generally more mature, active, and alert than male infants.[28]

Researchers have observed that fathers visiting their newborn children in hospital on the day of birth tended to spend more time holding and speaking to their sons than their daughters. Mothers, on the other hand, have been found to be more equal in their attentions to their sons and daughters, perhaps reflecting their initially more equal interest in the birth of either sons or daughters.[29] Moreover, this pattern of fathers being more stereotypical in their gender expectations than mothers has been shown to continue throughout children's upbringings.[30]

In everyday family life, mothers spend more time with their infants and do more and different things with them than do fathers.[31] Fathers tend to spend most of the time they do spend with their infants playing with them, while mothers spend the majority of their time taking care of them.[32] As a result, infants tend to get to know gendered adults as different kinds of people. The men in their lives come to be known as infrequent but fun visitors. Women, by contrast, normally come to represent the minutiae of daily life.

Mothers and fathers observed playing with their young children have been found to have significantly different styles of play. Fathers tend to play more physically active and less verbal games with all their children, but they tend to be most physically active, least physically affectionate, and least verbal with their sons.[33] Both parents, but especially fathers, tend to treat sons in ways which encourage them to think of themselves as tougher, more aggressive, more independent, stronger, and more intellectually competent than females. By contrast, female children are treated in a more protected manner. Sons are rewarded for exploring, taking risks, and solving problems, whereas daughters are encouraged to stay close to their parents and are praised for adult-oriented, help-seeking behaviours.[34] Thus parents communicate to their children that males hold the power to control situations, that males provide solutions to problems, and that aggression, anger, and vigorous physical activities are inappropriate to femininity.[35]

At the same time as youngsters are learning gender, they are also learning other basic lessons about how to survive and thrive in the world. The different gender styles of women and men communicate different lessons to children about the nature of the world at large. Children whose interactions with the world of adults are characterized by warmth, caring, and protection from external dangers will tend to develop more feminine personalities, whereas those whose experiences of the world of adults have been characterized by rough handling and a cool or distant caring, and who have been treated as responsible persons, will tend to become tough, independent, responsible, and more masculine people. The different experiences which sons and daughters have with their fathers are reflected in the ways in which they describe them. In one study, sons described their fathers as *aggressive, assertive, autocratic, confident, dominant, forceful, outspoken, strong, deliberate, enterprising, industrious,* and *shrewd.*

Daughters, by contrast, described their fathers as *forgiving, modest, praising, sensitive,* and *warm.* However, sons and daughters used similar sets of adjectives to describe their mothers, thus indicating that fathers may play a more decisive role in gender differentiated training of both boys and girls.[36]

As children mature and expand their social relations, their visions of their mothers' powers usually decrease because in patriarchal societies men are often dominant both inside families and in society at large. The credibility and desirability of mothers as role models thus is often diminished. In later childhood, fathers loom larger. Therefore fathers typically play a greater role in the development of gender in older, rather than younger, children. Starting in the second year of their sons' lives and increasingly as the years pass, fathers tend to spend more time with their sons and less time with their daughters.[37] The greater the amount of time which fathers spend with their sons, the greater the likelihood that their sons will use their fathers as gender models. The increased amount of time which fathers spend with their sons also increases the opportunities which fathers have for actively molding their sons' gender styles. Most often, fathers simultaneously make themselves less available to their daughters. This withdrawal of fatherly attentions, however, may intensify daughters' desires to please their fathers.[38] The significance of girls' fathers' responses to their gender displays may become further pronounced through the enhancement effects of intermittent reinforcement.[39] In the majority of situations, pleasing fathers requires of daughters that they exhibit conformity to feminine gender styles.[40] In some cases, daughters may find that they can get more attention from their fathers by acting like boys.[41]

Sibling Relations and Their Contributions to Gender Acquisition

Whether a person is an oldest, youngest, middle, or only child has been theorized both to have[42] and not to have[43] a great deal of meaning in family dynamics. The majority of research has focused on the patterns of oldest and youngest children. Middle children have been relatively little studied. Gender of children, when it has been taken into account in such research, has often been found to be an important factor modifying the apparent effects of birth order.

Oldest children pass the first years of their lives in a unique position. They live as only children until the birth of a second child, during which time they occupy a central role in their parents' lives. Parents who are learning how to parent with their first child have been found to be more anxious about their child-rearing skills and therefore more attentive to, and demanding of, their first child.[44] One result of this extra attention is that firstborn children have been found to have highly developed senses of what other people expect of them and a greater concern that they conform to those expectations.[45]

However, with the birth of a sibling, firstborn children often experience a rude "dethronement." In some children, the shock of no longer feeling like the most important person in the family can develop into a motivation to excel so as to regain the coveted attentions of parents. Dethronement anxieties might also translate into conservative desires to prevent change or a drive for power and authority.[46] Oldest children have also been found, more often than younger children, to have highly developed senses of responsibility and protectiveness toward others. That may be because it is common for oldest children to be called upon to partially assume the roles of surrogate parents to their younger siblings.[47]

Firstborn status does not always function in the same way for male and female children. Furthermore, in families which have only two children, one of whom is a boy and one of whom is a girl, gender may be an issue which overrides any birth order effects which may have otherwise been present.[48] In one study, firstborn children of both genders remembered their parents as having been stricter with them than did later children. Firstborn women, however, remembered that their fathers were stricter with them than were their mothers.[49]

Self-esteem and rational thinking have also been found to vary among both oldest and youngest children and on the basis of the gender of the siblings involved. In one study of young adults, firstborn sons earned the best ratings on a test of these qualities; youngest sons earned the worst scores. Girl children were ranked between these two extremes, with firstborn girls placing higher than youngest daughters.[50] Somewhat similar results were obtained in a study of dominance patterns. Oldest sons scored highest on a measure of dominance and youngest sons scored the lowest. Daughters again fell between these two extremes, although in this case youngest daughters showed more dominance than oldest daughters. Responsibility was found in this study to be a function of gender rather than birth order. Women were found to be more responsible regardless of their placement in their families.[51] Conversely, more men than women appear to have hard-driving, competitive, and work-oriented (type A) personalities. However, whereas birth order does not seem to matter among such men, it does appear to be a significant factor for women. Firstborn women have been found to be more likely to exhibit type A characteristics than later-born women. Perhaps in women such personalities reflect a gendered propensity for being more responsible combined with an oldest-child tendency toward achievement, whereas in men, gender socialization toward masculine competitiveness and dominance may be a more compelling explanation than birth order issues.[52]

Firstborn females in a patriarchal society nonetheless may have difficulties with the contradiction between their motivations for achievement and the prescriptions of femininity. In such cases, they may have problems with anxiety and self-esteem because of their heightened awareness of the demands of two sets of somewhat contradictory expectations and their inability to resolve them effectively within the confines of the dominant gender schema.[53]

Middle-born children have been characterized as nonconfrontational, noncompetitive, gregarious, and socially oriented. They are presumed to have these characteristics because their placements in their families encourage them to be peacemakers between older and younger children and because they have to work harder to gain attention than do oldest and youngest children.[54] Middle-born children of both genders have been found to be more often perceived by their siblings as popular and less often thought of as responsible.[55] They also appear to feel that they have received less parental support than other children in their families, possibly because parents have fewer resources available when they have larger numbers of children in their care.[56]

Youngest children have been described as carefree and affectionate as a result of being pampered and spoiled.[57] They are raised by parents who are at the end of their parenting careers, when they have more free time and more child-rearing experience, and who are more able to take the time to enjoy their last child.[58] Youngest children are said to make use of tactics of persuasion typical of weaker members of society. They are more likely than earlier-born children to pout, sulk, plead, cry, or appeal to higher authorities when they want something which is not immediately available to them.[59] Youngest females also have been found to differ both from older females and from youngest males in terms of their levels of dominance, self-esteem, and rational thought. Youngest sisters have been found to be more dominant, to be more rational, and to have higher self-esteem than youngest brothers.[60] These differences may be explainable in terms of the different patriarchal social expectations of men and women. Being the spoiled and pampered baby of a family is more incongruous with expectations of manliness than it is with stereotypical femininity. It may therefore be harder for youngest boys than for youngest girls to feel that they have adequately fulfilled the requirements of their gender.

Only children have been described as "super-firstborns" in terms of the kind of attention which they receive from their parents. They continue throughout their lives to be the sole recipients of their parents' full, uninterrupted, and anxious child rearing attentions. They also receive larger shares of familial financial and emotional resources than are available to any one child in larger families. One result of parental attentions is that they are thought to internalize their parents' values and expectations even more thoroughly than firstborn children and thus to exhibit patterns similar to, albeit even more pronounced than, those of oldest children. Only children have, indeed, been found to outperform all others on measures of educational and occupational achievement, on tests of creative thinking, and on standardized intelligence tests.[61]

In families with more than one child, older children often become role models for their younger siblings.[62] Sometimes when younger children imitate their older siblings they do so because they want to learn to be more grown up. At other times, imitation can be an expression of competition, with a younger child trying to outdo the performance of an older sibling. This type of competitive interaction is especially characteristic of younger brothers' attitudes toward older brothers who are relatively close to them in age. When there is a small age gap between siblings, there is a tendency for conflicts and rivalries to be exaggerated, especially between masculine children. Furthermore, parents may contribute to sibling rivalries by treating children differently when children are of different sexes as well as ages. When there is a larger age gap between children in a family there is less likelihood that they will compete with one another. When brothers in particular are more than four years apart in age there is a tendency for them to attribute their status differences to their age differences rather than their abilities. In such circumstances, older siblings will often take on a teaching or parental role toward younger siblings.[63] Older children may be pleased by the admiration of their younger siblings or enjoy their dominant role in their mutual activities—opportunities which may not be available to them among their age mates.[64]

When siblings spend a sizable proportion of their time in one another's company, the nature of their relationships can play a major role in shaping the quality of their upbringing. Sibling rivalries and coalitions can result in emotionally intense and intimate relationships which may or may not be correlated with the amount of fighting between siblings. In particular, later-born siblings appear to feel the influence of their older brothers and sisters more profoundly than do earlier-born siblings.[65] Siblings can thus contribute significantly to the personalities of their sisters and brothers.

Loss of a parent or parents through divorce, separation, or death can affect siblings in a variety of ways as they attempt to compensate for their losses.[66] In one study, sons in families separated by divorce were found to have higher self-esteem than either their own sisters or children in intact or divorced and remarried families. The same study also found that sons and daughters in divorced families harbored different feelings about their fathers. Sons were significantly more negative in their evaluations of their fathers than were daughters. By contrast, sons in families where there had been a remarriage were more positive in their evaluations of their fathers than were their sisters. Mothers were evaluated most harshly by young people of both genders in families where remarriages had taken place.[67] In light of the fact that the majority of children of divorces reside with their mothers,[68] these results might be interpreted as follows: Sons who become cast as surrogate fathers in their otherwise fatherless families may come to have more positive feelings about themselves because of their increased masculine responsibilities while, at the same time, harboring negative feelings toward their absent fathers for forcing them to grow up faster. Daughters, on the other hand, might feel more charitable toward their fathers because their departure might allow for the possibility of more undivided attention from their mothers. In families where a parent has remarried, sons feel more charitable towards their fathers because they once again have an adult male in the home to shoulder more of the masculine familial responsibilities. Daughters, on the other hand, might evaluate their fathers more negatively than their brothers, perhaps because they might see a new parent as an unwelcome interloper whose presence was occasioned by the departure of the birth father.

The introduction of step- and half-siblings into families rearranged through death, divorce, or separation can significantly change sibling relationships by altering age-graded hierarchies or otherwise disrupting hard-won power balances among siblings. Siblings who remain with their birth parents may take up the role of "landlords" and cast stepsiblings as having entered the family as "invaders." They may thereby resist losing their places in the hierarchy of their birth family if they perceive such an alteration to involve a loss of power. In some cases, step- or half-siblings may welcome the changes wrought by blended families because new siblings may relieve them of unwanted responsibility, may provide them with desired protectors and positive or negative role models or because it may prove to be easier to use step- or half-siblings as targets of strong emotions of love and hate.[69]

Thus it is important to bear in mind the immense influence which siblings can bring to bear on one another during the years that they live together. Siblings can be both friends and rivals. They can provide role models or practice grounds for more mature actions. They can offer comfort or create calamity. Furthermore, the number, order, genders, and timing of arrivals and departures of siblings can mark major transitions in the lives of children. Surely their contributions to one another's young lives can vary from minimal to monumental and can rival those of many parents.

Summary

Gender is a basic building block of social interaction. Knowing whether other persons are men or women, boys or girls, enables members of society to know how to behave appropriately in their social exchanges. Therefore one of the major lessons of childhood consists of learning how to recognize and enact gender according to the customs of one's society. Children learn such skills primarily from those people with whom they have greatest contacts. Thus children's foundational lessons about gender come from their observations of and the pronouncements made by their parents and siblings. From them they learn that men and masculinity are more highly valued than women and femininity. They further learn that masculine persons are supposed to be dominant, competent, forceful, competitive, and protective of what is theirs. They learn that women are supposed to be peacemakers and community builders who work through mutuality and cooperation. Through trial and error children learn from those around them how to fit themselves into this dominant gender schema as best they can.

4 | Family Scenes

THE RELATIONSHIPS THAT people have with other persons in their families during childhood are central in shaping who they are to become later in life. In this part, I discuss participants' gender learning experiences in their families up to the beginning of their teen years.[1] In doing so, I have chosen to take participants' recollections about their families as "factual." I have made no concerted effort to sort out the ways in which participants' memories have played tricks on them. What I had available to me to use as data were the stories which people told to me, as they remembered them. On the one hand, I had no reason to believe that anyone purposely fabricated stories to tell to me. On the other hand, I had every reason to believe that things did not occur exactly as they were told to me. No one has perfect recall; the years and events which passed between the original experiences and their retelling no doubt caused any number of details to twist and turn in the winds of time. However, unless I had the feeling that someone was deliberately embellishing for my benefit (I never had the feeling that anyone knowingly lied to me), I accepted the information presented to me as fact. I have proceeded in this fashion because, as W. I. Thomas pointed out, "If men [sic] define situations as real, they are real in their consequences."[2]

Who Were in Participants' Families

The individuals who are present in the early years of people's lives can play major roles in the formation of their personalities, attitudes, and beliefs. Mothers and fathers are, of course, usually the major players. Siblings, especially older brothers and sisters, can also be highly influential, as can aunts, uncles, grandparents, cousins, and family friends who, for one reason or another, supplement or supplant the centrality of parents' parenting. For these reasons, it is important to have a picture of the size and composition of the families in which participants grew up.

The number of children in participants' families ranged from those where Roger, Larry, and Grant were only children to Simon's family, in which Simon was the oldest of eleven children from three different combinations of parents and step-parents. The average number of children per family was 3.4.[3] Seventeen participants (39 percent) came from larger families of four or more children.[4]

Most parents, especially fathers, want at least one boy and one girl child and would prefer that their oldest child be a boy.[5] When a couple produces only girls, they are more likely to keep having children in the hope that they will have a boy the next time. When they have one boy and one girl, they are more likely to cease having children. Hence all-girl families tend to be larger families.[6] Participants' families tended to reflect these patterns. Eleven participants (25 percent) came from families where all the other children were girls,[7] seven of them being families with three or more children.[8] Ten (23 percent) came from families where all the other children were boys,[9] all but one of those ten being two-child families.[10]

The birth order distribution of participants in their families was roughly as might be expected in families averaging 3.4 children per family. Fourteen participants (32 percent) were the oldest children in their families.[11] Eleven (25 percent) were the youngest in their families.[12] Sixteen participants (36 percent) were middle children.[13] Roger and Larry were only children, as was Grant in her adopted family.

Separations, divorces, remarriages, and adoptions changed the size of the families of eight participants (18 percent) during their early years.[14] Parents, participants, and siblings came and went from their residences as a result of these alterations. As a consequence of such changes—and of two which occurred prior to Robin's and Fred's births—Simon, Bruce, Robin, Fred, and Hal came to live with half- or stepsiblings. Roger and Hal were adopted at birth and Grant was adopted at age five. Simon and Eli both lost siblings who moved away when their families were divided by divorce. Simon and Grant lost siblings to both adoption and death. Thus the composition of the families of ten participants (23 percent) were altered during their childhoods by divorces, separations, or adoptions. In addition, Keith's and Fred's older brothers moved out of their families' homes while Keith and Fred were still youngsters, and Harry's youngest sister was sent away when Harry was five years old. Although such shifts in family composition are not uncommon,[15] they may significantly alter family dynamics in families who experience them.

Unusual childhood illnesses may also influence how children are brought up in their families. Parents or siblings may treat participants with special care, thereby setting them apart from other family members and possibly from their peers. Thirteen participants (29.5 percent) experienced a major illness during their youth.[16] The problems which participants reported included extensive allergies, ongoing bladder problems, mild spina bifida, heart disease, asthma, a rare joint disease, hypothyroidism, scoliosis, polycystic ovarian disease, teratomatous cysts, diabetes, rheumatic fever, chronic ear and jaw problems, and scarlet fever. In addition, Simon and Grant suffered injuries from child abuse that were severe enough to require extensive medical attention.

In some cases, parents were absent or incapacitated for some portion of participants' childhoods. In such instances, participants either simply did without attention which they might otherwise have received or another family member had to fill the gap. Roger's mother suffered heart attacks. Darren's, Stan's, Alan's, and Dennis's mothers suffered from debilitating mental difficulties. Morgan's, Scott's, Brian's, and Grant's mothers were regularly impaired by misuse of alcohol or prescription medications. Simon's stepfather lied to her that her mother was dead, a lie which Simon believed from age six to twelve. Eleven fathers (25 percent) were alcoholic during participants' younger years.[17] Terry's and Bob's fathers were grievously injured in accidents; Roger's father died of cancer.

In total, ten participants' mothers (23 percent)[18] and thirteen participants' fathers (30 percent)[19] were unavailable to them during some or all of their childhoods due to physical or mental incapacity.[20] Thus in nineteen participants' families (44 percent), one or both parents were physically or mentally inaccessible to participants for some or all of their childhoods. Only four of these nineteen families were among those where participants lost one or more parent through separation, divorce, or adoption.[21] Combining these two sources of family disruption yields a total of twenty-three participants (52 percent) having suffered the loss of at least one parent to serious illness, incapacity, death, separation, divorce, or adoption before they had reached eleven years of age.[22]

It was not unusual for participants to be living with extended families. Sometimes such other family members took up some of the child rearing tasks to which absent or incapacitated parents were unable to fully attend. Twelve participants (27 percent) lived with other relatives during their childhood years,[23] either in their own residences or at the homes of their relatives, for a period of several years or more. All extended families except Roger's and Bob's included one or more grandparents; aunts or uncles, and the occasional cousin, accounted for the rest. In ten additional cases,[24] participants' relatives lived nearby and had frequent contact with them during their childhoods. The early lives of nine participants (20.5 percent) were marked by the loss of some of these significant relationships. The grandmothers of five participants died; all of them except Robin's grandmother had lived with participants' families.[25]

Eight participants (18 percent) or their families made changes of residence which participants felt as disruptive during their childhoods. They lost friendship circles and had to adjust to new social networks. Simon and

Bruce moved several times between the homes of divorced parents. Peter and Mel moved with their families to new areas which were different enough from where they had been living that they never felt adequately integrated into their new social scenes. Another four participants' families moved numerous times during their childhood years. Aaron and Eli simply said that they had moved "a lot"; Sam's family moved more than six times, and Ed's family moved seventeen times.

The overall pattern which emerges from these data is one which highlights potentially traumatic family disruptions and losses. Many participants' families were disrupted by physical or mental incapacity, by the death of close family members, or by displacement due to separation, divorce, or adoption. In addition, several participants felt that their childhoods were upset by changes of residence. In total, twenty-nine participants (66 percent) suffered from such losses or disruptions at some time during their early years.[26]

5 | Who Would Want to Be a Girl?

The Women (and Girls) in Participants' Families

Relationships with Mothers

PARTICIPANTS REMEMBERED HAVING a mélange of feelings about their mothers while they were growing up. When thinking about the comments which participants made about their mothers, it is important to keep in mind a few things about the context in which these mother-child relationships developed. Firstly, many of the homes in which these participants were raised were marked by marital discord. Twenty-one participants (49 percent)[1] recalled that their parents fought regularly during their childhoods.[2] In addition, although Eli, Bruce, Stan, and Phil did not specifically mention that their parents fought, their parents did divorce during their childhoods. It would seem safe to assume that there was also significant strife in the ambiances of those homes as well. If they are also included, then twenty-five families (58 percent) could be characterized as having suffered from marital discord. More often than not, participants remembered this discord in the form of their fathers emotionally belittling or physically abusing their mothers. Witnessing such events may well have affected participants' feelings not only about their mothers and fathers but also about the nature and possibilities for themselves as women in relationships with men.

Secondly, one of the major roles of mothers during their daughters' younger years is to teach them how to be girls and women in their society. However, many of the individuals who participated in this study felt their gender dysphoria from a very young age. One result of those feelings was that they were often in conflict with their mothers about issues such as household chores, deportment and clothing, play activities, and relationships with friends and family. Such continual power struggles certainly had the potential to taint even the most promising of relationships.

Finally, participants' relationships with their mothers were no doubt also coloured by their experiences with child abuse. It is a common reaction among abused children to be angry not only with those who abused them but also with those who were present but unable to protect them.[3]

In seven cases (16 percent), participants were physically abused by their mothers.[4] Sixteen participants (37 percent) were sexually or physically abused by their fathers or older brothers during their childhood years,[5] three of whom had also been abused by their mothers.[6] An additional seven participants (16 percent) told of having been sexually abused by older males who were not immediate family members.[7] In total, twenty-six participants (60.5 percent) had experienced either physical or sexual abuse before their teenage years. Even in those cases where participants' mothers were not perpetrators of abuse, participants' experiences of abuse may have had deleterious effects on their relationships with their mothers.

Taking Care of Mother: Mothers in Need of Protection

It is difficult for young girls to see their mothers as role models when those women appear to be weak, delicate, downtrodden, or otherwise in need of protection. Such views of their mothers led some participants to reject their mothers and women in general as role models. Others, rising to rather than retreating from the occasion, felt responsible for their mothers or attempted to become their mothers' protectors. More often than not, participants reacted in a combination of these ways.

Fifteen participants (35 percent) described their mothers in terms which implied that they were people in need of special care and attention.[8] In some cases, participants felt close to their mothers, of whom they felt protective; in others, they were angry or resentful about being prematurely forced to shoulder adult responsibilities. For instance, Walter described his relationship with his mother during his early years as so close that it was "absolutely symbiotic" despite the fact that, as a girl, she was largely raised by housekeepers and was in nursery school by the age of two.[9] When I asked him about some of the circumstances surrounding her feelings, he told me:

> I knew that, well, my mother was older because I was kind of a late-in-life baby. . . . And so like I knew she wasn't going to be around that long and I just wanted to spend every minute that I could with her. She was a saint. My mother was the most incredible person in the world. I know everyone says their mother was a saint, but mine really was.

Peter similarly said that, as a child, she thought of her mother as "a princess," as "somebody you took care of"; but when I asked Peter if he felt that he was in any way like his mother, he replied, "I hope not," and said that he had not been close to his mother when he was a young girl. His comment would appear to indicate that Peter had not identified with her mother as a role model when she was growing up.

Stan also felt responsible for her mother as a child, but for quite a different set of reasons. Stan's mother suffered from a severe mental illness for which she received drugs and shock treatments. Stan said that, as a child, she had "hated" her mother. He described her mother as "a zombie" and said, "she was like a nothing. In my mind she was not a person." Stan grew up being cared for by her grandparents, for whom she felt no love. Her grandparents taught her to hate and to fear her mother. By the age of four, she had begun to feel responsible for her mother's condition and everything else bad in the world. Stan described the situation in these words:

> When I was born I kept hearing stories of [how] I got to come home from the hospital before Mom did. And I think I might be responsible for that. I caused that. I probably didn't but, boy, you hear that stuff and yeah I wigged Mom out. I was the firstborn kid. . . . I had the responsibility of the world on my shoulders. And I don't know where that came from but I did take responsibility for far more stuff than I had any business doing. I was responsible for the divorce, and that Mom and Dad couldn't get along. That Mom was weirdest. . . . Yeah, I remember feeling really responsible for things and growing up . . . really quick. The worst part was not being comfortable at home with my mom like everybody else was. I felt a real longing for that. That everybody else had moms that would hug them and do little things for them and were moms. You know the classic mom. My mom was somebody to be afraid of. . . . and the older I got, the more I resented her, and the more I hated her.

Several participants felt protective of their mothers because they saw their mothers as unable to adequately protect themselves, or their children, from their abusive husbands. Bill spoke about the beatings which her father inflicted upon the family. As a girl, she worried that her father would kill her mother. Bill described his mother as "passive" and said, "She lets people use her and walk all over her." She had not felt close to her mother when she had been a girl and had not seen her mother as a positive role model.

Alan similarly talked about how, as a young girl, she had felt extremely protective of a mother whom she didn't like very much. This young girl felt compelled to "become a husband" to her mother because of a complicated set of circumstances which left her mother "wrapped up in her religion" and unable to cope with the rigors of life with a violent and alcoholic husband. Alan described the situation in her childhood home thus:

> I became more and more attached to my grandmother as my mother became more depressed and hopeless from my father's progressing alcoholism. I had to be strong for my mother, [but] I could be nurtured by my grandmother. . . . [My mother and I] became even closer. She started

to depend upon me more as my father's drinking got worse. I started to counsel her and reassure her that things would be better. . . . We drew even closer after the downstairs renter got drunk, fell asleep with a cigarette in his hand, and burned the house down. I was five.

My father started drinking very heavily after this happened and my mother would constantly come to me for advice about leaving him. I learned not to tell my mother my troubles as she didn't have time to listen. My parents also asked my grandmother to leave the household because the house was being rebuilt. With my grandmother absent, my father drunk, and my mother depressed and helpless, I learned to grow up fast. Then, when my mother's sister died of alcoholism and my mother informally adopted my three cousins, I stopped being a child at all. I was nine. . . . I got strong. I became a husband for my mother. . . . What I remember about childhood is NOT FITTING IN ANY-WHERE AND BEING ON CALL FOR MY MOTHER IN CASE SHE, ONCE AGAIN, DECIDED TO PACK UP AND LEAVE MY FATHER. I did not get much sleep as a child and my mother cried a lot about my father and encouraged me to "grow up" and deny my real feelings. In between all this, my father would be violent in blackouts and my mother would tell me that nothing had happened. By age nine . . . my mother considered me totally grown up. She didn't have time for me. What I remember as a child is not feeling like a child. I was worried and concerned about my mother and I wanted to marry her and take her away from all her troubles. (Emphasis in written original.)

Clearly, this child was forced into a "very close" relationship with her mother. Just as clearly, the relationship demanded that the girl place herself firmly in a masculine role. However, because of the pain and danger which she associated with her father, she did not have an easy relationship with the masculinity that her family circumstances demanded of her. Alan recounted the feelings she felt as a girl at the time: "I did not want to grow up to be a man. I wanted to stay as far away from men (aggressors) as possible. I wanted to be a man for my mother but I did not want to be in the presence of men." Alan grew up to be an adult with an unsteady gender identity who moved in and out of living as a man.

Other participants were less explicitly drawn into the power struggles between their parents. However, many of them felt compelled to take sides anyway. As might be expected in such circumstances, their allegiances were often divided. They saw their mothers as innocent victims in these domestic battles; but, being themselves female at the time, this put them in a difficult position. If they identified with their mothers, they were aligning themselves with persons who appeared relatively powerless and victimized. If they took their fathers' sides, they were validating the abuse of their mothers and, by extension, of the women whom they themselves might grow up to become. One solution to this dilemma was to take on the role of masculine protectors of their mothers. They could thereby avoid identifying with the vulnerability which they saw in their mothers' positions, and with the destructive violence in which they saw their fathers indulging while still being able to see themselves as doing something about the erosion of their familial peace and cohesion.

Mel, who remembered her mother as "the perfect mom," recalled that as a girl child of seven or eight she observed her father begin to drink heavily and become distant and emotionally demeaning to her mother:

> She got used and abused. Mentally abused. They never showed any affection towards each other and every time my mom would try my dad would tell her to get away. . . . But my mom was a very affectionate person, a kind of touchy kind of person, and my dad was just "shhooo, stay away." . . . He would be real negative to my mom. He would be real sarcastic to my mom in front of other people. . . . Insulting is putting it VERY mildly. . . . She always took it. She very seldom spoke back to him. He never hit her. She tried real hard. . . . I knew that if I said anything to her she would say, "Well that's just your father."

Mel said that although as a girl she had felt protective of her mother, she had not been close with her. She had been closer to her alcoholic father despite her mother's "perfection" as a mother. Apparently she chose to side with the man who seemed to control the household.

Dennis's memories were of a violent home. He talked about remembering her father being "like an animal out of control" when he beat her mother. Starting at the age of seven, Dennis began to feel responsible for helping her mother with her depressions. He told this story about that time:

> She always had big problems with depressions. After I was born it all started. And my father didn't want to recognize it, he didn't take care of her the way he should have. And so . . . I was the one she came to and talked to. Nobody would listen. Her family started giving her problems. . . . I listened and it took everything I had out of me. It took every ounce I had to have the strength to hear the same thing over and over. And it was desperate pleas for help. I didn't know—today I wouldn't even know what to do, let alone at seven and eight. I'd sit there and listen. That's all I would do. . . . In a way, it made me feel strong. Because I saw myself as the only one really doing that for her. Not that that was my reason. . . . But it gave me a sense of strength.

These themes continued to resonate in Dennis's life. When I met him, he, at age twenty-seven, was still living at home with his mother.

It was not clear to some participants whether their mothers had been innocent victims of circumstances beyond their control. For example, Harry, who had been sickly as a girl and was "considered my mom's suck," said that she went through the full range of emotions about her mother. Harry described how her feelings changed:

> One of my earliest memories is (I don't know how young I was): My mother was a very abusive person, but I was very close to her, and didn't relate to the abusiveness. Still saw her as a very wonderful person. I remember her taking one of my sisters, and literally throwing her over the chair, and at that point, something in my head snapped, and said this isn't right. There's no way I can still say this is a wonderful woman, and see that. And at some point I went from complete overwhelming love, unquestioning love, to overwhelming hate for my mother.

Another story told by Harry illustrated how complex a child's place in her family can become. This child was severely physically and emotionally abused by her mother, who in turn was emotionally and physically abused by her husband. The child was both "terrified" of, and fiercely protective of, her mother, while at the same time thinking of her father as an "angel."

> She used to make me sleep with her, which I didn't like doing. . . . I remember waking up in the middle of the night, and she was pushing the dresser up against the bedroom door, and screaming. And there was a knife coming in through the door, and it was my father. And I ran out of bed, and I pushed my back up against the dresser, and my feet up against the wall. I remember crying "Mommy, I won't let him in. He won't get in." But even now when I think of it, I still don't hate my father. It was like that was somebody else. It wasn't my father.
>   I'm told I came up against my father a lot like that—even very small. My mom said I was about three when her and my dad were having a fight once, and I walked up to him with a butcher knife, and said "Leave my mother alone." But my dad—he's so neat . . . he just looked at me and said, "Oh, for christ's sake, give me that knife." Even in the heat of anger. . . . So, I think because of my mom, the way she was, it made my dad seem more of an angel.
>   . . . . In the early years, yes, [I felt that I had to] protect her, yeah. Her and the rest of my sisters. I very much felt the burden was mine.

Tony remembered his mother as being entirely justified in her anger: "We spent most of our lives with my mother screaming and yelling at my father, and rightfully so." Nonetheless, although Tony felt that her mother was "probably the best person in the world" and "a great lady," her emotionality left Tony feeling very protective of, but not close to, her mother. He said of this time:

> She would be off to work. I used to worry about her terribly. I think back now there were times when I didn't sleep until she came home. . . . I don't know why. . . . but I just feared that something would happen, I

think when I was in grade school. And as I got older, the more I was afraid for her.

In sum, fourteen of the fifteen people who said that they had felt responsible for, or protective of, their mothers came from families where their parents fought regularly.[10] In particular, nine participants mentioned that fathers were violent or emotionally abusive toward their wives.[11] It seems likely that seeing their mothers so dramatically abused might have spurred on participants still further in their sense of responsibility for the protection of their mothers. As well, Stan's and Dennis's mothers, who also suffered from mental illness, must have seemed particularly vulnerable and in need of special care. In many of these cases, perhaps the participants were also motivated to come to their mothers' rescue because their fathers' alcoholism[12] or otherwise motivated absence from the family home[13] may have made it seem as though they had abdicated the masculine role as guardian of those who are vulnerable.

Missing Mothers: Lack of Affection from Mothers

Children have a right to expect love and affection from their parents. Unfortunately, there were many reasons why participants did not receive the amount of parental warmth which they desired. Peter's and Tony's mothers were often away from home at paid employment; Simon and Eli became separated from their mothers after divorces; Bob was sent away to live with an aunt and uncle; Roger was sent away to boarding school. Eight mothers were unable to provide affection because they were sick, withdrawn, or depressed.[14] In total, fourteen participants (33 percent) said that they felt that their mothers had been unable to offer them sufficient warmth and affection.

In addition to these reasons, ten participants (23 percent) specifically said that they felt that their mothers had favoured other children over themselves.[15] In eight of these ten cases, participants were disturbed by what they perceived as unfair advantages given to their brothers.[16] For example, Bruce, who as a child hated her mother, voiced this poignant complaint about favoritism:

> She sided with my brother. He was the only boy and he got his way about everything he did. It was okay for [him] not to share, but I had to share. It was okay for [him] not to do his chores, but I had to do my chores. It was okay for [him] to sit in the front seat of the car, but I had to sit in the back seat of the car. He always came sort of number one. . . . I thought why is he better than me? What's the difference?

Only Sam and Dale felt that their sisters had received special attention from their mothers and that they themselves had been neglected. Dale came from a family of six children. He had one younger brother and one older and three younger sisters. He said, "as far back as I can remember, I felt that they didn't want me . . . that my parents didn't love me." Dale reported that these feelings intensified when a younger sister was born. At that time, Dale started to do physical damage to herself as a way to try to muster some attention from her mother:

> I just looked at my mother, I think, a lot of times wishing she'd give me the love that maybe she showed to some of the others in the family. . . . I just withdrew. I can remember cutting myself on purpose so that I would get attention. I was desperate for attention. . . . Nobody went out of their way to really hurt me, but nobody made me feel accepted. Neither my mother nor my father. . . . I used to hurt myself a lot. Cut myself or . . . Bump myself, pound myself—I didn't do anything serious where I had any serious injuries, but yeah, I used to hurt myself a lot— hit myself. Give myself a bleeding nose. I took my anger out on myself. . . . I never did it in school for attention. I only did it at home for attention. . . . I was hoping they'd notice that I had a little bit of blood on me or something, just so somebody—my mom, I guess—would come and feel sorry for me or something. But she didn't notice.

Although this kind of acting out of feeling unloved was extreme, such feelings of being unseen, especially by mothers, were not at all unusual in this group. Only Steven, of all forty-five participants, felt that she had been her mother's favorite child.

Eight participants (19 percent) also recalled that their mothers had been emotionally icy or simply had not been affectionate with them when they were young girls.[17] Of the eight, only Morgan and Sam were also among those who reported that their mothers had favoured other children over themselves. None of them remembered their relationships with their mothers as ever having been close during their childhoods. Morgan, whose mother had suffered from a nervous breakdown, recalled that her mother was known among the local children as "the witch" because she was so "nasty." Morgan said that she "was like a sofa, with about as much personality," and remembered her as having said that "these parents who hug their children make me sick." Sam, who remembered her relationship with her mother as "painful" when he was a young girl, made these representative comments:

> I know she never held me. The only time I remember sitting on her lap was the day her mother died. I was six when my grandmother died, and I cried that day, and my mother was crying, and she held me in her lap. That's the only time I remember her hugging me, or really being close, or holding me, or anything.

Seven participants (16 percent) recounted episodes of their mothers physically abusing them while they were still in their childhood years,[18] most of whom were also among those who recalled that their mothers had favoured other children over themselves. As would be expected, none of these participants felt close with, or thought very highly of, their mothers. In fact, they tended to feel either fearful or very angry with their mothers. They used words like "terrified," "scared," and "afraid" to describe their sentiments about their mothers. Ron and Bob went so far as to say that they had wished their mothers dead. The abuse that prompted such feelings was generally quite severe. For example, Darren remembered:

> She'd get physically abusive sometimes. I used to get the brunt of it. . . . Pulling on the hair, pull up, you know, lifting off the ground. . . . Mostly at a very younger age. Not very frequently. Uhh, verbal swearing and other language. One time she grabbed me when I was eight or nine, on the neck here, and started to choke me, like. But let go, obviously, like I wasn't gasping for air, but there was marks and bruises, and I had to wear a brace.

Several other participants also told stories of serious physical abuse. Ron said that when he had been a child, she and her brother and sister "never wore anything like short pants or short sleeves because we always had this cable pattern in different places" from the daily beatings which they received from their mother with loops of electrical cable or garden hose. Bob reported that when he was a girl, her mother had often beaten her to the point where the woman would "collapse on the floor in a heap of exhaustion" from her efforts. Grant, who described her relationship with her mother when he had been a girl as a love/hate one, recalled one incident where her mother had beaten her so badly in the face that she had to have the lower half of her face surgically reconstructed and another in which she was scarred by an intentionally inflicted cigarette burn.

Several participants also spoke of the emotional abuse that accompanied such chronic physical abuse. For example, Harry told a story about her mother being both violent and emotionally sadistic with her children:

> She used to play this game where, if she was mad at us for whatever reason, she was going to send us to an orphanage—the three of us. And she would go into a big dramatic shpiel about it—how we'd be separated, and we'd never find each other again, and we'd never see each other again, blah, blah, blah. And then she'd put her hand down on the phone, and pretend to call the cab company. "Now you get out on the porch, and you wait for the cab to come," etc. So, we'd be out on the porch, crying, and making promises to each other that we'd try to find each other no matter what. Then she'd call us, and we'd come back in, and it was time to beg. We'd get down on our hands and knees, and

cry and carry on. She may say "yes," or she may say "no, it's not good enough," and send us back out on the porch, and on and on until she was appeased at some point.

Not surprisingly, Harry spent her youth being "terrified" of her mother.

In sum, twenty-four people (56 percent) reported that they had been denied the affection they had wanted from their mothers during their childhood years.[19] In some cases, the reasons had to do with maternal absences, ill health, or preferences for other children. More than one-third of these people who felt unloved simply felt that their mothers had never been warm with them. In seven cases, that lack of affection went far beyond neglect into the realm of physical violence.

Mothers Want Daughters: Battles over Gender

Many participants were eager for masculine friends, activities, and clothing from a young age. In more than one-quarter of their families, these interests were shrugged off as harmless tomboyism and indulged much of the time. Most commonly, as youngsters, participants were expected to look and behave like little girls at school, at worship, and on special "dress up" occasions. The rest of the time, mostly they were allowed to do as they pleased. In a few cases, parents seemed to actively encourage masculinity in their daughters, whereas a small number of parents were exceptionally disturbed by their daughters' masculine tendencies and made concerted efforts to eradicate them. However, few participants were exempt from some level of conflict with their parents over their gender styles. It seems likely that these conflicts, and the hostilities which they engendered, must have contributed to the dim outlook which many participants felt toward femininity as a viable option for themselves. Most frequently such conflicts were with mothers.

Sixteen participants (37 percent) described their childhood attitudes toward a girlish appearance in strongly negative terms.[20] For example, Dennis called it a "torment," and others made comments along the lines of "It was just a total nightmare," "It was a killer. I hated it. It was disgusting," "It was like puke." Jack said that, as a child, she had "felt like a moose in a cow barn." Tony described what happened whenever an occasion required a dress: "I would yell, and they would yell. I would cry, and they would yell. And it didn't matter. I never won. I always had to put on the dress."

Only Ken and Eli were fairly moderate in their reactions to their mothers' pressures on them to dress and act femininely. They simply accepted that those were the rules. They knew they were female and, at that point in their lives, assumed that there was nothing much that could be done about it. Consequently, they begrudgingly accepted their fate. Ken summed it up nicely:

> Girls were girls and that's the way it was. It didn't matter whether you liked that dress or not. It was one of those things. There were no ifs, ands, or buts. It was just like black is black and white is white. . . . I didn't tell others about my feeling then. It's really irrelevant at that age. You really don't know what's going on in your life.

Several participants specifically said that they had learned from observing their mothers and other elder females in their families that being a woman or a "lady" was not what they wanted to be. Instead, they were eager to learn the ways of men. Ron, whose mother had been extremely physically abusive, said this most succinctly: "when I'm looking back, in ways I'm still grateful, you know, for her having been a role model like that, showing me a lot of things that I don't want to happen in my own life."

Brian also expressed similar sentiments. Very early in life, she began to learn to regard femininity as off-limits to her. Brian told this story about an incident which stood out in his mind as symbolic of her girlhood relationship, both with her parents and with femininity. Brian recalled that although she was supposed to be a girl, she was punished for taking an interest in feminine accoutrements:

> I was probably not yet three. . . . My mother was using make-up and jewelry and I was watching her. I became very curious of these objects. . . . I had to take a nap. My mother put me in crib. When things were quiet, I got out of crib and went to mother's dresser. I was able to reach some of the cosmetics and small objects and gathered up fistfuls. I put these in my crib, under the pillow, and climbed back in. I was looking at one of these bright objects when I heard my mother coming. . . . I hid the object and was scared of her. She noticed something and discovered what I had under the pillow. She was very loud and angry and called me "thief" and called for my father. He was very loud and angry and said I could not be trusted and he would make sure I stayed in the crib. He got a long rope and tied me in the crib. They left and I was afraid to move for a long time. I can always remember that rope very vividly. After a while I inspected the rope and realized that I could wiggle loose from it—it was wrapped across my body many times, around the mattress. I was afraid that if I crawled loose they would punish me again.

Brian further described her mother as "a distant person to be avoided" who personified all that later became repulsive to her about femininity:

I was not permitted to do certain things "because girls don't do those things," or it's "not lady-like." I learned at a very early age to despise girls and girl things as much as adults seemed to. . . . Life made no sense at all to me. I always heard grown men constantly criticizing women for being weak, stupid, helpless, "damned" this and that, yacking too much, always complaining. Women and girls were "useless." . . . I think [my mother] justified her helplessness and self-pity as being "lady-like." She was always demanding that my sister and I act "like ladies." I truly and deeply despised that word. A "lady" is a weak, helpless, and worthless creature.

Consequently, Brian never felt much incentive to adopt feminine ways as her own and took whatever opportunities she could to acquire masculine ones.

Fourteen participants (33 percent) were allowed to indulge their masculine predilections within limits or were actively encouraged in their masculinity by their mothers.[21] These participants held generally positive attitudes toward their mothers,[22] except in those cases where their mothers were cold to them, beat them, or raged at them on a regular basis.[23] Aaron's recollection of her mother's attitude toward masculinity in girls was fairly typical of several others:

My mother knew that what she called a tomboy was what I preferred. She knew I preferred boy's clothes, but she also was very realistic and knew what had to be to survive in the world. I mean you had to wear a dress and act like a lady to go to church, to go to school, to go to a restaurant. So that's what was required. . . . It was okay for me to be a little boy at the summer place. I swam in a boy's bathing suit 'til I was fourteen, helped build a summer place, built tree houses and all this and there was no conflict with the family. When company came, I had to conform.

Aaron also recalled, "when I was a child, the word lady was never used alone when spoken to a little girl. It was 'ladies don't.' You see ladies were people who didn't cross their legs. Ladies don't bite their nails. Ladies didn't swear. . . . Women were people who did." The girl who learned these lessons grew up to be a woman (but *never* a lady) who married and had four children before deciding to make a transsexual transition in her late 40s. She, at least, learned that there was an acceptable feminine role option called "woman." Not surprisingly, Aaron had quite a positive attitude toward his mother, and said that she had been "an excellent mother."

Eli was similarly allowed to indulge in a masculine presentation often enough that she was willing to permit her parents also to make her pretty from time to time. Eli said that her mother had been "the perfect mom" and recounted this story about their relationship:

[My mom] bought me what I wanted. I always wanted boys' clothes from the boys' department. . . . they fit me absolutely perfectly. . . . She and my dad just let me be. Then I'd dress up in pretty little girls' clothes and do my hair. . . . That was ok because I could have my way. I could enjoy that because it pleased them and I loved them. So I did that . . . But my preference was boys' clothes when it was my choice.

A few participants felt that their parents had been tacitly encouraging them in their masculinity since they had been very young girls. The recollections of Walter, who had referred to his mother as "a saint," were typical of those who felt this way:

As soon as I was old enough to talk I was telling people that I should have been a boy. That this was a mistake, that God made a mistake. . . . basically, [my parents] humored me. They humored me to the degree where I felt that they probably also felt that God did make a mistake. . . . That's one thing about my parents, they did almost, I really am hesitant to say this, but they almost encouraged my crossdressing. . . . It was really like they accepted it . . . and so on the surface it would appear that they were encouraging it, but they really weren't. They just weren't discouraging it. But they treated me like a normal boy.

Similarly, Bob said that when she was a girl, she and her mother had at first fought about her lack of femininity. Later, after the birth of a younger sister, Bob's mother displaced her feminizing energies to the new, more receptive daughter and allowed Bob to pursue her masculine interests relatively unfettered:

By this time, my mother had given up trying to make a little mademoiselle out of me. And I was allowed to wear jeans, I was allowed to play rugby, I was allowed to be a cowboy, I was allowed a bike; all the things that my brothers did, I was allowed to do. Totally.

Although Bob had been allowed to pursue her interests as she wished, she also had been regularly beaten by her mother. Unlike other participants whose masculine interests were allowed free reign, Bob harbored intensely hostile feelings toward her mother. He recalled having wanted to kill her mother when she was a girl.

Even more pronounced was the situation of Alan, who, as a child, felt that she had to become a husband for her mother. Rather than simply having been given permission to follow her own propensities, Alan recalled having been groomed to masculinity by her mother: "I didn't want to be a boy, because I already was one. I was treated exactly like my brother. My mother dressed me as a boy. I had short hair, I was a tomboy. . . . unlike my masculine brother and my feminine sister, my family role was counselor/neuter."

In contrast to those participants who felt that they had been given some room to follow their own preferences were the seven participants (16 percent) who remembered their mothers being highly critical of them for their resistance to or lack of talent at being feminine.[24] They felt that their failure to be proper young ladies resulted in their mothers being sorely disappointed in them. None of these participants felt close to their mothers when they were children.

Bruce said that when he was a girl, her mother had repeatedly called her an "ugly duckling." Her mother's continual remonstrations left her feeling unhappy with her body and inadequate as a female:

> I had a very negative body image, as a child, from my mother saying to me, first of all, that I was an ugly duckling and that someday I would be a beautiful swan. And I remember my mother always saying "You walk like a truck driver. You don't eat like a lady; you don't sit like a lady. . . . You don't set a good example for your sister." And I remember feeling like I was never competent at being a girl. It just didn't fit.

More dramatically, Dennis said that when she was a child, her mother felt "utter confusion and disgust" and "shame and embarrassment" about her because of her masculinity. She lived daily with this "ever present" feeling of causing pain to her mother. Her inability and unwillingness to change this source of pain to her mother created emotional conflicts in this child who also felt very protective of her mother. Grant and Pat both reported that their parents were so disturbed by their interests in all things masculine that they were sent to child psychiatrists for treatment.

In sum, there was little pleasure for participants in the feminine socialization bestowed upon them by their mothers during their youths. For the most part, their mothers seemed to be trying, to little avail, to teach them to be appropriately feminine young girls. The conflicts which they had over these issues often served to further erode relationships which were already stretched thin by other stressors. The most successful mother-daughter relationships seem to have been those in which the mothers largely abandoned the project of feminizing their reluctant daughters. Those daughters who were granted such leave were those who recalled their childhood relationships with their mothers in the fondest terms.

Before Gender Mattered: Good Times with Mother

Despite, and sometimes in addition to, the many sources of pain and conflict in these mother-daughter relationships, nine participants (21 percent) remembered having passed much gratifying time in the company of their mothers.[25] Most of their tender memories were of their preschool years, before they began to battle with their mothers about gender issues.

For some people, the best thing about their mothers was that they provided the safety of a warm and stable home. Several people also enjoyed being close to their physically feminine mothers. For instance, Hal remembered her mother this way:

> My mother was petite and pretty. She was soft-spoken, gentle, and well-organized. She would play word games with me, and taught me about the material world: colors, sizes, numbers, the way things felt or smelled or tasted. The best thing about her was that she was always there. It seemed like I could go out and roam around or play some game, or enter some imaginary world, and whenever I returned my mother was always there, always at home, making something, putting something away, getting ready for dinner . . . and it was always like I'd never been gone. She would always give me something good to eat. I liked this "constancy" best about her because it made me feel warm inside.

Alan similarly remembered that before she was prematurely forced to grow up, she was enthralled by her mother's physical femininity:

> I do not remember much about my preschool years except being fascinated with my mother's smell, pale blue eyes and pale, long blonde hair. I remember that she held me a lot. She'd let me play with her hair. I still have a fascination with pretty, long-haired, blue-eyed blondes. I was entranced when my mother would get made up to go out with my father in the evening. I still have a fascination for women who wear makeup and dress very femininely. . . . The sweet womanly smells and sights (perfume, clothes) were the best things I remember. The smells and sights made me feel secure.

Other participants fondly remembered that their mothers took time to give them special attention when they were still young girls. Steven, the only participant who felt that she had been her mother's favorite child, said that her mother was "the most generous woman I've ever met. She's very maternal. They don't make mothers nowadays like they made her." He described their relationship at the time as "exceptionally close" and went on to explain how her mother had lovingly cared for her when she had scarlet fever. Jack similarly recalled getting special attention from her mother because of illness:

> I always loved my mom and that's from a very early age, because she was always caring, loving, she was always my rock. Being the youngest too, it made us close. Because I was born nearly a month premature, and so she had to take special care because of that, and I think that was probably what made us so close too. And I was allergic to bees, and so she always kept a close eye on me, always afraid I'd get stung or something. . . . And she would always talk to you. . . . if Mom said it, that's like

God saying it. But you know because I love my mom, I respect her. . . .
And from a very early age.

Others illustrated their feelings about their mothers by telling stories about the highly enjoyable things which they did together. Eli's story summed these feelings up nicely:

> She is the most perfect, sane and beautiful person that ever lived or will live. . . . She was just loving. Ubiquitous. . . . My mother would stop and take time if I had a little project I wanted to do. . . . I loved my mom, we have always laughed together and sung and played together. We didn't have time to fight. There was no reason to fight because we had too much fun.

Thus for several participants their preschool years were an oasis before gender became an issue for them. During those few years they could enjoy an unencumbered freedom, and an unconflicted closeness with their mothers. However, their school aged years and later maturity brought issues of gender conformity more sharply into focus in their lives. For most participants, their best years with their mothers were their youngest ones before they began to chafe at being girls.

Summary and Commentary

In families where girl children grow up to be women who are relatively satisfied with their femaleness, daughters usually look to their mothers as role models. The stories which participants told about their relationships with their mothers during their childhood years conveyed a picture of strained and antagonistic interactions in which few participants felt able to use their mothers as role models. In some cases (33 percent), the distances between mothers and daughters were matters of physical separation or mental incapacity.[26] More often, the issues were more complex.

Overall, times of conflict loomed larger than interludes of warmth and affection. Almost three-quarters (79 percent) of the families in which participants grew up were marred by marital discord or violence.[27] Almost half (46.5 percent) of participants fought with their mothers about their resistance to being forced into femininity.[28] A similar number (44 percent) felt unloved by their mothers.[29] Sixteen percent were physically abused by their mothers.[30]

Participants grew up, for the most part, feeling distant from their mothers. Those who reported warmth and closeness with their mothers did so within fairly narrow parameters. They fell loosely into two groups. On the one hand, there were those who remembered their youngest years as blissful times before they began to have gender conflicts with their mothers and in the larger world around them. On the other hand, there were those participants who cherished their mothers as vulnerable, and pretty, feminine women who were in need of their protection. They seemed to romanticize their mothers and fall in love with the images they had created of them. These participants cast themselves in equally idealized masculine counterpart roles to complement the ones which they saw their mothers as occupying. In neither scenario did they identify with their mothers and take them as role models.

Furthermore, throughout most of their childhoods, most participants seemed to have identified females and femaleness as powerless and vulnerable positions. Many participants were themselves victimized by older males, from whom their mothers did not protect them. They also saw their mothers being physically and emotionally hurt by their husbands. They learned from watching their mothers' roles in their families that their mothers were either unable to protect themselves or their children from the dangers to which they were exposed or that their mothers were themselves sources of pain and frustrations. They appeared to take from this the message that were they to grow up into women, they would likely become wives who would be as overpowered, belittled, and hurt by their husbands as their own mothers too often had been. Simultaneously, it seemed as though they envisioned that were they to grow into men, they could have before them the possibility of controlling, at the least, their own environments. They imagined that they would then be able to protect themselves and the women and children whom they might come to love. It would seem that many participants began moving in this direction quite early in life.

Finding Refuge with Grandmothers and Aunts

More than one-third of participants had grandmothers who played significant roles in their upbringings.[31] Sixteen participants (37 percent) considered their grandmothers as having made an impression on them during their young lives.[32] Nine participants (21 percent) lived with their grandmothers at some point during their youths.[33] Another seven participants (16 percent) regularly spent time with their grandmothers who lived nearby.[34] In addition, Bruce, Grant, and Hal remembered their grandmothers coming to visit them when they were young. Often their grandmothers provided some alternatives to their relationships with their mothers. For the most part, participants' memories of their grandmothers were fond ones.[35] Only Bill, Harry, Darcy, and Nathan remembered their grandmothers as unpleasant presences in their young lives, but none of them had held a particularly pronounced role in their upbringings.

Peter's story was typical. Peter's mother, who Peter said was rarely home during her daughter's youngest years, was recalled by Peter as being very feminine. Peter, who was her grandmother's favorite grandchild, found a welcomed parental proxy in her grandmother, who often babysat for her. Peter "loved" her grandmother and called her "neat" because, unlike her mother, she "showed an interest in me, in the things that I liked. She'd listen to me. She'd take time. She took me seriously" and she was tolerant of Peter's tomboyish behaviors. Ken likewise remembered both of her grandparents as "very important to me because they believed in me. They listened and that made a difference. I felt like someone else cared. They knew I was alive. I wasn't the oldest. I wasn't the youngest. They just liked me for being me."

Sam, Robin, Brian, and Gary similarly recalled that their grandmothers had, in some ways, taken the places of their mothers. For example, Sam, who remembered her grandmother as more affectionate and accepting of her than was her own mother, lived with her grandmother for only one year, between the ages of four and five, but was so close to her grandmother that after she committed suicide a year later Sam was distraught about it for years. Similarly, Robin's grandmother took care of her during the days while her mother worked full time during the first three years of Robin's life. Robin grew "really close" to her grandmother and, like Sam, was tremendously upset by her death when Robin was six years old.

Brian, who thought of her mother as cold and distant and used her as a negative role model of feminine helplessness, lived with her grandparents when she was a child. He remembered her time with her grandmother as among the "best parts" of those years:

> About mother. She was nervous, impatient, frequently yelled or cried. . . . Mostly I saw her as a distant person to be avoided. I remember my grandmother more because she was smiling and friendly and liked to rock us in her lap. My grandmother would show us things and take us on walks. My grandmother was more friendly and patient. . . . She gave us the attention our parents didn't.
>
> I reckon I argued some with my mother about the issue of my behaviour and total lack of interest in being a "young lady." Sometimes my grandmother was supportive, allowing that letting me be a tomboy wasn't a bad thing. She figured she'd been a tomboy as a girl herself and her father had said that wasn't a bad thing, that tomboys generally grew up to be hard working and more reliable women than girls who were spoiled.

Alan's grandmother's attentions also provided a haven in an increasingly unbearable family home life. This sanctuary was interrupted first when her grandmother was asked to leave the home when Alan was nine years old, and later by the grandmother's death when Alan was eleven. During those years, when Alan's mother came to lean on her more and more, demanding that she fulfill the role of protector and husband for her, Alan's grandmother allowed Alan to have time off from the burdens of surrogate husbandry:

> I was very close to my father's mother. I became more and more at-
> tached to my grandmother. . . . We read stories together and talked like
> adults. We did crossword puzzles or looked at the view together. We
> rocked in the rocking chair. She let me touch her delicate glassware and
> touch her jewelry. She listened to me. I felt safe and loved by my grand-
> mother.

Stan's relationship to her grandparents when she was a girl was unique among the participants in that, because Stan's divorced mother was incapacitated by mental illness, Stan came to be raised by her grandparents. Stan's grandfather ruled the home with a patriarchal iron fist. Stan said that she had "loved" her grandmother, but he described her as "very, very passive," "milque toast, like nothing. . . . She would nag you though." Stan ended up spending a fair bit of time with her grandmother because "she was the only one I had left." Stan's father was gone, she was "afraid of" her "crazy" mother, and her grandfather was entirely partial to her brother. Consequently, Stan's grandmother became "my buddy kind of by default more than anything."

Thus, with the exception of Stan's grandmother, who raised her in the place of her mother, participants' experiences with their grandmothers were generally gratifying ones. Their grandmothers supplied them with more congenial and appreciated female elders than did their own mothers, but their closeness with their grandmothers tended to be short-lived.

Simon, Roger, Bob, Gary, and Phil lived with their aunts while they were children, and Grant and Hal had aunts whose annual visits were important to them as children. Simon remembered very little about the time she spent with her aunt while she was still preschool age. Likewise, Roger, Gary, Phil, and Hal also had little to say one way or the other about their aunts. Grant remembered his aunt's visits fondly. Howie, who as a child had been close with her mother, and Dennis, who had not, often visited at their nearby aunts' houses. Both said that they felt as though their aunts had adopted them as the "surrogate" children whom they had never had. Dennis remembered his aunts as people who compensated for some of the "disgust" which Dennis thought that her mother felt toward her. Dennis said that, as a child, she had liked her aunts better than her own parents because of the affection and acceptance of her masculinity which she received:

> They were fun. I had great times with them. I was more with them than
> I was with my mother, and they gave me attention that my mother
> didn't give. And they taught me how to be affectionate, I think, because

this family here is not affectionate. . . . But my aunt, she was big and fat, and she always used to hug me. I never got hugs from anybody else.

I remember every week we used to go to the five and ten and I'd pick out a new rocket. . . . I loved those things. And then there was [a toy] called Union Station. It was a huge train station. I loved it. . . . And then I used to have gas pumps and . . . hot wheels cars and shaving kits. I was four and five [years old].

Unlike other participants, whose memories of their aunts were either fond or neutral ones, Bob's relationship with her aunt stood out from the others in that, when he was a girl, she hated the aunt with whom her parents sent her to live. The aunt, for her part, also differed from the others in that she was abusive rather that loving.

I was ill from about seven years to about nine years old, and my parents, after coming back from hospital, sent me to live with my auntie and her tribe. . . . The only person I disliked immensely was my auntie. . . . She was an idiot. And I thought my mother was physically violent, but my auntie was extremely. It was like a child was a slave. You did everything. You were there at her beck and call. If you didn't do it, she'd just about beat the shit out of you. . . . This was a woman who subjected some really inhumane treatment on children. I couldn't believe that a human being could do that to a child.

In sum, more often than not, the relationships which participants had with their aunts and grandmothers injected some small antidote into the negative attitudes which participants seemed to be developing toward their mothers and toward women in general. Their grandmothers and aunts for the most part provided female solace and acceptance. There were, however, a few notable exceptions to this pattern. Nonetheless, the overall effect of these women on most of their granddaughters and nieces was an ameliorative one. Unfortunately, five participants' beloved grandmothers died during their childhood years.[36]

Relationships with Sisters

The relationships which girls have with their sisters can take many forms. Older sisters in particular often play the role of surrogate or assistant parents, especially when they are somewhat older than their siblings, when their primary caretakers are detached or distant figures, or when they are members of larger families.[37] When older sisters do perform this function, they tend to be perceived by their younger siblings as more tolerant and fairer arbiters than parents.[38] Younger sisters in turn may follow after their older sisters, eagerly absorbing important information about how to negotiate their own feminine placement in the world, or they may strike out on their own to forge their own independent identities.

Sometimes sisters who are close in age share so many similar experiences that they may come to feel as though they are twins. Conversely, some sisters may find their similarities to their female siblings stifling and may move to differentiate themselves from their sisters. Such young girls who feel unwilling to merge their identities with those of their sisters may interpret their worlds in terms of "hers" and "mine," thereby dividing up possessions, relationships, and attributes into those belonging to one sister and those belonging to another. Parents may inadvertently contribute to such sisterly behavior by setting up one sister as an example for others to follow. Some girls take the bait; others rebel against it.[39]

The relationships between participants and their sisters fit most of these patterns to some degree. Most commonly, however, participants were fairly distant from their sisters and were more often in revolt, either against following the examples set by their older sisters or against the requirement that they should set proper feminine examples for their younger sisters. In those instances where participants reported having been close with their sisters during their youths, they were more likely than not to have said that they felt more like a brother than a sister in their sibling relationships. The single overriding theme that echoes throughout most of their stories is that of participants' sisters willingly fulfilling their feminine role while participants grew into masculine ones.

Who Had Sisters

Thirty-one participants (70.5 percent)[40] had sisters;[41] nine were from families in which all of the children were females.[42] Robin, Terry, and Pat, who had sisters, did not have any brothers who were close to them in age. Thus twelve participants (27 percent) grew up in families in which sisters dominated their sibling world.

Fifteen participants (34 percent) had older sisters.[43] Of these, Ed's, Eli's, Walter's, Terry's, and Dennis's sisters were five or more years older than they were and only Dennis had any other siblings closer in age than six years. All other participants who had older sisters had at least one older sister who was close to them in age. Thus ten participants (23 percent) had older sisters who were close to them in age.[44] Seven of those with older sisters were themselves the youngest in their families.[45]

Twenty-one participants (48 percent) had younger sisters.[46] Nine participants' closest younger sisters were five or more years younger than themselves.[47] Thus twelve participants had younger sisters who were close to them in age.[48] Eight of those participants who had younger sisters were themselves the oldest in their families.[49]

Only six participants had both younger and older sisters.[50] Brian's younger sisters were seven and ten years younger; Dale's younger sisters were six, eighteen, and twenty years younger; Colin's younger sister was nine years younger; and Dennis's older sister was five years older. The net result therefore was that only Bill and Harry had both older and younger sisters who were close to them in age. Tony had a nonidentical twin sister.

The age spacing in participants' families resulted in twenty-one participants (48 percent) having been raised in families where they had sisters close in age to themselves.[51] Twelve (57 percent) of those participants' early sibling experiences might be said to have taken place in virtually an all-girl environment in that they were either from families where there were only daughters or where there were no boys close to participants in age during their younger years.

Tattletales and Bad Examples: Distant Relationships with Sisters

It was most common for participants to remember their relationships with one or more of their sisters as cool or distant. Fourteen participants who had sisters close to them in age did not warmly remember them from their youths.[52] Another five participants also complained that they had difficult relationships with sisters who were more distant in age.[53] In addition to these, another five participants felt distant from their sisters simply because of age differences.[54] In total, twenty-five of the thirty-one participants who had sisters (81 percent) recalled their relationships during their youths as having been distant or strained. Only five of these people had the counterbalance of a close relationship with another of their sisters.[55]

Sam's, Ron's, Nathan's, Ken's, and Harry's relationships with their sisters were strained by a "tattletale" younger sister who regularly got participants in trouble with their parents. Sam "very seldom talked" to her only sibling, a younger sister "who was very willing to tattle." Ron "beat up" her only younger sister "a lot" "because she got everything she wanted. . . . She would tattle . . . and we'd get beaten. You know, her word against ours, but we'd still get it." Nathan recalled that she and her brother used to "pick on" and "tease" their "spoiled" baby sister "a lot." Nathan remembered that when they were young girls together, her sister "would tattle on me constantly and I would be whipped for things I often didn't do." Not surprisingly, Nathan was "not close" with her only sister. Ken's older sister "told a lot of lies," which Ken said "got me in trouble a lot."

Harry, on the other hand, was the tattle in her family of five girls. During most of her childhood, only the older two of her four sisters were at home. Harry's oldest sister took over parenting Harry to save her from some of their mother's abusive punishments. Harry "didn't agree with her rules" and "hated it" that her sister had taken over parenting her. But Harry also remembered that her sister seemed "much fairer" and more "consistent" than their mother, of whom Harry was "terrified." Harry obeyed her sister's rules because she assumed that if she didn't she "was dead meat" at the hands of their mother. Although a bond was forged between them in their common experience of their mother's abusive behavior, Harry's tactics also drove a wedge between them:

> My sisters would be mad sometimes. And they'd be mad sometimes with just cause. I mean, if I was going to get in trouble with my mom, I never liked getting my punishment, whether it was justified or not. And I'd often try to tell stories about my sisters . . . and they'd get in shit, so I wasn't really close to either one of them, the two older ones . . . in the sense to know them, to talk to them, to be with them. I felt a bonding with them, especially because of [mother's abuse]. . . . I lived in my own world, had my own friends, did my own thing, and they did theirs.

Another six participants recalled resenting their sisters for the special treatment they remembered them as having received in their families.[56] For example, Brian, who had one older and two younger sisters, derisively recalled her younger sister as "pretty" and a "pet." Dennis, who had two siblings, one older and one younger sister, remembered them as having been spoiled by their father.

Dale had three younger and one older sister. Dale, too, remembered the youngest of the sisters with whom she grew up as "spoiled" and hated her for the special privileges she was afforded:

> And then the next child came along. I was six. And I hated her. I hated her so bad I wanted to kill her. Because she got all the attention. Mom took her dancing and everything else, and she had a little purse with money in it. We never had a nickel. I used to steal out of it. A nickel was a lot of money in those days . . . and she didn't have to work like we did in the fields. . . . But I hated her, and I used to have to sleep in the same bed as my oldest sister and her, and my oldest sister used to have to sleep in the midst, because believe me, if I could have gotten my hands on her . . .

Bruce, Luther, and Colin were unhappy in their relationships with their sisters for still other reasons. They remembered being plagued by their mothers' insistent comparisons between their own and their sisters' levels of femininity. For example, Bruce recalled, "My mother would get really upset at me. My mother was always telling me 'Now you have to be ladylike because you have to set an example for your sisters.' " Bruce said that as a result of these remonstrations, she always had a "very negative body image" as a female. Luther and Colin were both urged to act like their more feminine older sisters. Luther recalled that her mother "would always scream and yell about . . . why wasn't I like my older sisters." Colin considered "pressure to act like my perfect older sister" to be a form of "emotional abuse" and dismissively characterized her sisters as "silly girls."

Tony's childhood relationship with her nonidentical twin sister was also a strained one. Tony remembered the twin sister of her youth as "just a nasty person" and "totally different." Likewise, the odd power dynamics in Darcy's relationship with one of the two younger sisters of her youth, although intense, were certainly not warm. Darcy remembered her youngest sister as "an ugly little bug-eyed kid" who liked to play with dolls and clothing. Darcy recalled the other sister as smart but not "normal" and "always off in left field." When they were children, Darcy grossly dominated the sister who was two years younger.

> I was the boss, and she was my slave. We had a very strange sort of, almost like an S/M type of [relationship]. . . . Like, I'd make her pull me around in a cart. . . . Or she'd be the dog, and I'd be the dog trainer, or whatever. Or I'd be the knight, and she'd be the person who'd follow me and carry my stuff.

In sum, more than three-quarters of participants (81 percent) had difficult or strained relationships with one or more of their sisters during their youths. In a few cases, such feelings were somewhat balanced by warmer relations with other sisters. On the whole, however, indifference and alienation seemed by far the most common emotions in participants' relations with their sisters.

Sisters Who Care: Close Relationships with Sisters

Twelve people remembered having warm relations with at least one of their sisters when they were children.[57] In half of these cases, their closeness was based on one of the sisters having performed a goodly amount of child care for the other.[58] Jack's and Eli's older sisters looked after them when they were young, whereas Bruce, Alan, Dennis, and Steven took care of their younger sisters. The nurturant quality of the time they passed together was fondly remembered by participants. However, participants tended to put a brother-sister cast to it.

For example, Eli remembered that when she was young, she had looked up to her older sister. Eli's sister, who was her only sibling and ten years older than Eli, had "looked after me sometimes when my mom had to be away." Eli recalled about that time:

> We were great pals, except she was a real girl. . . . Basically we had fun, she was probably a little stricter with me than Mom. . . . We would argue sometimes about some things, but I think we are about as close as any siblings can be. But I did feel more like a brother.

Dennis had few childhood memories of his sister who was five years older. However, Dennis did remember feeling close to her only other sibling, a sister who was three years younger. Dennis characterized the closeness that he recalled as that of an older brother protecting a younger sister. He said of that time:

> I just remember I thought she was the cutest baby. I liked playing with her as a baby. But I used to take care of her. Walked her to school. I used to feel proud to pick her up from kindergarten and wait for her.

The remaining six participants who said that they had been close to their sisters explained their closeness in a variety of ways. Dale had an older sister with whom she had shared a bed as a child. Dale remembered their relationship as "very close" and described that sister as someone whom "everybody seemed to like" because "she was bubbly and outgoing." As children, Darren and Bill both shared bedrooms with their sisters, which seemed to have brought them closer together. Darren remembered being closer to her younger sister than with any of her other siblings, even though Darren was an outdoors type and her sister was "reclusive." Bill remembered that, as a girl, she both "sewed doll clothes" and "played football and softball" with her sisters. Neither Gary nor Phil said much about their relationships with their only sisters but they did characterize them as close. Gary said of his sister: "we can talk about anything." Phil said: "we did everything together."

Keith's relationships during her girlhood with each of her only siblings, two younger sisters, typified the relationships which many participants had with their siblings. In Keith's family, as in those of many participants, Keith took on a decidedly masculine role while one sister played out a clearly feminine one. Keith warmly remembered one sister as the "perfect woman" and the other sibling as a rival in masculinity:

> I'm the oldest, and my middle sister was the complete opposite of myself . . . extremely feminine. I can't say enough good things about her. She was the perfect woman in my mind. If she wasn't my sister, I'd marry her in a minute. She was just the sweetest, and most loving, and kind of a little bit scatter-brained. But you could never ever get mad at her be-

cause you loved her too much. Sweet, good hearted, not funny in a witty way but just the way she would tell things, so cute. . . . I love my sister dearly.

And the youngest one is just like me. . . . We see ourselves in each other. And for that reason we never got along when we were kids because we always clashed. It was always a struggle for dominance. I was rather hard on her, I'm sorry to say, when I was a kid. . . . I disliked [her] most . . . both being very masculine. She . . . is just a real masculine woman. . . . But we used to fight because of that.

Although a sizable minority of participants remembered being close with their sisters when they were children, none said that they were inclined to use their sisters as any kind of role models for their own behaviours. They instead seemed to see their sisters either as idealized models of femininity to whom they were romantically attracted, or they disparaged their sisters' femininity and distanced themselves from it and from them. Either way, in most cases they responded to their sisters from perspectives grounded in increasingly masculine self-identities.

"Hers" and "Mine" Gender Styles

Twenty of the thirty-one participants who had sisters (64.5 percent) described their relationships with their sisters in terms which either explicitly or implicitly indicated that they saw their sisters as the girls in the family and that they saw themselves as among the boys.[59] In many cases, they remembered their parents as having helped to train them and their sisters into their different relationships to femininity. In some cases, as I have already described, they either veered away from their sisters with some animosity or enjoyed their sisters' femininity without wishing to emulate it. Most often, they seemed disinterestedly to go their separate ways from their more feminine sisters.

Eight participants remembered that their parents had treated them differently from their sisters.[60] For example, Jack, who was the youngest of four girls in a farming family, recalled that when they were children, her father usually came to her for help with farming chores over and above any of the other girls. He said of this time: "I have three sisters and I didn't want to do anything they wanted to do. This playing with dolls crap and all that was not for me."

In Dale's memories of childhood, both of her parents contributed to Dale's being cast as one of the boys of the family. When Dale was a girl, she had an older and a younger sister and a younger brother at home. Dale remembered the contrast between the ways she was treated and the ways her sisters were handled by her parents:

> My mother would take my sister shopping with her or to a movie, and all I ever felt good enough for was doing the work around there. Now, I worked hard. I did a man's job as a kid. . . . My sister did the baking and cooking. . . . She got more the indoor chores, and I was outside packing the water, chopping the wood, and she got to . . . help Mom. . . . I would have hated to do it anyway.

Sam similarly recalled that when he was a girl, her parents had contributed to dividing their two offspring into one masculine and one feminine. Sam felt that her father had favoured her while her mother had favoured her sister. Sam recalled her father's gender socialization efforts this way:

> My father treated me totally different than he did my sister. With my sister it was all joking, laughter, fun and games. With me, he pushed me real hard to achieve. He knew I was intelligent, and he pushed that real hard. No excuses acceptable. And I was told many times that if I wasn't the top of my class, or couldn't do better than everybody else, I had to work harder.

Another nine participants likewise remembered their sisters as being interested in feminine pursuits while they preferred boys' activities. However, they made no mention of their parents' roles in this regard. In some cases, participants and their sisters played together, with the participant taking masculine roles in their play and their sisters taking the feminine ones. In other instances, participants and their sisters shared so few common interests that they had little to do with one another.[61]

Bill, who came from a family of five girls, made a typical comment: "They all . . . enjoy being females. They all like to wear make-up and do their hair and dress up. I never wanted any part of it." Walter explained, in a little more detail, some of the childhood differences between Walter and her sister who was ten years older. When they were children, there was some distance between them because of their ages and because Walter's older sister teased her about her weight. Walter also remembered that they did not have many interests in common because:

> I was more into playing like boys' games, like army and stuff. And she wasn't into that. I was heavily into army, I had whole uniforms . . . I was a military strategist at the age of six. . . . I was socialized as a boy a lot. I got a lot of things that . . . I don't think my sister got.

Luther similarly remembered the nature of her relationship with her only sibling who was close to her in age, a sister who was four years older.

> I played exclusively with boys my own age. My sister played with girls her own age. . . . I just did not want to do the same things my sister did.

I never wanted dolls so I never wanted to play with my sister. . . . [my playmates] never included my sister because she just was not interested in jumping over fences, and playing Kamikazie pilot, and reenacting the invasion of Normandy. . . . I was born right after the war, so those games were games that kids played. And she was not interested in that, and I was. So I never played with her.

Pat's story also reiterated the same theme of one sister taking on a boys' role while another sister enacted a feminine one. Pat described the relationship in these terms:

My sister was just real femmy in a lot of ways. And I didn't like that about her. And we would play together because we were close in age, but it was like we were really very different. . . . I was not close with my sister. . . . I took on more of the male type roles, especially since my brother was so much younger. . . . I would do the boy things and she would do the girl things. I would lift the heavy stuff and she would help clean up, or things like that.

When Dennis and Steven were girls, they too would never play with anything which seemed girlish to them. They left that to their sisters. Dennis recalled that, as a child, the only time she would play with her older sister was when her sister played with a Barbie doll and Dennis acted the part of a Ken doll. Although Steven differed from Dennis in that he remembered being "extremely close" with the sister nearest in age, Steven was similar to Dennis in that, during childhood, Steven rejected anything in their playtime that smacked of femininity.

[My sister] liked to play dolls, but any dolls that were given to me, I used to tie a rope around their necks, strip them, and beat them up as a punching bag in the cellar. She would feel sorry for my dolls and adopt them. . . . I didn't want these damn things. I didn't like them. So, I had to find a use for them, and they were good punching bags.
We used to have . . . two statues. One was a Christ statue, and one was a Virgin Mary statue. . . . And I can remember that she said "Well, you take the Virgin Mary." I said "No. I'm the Christ. You're the Virgin Mary." And we used to play with these two statues . . . like puppets or something. And to this day she says "I remember you would never take the Virgin Mary. The Christ was you. You had to be the Christ, and you would not take any female thing at all". . . . So, there were certain things that were more feminine that she would do and I wouldn't do.

Close or distant in ages or in emotional bonding; playing together or refusing their sisters' company: approximately two-thirds of participants (64.5 percent) seemed primarily concerned with differentiating themselves from their more feminine sisters and claiming a masculine role as their own. None of them took their sisters as positive role models. Most often they seemed to prefer to see their sisters as contrasting personas whom they used as foils to help them to bring their own developing masculinity into sharper relief.

Summary and Commentary

Two refrains appeared to permeate most of the relationships which participants recalled having had with their sisters. Firstly, more than three-quarters of participants (81 percent) reported that they did not recall being close with their sisters during their childhood years. The distance in their relationships came from a variety of sources: age differences, conflicts over dominance hierarchies, resentments over special treatment, unwelcomed comparisons made by parents, or divergent interests. Not one person said that she had turned to a sister as a role model. Secondly, approximately two thirds of participants characterized themselves as having been more masculine than their sisters during their childhoods. Most of the people who remembered their relationships in this way also remembered having few common interests with their sisters. In those cases where participants did recall enjoying their sisters' company, participants said that they had thought of themselves more as brothers than as sisters to their sisters.

Together these two motifs account for each and every participant in this study who had a sister. In many cases, both factors were present. In some cases, only one of these two types of sibling relations was reported. The overall effects of these circumstances seem to have been twofold. In the first instance, many participants spent little time with their sisters, thereby minimizing the feminine gender socialization effects which their sisters might have had on them. In the second place, those who did interact with their sisters did so largely within a context, in their own visions of themselves, of brother-sister relations. Thus it seems likely that those participants who did share time with their sisters only became more confirmed in their own beliefs that they were unlike other girls. Any contribution that their time with their sisters made to strengthening their identities as girls was probably minimal.

Summary and Commentary:
Relationships with Female Family Members

The relationships which participants had with the women and girls in their lives typically were neither warm nor close. In a few cases, under particular circumstances and for relatively brief periods, participants felt close to female family members. Those participants who had relatively warm memories of their mothers from their early years were of two types.

Most often they were those who felt that their mothers had treated them fairly with regard to gender issues, i.e., their mothers had generally allowed them to dress and act as masculinely they wished. In a smaller number of cases, participants briefly had warm relationships with their mothers during their youngest years, before gender conflicts began to interfere with their intimacy. Most often they were alienated from their mothers and indifferent to their sisters.

The vast majority of participants recalled that their parents often fought and that their mothers were rarely able to defend themselves successfully in these conflicts. Such perceptions led many participants to feel that their mothers, rather than being people to whom they could turn for maternal support, solace, and protection, were people who were themselves in need of such ministrations. Furthermore, another lament which regularly arose was that they felt unloved by their mothers. Some mothers were described as being unavailable due to illnesses; others were lost in intoxication; some were away from their children due to the necessities of earning a living. However, the main sources of such feelings were their memories that their mothers favoured other children over themselves or that they were cold and rejecting, sometimes to the point of physical and emotional abuse. Such feelings of distant and unloving relations between participants and their mothers during participants' youths were no doubt amplified by the ongoing clashes about femininity in which they engaged with their mothers.

It might be expected that young girls who felt that they had so few circumstances in which they might turn to their mothers for support, shelter, and solace would turn to other female family members for the nurturing and role models that children seem to naturally desire. Although most participants did have sisters, few turned to them in any significant way for any of these needs. Most often their relationships with their sisters were distant, sometimes benignly so; sometimes they lived together in a climate of outright hostility. What participants seemed to find most useful about their sisters was the role which they could play for them as they tried out their budding masculine skills. The most frequently described types of interactions between participants and their sisters were ones in which participants remembered themselves as being in brotherly-sisterly relations. Some participants recalled their brotherly connections with their sisters as gratifying; some remembered their more feminine sisters with disdain. In any event, few participants found much reinforcement for feminine behavior patterns in their relationships with their sisters.

This seemingly unbroken and bleak emotional landscape was periodically interrupted by the presence in participants' lives of older female relatives with whom they found comfort. Most often grandmothers but occasionally aunts provided places of feminine warmth and connection for some participants. The women who provided these islands of safety were appreciated by participants for the behavioural latitude which they allowed them and for the warm, respecting, and accepting attitudes which they conveyed to their granddaughters and nieces. Unfortunately for those participants who enjoyed such relationships, they were, with few exceptions, only punctuation points among their otherwise principally unsatisfying relationships with the women and girls in their lives.

The overall picture that emerges from the reports which participants supplied about their relationships with their mothers, sisters, grandmothers, and aunts is one in which alienation from identification with femininity is the overriding theme. In those families where participants did not feel excessively forced to conform to feminine role expectations and where participants did not feel otherwise abused, it was not uncommon for participants to feel affection toward their more feminine female relations. In such cases, participants seemed to prefer to cast themselves in more masculine roles in relation to those to whom they felt fondly attached. When they were not allowed this freedom, the result was alienation and hostility toward those women and girls in their lives whom they felt were intent upon forcing them to be the feminine creatures whom they had no interest in becoming. In neither scenario were participants inclined to model themselves after the feminine aspects of the women and girls in their lives.

6

Men Rule

The Men (and Boys) in Participants' Families

Relationships with Fathers

THE RELATIONSHIPS WHICH participants had with their fathers were often of a very different valence than those which they had with their mothers. Whereas the difficulties which participants had with their mothers tended to alienate them from their mothers, most expressed much more positive attitudes about their fathers than they did about their mothers. The ways in which participants described their fathers made them seem to be powerful, enigmatic men who commanded admiration from their young daughters. They were often scarce in participants' young lives, but when they did appear they tended to be either violent and dangerous or exciting and fun people. Many fathers were away at work or lost to alcoholic rages and stupors during participants' younger years. A sizable number of fathers were also physically, emotionally, or sexually abusive to their children. Despite these paternal shortcomings, or perhaps because of them, when their fathers did appear in their lives, many of those participants who were not chronically abused by them seemed to take their fathers as role models. For their own part, many fathers seemed to be willing to facilitate such identification by encouraging participants to share in their masculine activities as if they were sons.

Fathers as a Scarce Commodity

When a father is a relatively rare visitor to a child's life, he may become a kind of mythical figure of great importance. His arrival can become a heralded event surrounded by a mystique of potency. If, when such a father is present in the family home, he dominates other family members, his role as sovereign may be further confirmed in a young mind. Approximately one-third of participants remembered their fathers as infrequent visitors in their lives during parts of their childhood years.

Thirteen fathers (30 percent)[1] were away at work for significant periods of time during participants' youths.[2] Although this kind of absence was not unusual for families of the 1950s, 1960s, and 1970s, it is nonetheless likely that such a pattern made the times that these fathers did spend with their children disproportionately memorable and influential. In a few cases, participants specifically described their fathers as "workaholics."[3] In others, participants remembered that their fathers' jobs caused them to travel a lot or left them few free waking hours which they might pass with their offspring. For example, Tony remembered her father as a "hard worker" who "worked a million hours" and had little time for his family:

> We never did anything together. My father rarely took us on vacation. He rarely took my mother . . . anywhere. My father, he was a hard worker. When he was working manual work he'd leave at six in the morning and he'd come home six at night. But the biggest thing was . . . he was always sleeping on the couch. He'd snore through our TV programs and everything else.

Tony went on to describe his father in glowing terms despite the fact that the man was a "compulsive gambler" who "didn't take care of his family the way he could have" because of his "big problem." Still, Tony called him "a really nice guy," "a great guy," and a "wonderful man" even though he also said that, as a girl, she and her siblings all "saw what my father was like and we all swore we'd never be like that."

Steven similarly recalled that her father seemed to work all of the time:

> And my father worked sixty hours a week. He had two jobs, and it was rough. The government was his main job, but he also worked for a private firm . . . at a moonlighting job. He worked on the weekends and a few nights a week. He was always busy taking care of some kind of responsibilities. . . . Sundays was really the only time that I can remember seeing him a lot.

Steven also had good things to say about her father. He called him a "very responsible" and "very good father" whom she thought of as "a tower of strength." He also said that, as a girl, she had "an exceptionally good childhood" even though her father had been physically and emotionally abusive to both her and her mother throughout her childhood.

Another five participants lost their biological fathers while they were still quite young. Simon's, Eli's, Stan's, and Phil's fathers left their family homes due to divorces when they were six years old or younger. Grant's father died when Grant was five years old; he had few memories of the father of her childhood and spoke mostly of her adoptive father. Simon and Stan had little or no memory of their biological fathers. Eli continued to see her father irregularly during her childhood and described the father of her youth as "a very masculine man. . . . He had a profound presence.

People had to respect him when he walked into a room." Eli described her father as "like God" even though this father was a somewhat tarnished man of God, a minister, who was "forced" to divorce his wife because "he was having affairs left, right, and center all the time." Phil, who remembered his father fondly, put this into perspective when he said that "he was not around long enough for me to dislike him."

Participants' fathers were largely absent from participants' early lives in approximately one-third of the families about which I was given information. Although this is not an unusual situation even in contemporary families, it is not without consequences. That which is not readily available often increases in value. When parents who are scarce are also persons who are afforded relatively higher status and authority, both within their families and within society at large, simply by virtue of their gender and sex, their value may become further inflated in the eyes of young children. If such parents also rule arbitrarily and harshly, their children may feel more highly motivated to shape themselves to become the people whom they expect will most please the visiting paternal dignitaries in their lives.

Dangerous and Distant Fathers: Child Abuse

Child abuse is a way of life for far too many children.[4] Brutal beatings, harsh physical punishments, debilitating emotional insults, and sexual use of children by adults were all experienced by the participants in this study before they reached the age of eleven years. Fourteen participants (33 percent) remembered their fathers having beaten them badly and often or having been sexually abusive to them when they were children.[5] Another nine people (21 percent) recalled their fathers inflicting harsh physical punishments or subjecting them to ongoing emotional humiliation and shaming.[6] In total, twenty-three participants (53.5 percent) said that their fathers had treated them in abusive ways at least some of the time. In most cases, those who were badly beaten were profoundly fearful of their fathers. In some instances, the abuse seemed to make the youngsters try harder to win their fathers' love and approval. In a number of situations, participants responded in a complex interplay of both of these ways.[7]

For example, Morgan described her father as an alcoholic who "worked seven days a week" and "was right out to lunch" much of the time, whereas Morgan's mother had mental problems and was often incapacitated by her illness, prescription drugs, and alcohol. Not surprisingly, Morgan recalled that her childhood home was a "horrible" one in which there was "no affection at all." Morgan recalled that, as a young girl, she and her younger brother lived in constant fear of their father's abuse:

> I remember his temper. By the time we were seven or eight . . . my brother and I shared a room, and my mother instituted this thing. Like, if my father was at work and we did anything bad, when he got in it was, like, a regimented thing. He would come in and beat us up. I can remember . . . we did something, and . . . we were lying in bed and we heard him come in, and both my brother and I were just screaming and crying because we knew for sure that she was telling him and he was going to come in and hit us both. And we were just terrified. I can remember that terror of knowing that there was someone that was going to come in and beat you up.

Despite this fear, Morgan recalled that she had been closer to her abusive father than to her "crazy" mother because her father "had more of a personality than my mother."

Ken was the victim of what seemed to be almost constant torture at the hands of her alcoholic father. Ken repeatedly said that "emotional and physical abuse were a way of life." Ken told of many abysmal forms of physical, sexual, and emotionally sadistic treatment which her father meted out to her, her mother, and her siblings. He characterized her grade school years as a time when she endured all of these types of domination. He told this story through tears:

> We got slapped around a lot. But these are the years when the sexual abuse was something that I didn't know how to cope with. . . . I know it was during . . . fourth or fifth grade that I remember the incidents, but everything else is gone. I remember my mom worked two nights a week. She'd go later on in the day and she'd come home later. . . . I'd usually finish eating first . . . and then, when the chores were done, I'd go to my room. When my sister and brother finished eating my father would come up to my room and yell at me.
>
> We all had desks in our rooms and a chair. . . . I'd be sitting in that chair when he'd come in and I'd try not to look at him. Well, one day when he came in, he was standing behind me and he had his one hand on my shoulder and he was talking. I don't remember what he was talking about but I remember that I heard something and he unzipped his zipper. And I didn't know what he was doing. And I don't remember whether he asked me to turn around or whether he pushed the swivel chair around but he took my hand and he put it on his penis. Today, I know what he was doing, but then I didn't. He was masturbating, and when he was just about to come he put his penis in my mouth. He just told me to lick it like a sucker. He'd come to my room a lot. He'd jack off and then he'd put his penis in my mouth and ejaculate and, well, what do you do?

What, indeed does a child of this age do in the face of such abuse? First of all, Ken reported that he had blocked out much of what happened to her during those years. Secondly, she became quite "confused." He recalled,

"I didn't know if I would grow up to be a man. I knew that I didn't want to be like my father, but I wanted to be in control. Yes, I wanted to be a boy."

Simon lived with a stepfather when she was between the ages of six and twelve. During most of that time, she was convinced by her stepfather that he was actually her biological father and that her mother was dead (which she was not). He described the man as "really evil, in the true sense of the word" and illustrated his point with this description of just some of what this man inflicted upon those who had the misfortune to live with him:

> He had threatened to kill [mom]. She, to this day, keeps her number unlisted and unpublished because of that. And I think that the man would. I know that he killed one of my stepbrothers. He also killed [a previous wife]. . . . He killed one of her children. He hit him in the stomach. He was three years old. His appendix burst and he didn't take him to the hospital until he was so physically sick from the appendix rupturing that he had to be hospitalized and at that point it was too late and he died from the poisoning. And nothing happened from that. . . . Then the woman that he was married to was an epileptic and I saw her have two grande mals. She got real gutsy and left him shortly after her son had been killed—shortly after the funeral. Her medication was found outside of her apartment, on the ground, and she died of a seizure. All the circumstantial evidence pointed towards him, but it was circumstantial evidence.

As a child, Simon was overwhelmed by her stepfather's power to do whatever he wished and suffer no consequences for his actions. She recalled feeling this way about him:

> Oddly enough I had a great deal of affection for my stepfather. . . . I was very much in awe of his body. He was about six feet tall and he was one of these people that, even while he ate, his muscles rippled. I was fascinated by that. He was very, very strong. . . . To me he was huge. He was a giant. He was awesome. . . . I wanted to grow up to be just like him. So, in some ways he was a role model for me at the time. . . . I've never quite understood that but, you know, I read something recently about the tortured identifying with the torturer and I think it's that kind of syndrome that you get into.

Alan told a similar story about being both attracted to and repulsed by her father's apparent ability to control all that happened around him. She too wanted to become like her father, at the same time as she both feared and loved him. Alan described the relationship she had with her alcoholic father this way:

Before school, I got up and hid from my father. . . . After school, I went to my room and hid from my father. He had his own business and worked different shifts so I never knew when he'd be home or in what mood or how drunk. I hid in my room and read books. . . . I remember being poked with forks at the dinner table because my father "owned" me. I remember learning to say nothing, to not cry, and to be as passive and unobtrusive as possible in order to avoid physical and verbal abuse. I remember "glazing over" my eyes to look as unthreatening and as uncompetitive as possible to my father. I remember being brutally shaken by my father while he was in blackouts. I remember vomiting after dinner quite a bit, knowing that I would be further abused during the evening because of my father's alcoholism.

I looked up to my father because he had the power in the family. I feared him but also wanted to be like him. . . . I feared my father and I was jealous when he gave my mother attention, but I don't remember being able to dislike him because I didn't know what a normal father-child relationship was supposed to be like. . . . I wanted to be a father/husband. I equated power with being a father/husband.

Jack, Bill, Dale, Nathan, Dennis, and Steven, all of whom suffered abuse from their fathers and watched their fathers similarly abuse other family members, described their fathers in terms such as "real mean," "scary," someone to be "petrified of" and "hate." Unlike the previous participants, none of these people remembered feeling admiration for their fathers while they were young girls.

Those who were only occasionally beaten or whose fathers were emotionally rather than physically hard on them, their mothers, and their siblings were likely to have appreciated their fathers' roles in their young lives. They tended to see the treatment they received from their fathers as fitting to the circumstances under which it occurred. Concomitantly, they were likely to describe their fathers in complementary or at least relatively neutral terms and to see themselves as in some ways similar to their fathers.

For example, Peter remembered only a few severe beatings from her father while she was a youngster. In retrospect, Peter felt that he was able to understand why her father had reacted the way he had to her childish transgressions, although at the time and for many years afterward she felt deeply wronged by the events. Peter remembered spending many enjoyable hours being very close with her father while her mother was away at work. He remembered the father of her youth as "my buddy" and said emphatically that at the time "I wanted to be just like my dad."

Mel likewise felt that the dozen or so times that her father had beaten her and her brother with a belt were justified. Mel recalled a mixture of emotions about her childhood relationship with her father. Her father was an alcoholic who had good periods and bad periods. During the good times, Mel recalled that she and her father "got along great" and that she was her father's favorite child. At other times, Mel recalled, "he was a good provider but he was a fucking asshole. Every time you needed him to be a parent, he was drunk."

All of the others who were physically punished or severely emotionally criticized did not consider themselves to have been abused by their fathers. Nonetheless, all but one of them felt that their fathers had been distant when they were girls. They seemed to accept this, albeit with some irritation. Terry, for example, remembered the father of her youth as having been taciturn. Terry felt that she had been emotionally abused by her parents because they "would tell me that I was no good, that I had failed them, and what the hell was wrong with me (because I did not want to wear dresses and so on)." As Terry remembered it, she had no other interactions with her father besides such fights over gender. However, Terry was able to describe her "unemotional" father somewhat sympathetically as a man who at times could "show his tenderness for his children." Howie remembered the father of her childhood as mostly a "timid" man who was "happy to just get by" and who "let others use him." Nevertheless, Howie felt that the times that her father had physically punished her were justified and that overall her father was a "very nice and gentle" and "generous" man.

In sum, many of these children grew up in environments which were charged with violence, humiliation, and abuse. Fifteen participants (35 percent) lived through their childhoods watching their mothers[8] or siblings[9] being beaten or humiliated by their fathers. All but one of them[10] plus another ten participants[11] (56 percent) were themselves subjected to violence or humiliation by their fathers. In total, twenty-four participants lived in environments of violence or humiliation which they perceived to be largely under the control of their fathers.

It seems likely that many of these children followed a pattern of identifying with the aggressor which is sometimes found among oppressed people.[12] When people are subjugated, their natural desire for dignity may lead them to search out ways to redeem their senses of themselves as valuable human beings who are not subject to arbitrary violation by others. Unfortunately, often the most salient examples of inviolate strength and power which are readily available to them are the seemingly omnipotent images presented by their dominators. In striving to rebuild their self-respect and reestablish their boundaries, they may imitate the most compelling figures of authority and power to which they have access. When they thus identify with and then replicate the behaviours of their oppressors, they may begin to feel strong again. However, the price for doing so, under the conditions of patriarchy in general, and under the conditions of families such as those of some participants, is the necessary rejection of the potential for seeing femaleness as a position of strength. Such participants were instead drawn to model themselves after the actuality of male patriarchal power.

Daddy's Girls?: Fathers as Agents of Gender Socialization

A number of participants' fathers seemed to take special interest in their daughters while they were young, taking them with them as they did the masculine things of which their everyday work and recreational lives were comprised. Such fathers seemed to be more or less following the pattern of behavior which fathers more commonly exhibit with their sons. They spent more time with these girls than with their other daughters and in some cases more time than with their sons—so much so that Morgan, Eli, Harry, and Dale said that when they were girls, they believed that their fathers had wanted them to have been boys.[13]

Thus many participants' fathers seemed to relate to their daughters as companions with whom they might share the pleasures of their masculine interests and the burdens of their masculine responsibilities. They expected participants to accompany them in their activities with the uncomplaining attention which fathers usually demand of their sons. It would almost seem that many of those fathers who were not guilty of alienating their daughters through their violence were busy grooming them to be their young replicas. In some cases, a combination of these effects seems to have bound fathers and daughters together in intense love/hate identification processes,[14] so much so that fifteen participants (35 percent) made comments indicating that they had adopted their paternal figures as role models.[15] This stands in stark contrast to the attitudes which participants expressed about their mothers, of whom they were often protective and sometimes complimentary but whom they rarely wanted to emulate in any way. In addition, nine participants (21 percent) said that they felt that as young girls they had been their father's favorite children,[16] versus only Steven, who felt that she had been her mother's favorite. All participants who had been their fathers' favourite children except Robin, whose father was much older and reserved, either said very positive things about their fathers or reported that they had, as girls, wanted to model themselves after their fathers.

Alan's angry declaration was the most negative of the comments made by those participants who felt themselves to have been their fathers' favourite children. Alan said that even though, as a girl, she thought her father to be "cruel" and was "scared to death of him," she still wanted to "respect and imitate him" because "he seemed powerful." Warmer feelings were expressed by Scott, who thought her father was "kind of special," and by Mel, who was often angry at her father for his irresponsibility when he drank but felt that he was "great" at other times. On the most enthusiastic end of the spectrum were Sam, who remembered her girlhood father as "the best in the world"; Darren, who "hero-worshipped" the father of her youth; Bruce, who remembered her father as a "handsome," "honest," "hard-working," and "wonderful" man; and Bob, who repeatedly referred to her childhood father as her "hero" and her "knight in shining armour."

One of the major ways in which fathers are influential in socializing their sons to be properly masculine and their daughters to be appropriately feminine is by selectively reinforcing and discouraging stereotypically gendered behaviors and attitudes. Not surprisingly, many participants recalled their fathers as either tolerating their masculinity or actively helping them to become masculine. Approximately two-thirds (63 percent) of the participants remembered their fathers as either having been unconcerned about their masculine pursuits[17] or having actively encouraged them to shoulder masculine responsibilities or to enjoy masculine activities.[18] Another eight participants (19 percent) said that they had received mixed messages from their fathers about their gender training; sometimes their fathers encouraged them to adopt femininity, sometimes they were apparently placid about gender, and sometimes they encouraged their growing masculinity.[19] Six other people (14 percent) made no distinctive comments about their fathers' roles in this regard.[20] Only Morgan and Ken felt that their fathers actively and exclusively had trained them toward femininity.

Most of the participants who felt that their fathers had been supportive of their masculinity also remembered feeling warmly toward their fathers and having wanted to be like them when they were young. Many of them had ample opportunities to imitate their fathers. Some fathers took their daughters with them while they worked; some fathers allowed their girls to help out as they did their household chores; some fathers spent recreational time with them doing typical masculine pastimes; some fathers did all of these things.

Roger's story illustrates several of these themes. Roger was an adopted only child. Her mother was away at work most of the time that Roger was a preschool girl. Therefore Roger's father did most of the child care during this time. Roger fondly remembered these formative years during which she and her father were alone together every day on her father's ranch. Roger remembered her father making fun out of most chores which they did together. For example, she thought it was a treat when she got to "drive the truck in the hayfields when it was hay cutting time." Roger said that she and her father were "inseparable" during these years. He was her "idol" until his early death when she was eleven years old. Roger remembered her father as a very special person:

> For a man back in the 1940s, he was very warm, very sensitive, very caring person. Back in the 1940s, men didn't take charge of their kids. They didn't change their diapers, they didn't feed them. He did. He was not a stereotypical man of the 1940s. And yet he was a very macho man, a man's man. He was six foot tall, weighed 220 pounds, very active, hard worker, my favorite person.

As an example of how much she admired her father, Roger explained how she had imitated the way her father looked and moved:

> I was a little girl at the time, and girls weren't supposed to dress the way I was. . . . Just like my dad. Work boots, jeans, and a shirt, with gloves hanging out of my ass pocket, just like him. . . . My mother dressed me the way I wanted to dress.

In addition, her father called her by a boyish nickname.

Bruce likewise remembered that her father had shared masculine activities with her and was supportive of her wish to dress and move like a boy. He even defended her right to do so against Bruce's mother, who wanted her to be more feminine. Bruce described the dynamics as follows:

> He always included me in everything. . . . "You can hammer that nail . . . sure you can, you won't know if you don't try." And . . . like, if I got a dress dirty, he was okay. My mother would get really upset at me. My mother was always telling me "Now, you have to be ladylike." . . . My mother would say "Stop walking like a truck driver." And . . . I'd hear him say, "Let her walk any way she wants to walk." He was always supportive. . . . My mother always tried to make me a girl. And my father would say, "What would you like for Christmas?" And I would say, "Well, I would like a football helmet, and I would like shoulder pads, and I would like boxing gloves." And that's what he would go out and get. And my mother would get me this easy bake oven. I blew it up. . . . Being male came very natural to me. I think it's because my father had a very positive male image, and he was always giving me good strokes about being whoever I was, no matter what that was. And my mother was always subtracting, my dad was always adding to who I was.

As might be expected from a child who felt so strongly supported by her father and thwarted by her mother, Bruce said that she had been "in love with her father" and had "hated" her "weird" mother. When she was eleven years old and her parents divorced, she held her mother entirely culpable for causing the rift and "hated her for hurting him."

Several participants recalled being brought along or following their fathers as they did their work.[21] Ed's father was a trucker, and when Ed was a girl, she "always used to go on the trucks with him. And that was great. Right up on the sleeper and read comic books about picking up little girls. That was fun." Similarly, Luther's father, who was a property manager, took his preschool daughter "around with him" as he worked. Luther recalled that these times together were almost the only times that she got to see her father. They must have made a significant impression because Luther turned out to be "very much like him."

Jack's and Dale's stories about their fathers were almost identical to one another. When they were young girls, they both spent a lot of time with their fathers, who were farmers. Jack said that her father was a "very, very distant," "angry," and "frustrated" alcoholic man who beat his children with a horsewhip. Dale remembered her father as a violent man who "scared the living shit out of us." Jack, who was the youngest of four girls, was "all the time" drafted by her father, as if she were a son, to help with the "men's" work on the farm:

> My father, I love him, but I don't like him. He is real mean. He would never ask us to help him, it was always, "You son of a bitch kids come out and help now." . . . He usually came to me. I always loved to operate farm equipment, and I got pretty good at it. And so, him and I were always, him on one tractor and me on the other, and so that worked out fine.

Dale said that she "did a man's job" and that her father made her "get out of bed at four in the morning. We'd work 'til ten at night. We worked, worked, worked." As girls, both Jack and Dale learned to work "like a man," and to take abuse "like a man." Although neither ever felt any fondness for their fathers, clearly the lessons of masculinity were pounded home.

A number of other fathers also liked to play or relax in traditionally masculine ways with their daughters. Scott, Sam, Colin, Nathan, Dennis, Steven, and Peter all went camping out in the woods, hunting, or fishing with their fathers or spent time with their fathers playing ball or watching ball games on television. Peter's father, for example, did a lot of the child care for her when she was preschool age and throughout her childhood. Peter, who recalled being her father's favorite, liked to play catch and go fishing with her father. As Peter remembered it, their games of catch taught her more than one lesson about masculinity:

> Dad would take me outside and we'd play catch with the hardball. And he didn't hold back. . . . And my hand would be red and swollen. He'd say, "Don't you cry." He'd just go, "Catch that ball. You don't be afraid of that ball." And I'd play.

It would seem that her father was teaching her to be physically tough in a stereotypically masculine way. Peter remembered that her father used to say to her, "you're my kid," in a very proprietary way. Peter, as an adult, said of their relationship: "I am more my father than anything, and he knows it. We are alike!" Apparently Peter's father's educative efforts were well rewarded.

Some fathers seemed not to be emphatically masculine in their interests. The interests which they nurtured in their children were thus perhaps less distinctively masculine. However, the salience of the time which they spent with their daughters may still have been important in encouraging them to identify with their fathers, people with whom they spent many special and enjoyable hours.

When Eli was a girl, she and her father spent many enjoyable hours together before a divorce forced them to be apart more of the time. Eli remembered her father as a sensitive, artistic man whom she strove to emulate, as would a son:

> He was terrific, he was a pal. He was a neat dad to have, he used to sing me to sleep, we used to have fires, and go for long walks up in the woods, and chop wood, and build things together. I'd play music for him, and he would sing to me, and we would play chess by the fire. . . . I think the best of all was just walking, quietly, with my dad, going for long walks. . . . He was a poet too, and he would say beautiful things. . . . We had great times. . . . To me, he was just a lovely dad. He was the kind of guy you want to sit on his lap. I remember I used to crawl into bed with him. I remember . . . it was warm, and it was safe. . . . I admired him intensely. . . . I felt like I was like him. . . . We were great pals, even though he says I was a nice sweet little blond haired girl, I still think we were as close as a father and son could get.

Darren lost both of her parents in a car crash when she was sixteen years old. Darren did not think very highly of her mother, who was violent and suffered from mental illness, but "hero-worshipped" her father, who favoured her over her four brothers and sisters. Darren remembered her father more for his highly moral character than for anything else:

> I thought he was the greatest. . . . I guess probably the biggest thing was he was very individualist, which I am, which is a very important thing to me, which I feel very few people are. . . . It means standing by your principles, your values. Not being afraid to be ridiculed, you know. And making a departure from the crowd, from the masses. . . . I guess I really learned that individualism from my father. He wasn't afraid to say, or do, or think what he felt. And I'm sure he did get ridiculed, because he was from a different culture in this country, and [our city] was kind of conservative. Short, and dark-skinned and wore a French beret

and looked kind of silly to other people. And a silly accent to them and, you know, probably got laughed at and stuff. I think he was an eccentric, but he didn't care, and I inherited some of that. Quite a bit of that. And thank God, because I value that individualism very highly. That was one main thing. . . . The other thing, I think, which sort of comes related to that is integrity. I value integrity very highly, and living by your principles, your values. I think my father did that, I mean, obviously he fell short, and I do too, but I think there was a real striving for integrity.

Keith also felt that, as a girl, she had "always been close" with her "family oriented" father, with whom Keith felt "very much alike." Her father took her and her sisters to classical music concerts and museums, to botanical gardens and theme parks. Keith remembered him as "a good father":

There was a lot I liked about him. I'd say the best I liked about him was his philosophical constant thinking, constant trying to understand things. And being an intelligent person like he was he did have a great deal of understanding of things. Not just physical things, philosophical things, you know religious things and moral questions. . . . He always did everything in the best quality way that he could do. That's the best way to describe him. Extremely sensitive, fairly emotional, romantic kind of person. A little on the quiet side, but able to express himself very well—something I've always admired. . . . And also another thing about him which I picked up . . . was his taste for the arts. . . . I'm like my father in almost everything really.

Keith grew to be a man who consciously and purposefully modeled himself after his father:

I succeeded in many ways of emulating what type of role model I wanted to emulate. One of the most major ones was my dad. . . . And I think that [Dad] was very much a positive influence on me as a person, and most certainly as a male. Whenever I'm in doubt as to the proper way to handle a situation—I mean proper in the sense of being morally correct and in being the best, the most positive and the most right way to handle the situation—I ask myself what my father would do. And usually that dictates to me the proper course of action that I feel comfortable in following.

Thus most participants (63 percent) remembered the fathers of their childhood years as larger-than-life figures. They recalled their fathers in generally favorable terms ranging from begrudging to outright admiration. The basis of their fond feelings seemed mainly to lie in their recollections of time spent with their fathers sharing the enjoyment of stereotypically masculine work or recreational activities.

Aaron, Bill, Jorge, Terry, Brian, Grant, Pat, and Hal all remembered getting mixed messages from their fathers about whether they should act more like boys or more like girls. These participants remembered their fathers as demanding femininity from them but also conveying to them the message that they actually thought more highly of masculinity. Thus these participants were also given incentives by their fathers, albeit covert ones, to emulate masculinity. As might be expected, the people who received such ambivalent gender training from their fathers also expressed an assortment of feelings about their fathers.

Aaron told a few stories which illustrated this kind of predicament. Aaron's father wanted a son with whom he could share his interests. Aaron did have a brother who was two years older, but even when they were children, the brother leaned more toward femininity while Aaron tended toward masculinity. On the one hand, Aaron's father "dogmatically" insisted that she dress and act in a feminine manner when company came to visit. There were times when Aaron felt that her father had been exceedingly insensitive to her youthful feelings:

> I saw a movie taken of me on my three year old birthday, I was forced by my father . . . to get up on a picnic table (we were outdoors, June birthday) and dance for this movie camera. And . . . I was crying. I was three, I was dancing being cute again for the adults, which I resented very much, and I was crying and dancing. . . . I'm saying this man was cruel. And at later times, I was dressed up and asked to perform on the piano and so on. This was why he paid for the lessons, so he could show us kids off. And I resented it terribly and a lot of it had to do with being dressed up and shown off.

On the other hand, there were times when Aaron's father seemed to accept his daughter's proffered willingness to take the place of the son who demurred from engagement in more rugged father-son activities. Aaron recalled one such incident as one of the few times when Aaron's "uninvolved" father paid attention to her:

> The summer I was nine we got away from everybody as a family in a way that's never happened before or since. There was a resort that was not used because it was Second World War and somebody gave it to my dad for two weeks. . . . We got in there by bus. . . . There was no place for him to go, and no telephones. He had no chance to relate to his business, and he was lonesome. So, he and his boy were going to fish. Well, unfortunately, his boy didn't care that much for fishing. And he didn't care at all for going out and catching the little bitty green frogs and putting them on the hooks. And I did. I thoroughly enjoyed it. . . . And we spent two weeks that not only stayed in my mind as the way it should have been between father and son, but also stayed in his mind.

When Brian was a girl, her father seemed to be willing to allow her to follow along and attempt to be helpful as he did his chores. However, it felt to Brian as if her father always expected her to fail at these things because she was "only a girl." Brian felt ignored and demeaned for being female and sorely resented being considered to be a member of what she thought was an inferior group. Brian remembered a particular incident with her father as having painfully driven home this point:

> I became more aware that I was discounted in worth because I was only a "girl." Once, when I was about ten, he took my two brothers fishing to the pond. He never mentioned or invited me and my sister. I was bitterly enraged and angry. I liked to fish very much and I was older than the brothers. . . . I complained to my mother and she told me it was because they were boys and my father wanted to do something with just the boys. The matter burned in me like fire. It was one of the fiercest feelings I felt about any incident when I was a kid. . . . All that summer, the matter of the fishing trip burned in me. In every aspect of my life, my belief that I should have been born a boy, that I might yet somehow become a boy, were very powerful parts of my consciousness. Because I was a "girl" no one credited or encouraged my accomplishments. . . . My father never kept his promise to take us fishing like that day. Somehow, he never had time.

Hal was particularly articulate in describing the tensions in the relationship she had with her father as a child. As a girl, she wanted to please her father, whom she thought of as tremendously handsome and likely to become president of the United States. Her father expressly advocated femininity for Hal but, through example, seemed also to nourish some of Hal's masculine tendencies. Hal outlined the dynamics thus:

> My father was tall and handsome, very self-confident, with highly developed social skills. He was also quiet and reflective. He liked to read a great deal, and to work in the garden. . . . On the weekends he would always let me help with chores, and he taught me how to do many things and how to use tools that Mom didn't know how to use. He made me feel very special, and that's what I liked best about him; not that he put me on a pedestal, but that he included me and taught me things so that there was always a special kind of bond between us. It made me feel acknowledged, seen for who I was.
>
> There wasn't anything I disliked about him, even though we would fight sometimes. . . . When we fought, it was usually about a conflict in agenda or attire. It was easier for my father to get me to put on a dress because he would tell me how nice I would look and how proud of me he would be. . . . Looking back on it, I can recall the pressure I felt knowing Dad liked pretty little girls in dresses and wanting to

please him, wanting to preserve that feeling of acknowledgment I got from being with him, all the while knowing that when I wore a dress I was not projecting the image of who I really was. So there I was getting acknowledgment for something that wasn't me. Of course, I didn't understand all that then; I only felt the pressure of it.

Hal therefore felt that although her father's actions seemed to say "be like me," his words said "be a pretty little girl."

Grant had a love/hate relationship with her physically abusive adoptive mother but felt closer to her adoptive father, who she felt was more consistent in his treatment of her. Grant remembered her adoptive father as being "supportive" of her proclivities as a child.

> I could get through to my dad that I didn't want girls' toys exclusively.
> . . . I had an operating garage. You could crank up the little elevator, wheels moved on the cars, it was great. . . . I was a Civil War buff for a long time. We went to Gettysburg. I came home with a reproduction of both the pistol and the rifle and taught myself to shoot. . . . They put up with it; they tolerated it. . . . I remember one year I got . . . building sets. . . . I was getting this from my parents. . . . I remember western toys. I remember six shooters, and one of those rocking horses on springs. God, that was great. I remember being very upset when I got my bicycle because it was missing the bar. That annoyed me. But they at least got it for me in blue. That was a plus. . . . it was funny. I wanted things like this, and it was acceptable. That was no big deal.

Grant became convinced from a very early age, however, that she should have been a boy. When she told her adoptive parents about her convictions and began to have social problems related to her gender, they no longer were tolerant of her masculinity and sent her to a child psychologist for gender related counselling starting when she was six years old.

Pat also remembered getting mixed messages about gender from her father when she was a girl. Pat recalled being close with the father of her youth who "had some primary parenting responsibilities for me . . . bathing me, feeding me, that kind of stuff." Pat also remembered, "my father treated me much like a boy, I think. In terms of encouraging athletic stuff and how to fight and things like that." However, her parents were also sufficiently concerned about her budding masculinity that, like Grant's parents, they sent their daughter to therapy while she was still in grade school in the hope that it might cure her of the gender nonconformity in which they had previously encouraged her.

In sum, approximately one-fifth (19 percent) of participants remembered their fathers as having both encouraged and discouraged masculinity in them during their childhoods.[22] They recalled their fathers as men who clearly valued masculinity more than femininity but also as men who seemed to believe that their daughters ought to be feminine. Participants thus seemed to have been caught between wanting to be good girls and trying to perform in ways which would gain their fathers' respect.

The only two participants who recalled their fathers as having consistently demanded femininity from them were consistently negative in their evaluations of their fathers. Morgan remembered that when she was a girl, her father was mostly an absent figure from her young life, but that when he was there he expected her to act like a girl. In addition to their battles about gender, Morgan also recalled having been physically abused by her father. Ken, who as a girl was severely physically and sexually abused by her father, said that there was no tolerance for gender variance in her family at all. Beyond this abuse, Ken remembered doing very little with her father, who was drunk and angry much of the time. Ken felt as though she had been her father's "scapegoat" and that they had never been close.

Overall, the vast majority of participants felt that their fathers had at the very least been unconcerned about their budding masculinity during their childhood years. Most participants reported that their fathers had, in many ways, encouraged and condoned their masculinity. It would seem from the stories told by these participants that many fathers were happy enough for the interests which their daughters took in their pursuits and were willing to share with them the pleasures and pains of manhood. The children, for their part, seemed happy to follow their fathers' leads.

Summary and Commentary

The relationships which participants had with their fathers cannot be understood in isolation from the context of the larger social relations in which they were played out. Their families were organized in accordance with the practices of European and North American patriarchal capitalism of the late twentieth century. Thus they were members of societies which presumed that fathers would hold more authority, power, and respect than mothers by virtue of their paternity alone and that those people who earned the most money by selling their labour, or the products of their labour, would likewise be afforded greater power, status, and authority. The terms of participants' relationships with their fathers were therefore set by default to favour participants' admiring their fathers for their greater mastery in those areas of life afforded higher social statuses.

The fact that many fathers were away from their homes or otherwise unavailable to their daughters much of the time may have served to reinforce their value in their daughters' eyes. Many of them came to see their fathers as important people who were engaged in serious business which took them to more interesting and exciting places than their own homes. When they had time to devote to their children, their time came as a scarce and therefore very valuable commodity. This may have meant that the time which these fathers spent with their daughters became especially salient to their daughters, that the messages about gender which the fathers communicated to their daughters also became especially weighty in import, and that participants were more highly motivated to please these important men who had so little time for them in their busy days. Similar effects seem also to have followed from some fathers' absences which came about for less noble reasons.

Many participants' fathers were also violent men who imposed their wills upon their family members through terror, humiliation, and abuse. Although in most cases this type of treatment alienated participants from loving or otherwise feeling close to their fathers, it did not prevent them from wanting to possess the power which they experienced as adhering to manliness. They generally perceived these fathers as largely invulnerable men who could do as they pleased in their own worlds. For those who were on the receiving end of their controlling and abusive behavior, such freedom and hegemony must have seemed exceedingly tantalizing. Many of those who suffered under their fathers' reigns spoke of wanting to hold power like their fathers when they were older.

Fathers also usually socialize their daughters to be feminine by selectively rewarding feminine behaviors and discouraging masculine ones. The majority of participants recounted stories which indicated that their fathers either encouraged or benignly tolerated participants' interests in emulating masculinity. In some cases, participants felt quite strongly that their fathers had wanted them to be boys. They relayed stories in support of these beliefs which illustrated some of the ways in which their fathers had seemed to be actively training them to adopt the ways of men. In a few cases, circumstances were such that fathers had primary caretaking responsibilities for their daughters during some of their younger years, thus facilitating a masculine identification process. Others encouraged their daughters to model themselves in their images by taking them with them wherever they went, sharing with them their workaday and recreational lives, and specifically instructing them in the skills of masculinity.

Overall, participants seemed to absorb quite readily the lessons they learned from their fathers. They appeared to have learned that men are people of great importance and power who can hurt and control others but who can rarely be hurt or controlled themselves. Participants learned from their fathers that what men do can be interesting and fun and that when men have to do things which are less than enjoyable, they are highly rewarded and valued for their efforts. They learned that the lives of their fathers, difficult as they may have been, were good ones to have in a patriarchal world.

Relationships with Grandfathers and Uncles

Sixteen participants (37 percent)[23] said that to some degree their grandfathers[24] or uncles[25] had played parts in their youths. Six people lived with their grandfathers for a period of time during their childhood years;[26] Ken, Bill, Harry, and Nathan all had grandfathers who lived nearby and with whom they visited often; Grant's and Hal's grandfathers' visits from out of town were memorable for them. All of these participants except Stan remembered their grandfathers warmly from their time with them when they were girls.

Ken, Bill, Brian, Darcy, and Nathan all spoke of their grandfathers in considerably kinder terms than they had used for their fathers. Ken's case was particularly dramatic. Ken's father had been brutally abusive to her as a girl: emotionally, physically, and sexually. Ken said that he "had nothing positive to say" about the father of her youth and that "the number one person I especially disliked was my father." By contrast, when Ken spoke of his grandparents he called them "caring and concerned" and said of them: "I liked someone to talk to, and I remember them taking the time out just to talk to me. It made me feel important."

Bill similarly remembered the father of her youth as "a very angry and violent man" who beat her often enough that she tried to "avoid him as much as possible." Both Bill's young grandparents and great grandparents lived nearby when she was a child. Bill saw them regularly and remembered both her grandfather and great grandfather as providing her with examples of men who could be "kind but stern." She was "a little afraid of" and "looked up to" both of them, but, in contrast to her feelings about her father, she enjoyed spending time with each of them. Bill said of the grandfather of her youth, "I looked up to my grandpa. . . . I was very comfortable in his company," and of both of her grandparents, "They were very important in my life because I loved them both and learned a lot about how I wanted both to, and not to, face life's challenges."

Brian also talked about her grandfather as a better masculine role model for her than her father had been. As a girl, she lived with her parents and grandparents on the family farm. Brian remembered her father as a "loud and angry," "impatient," "stern," "distant and silent, often disgruntled person" whose motto seemed to be "keep your eyes open and your mouth shut." Brian remembered her grandfather as also being a silent man but a more kindly one, from whom she learned lasting lessons about how to conduct herself in the world.

> I remember my grandfather as an intermediary. We spent a lot more time with our grandfather than our father. My grandfather was . . . more soft-spoken. He didn't really express affection or emotions either and didn't allow kids to be crying or whining around him. Mostly, I guess I learned from my parents and grandparents that people keep a lot of distance from each other. Work is serious. Expressing emotions is weakness. . . .
>
> I [felt] a lot closer to my grandfather. My grandfather was always there, yet somehow a stranger too. He rarely answered questions or talked more than a few words at a time. Sometimes, if I tried to ask him things he'd tell me that if I wanted to be with him I should be quiet. He didn't say it like my father, just quietly and always seeming distant in his own thoughts. . . . My grandfather started to have a greater influence on me. He would point things out to me . . . but the rule was, don't talk, just look and listen. As I look back, I sometimes feel I learned a lot from my grandfather, other times I feel I scarcely knew him. He rarely shared his thoughts.

The other enduring lessons which Brian took away from these men were the value of maleness and masculinity and to "despise girls, and girl things."

Stan's relationship with her grandfather differed from other participants' relations in that she was raised by her grandparents after her father separated from her mentally ill mother. Stan's Christian fundamentalist grandfather "was a very powerful figure" in her young life who "was really strict that I'm not your father, I'm your guardian," and who ruled the family with "an iron fist." Stan's grandfather convinced her that she should be afraid of both her mother and father but offered her no affection himself. In fact, he very clearly communicated to her that she was of very little use to him at all. Stan remembered it this way:

> I was really jealous that he liked my brother better. . . . The first grandchild was me, and then [my brother]. [My brother] was so wonderful. I was so jealous of that. . . . I really thought Grandpa overdid it. I mean, "do you have to be so obvious about liking him more than me?" . . . I hated my mother because she didn't defend me. . . . And it was obviously not parity at all.
>
> [My brother] was a boy and that was the only difference between us. I was just as smart. I had absolutely everything going for me, but I just wasn't a boy. And that was my only fault. . . . I was angry at Gramps. . . . I was doing all I could do. . . . I was making good grades, I was taking piano lessons. . . . I was doing everything that I could do

and it still wasn't working. So, it was out of my control. So, all I could do was be angry.

It would seem almost as if Stan's family pattern was actually designed to teach her that males were, by virtue of their maleness alone, destined to be the most prized and powerful members of her world.

Roger, Gary, and Phil each lived with uncles while they were young. Dennis and Steven both lived close to uncles who played important roles in their childhoods. Grant and Hal visited with uncles who impressed them favorably during their girlhood years. Roger, Grant, Hal, Gary, Dennis, and Steven had gratifying memories of the time which they spent with their uncles when they were girls. Gary had little to say about her father, but from what Gary said of her uncle it can be surmised that her father was a distant figure in her young life and that her uncle took his place in her heart: "My uncle was the father I could talk to. . . . He helped us with homework and problems we had. . . . I looked up to my uncle. I wanted to be like him."

Dennis and Steven each latched on to their uncles as lifelines to offer them masculine but safe havens away from their abusive fathers. Dennis recalled the father of her youth as "a real bad guy" who "would go crazy, absolutely crazy" over "the least little thing." Dennis "always felt, when I was a kid, that we would never wake up the next day. I thought he'd kill us all. A lot, I used to think that." Dennis would sometimes think that she would like to kill her father, whom she felt was responsible for her "house of hell" home environment. Dennis went to her uncle's house as often as possible to escape this miserable situation. He told me about her uncle:

> I had an uncle, a godfather. . . . he used to take my father's place and do things with me, and spend time with me. . . . I saw him a lot. He used to pick me up from kindergarten . . . three or four times a week. . . . He was a bachelor. . . . He had a big influence on those early years, because he was like . . . a buddy to me. . . . He taught me a lot. . . . He was very mechanically inclined. He always used to have projects for us, for me and him. And when I was like six and seven, I would work beside him, and we did major construction on his house, and it was one of the high-lights of my early years. He was like a role model for me. . . . In some ways I wanted to be like him when I grew up. I was always compared to him. Up till this day they say we're two of a kind. . . . When I was younger, that made me feel good when people said that.

Steven similarly remembered that her father was physically and emotion-ally abusive to her. She "hated" him and was "afraid of" him. Steven too had a "special" uncle who had never had children and who seemed to adopt her "sort of like a father."

With the exception of Stan's grandfather, who was legally "in loco parentis," the influences that these elder male relatives had on their grand-daughters and nieces served to further reinforce any positive feelings which they were developing about men and masculinity. In some cases, they provided sanctuary and role models for a few young girls who were frightened and alienated from their own fathers. In others, they simply further confirmed the high value which participants already placed on men and masculinity in their lives.

Relationships with Brothers

Siblings are frequently young children's primary companions and playmates. As such, they can offer many forms of assistance in doing things for one another which they are unable or unwilling to do for themselves, or they may become one another's arch rivals. They may act as comrades in difficult situations, closing ranks to help each other to stay out of trouble with other children, parents, or social institutions,[27] or they may experience conflicts over such issues as status and power afforded to children on the basis of birth order, age, or gender.

Older children can feel sorely neglected when younger siblings first arrive on the scene, or they may feel prematurely promoted to responsibilities for which they are ill-prepared and loathe to undertake. Younger children may feel highly competitive with their older siblings, wishing to prove that they are every bit as able as their senior siblings.[28] Such competitiveness is often especially pronounced between brothers, and even more so for brothers who are close in age.[29]

Girl children with older brothers,[30] especially those in families with few girls and many boys, have been found to be more likely than other girls or than boys with older sisters to play with, imitate, and compete with their brothers in masculine ways.[31] The relationships which the participants in this study had with their brothers during their childhoods appeared to be more similar in nature to those that boys typically have with their brothers than to those which girls usually have with their brothers. They were largely characterized by competitive jockeying for position, masculine styles of play, and the formation of protective coalitions under conditions of threat.[32]

Who Had Brothers

Thirty participants (68 percent)[33] had brothers.[34] One-third of the families of these thirty participants had no other girl children.[35] In another seven families, participants had sisters who were five or more years older or younger than themselves.[36] Therefore a total of seventeen participants (39 percent) came from families in which brothers dominated their sibling worlds. In six additional families, participants either did not have any friends outside of their families or had brothers who were their closest friends during their childhood.[37] Thus in twenty-three (77 percent) of the thirty cases where participants had brothers, these brothers loomed large in their childhood lives.

Sixteen participants (36 percent) had older brothers.[38] Six participants had brothers who were closest in age to them but nevertheless were five or more years older than themselves;[39] only Luther had a sister who was any closer in age. Therefore five of those who had older brothers grew up in homes where they were more or less only children, and ten participants (23 percent) had older brothers who were of an age similar to themselves.[40]

Eighteen participants (41 percent) had younger brothers.[41] Darren's, Tony's, and Pat's younger brothers were five or more years younger than themselves. Darren and Tony also had older brothers who were close to them in age. Thus fifteen participants had a younger brother who was close to them in age.[42] The majority of the eighteen who had younger brothers (61 percent) were also the oldest children in their families.[43]

Only Darren, Tony, Bob, and Phil had both older and younger brothers, but Darren's two younger brothers were seven and thirteen years his junior; Tony's only younger brother was eleven years younger; one of Bob's younger brothers was seven years younger. Therefore only Phil and Bob had both younger and older brothers who were close to them in age.

The pattern which emerges, in terms of either number of brothers or number of brothers close in age, is that more participants were older sisters to younger brothers than the reverse. In addition, eleven (37 percent) of the thirty participants who had brothers were themselves the oldest in their families.[44] Six of them had only their one younger brother as a sibling.[45] Only Aaron and Lee had an older brother as their only sibling. Jordie also had only one older brother, and two sisters, eight and ten years his junior. Thus twenty-two (73 percent) of the thirty participants who had brothers were close to them in age.[46]

Rivals from Birth

A handful of participants reported that their feelings of competitiveness with their younger brothers began at their births. Five of those participants who were older children reported having suffered from resentment toward their younger brothers for the feelings of dethronement which they experienced shortly after their births. Scott, Morgan, Stan, Alan, and Brian each complained about the arrival of their younger brothers into their families. Each of them, except Brian, was the eldest child in their families. Their feelings of displacement may have been exacerbated by the extra welcome that their brothers received on account of their maleness.

Scott's only younger sibling, a brother, arrived when Scott was only two years old. Scott remembered feeling as though her violent and verbally abusive alcoholic mother favoured her brother when they were children but that her father favoured her.

> When my brother was born, I have a feeling that my mother basically ignored me after that. . . . when I look at pictures of my brother, my mother, and I together, I'm always away from the group and I look very sad. . . . I was probably feeling bad about myself, and feeling left out, and feeling really distant from my mother at that point.

Morgan also had only a single sibling, a brother, a year and a half younger. Morgan's mother said that "when he came into the family I changed completely." Morgan remembered that "I used to beat my brother up a lot" and that they were not close as children. Morgan also recalled feeling that when they were young, "it was obvious" that her little brother, like Scott's, was her mother's favorite child.

Stan likewise had a single younger sibling, a brother who was one and a half years younger than Stan. Stan remembered her brother being blatantly and relentlessly favoured simply for being born a boy. Stan said that although as a child she did not hold her brother directly responsible for the situation, she was always very angry about this. In reaction, Stan strove to be the best at everything she did in the hope that she would win some measure of praise for her efforts.

Alan also remembered that the arrival of younger siblings cost her the comfort of maternal warmth, security, and protection. Alan had one brother, who was two years younger, and one sister, who was four years younger. When Alan was a girl, she, like Stan, did not hold her younger siblings responsible for the way her mother changed with her. Alan said, "I only remember her being gone and feeling loss. . . . when my brother and sister were born, my mother started calling me 'grown up.' "

Brian, who had two younger brothers and one older, close to him in age, also remembered the arrival of one of her younger brothers as especially upsetting.

> I liked people to read to me. I was about four. My mother used to read books . . . to my sister and me at bedtime. . . . Then our little brother began to want to join us. He was too squirmy. I had to sit further from our mother because he got to be next to her. He was talkative, prevented me from seeing pictures. We all fought. Our mother stopped reading bedtime stories completely. She never took time to read us books after that.

Thus five participants (11 percent) recalled having felt resentment at the arrivals of their younger brothers into their family constellations. Their discomfort at losing their special positions as babies of their families seemed to have been further compounded by the differences in parental attentions afforded to older girls versus baby boys. As older girls they were expected to take back seats to their baby brothers, perhaps even to act in their service. Participants did not recall these changes fondly.

Playing Together

Most participants who had brothers who were close to them in age spent a considerable amount of their time playing with them when they were young. When those brothers were older brothers, participants often followed after them, mimicking or competing with them. In some cases, especially when their brothers were considerably older than themselves, participants used their older brothers as idealized role models. Eighteen of the thirty participants who had brothers (60 percent) said that as children they had often played with their brothers.[47] Seven (23 percent) of them also looked up to their brothers as examples of how they would like to be if they could somehow have become boys.[48]

Jorge's and Phil's memories from their childhoods were similar to those of several others. Phil simply said, "my brother and I did everything together." Jorge remembered that when she was a girl, she was "real close" with her only sibling, her brother who was four years younger than she. Her brother was "the main person I did things with" and what they did together was they "played sports and typical 'male' games."

Robin, Luther, Howie, and Fred all looked up to their much older brothers and wanted to be like them. Robin said that she had "idolized" her older brother "because he was a boy" and that she had wanted to be "just like him." She "tagged along with him" whenever he would allow it. When Luther, Howie, and Fred were girls, they were not able to follow after their brothers very much, but they too "looked up to" their brothers and used them as role models. Luther wanted to be "just like" her only brother, who was five years older than herself. Howie said of his brother, who was nine years older and his only sibling, "I worshipped my brother. He was my mentor. . . . For me, my brother (rather than my parents) was my role model."

Bruce, who had one older brother and two younger sisters, also remembered preferring to be with the boys doing whatever the boys enjoyed most:

> I always remember feeling like the things that my brother did, or the boys in the neighborhood, the things that they did, were much more

exciting and fun than what girls did. Girls played with dolls and Easy Bake ovens. Yuck. And boys played with Matchbox toys . . . and they played in the jungle. . . . And boys were not afraid. And boys would touch spiders. And boys were bold, and girls were not supposed to be. And boys did not have to wear shirts, and girls had to. . . . I think I envied that.

Aaron similarly recalled:

I tried to get into my brother's group of boyfriends. All I remember is being one big mass of skinned knees . . . because I was always running after these kids that were bigger than I was, trying to keep up. . . . But I wanted to be with my brother's friends.

Dale, who had one younger brother and four sisters, had felt unloved and unwanted by her parents. She felt that her only brother, who was treated "like a god in the family," was the sole person to whom she could "reach out" in her "really, really lonely" early childhood. Dale remembered their relationship this way:

I think I can remember, before I went into grade one, that I wanted to be a boy. Like, I wanted to be like my brother. I was just more interested in boy things than girl things. And actually, we were inseparable as kids. I used to envy him when he would get the boxing gloves for Christmas and the boys' things, and I would get a doll or something. . . . I was a very, very shy child. I was so quiet everybody used to call me Mouse. But my best friend, and the person I was closest to, was my brother. We did the outdoors stuff together and roughed it up. We wrestled, we boxed. . . . We played in the bush all the time. We had our own forts out there and what not. . . . I was just like my brother, I guess. I guess I just thought of myself as a boy then. . . . I just wanted to be like my brother.

Unfortunately for Dale, her brother also had a "very mean streak," and by the time Dale was ten or eleven years old her brother "got very brutal with us. . . . He chased us with knives and he used to beat the living shit out of me. Lumps all over my head and everything else." Dale became "petrified" of their brother and started keeping her distance from him.

Whether or not participants were welcomed by their brothers, whether or not participants admired their brothers, most of those participants who had brothers (60 percent) spent a lot of time in their company. Unlike their relationships with their sisters, participants were well positioned to learn from their brothers and from the other boys in their play groups how to sharpen their proficiencies at masculinity. In addition to those participants who clearly stated that they used their brothers as male role models, it might be inferred from participants' preferences for the companionship of boys that participants who played with their brothers and with other boys were also engaging in actively absorbing the skills necessary for making themselves acceptable among boys. Thus, at the same time as they were isolating themselves from their sisters, the majority of participants happily accepted masculine socialization in the company of their brothers.

Tomboys: Competing for Fathers' Attention

Thirteen of the thirty participants who had brothers (43 percent) talked about competing with their brothers for their fathers' attention.[49] Part of this kind of competition for paternal acceptance involved participants putting a great deal of energy into attempting to outperform their brothers at masculine activities. For most of them the contest was relatively easily won. Many of their brothers were either unable to compete effectively or were simply not interested in taking up the challenge.[50] Thus the girls often won over their fathers' affections, whereas their mothers more often aligned themselves with participants' brothers. Nine participants felt that they had been favoured by their fathers over and above their brothers,[51] and six of them remembered their mothers as having favoured their brothers over themselves.[52]

Aaron and Ron each had only one brother, and both brothers later became gay men. Neither brother was interested in masculine activities as a boy, and they happily let their sisters fill their expected roles in their families. Aaron remembered following around after her older brother, playing with his friends, and being more macho than he. Aaron recalled:

> Okay, so what happened was my folks bought sports equipment for my older brother, he didn't play with it, so I'd swap him things for it. So I ended up with the sports equipment. We had a little more money than a lot of the neighbour kids so I had the football, I had the hardball, I had a couple of mitts. If they wanted to play, they had to let me play. So I bought my way in to start with. And then when I got into it, if somebody would belittle or put me down because I was female in any way, then I would get into a fight.

Ron remembered that in the family of her youth, her older brother was the favourite child of her violently abusive mother precisely because "he was always hanging around her, and cooking with her, and was interested in all her stuff. And he wore her dresses." However, Ron recalled that her father was not happy with the situation: "My dad was quite upset with my mom. He told her not to let him dress up. She thought it was cute. It was her boy." Filling the void left by her effeminate older brother, Ron took on an older brother role in her family. She helped her father with masculine chores around the house, dressed in her father's clothes, and protected her older brother from neighbourhood bullies.

> He was never my big brother. I used to escort him to public school, and sometimes pick him up—wait an extra class until he was finished, so he didn't get beaten up. I protected him all the time. And he was four years older, too. I was ten, and he was fourteen. The other guys respected me too, because I was really strong. And a lot of them I knew from . . . the street gangs, and they knew I could scrap. I had a vicious streak, too. I guess part of my upbringing. . . . He was weak. . . . He was a good runner. . . . He used to dress up, and. . . . he was always talking about himself as she.

Peter's older and only brother was "different" because he was "a genius" who preferred studying science to playing ball. Peter remembered her mother as favouring the intellectual boy. However, Peter's father was a masculine man who enjoyed sports. When his only son appeared uninterested in such activities and was appropriated by his mother, Peter's father accepted his daughter's offered companionship. Peter enjoyed her father's attentions as she slipped into being a "buddy" to her father.

Sadly, Peter's relationships with both of the older males in her life was soured by her brother's sexual abuse of her between the ages of eight and fourteen years. Peter was reticent about the details of the abuse and protective of her abuser brother. Peter did, however, say "it was a big deal" and "I lost my virginity to my brother." He said that it went on for so long because she didn't think that anyone would believe her and because she "liked my brother" and "it was about the only thing my brother and I ever did together." It ended because, at some point, her father figured out that something was going on. There was never any direct discussion of the situation and both children were beaten by their father. Peter, despite the years of abuse, continued to be sensitive to his brother's needs. At the time of his interview he emphasized that his brother was "a brilliant guy."

Tony's two brothers were also both exceptionally bright. Tony described his older brother as "a wonderful guy" and "a genius" and his much younger brother as "the smartest of us all." Tony's younger brother was eleven years younger and severely disabled by "very violent" epileptic seizures. His older brother was "legally blind." As a child, Tony always seemed to feel in the shadow of her older brother's intelligence. She thought of him as "a tough act to follow" all through school. Probably as a result of Tony's ongoing failure to be able to effectively compete intellectually, the two children often came to blows. In these contests, Tony did very well:

When we fought, the difference between him and me was he was much larger than I was, and the difference was he didn't really want to hurt me and I wanted to kill him. He has very bad eyesight. He's legally blind. The first thing I did was knock off his glasses and just dance around and beat him up. And he couldn't even see me. It was terrible, I took terrible advantage. One time I beat him with a stick. It was wild stuff. He never really wanted to hurt me. I wanted to kill him.

Tony, who felt competitive with her brothers, was able to physically dominate them both. She was thus able to appropriate, to some degree, a role of masculine dominance among the children in her family.

Hal, Mel, and Bruce were also easily able to top their brothers in many masculine endeavours. Hal remembered her younger brother as "a sweet little boy who always wanted to do everything I did." Mel won her father's favour by surpassing her only sibling, a brother one year younger than she, at sports and at school.

My dad . . . thought that my brother . . . belongs with Mom and I belong with you. [My brother] was a real awkward kid. If there was something that was worth any money and he had it, he lost it. I watched everything. I did stuff with my dad all the time. My mom used to get upset with my dad because he would get things for me and not really pay a lot of attention to [my brother]. . . . My brother was just a real natural klutz, it came easy to him. If you wanted something torn up just give it to [my brother]. He'll either lose it or tear it up, you know. My mother protected [my brother]. I'm finding out in the last month or so that [my brother] had always been afraid of my dad. I think because he wouldn't measure up to me, and Dad would say something to him or make him feel guilty for not measuring up. . . . He compared us. . . . He always thought that I had the brains. He always thought that I could do anything that I wanted to do. My brother, in his opinion, was a klutz.

Bruce similarly remembered that her father and her only brother "never got along." She figured that the tension between them was because her mother so obviously favoured her brother. Bruce tried to fill the gap by working to earn her father's affection:

My father expected him to be perfect. I think that was not right. He didn't expect me. I strived to be perfect, I did everything I could to be the best. I made my dad happy. . . . If my dad was going to cut the grass, he said, "Well, who wants to help?" And I'd always. . . . So I sort of became my dad's favorite. . . . My brother was never good enough. Well, I was always better than my brother. Like, I could run faster, and I could always do things better than him. And he was always sort of clumsy. . . . And we had a real sibling rivalry . . . that started right from as little as I can remember.

Not all participants who attempted to win their fathers' affections away from their brothers were successful. Brian also competed vigorously with her brothers for her father's favour, but Brian was unable to convince her father of her worthiness. Brian remembered with a great deal of pain the difference between the way she was treated and the way her brothers were favoured. She dedicated herself to being better at boyish things than either of her two younger brothers. However, nothing she could do managed to shake her father's deep misogyny. As long as Brian was female, Brian knew that her father would always see her as inferior to her brothers. Brian recalled:

> I was also very jealous that my brothers got more attention and privilege because they were <u>boys</u>. . . . This whole period of my life is very vivid and I was very conscious that I could not get any support or approval because I was only a girl. Doing things my brothers might get encouraged for, won me extreme disapproval. . . . I learned that girls were <u>worthless</u>. I knew I wasn't a girl. I knew I was bigger, older, and smarter than my brothers and I was extremely jealous and hurt. . . . I thought that I rightfully should be a boy, because I preferred boy things, proved myself capable of doing them, proved myself better than my brothers. I believed that if I willed it, and prayed hard enough, I could somehow grow a penis and prove I really was a boy. (Emphasis provided by Brian)

Thus it would seem that even in childhood many participants were already acting in ways more typical of male children. As brothers commonly do, they competed with the boys in their families for their fathers' attentions. However, they did so only in those arenas which they perceived as masculine ones. Fathers who might have been pleased by more feminine daughters were not catered to by these participants. Rather, participants strove to be the best at masculine pastimes. Participants who found the greatest success with such endeavours were those whose brothers were not particularly interested in or adept at masculine pursuits. Thus participants were able both to outdo their brothers and to find receptive audiences in their fathers whose desire for the companionship of a masculine offspring might otherwise have been thwarted.

Building Brotherhood: Forming Alliances

Some relationships which participants had with their brothers displayed another common aspect of brotherly connection, a bonding together to form alliances when threatened by an outside danger. It is not uncommon in brothers' relationships for such alliances to coexist with tense competition on other fronts. In some cases, the hazard was in the form of a violent or threatening parent. In others instances, participants protected their brothers from neighbourhood children.

Simon, Ron, Bob, Dale, Alan, and Steven all felt some sense of solidarity with their brothers in the face of abuse from their mothers or fathers. In each of these cases, participants felt particularly responsible for the protection of their younger siblings. Obviously, it was well beyond the capabilities of the young children whom they were at the time to actually succeed at such projects. This incapacity often left them feeling guilty and may have prompted some of them to redouble their dedication to becoming the protectors of their loved ones. For example, Alan's description of the relationship she had with her brother when she was young was typical of the others who formed such self-protective coalitions. Alan recalled, "we were especially close because we all feared my father. . . . We tried to protect each other from my father." As they grew into adults, Ron and Alan also battled to protect their less able brothers from bullying by other local boys.

Simon felt guilty about being unable to protect the younger children in her family. He said that as a girl she was forced to witness some terrible abuse of her step- and half-siblings, including what she believed to be her stepfather's murder of one of his children. For years Simon felt both powerless and responsible. Simon told about one such incident and her attendant feelings:

> [My stepmom] wasn't as mean as [my stepdad], but she's pretty cruel. She wasn't evil but she was cruel and I think it was because [my stepdad] mistreated her and she took it out on the kids. The only real vivid memory that I have of that is my youngest half-brother . . . was about five and he was playing with some matches. And she caught him and took him into the gas stove, turned on the burner, and held his hand over the burner until it blistered up like this. And she made myself and my other half-brother watch. I had all kinds of guilt things about my inability to stop that. You know, I was the oldest kid and I always felt up until a few years ago, working it out in therapy, I always felt that I should've been able to do something. . . . I felt a real sense of responsibility, and a real need to protect them, and a real inability to do so.

Bob similarly recalled that as a ten year old she felt responsible for the protection of her younger brother:

> [My brother] was a very passive child. . . . My mother was still prone to severe outbreaks of violence. And there were times when my mother used to bale my little three year old brother up in the corner, and beat the living daylights out of him. And quite often I used to get between him and my mother, and I used to threaten her, that if she ever hit him again, I'd kill her. So, it came to a point where I used to protect him.

The protectiveness which these youngsters felt toward their brothers could be seen simply as the heightened sense of responsibility commonly found in eldest children, especially in elder girl children. However, these feelings must be viewed against the backdrop of their relationships with the other significant people in their lives. These children were displaying masculine propensities in all areas of their lives, and so their protectiveness toward their younger siblings easily could have been felt by them as entirely in keeping with the masculinity which they were developing in other aspects of their lives. However, had their lives unfolded differently, these same memories might be interpreted as descriptive of motherly rather than brotherly behaviours. Such is the flexibility of memory, hindsight, and gender styles.

Summary and Commentary

Two main factors in participants' relationships with their brothers may have encouraged them to lean toward masculinity. All thirty participants who had brothers fall within one or both of the sets of circumstances described by these two factors.

Firstly, the majority of participants appear to have been thrown together with their brothers a great deal of the time. Approximately three-quarters (73 percent) of the thirty participants' families in which there were boy children were families in which the participant was the only girl in the family,[53] in which other girls in the family were distant in age,[54] or in which participants had few friends other than their brothers.[55] Spending copious amounts of time with their brothers may have contributed to their appreciation of and abilities at masculine ways. They learned to compete or bond with their brothers according to masculine standards and styles.

Secondly, it seemed as though most fathers wanted to have at least one child in the home at any given time who would perform the role of son. In eight families, there were age gaps of five or more years between participants and the nearest male child,[56] which might have been a factor in causing some parents to cast one of their female children into the role of son. In addition, there were another eight families in which the only boys who were present in participants' homes were for some reason unable or unwilling to shoulder the full responsibilities of their son role as it was defined in their families.[57] As well, in several cases, both fathers and mothers seemed to play parts in a process of shifting some participants into the roles of sons within their families. In such cases, they seemed to have divided up their children into "his" and "hers." In six instances, participants' mothers adopted their sons as their favorite children, while fathers took on their daughters in that capacity.[58] In addition to these six, Robin, who was the first child whom her remarried mother had with her older father, and Alan, who thought of herself as her mother's "surrogate husband," also both felt that they were chosen by their fathers to be their favorite children. A total of nineteen of the thirty participants who had brothers (63 percent) fell into this second grouping.

Thus all thirty participants who had brothers seemed to have been subjected to masculine socialization from either their brothers or their parents. Most participants played extensively with their brothers either by preference or because gratuitous circumstances threw them together. Furthermore, most participants also either fell into, were coerced, seduced, or eagerly dove into being their father's favorite children who mimicked their paternal role models. It would therefore seem from participants' stories that having male siblings was often auspicious for participants' budding masculine identities and rarely constituted a major impediment.

Summary and Commentary: Male Family Members

Two issues stand out above the rest in the relationships which participants had with the men and boys in their young lives. Firstly, the men and boys who were in participants' lives during their childhoods most often functioned as role models for them. Secondly, this appears to have been true even though the relationships which participants remembered having had with the males in their families were frequently infused with fear, violence, and antagonism. It also seems as if these two issues were often closely related in a single, complex dynamic in which male violence against women and children within a male dominated society can be simplistically understood as an expression of individual men's rightful power. When seen this way, the desire of children to emulate those men who fill them with fear might just as well be interpreted as the more easily understandable aspirations of youngsters to imitate those whom they hold in awe.

The relationships that participants recalled having with their fathers exemplified these dynamics. The vast majority of participants indicated either that they had themselves chosen to use their fathers as examples to emulate or that their fathers had provided participants with both opportunities and incentives to mimic them in many aspects of their masculinity. Several participants eagerly courted their fathers' favour; some participants believed themselves to have been chosen by their fathers to be their favorite children; some believed that their fathers had always wanted them to have been boys; many participants reported that their fathers extended their time and energy to them, specifically teaching them to take up the ways of men as their own. All of this took place within contexts which underscored the social power and advantages of maleness.

At the same time, much of this modeling took place within environments which were often charged with emotional, physical, or sexual aggression. When participants were youngsters, the majority of their fathers attempted to control their wives and children through belligerently authoritarian measures which ranged from manipulative, hostile silences, through angry emotionality, to vicious sexual and physical abuse. Although it was the case that when participants were themselves on the receiving end of such treatment they did not necessarily admire their own fathers, they nevertheless learned the social value accorded to the people who were given license to so disregard the rights of others.

Participants also appeared to have received similar messages from the time which they spent in the company of their brothers. It would seem that they learned from their playtime with their brothers that men and masculinity were more desirable social statuses than women and femininity. In a few cases, participants followed after their brothers, admiringly mimicking them in their masculine ways. A few other participants banded together with their brothers to form alliances in the face of what seemed to them at the time to be unrelenting abuse from their fathers. More often, participants became rivals with their brothers for their fathers' approval. They entered into competition with their brothers in masculine quests for achievement of dominance in their sibling hierarchies, and they vied with their brothers for their fathers' love and attention. They related to their brothers more in the mode of brothers with brothers than of sisters with brothers.

Similar but more gratifying refrains can be seen in the relationships which participants recalled having had with their more distant elder male relatives. Only one participant had a difficult relationship with his grandfather, a man who stood in loco parentis. All other participants who commented at all about their relationships with their grandfathers or uncles remembered them as men who provided them with positive models for the sorts of people they wished one day to become.

The overwhelming pattern in participants' relationships with men and boys during their early years seems to have been one of participants' identification with the social and cultural roles of men and boys. The affinity they felt with masculinity seemed to have been the result of a number of factors in their relationships, sometimes working in concert with one another, sometimes not. In the end, they all seemed to be reducible to a single compelling consideration. It looked to most participants as if boys and men had more fun and more power than did women and girls.

7 | Lessons Learned at Home
Summary of Family Relationships

THE TRANSSEXUAL PERSONS who participated in this study grew up in homes which were constituted in consonance with the overarching canons of the societies within which they lived. In addition, they were also exposed to the ideologies of patriarchal capitalism through their contacts with their friends, their schools, their religions, and the media. Thus, like other members of society, they learned that males should have, by birthright, greater power, prestige, and authority than females. In most cases, they also learned this by example. They saw in their families that their fathers, grandfathers, and uncles ruled their families either by virtue of their authority as males, by their power as breadwinners, or by the force of the threat and actuality of their violence. They saw that their brothers were offered the mantle of power and the privileges of prestige solely because they were born as males. They also observed that in many cases their mothers, grandmothers, aunts, and sisters seemed to be either pleasant but ineffectual and victimized people in need of protection or unpleasant people who enforced repugnant restrictions upon them, sometimes through the use of violence.

Many of these children thus seemed to have been raised from a very early age to preferentially identify themselves with men and boys and to dismiss women and girls as viable role models. Participants reported feeling alienated from their mothers, grandmothers, and aunts for a variety of reasons. Their explanations largely had to do with frustrations participants experienced as a result of their mothers, grandmothers, or aunts either seeming unable to adequately care for or protect them or as a result of their ongoing insistence that participants submit to the demands of stereotypical femininity. In some of these cases, participants' frustrations had to do with their mothers, grandmothers, or aunts being present in their lives but inaccessible to them because of illness, drugs, alcohol, or some form of incompatibility between adult and child. In other instances, participants felt that outright anger, hostility, and violence were directed at them from their maternal figures. Understandably, they retreated from it and from them. None of the participants in this study indicated that they wanted to pattern themselves after their mothers, grandmothers, or aunts in any but the most peripheral of ways.

Concurrently with the process of coming to reject females as their role models, they turned to the males in their lives as possible prototypes for themselves.[1] The men who filled fatherly roles in participants' lives were more inclined to be permissive or encouraging of masculinity in participants' girlhoods. One result of this state of affairs was that it was not uncommon for participants' mothers and fathers to communicate different messages to their daughters about gender and about what gender performances were expected of them. When this did occur, fathers tended to be engaged in wooing their daughters away from identification with femaleness and encouraging the development of an affinity for masculinity in their daughters. Participants' fathers' energies bore fruit and earned them the admiration and appreciation of their daughters, while participants' mothers' efforts at feminization remained largely barren.

In many cases, participants' fathers, grandfathers, or uncles seemed happy to take them under their tutelage and impart to them the benefit of their masculine knowledge of the world. In such cases, these men became involved in participants' gender identity development in ways more typical of father-son relationships, and the outcomes seemed to follow logically. In other cases, participants' fathers or father figures were infrequent and harmless visitors to their lives. Some of them thereby tended to become merged in their daughters' minds with their society's fantasy of the ideal good, hard-working masculine provider. In still other instances, participants' fathers were violent and dangerous presences in their daughters' lives. Ironically, this kind of treatment did not necessarily drive these girls away from identification with men. In fact, in many cases, participants who remembered their fathers as physically or emotionally intimidating also felt that they had either received some kind of preferential treatment from their fathers or had otherwise been the object of particular encouragement toward masculinity from their fathers. Such a combination of psychological influences may have led them to feel an especially pronounced identification with these aggressive men.[2] A few of these same participants, as well as a few others who also suffered from abusive fathers, found attractive alternative father figures in the persons of their grandfathers or uncles, whom they instead chose to emulate.

Furthermore, the contrast between the nature of the relationships which participants remembered having with their brothers and sisters was also striking. Participants recalled intense relationships with their brothers. Some of them turned to their brothers for relatively amiable fraternal companionship. Others fought with their brothers for dominance among siblings and recognition from their fathers. A few bonded with their brothers under conditions of danger. Consistently, their relationships were significant and carried a strong valence. Subsequently, many of those who felt that they had acquired some skill in that regard entered into competition with their brothers to prove that their own prowess at masculinity exceeded that of their brothers. These patterns resulted in participants, when they were girls, increasingly avoiding all things feminine and sharpening their skills at masculine endeavours.

Their relationships with their sisters, by contrast, seemed to have been mostly inconsequential to participants. They played with some, they fought with some, and they formed alliances with some, as they had done with their brothers. However, the emotionality with which they did so was considerably more temperate than that which they recalled about their links with their brothers. They seemed to find the affairs which preoccupied their sisters to be irrelevant to the matters which were of utmost importance to them. Although participants seemed to find the lives of their brothers compelling at best, they seemed to consider those of their sisters either with indifference or with the romantic curiosity of brothers fascinated by the delightful otherness of their charmingly feminine sisters. At worst, they seemed to see their sisters as foolishly complicit participants in a social system designed to benefit men and boys and to leave women and girls powerless and excluded from the more consequential concerns of the world of men and boys.

The overall effects seemed to have been that participants became incrementally more adept at masculinity and less able to perform in the feminine ways that their families ostensibly expected of them. As they found themselves failing at girlishness, they simultaneously discovered that they were becoming more proficient at boyishness. The scene was being set: not only were they having problems with being girls, but also they were socially and psychologically much better equipped to be boys. The "obvious" conclusion, which they were all one day to reach, was that they would do much better in the world if they were to become males.[3]

The stories which participants told about their early childhood upbringings in their family homes would seem to make a fairly solid case for attributing their increasingly strong gender dysphoria to familial socialization dynamics. Clearly, such patterns were present. It is important to bear in mind, however, that the existence of familial tolerance for, or encouragement of, masculinity in girls does not necessarily establish causation. It remains entirely possible that family members were responding to an innate predisposition toward masculinity in these girls. These may have been children who virtually demanded of those around them that they be treated as boys. The evidence is inconclusive.

8 | Childhood Friends and Foes

Relationships with Non-Family Members

Other Adults Who Mattered

THERE ARE USUALLY only a few adults of any influence in young children's lives who are not family members. Those adults are usually teachers, religious leaders, neighbors, or an occasional family friend. Few participants mentioned any such adults in response to interview questions about important relationships with nonfamilial adults. Those who did, made only the briefest of comments. It would seem safe to assume that in most cases, their influence on participants' lives was marginal. There were, however, a few notable exceptions: a few teachers, one family friend, and several adults who sexually exploited participants.

Sixteen participants (36 percent)[1] specifically mentioned elementary school teachers or religious leaders whom they remembered because they either had inspired them to like school or had made the opposite impression upon them.[2] For example, Simon spoke of a lifelong love of learning which began in elementary school. Simon's childhood home life was often chaotic and violent, and she was forbidden to have any friends. Simon's favorite teachers provided a welcome respite from domestic distress and offered some human warmth. He remembered:

> The only people I remember from elementary school are my teachers. I can name every single one of my teachers. . . . I think they all took a liking to me because it was a small town and I think they knew what was going on. And they all sort of took me under wing. Each gave me some special little thing, concentrated on some particular area with me. . . . They were all female. And my principal also had a real interest in me. It turned out that he was related to my second stepfather and that maybe was part of the reason he used to just have me come down to the office to talk. . . . It was like he knew. . . . I think that because it was a small town they all knew what was going on and in their own individual ways they were reaching out and trying to alleviate some of that.

Nathan, Brian, Peter, Mel, and Larry also fondly remembered teachers and principals who were warm and helpful. Nathan, like Simon, was unhappy at home. Nathan remembered having "some great teachers" who were instrumental in making school into "an escape from home." Brian, who found it difficult to trust anyone and had few friends as a result, had one favourite teacher for two years during grade school. Brian remembered the teacher as one who "adored me and used to praise me a lot" and who "gave me a sense of importance that no one else did."

Darren and Harry were also fond of their elementary school teachers, but their fondness was in the form of schoolboy crushes. Both of these individuals recalled having been lonely children who had few friends. Both envisioned themselves as males in their fantasy love of their women teachers. Darren said that she had crushes on "nearly all" of her grade school teachers, whereas Harry's romantic interest was focussed on one particular teacher.

Morgan, Grant, Bill, Jorge, and Steven all complained about teachers with whom they clashed as children. In addition, Walter said that when he was a girl, she had a love/hate relationship with her teachers which tended more toward hate. Morgan and Grant were the most critical. Both of them remembered school as a place where children went to have their spirits broken. Morgan said, "You can't even treat a dog like that now." Bill remembered being so terrorized by a combination of a rampaging father and a series of hostile teachers that she developed stomach ulcers at age six. Steven had similar memories of being frightened by the teachers she had as a child. He told of it this way:

> I was very afraid of the nuns, the structure, the discipline. It was almost militaristic. . . . This nun used to come barreling down the aisle and beat the crap out of this guy in front of me. And I thought she was always coming after me. My stomach was in knots for a year.

Fred and Stan each mentioned finding some valued adult approval from religious leaders. Fred remembered her minister and Bible teacher as "the kind of people I wanted to be around." Stan, who felt unloved at home, found confirmation of her worth from her activities at church:

> I more related to the older people of the church, that were more my grandparents' peers and contemporaries, looking for their approval. I wanted to be the good kid. The one that did the stuff, and that's how I got approval from them.

Only one participant, Simon, told a story about an adult friend who was unequivocally a positive influence in her young life. This friend provided a welcomed escape from the difficulties of Simon's very strained home life. Simon remembered him as a major influence on her young life:

> I don't remember how I met the man. . . . He was probably, when I met him, fifty-five–sixty. He had retired early and he had two ranches . . . for the summers that I was eight, nine, and ten, he took me out to his ranch. That was heaven because I was away from my stepfather. I was totally under his guardianship and he was pretty liberal. He set rules. He was affectionate. But he wasn't somebody that was trying to molest me. He was like a father to me. If I really have role modeled after anyone, it's been him and my grandfather, who were both very gentle men and totally different than my stepfathers. I have very fond memories of those summers with him.

Simon and six other participants (16 percent) told stories about sexual encounters during their childhood years with adult men who were not members of their families.[3] Only two of the participants who recounted these incidents seemed to have considered the episodes to have been of major importance to them at the time of their occurrence.

Simon said that at age ten she was molested by a school janitor. Apparently the attention was more gratifying than the molestation was traumatic. Simon recalled:

> I actually did enjoy it. . . . It was a janitor at my elementary school. For a while I went back to him and I think it partly had to do with he gave me affection and attention that I wasn't getting elsewhere. So, I don't feel particularly bad about him molesting me. . . . I never even saw the man's penis. It was all hand fondling, and that kind of thing. I mean, he definitely played with my genitals but beyond that he never tried anything.

Stan was also more moved by the "neat" things that she got to do with the man who sexually touched her than by the sexual manipulation itself. Stan told the story this way:

> When I was a kid, probably under second or third grade, I remember going down to watch this painter [at a neighbour's house]. . . . I remember . . . he would carry me up the stairs and he was feeling me up. He was using manual manipulation of a little girl's genitalia. And I kept going back. . . . It felt kind of funny, but it didn't really hurt that bad and he was a neat guy anyway. He would laugh and joke and he would let me paint and watch him and all that stuff. . . . I liked the guy. . . . I was actually probably more curious about it than anything. . . . It was a minor thing to tolerate because I got to do the other stuff that was neat. It may have happened maybe four or five times.

Eli similarly remembered being sexually used by an adult man but not being particularly upset by it at the time. When Eli was a girl of four years, her parents separated and she went with her mother to stay with friends. While there, her host asked her to perform fellatio on him.

> I was so little I didn't know anything. I remembered this shower. It was probably an average shower but it seemed like a huge room. . . . It must have been the husband had me in the shower, and I knew there was something wrong with it, but I was so innocent. . . . He asked me to suck him, his penis. I remember the taste of it. And when I think back on it, rather than being horrified, I'm a little bit, not exactly proud, but [it was like] a kind of initiation or some kind of thing to do with being masculine. . . . I just remember thinking it was weird and odd. . . . but I don't remember being upset or crying. . . . I just did it. He proffered this object to me and told me to [suck on it]. . . . I didn't think this was right. I just kind of did it anyway. . . . I don't remember being particularly upset. . . . I was curious, it was weird. . . . I did have this kind of danger feeling you get in here [when] you know it's wrong. I probably did say something to my mom but I don't remember.

Ed told a story about a neighbour man that he said had been recounted to him by his mother. He said that he had no memory of the sexual incident itself but that he believed his mother's version of the tale, which centered on the man's exposing his genitals to Ed when she was a five-year-old girl. Ed also seemed to think that the encounter had some effect on her gender identity. Before that time, Ed remembered being a typically feminine little girl. After the incident and a move to a new neighborhood, Ed always insisted on playing the part of a boy in all ways.

Walter's story was also less than clear-cut. Looking back on the situation as an adult, Walter thought that the doctor she went to as a child had acted inappropriately. Walter remembered "every time I went to the doctor, the doctor wanted to seriously examine my private parts. If I would go in there for a cold, a runny nose, I would be up on the table." Walter said that as a girl she had "never felt uncomfortable about it. . . . It just seemed OK."

Jordie was disturbed by the sexual exploitation which she endured while she was a girl. As a child, she had been "repeatedly sexually abused by a neighbour man" for two years while she was between the ages of seven and nine. The man "touched me on my genitals, talked in sexual terms, used objects to penetrate me, made me touch him." Jordie's parents did not know about the abuse. "They thought he was nice." The abuse stopped only after the family moved away, but Jordie was still forced to go to visit the "nice" man.

The sexual assault which happened to Bruce was also traumatic. However, the magnitude of the distress which Bruce felt as a child was

amplified by the way her mother handled the situation. The incident occurred while Bruce was in grade school. Bruce described it in these words:

> I was playing in the schoolyard. . . . I was playing hide-and-go-seek with
> my brother and my friends. And I remember having my pink dress on,
> and some shorts. . . . I knew where to hide that nobody would find
> me. It was underneath the first-grade building. . . . So I went under this
> building and there was this man laying there on the ground and he had
> a bottle of Jack Daniels. . . . I was a Mormon at the time. And he said
> to me, "Come here little girl. Help me." And my immediate thought
> was God would be happy if I helped this man. . . .
>
> And so I went over to help him and he grabbed me by the ankle, and
> he pulled me down, and he rolled on top of me and he jacked off. . . .
> And I felt his penis hit me, I had shorts on so he didn't penetrate me. . . .
> It happened so quick. . . . And he rolled off me and there was this yucky
> shit all over the front of my dress . . . I thought, "What is this?" I had
> no idea. . . .
>
> And I got up and I ran to the water fountain. . . . I was upset because.
> . . . I knew I would catch hell from my mother if I went home with
> a filthy dress. So I thought, "I've got to get this mess cleaned up quick."
> . . . So I went to the water fountain and I tried to wash this stuff off and
> I sat down and [thought] . . . "I've got to tell my mother what hap-
> pened." . . . I came to the back door and I was . . . hysterical at this
> point. And my mother said, "Get a hold of yourself. What's wrong?"
> And I tried to explain to her. I didn't even know what it was. And she
> punished me for making something up.

But Bruce was a child with a great deal of spirit. She did not let this
injustice go unanswered. This is how he described what happened next:

> I started to get mad. . . . I thought . . . "What did I do wrong?" So I got
> myself together and I changed my clothes and my mom let me go out
> and play. . . . I went back to the school and . . . I knew where they
> stored all the old dried paints, water colors, big thick heavy gooey
> paints. So I got a coffee can from behind the cafeteria and I mixed all
> these paints up. In the meantime, this guy had gotten out and he was
> paying boys a dollar to touch him. . . . He was sitting on the stairs and
> there was like eight kids there. . . . And I took this coffee can and I put
> it behind my back and I saw this guy and I saw this thing sticking out
> of his pants. . . . So I walked over to the man and I took this whole can
> of paint and I dumped it right on his dick. Right on his dick! And we
> all ran. Everybody thought it was just the greatest thing. Well, the next
> day I got called into the office because the man had tried to sodomize a
> little boy. The little boy went home and told his mom and they got
> the guy from the paint all over the little kid. So it was like the evidence.
> But they didn't ask if anything happened to me. I was so ashamed at

what had happened and thought, "Why would these people believe me
but my mother didn't believe me?" I thought, "I can't tell them."

It would seem clear that participants had few remarkable contacts
with adults outside of their families and formal institutional contexts during their childhood years. With only one exception, those few who did
remember informal contacts with adults (16 percent) remembered adult
males who sexually took advantage of their naiveté. However, only Jordie
and Bruce remembered being upset by the sexual contact, which, in
Jordie's case, was severe and ongoing.

Summary and Commentary

A total of twenty participants (45 percent) mentioned adults other
than family members whose impact on their lives was sufficiently memorable to warrant comment. Most of the adults who were remembered
had pedagogical relationships to participants, as either teachers or religious leaders. In two cases, these roles overlapped, in that two of the nine
participants who attended Catholic schools[4] were among those who commented about their teachers. As might be expected, participants' experiences with their teachers were varied. In some cases, their teachers encouraged them and thereby helped them to feel good about themselves. In
other cases, the disparagement of teachers left emotional scars. In only
two cases did gender issues appear central to participants' recollections
about their teachers. In both instances, teachers served as the objects of
participants' childish crushes in which participants envisioned themselves
as male.

All but one of the other adults spoken about by participants were
adult men who sexually used participants while they were children. These
were men with whom participants came into contact through family or
friends. In all but one case, participants remembered their sexual experiences as being discomfiting but neither physically painful nor emotionally
traumatic. In five cases, their experiences seemed to have made little lasting impression beyond the curiosity which they aroused in the children.
Indeed, most participants seemed glad of the attention which they received
and seemed to have considered the sexual contact to have been only a minor price to pay in exchange for the opportunity to spend time in the company of the otherwise fascinating men who sexually used them. However,
Bruce, although not extremely upset by the actual sexual assault, remembered the aftermath in her family home as very emotionally painful. Jordie
was the only participant who told of ongoing sexual assault and exploitation by a male friend of the family. Jordie was alone in claiming a negative
emotional significance to what had happened to her as a young girl.

Thus it seemed as though Simon was the only participant who believed himself to have significantly benefitted from contact with nonfamilial adults. Simon learned to love books and educational pursuits from a series of beneficent teachers and found a kindly and gentle masculine role model in the man with whom she passed several summers. Other participants' memories of positive adult influences beyond their family spheres seemed minor.

Of Boys and Tomboys

The interactions which children have with their peers during their childhood years can leave lasting impressions. In some cases, the experiences which children have among their peers may reinforce family dynamics. In other cases, they may perform an opposite role, by serving as welcomed antidotes to stressful and debilitating family tensions or by undercutting strongly empowering familial supports. In either event, it is not unusual for occurrences which may seem insignificant to adult observers to hold great emotional value for the children involved. Certainly, when peer relationships follow relatively consistent patterns over extended periods of time, they will, for better or for worse, remain embedded in the psyches of the adults whom children later become.

The stories that participants told about the time which they spent with other children in their neighborhoods and with their age-mates at school exhibited several commonalities with regard to their gender issues. Some participants reported having varied experiences during their childhoods due to changes of school or home environment which catapulted them into new peer groups. Other participants said that their relationships with their peers changed as they grew older and the social expectations for young girls became more narrowly defined. Thus, as the rules of the game changed, their roles as players were also redefined and, in many cases, their abilities to perform the new parts demanded of them were insufficient to retain for them the statuses they had previously enjoyed.

Most participants, as they described themselves as children, can easily be seen to have been tomboys. Many of them most emphatically and specifically used that term to describe themselves. As such, they much preferred the kinds of play activities in which boys stereotypically engaged. A number of those who called themselves tomboys engaged in these activities with an intense fervor. Perhaps they were, on some level, striving to prove that they were truly and unequivocally as much boys as were their male peers. Whatever the reason, many participants recalled having excelled at their boyish pastimes. They were so highly competitive at their masculine activities that seven participants (16 percent)[5] recalled that they had taken leadership positions among their male comrades.[6]

Most of them also recalled having felt a pronounced aversion to stereotypically feminine activities. A number of participants said that they had not placed much importance on the anatomical differences between the sexes. They recalled that although they were aware of the fact that they were not physically male, that was of little consequence to them as long as it remained of little consequence to their playmates. Thus a number of individuals fondly remembered engaging in roughhousing and sports activities with both boys and girls. For them, the issue was the ability to play as they wished, rather than the genders of their playmates. For many of them, this remained the case until such time as gender based restrictions began to limit both what their diversions might be and with whom they might be friends.

Those few participants who told of having enjoyed their time with other young girls their own ages were relatively uniform in their assertions that although they may have enjoyed playing with girls, they did so as boys. They claimed that when they were playing at what seemed to be girls' games, they were in fact playing the masculine parts in those games. They either recast themselves as masculine suitors of their more feminine girlfriends or else they explicitly took on male roles in play-acting games of fantasy. Thus even those participants who seemed to be playing as stereotypical little girls did not see themselves as doing so. In this way, the development of their masculine identities paralleled those of their more tomboyish counterparts. In each instance, they perceived themselves to have been "one of the boys." In some cases, they were boys playing with boys. In other situations, they saw themselves as boys playing with girls. Only rarely did they remember themselves as having been girls in any way that was meaningful to them until such time as that identity was forcefully imposed upon them by the adults and children around them.

Still others remembered having strained against gender definitions from the beginning. Those participants who recalled having been unable to play freely with the boys, or at least with other girls who were tomboys and wanted to play at more masculine pursuits, recounted tales of loneliness and alienation during their childhood years. They were generally uninterested in the pastimes which engaged the attentions of their more feminine peers. On those few occasions when their desires for human companionship drove them to attempt to join in the girlish games of their more feminine friends, more often than not they recalled having either been unwelcome or so inept at their endeavors that they never wished to return to the scenes of their humiliations. A few participants recalled that they had simply been "withdrawn" or "terribly shy" as children and had not made any earnest attempts at making friends with their peers.

Boys Have More Fun: Playing with Boys

Three-quarters of participants recalled having played with boys most of the time that they played with other children.[7] Their involvements ranged from those of Aaron, Ron, and Jordie, who had been members of "boys-only" gangs, to those of participants who simply recalled that they preferred the company of boys and played with them whenever they could. In some cases, participants' preference for the company of boys seemed to be based primarily on an appreciation of more masculine interests and the freedoms usually afforded to boys. In others, their interest in boys' companionship was to the exclusion of almost all positive feelings about their feminine peers.

The kinds of activities which participants recalled having enjoyed in their younger years included most stereotypically masculine childish pursuits. Sports were high on many people's lists. Among other things, they mentioned tackle football, baseball, basketball, soccer, hockey, fishing, and playing marbles. Make-believe play with masculine characters and themes, such as cops and robbers, war, cowboys, trucks and cars, explorers, and superheroes, was also popular among participants when they were children. In addition to their other masculine predilections, ten participants (23 percent) spoke with pride of being "tough kids" and seemed to relish their memories of their prowess as fighters.[8]

For example, Aaron recalled that as a child she had never thought of herself as a girl. In fact, she took being called a girl as a slur and fought anyone who dared to so insult her.

> I had a male identity as a child. . . . I'd wear my brother's outgrown clothes, I was out fighting almost every afternoon, playing tackle football and all this. Okay, at that point, I was somebody with a girl's body and the boys knew it. But they didn't dare call me a girl because they knew what would happen. They'd get the shit kicked out of them. . . . I had the group orientation of a gang of boys and until I was in puberty . . . I ran with a tough gang, about eleven boys. . . . I fought my way up to the top and ran that gang for a few years. . . .
>
> You see if you call somebody a girl that was an insult. It was equivalent of calling somebody a sissy. . . . I was the only female in this little gang. They didn't play with girls. . . . But I wasn't a girl when I was wearing boys' clothes and playing tackle football with them—in their eyes and in mine. They knew I was physically female. . . . you didn't say, "girl," you said, "girrrl." It was an insult. And that was fighting words. . . . You had to fight. . . . That was part of the code.

Darcy, as a child, likewise always thought that she was a boy and took a leadership position among them. Apparently, others shared her perception:

> I felt I had lots of power, and enjoyed wielding it. I had a little gang I was in charge of. . . . All boys. I wouldn't even talk to girls. You don't talk to girls until you're a certain age. . . . I went to shop class with the boys because I didn't know I was a girl. We went to a different school. They didn't know I was a girl, so I was in shop class. It was too late to pull me out.

As a girl, Harry also prided herself on being one of the boys. He remembered: "I hung around with the boys. I was considered one of the boys. . . . It just didn't come into question about biological differences meant anything. So, for all intents and purposes, I was one of the guys." Jack similarly said of his girlhood: "I did everything with the guys. I was usually the leader of the army, the general. So I was always right up there in front and I was always telling everyone all the moves to make." Like Aaron, Jack said that she "would have busted" anyone who challenged her right to her place among the boys.

Analogous sentiments were remembered by many participants. For example, Fred said that he remembered feeling like a boy when young:

> I never thought I was anything other than a boy. I thought I would grow up to be a man. When we played house or something, I was always the husband or the daddy. I was a boy in my fantasy life. I was always running, and jumping, and playing, and doing something special, but I was always a boy.

Thirteen participants (29.5 percent) went so far in their feelings of being boys as to use boys' names for themselves.[9] Some of these children were nicknamed by their friends because of their marked similarities with boys. Others chose their boys' names as a way of confirming their own innermost feelings of masculinity. For example, Ed was called "Son" by her friends because she "always got kids saying, 'Are you a boy or are you a girl?'" Similarly, Eli had "a whole string" of masculine nicknames which she and her girlfriends used to refer to her; so did Walter and Dennis.

A few kept their self-selected masculine names as their own comforting secret identities. Both Pat and Peter kept secret masculine names for themselves when they were girls. Peter consciously developed an alter personality through which she could live out the life that seemed closed to her as a girl.

> As far back as kindergarten I remember having another personality . . . I was another person in my mind. . . . Because I couldn't live it in reality.

I did it in my fantasy, in my dreams, in all my private thoughts. I wasn't who you thought I was. I was this other person. . . . And this other person was a boy. . . . Which means he had the freedom. . . . No one was going to make him wear a dress. . . . If he wanted to go fishing, he could go fishing. If he wanted to play baseball, he could play baseball. He doesn't have to do this, that, and the other thing. He doesn't have to act a certain way.

In sum, it seems clear that a large majority (73 percent) of these children had very strong commitments to masculine behaviour patterns even as young children. In several of these cases, their involvement in masculinity was such that on some level they believed themselves to be boys. They did this either in their fantasy lives, where they vividly imagined themselves to be male, or by willfully retaining, as long as possible, a fiction that their female bodies were inconsequential to both their own gender identities and the genders which their peers attributed to them.

Girls Are Dumb: Aversions to Feminine Activities

At the same time that these youngsters were drawn to masculine play and playmates, they were also seemingly either oblivious to or repelled by more feminine girls and their interests. In some cases, their disinterest was mild and extended only to feminine play. Those participants who recalled such feelings were quite content to play masculine games with other girls who were tomboyish like themselves. Other participants recalled having felt a more intense distaste for femininity, which led them to also disdain other girls.

Eleven participants (25 percent) said that as children they had preferred the company of boys in general but were willing to play with other girls who lived up to their standards of masculinity.[10] Eli's remembered feelings typified the sentiments of those who felt this way:

I didn't have any preference about the sex of my friends. They were just people. . . . I never saw any [of my girlfriends] as girls. They were like boys to me. . . . I could see that they were girls, but that didn't matter. . . . They weren't all tomboys, but their boy part was very well developed. They were not girly girly to the point where we couldn't be friends.

An additional fourteen participants (32 percent) spoke about feminine play with a sneer in their words.[11] Their point seemed to be that feminine activities, such as playing with dolls or other wife and motherhood rehearsal play, were entirely foreign to or beneath them. Steven typified these emotions when he recalled the feelings she had when she found herself in an all girls' school: "So I was forced into being with girls. And I didn't even know what you were supposed to do with them." More striking were the memories of Brian, who said that as a girl she had considered girls "worthless" and "hated God for making me a girl." She reported that she had "made every effort . . . to avoid doing girl things" and that "in public, I could only be sulky, uncommunicative, just refuse to do things which were girl things, or distance myself internally if I was forced to do such things." Brian explained her refusal by saying, "It's a matter of it didn't fit. I'm not a future female impersonator."

Those participants who did concede that they had played feminine childish games distanced themselves from those activities by saying that they had done so to please their girlfriends and that such activities were their least favorite diversions. The only pleasures which participants claimed to have taken in such play were when they took distinctly male roles in their fantasy enactments of domesticity. Twelve participants (27 percent) mentioned having felt this way.[12] Ed's comments on the subject were characteristic of those of many in this group. He remembered that she was "very set on the fact that if I was going to play house, I was the father, or I was the brother. I wasn't the girl. I wasn't the mother." Howie also said that as a girl she had always played the part of father when she played house. Howie remembered, "that's when I was the happiest—pretending to be male."

In sum, twenty-five participants (57 percent) clearly remembered having done what they could to avoid the company of other young girls when they themselves had been children.[13] Furthermore, twelve participants (27 percent) recalled that when they did play with other girls, their enjoyment was contingent upon their being able to do so as if they were males.[14] Thus thirty-two participants (73 percent) could be said to have had a general pattern of preference for boys' company and games to the relative exclusion of almost any voluntary and pleasurable interactions with girls. Many of the remaining participants described themselves as solitary individuals. A few said too little on the subject to draw any conclusions one way or the other.

Loners

Approximately half (52 percent) of the participants in this study said that at some point during their childhood years they had felt lonely among or isolated from their peers.[15] For some, this was the sum of their experiences among their age-mates; they had held themselves back from making friends. For others, alterations in social standards brought about by changes in home or school venue, or by maturation processes, were responsible for a shift in their sense of social belonging. In such cases, their alienation from their peers can be traced to their failure to fit in with their more feminine peers. All who suffered from this malaise had in some way found that their access to boys had become restricted. Some therefore found themselves with no friends because of their own unwillingness to mix with other girls. Others were simply unwelcome among more typical girls because of their oddly boyish ways.

Eight participants (18 percent) reported that they had almost always felt lonely as children.[16] For example, Simon was forbidden to have any social life at all and was "a real quiet kid" at school. Likewise, Dale would have liked to have made friends with some of the other children, but a number of things stood in her way:

> We couldn't have friends. We lived so far from school. I can't remember having special friends in class, really. I was very self-conscious at that age too, because we were so poor. Like we didn't have lunches like everybody else, and we wore hand-me-down clothes, and it all had an effect on me. I was really quiet and . . . I was very self-conscious about it.

Pat said that as a youngster she "really didn't have a lot of friends" and that she "felt I didn't really fit in." Certainly, the way the other children treated her must have contributed to these feelings. Pat recalled that "some of the kids were OK, some rejecting and jeering." Pat conveyed the feeling that she "basically felt very lonely a lot of the time."

Other participants had male friends when they were younger but lost them as they matured. After pleasant preschool years playing with local boys, Roger was sent away to a series of girls' boarding schools, where she made few friends. Similarly, Sam's mother forbade her from playing with boys and Sam was unable to relate well to the girls. As a result Sam remembered being a loner:

> At that point in my life I didn't have friends. I just wasn't comfortable with people. . . . I didn't make an effort to make friends. It was just too uncomfortable with the girls. I was simply not interested in the same things. . . . I don't think I gave people a chance. . . . They weren't really mean to me. Just, I ignored them and they ignored me. . . . I don't think I ever sensed any real loss from not being with other kids.

Another ten participants (23 percent) recalled their childhoods as lonely even though they did have a few friends.[17] When Peter was a girl, she did have some friends but lived mostly through her fantasy life. Peter recalled being so "very shy that if somebody came to the door, I'd run and hide behind my mother's leg." Darren also managed to make a few friends despite the fact that she had been "a kind of a loner" who was "somewhat emotionally repressed." Morgan, who also had few friends, recalled that she would have preferred to play with the boys but that the boys she knew "just don't accept girls." At the same time, Morgan was "quite quiet and too self-conscious" and "withdrawn" to reach out enough to make many friends of either gender.

Several participants were able to find playmates but never were able to feel comfortable among them. For example, when Bruce was a girl, she did make friends but always felt somewhat out of place nonetheless:

> The girls made fun of me for playing with the boys, and the boys didn't think it was OK for a girl to be playing with them, although they enjoyed playing with me. . . . But I played alone a lot. I had this big fantasy world.

Howie, Brian, Nathan, and Phil also "felt different from all the other kids" when they were children. They remembered childhood as "a scary and lonely time" when they "often felt out of place" and during which they were often "teased and picked on by the other kids." Brian said of this time:

> I learned immediately in the first grade to avoid other kids. . . . I stayed by myself on the playgrounds. . . . I was very scared and cried a lot during grade school. . . . I hated the kids at school because I was different and they picked on me. . . . It seemed to me that no one could be trusted in the world.

Grant too felt "different," and she was frequently picked on by the local boys. However, Grant remembered taking pride in her differences. Grant said, "I didn't fit in with the boys. I didn't fit in with the girls," but she also "did not see the point in trying to fit in. They seemed very shallow to me. . . . Thank God I didn't fit in."

A few participants' stories were about lonely lapses in childhoods otherwise agreeably filled with companionship. Jordie was one such person who attributed her isolation among her peers to the fact that at a certain age her extreme tomboyism was "no longer acceptable" to either the boys or the girls whom she knew. Dennis, who had made male friends in the neighborhood near her home, told of having been unable to make friends among her schoolmates because of her ambiguous gender appearance. Stan, who had been a leader among her girlfriends at her old school, went through a period of several years of feeling "really foreign" when she moved to a new school in a smaller town. Steven also seemed unable to successfully make the adjustment to her new Catholic girls' school.

> I was a very quiet introverted kind of person, and I was scared. I was very afraid . . . of people. I was afraid of new situations. . . . I felt I was totally different. It was anxiety to be different. . . . People did make fun

of me. . . . I don't know if they detected anything different or just thought "What a queer kid."

It would seem from these stories that many participants felt that they did not have a comfortable place among their peers. Certainly many children feel this way. It seems striking, though, that so many participants recalled feeling lonely and out of place among their peers due to gender issues. Sixteen of those twenty-three participants who remembered such lonely periods during their childhoods (70 percent) were among those whose recollections included enjoyable playtime among boys.[18] However, slightly more than half (52 percent) of participants who had trouble socially fitting in with other children largely attributed their differences to their own gender concerns and those of others.

Summary and Commentary

It would appear from the stories told by participants that their inclinations toward masculine gender expression were a major influence upon the relationships which they developed among their childhood peers. Close to three-quarters (73 percent) of participants reported that as children they spent a large proportion of their interpersonal play time among boys. The reasons they gave for having passed their days in this way did not vary greatly. They did so because boys did the kinds of things which most appealed to them. Some participants played with boys as girls; some played as honorary boys; and some genuinely and naively believed themselves to be boys during their earlier years. It seems self-evident that these girls, who were so often among boys, were also subjected to intensive masculine peer socialization while they were being "one of the boys."

Most participants remembered that when they were children they played with girls as well. The kinds of play in which they engaged with girls could be characterized in two often overlapping ways. When participants played with females, they usually did so without breaking from their masculine patterns. They either played with other tomboyish girls who shared their masculine interests or they took on male roles in their play with other girls. In many cases, these were explicit conditions of their willingness to play with girls at all. To do otherwise, according to participants, would have felt like violations of their young identities.

In addition, many participants described some or all of their childhood years as lonely and lacking almost any friends of either gender. The explanations which they offered for their isolation were varied. Some participants were restricted in their social lives by changes in parental decrees, residences, or school attendance. They were unable to play with boys and were not drawn to play with girls. Other participants, finding themselves cut off from boys, tried to make friends with girls but found that the girls didn't want to play with them because they were not adept enough at feminine activities. Still other participants were simply so shy that they held themselves back from trying to make friends of either gender.

Thirty-eight participants (86 percent) indicated that they would have preferred to have spent most of their childhood time with boys rather than with girls.[19] Most of those who indicated that they had felt this way were relatively successful at achieving such arrangements. A handful of participants went so far as to completely reject the companionship of other girls. It seems clear that participants' masculine gender behaviour was a major factor in their choice of friends and the activities in which they engaged during their childhood years.

PART III

Adolescence

David Harrison

9 | Adolescence Is about Change

DURING ADOLESCENCE CHILDREN turn into adults. Because of individual variation and the range of maturation tasks to be accomplished during these years, it is useful to think of adolescence as a three-part process consisting of early, middle, and late adolescence. Early adolescence (approximately ages ten to thirteen years) is the period during which young people grow out of childhood and enter adolescence. In girls, early adolescence roughly coincides with the early phases of puberty. Middle adolescence (approximately ages fourteen to sixteen years) is the time during which girls usually complete puberty. In late adolescence (ages seventeen to twenty years), young people embark upon the final stages of their transitions from youth to adulthood.

Welcomed or not, adolescence compels young people into new tasks by the undeniable changes which their bodies undergo. These changes signal to them and to others that the time for learning new ways of being in the world is upon them. Those children whose pubertal development is ahead of that of their peers encounter new pressures earlier than their age-mates. Children whose pubertal development lags behind may, with some reluctance, find themselves subjected to pressures to move along with their peers before they are eager to do so.

The major developmental issues for adolescents, their families, and their peers revolve around the attainment of adulthood. As such, it has been suggested that adolescence constitutes a second separation-individuation period as important in personality formation as that of the first few years of life.[1] It is during this interval that teens must relinquish their childish identities and grow into adult responsibilities. Parents, teachers, peers, and siblings all expect new behaviours along with the new bodies into which adolescents grow. Adolescents must learn how to deliver what is expected of them. For most teens, adolescence is a time of many false starts and experiments, often fraught with insecurities.

It is inevitable that teens will be unsure of themselves as they encounter new expectations and learn to live within the contours of their new bodies. Many teens periodically turn away from their parents in an effort to establish themselves as independent adults, only to return to them for comfort and support when they discover that they are not yet fully able to function as adults. Conventional wisdom says that adolescence is a time during which teenagers fight with their parents more than at any other time in their lives. Although this may be true for many young people, such sentiments most certainly overemphasize the level of conflict and distress found in most families in which there are teenagers. Research shows that adolescents act in accordance with the values of their parents far more often than in defiance of them.[2]

Nonetheless, dependence upon parental support and guidance is part of the yoke of childhood. Thus as teenagers progress through their adolescence they usually have many occasions on which to assert their independence from their parents. Parents, for their part, often have many reasons to be concerned that their teenaged children may not have sufficient maturity to safely undertake the endeavours which they propose. Conflicts over autonomy are therefore an inevitable part of the adolescent years.

In particular, conflicts between mothers and daughters are often among the most acute. Mothers are traditionally charged with the everyday supervision of their offspring, and so they are most often in positions to be the ones making rules which are deemed by teens to be too narrow. In addition, the teen years are generally a time of increasing freedoms for teenaged boys, whereas for many girls their entry into sexuality usually marks the beginning of a circumscription of their lives. Those girls who have become accustomed to the relative freedoms of tomboy life may find the required adjustments especially onerous. Thus, although conflicts about autonomy will inevitably arise between mothers and daughters, the intense and intimate day-to-day basis of their relationships are often such that mothers and daughters have opportunities to reach mutually satisfactory solutions to their differences.[3]

Most teens also become extremely conscious of the opinions of their peers. At a time when adolescents must accomplish a great deal of psychic and social restructuring, most teens feel that it would be childish to rely too heavily upon parental assistance in the quest to become adults. Therefore teens increasingly turn to their peers for both the succor of intimate dyadic friendships and the confirmation of group popularity.[4] They turn away from their parents and toward their friends to serve as "looking glasses" in which they can appraise their progress into and through adolescence, and later, out of adolescence and into adulthood.

A Social Context for Adolescence

During childhood, gender requirements for females are more relaxed than they are during adolescence. Many young girls are indulgently allowed by peers, parents, and other adult representatives of society to be somewhat nonconforming in their gender styles. The appellation of tomboy is by no means an insult to a young girl. As many as 59 percent of female adults recall that they considered themselves to have been tomboys as children. This figure rises as high as 75 percent when lesbian women are considered as a separate group.[5] Because the onset of physical maturation often marks a sharp dividing line between the relative gender freedoms of female childhood and the more stringent gender style demands of female adolescence, it is not unusual for girls whose tomboyishness has been benignly accepted or even tacitly encouraged by parents to find that upon reaching adolescence they are expected to conform to new and more exacting standards of femininity. This can come as a rude shock to some girls.[6] For others it is only as had been anticipated, and they welcome the change of social roles expected of them as a sign of their new maturity.[7]

During the teen years, girls are expected to identify their life goals and begin to work toward achieving them. Social standards as to what constitute appropriate life goals for females vary with such factors as historical period, social class, ethnic or racial membership, and religiosity. Nonetheless, it is generally accepted by most members of society that major components of the adult lives for which female adolescents should be preparing are heterosexual marriage and child rearing. Because job or career concerns are usually regarded as secondary to family commitments of adult women, educational goals are often downplayed to and among teenaged girls.[8]

Thus heterosexuality is the main driving principle behind many of the behavioural and attitudinal changes which most adolescent girls are expected to undergo. Teen culture emphasizes appearance and encourages girls to become more feminized and sexualized because adult women are supposed to be both (hetero)sexual and maternal. As girls become women, their male peers are supposed to be gradually transformed from playmates into dates, and their female peers are supposed to become co-conspirators or rivals for male attentions. Parents become concerned with regulating their daughters' progress into women, sometimes encouraging greater femininity and at other times attempting to slow their daughters' sexualization.

At the same time as social compulsions encouraging femininity are brought to bear on teenaged girls, other pressures are exerted by family and friends to discourage adolescent females from behaving in masculine ways. Normally, any previous support or tacit encouragement which was available to tomboys is terminated. Stigma, ridicule, ostracism, or punishment are proffered in their stead to those girls who refuse to abandon their childhood fascinations with masculinity. Therefore those who cannot or will not turn their backs on boyish ways of life which have brought them satisfaction will often find themselves isolated and lonely.[9]

Some such girls may find that they feel sexually or romantically attracted to other girls. If they are fortunate enough to have access to others of their persuasion, they may find some support for a tomboyish gender expression among lesbian women. Other tomboyish adolescents may avoid sexuality altogether, opting instead for more gender-neutral identities as athletes or intellectuals. Again, they may be lucky enough to find a community of like-minded others with whom to pass their adolescence. Those who do not will almost inevitably have to resign themselves to being outcasts among their peers, disappointments to their parents, and generally ill at ease with their places in their social world.

Puberty: Physiological Maturation

Physical maturation constitutes a dramatic alteration for most girls. Some of the changes which take place in their bodies, such as changes to body hair and menstruation, are markers of growth which can be concealed from others. The growth of breasts is a process which will, in most cases, be impossible to conceal. Thus it is breast development which most publicly marks the waning of childhood and the beginning of the march into womanhood.

Among contemporary North American females of European heritage puberty normally starts between the ages of eight and eleven years and continues for about four or five years. The first sign of physical maturation which is apparent in most of these girls is the beginning of breast growth. The average age at which breast budding starts is 10.5 years; it is generally complete by the age of 15.5 years. Because breasts often feel like an entirely new part of the body, their appearance may prompt girls to start to think of themselves in entirely new and different terms, to move away from being girls and into being young women. Breasts also carry with them a heavy social coding as sexual objects in European and North American societies. Thus their appearance also propels girls into an awareness of themselves as sexual beings. It is therefore not surprising that many girls go through an initial period of alienation from their budding breasts, which may at first feel like awkward and uninvited guests.[10]

Menarche, the beginning of menstruation, comes late enough in the puberty of most girls that they are usually well into early adolescence by the time this major transition occurs. The average age at which this milestone occurs for girls of European heritage is 12.8 years.[11] The contours of their bodies have usually already begun to change in obvious ways and thus the more private event of menarche is often somewhat anticlimactic.

Although adolescent girls commonly greet this maturation with a variety of emotions, most find it to be less burdensome than they had anticipated and take pleasure in it as a sign of maturity.[12]

Although the goal of adolescence may be posited as maturity, it would seem that girls who reach physiological maturity ahead of their age-mates are vulnerable to a number of emotional and behavioural difficulties. They are more likely than either on-time or late maturers to be dissatisfied with their bodies and to have negative feelings about their menstruation and about puberty in general. They are also more likely to suffer from eating disorders, to have conflicts with their parents, and to become depressed by problems which they encounter during this period.[13] Late maturing girls, by contrast, have been found to have no particular social difficulties associated with their later pubertal development. This may be because, although they may be late compared with other girls, their developmental timing is synchronous with that of their male peers, who typically enter puberty approximately two years later than do girls.[14]

This combination of physical changes can be unsettling; and because societal ideals of feminine beauty are mostly unrealistic and unobtainable, few teenaged girls seem to be entirely satisfied with their new bodies. In one study of white teenaged middle-class suburban girls, most said that they wanted to be thinner and have smaller physiques. The single notable exception was in their attitudes about their breasts. Most girls wanted their breasts to be larger than they were.[15] There was, however, a tendency to greater body satisfaction among those girls who were more physically active, indicating that those girls whose bodies performed well for them were less susceptible to feelings of physical inadequacy. However, by the time most girls have successfully negotiated puberty and adolescence, most of their uneasiness with their bodies has subsided. Few adult women are perfectly happy with their bodies,[16] but most come to accept with equanimity, if not with joy, the unique aspects of being female.

Friends and Lovers: Emotional and Sexual Maturation

As the beginnings of physical maturation signal to young teens that it is time to cease to be children, they are presented with the dual enterprises of beginning to disengage from their dependency upon their parents and learning how to relate more intensely to their peers. In service of these projects, teenagers commonly spend twice as much of their free time with their peers as they do with their parents.[17] What teenagers lose in intimacy with parents they would seem to attempt to recoup from their increasingly emotionally intense peer relations.[18]

In the process of finding their own maturity, many teenagers go through periods of disparaging the value of their parents. Nonetheless, although teenagers prefer the advice of their peers on issues of appearances and peer culture, they still turn overwhelmingly to their parents for factual information and assistance in making decisions about moral issues.[19] When adolescents do disagree with their parents, it is usually over such things as household responsibilities, limitations on teenagers' activities and friendships, schoolwork, and teenagers' appearance. Adolescents tend to see their parents as inappropriately restricting their personal freedoms in these areas, whereas their parents tend to understand their own concerns more in terms of wanting their offspring to behave in ways which are consistent with social conventions.

By early adulthood, most young people have turned from their parents to their peers for emotional intimacy and support. The intensified peer relationships in which young people engage during their teen years serve a number of important purposes for their emotional development. Being popular with groups of peers or having individual friends helps young people to feel good about their own value. Friends provide opportunities for adolescents to develop and exercise their intimacy and affectional skills, while peer groups and friends provide the security of companionship and alliances. In addition, adolescents can try out tentative new identities in relative safety among their friends.[20]

The adolescent peer groups which serve these purposes tend to fall into three types: crowds, cliques, and dyads. Crowds are groups with which teenagers become identified on the basis of their reputations as particular types of people (e.g., jocks, nerds, popular kids). Crowds act as reference groups, providing a kind of generalized sense of how people of a similar type behave. As such, they can provide norms of behavior to the degree that particular adolescents identify themselves with a crowd. Cliques play a more important and direct role in regulating adolescent behavior. Cliques, smaller sets of chosen friends, form close-knit associations of like-minded persons. The opinions of these more intimate affiliates weigh more heavily in adolescent decision-making than do those of more generalized crowds of more distant peers.[21]

Another main learning task of early adolescence is the shift from childish playmate friendships to emotionally close and intense dyadic friendships.[22] Adolescent one-to-one dyadic friendships are organized on the basis of intimate reciprocal conversations about private internal emotional states. Teenage girls especially value such friendships for their openness, closeness, and sharing. Moreover, girls, who on average mature earlier than boys, shift their friendships in this direction at an earlier age than do boys.[23]

As many as 20 percent of adolescent girls nevertheless have difficulties attaining satisfactory peer relationships.[24] Sometimes young people have few friends because of various forms of discrimination and bigotry over which they have no control. Sometimes teenagers are loners because they choose to remove themselves from the social milieux of their peers. Generally, those who are excluded from membership in any adolescent group have lower self-esteem than those who are members or who voluntarily choose to remove themselves from the mainstream of their peers.[25] Research also suggests that those teenagers who either have few friends or have strained relationships with their peers are also more likely to have difficulties in their social relationships as adults.[26]

These many changes in the lives of adolescents can prove to be very trying to them. In one study, 29 percent of adolescent girls were found to suffer from depression; 27 percent reported feelings of anxiety; 4.5 percent had eating problems; 17 percent had alcohol problems; and 15 percent had considered suicide. In all of these areas except drinking, adolescent girls were significantly more likely to report these emotional states than were adolescent boys.[27] Depression and moodiness among teenagers appear to peak in the middle adolescent years, with girls being two to three times more likely than boys to say that they have such feelings.[28] The severity of feelings of depression among teenaged girls has been found to be related to the cumulative number of stressful life events experienced during early adolescence. Girls who experience changes in school attendance, peer group, or family situation during adolescence have been found to be more likely to become depressed and to suffer from lower self-esteem than their peers whose lives are less labile.[29]

As children grow into teenagers they also become increasingly aware of their own sexual and romantic urges; their peers increasingly expect sexualized interactions of them; and their parents increasingly become concerned to regulate the sexuality of their children, especially that of their daughters.[30] Although for many teenagers their sexual and romantic feelings can be the source of satisfaction or even euphoria, they can also be the cause of adolescent anxieties. One study of middle adolescents found that their feelings about "single individuals of the opposite sex" accounted for the largest proportion of all of their negative emotions. Once again, this effect was more pronounced among girls than among boys,[31] perhaps because of the tendency among adolescent girls to focus on their feelings, whereas teenaged boys tend more to avoid examining the sources of their unhappiness.[32]

Most young people begin to date during their adolescent years, and some of them engage in sexual intercourse. Estimates of the ages by which teenaged girls in the 1970s had experienced heterosexual intercourse are as follows: 6 percent of those under age fifteen, 30 percent of 15 and 16 year olds, 40 percent of 17 and 18 year olds, 55 percent of 19 year olds, and 85 percent of those in their early twenties.[33] It has been suggested that younger teenaged girls who become heterosexually active do so to enjoy greater masculine approval, whereas older teenaged girls' heterosexual activity reflects their greater independence.[34]

Some adolescents also have sexual and romantic feelings for people of their own gender and sex. One study found that 11 percent of teenaged girls had one or more lesbian sexual experience.[35] Many of those who experiment with lesbianism as adolescents probably go on to make a commitment to a lesbian way of life. One survey of close to 600 middle-class white lesbian women found that 45 percent of them had begun having sexual relations with other females before the age of twenty-one and that 36 percent had begun to call themselves lesbian by that age.[36] However, some teens who have been homosexually active have been reluctant to attach the designation of lesbian to themselves. This probably has been due in some measure to the fact that lesbianism was and still is stigmatized in North American and European mainstream societies.

The most common negative stereotype of lesbian women during most of the twentieth century has been that of the "mannish woman." The image of the mannish woman includes both the idea that lesbian women want to be as much like men as possible and the belief that masculine women are lesbian. Thus female teens might feel that if they are sexually or romantically attracted to women, they should cultivate masculine images; or, if they are already masculine, that they probably are lesbian. These feelings can be exacerbated by the reactions of peers, who may also interpret tomboyish appearances as meaning that adolescent girls are lesbian and treat them accordingly.[37]

Furthermore, most adult lesbian women have reported that they were tomboys when they were young;[38] that they took on male roles in fantasy play;[39] and they reported such histories more often than their heterosexual counterparts.[40] As well, as many as one-third of adult lesbian women recalled that they occasionally had wanted to be boys when they were children.[41] However, most lesbian women also reported that upon reaching adolescence they accepted the physical aspects of their womanhood with equanimity.[42] Thus very few adolescents who later became lesbian women have been found to retain their childhood wishes to be male,[43] although a sizable minority continued to be tomboyish teenagers.[44]

Adolescence is always a difficult transition to negotiate. Rapid physical, social, and emotional changes characterize the period. It seems inevitable that adolescents will experience some confusion and anxiety in the face of so many, so intense, and such fast-paced alterations of their world.

Self-absorption, conflicts with parents, and oversensitivity to the opinions of peers are normal for this age group. For most adolescents, the volatility and turmoil of the teen years is simply to be expected and endured until the passage from childhood to adulthood is complete.

Gender and Sex Dysphoric Adolescent Girls

Gender and sex dysphoric adolescent girls react quite differently to the arrival of their puberty than do most other girls. Many gender and sex dysphoric girls maintain a secret hope that at puberty their bodies will mature into male ones, thereby self-correcting what they hold to be a biological error in their sex.[45] The first sign of puberty, the budding of their breasts, rather than being a somewhat alien but generally welcomed event is usually greeted by gender and sex dysphoric teenagers with horror.[46] The development of breasts is for them the first absolutely undeniable sign that they will become transformed from boyish children into adult women. Many respond to the growth of their breasts with diversionary tactics. They may take to slouching and wearing oversized clothing in an attempt to hide their physical maturation from others. Some adolescent girls go so far as to devise ingenious methods of binding down their breasts in the hope that they will either stop growing or at least not be obvious to others.[47]

The alienation which gender and sex dysphoric adolescent girls feel about their bodies extends also to the new social demands which are placed upon them by their peers at this time in their lives. To their dismay, they often find that the boys with whom they previously were chums either reject their companionship outright or begin to relate to them in a sexualized fashion. Thus they lose their prized status as "just one of the boys." Simultaneously they may become even further disaffected from their female peers as their female age-mates become increasingly preoccupied with enhancing their feminine appearances and attracting the sexual and romantic attentions of boys. Despite these pressures, many gender and sex dysphoric adolescent girls tenaciously cling to their tomboyish ways.[48] Even more so than for many other teenagers, adolescence can be a time of loneliness and isolation for gender and sex dysphoric girls.[49]

During the adolescent years, many girls who later go on to become transsexual become even more dedicated to their hopes of becoming male.[50] These feelings are often exacerbated by their rising sexual feelings. As teenagers, most female-to-male transsexuals-to-be find that they are sexually attracted to other girls but that they imagine themselves to be boys in their fantasies.[51] On average, female-to-male transsexuals report that they began their sexual involvements at younger ages than did lesbian or straight women, more than three-quarters of them having begun by age eighteen.[52] They also differ from lesbian women in the nature of their same-sex sexual practices as they relate to their gender and sex identities. Young women who are later to become transsexual tend to insist that their female sexual partners *not* be homosexual and that their partners relate to them as if they were male. Thus most gender and sex dyphoric females, unlike most lesbian women, have been found to generally prefer that their sexual partners not touch them on their breasts or manually penetrate their genitals, as this would call attention to their persistent femaleness.[53]

Some gender and sex dysphoric teenaged girls become confused or frightened by their feelings for others girls and try to deny them in order to avoid the stigma associated with lesbianism. Some may avoid sexuality altogether.[54] Some may engage in exploratory heterosexual relations during adolescence or young adulthood in attempts to take refuge in conformity with the sexuality that is expected of them.[55] Religious affiliations may contribute to such reactions.[56] As well, a small minority of girls who are later to become transsexual find that they are sexually interested in men but fantasize themselves as gay men rather than as women.[57]

In sum, adolescence is usually a time of crisis for girls who go on to become transsexual. Not only do they find social demands for femininity increasingly difficult to evade, but their bodies also seem to betray them. As children, they were able to take refuge in the relatively acceptable tomboy style. Come adolescence, the viability of that style becomes all but nil. The boys with whom they used to play cease to accept them as one of the boys; the girls with whom they used to play grow into young women. Perhaps most difficult of all, their physical selves relentlessly proclaim to all that they live within the bodies of young women.

Summary

Adolescence is a time of flux. Young people are confronted with the task of leaving behind their childhood lives and negotiating their transitions into adulthood. Old allegiances and strategies must be reworked, if not abandoned. Parents may sometimes seem like teenagers' best resources, but often they are viewed by their children as stumbling blocks in their race for maturity. Peers take on a new importance at this stage of life. They become the measure of almost all things. Peer approval becomes the authority before which all must bow. Peers of the opposite sex take on a special importance for most adolescents as they propel themselves headlong into their first consensual sexual experiences. For a smaller number of teenagers, same-sex peers come to occupy a similar role. For all adolescents, these social, sexual, and psychological changes are prompted and accompanied by profound physiological maturational processes. Clearly, adolescence must be both an exciting and awkward time.

10 | Crises at Puberty

MANY GIRLS FIND that puberty can be somewhat unsettling at first, but generally they come to accept, if not celebrate, their physical womanhood. The participants in this study, however, overwhelmingly reported that they were not able to make peace with their physical maturation during their adolescence. For the most part, they reacted to their increasingly womanly bodies with pronounced aversion. Many began to make mental commitments to later pursue gender and sex reassignment; some began their transitions while still in their teens.

No Way, Not Me: Menstruation

The average age at which participants reached menarche, 12.9 years, was consistent with typical pubertal development for North American girls of European heritage. Where they differed from the norm was in the number of participants whose experiences of menarche and menstruation were extreme. An unusually high number of participants began their menstrual periods either younger or older than would be expected. In the population at large, 95 percent of all girls reach menarche between the ages of eleven and fifteen years.[1] In this group of forty-five female-to-male transsexuals, 11 percent, or 2.2 times as many as normally would be expected, reported that they reached menarche either at nine[2] or seventeen[3] years of age.

Another way in which these participants were atypical as adolescent girls was in the variety of physical difficulties associated with their menses. Approximately half of all participants (47 percent) had complaints, the most frequent of which was extreme menstrual pain.[4] The remaining twenty-four participants (53 percent) either said that their menses were normal or did not mention any physiological difficulties.[5]

Eleven participants (24 percent) said that during their adolescence they found their menses to be painful to the point of debilitation.[6] Many of these individuals also had other complications related to their difficult menses. Jack, for example, who said that as a teenager she had such pain that "there would be many times that I couldn't get up off the floor—I was on my hands and knees," also had to take birth control pills to regulate her menstrual periods; without medication, she suffered with an almost continuous flow.

Three participants also told stories which indicated that their doctors had informed them that they had some virilization of their internal reproductive capacities. Eli said that although as a adolescent she had not particularly suffered with her menstrual periods, she was hairy and had a masculine body build. Later in life Eli had a cyst removed which Eli described as having been located on a "male vestigial canal . . . the sperm carrying canal." Sam attributed the unusually early onset of her menstruation to the hyperthyroidism from which she suffered. Later in life Sam had difficulties bearing children and eventually had to have a hysterectomy. After the hysterectomy, her doctors told her that she had been "all male-formed inside." Bruce also had painful menses. Bruce's menarche was exceptionally late, arriving when she was seventeen years old; it did not happen again for another year and thereafter only every two months. Like Sam, later in life, severe menstrual cramps brought Bruce to exploratory surgery. Her doctors detected three ovarian cysts, one of which was a male teratomatous growth "the size of a tennis ball."

Walter suffered from polycystic ovarian disease which Walter claimed elevated her childhood and adolescent androgen levels into the typical male range. As a result, Walter both "spontaneously virilized" at puberty and endured painful and infrequent (once or twice a year) menses. As a teenager, Walter was wide shouldered, narrow at the hips, muscular, tended to deposit fat in the stomach area, and had "more than average" facial and body hair.

Howie also experienced irregular and painful menses, accompanied by a number of masculine secondary sex characteristics. Howie described puberty this way:

> When I was female, I always had total male weight distribution: no waist, flat rear-end, no hips, no curves, flat chested, broad shouldered. I was referred to as "lumberjack" once. I also had total male hair distribution. After puberty, at age eleven, I had beard, mustache, sideburns, chest hair and stripe of hair down stomach area. It increased and darkened with age. I had a very irregular menstrual cycle. I'd go without menstruating for eight–ten months and once menstruated an entire summer long! Talk about a mistake of nature! . . . This was very traumatic for me and I was always self-conscious. . . . I considered my excess facial and body hair to be a real curse.

Steven, too, had painful and irregular menses. When Steven was in her late teens, a doctor who performed a gynecological exam told her that "my internal organs were very much underdeveloped, like prepubescent.

Even though I had menses, I had very small internal reproductive organs."
Steven, like Walter and Howie, also said that when, prior to commencing transition, she had her hormones tested, the results showed that her androgen levels were elevated. Steven said that she had the androgens of a 17 year old male.

In addition to those already mentioned, another six participants (13 percent) had nonpainful but particularly irregular menses.[7] Stan's adolescent menses were irregular enough that she had to take estrogen therapy to stabilize them. Luther probably should have gotten medical attention but did not. Luther's menses started at a normal time in her life, but shortly thereafter she ceased to menstruate for approximately five years. Terry's puberty sounded like she too might have had hormonal irregularities. She menstruated only once a year, had "large amounts" of facial and body hair, small hips and breasts, and was "rather muscular."

Ron and Dennis each had irregular menses because of external interventions. At the time of her puberty, Ron was a competitive athlete in a European country with very lax policies concerning the use of performance-enhancing drugs. Ron took steroids over a period of two years in her midteens, and they caused her to have a delayed puberty and infrequent menses. Dennis, as an adolescent, was so traumatized at the thought of menstruating that she almost killed herself in her efforts to stop her menstruation. At the advent of her menarche, Dennis set out to obtain a hysterectomy. The story of how she managed her menses is a harrowing one:

> Well, all it took was once, for me to know that no matter what it took in this life, this was not going to happen to me. . . . It's like I would deal with the devil, I'd do anything. . . . I would just get obsessed with finding a way to stop it. I knew . . . if hysterectomy is what it would take, then . . . I would find a way to have that done. And until then . . . I read in a magazine that excessive running and dieting will stop it. And I had always been into exercise, and that's what I did. I started running and dropping weight. . . . Then I lost it. I couldn't control what I was doing anymore. And I eventually got to sixty-two pounds. . . . and here I am not realizing what the hell I look like. All I know is that all my pants are falling off me. And I used to get so cold that I would have to come home and run hot water . . . over my feet and my hands because I couldn't stop shivering. And then I grew all this hair on my back like an animal would grow hair. Long hair. . . . Like coarse. Like a weird thing. . . . And I start losing hair [on my head]. . . . I was detached from those things because nothing mattered except that one thing—the reason I started this.

Dennis's uncle found a doctor who managed to convince Dennis to maintain her weight at a level which assured her survival but still eliminated

her menses. Dennis kept to this regimen for several years until an accidental injury interfered with her exercise programme. At that point she had
her fourth menstrual period and became suicidal. Another doctor prescribed birth control pills in a strength which suppressed Dennis's menses
until she was a young adult and was finally able to obtain the hysterectomy for which she so hungered.

Not all participants were as perturbed about the coming of their
menses. Twelve participants (27 percent) said that they had either simply
accepted their menses when it began or had chosen to put it out of their
minds as much as possible so as to avoid dwelling on something which
they could not change.[8] Approximately half of all participants (51 percent), however, did state that they had felt intense emotional discomfort
about their menses while they were adolescents.[9] They frequently resorted
to very strong language to capture the force of their reactions; they used
terms such as "shameful and disgusting," "degrading," "humiliating,"
"abhorrent," "repulsive," "a nightmare," "doomsday," and "pure hell" to
describe their feelings about menstruation.

As participants explained the situation, there were two interlocking
reasons for their passionate reactions. One was that, concurrently with
their attainment of adolescence, they began to be subjected to unrelenting
social pressures to abandon their tomboyish ways and join the ranks of
womanhood. They perceived these initiatives as curtailing their freedoms
and as inimical to their natures. The other reason was that for many participants, their menses were insurmountable proof that they were not boys
and would not grow up to be men. This was a devastating blow to many
participants.

Morgan described puberty as the time "when the hatchet came down.
Suddenly, I wasn't allowed to do things." Jorge said, "the onset of puberty
was horrible and depressing. Being a woman was scary to me. I wasn't
comfortable being treated as a female by others." Bob described analogous
feelings in these words:

> It was pointed out to me on many occasions that I should learn to be
> more feminine. . . . I had come to grips with the fact that I was female,
> that I was not born a male, and there would be only one way to be a
> male. And that was to have surgery. So, I had come to grips with the fact
> that I was born a female and it wasn't a fluke. That I was a male inside
> a female's body. . . . I had to realize that I would not grow up to be a
> man.

Harry saw that not only was her body changing but so too were the
social dynamics between herself and her peer group.

> I knew, in my terms, something was wrong. . . . It's not just that I was
> changing. The guys were changing too. I mean, they started to become

attracted to girls. So, they would talk to me, and hang around with me in the sense that they wanted me to go to this girl, and say that they liked them.

Ten participants (22 percent) reacted to these new social demands with depression and a withdrawal from the social world around them. They seemed to feel that there were no longer any suitable social positions for them to occupy. They felt forbidden to be boys and unable to be girls. Many resorted to spending a lot of time alone, withdrawing from normal adolescent social interactions.[10]

Simon's expression of desperation was perhaps the most dramatic. Simon attempted suicide on the night of her first menstrual period. Others were only slightly less extreme in their withdrawal. Jack described menarche as "probably the most traumatic thing that ever happened in my life." At the time, she felt "This is it! My life is over!" and became so depressed that she suffered from insomnia. She used to tell her friends, "I am basically a depressed person. Depression is my middle name." Luther echoed the same sentiments: "My life was over! . . . My freedom to be me was over." Fred became so anxious over puberty that she was hospitalized with a nervous breakdown at age sixteen:

I was withdrawn and didn't really care about a whole lot. I had a lot of friends, but didn't really care about socializing or anything. . . . I didn't know how to really relate to anyone so I began to become quiet and shy. . . . the stress became so great for me trying to fit into the norm and I just couldn't deal with it any longer, and I remember Mom had to come to school to pick me up. I was sick to my stomach. That was all the time. I wouldn't eat. If I did eat or drink anything, it came back up. So, she was very frustrated and disgusted with me, and had taken me to the doctor probably hundreds of times to see what was wrong physically. They found nothing physically.

Harry found the whole idea of becoming a woman so distressing that she too withdrew from everyday social relations with her peers:

I just didn't like it because of what it meant. . . . It meant, "I'm getting more and more proof that these people thinking I'm a girl are right." . . . It didn't mean I really was female. It meant more evidence was coming in. . . . I wasn't convinced yet. . . . I stayed mostly to myself. I was quite introverted. . . . And then I started looking at myself biologically, and then I guess one day it dawned on me. It was, "Oh, oh my God! This means this! Oh-oh. Christ! I'm a girl! Jesus Christ, I'm a girl!" . . . It all started to fall into place. . . . I was really upset. . . . I got incredibly depressed. . . . It was like, "What the fuck am I going to do?" . . . There's nothing I can do. And I just lived with that thought. I became a zombie.

Seven participants (16 percent) were so alarmed and ashamed of having their menses that they kept their menstrual periods secret whenever they could.[11] For example, Bruce had been educated at school about menstruation but had persisted in the hope that it would never happen to her. When she finally reached menarche at age seventeen she thought:

> I'm dying! I'm bleeding to death! And I couldn't tell anybody. And I thought this is what it was they talked about, God didn't hear me. . . . I took care of myself, I never told anybody.

Steven had similar feelings about her menstrual periods:

> They were very physically painful and emotionally traumatizing . . . devastating. . . . I wasn't growing up the way I thought I was going to grow up. . . . When my mother told me about it, I said, "Bullshit. I ain't going to get this thing." . . . And when I did get it, I could not bring myself to admit it to myself, let alone tell my mother. It was embarrassing. It was humiliating. It was deplorable in my mind. It was just the most disgusting thing I could think of. I thought I would rather be dead than have to go through this every month. It was like sheer torture.

Irregular, extremely painful, or otherwise physiologically abnormal menses seemed to have been unusually common among participants when they were teenagers. A total of nineteen participants (42 percent) had physiological difficulties with their menses during their adolescent years.[12] Emotional resistance to menstruation was also a common theme among participants. Intensely negative sentiments were most common; about half of participants (51 percent) reported a high level of emotional discomfort about their menses.[13] In some cases, these feelings were more connected to the social implications of physical maturation. In others, participants seemed to feel that the physical aspects of menstruation were both inappropriate to them and intrinsically defiling to them as human beings. When all of these sources of alienation from menstruation are taken into account, more than two-thirds of participants (69 percent) were very distressed by their menses during their adolescence.[14]

Body Betrayal: Growing Breasts

Even more so than menarche, the emergence of breasts on an adolescent girl's body heralds her femaleness. Menses can be a private affair. Breasts are much more a matter of public record. The participants in this study overwhelmingly reported that their breasts were a source of anxiety for them. For the most part, they, unlike most teenaged girls, just wanted their breasts to disappear.

During their adolescence, twenty-eight participants (62 percent) took steps to hide their breasts so as to make themselves appear more boyish.[15] Six additional participants (13 percent) were fortunate enough to have developed very small breasts and so were unconcerned with their effects on their appearances.[16] Participants who did not try to hide their breasts were not necessarily pleased with them either. Another six participants (13 percent) reported that they either felt extreme discomfort about their breasts when they were teenagers or just tried to dissociate themselves from them as much as possible.[17]

The reasons which participants gave for wanting to obscure their breasts were similar to those they cited in objection to their menses. The new body image was not right for them. They did not want to be identifiable as female because it was in conflict with their visions of themselves as boys. Were their breasts to show, they felt that they would be exiled from their boys' world and relegated to the company of girls.

Rick's comments exemplified the feelings of many participants. He talked about how, as an adolescent girl, she could not find any way to comfortably reconcile her new contours with her gender identity:

> That was extremely disturbing and stressful. From that point on was the worst, because you do get a body shape or form that is traditionally one way or the other. So that was a lot more difficult, practically impossible actually. My stress level was enormous. Absolutely no sense of self-comfort at all, even privately. Just kind of a constant warfare with yourself.

Mel similarly found that the changes to the shape of her body made it impossible for her to go on behaving as if she were an unremarkable boy. Mel remembered the alteration in her status this way:

> You get to puberty and then just everything blows apart because you delude yourself, you put yourself in situations where you can deal with it. It's your own little secret, but you're dealing with it. You get to puberty and . . . now you have to deal with . . . that little lie I've been telling myself all this time. . . . That I'm really a boy and that this is really a big nightmare. It's really a dream, but as long as I keep my thoughts to myself I'm safe. Then your body starts screwing you up. Because, before, as long as you had your pants on it was OK. . . . And then you have to just figure out what the heck you're doin'. You have to come up with a new game plan to exist.

Stan's testimony was along the same lines:

> I guess that was evidence that I was going to grow up to be a woman. The decision was being made. . . . Up to that point I could fake it. I could walk the fence. I really didn't have to tell the world, "Hello. I am a woman." I could do what I wanted to do. I could play the games I

wanted to. I could wear pretty much the clothes I wanted to wear. Hang out with the kids I wanted to hang out with. . . . And as my body started to change, that's when the social pressures started coming on.

Scott pinpointed the day that she got her first bra as a turning point for the worse:

Ever since I've been twelve, I've felt like I was in the wrong body. . . . In fact, I remember when I was about thirteen my mom . . . came home and said, "I have a present for you." . . . And she bought this bra. And that was the worst day of my life! . . . I think from then on I was pretty unhappy about my gender. I felt restricted in my activities. I couldn't play football any longer. I was real upset that I couldn't . . . play baseball. I had to play softball. It just didn't feel comfortable for me at all.

Brian felt even more strongly that becoming a woman was a major step down in the social hierarchy. Brian seemed to feel that women were almost subhuman and was not pleased about being expected to be one of them:

The feelings were especially strong when I hit puberty and my body completely betrayed me and became even more filthy and degrading by growing breasts. I felt God had betrayed me or didn't care about me. I argued with others that I hated being a girl and didn't want to be one. They were critical and unsympathetic. They demanded more than ever that I should behave in degraded ways, act feminine. . . . I hated my body and used to beat on myself with my fist. It did not belong to me. It was a prison and I wanted to be rid of it.

Most of those people who felt so badly about having breasts took some steps to make their breasts as unobtrusive as possible. Twenty participants (44 percent) bound or hid their breasts during their adolescence in an attempt to continue to pass as boys, or at least as neuters, for as long as possible.[18] Frequently their efforts resulted in their being intermittently taken as boys by people who didn't know them. As well, Darren, Bruce, and Luther privately crossdressed as a way to alleviate some of the stress of feeling like boys when everyone else thought of them as girls. Simon, Jorge, Alan, and Grant began to crossdress full-time in late adolescence, having already begun to think of themselves as men.

The techniques which participants used to mask the shape of their breasts were twofold. One way they concealed their breasts was to flatten them against their bodies. They utilized various methods involving tight undershirts or binding strips of their own devising. A few participants also used variations on these methods to try to stymie the growth of their breasts. The other common approach was to hunch their shoulders forward and to wear baggy clothing so that their breasts would not protrude in any way. Some people used both methods.

Walter's story illustrates one of the more benign approaches to this issue:

> In my teens, it was the sixties, so we all dressed the same. We all wore jeans and work shirts. . . . I thought of those as men's clothes. . . . even when other women would be wearing those clothes, I would still think that. . . . I would sometimes get the "Are you a boy or a girl?" like they would say to any guy with long hair. . . . I was always taken as male.

Bruce's distress at her puberty was considerably more intense. At age thirteen, Bruce had a male identity that was so at conflict with her budding breasts that she attempted to stop their growth. Around the same time, Bruce also began to crossdress and told her mother that she needed a sex change. Bruce explained these activities in terms of body identity issues and social practicality:

> My mother had really large breasts. Nice looking tits. And she would say, "You're going to have breasts just like mine. Look what you have to look forward to." And I'd go, "I'd die if I had to have tits like that." . . . So I would lay on my back and sleep and hope gravity would make my tits not grow. And then it wasn't working so I'd lay on my stomach and so that would make them not grow. . . . I started binding myself down, even though I had nothing. . . . I had T-shirts . . . I had sewn . . . very, very tight. . . . or I would pull my undershirt, and just pin it to my pants or a skirt. . . .
>
> I started to . . . identify as more male, and I noticed that men had bulges in their pants. . . . So I tried to create that. And the only thing I could think of was balls. And the only thing small enough were croquet balls. . . . I would do it in the privacy of my own room. I would dress up and do this, and then I would shave with a pencil. I'd lather up with soap, and I'd pretend like this pencil was my razor blade. . . . And I remember packing my pants for school . . . I just created it out of toilet paper. And that was really important because that's what boys did. They had dicks. . . . It was easier to pass as a boy than a girl because people always thought I was a boy. When I had to explain that I was a girl it was more of an embarrassment.

Grant, too, wanted to be taken as a male, and crossdressed to gain that outcome. She didn't know that female-to-male transsexualism was a possibility until she was twenty-two years old. As a teenager of eighteen years, Grant felt the need to express her inner identity by passing as a gay man:

> I worked part time in a gay bar [cross]dressed. I worked as somebody's kid brother is what I looked like. This was before hormones. Thanks

to some six-inch ace wraps and short, short hair. . . . I did that part
time. . . . I learned about the fact that you could take a thin knee high
sock, roll it the right way, stuff it in the right place, and people would
be all over you.

In her early and midteens, Darren too, knew that she wanted to be a
man but didn't yet know about transsexualism. She would often put on a
jacket and tie of her father's in the privacy of her own bedroom and revel
in her appearance in the mirror. Darren decided to pursue sex reassignment surgery shortly after the accidental death of her parents when she
was sixteen years old. Darren then occasionally crossdressed in public. It
was only after being officially diagnosed as transsexual, however, that
Darren dressed as a man all of the time.

Alan met some transsexual people after she ran away from an abusive
home and became a street prostitute during her teen years. During her
time on the street, Alan had already begun to crossdress and to consider
that she might be transsexual. She became convinced that this was the
appropriate course of action after spending her fifteenth year successfully
passing as a young male prostitute on the street.

When she was in her teens, Luther also knew that one day she would
undergo gender and sex reassignment. Until that time, she lived a double
life. In her everyday world, her large breasts made it impossible for her
to try to pass as a boy, so she tried to appear as an acceptable-looking
woman. To satisfy herself, she crossdressed in private. She started soon
after her breasts developed:

It really did affect my identity. I was, in fact, very shaken. I was turning
into a woman. I had a fairly well shaped body for a woman. I didn't like
that very much. I tried to hide the changes in my body. When I was
home [alone] . . . I would spend lots of time in the mirror combing my
hair and restyling it like a man. And I would tie my breasts down. And
I would wear men's clothes. And I liked that very much.

Like Darren and Alan, Simon decided that she was transsexual when
she was sixteen years old. Simon had always worn boys' clothing as often
as possible. When she grew breasts she took to using layers of clothing to
disguise her figure until she met a female-to-male transsexual who taught
her how to bind her breasts. At that point, Simon began to live as a man.
Simon recalled:

I used to wear real tight T-shirts, and like a flannel over that (and this
was year round) and a coat of some kind, a jacket, you know real
hunched with the shoulders and everything so that nobody could really
tell.

In sum, participants' reactions to the growth of their breasts during their adolescence can only be described as aversive. No one was happy about the emergence of these unequivocal insignia of femaleness. A total of thirty-four participants (75 percent) actively concealed their breasts,[19] crossdressed,[20] or had small, inconspicuous breasts which did not interfere with their efforts to downplay their femaleness.[21] An additional six individuals reported that they too had been unhappy with their development of breasts but had, for a variety of reasons, learned to live with them without resorting to subterfuge.[22] Thus forty of forty-five participants (89 percent) reported that they did not want their breasts to be obvious enough to mark them as female.

Trying to Conform

Eleven participants (24 percent) went through periods of their adolescence during which they tried to take more conformist routes. They tried to acquiesce to what was expected of them and went through girlish phases.[23] Eventually, all of them were to conclude that this was not appropriate behaviour for them. Most participants came to this conclusion after relatively brief forays into femininity.

Aaron took an interesting approach to her physical maturation. She had a flat-chested, boyish body throughout her adolescence and uneventful menses. When she reached menarche, she welcomed it while still seeing herself as a boy:

> You got to realize that I loved babies. . . . I was . . . almost fifteen when I finally had a period and my reaction was such that I actually wrote it down in a diary. And it says very simply, "Wow, I'm the only guy here that can have babies!" That was my reaction. . . . I was slow growing up. . . . I was glad to be growing up. The other females were starting to grow up too. Leaving me behind. . . . But let's face it . . . periods didn't offend me. I saw sex and periods towards one goal, and that was having babies. I didn't see it in terms of getting married as much as I did in terms of having children.

Aaron went on from that point to live as a relatively gender-conforming woman until she was in her late twenties. During that time she had four babies.

Keith described her teenaged self as "an obedient child" who "knew what I was supposed to do and did it." For a time Keith was "a pretty girl" outwardly, while inwardly she "had a fantasy identity that no one ever saw" in which she was a boy. But even while she was being a girl, she did what she could to minimize the obviousness of her breasts.

Eli also wanted to be cooperative. She assumed that everyone knew that she was really a boy and that she was only dressing as a girl because she somehow had a woman's body. Eli was able to discount this contradiction in her own mind until she was in her forties.

> I had a girl's body. So, I figured fair's fair. This is the kind of body I got, and at the time I didn't have any problem with it, because I never [emotionally] went through adolescence. I had the female puberty, and I kicked up a little bit about that, but then, in a very manly way I announced I was going to really try and do the girl thing when I was supposed to do it, like shave my armpits, shave my legs, wear lipstick. . . . And then I'd come home and put on my good clothes and have my bicycle gang, and pretend I was Marlon Brando. . . . as long as I knew that I could do what I wanted to, I'd play their game and do the girl thing. . . . I just knew that being a fair and good person, I should do what was right from their point of view, and not rock the boat.

Scott, Robin, Steven, Hal, Luther, and Simon also went through feminine phases because they felt that was what was expected of them and there was no way out of it. Scott wore makeup and had a curvaceous body and long blonde hair. Robin tried to look like a girl, but she was less than completely effective in her femininity and was an "outcast" among her peers. Steven "hated" wearing long hair and appearing to be a girl but "felt that there was no other way." Hal allowed her girlfriends to "inflict abominations" upon her visage because she "wanted to be included," but she ended up feeling "really stupid" and "ridiculous" and later avoided such experimentation. Luther, who crossdressed in secret, recalled her feminine phase this way:

> I was willing to try and be a girl. . . . I didn't know how to get out of it, and so I may as well at least try. Maybe I could be happy if I was like everybody else. . . . I curled my hair, and I learned to wear makeup. . . . By this time, I had developed pretty large breasts, so I couldn't really disguise myself.

Simon, too, went through a short period of experimentation with makeup because of "peer pressure." Simon remembered:

> What always surprised me was that men found me attractive. Peers as well. I didn't understand why. . . . I've since decided that that was because most of them were actually gay or the kind of men who are attracted to very masculine women.

Morgan was "disgusted" with her body as a teenager, but she was also so embarrassed when people teased her about looking like a boy that she experienced that period as "the worst time in my life." In response, she tried to look more like a woman. Nevertheless, she chronically hunched her shoulders to hide her breasts even as she adopted a colorful feminine look:

I could look feminine but I was always a bit weird, like eccentric. Like I got into really weird . . . heavy black makeup. And I had my hair parted really long and in ringlets. . . . Like this was at the height of the hippy thing . . . I'd wear a black top hat and a long cape. . . . And that period lasted for quite a while. . . . [Later] I became more masculine in an offbeat way. Like I wore this huge belt, but I still wore lots of make-up. But I looked more like a guy, except that I was wearing makeup. So I was really into wearing like a lot of makeup, because without it I looked really young.

Each of these people did eventually decide that they were unable to continue to indefinitely accept themselves in their female form. It is interesting to note, however, that Morgan, Eli, and Robin were three of only six participants in this study who, at the time of their interviews, had not yet embarked upon any surgical or hormonal steps to masculinize their bodies. A fourth person among them, Aaron, did not start his transition until she was a grandmother in her middle forties.

Summary and Commentary

Puberty can be a rough time for any adolescent girl. The physical changes which the contours of girls' bodies undergo can be unsettling. Menses can be uncomfortable or painful. Learning how to deal with menstrual periods can be a vexation. However, after an initial adjustment stage, most teenaged girls come to accept their altered bodies. They learn that the physical changes which they have undergone also usher in access to life as adult women. For most adolescent girls, this is adequate recompense for the inconveniences of puberty.

The people who participated in this study reported that they reacted quite differently to their pubertal changes. Some were perturbed by their menses. Others were outraged at the exposure of their femaleness which the growth of their breasts entailed. As adolescents, these people were unable to find comforting compensation in the social world of women which was opening up before them. To the contrary, they seem to have rebelled almost universally against the prospect of taking their places among the sorority of women. Significantly, almost all participants (91 percent) reported that they suffered through their puberty with ongoing and relatively intense anxiety specifically about their breasts[24] or their menses.[25] Only four participants seem to have sailed through their adolescence with no more than the typical amount of female teenaged puberty trauma.[26] Clearly, puberty was an occasion for increased gender and sex dysphoria among the participants in this study.

11 | Adolescent Friendships

As young people move into and through adolescence, they increasingly turn to their peers for their close relationships and as arbiters of their social mores. The companionship, opinions, and acceptance of their peers thus commonly take on higher value for teenagers. Therefore adolescents' abilities to establish themselves as members of particular crowds, of small, close-knit cliques, or to make "best friends" often comes to feel, to teenagers, like measures of their worthiness and success as human beings.

Trouble Fitting In

Many participants reported that their peer relationships during their teenaged years were trying to them. Half of them (50 percent)[1] recalled that they had trouble fitting in with their peers during some or all of their teen years.[2] Most often, the source of their difficulties lay in their gender presentations. A common refrain among participants was the lament that other teenagers teased them or ostracized them because they didn't look and act in ways which their peers found acceptable. Fourteen participants (32 percent) remembered being treated in this fashion.[3] They said that as teenagers they had often felt like "misfits" or "outcasts," and they remembered their peers as "cruel."

As participants moved into their teens, some were forced out of their childhood peer groups. For example, Morgan suffered ridicule from both boys and girls for not looking right. At first, she had a lot of girl friends who encouraged her to play at being a boy. However, after a while, it was no longer amusing, and Morgan decided that she would be better off if she tried to look more like a girl. However, that brought heterosexual attentions with it, something which Morgan found intolerable. Morgan tried to walk a thin line between looking feminine enough to avoid derision and not looking so feminine as to signal an interest in heterosexuality. Morgan described how she made her decision:

> People were saying . . . "Oh, you make such a good guy." . . . But after about a few months . . . it was not getting funny anymore. . . . It's too

unusual. . . . I was sitting in a class once, right? And they brought in another class to watch a movie. And the lights were off. And these people, they stuck a compass in my leg, and they were pulling my hair. And people started to bug me, threatening to beat me up. . . . It was starting to get too uncomfortable and I was starting to lose friends and stuff, right? Because then they thought you were a lesbian, right? And they didn't like that. . . . So I decided it was time to fit in.

A number of participants responded to changes in their peers' expectations by withdrawing into themselves. Dennis did not want to be a girl but, at the same time, she didn't want the ignominious attention which her ambiguous gender appearance brought to her. Both her peers and her teachers were constantly confused as to her gender. She began to withdraw into herself. Dennis recalled:

> I was ostracized to a certain extent by the . . . girls. And I hadn't [developed any breasts yet]. And . . . as much as I didn't want anything on my chest, I just wanted something to show so that I wouldn't be totally embarrassed everywhere I went. Everywhere. In school, teachers never knowing what sex I was. I couldn't make friends. I was always on guard, always afraid, never able to relax. . . . I just felt like I was at everybody's . . . fucking mercy! . . . They would say, "Well, what are you? Are you a boy?" . . . I started withdrawing. . . . It was just that sense of confusion. . . . I didn't understand at first why it was happening. Because . . . even though I wore this school uniform every day, I thought that it was like you could see right through and see the person that I am. . . . a boy.

Harry remembered being pushed away by her childhood male friends as the gender demands of adolescence began to predominate. Harry wanted to keep being part of the boys' crowd, but the boys she knew brought it home to her quite forcefully that she was no longer one of them. When Harry understood what was happening, she withdrew from most social contact.

> I hung around with the guys till early teens. . . . And then it was like, "We can't do this anymore," and "We can't do what? What the hell is going on?" . . . And when some of the guys would say, "Well, you're a girl." . . . And I still didn't put that together. It's like, "No, I'm not. No, I'm not. What the hell are you saying?" And . . . it's like, "Either you're a girl, or you're crazy." And by the age of thirteen, I went right inside. . . . It was more weapons against me. They could start teasing me with this. . . . The fights were quite constant.

Jorge similarly went from being "very popular" in elementary school to being "very distant" in junior and senior high school. Jorge said of this time: "People would laugh at me and make bets as to if I were a boy or a girl. I became more shy and withdrawn. This was just not a good time of life. I started thinking about suicide."

Robin, Keith, and Grant recalled that their gender issues were further compounded by other things about them which set them apart from their peers. Robin remembered being a "total outcast" in high school. She had recently immigrated to the United States from Europe and entered her new school with different cultural standards as well as her gender issues. Robin recalled:

> I hated high school. . . . I was made fun of because I looked different. I wasn't your typical . . . American girl at age fourteen. . . . And so throughout high school years I was a total outcast. Totally. . . . I never felt accepted. I never adjusted. . . . I found one or two friends. . . . They were also outcasts. . . . I lived a very lonely, lonely life. . . . I didn't make any effort to meet people.

Keith also remembered being an outcast whose gender discomfort was compounded by her bashfulness.

> In . . . every class there's always some kid that's the butt of the class . . . the one that nobody likes. And I was one of those. . . . This was when all the girls were wearing miniskirts . . . were wearing makeup. . . . Fishnet stockings were really big that year. . . . And it just wasn't in me. I didn't have the interest. Seventh grade was a hard year because I was . . . naturally shy and sensitive. Any time I had to stand up in class and speak or anything else I'd just die because I had the cruel jibes of my schoolmates.

Grant was additionally stigmatized because she was seeing a school psychologist for her gender issues. This marked her as a "psycho" and further set her apart. Grant recalled, "Nobody wanted to have anything to do with me." Resiliently, Grant decided that her peers were "shallow" and that she "couldn't relate" to them. Self-protectively, Grant "shut myself off" from them and threw herself into other things.

Other participants also recalled that they voluntarily withdrew from the fray of adolescent peer relations. Eight additional participants (18 percent) described themselves as loners.[4] They remembered having felt unwilling to join in with others in the types of activities which were open to them as teenaged girls. Jordie "dropped out of life." Bill also turned away from socializing: "I didn't fit in at all and began to gain weight, focus on academics, and isolate myself socially."

Nathan and Brian were also withdrawn as adolescents. The one time that each of them reached out to another person, it proved to be painful. Nathan had a dear best friend, but he died when they were fourteen years old. Nathan was not again able to trust enough to make another friend during her adolescence. The one time that Brian started to make a friend with a troubled young man, their teacher berated her in front of the whole class for "associating with a bad influence like that." After that, Brian "avoided people for the most part" and had "no significant friends."

Fred and Howie felt it necessary to hide who they were from their teenaged friends. However, Fred remembered that her facade was popular:

> I wanted to fit in, and I wanted to be part of the norm. So at this time . . . I felt like, to appear normal, I needed to act female. . . . I felt like I never could be me. I had to act and be someone else. But yet, at the same time, I had to keep myself smiling and happy. People seemed to like that, so that's what I did. . . . I was shy, bashful, and backward, but I still tried to stay involved in things.

Thus, a total of twenty-two participants (50 percent) reported that during their adolescence they either were harshly rejected by their associates or voluntarily chose to withdraw because of their own discomfort. In some cases, there appeared to have been any number of sources of this conflict and discomfort, but the clear theme which either underlies or co-exists with other conducers of conflict was that of participants' inability to conform satisfactorily to adolescent feminine gender style expectations.

Finding a Crowd

Twenty-eight participants (64 percent) had extracurricular interests which brought them into contact with similarly disposed others.[5] Those participants who had such interests were able to overcome some of their own alienation, as well as that of their peers, by focusing on their mutual concerns. Thus, even if they were unable to have close friendships with other adolescents, they were at least able to enjoy the companionship of a crowd of other young people. They therefore were also able to benefit from a feeling of belonging which was not necessarily predicated on being female. Aaron basically said as much when he recalled that "cliques and things like that didn't bother me because I had my own support system through the music department."

Sixteen participants (36 percent) found solace in some kind of creative endeavour.[6] Grant perceptively wondered about the prevalence of this type of relief for gender troubled people:

> I looked back a few years down the road and I was thinking, "Gee, I wonder how many of us go into music to get it out of our systems. To try to find a catharsis." . . . For me, if I sat down at the piano, or played flute, and I was playing Bach, people left me alone.

Steven's story of joining the school band seemed to bear out Grant's musings. Steven recalled the satisfaction which she derived from music and the companionship she gained through it:

> It was giving me a feeling of belonging because that was something I really needed at this time. . . . I felt so different, and yet now I had something in common with people. . . . And I started to become friends. . . . This was some kind of turning point . . . because the music became an outlet for years of loneliness and frustration and being alone. . . . Music became my life. It was literally consuming.

Eli's involvement with drama also brought her friendship and relief from mundane reality. She and her girlfriends indulged in ongoing fantasy enactments in which Eli always took a dominant male role. Her skits provided her with an immense fountainhead of imaginary alternatives to her life as a teenaged girl. Eli reminisced:

> I would turn into Marlon Brando . . . with my friends, who were girls, but we were all dressed like Marlon Brando. . . . and we had a motorcycle club . . . like a gang of boys would have except we didn't have the rivalry. . . . Oh, we had Roman parties, and we did *On the Waterfront* parties, and Napoleon parties, and we'd be Egyptians. We'd make movies of all these things and we'd read poetry. Oh, we did all kinds of neat stuff.

For other participants, their involvements with the arts were more double-edged. Simon was attracted to the stage and entered a drama program at her university but left it as soon she found out that she was expected to play women's roles on stage. Instead, Simon became a technician and was able to retain her connections with the theatre that way. Similarly, Peter "loved" her six years of ballet because she "could just get carried away" in it, enjoying "a tremendous escape." Unfortunately, Peter's parents decided that Peter was "getting too damned serious" about it all and cancelled her lessons when she was fourteen years old.

Morgan found that art school was a source of both satisfaction and frustration. Her parents and other students created anxieties:

> It was like a double whammy. [My parents] would buy me paints and stuff . . . but on the other hand, "You're never going to amount to anything." . . . [At] art school . . . there was an eraser called a kneaded eraser and the [male students] were always, like, making it into little cocks and putting them on my desk. And one time I came back from lunch and . . . they'd made this huge clay penis and put in on my chair. It was actually a lot of fun. There was just stuff like that. I had my hair tied back, right, and a guy comes up and says, "Hey man, get a haircut"

kind of thing. There was always things coming up. It was just little things.

Brian's artistic talents brought her feelings of pride and accomplishment, but only for a while. When her art teacher separated her from her only friend, Brian said, "I began to hate art. I stopped drawing much. I could hardly pick up a pencil or brush without feeling rage about the incident, and that even my art had betrayed me."

Sports were another interest which many participants found satisfying as teenagers. Thirteen participants (29.5 percent) were active in sports.[7] Most participants found sports to be a rewarding way to gain entry to a world of women where they were less likely to be stigmatized for their masculinity and where they were often rewarded for it. As a bonus, some also found that other tomboyish girls like themselves tended to congregate in girls' sports. However, a few participants looked at sports in a different light. They felt that girls' sports were sissified and beneath them. They preferred the company of boys on the playing fields.

Dale found that her entry into sports at age fourteen provided her with a ready-made clique of friends. Whereas before then she had suffered from "very, very low self-esteem" and was shy and "withdrawn," when Dale joined the women's basketball team to be like her "heroes," the boys whom she "admired" and "wanted to be like," Dale became "a star" and was soon happily "very popular."

Bob and Ron also gave sports a central place in their lives as teenaged girls. Bob was an all-around award-winning athlete. Ron excelled in competition and teamwork with both girls and boys:

> Sports were very important to me. . . . I played soccer, and I did shot put. . . . I also did horseback riding, and then I had about six hours of martial arts every week. So, it was my life, basically. . . . I just played with the girls at school, but outside school I played with the boys. . . . I was always top dog, even in the boys'. . . . I won many trophies and awards.

Bruce and Ken were less enthusiastic. Both disdained girls' sports. Bruce called girls' sports "foofi games" in which "you couldn't be aggressive" and preferred to play with boys after school for as long as they would accept her. Ken recalled, "I always felt slighted that I was on the girls' volleyball team and the girls' softball team. I wanted to play football. My friends were male. . . . And I felt like I was being left out." Although both Bruce and Ken played girls' sports and found a place for themselves there, they were still happier when they were among boys.

Nine participants (20.5 percent) found companionship through their religious connections.[8] Aaron was probably the one most drawn to religion as a teenager, but being female cut short Aaron's ambitions. Aaron explained what happened:

> When I was . . . in high school, I was very active in the church. . . . And I felt, with my people skills, and my speech skills, and some of the other skills I had . . . that I would make a very good minister. And I felt called to the ministry. And made a public commitment to this effect, only to find out that [my church] . . . would not accept female ministers. . . . And I was very devastated. . . . Well, when I found that out, I was just starting college, planning towards that. . . . That was one of the reasons I dropped out of college.

Bruce started out life as a Mormon but was excommunicated when she was fourteen years old over a disagreement with the bishop. A couple of years later, when Bruce was feeling troubled over gender issues, she joined a Pentecostal church and "tried to get healed." Bruce remembered her desperation to be "rid of whatever this was that was making me uncomfortable and not happy":

> It was very oppressive. . . . I remember . . . them telling me, "Now, you remember this. You are God's little princess, God's little girl." . . . And I tried very hard to please God. . . . It didn't work. And I tried to have them exorcise demons out of me, but that didn't work. And I went on a mission . . . and that didn't work. . . . I left the church. And then I got involved with women, thinking "This is it."

Darcy and Dennis found real comfort in their religious beliefs during their adolescence. Darcy, who had been raised in a fundamentalist Christian home, remembered how her faith sustained her through her confused adolescence:

> I still had the faith that everything would fall into place. So, nothing hit me until the last few days of grade thirteen, and I realized that things weren't going to fall into place. . . . And so, high school, actually, wasn't that bad. When I'm looking back on it, I thought if I didn't have faith that something would happen, I would have been having a horrible time.

Dennis, who was a Catholic, said that during her adolescence she spent a lot of time "on my hands and knees praying," asking Jesus to terminate her menstrual periods. Dennis saw her plight as a test of her faith, a contest between "good and evil," "the Devil and God." When her prayers were not answered as quickly as she would have liked, Dennis appealed to the "healing" powers of a television evangelist. Dennis recalled:

> I found one of those stupid shows, those TV evangelists. . . . I didn't know what to do. I went to an event. You know, "miracles, miracles,

miracles." And I was torn. . . . Should I do this? . . . And I called one of these hot lines. I don't know how I ever told them, but . . . it must have blew their fucking minds. . . . They were not helpful, but I didn't give up. I had this faith. I had this great faith. And then in the month following that, I went to, like, a healing service.

Clearly, Dennis was not healed through religious faith alone. Medical technology was to be Dennis's ultimate savior when it came to her gender needs.

In sum, a total of twenty-eight participants (64 percent) found either some companionship or consolation in the arts, sports, or religion. These avocations gave participants the pleasure of being part of something larger than themselves, a feeling of being part of a community of like-minded people. As well, participants were gratified by their commitments to these interests because they were areas in which their gender did not need to be of paramount importance. For them, fiction, physicality, or faith brought them some respite from the otherwise unrelentingly gendered demands of adolescent life.

Buddies and Best Friends

In adolescence, in contrast to childhood, participants tended to count their closer friends more among girls than among boys. Nine participants (20.5 percent) remembered having both male and female friends during their adolescence.[9] However, more than twice as many people, twenty-one participants (48 percent), reported that they had spent their adolescent years predominantly with female friends.[10]

Three dynamics appear to have been largely responsible for the shift in participants' peer groups from mainly male to mainly female ones. A first theme, which underlaid the other two, was the pattern of social expectations that peer interactions should become increasingly heterosexually oriented as young people mature from children into adults. As participants' male peers absorbed this message, they began to reject those relationships with girls which they could not sexualize. For their part, participants also shied away from most relations in which they were expected to behave like straight women. At the same time as participants' relations with their male peers were becoming more distant, many participants also began to see their female peers in a more sexualized way. Many of them began to do to their girlfriends what they didn't want the boys to do to them: find them romantically attractive. Thus many participants experienced a push away from boys at approximately the same time as they began to feel a stronger pull toward other girls.[11] Finally, some participants postponed their entry into the highly charged sexual rituals of adolescence by forming alliances with other tomboyish girls who were similarly inclined.

Several participants nonetheless found a variety of ways to retain some male friends while beginning to shift their focus to other girls. For example, Roger adapted to the shock of going to an all-girls' boarding school by becoming involved in sports and finding a group of tomboyish girls on the teams which she joined. However, when Roger returned home between school terms, she found boys who were happy for her companionship in their adolescent misadventures.

Ken lived a Jekyll and Hyde kind of existence for part of her adolescence, moving between the worlds of the two genders. Ken mostly preferred the company of boys in her everyday life as a teenaged girl and, in that context, was disdainful of femininity. For a number of years, however, she "loved" her "very important" excursions to Girl Scout summer camp because she found that she felt free there to express "a feminine side that I enjoyed."

Morgan, too, moved back and forth between having girls and boys for friends. First, Morgan's mother forbade her to play with the boy next door when they were twelve years old because of the sexual overtones which her mother read into their relationship. Then, when Morgan was fourteen years old, she found herself in an all-girls' class at school. She became the "boy" of the class for their entertainment. They called her by a boy's name, assumed she was a lesbian, and laughed at her jokes. Later still, after all of that went stale and Morgan dropped out of school, she found a group of boys with whom she took LSD and went to rock concerts. As long as they treated her as one of them, Morgan was happy.

Part way through adolescence Jack and Darren both unwillingly switched from male to female companionship when the boys they knew started teasing them about being boyish. They each found a small group of tough girls with whom they could find refuge. Jack missed the boys with whom she had played as a child but, as she said, when one reaches a certain age "guys all of a sudden don't want to play army with you any more." Darren described her strategy at the time, saying, "It's like the losers would find each other." For companionship, she paired up with another tomboyish girl whom he remembered as an "ostracized . . . misfit" like herself.

Harry spent time with both boys and girls during her adolescence but never felt close with either group. On the one hand, the boys she knew had become interested in girls and only wanted to use Harry as an informant and messenger in their romantic intrigues. On the other hand, Harry was alienated from the girls she knew because they had become romantically interested in boys. Harry had access to her peers if she wanted to cooperate, but she came to prefer her own company. Harry remembered:

> I had spent some time with some female friends. I wouldn't really say I really tried to integrate myself with them. . . . But some times, you know, if we were sitting around talking, or whatever, and then they'd get into things like plucking their eyebrows and doing all this stuff, and they'd say, "Oh, let's pluck your eyebrows. Let's see what it looks like." You know, all that shit. And, of course I'd say, "No, thank you." . . . Really, I mean, I spent a lot of time by myself.

Stan took a different tack. She aligned herself with two similar cliques of teenagers, both of whom largely absented themselves from gender. Stan recalled how she handled her peer relations during her teen years:

> I did hang out with people that weren't ultra feminine, and stayed neutral . . . we were the nerds. We were the brains. And we didn't have to have dates, and we didn't have to be girls. We were just brains. And we were competing on an entirely different level with the boys. Not as girls, but on doing the project. We could answer the math questions, we could figure out the equations. And that's how we competed, rather than being prettier and more feminine. . . . It was asexual. . . . I ran in two different circles. With the female nerds, we hung out at lunch. There were three of us. . . . But during class I drifted more with the guys.

Eli went another route as a teenager. Like several other participants, she allied herself with a group of girls who rejected femininity, but Eli seemed to have been entirely pleased with her little clique of thespians. Eli was quite adamant about her rejection of femininity as a teenager. Eli remembered what her peer group was like then:

> Boy, I'll tell you one of the great shocks of my life was one day in junior high seeing a nice looking girl with this regular face, and regular eyebrows, and regular hair, and the very next day, literally, she came back and her eyebrows had been shaved off, and there was these thin little pencil lines, and she did some weird thing with her hair and her face, and I didn't know who she was. I mean, I knew it was the same person, but it was this horror. . . . It was . . . like somebody had cast a spell on her and she was dead to me. . . . she wasn't even acting the same way any more. . . . My friends didn't do that. . . . One day you're talking to somebody and you think you know who they are, and the next day it's as though they had been possessed! It was horrible! Horrible! Disgusting! . . . They were acting false and phoney. . . . I felt betrayed by these people. . . .
> Some people were girls and they sort of would hang around the fringes of our group. They couldn't really be in it because they weren't full people, you know, they were too girl. I felt a little sorry for them.

Maybe I felt a little superior. . . . I just couldn't understand why they were so undeveloped. . . . I mean . . . my pals, they weren't women. I always looked upon them as a guy would look on other guys.

Several participants had only one or two close female friends during their adolescence who also tended to be tomboyish like themselves.[12] Lee was somewhat embarrassed to describe her only friend during high school as a "butch . . . buddy." Hal more fondly recalled the best friend of her adolescence who shared her more masculine interests:

In junior high I met another girl who shared all the interests I had. . . . We were accused of being lesbians in high school, but she was (still is) straight, and I channeled all my sexual energy into my writing. (I didn't even know what "lesbian" or "homosexual" meant until I was in college.) . . . [She] and I would roam around and just talk about ideas we had for stories, or we would play pretend games in the hills in which we were cowboys, or soldiers, or Tom Sawyer and Huck Finn. Or we would practice our music, or build model trains, or ride bikes, or work on our writing. . . . [She] and I were the only girls on our high school ski team, and I was on the gymnastics team. . . . [She] and I started playing folk-rock. . . . We used the money we earned playing music . . . to purchase items of boys' clothing which our parents refused to buy for us.

In sum, approximately two-thirds of participants (68 percent) were able to find a few adolescent friends who accepted them as they were. Clearly they were not eager to make the switch from the companionship of boys to the friendship of girls. They only reluctantly transferred their friendships to other girls as their fellowship with boys became untenable. However, there were compensations and compromises to be had. Whenever possible, participants held onto what contacts they could among boys. Among girls, participants gravitated to other boyish girls like themselves until such times as they were overcome with romantic feelings for females.

Summary and Commentary

Developing friendships during their adolescent years proved an especially difficult task for many participants. Fully half of them reported that they had trouble fitting in with their peers.[13] Some participants were ostracized or ridiculed; others more voluntarily withdrew from adolescent socializing without having suffered many barbs; still others persisted despite feelings of alienation and anomie.

There appear to have been several reasons for the awkwardness which participants felt among their age-mates, but most of their difficulties can be traced back to their gender discomfort. Participants entered adolescence as young people who were primed for masculine adolescences. They were expecting and ready to grow into young men in mind, if not in body. They were thus ill-prepared to perform the ritual enactments of adolescent femininity which were expected of them. They were also largely both unwilling and inept at feminine friendship skills. Thus, although they may have been able to do better among the boys, few were given much opportunity by their male contemporaries to demonstrate their masculine skills once their bodies indicated that they were so obviously *not* boys.

Most participants found ways to survive adolescence without succumbing entirely to an unwelcomed isolation. They found companionship through their involvement in activities and interests which they shared with other young people. In some cases, that allowed participants to enjoy the company of young men free of sexual overtones. More often, they found their friends among other girls, some of whom were also gender rebels like themselves. Only rarely, however, did participants form intimate one-to-one relationships of the kind which so specifically characterize female adolescents. Rather, it seemed as though even their female "best friends" were more like adolescent masculine-style buddies than highly self-disclosing girlfriends. Most often they tended to form looser friendships with groups of young people which were predicated on doing things together, i.e., the kind of masculine-style, side-by-side friendships typical of teenaged boys.[14]

Thus it would seem that even though participants as adolescents were more often thrown together with females than they had been as children, they were resistant to feminine peer socialization. They either kept to themselves or kept their relationships with others at safe emotional distances. This level of emotional self-containment allowed them to preserve some sense of themselves as boys even as so much around them was telling them otherwise. It also left the door open for them to develop romantic attachments to those creatures whom they persisted in seeing as "other" — girls.

12 | Women Are Different
Relationships with Female Relatives

Relationships with Mothers

Most participants' relationships with, and attitudes toward, their mothers continued in the same vein as they had during childhood. Participants generally entered adolescence tending to see their mothers as relatively powerless people whom they were not inclined to use as role models. Participants' relationships with their mothers did not improve during their adolescence.

Approximately three-quarters of participants (74 percent)[1] reported erratic or antagonistic adolescent relations with their mothers.[2] The sources of their difficulties lay in several often overlapping areas. A handful of participants recalled their mothers as having been abusive toward them during their adolescence. More often, participants' mothers had problems of their own which made them somehow unavailable to their daughters during their teenaged years. In some of these cases, participants felt protective toward their mothers; others resented their mothers' virtual absence from their lives. Most commonly, however, the source of friction between teenaged participants and their mothers lay in participants' strivings toward independence. In particular, participants and their mothers most often came to a parting of the ways over issues of gender presentation. Participants' mothers wanted them to look and act more femininely than participants wished for themselves. They frequently came to harsh conflicts over this issue.

Whereas many participants reported difficulties with their mothers, one-third of them also recalled having been close to their mothers at some point during their adolescence[3] and only six participants (14 percent) recalled having experienced both types of emotions.[4] In most cases, when they were close it was either because participants felt protective toward their mothers or because participants felt that their mothers had been supportive of their gender expression.

Abusive Mothers: Losing Battles

Six participants (14 percent) reported that they had experienced their mothers as actively and aggressively abusive to them during their teen years.[5] Bruce was sexually abused by her mother during her adolescence;[6] the others were physically and emotionally maltreated. Understandably, these participants reported that they felt alienated from the women who inappropriately used their power over them.

Grant's adolescent experiences of physical abuse and neglect at the hands of her mother, which were among the worst reported, were a continuation of her childhood experiences. Two incidents in particular precipitated Grant's decision to leave home at age fifteen. Grant recounted these stories about those events:

> My mother decided . . . that I could be cured of my homosexuality. And I was taken to see a doctor at a psychiatric hospital. He prescribed two medications that should not be given together. . . . I don't remember the next three months. . . . I was sleeping most of the day. . . . I wasn't interested in sex. I wasn't interested in food. . . . I dropped serious weight. I was more or less in a vegetative state. . . . My mother was feeding me the pills. . . . She didn't care as long as those pills went down twice a day. . . .
>
> I was taken to a hospital [by my girlfriend]. . . . I was reaching toxicity levels. . . . [My girlfriend] wanted blood work done. . . . We flushed the pills. I wasn't taking those pills again. She saved my life.
>
> The Labour Day that I left, I had been at work with [my girlfriend]. The air conditioner broke down in the building. . . . After a while you start thinking of a dry sauna. We come home. . . . We come in, my mother is making stew. That's all I need. Could I please have a wedge of lettuce? I'm going to go upstairs and shower. There was no air conditioning. I'm miserable. I'm hot. I have peeled down to my underwear. My mother comes up the stairs. Leave the rest to your imagination. She comes down, she goes into the TV room, opens the liquor cabinet, pours herself a tall scotch straight up. . . . I'm upstairs curled up like a fetus on the bed, welts on my body, crying. . . . .Well, [my girlfriend] got me dressed, took me to the hospital. The social worker asked me what happened. I told her. The idiot calls my mother. "Did you do this?" My mother said, "No." What was she going to do? Admit to it? If I walk in the door, I get more of the same. We left that night.

Harry's mother had also been extremely physically abusive when Harry was a child, but by the time Harry had reached adolescence her mother had switched over "really heavily into the emotional stuff." Harry remembered thinking that her mother had "control" over her until her mother's nervous breakdown showed Harry that her mother could be vulnerable and weak. After her mother's collapse, Harry recalled having mixed emotions about her mother. "When I got into this period of hate, it was a torn thing. There was a piece of me that felt a connection. . . . I couldn't completely say that she was . . . an awful person."

Bob and Ron told similar stories about their adolescent battles with their mothers. Each had been beaten by their mothers since childhood. Although, in each case, their mothers became less physically abusive to them as they grew older, the hostilities between them did not otherwise abate. Bob described her relationship with her mother during her teen-aged years as one of "combat," although, during Bob's adolescence, her mother's attempts at discipline became progressively less effective. Bob recalled:

> After a while, the hidings became of no importance. She couldn't make me cry. She couldn't hurt me. My mother used to collapse on the floor in exhaustion, and I used to just walk right over the top of her, and just laughed at her.
> My mother hit me for no reason one day, and I turned around and punched my mother out cold. That is what the relationship had come to. . . . My mother continued to blame me for everything that went wrong. So, I retaliated, and I struck out. . . . I never hit her before this, and I never hit her again after. . . . I was shocked. I really was. . . . I was physically able to knock my mother down to the ground with one blow. . . . I almost broke her face. . . . .[After that] she no longer threatened me.

Ron's mother had been extremely physically abusive to her as a child. When Ron grew into a strapping adolescent, things changed somewhat between them. Ron also hit her mother back one time, after which Ron's mother turned to manipulating her children through "emotional or psychological blackmail."

Darren's relationship with her "manic-depressive" and "emotionally repressed" mother had always been characterized by physical abuse during Darren's childhood and adolescence. Just at a point in their relationship when Darren felt that they were starting to see the possibility of some closeness developing between the two of them, Darren was orphaned at age sixteen. Darren recalled going through a panoply of emotions after her parents' untimely deaths; but mostly Darren remembered feeling anger, a little sadness, and relief. She felt relief because whenever her mother had come near her, Darren had feared violence. After her mother's death, Darren recalled, she "could finally relax."

No One Was There: Emotionally Distant and Alcoholic Mothers

Eight participants (19 percent) remembered their mothers as being lost to them during their adolescence because of their mothers' emotional problems.[7] Simon, who lived with her mother only during three years of her adolescence, remembered that her mother was "so wrapped up in her own problems" that Simon didn't even try to turn to her when she felt in need of maternal support or guidance. Ed similarly recalled that she rarely turned to her mother for solace or support because her mother was "always crying."

In addition to being physically and emotionally abusive, Harry's mother went through a period during which she was lost in her own emotional problems. She leaned very heavily upon Harry during that time and became even more emphatically not someone to whom Harry could turn in her own times of need. Harry remembered how it was during her mother's nervous breakdown:

> About the time I was thirteen was when my mom . . . was pretty psychotic. . . . She went off the deep end. As an example . . . she was freaking out in the living room one day . . . and she said that she could see the Devil, and he was standing right over there. . . .
>
> By the time I started high school, Mom had gotten really sick, mentally. . . . and she asked that I stay home from school. . . . Between September and December, I was away sixty-four days . . . because my mom wanted me to. . . . What we did, I couldn't tell you. Because, I mean, I remember I'd just sit there and listen to the radio. . . . And she must have just sat there and watched TV. And I remember thinking a few times, "Why am I here?" . . . I did manage to pass most of my classes. . . . And I do remember . . . the guidance counselor interviewing me. . . . And at some point she twigged on my mother, and I remember this, all I did was I just kept crying. I just kept crying and crying and crying.

Dennis and Stan also remembered their mothers as consumed by mental illness. Their mothers' troubles began with postpartum depressions following Dennis's and Stan's births, for which both participants felt responsible. Dennis remembered that there were "very frequent" times when the drugs which her mother took did not do their job and her mother had to be hospitalized for weeks at a time for her depression. Dennis "felt bad for" her mother and tried not to bother her with her own adolescent angst.

Stan's mother was even more disturbed. She was totally unable to function as a mother. Stan was therefore raised by her maternal grandparents, who taught Stan to fear her "crazy" mother. Stan recalled, "the older I got, the more I resented her, and the more I hated her." As a teenager, Stan grew increasingly hostile toward her mother based on two ways in which Stan felt that her mother had let her down. In the first instance, Stan was angry at her mother for not having helped her through the "horrible, horrible change" of puberty. In the second place, Stan was angry because, as a teenager, she saw her mother's condition as a premonition of what she might become if the changes begun by her puberty were allowed to follow their course.

Luther, Jordie, and Alan also concluded that it would have been futile to try to rely emotionally upon their mothers. Luther felt that it would be fruitless to turn to her mother with her own needs because "I was always wrong. I was bad. . . . The relationship never changed. . . . Just a constant coldness from my mother." When Jordie's father started to abuse her during her teen years, she turned to her mother for help. When Jordie's mother refused to believe that her father was sexually using her, Jordie "felt abandoned" by her mother and was no longer able to turn to her for any sort of comfort.

Alan also suffered from sexual assault as a teenager, but Alan didn't even bother to try to seek solace or assistance from her mother after being raped. Alan already had become convinced that it would not be forthcoming. Alan, who had been acting as a husband to her mother since age nine, remembered:

> My mother never healed from her adult-child-of-an-alcoholic issues, so . . . I knew with utmost certainty that my mother wasn't ever available to me when I was raped at sixteen. . . . I didn't tell my mother because I didn't want to worry her. I sensed that she wouldn't know what to do. . . . I didn't want to be weak because she needed me to be strong for her.

Another seven participants (16 percent) remembered that during their adolescence their mothers had drinking problems.[8] In some cases, participants' mothers were angry drunks for whom participants felt little empathy. In other cases, they responded to their mothers' infirmity with sympathy and warmth. In neither circumstance did participants feel that their mothers were people to whom they could turn for assistance with the trials of adolescence.

Like Jordie and Alan, Ken and Grant were both sexually abused as teenagers, and they too felt unable to go to their mothers to ask for help with the sexual abuse to which they were subjected. Ken recalled the incident which started her mother's drinking:

> My grandfather had come to town one night. . . . My mom called [my dad] and said, "I'm going to go see him. He's only going to be here one night." . . . My dad told her, "No." . . . Mom went. And when she got home that night my dad beat the shit out of her. I never forgave him for that. . . . Well, the next day my mom tried to commit suicide. She took a lot of pills. . . . I wanted to know how she could be so unhappy and how she could do that. It hurt me. She was tired and scared. . . . She

worked, she worked at home, she put up with these kids who wanted more. . . . She'd get paid and my dad would take her money. It went to drinking and booze. My mom started to drink.

Considering her mother's emotional condition and alcoholism, Ken "didn't want to hurt her" mother by exposing her to the awful truth about being incestuously used by her father.

Grant tried to go to her alcoholic and abusive mother for help when she was raped at age fifteen, but Grant's mother refused to believe that the source of her injuries was a rape. Instead, Grant's mother attributed Grant's physical condition to a fight with her girlfriend. Grant's mother's treatment of this incident only contributed to Grant's hatred of her mother, which was already well fueled by numerous previous incidents of abuse and neglect.

Roger began life relatively happy in her relationship with her mother. However, Roger's relationship with her mother altered drastically after Roger's father's death when Roger was eleven years old. At that point, Roger's mother "went down the drain" and began to drink heavily. Roger stepped into the breech left by her father's death and "took over as father and husband" because Roger felt that her mother "really needed someone to take care of her for a while." As it turned out, the "while" turned into the remainder of Roger's mother's life. In contrast to their more distant relationship when Roger had been a child, they became "very, very close," but in a way which cast Roger as the dominant member of the family. Consequently, Roger was left devoid of a maternal figure to turn to for guidance, care, or support.

Clearly, these participants felt abandoned by their mothers during those years in which they were growing from children into adults. Their mothers, who had their own persistent and unresolved issues, were perceived by participants to be ill equipped to assist them in negotiating the difficulties which they were experiencing in their adolescence. No doubt this contributed to the feelings of isolation from which so many participants suffered as teenagers.

Act Like a Lady!: Conflicts over Femininity

A sizeable number of participants struggled with their mothers over their appearances during their adolescence. Nineteen participants (44 percent) said that during their adolescence they had often had problems with their mothers about gendered aspects of their appearances.[9] For some participants these fights loomed large in their adolescent relationships with their mothers. For other participants, they represented more minor aspects of their complex relationships with their mothers.

Aaron's and Peter's reactions to their mothers' exhortations to become more feminine were typical of those of many other participants. Aaron remembered:

Oh, I resented wearing a dress or shopping for girls' clothes and so on. It was always a fight. To be taken to a beauty parlour was sheer torture. . . . [I felt] mortified. . . . Like any other . . . boy would have felt.

Sam even seemed prone to understatement when he reported that her mother considered it "important" for her "to be like other girls." Sam said that her mother pressed her so intensely about this issue that it became a major bone of contention between them:

It got to the point where, by the time I was twelve, I was told I either conformed and was like the other girls or I was going to be kicked out of the house. . . . I had to have a boyfriend. I had to go to parties and to do all the things other girls did.

Whereas Sam complied with her mother's demands, Bob openly fought about femininity with her physically disciplinarian mother. Bob remembered the conflict between them becoming increasingly malicious during her adolescence:

My mother wanted me to be a sucky, pandered, stupid girl, and I wanted to be what I wanted to be . . . tomboy. I just had no interest in girlie things. . . . I was fifteen, and I had to go to the school dance. And my mother made me the most hideous, horrible, bloody dress you've ever seen. . . . And it was embarrassing, I can tell you. I hated it. . . . Oh, mother thought I was the cat's whiskers. And I took one look in the mirror, and I thought "Good god! How could she do this to me?" . . . I tell you, if I'd had a knife, I would have cut her throat.

Although Simon and Bruce also fought with their mothers about clothing, other issues were probably more influential factors in their relationships with their mothers. Simon's fights with her mother about wearing dresses were significant enough that they motivated Simon, who loved studying, to drop out of high school and leave home a scant two weeks before graduation. Simon, however, felt a need to protect her mother which seemed far more central to their relationship while Simon was a teenager. Similarly, Bruce's battles with her mother over femininity, although important in and of themselves, were only a small part of the complex web of mother-daughter dynamics which Bruce felt may have been largely responsible for his transsexuality. The family therapy which Bruce's mother instigated in response to Bruce's expressed desires to be a man appeared to have had little salutary effect on Bruce as a teenager. Rather, the sexual nature of Bruce's adolescent relationship with her mother seems to have had a more lasting effect than any maternal encouragement toward femininity.

A few participants had a somewhat different problem about femininity with their mothers. Rather than having mothers who propelled them into being young women before they were ready to make the move themselves, Morgan, Mel, and Harry seemed to resent their mothers for having embarrassed them by delaying their entry into adolescent womanhood. Morgan remembered being laughed at in the locker room at school because she had not yet received her first bra from her mother. Mel and Harry likewise both felt that they had to push their mothers to purchase their first bras for them. Although none of these individuals were happy about the physical changes which puberty brought, neither were they pleased to be the object of ridicule for the unrestrained prominences protruding from their chests.

Such conflicts between mothers and their teenaged daughters over how young women should dress are certainly common. The conflicts which participants had with their mothers, however, were of a different timbre than is usual. Slightly less than half of participants wanted to continue in their tomboyish masculinity past the point where their mothers, as socializing agents, deemed it time for them to grow into feminine young women. As tomboyishness thus became increasingly incompatible with female physiological and social maturity, conflicts between participants and their mothers intensified, further estranging these participants from their female parents.

Standing on Guard: Mothers in Need of Protection

A large minority of participants entered adolescence feeling responsible for their mothers' safety or emotional equilibrium. All of these people had begun to feel this way during their childhoods and found continued reason to do so as adolescents. One-third of participants recalled that as teenagers they had felt protective toward their mothers.[10] Eleven of these fourteen participants (79 percent) had witnessed their mothers fighting with, or being badly treated by, their male partners.[11] The stories which participants told indicated that they felt that it fell to them to protect their mothers from the men who victimized them. Whatever their reasons, in all cases their feelings resulted in close interdependency with their mothers. The nature of such connections precluded participants' identification with their mothers as role models and instead fostered their adoption of protective masculine attitudes toward their female parents.

Simon told a particularly dramatic tale illustrating this theme. This story comes from the only period during which Simon lived with her mother. Simon recalled about those years:

I fell very much in love with my mother quickly, which surprised me because I didn't have any strong attachments to anybody at that point. . . .

I became my mother's protector because [my stepdad] battered her. . . . When I was fifteen I was old enough, I felt, to do something about that. . . . I pulled a gun on him once when I was sixteen. I came home from my part-time job and I heard one of my other brothers screaming, and I went down to where the scream was, and my stepfather was choking my mother. He was big. He was 6'2" and at that time he probably weighed 240. I probably weighed about 120. . . . I took him by the shoulders and I threw him across the room. I yelled at my brothers and my sister and my mother to get upstairs. I had to help my mother upstairs cause she was turning blue when I walked into the room from him choking her. . . . .I knew where he kept his pistol and I went and got it. When he came up the stairs, just as his head came in sight I pulled the trigger. Which scared the shit out of him; scared the shit out of me. . . . There wasn't a bullet in the first chamber. Everybody was terrified by that click, including him. It was no threat. He had taught me how to use guns. . . . I was gonna kill him. I was determined to kill him. I was surprised that there was a click rather than a boom.

After that I could say, "Sit down," and he would. It was an awesome power. Seriously, they'd start to get into a fight. He would go out, and he would drink, and then he would come home. . . . I would sleep on the couch until he got home because I knew that when he walked through the door he was going to start picking a fight with my mom. I could just sit there on the couch, and he would start to come towards her, and I would say, "Sit," and he would sit. . . . It was just like a dog. He was scared.

Bill also quite explicitly remembered having felt responsible for her mother's well-being in the face of a rampaging husband and father. Bill recounted this version of those years:

My parents were divorced when I was thirteen or so for about a year and a half prior to remarrying. I was very protective of my mother during that time because I was fearful that my father would come back around and kill all of us. We had already had a couple of what I thought of as close calls. Once he had pulled a knife on my mother during an argument when she had told him to get out. Another time Mom, [my sister], and I had gone for a long walk one Sunday when Dad was buried in the sofa with his beer watching football. We were all three trying to lose weight and were walking for the exercise when we became thirsty and bought a quart of orange juice to drink. We were seated by the football stadium in the park when my Dad came driving right onto the grass in his truck and came so close so fast that he almost hit us. He got out with my littlest sister and had purchased a pie which he tried to rub in my mother's face. . . .

Things had changed a lot between us. I think the boundaries between parent and child had been severely breached as she took me too much into her confidence and I began to take on too much responsibility for her health and happiness.

Alan, too, became her mother's caretaker. Alan's father was a violent, alcoholic man who terrorized his family; both Alan and her mother retreated from him into an unhealthy symbiosis. Alan quite emphatically stated that the relationship between herself and her mother was an overheated one:

> I was psychologically locked into rescuing my mother. I was overly close with my mother. I did not fight with my mother. She was too dependent upon me. . . . I wanted to be my mother's husband emotionally, physically, and sexually.

Tony also remembered that as a teenaged girl she wanted to take care of her mother. In Tony's case it was because her "compulsive gambler" father seemed unable to do so. Tony recalled how she attempted to compensate for her father's failures by becoming a first-class provider for her mother:

> I got a job at fourteen. I had my own money in my pocket. I would go to the meat market and come home with $100 worth of meat for my mother and put it on the table and say, "here." . . . I remember my very first pay cheque, I bought my mother a sewing machine. . . . She was so thrilled. . . . It was one of the happiest times I can remember. Being able to give this to my mother.

Tony also felt that the protection and companionship which she provided to her mother gave her mother peace of mind:

> As I got older, the more I was afraid for her. And then once I got my own vehicle, I started driving, I would go get her all the time. . . . I didn't like the idea that she had to take public transportation. I was always afraid that something would happen to her. . . . I was her stability for a long time. . . . I would sit there and read the paper and listen to her with one ear. And it made her feel better, and it didn't do me any harm.

Most other participants' referents for their protectiveness of their mothers were more diffuse memories of intrafamilial strife in which they perceived their mothers as having been victimized. For example, Ken recalled having felt that her mother was a victim of her father's abusiveness. Ken tried to help by calling the police several times—but to no avail, as Ken's paternal grandfather was an officer and "it was like, my dad does no wrong." Jorge remembered her mother as a woman whose entire marital existence was passed in fear of her husband's vindictive temper. When

Jorge's father left her mother for another woman, Jorge recalled her protective feelings, "I wanted to kill him, and all I could think was 'how
could he do this to my mom?' " To Jorge's dismay, they later reunited.

The degree of intense intimacy which these participants experienced
with their mothers during their adolescent years is striking in both its form
and its content. Adolescence is a time when most girls are beginning to
flirt with independence and femininity. When they do crave intimacy with
their mothers it is most often for assistance with their forays into femininity. The participants in this study told quite a different story. They felt
compelled by their families' dynamics to become their mothers' confidants
and protectors. Thus they found themselves in dominant positions vis-à-
vis their mothers, and the attitudes with which they did so carried a decidedly masculine flavour.

I'm OK, You're OK: Good Feelings about Mothers

Amongst all of these roiling emotions, one-third of participants reported that they felt warmly toward their mothers during adolescence.[12]
Half of the people who remembered feeling this way were among those
who also felt protective of their mothers.[13] It seems likely that those participants found their protector role gratifying and congruent with their
masculine self-images. As well, Walter, Roger, Ed, and Jack said that their
appreciation of their mothers during their adolescence was based in part
upon their mothers' more explicit support of them in their ongoing commitment to their masculine personas. The remaining persons who recalled
positive emotions about their mothers during their teenaged years made
nonspecific comments to the effect that they loved their mothers. Such
statements seemed to reflect little more than a habitually polite respect for
one's parents.

Walter recalled both warm and protective feelings toward her mother.
As both a child and a teenager, Walter had a high opinion of her mother,
whom he remembered as "pretty well a perfect mom," and a "lovely, wonderful person" with whom she had always been "very, very close." One
testament to his mother's exceptional personality proffered by Walter was
her handling of the issue of Walter's hormonal imbalances during puberty:

> When I reached maturity, when I started to menstruate, they could have
> treated me with female hormones and it was actually recommended . . .
> but I was just so resistant to it. And my mother respected that. . . . [She]
> didn't try to push me into that female mold.

When Roger was an adolescent, her protectiveness and fondness for
her mother was enhanced by her mother's willingness to foster Roger's
masculine disposition. Roger remembered her mother as being the per-

son who first introduced her to a lesbian subculture as a teenager. Clearly Roger's mother's acceptance of her daughter's sexual orientation as a butch lesbian was a bonus on top of the satisfaction which Roger derived from being able to care for her mother when she was incapacitated. Roger told this story about her mother:

> When I got out of high school I came to [the city where I] had my first job. Mom had been living here for some time . . . and she was hanging out in the gay bars because she liked the way that the gay guys treated her. It was safe, and they adored her, and she adored them. And she started taking me to the bars with her. . . . I was seventeen, 1958, '59. . . . In those days it was called dyke. I was just a rompin' stomper. . . . Mostly, Mom didn't have any trouble with that. . . . And she sat me down one time and she said, "You know, you've chosen the most lonely lifestyle in the world that you can choose." And she said, "If you're going to do it, do it right and make something of yourself." . . . She was that progressive.

Jack also found support for her masculinity from her mother. When Jack was a girl of sixteen, she went to her mother and told her how she felt about being female. Her mother's response pleased Jack so much that he remembered her as "my Rock of Gibraltar" and as an "exceptional" woman. Jack described the scene thus:

> When I was about sixteen, I talked to my mother and told her. And she said, "Well you have to do what pleases you in your heart." She said, "You can't go around pleasing everybody else because it'll make you crazy. So do what's needed in your life to make you happy, and I'll be happy for you." So, that's why I say my mom was always my rock. . . . I said, "Mom, I do not feel female and if I ever get the chance I'll change it." . . . She said, "Well, it isn't what I want, but." I said, "Well, I'm not doing this to hurt you this is just how I feel, and I can't get rid of it."

Ed also went to her mother about her gender dysphoria. Ed first announced to her family that she thought that she might be transsexual in her late teens. In retrospect, Ed considered her mother to have been entirely backing her in her quest to become a man. Ed appreciatively recounted this story about her mother's response to her desire for a sex change:

> When I told my parents what was going on I was pretty much to the point of being very suicidal and just totally depressed. My mother was really happy to think that there might be something that I could do to make myself feel good about myself. Because I think, in general, I was pretty miserable growing up and she knew something was wrong. And when I finally told her what I wanted to do she was very supportive.

Ed's mother went on to find a counsellor who facilitated Ed's entry into a gender clinic program leading to gender and sex reassignment.

Howie's situation was both analogous and anomalous in this group of individuals. Howie, too, remembered having a loving and warm relationship with her mother when she was a teenager. Like the others, this warmth was based in part upon Howie's mother's assistance with Howie's gender discomfort. Howie's difficulties arose because puberty brought with it an excess of masculine secondary sex characteristics at a time in Howie's life when she had not yet made an identification as transsexual. Howie remembered feeling like a "freak" because of her adolescent sprouting of mustache, beard, and body hair and was appreciative of her mother's efforts to find a medical solution to her premature masculinization. Howie described her adolescent relationship with her mother as "loving."

In sum, as had occurred during their childhood years, those participants who remembered having warm and loving relationships with their mothers during their adolescence largely did so in a context which allowed them to have sufficient psychological room to maintain a satisfactory level of masculine identity. This took place in two main ways: either participants' mothers tacitly relied upon them to take on masculine protector or provider roles, or their mothers were overtly supportive of participants' chosen avenues of gender expression.

Summary and Commentary

Participants expressed a range of attitudes when they recalled the relationships which they had with their mothers during their adolescence. As would be expected of any group of people, some remembered their teenaged interactions with their mothers with great warmth, others recalled having been relatively indifferent, and still others' memories were filled with pain. What stands out as noteworthy is that no matter how well they thought of their mothers at the time, none of them said anything to imply that they had wanted to grow up to be like them in any ways which could even vaguely be associated with womanliness.

Two dynamics of their relationships seem particularly salient in this regard, Firstly, nineteen participants' mothers (44 percent) were remembered by participants as being women who were either unwilling or unable to provide them with maternal care or guidance. Their mothers suffered from pronounced psychological problems,[14] were alcoholic,[15] or were abusive to their daughters.[16] In some cases, participants took pity on their mothers in their incapacity and took on the role of protectors or providers for their mothers.[17] In other cases, they had little sympathy for their mothers and distanced themselves from them by whatever means were available to them. Either way, feminine role modeling was not an outcome.

A second significant factor can be found in participants' interactions with their mothers concerning the gendered aspects of their appearances and social behaviours. Many participants' mothers (44 percent) pressured their daughters to conform to the dominant social expectation that they would grow out of their childish tomboyism and feminize themselves.[18] Those mothers who made such demands of their daughters were generally rewarded with antagonism and hostility. The few mothers who allowed participants to follow their own tendencies to further masculinize themselves were consistently appreciated by their adolescent daughters.[19] Thus mothers either pushed for femininity and lost their daughters' allegiances or allowed them their masculinity and retained their affections in styles more akin to those of mother-son relationships.

In the end, most participants (70.5 percent) pulled further away from their mothers during their adolescence. They did so either because of their mothers' dysfunctional behaviours or because they could not abide their mothers' insistence on their becoming more feminine. A few participants also became, or continued to be, close with their mothers during their adolescence. In some cases theirs was a suffocating closeness in which participants' mothers' actions elicited masculine protector or provider patterns of behaviour from participants. In others, their closeness was based on participants' mothers' outright support of their masculinity. Clearly the courses which had been set in participants' childhoods were not set aside by the events of their adolescent relationships with their mothers.

Relatively the Same: Relationships with Grandmothers and Aunts

As participants matured through adolescence, the influences of their grandmothers and aunts dwindled in importance. In part this was because adolescent participants became more independent of their families; in some cases, beloved grandparents died; in other families, intergenerational living arrangements gave way to nuclear family domiciles. Ten participants (23 percent)[20] did, however, live with or very near their grandmothers during their adolescence.[21] As a result of their proximity, those participants' grandmothers were available as alternative maternal figures. Another eight participants (19 percent) reported that they had memorable relationships with aunts[22] or grandmothers[23] who visited them on occasion.

Throughout their teenage years, Stan, Brian, Colin, and Gary continued to live with their grandparents, and Bill's maternal grandparents, who lived across the street, continued to be constant presences in Bill's life.

However, only Stan and Brian commented extensively on the influences which their grandmothers had on them as teenagers.

Stan's grandparents continued to act in loco parentis for Stan's mentally ill mother and absent father during Stan's adolescence. Stan also had a favourite aunt who made herself available to Stan during those years. What Stan recalled most prominently was that her grandmother and aunt tried to convince her to become more feminine as a teenager. As Stan remembered it, she did not take well to their urgings:

> Grandma would sort of try but she was just so uncomfortable. She just couldn't do it. That was just too much worldliness. . . . my best favourite aunt . . . finally did it. She just took me aside and we went for a walk and like it was . . . you need to start wearing a brassiere, and you need to start doing this now. And I hated her having to tell me that. . . . she had to do the dirty work and enforce it. . . .
>
> It was bad news because I was going to grow up like Mom. And I was going to grow up like Grandma. . . . That was the role model that I looked forward to. That I was here now, and then I would be like Mom, and then I would eventually fade out into nothing and be like Grandma. I didn't want that. . . . They don't do adventures. They didn't drive cars. . . . [My aunt] was being a mom. She had two kids and was struggling through that. I had a lot more respect for her as a person but I didn't relate to wanting to be like her. . . . they didn't have control of money. They didn't have a say in getting anything done. . . . And they didn't get to be leaders. They were all very passive followers, and never got what they wanted it seemed like. . . . I didn't want to be that way.

Neither Stan's mother, grandmother, nor aunt provided a female example which Stan was inspired to follow.

Brian also continued to live with her grandparents as a teenager. As a child, Brian had found solace in her grandmother's company because of her grandmother's acceptance of her as a tomboy. However, once Brian became an adolescent her grandmother withdrew that support, and Brian, feeling "deeply betrayed," also withdrew.

Simon was sent to live with her maternal grandparents after the courts removed her from her stepfather's custody because of his abusiveness. Simon was not happy under her grandmother's sway because her style of child rearing was so much more permissive than that to which Simon had become accustomed. Simon recalled the circumstances thus:

> I didn't like my grandmother. And that partly had to do with she knew what kind of environment I had been living under and she said, "You don't have to live that way any more." But she didn't give me any skills to be able to adjust from a total totalitarian environment to one in which I had rights and freedoms. And I didn't know what those things were, and I went pretty wild.

Simon became a "passive resistor" against her grandmother's attempts to feminize her until she ran away from her grandparents to live with her mother and second stepfather. Simon's grandmother died two years later.

Bruce and Ken found their contact with their grandmothers considerably more satisfactory. Bruce's grandmother lived on the same street as Bruce's family for one year shortly after Bruce's parents divorced. Bruce remembered her grandmother as her "favourite friend" who doted on her and provided her some comfort to cushion the blow of the divorce. Ken similarly found refuge from the violence and chaos of her family home with a grandmother, with whom she lived during her last year of high school. Ken remembered about her grandparents: "I still looked up to my grandparents. They cared."

Peter's, Darcy's, Alan's, Howie's, Dennis's, and Hal's recollections of their female relatives' visits to their lives were also warm ones. Peter remembered her grandmother as a kind and understanding woman who intuitively seemed to know that Peter should not be rushed into maturing into a woman. Howie and Dennis were "very close" with aunts who adopted them as surrogate children and treated them royally. Alan perhaps benefited the most from having a grandmother who provided one of the few safe and sane havens in Alan's young life. Alan marked her death when Alan was eleven years old as one of the worst events in an extremely grueling adolescence.

Other participants had less than rosy memories of their time with their aunts. For example, Tony mentioned an aunt whom she "really hated" for having told her mother that Tony was a lesbian before Tony herself had figured it out. Eli displayed her distaste for an aunt with whom she briefly lived as an example of why she didn't want to become a woman:

> I certainly didn't like women. . . . Like my aunt . . . she'd run around the house in her bra and panties. I mean, she had no shame! You know, her woman kind of shape was particularly repulsive to me. Just the way she walked, and the way she looked. . . . She'd come and spy on me when I was changing my underwear and say things like, "How cute." And her daughters were kinda strange. They were always talking about having breast cancer and talking about body parts. That always seemed very repulsive to me that they were always relating to all their body parts all the time. . . . always, "What kind of bra do you wear, or what girdle, or panty girdles?" You know, all that crap still drives me wild. Ooh, it was pukeworthy!

When looking at the group of participants as a whole, it would seem that although a few participants had older female relatives who provided relatively attractive examples of adult females, their effects on participants' gender development was minimal. At best, they appear to have provided some escape from participants' difficulties at home. At worst, they only served to reinforce participants' estrangement from the idea of themselves becoming women.

Relationships with Sisters

The main theme emphasized by participants when speaking about their relationships with their sisters during their teenaged years was distance. Their lack of closeness with their sisters was largely the result of differences in ages and a divergence of interests. Participants tended to enjoy masculine pastimes, while their sisters were more likely to prefer feminine ones. As a result, participants tended to find that they had little in common with their more feminine sisters and to use that as reason enough to eschew their companionship. Some used that same condition as a rationale for feeling responsible for their sisters' welfare.

Twelve (39 percent) of the thirty-one participants who had sisters said that during their adolescence they saw very little of any of their sisters. Robin's, Keith's, Jordie's, Bob's, and Colin's sisters were too young for participants to want to share much time with them. Nine participants and their older sisters became separated because one or the other of them moved away from their family homes during participants' teen years.[24] Simon's, Darren's, and Bruce's families broke apart, separating them from one or more of their sisters, and Alan left home when she was seventeen years old. Thus only eighteen participants had sisters at home with whom they had any significant level of interaction during their adolescence.

Why Bother?: Cool or Distant Relationships with Sisters

Fifteen participants who had sisters in their homes during their adolescence (48 percent) remembered their adolescent relationships as having been either indifferent or hostile ones. For the most part, those who were indifferent reported that they simply were not interested in the girlish preoccupations of their sisters,[25] whereas hostilities between participants and their sisters were generally continuations of conflicts begun in more youthful times.[26] In addition, Bill and Alan found that their previously good relationships with their sisters soured during their adolescent years.

Bob's recollections about her relationship with her only sister typified the detached attitudes which several participants remembered holding about their sisters during their adolescences:

[My sister] . . . matured into a female. All the mature things that females do: changing styles, changing hairdos, her girlfriends were girlfriends, as such. . . . She was boy mad, as such, and teenage girls, they giggle with one another. They held these funny little secrets. She became a female. . . . I went about my things my way, and [my sister] just went about her things . . . her way, and there was no resentment on either side by us. . . . I never wished I was like her, and she never wished she was like me.

Other participants recalled that their already tenuous relationships with their sisters deteriorated still further during their adolescence. For example, Ken's unhappiness with her sister was founded upon what Ken perceived as her sister's ability to manipulate their father into providing her with special privilege at the same time as Ken's father was sexually abusing her.

I wasn't close with my sister. This was a very bitching time. I bitched at my sister about everything. I hated her. . . . We fought about everything. She was allowed to stay out late. . . . She was allowed to watch TV whenever she wanted to. My sister got her first car. It was just given to her; she didn't even have to ask. She could do everything. She didn't have to do anything. She got away with murder. I had to stay home and do chores. That was my job. . . . I guess she was more self-centred than she had been before. She got whatever she wanted. She had my dad wrapped around her little finger. . . . My sister lied to get whatever she wanted.

Bill, who had three younger sisters and one older one, also became more antipathetic toward her sisters during her adolescence. Bill had never liked her younger sister who was closest to her in age but had been quite fond of the others during her own younger years. Bill began to "avoid" one of her younger sisters when the sister began to exhibit psychological problems during Bill's adolescence. Also during that time, Bill's oldest sister had moved out of the house and had thereby left Bill in the position of "the one now responsible for looking after the youngest ones." Bill remembered feeling some resentment toward her oldest sister, whom Bill had previously described as her closest sister.

After she got married, I missed her but would not allow myself to feel it. I often spent my spring break or Christmas vacations visiting her and her new family. I sometimes felt angry with her because she often used a "poor me" line with my parents and manipulated them into buying her groceries, a washing machine, lending her money. I felt very judgmental toward her because I felt she had chose her life, married at nineteen and had three girls ten months apart in age. She laid guilt trips on the rest of us because my parents finally were in a position to take us on vacations to Florida to visit my grandparents. She also brought her babies to the house almost every night and I used to think we would never know anything but chaos.

Alan's attitude toward her sister also changed while they were teenagers. As Alan became more entrenched in living publicly as a man, his younger sister felt abandoned when Alan left home at age seventeen. Alan recalled:

> My sister had problems with my crossdressing. She wanted a female figure (mother) in her life that she could depend on. She said she could accept my gayness but not my transsexualism. My sister became more needy. She wrote me letters and begged to live with me. . . . It was easier for me not to answer her letters, to try and forget that I had a family.

Although Alan was unsuccessful at forgetting about his sister, he never did return to the bosom of his family.

In sum, almost half of participants who had sisters recounted stories which highlighted their disinterest in their sisters' lives. In a few cases, they expressed these sentiments quite strongly. However, an unspoken message emerged in the paucity of commentary which most participants offered about their relationships with their sisters during their own adolescences. Apparently they were so disengaged from their sisters as to have almost nothing at all to say about their sororal relationships during those years.

Sisterly Supports: Closer Relationships with Sisters

Twelve participants (39 percent) reported that they remembered feeling close with one or more of their sisters when they were adolescents. As was the case with those participants who were close with their mothers during this phase of their lives, participants either recalled having felt protective toward their sisters[27] owing to intrafamilial abuse or made nonspecific comments to the effect that they felt fond of or responsible for their sisters.[28] However, even those participants who spoke well of their sisters were fairly reticent on the topic. It would seem that their attentions had been more fully occupied elsewhere.

Harry and Jack both remembered feeling responsible for making sure that their sisters' boyfriends were of a high calibre. One story told by Jack graphically illustrated the kind of role which many participants took in relation to the female members of their families.

> My oldest sister . . . she's one of these people who can always attract the worst men, and if you lock the girl in a closet she'll still get in trouble, you know, that kind of thing. And she would find the worst scumbags, you know, and of course she brought them up to my folks' house all the time. Well, this guy happened to be a drug pusher and that kind of thing. And she's one of these that, "Oh, I can change him. I can change

him." I mean this guy would even give drugs to his kids and that just irked me.

And they had an argument one night and what does she do? She comes to me and says, "Will you take care of this?" I'm eighteen. I said, "What do you want me to do?" "Well, just talk to him." . . . So I set him down. . . . I said, "Well, you know, you and [my sister] are having problems and I really don't like the way you're treating her." He said, "Well, it's none of your business." I said, "You're in this house. It's my business." And he just kind of laughed it off, and he went . . . upstairs.

But dad always keeps a rifle loaded. I grabbed one and I went up after him and I put a bead right on him and I said, "You got five minutes to get your fucking ass out of here." And he kind of laughed it off, he didn't think I'd do anything. And I came very close, that's probably the maddest I have, or ever will be, in my life. I raised it up to the window and I laid a shot. I said, "The next one goes right between your eyes bud. You move now." He was out in five minutes. I even hit him a couple of times. He was huge, linebacker size, you know, and I hit him and he said, "I don't want to hurt you." I said, "You want to hurt me you idiot. Come on." I hit him in the jaw I had blood blisters where my ring hit him. Then he said, "You ain't a woman." I said, "If I'm not a woman come on." He probably would have killed me. . . . But anyway, I ran him off.

Other participants were less forthcoming in their comments about their attitudes toward their sisters. For example, Bill and Darcy simply said that as teenagers they had felt responsible for their younger sisters, whereas Brian recounted that she had wanted to help her sister get a good start in her life when she left home.

Eight participants (26 percent) reminisced about the closeness, warmth, or admiration which they felt for their sisters during their adolescence.[29] As with their reports about their relationships with their mothers, most of their remarks on this subject were only vague assertions. Where participants went into more detail, it was to point out that their sisters had been useful to them in their quest for manhood.

Dale had very strong feelings for her sisters. In addition to the older sister, whom Dale "really loved" and wanted to protect from their father's and brother's violence, and a spoiled younger sister, Dale had a baby sister upon whom she doted. Dale lamented:

It just about killed me to leave home. . . . My little sister . . . she was two years old. I loved her more than I loved anything in my life. 'Cause she loved me. She was so damn precious.

Jack's opinion of one of her three sisters was also exceptionally positive, so much so that Jack may have used her as something of a role model, albeit not a very feminine one. In addition to the sister whom Jack protected and the sister whom Jack disliked for being spoiled, Jack had one other sister whom Jack respected for her great size and strength.

> Me and my second to the oldest sister are . . . built very stocky. . . . And she's taller than I am, she's bigger than I am. She's two hundred pounds, five six, and solid as a brick. And . . . [she] was so strong that twice she was in taking a bath . . . and the tap kept dripping. She said, "Mom, it won't shut off." So, she reached up there and twisted it right off. She did it twice, and finally my dad said, "I'm not fixing those damn faucets again till these kids leave home." . . . She used to milk cows, and had forearms on her like, you know. So, her and I were always strong. . . . And I was always proud of my strength.

Darren and Steven liked their sisters because they were supportive of them in their first steps at coming to terms with their gender and sex dysphorias. Darren had always been "especially close" to her only sister during their childhood. When Darren started to crossdress in her early teenaged years, she was sharing a bedroom with her sister. Darren appreciated that her sister "kept quiet about" Darren's unusual behaviour.

> She cared about me. She cared enough not to tell my parents. I told her, "Don't mention this to anybody else." And she didn't grill me, or make fun of me, or laugh at me. She let me go ahead and do it. She didn't know what the hell was going on, but she knew this was important to me, and so she let me do it. . . . She condoned it.

Steven, too, retrospectively treasured the sympathetic kindness which characterized her sister. Steven remembered the day that she and her sister went together to see a film about Christine Jorgensen.

> I was, I'd say, maybe sixteen, seventeen. . . . And the audience was hilariously laughing, and I felt such pain for myself and for Christine. And I said, "This is the type of way people will relate to me. This is what I'm going to have to put up with if I ever, ever had the possibility of going through with a secret desire of changing sex." My sister, I later learned, also felt an empathy towards Christine and thought that it was horrible that people would sit and laugh at such a moving and sad life experience.

In all, approximately one-third of participants remembered feeling close with one or more of their sisters. However, it seems as though participants were able to sustain positive feelings about their sisters only if they were able to construe their relationships as ones in which they played brotherly roles. They either cast themselves as brave protectors of their more defenseless sisters, or they had sisters who were otherwise agreeable to indulging participants' needs to express the masculine sides of their natures. Either way, participants were able, in their own minds, to see themselves as boys in their relationships with their sisters or else they saw very little of their sisters.

Summary and Commentary

Three main observations can be reasonably drawn from the information offered by participants about their adolescent relationships with their sisters. Firstly, it was noteworthy that few participants were loquacious about their sisters at all. This in itself would seem to indicate that most participants' sisters were not influential in their adolescent lives. Secondly, 87 percent of participants reported that they either had nothing whatsoever to do with one or more of their sisters or that the contacts which they did have were either distant or hostile.[30] Thirdly, 39 percent of participants did have at least one sister with whom they recalled having had amicable relations.[31] As in other areas of their lives, participants were able to appreciate only those relationships in which they could behave in accordance with their inner sense of maleness. Thus they fondly recalled their sisters who either tacitly or actively cooperated with their desires to be in the world as if they were teenaged boys. In all, it would seem that participants' sisters either played minor supporting roles in participants' adolescent gender dramas or participants wrote them out of their lives altogether.

Summary and Commentary:
Adolescent Relationships with Female Family Members

For the most part, participants' patterns of relationships with their female family members changed little during their adolescence. Participants were disinclined to use their female family members as role models and generally were not exceptionally close with them.

However, there were two conditions under which participants seemed to be willing to become quite intensely engaged with their mothers and sisters. On the one hand, a number of participants felt obliged to become husband-like protectors or providers to their mothers or sisters. By so doing, they could retain a sense of intimacy with them and simultaneously feed their images of themselves as valiant young men growing into responsible adults. They could thus use these relationships as practice arenas for the future romantic or familial roles which they envisioned for themselves. On the other hand, participants felt free to indulge in close familial relations when their mothers, grandmothers, aunts, or sisters provided participants with safe space in which to display their masculinity as expansively as they wished. A few participants also recalled feeling warmly toward grandmothers or aunts who provided haven from chaotic or violent homes, as long as that succor was not accompanied by high demands for femininity.

More frequently, participants reported that their female family members expected or demanded increased femininity from them as they suffered through their adolescence. Some participants fought violently with their mothers over this issue. Most were more reserved in their resistance; they simply withdrew as much as they were able from any exchanges which required feminine appearances or behaviours from them. If this meant that they were left with only angry, sullen, or silent relationships with their mothers, grandmothers, aunts, or sisters, participants' attitudes seemed to say, "So be it!"

Participants' adolescent relationships with their female relatives thus seemed to foreshadow the emotional conundrum in which many transsexual people eventually find themselves. Participants' actions indicated that they would rather not live in relationships which required them to play at being a gender which did not suit them. Either they could be in their worlds in accordance with their own inner gender needs or they would prefer not to be in those worlds at all. Because they were adolescents, they had little choice about where they would live or with whom. The results, then, with those whose family members would not obligingly cooperate, were fights or frozen silences, followed by expedited exits.

Access Denied, Restrictions Apply

Relationships with Male Relatives

Relationships with Fathers

On the whole, participants' relationships with their fathers were less satisfying to them during their adolescences than they had been during their childhoods. A number of circumstances contributed to this decline. Many participants felt alienated from their fathers because they endured or witnessed ongoing abuse meted out by their fathers. As well, in comparison to when participants were children, fewer fathers (32.5 percent vs. 63 percent)[1] engaged in masculine pursuits with their daughters[2] and more of them (20 percent vs. 5 percent) began to apply pressures in the direction of femininity.[3] As a result of these factors, fewer participants (17.5 percent vs. 35 percent) felt inclined to use their fathers as role models than had done so as children.[4]

Compounding these factors, many fathers were also unavailable to their daughters during their adolescences. Roger's and Darren's fathers died when Roger was eleven and Darren sixteen. Eli's, Bruce's, Bill's, Nathan's, and Phil's parents were divorced or separated during this period, partially removing their fathers from their lives. Another eight participants recalled that their fathers were so occupied with their work that they had little time left for their families.[5] Sixteen participants' relationships with their fathers (40 percent) were also impaired by their fathers' alcoholism.[6] Thus a total of twenty-seven participants (67.5 percent) either saw little of their fathers during their adolescence or saw them mostly while their fathers were under the influence of alcohol.

Fewer than one-quarter of participants (22.5 percent) reported that their already warm relationships with their fathers continued to be comforting to them during their adolescence.[7] Participants who remembered their fathers in this light also tended to remember them as men who were not abusive to their family members, who were often understanding about participants' gender issues, and who sometimes favoured participants over other children.

Finding Faults in Fathers: Abuses and Abandonments

More than three-quarters of participants (77.5 percent) reported that their relationships with their fathers during their adolescence either continued to be dissatisfying ones[8] or became less gratifying during their teen-aged years.[9] Some participants said that they had lost respect for their fathers during this period of their lives; others spoke of "fearing," "loathing," "hating," or wanting to kill their fathers. Participants described their opinions of their fathers during this phase of their lives using terms such as "sleazy," "evil," "fucking asshole," and "an animal out of control." Clearly, many of their fathers seemed less than ideal to them during participants' adolescence.

It would seem that in many of these cases, their opinions could be largely attributed to the abusiveness of their fathers. Fourteen participants (35 percent) reported that they had been abused by their fathers while they were adolescents.[10] Simon, Ken, and Jordie were sexually abused by their fathers during their teenaged years. All other participants who reported having been abused, except for Walter and Jorge, complained of both physical and emotional maltreatment. Walter and Jorge complained only of emotional torments. In all cases except Brian's, their fathers' abusiveness toward them was a continuation of practices begun while participants were still children. In addition, six participants who were abused and three other participants witnessed their fathers being abusive toward their mothers and sisters.[11] In all cases, participants' fathers' abuse of mothers and sisters was ongoing since participants had been children.

Several participants told tales of episodes in which their fathers shamed and humiliated them in conjunction with subjecting them to other forms of abuse. As teenagers attempting to establish themselves as independent and capable young adults, they must have found these incidents especially galling. Peter was one participant who recalled such treatment. Peter's father had always used physical punishments to discipline her. The frequency of these beatings increased during Peter's adolescence at the same time as the compensations of father-son-style time together decreased. Peter remembered that her father instead began to focus on her femaleness when she reached puberty:

> There wasn't any more "Hey, do you want to go fishing?" . . . "Do you want to go out and play catch?" That sure as hell stopped. . . . We weren't doing anything anymore. . . . He started teasing me when I started developing this chest. He was always teasing me about it. I felt bad about it. I didn't want it. . . . And I got hit a lot when I was a . . . teenager. Sure. Because I was real rebellious. Mostly my dad, but they

[both] thought I was nuts. They were ready to have me committed because I didn't want to go along with their program.

The message from Peter's father seemed clear. Her father was prepared to use physical force and the power of the state to make Peter into a woman, and being a woman meant that there would be no more father-child interactions of the kind which Peter liked.

Morgan recounted a number of stories about being beaten almost daily and regularly humiliated by her father.

> This was when my father used to go inside by the dining room table, and he used to get at one end and I got at the other. And then I'd have to take off into my room and have to lean against the door so he wouldn't get in. And I'd be sliding in my socks as he forced the door open. And he'd get my head and hit it against the wall. And he'd get me with my face and just . . . throw me against the wall and scream. . . . There was [also] a lot of incidents like where I was just embarrassed. . . . This was happening a lot. And . . . once . . . his blood pressure was up, and he turned to me and said, "It's because of that thing there," meaning me. But it didn't hurt by then because he was like that so consistently.

Morgan's father also repeatedly humiliated her by hacking off her hair as a punishment for what he thought was Morgan's sexual promiscuity. According to Morgan, such libertine behaviors were a figment of her father's imagination. Not surprisingly, Morgan remembered being "terrified" of her "schizophrenic" father. Sessions such as these continued until Morgan reached the age of sixteen years, at which time her father became ill enough that he apparently decided that she could do as she pleased.

In addition to severe sexual abuse, Ken suffered physical and emotional abuse at the whim of her father. For example, Ken said that one time her father kicked and punched her down two flights of stairs. Ken also reported that her father regularly called her "dumb" and "stupid" and thwarted everything which might have brought her pleasure.

> I wanted to stay after school one day [to play sports] . . . and I called my mom, and she said, "Well, you know what your father thinks. I'd love to let you stay." Well, I stayed anyway. When I got home, my dad put me through a drill. He said, "So, you want to do sports?" And for about two hours—now we had a three story house. . . . It was a summer, it was hot, humid—he made me go from the cellar up all three flights of steps, plus the split type level, and get one thing and . . . run all the way back downstairs, and then back and forth. And he said, "Now, if you'd like to go do sports, you can do this all night long. That way we'll wear you out, if you have so much excess energy." And the next morning he woke me up at like five o'clock and had me cut the grass. And he said,

"Now you can go to school, and I doubt if you'll have any energy to stay." He was that kind of perverted type person.

Ken, who held her father responsible for her mother's suicide attempt, said that her father became a symbol to her of all that she never wanted to become.

Bill was never able to forgive her father for the abuse which he first showered upon Bill and then later, during a marital breakdown, upon Bill's mother. Bill thought that her father was capable of killing her or her mother in his anger. After witnessing her father's performance during a temporary separation of her parents, Bill completely wrote off her father as any kind of example of admirable humanity. Bill recalled:

> I loathed and feared my father during this time. Even though he was "well behaved" for a year or so after my folks got back together, I never trusted him, avoided him, rarely even spoke to him. . . . Things had changed because I saw him as pathetic and weak as well as very manipulative. He had cried once outside the house when my mother had chucked him out, begging to be let in and promising not to hurt anyone. It had turned my stomach. I felt no pity for him but just wanted him OUT!

A few participants became bolder during adolescence and started to stand up to their fathers. Tony reported that when she was a teenager she "took the brunt of his problems. Between my seventeenth and nineteenth birthdays, my father hit me more than he hit all four of us put together." Tony illustrated the nature of their relationship with this story:

> He'd come after me physically. And I remember punching him in the face one time, punching him so hard that he stepped back. He couldn't believe I hit him. I remember one time he picked up one of my mother's heavy old-fashioned pots and whacked me in the head with it. . . . I told him one time, "Don't go to sleep because I'm going to kill you in your sleep." It was funny because a couple of months later my mother said to me, "Oh please, tell him you're not going to kill him because he hasn't slept a day since you said that and he twists and he turns and he keeps me awake." So I told him, "I'm not going to kill you in your sleep." One time I opened up all the lugs on his car hoping he would drive off and get killed. The only reason I tightened them back up was because my mother stood there crying.

In addition to these battles, Tony resented her father for gambling away all of his income and therefore not properly supporting their family. Despite these protracted and pronounced hostilities between them, Tony described his father both as a negative role model and as a "really nice guy" who had a problem.

Brian was only badly beaten by her father one time, but that single instance of physical abuse was pivotal in the relationship. Even though Brian endured a brutal beating in a test of wills with her father, he recalled feeling as though she had won the contest. After her "victory," Brian felt no further allegiance to her father. The altercation began over what Brian felt was an unfounded accusation.

> I was in a rage about his suggestion. Then my youngest sister . . . piped up repeating one of his remarks against me. I snapped, and leaned over the table to slap her in my anger. My father grabbed me and was completely in his own rage. He took off his belt and took me into the next room. . . . He made me stand and began to whip me with his belt across my back and butt. I was really ornery and refused to cry out, although it hurt a lot and it was hard to keep tears out of my eyes. . . . I counted the blows. My brothers and sisters were nearly hysterical at the whipping I was getting. My mother was timidly protesting and asking him, "Isn't that enough?" My father was in a really burning rage and I absolutely refused to buckle. I counted thirty-two blows before my mother's protests finally got to him. When he did stop, I demanded, "May I go to my room? I need to do my homework." He finally let me go. He was the one who had to go back to the supper table to face the rest of the family. Of course, I couldn't even study. When I was safely alone, I could bury my head under my pillow and cry and explore my bruises. Somehow, I was as much privately proud of my endurance as hurt by the incident. After that, I knew I was much stronger than my father. Ever since, I've never felt much that I wanted anything from my father. I had entirely lost respect for him.

A few participants reported that, as they matured, their feelings about their fathers' abusiveness were more equivocal. Although they and their mothers and siblings continued to suffer the consequences of their fathers' aggression, they came to empathize more with their fathers and were less resentful of them for their inappropriate behaviours. For example, Walter remembered that while she was a teenager, her father's irrational rages became worse. However, Walter began to rationalize that her father's crazed outbursts were "really just a convoluted expression of his great, incredible love for us." Thus Walter both endured more of her father's fury and forgave him more for it.

Harry too had mixed feelings about her alcoholic and violent father. Harry went through a childhood period of both idolizing her father and feeling that her mother needed protection from him. As a teenager, Harry watched her father sometimes beat her mother to the point of her needing to be hospitalized. However, Harry also remembered thinking about her violent and mentally unbalanced mother, "I wish he would just punch her lights out so it would shut her up for a while." Thus, although Harry was mostly upset by her father's violence, she sometimes secretly empathized with her father's anger.

Colin's, Mel's, and Darcy's relationships with their fathers also went downhill when they lost their fathers' attentions as their fathers came to prefer the company of "real" boys. Colin continued to want to be "just like" her father even though she was confused when her father decided that it was no longer "proper" to take her hunting and fishing with him. Similarly, Mel's father had favoured her over her younger brother while she was still prepubescent. However, once Mel started to look more like a woman, Mel's father both stopped beating her and stopped spending any significant amount of time with her. Mel didn't miss the thrashings but was sorely disappointed at the loss of her father's attentions. Darcy, too, had enjoyed more of her father's companionship as a child than as a teenager. Darcy, who had no brothers, was dismayed when her father seemed to be no longer able to relate to her when she started to become a young woman.

> That's when he started switching over to being friends with my boyfriends instead of me. . . . I fixed the cars, and he gave them to my boyfriends. . . . He says, "Well, they're boys. They should have a car." . . . And I couldn't figure out why he would pay them to do things that I was doing for free all along. And then I couldn't do them anymore.

It was only as an adult that Darcy discovered that her father had spent a great deal of his time away from home around gay men during Darcy's youth. This information seemed to somewhat clarify, for Darcy, the mystery of her father's allegiances.

Other participants' memories about the reasons for their unsatisfying relationships with their fathers during their adolescence were more varied. Fred and Hal withdrew from their fathers because they were so unhappy with themselves that they did not want to impose themselves on their fathers. Ron, Howie, and Robin were disdainful of their fathers for what they interpreted as deficiencies in their masculinity. Ron considered her mostly absent father to be "very passive," "weak," and "unmanly" because "he didn't stand up for himself" to Ron's violent and controlling mother. Howie similarly had little respect for her father, whom she characterized as a man who "was not really a participant in life. He was very timid and quiet and was always off in a private daydream." Robin, too, resented her father for his sensitivity and was embarrassed by her father's advanced age. Robin described the situation this way:

> When I was growing up, my father was very . . . to himself. . . . Also, I have to point out to you that . . . when I was born he was already in his fifties. And so he didn't do much with me, which I resented. . . . I felt he

wasn't there for the kids. . . . Also . . . I used to be embarrassed about my father because . . . when I was eleven, twelve my friends used to say, "Is that your grandfather?" . . . He was a very emotional man too. If he listens to really good music, he cries. . . . And sometimes I got embarrassed by him showing his emotion, I didn't know how to handle it myself. I felt uncomfortable.

In sum, it seemed as though the men who had appeared so powerful and above reproach to participants when they were children had lost some luster in participants' adolescent eyes. Part of this diminishment can probably be attributed to the normal disengagement from their parents which most teenagers undertake as they strive for their independence. Some might easily be explained as the hypercriticalness which many adolescents feel toward their parents. However, there did seem to be other significant forces at work in these people's lives.

Once participants had reached adolescence they had developed more acute analytic faculties than they had as children. They were therefore less likely to blindly accept their father's drunkenness or abusive behaviours as normal, acceptable, or deserved. They were also more likely to understand that their fathers were not all-knowing, all-suffering princes who were always motivated by noble concerns. In short, many participants started to see their fathers more realistically.

There were also a handful of participants who, still yearning for their fathers' beneficence, were abandoned by them. Some fathers found the physical changes wrought by puberty impossible to ignore. They ceased to treat their daughters as if they were sons and instead, turned their attentions either to training participants to be proper women or to enjoying other young people who were indeed boys. Finally, a few participants became more confirmed in their childhood impressions that their fathers were inadequate as men. They, too, felt distant from their fathers.

A Parent to Love: OK Fathers, Problem Mothers

Nine participants (22.5 percent) remembered their relationships with their fathers as having been good ones during their adolescence; all of these relationships had also been gratifying to them as children.[12] Participants who felt warmly toward their fathers reported two main ways in which their fathers endeared themselves to them. Firstly, Sam, Darren, Bruce, and Bob all felt themselves to have been favoured by their fathers over their siblings. Secondly, Eli, Darren, Bruce, Bob, Phil, and Grant all credited their fathers with having been understanding or supportive of their gender needs. Five of those participants who were fond of their fathers during their teen years were so enamoured of them that they persisted in using them as role models throughout their lives.[13]

A necessary but not sufficient condition for participants to have felt warmly toward their fathers seemed to have been that they also remembered a dearth of paternal abusiveness in their family homes. They or their siblings may have been physically disciplined, but they considered the punishments to have been commensurate with the offenses. They may have witnessed their parents fighting, but they did not perceive their fathers as having taken unfair advantage of their mothers. In addition to the absence of unwarranted abuses of power, most participants who praised their fathers also disparaged their mothers. This would seem to imply that these participants turned to fathers who were either kindly or relatively benign in order to satisfy their needs to feel that they had at least one "good" parent.

To illustrate, Bruce and Bob both reported that their fathers were men who often took their sides in family battles and who also made no demands upon them for femininity. By contrast, both of their mothers had been abusive to them. In a similar vein, Darren's father was kindly when she tried to talk with him about feeling "like a male on the inside," whereas Darren's mother was physically abusive to her. Grant likewise remembered her father as having been more accepting of her lesbianism than her often brutal mother.

The contrasts between Sam's, Keith's, and Luther's memories of their mothers and fathers were perhaps less dramatic but were consistent with this same theme. Sam remembered her mother as imposing harsh gender demands upon her in her adolescence, whereas her father just continued to provide some of the "best times" of her youth. Keith fought with her mother about anything and everything, whereas Keith continued to feel close with her father, whom Keith continued to idolize even though they spent little time together during her adolescence.

Luther remembered her mother as being sharply and unfairly critical of her during her adolescence. Luther's memories of her attitude toward her father, however, were vividly disparate from those she held about her mother. Luther characterized her father, who "never sounded angry, never sounded judgmental," as being "not like my mother." Luther recalled that although she and her father did disagree on some things, it had no deleterious effects on their relationship:

I think we began to fight now because it was during the years that I became politically more aware. . . . It was the height of the civil rights movement. . . . My father was a Republican and I was a Democrat, and

I couldn't understand how a Black man could be a Republican, and we'd have these fights about that. . . . But essentially the relationship didn't change very much. Even though we fought there was never any acrimony. I never came away from a conversation with him at this time feeling bad.

Luther also learned to have a great deal of respect for her father's achievements as she became old enough to understand their import:

And here was a man who . . . had what would be the equivalent of a third-grade education. And who had put, by the time I was a teenager, two daughters through college, presently putting one son through college. All of them had private high school and grammar school education. And I was living in this suburban life and just beginning to see a difference between myself and other American Blacks. I began to see, "Wow, it's a hell of a thing what he has done that he's carved out for himself!"

Luther said that his father had served as his role model ever since.

It would seem from these stories that although participants didn't see a lot of their fathers during their adolescence, 22.5 percent of them found sufficient reasons to entertain warm feelings toward them. Four participants felt that their fathers favored them over their siblings; none of the nine fathers applied stiff demands for femininity; and none of them were perceived by participants as having abused their power over them. Perhaps more importantly, most of those fathers who were well remembered were married to women whom participants remembered as having made their teenaged lives miserable. By contrast, their fathers seemed to be kindly and worthy men. A few participants were thus able to secure for themselves the comfort of having one parent with whom they felt a close connection during their adolescence.

Summary and Commentary

For most young people, adolescence is characterized by greater distance between themselves and their parents. More than two-thirds (67.5 percent) of participants recalled that their fathers were unavailable to them during much of their adolescences.[14] Some fathers were occupied with their work. Some passed most of their hours at home in an alcoholic haze. A few were absent due to separations, divorces, or death. Only a few participants were left with the option of initiating their own withdrawals from their fathers' attentions.

For many participants, this distance allowed them to have sufficient perspective to be able to see their fathers in more realistic terms. As a result, more participants came to hold more critical opinions of their fathers; 77.5 percent of participants reported that they were unhappy about the states of their relationships with their fathers during their adolescences.[15] Their dissatisfaction seemed to have stemmed from two main sources: the abusiveness of their fathers and the withdrawal of their fathers' tacit support of their masculinity.

In the first instance, a number of participants had always been scared of, or angry at, their fathers for the violence with which they ruled their families. These people were joined by other participants who became less in awe or forgiving of their fathers' aggressiveness as adolescents than they had been as children. They became more judgmental of their fathers' assaults as unjustified. In a few instances, participants also became less tolerant of their fathers' uncontrolled ire and vindictiveness as participants came to feel increasingly responsible for caring for their mothers who were on the receiving end of their fathers' outbursts.

The other main factor which seemed to have contributed to participants' grievances about their adolescent relationships with their fathers was their fathers' failure to support them in their masculinity. It seemed as though many of those fathers who had so happily allowed their younger daughters to pal along with them in their men's worlds abruptly abandoned them as participants started to physically mature. Perhaps their fathers believed, as do many other people, that young females do not really acquire their gender or sex until they reach puberty. Before that time, they exist as a kind of neuter; after that time, they become women. Before that time, they may pass freely in either the worlds of women or men; after that time, they must be only women. Thus as participants began to show signs of physical maturation, many fathers quietly averted their attentions from their offspring whom they now saw as young women. Even worse from the point of view of the participants, some fathers continued to attend to their daughters; but instead of treating them like buddies, they began to treat them like female chattel which needed to be trained and contained.

Fewer than one-quarter (22.5 percent) of participants reported that they were able to maintain positive attitudes toward their fathers during their teenaged years.[16] Those who were able to sustain these feelings shared a number of common memories. Firstly, none of them remembered their fathers as violent men. Secondly, half of them remembered having been favored over other siblings by their fathers. Thirdly, none of their fathers were among those who ceased to be tolerant of participants' continued adolescent tomboyishness. These circumstances add up to a picture which portrays this group of fathers as, at the least, benign and, at the most, beneficent.

Context and contrast also seemed to play roles in enabling a small number of participants to remember their fathers in a good light. Over and above the fact that participants remembered their fathers as, in the first place, doing no harm were seven participants' memories of their mothers as women who had abused and berated them. Thus their fathers, by comparison, seemed that much more worthy of their admiration. Furthermore, four participants' fathers were absent from their family homes for some part of participants' teen years. It was therefore more possible for participants to both ignore their fathers' shortcomings and to dwell on their more commendable attributes. In contrast to their mothers, who were very present and very unpleasant, their peripatetic fathers must have seemed that much more preferable.

In sum, participants' adolescent relationships with their fathers seemed on the surface to contribute less to their incipient masculine identities than had their childhood relationships. However, it seems unwise to neglect the powerful effects which often result from deprivation and adversity. These individuals did not enter adolescence as blank slates. Most had already been thinking of themselves as boys for years. Their fathers' behaviours may in fact have spurred them to try still harder to fit themselves to masculine molds. Their fathers' abusiveness may have motivated them to want either to become gentle and considerate men or the obverse, to become tough enough to earn back their fathers' respect. Rather than encouraging femininity, their fathers' withdrawal of collusion with their youthful masculinity may well have had an opposite effect: participants may have taken their fathers' withdrawals as messages that they needed to try harder, to do better, to become more manly still. Finally, those fathers who continued to respect their daughters' gender choices, of course, only added their encouragement to already established patterns. It would seem that if participants were set on seeing themselves as boys, they might construe any range of paternal behaviours as reasons to strive harder to be seen by others as they saw themselves, to be seen as young men.

Adolescent Relationships with Grandfathers and Uncles

Few participants recalled any of their elder male relatives as having played any significant role in their adolescent lives. Although fourteen participants (31 percent) did mention a grandfather[17] or uncle,[18] half of them also made comments which suggested that their influence was minimal. When Grant, Hal, and Darcy spoke of their relatives they were talking about people whom they saw on infrequent visits. Another four participants who briefly lived with or near older male relatives during their teen years seemed to have been little touched by their experiences. Simon lived with her grandparents between the ages of twelve and fifteen; however, Simon made no mention of her grandfather's presence in her life during those years. Harry also lived with her grandparents for one year during her high school years. However, Harry remained aloof from her grandfather. Eli made only a single passing mention of the uncle with whom she had lived briefly. Bruce's grandfather, who lived down the street from her, "wasn't that important" to her. Clearly these participants' grandfathers had been relegated to the peripheries of their psychic lives.

Gary and Stan were on the other end of the spectrum with regard to the intensity of their relationships with their male relatives. Each had a man who stood in for their fathers in their lives. Gary lived with her parents and a large extended family when she was growing up. Gary had little contact with her "hard-working" father but did relate to one of her uncles as "the father I could talk to" and the man whom she "wanted to be like."

Stan's maternal grandfather took over her upbringing when Stan's father disappeared from her life when Stan was a young child. The man always made it clear to Stan, however, that he was her "guardian," not her father. Stan never felt loved by her grandfather and in fact always felt sorely slighted by him in favour of her younger brother. Stan remembered that her grandfather's favouritism only got worse as she and her brother got older. Stan recounted this story to exemplify the nature of her position in her grandfather's affections during her adolescence:

> When I was sixteen and I wanted to drive so bad I couldn't stand it. . . . I wanted my own vehicle. Somehow it didn't seem feasible to get a car; I wanted a motorcycle. So I remember working all summer long. Working my butt off. Not going to the movies when everybody else was. Not going to the lake. Not hanging out or going to town. I worked at a hospital at nights. . . . But, by the end of the summer I had $350 . . . and I got this motorcycle. Well, when [my brother] turned sixteen, it was about that time that Gramps decided we needed a new family car and he went out and bought a new car. And guess who just got the old car, just got it?! Oh, I hated! I was so angry! And I still had my motorcycle, but I couldn't take my friends out. It was just for me. I got around with it but, oh, that hurt! That really really hurt that he just got the car.

As angry and hurt as Stan remembered being at the time, she was already so alienated from her grandfather that Stan said that her relationship with her grandfather was made no worse by such events.

Ken, Bill, Brian, Dennis, and Steven remembered their elder male relations as people who significantly improved the quality of their lives. In all of these cases, the men in question lived close enough to participants to make frequent access to them easy to obtain. Ken, who despised her viciously abusive father, found some comfort in having her caring and generous grandfather living nearby. However, because he was her father's father, she felt unable to tell him how abusively her father took advantage of her. Bill similarly reminisced that her grandfather had been "very important" to her in her youth because, unlike her hated father, he provided her with an example of a man in whose footsteps she would have been proud to follow. As Bill became more and more disaffected with her father, she spent more time with her grandfather at his nearby home. Brian's grandfather also provided an appreciated alternative to an often angry father. Brian's grandfather lived and worked on the same farm land as her own family throughout her youth. Brian remembered her grandfather as a quiet and distant but comforting man who did not seem to find her femaleness to be an impediment. After his death when Brian was fifteen years old, Brian tried to take her grandfather's place around the farm whenever she could. This, however, only led to more fights between Brian and her father over the proper role for her as a girl—conflicts Brian rarely had had with her grandfather.

Dennis, who remembered her father as a dangerously violent man, remembered one of her uncles as a life saver. When Dennis was near to death from self-starvation, her favorite uncle found a doctor whom Dennis would trust enough to respond to his ministrations. However, her uncle was only able to convince Dennis to make an initial visit to the doctor by threatening "to tie me up and pull me there in chains." Dennis frankly appreciated having a caring male alternative to her father in her life.

Steven, too, had a favorite uncle who gave Steven special attention when she was a teenager. Steven remembered that her childless uncle sometimes seemed to take the place of her workaholic and "demeaning" father. In particular, Steven remembered with gratitude the time that he took her to a special baseball game:

> My uncle took me to a "father and son" baseball game. The Yankees were playing the Baltimore Orioles. I was about thirteen I guess. And I was on the bus with him, and I knew more about baseball than any. . . . male there. . . . My uncle didn't have any sons of his own. So, therefore, being that I was sort of masculine and desired to be going to the games, he took me. And it gave me a feeling of being male for the day.

For the most part, it would seem that with only one exception, participants' contact with their grandfathers and uncles during their adolescent years either made little impression upon them or left a favourable one. Half of the fourteen people who said anything at all about their grandfathers or uncles indicated that their presence in their lives was both benign and peripheral.[19] Only one participant, Stan, reported an unrelieved negative experience of her grandfather. However, as her legal guardian, Stan's grandfather was also the only one who did not have the grandparental luxury of being able to choose to avoid difficult confrontations with his granddaughter. Because of both the circumstances of Stan's family constellation and the prejudices of Stan's grandfather, Stan was left with no positive role models in her immediate family sphere during her adolescence.

Six other individuals recalled that although their grandfathers or uncles were not generally positioned so as to displace participants' fathers as participants' primary male parental figures, they seemed to act as positive role models for participants. As noncustodial relations, they were able to exercise their options of only showing these girls their best sides and vacating when more trying times loomed ahead. By so doing, they made it more possible for participants to imagine that a man might be a decent kind of person to aspire to become.

Relationships with Brothers

As was the case with their other family members, participants' relationships with their brothers also generally became more distant during their adolescent years. In some cases, the distance between participants and their brothers was simply due to changes in residence which occurred during participants' adolescences. More often, the increased distance between participants and their brothers was a result of the greater divergence which is commonly found between the activities and interests of adolescent boys and girls. Many participants found that, as adolescents, they were either increasingly excluded from boys' peer groups, or that they preferred the company of girls about whom they could indulge in romantic fantasies. Therefore, although few participants reported that they had significantly changed their feelings about their brothers during this stage of their lives, the intensity of participants' involvements in them probably lessened to some extent.

For twelve of the thirty participants who had brothers (40 percent), physical distances intervened as one or more of participants' brothers left their family homes during participants' teen years. Simon, Darren, Bruce, and Phil lost brothers in family breakups; and another eight participants' brothers left home to pursue their own goals while participants were still teenagers.[20] These changes left Simon, Robin, Luther, Terry, Howie, and Fred as only children in their homes. In total, twenty-four participants[21] lived with brothers during all or most of their adolescence, including Alan, Darren, and Bob, who lived with their brothers only until they reached the age of sixteen or seventeen, and Bruce, who sometimes lived with her brother.

Brothers as Buddies: Close Relationships with Brothers

Nine of the twenty-four participants who had brothers at home (37.5 percent) said that they had continued to get along fairly well with at least one of their brothers during their adolescent years.[22] Participants remembered closeness with their brothers appeared to have been based upon a sharing of adversity or upon participants' feelings of responsibility for younger and more vulnerable children.

Ron, Aaron, and their brothers were homosexual at a time when to be so was to be marked with a major stigma. Both participants felt that this helped to bring them closer to their brothers. When Ron began to feel that she was in the wrong body, she went to her gay brother to talk about it. Ron remembered that her brother's counsel "made me feel better about loving women" but that he didn't quite understand what Ron was trying to communicate. Ron remembered that she appreciated being able to talk about her feelings.

> He could empathize with some of it, because we had crossdressed together as children. And I remember him when he was fifteen, sixteen, we were going over porn magazines, and he was telling me about his feelings, how much he wanted to be this woman or that woman. So, he did understand my feelings, but he had decided on a homosexual lifestyle, so. . . . He just thought I'd probably be butch or something like that.

Aaron's adolescent relationship with her gay brother continued somewhat along the same lines as it had taken when they were children. They began sexual exploration together when they were quite young and took it up again when they were adolescents. Aaron recalled, "My sexual relationship with a male was with a person with both components, male and female. He had a male penis and a very male body, but was more like an older sister in terms of the way he acted and touched, his lack of aggression." Aaron had only the fondest of memories of her teenaged relations with her brother, wherein she was afforded the opportunity to explore gender and sexual fluidity.

As had happened when they were younger, a number of participants formed alliances with their brothers in order to protect them from the myriad difficulties inherent in their everyday lives. For example, Bob, who had three brothers, fought with her two older brothers but felt protective of her youngest siblings. Bob made sure that they were properly fed, and she stood up to their mother when the little ones seemed in danger of receiving beatings. Alan, too, stayed close with her brother while they were both in their family home and thereby vulnerable to their father's outrages. While Nathan was a teenager, her parents dissolved their marriage. Nathan recalled that her brother and sister were the only people to whom she felt close at the time because their "parents were impossible." Phil similarly remembered becoming closer with her remaining brothers after their parents divorced and her older brother moved away with their father.

Darren and Steven both had younger brothers of whom they felt protective and for whom they provided child care. Although neither of them were friends with their little brothers because of their age differences, they nevertheless felt a warmth toward them born of their sense of responsibility for their well-being when they were young.

In sum, 37.5 percent of those participants whose brothers were part of their lives during their adolescences remembered having benefited from their presence in their family homes. The main area in which they gained was in the solidarity which they felt with their brothers. Two participants were glad to have gay brothers. In some cases, participants and their brothers banded together as comrades fortifying themselves against the storms of rampaging parents. In other instances, they took solace in commiserating with one another when their parents separated or divorced. A few participants also fondly recalled their younger and needier little brothers whom they cared for and protected. Such warmth between participants and their brothers must have provided a small island in the midst of their otherwise stormy adolescent years.

Left Behind: Distant Relationships with Brothers

More participants remembered having rocky relationships with their brothers who lived with them as teenagers, than did not. Two-thirds of participants reported that their adolescent relationships with at least one of their brothers left them cold.[23] Most of the participants who remembered having felt this way attributed their feelings to memories of fights over dominance and jealousies or uneven gender privileges accorded to them by their parents.[24]

Mel, Morgan, and Ken all remembered being especially angered when their younger brothers suddenly became young men who could outdo them in physical prowess, displace them from prized positions, and surpass them in freedoms. Mel had always been competitive with her brother. As a child, Mel had easily bested her "klutzy" brother in most areas of endeavour. When they became adolescents, however, the tables turned and her father turned his attentions away from Mel to her little brother. Suddenly her brother seemed considerably more competent.

> I envied him when we got to high school because he was all the things that I wasn't. All the physical things. I used to get mad at him constantly because he wasn't going out on dates and that was the thing I wanted to do so damn bad. We fought constantly. I dropped out of whatever competition there was in seventh grade, everything with my brother. I just decided I was going to do my own thing. . . . He was starting to get a little bit taller, finally. I couldn't beat him up quite as easily. Essentially

we both went our separate ways and when we got together we fought is what it amounted to.

Morgan similarly recalled that as she and her brother who was one and a half years younger reached adolescence, the restrictions and punishments imposed upon them by their parents began to differ dramatically. Morgan attributed part of the difference in their treatment to her brother's less argumentative character but nevertheless remembered her teenaged family dynamics with some resentment:

> My brother was allowed to stay out at night because he was a boy, and I wasn't. I had to be in really early . . . by seven o'clock, and stuff like that. So I was just seething with all this energy and I couldn't do anything with it. . . . My brother started getting some [abuse] as he got older, and his grades were really bad and he started getting into trouble with the law. And then he wasn't too sweet around the house either. But he didn't get the physical stuff that I did. . . . [Dad] hardly ever touched my brother.

Ken, too, recalled that she lost ground in her competition with her brother, who was four years younger. As an adolescent, Ken became increasingly alienated from her brother and jealous of his relationship with their father. Ken remembered how it was then:

> I fought with my brother . . . about just about everything. . . . There was really nothing there. My brother was self-centred. He was lazy. He always wanted something. . . . He was pushy. . . . I think the hardest times were when my dad and his buddies from work would come over and they'd take my brother to the ball games. I was never asked. . . . and, boy, I knew everything there was about baseball. My brother could have cared less. He just went to eat hotdogs and popcorn. . . . and that was rough. I felt really left out.

Bob did not complain of inequality in the way that she and her brothers had been raised because, basically, they had all been afforded the same privileges and obligations. However, this did not prevent Bob and her brothers from coming to blows in a family which was run by the imposition of regular corporal punishment. Bob recalled that she and her two brothers closest to her in age were "extremely stubborn, self-willed, and . . . extremely bad tempered." In addition, Bob remembered both of those brothers as being "extremely violent" in their expressions of their anger. Once Bob's older brother joined the army, Bob became the "top dog" among the children and used her position to impose some kind of order. Bob recalled:

> As for [my next younger brother], well, [he] and I used to have physical combat quite regularly. We used to have some real big punch ups. . . .

> [He] still caused a lot of trouble. . . . He used to pick on my youngest brother, so I used to sort him out. And the only way to sort him out was to give him a hiding, and threatening if he touched him, I'd kill him.

Dale's brother, who was three years younger, became violent and abusive as he grew older. Dale went from admiration for her brother when she was a child to "hate" of him when she was a teenager. Dale had a number of causes for her turnabout. Her brother and father drank together and "teamed up" to "pick the shit out of" and physically push around their mother. Dale also remembered her brother as the one who "got everything." For example, Dale's father gave her brother a new car when Dale "dreamt about driving" but was only allowed to drive the tractor. Overarching it all were Dale's memories of her brother's incessant and excessive violence:

> My brother just got mean. He would beat up the neighbour kid who was the sweetest little guy. He was much smaller than my brother. My brother just was brutal. And I hated him. . . . He just got away with hitting us. . . . and he was mean to things. One time we did something which wasn't very nice. We played baseball with some baby birds. . . . My brother enjoyed it. I can remember him stabbing a great big frog right in the middle and just letting it suffer away. . . . But he just was a "Me, Myself, and I" guy.

Dale learned to keep her distance from her increasingly malevolent brother.

Those other participants who were not close to their brothers during their adolescent years cited a number of reasons for their distant relationships. Peter and Bruce were sexually used by their brothers during their teenaged years;[25] and Ed, Jordie, Tony, Bob, and Pat had brothers in the house with whom they had little contact because of age differences between them.

In total, almost two-thirds of those participants who had brothers who were present in their lives during their adolescent years remembered their relationships as having been distant ones. As participants and their brothers reached adolescence, many of their parents began to differentiate between them in a more sexist way. They allowed their sons more freedoms in accordance with their maturation, whereas they seemed to grant few such allowances for their daughters as they grew into young women. In those homes where participants' younger brothers were given more freedoms than themselves, participants especially tended to resent their younger brothers.

Some participants also found that their dominance over their younger brothers was upset by the physical changes which puberty brought to their brothers but failed to bring to them. Thus a number of participants lost their ability to physically overpower or outperform their younger brothers at the same time as they jealously coveted the bodies into which their brothers were growing. These developments also contributed to an increased level of strife between participants and their brothers. Clearly participants' brothers played a less salutary role in their adolescent lives than they had done in their childhood ones.

Summary and Commentary

Things changed between many participants and their brothers as they made their way through the trials of adolescence. Their physical bodies changed. Their peer groups changed. Their relationships with their parents shifted. Brothers moved away. Each of these alterations contributed to an overall trend toward greater alienation between participants and their brothers during participants' teen years.

As participants physically matured into women, their brothers also matured. In a few instances, participants who had easily overpowered and outperformed their brothers found themselves at an insurmountable loss against the testosterone enhanced physiques which their brothers began to sport. In addition, as participants began to look less like boys and more like women, they found that they were increasingly ejected from the male peer groups in which they had previously enjoyed membership. For a number of participants this also meant they had lost the pleasure of their brothers' companionship. Participants' parents were also cued by the physical transformations which puberty wrought in their offspring. Fathers who had previously enjoyed their daughters' boyishness turned instead to the company of real boys. At the same time, participants found that they were held under tighter restrictions even as their brothers were being encouraged to explore the world and taste new freedoms. These factors also added to the distance between participants and their brothers during adolescence.

As compared to their memories of their childhoods, a smaller number of participants reported that they had been close with their brothers or otherwise felt warmly toward them. Their closeness continued to prevail under three conditions. Firstly, participants and their brothers drew together when they were mutually faced with greater threats than those which they posed to one another. Secondly, participants remembered having enjoyed their brothers when they were so much younger than themselves that they posed no threat at all but rather were cute, cuddly, or vulnerable youngsters in need of their big sisters' care and protection. Finally, a couple of participants' brothers left their immediate lives before participants were old enough to garner any reasons to question their near perfection.

Thus the stories told by participants would seem to indicate that for the most part, participants' adolescent relationships with their brothers probably contributed to participants' general dissatisfaction with the social ramifications of becoming more unequivocally female. The overall effect of their adolescent relationships with their brothers seemed to have been to drive home contrasts between the potential freedoms socially offered to females and males as they matured. Participants were generally not pleased to find that simply being male seemed to put their brothers in advantageous positions, whereas being female was becoming increasingly an impediment to their self-expression. The admiration, amiable companionship, or fair fights of their childhood relationships with their brothers largely gave way to jealousy as participants realized how many doors were closing for them as they were simultaneously opening for their brothers. The few participants who did not fall prey to these dynamics were largely those who were exempted from them because of more pressing concerns or because of their cushion of larger age differences. Overall, participants' adolescent relationships with their brothers would therefore best be summed up by the words contrast and envy.

Summary and Commentary: Adolescent Relationships with Male Relatives

The relationships which participants had with their male relatives during their adolescent years were generally less than optimally satisfying to them. As teenagers, participants had better perspectives from which to judge the value of their relationships with fathers, grandfathers and uncles, or brothers, and most of these men and boys lost ground in participants' teenaged eyes. Three main elements seem to have been central to the quality of participants' adolescent relationships with their male relations: proximity, violence, and contrast.

Proximity was an issue in all three classes of male relations. On the one hand, if fathers, grandfathers, uncles, or brothers were physically absent or only rarely present in participants' teenaged lives, participants tended to feel emotionally cool toward them. In such cases, those men and boys seemed to have little influence on participants' adolescent gender development. There were, however, a few exceptions to this general trend. In some cases, participants were able to maintain high opinions of male family members who were only rare visitors to their lives, and they did so unimpeded by any rudely unflattering input. Therefore those participants who needed or wanted to be able to continue to uncritically value an older male role model were sometimes able to do so in such a manner. On the other hand, when male family members were daily physically present in participants' adolescent lives, their blemishes were harder for participants to ignore. Thus as participants went through the throes of adolescence and scrutinized with greater sophistication the men and boys around them, most participants found that the enthusiasms of their childhood years were less firmly grounded than they had once thought.

The level of violence in participants' family homes was one of the most imposing factors in participants' attitudes toward their fathers. In a number of cases, participants ceased to be in awe of their fathers' abilities to rule their homes through coercion and instead became contemptuous of their fathers for their heavy-handed methods. Violence also appeared to be a pivotal factor in those cases where participants appreciated their fathers' humanity. In several homes, the contrast between participants' fathers' lack of violence and participants' mothers' indulgence in it veered participants' allegiances toward their fathers and away from their mothers. Thus it would seem that as teenagers, participants were more likely to disapprove of violence as a method of discipline or problem solving than they had been as children.

Contrast came into the picture in several ways. Participants often made comparisons between the behaviours of their mothers and fathers. When one parent ended up looking better than the other, that parent received participants' greater respect and admiration. In a number of families, participants were dissatisfied either because no parent provided them with the role model for which they were looking or because participants specifically felt the need for a male example of humanity whom they could admire. Thus, where possible, a few participants found that the contrast between the apparently exemplary treatment afforded them by their grandfathers, uncles, or absent older brothers and that of their fathers allowed them the luxury of employing them as idealized elder male figures in their lives.

Participants' relationships with their brothers further revolved around issues of contrasts during participants' teen years in two main ways. Firstly, participants were almost universally distressed at the direction in which their puberty was taking them. The contrast between their own undesired pubertal changes and the coveted ones transpiring in their brothers' bodies served to sour several participants' feelings toward their brothers. To make matters worse, those same differences meant that when participants expressed their frustrations by picking fights with their unsuspecting brothers, participants were that much more likely to lose those contests.

Many participants also became increasingly distressed at the contrast between the ways in which their parents, other family members, and peers reacted to participants' attainments of adolescence and their brothers' accomplishments of the same maturity. Many participants were outraged to discover that their own adolescence signalled to others that they had become sexual beings and therefore were either to be sexually exploited or to be carefully curtailed so that they could explore neither their own sexuality nor the world at large. By contrast, their brothers' adolescence heralded their initiation into the world of men, with all the additional rights and freedoms attendant therein. Watching the world open up for their brothers as their own shrank only served to sharpen many participants' discontent with themselves, their family members, and their futures as women.

Thus the overall picture which emerged of participants' relations with their male relatives was one wherein participants still wanted their male relations to serve as role models for themselves but found it increasingly difficult to cast them as such. Participants reported that their adolescent years were mostly times during which the distances between themselves and their male family members grew. In some cases, their increasing distances were due to choices which participants made as a result of their greater adolescent criticalness. In other cases, participants felt that their choices had been made for them. They were no longer welcome at the club. Either way, their gender and sex dysphorias were heightened. It was becoming very difficult both for participants, and for those around them, to act as if their femaleness was of no consequence.

14 | Looking for Love, Groping for Identity
Adolescent Sexuality

THE LURE OF sexual exploration is a cornerstone of adolescence. Some teenagers resist the challenge; some charge headlong into it; others haltingly test the waters. Sadly, many young people do not get to experience the intermingling of delight and anguish which comes of gradually exploring one's own sexuality. Sexual assault and sexual abuse are dauntingly widespread and many girls' first experiences of sexuality are under conditions of coercion and pain. For them, sexuality is something imposed upon them. It is only later in their lives that they can struggle through the aftermath of their prematurely forced introductions to sexuality to find what best suits them. Although few people are ever able to cleanly weed out the residues of such experiences, many people who experience sexual abuse go on to lead happy and satisfying sexual lives.

In the common course of events, most girls experience an increase in libido during adolescence which, along with myriad social cues, prompts them to begin to think about themselves and their peers in more sexual terms. It is under such impetuses that many young people first masturbate.[1] Usually such autoeroticism in girls is accompanied by romantic fantasies about the mates of their dreams.[2] Furthermore, as the sexualities of adolescent girls are shaped by social forces which impinge upon them from many directions, many aspects of their social world begin to communicate to them that they should become heterosexually active. For most girls, their first forays into the world of heterosexuality consist of romantic fantasies about glamorous males. Later, most adolescent girls begin to date and fall in love with male peers. By late adolescence, many teenaged girls have experienced heterosexual intercourse at least once.[3]

At the same time that most girls are encouraged by their social environment to become sexually and romantically interested in boys, they are discouraged from thinking of their female peers in such terms. It has been only very recently that lesbian liaisons have become in the least bit socially acceptable. Certainly in the 1950s, 1960s, and 1970s, the decades during which most participants were in their teens, female homosexuality was highly stigmatized and suppressed. Few teenaged girls experimented sexually with their female peers, although passionate romantic friendships between teenaged girls were not uncommon. Most young girls who did have sexual contact with other girls during their teen years kissed and fondled one another in preparation for anticipated heterosexual activities. Genital contact appears to have been quite rare.[4]

Some teenagers attempt to avoid the complexities of sexuality altogether. They may do so as a result of their own conscious choices or as a result of feeling that there is a paucity of available and desirable partners. Others may simply be unaware of how to go about becoming romantically or sexually engaged with the objects of their desires. Eventually, however, one way or another, almost everyone falls into either love or lust and thus joins the fray.

Learning about Sexuality at Home: Adolescent Intrafamilial Sexual Experiences

Nine participants (20 percent)[5] had already had sexual experiences imposed on them by older males by the time they reached their teens.[6] In two cases, the sexual abuse continued during their adolescent years. Peter's brother, who began raping Peter when she was a girl of eight, continued to rape her until the situation was stopped by their parents when Peter was fourteen years old. Peter had no other sexual experience before reaching adulthood. Ken's father sadistically sexually abused her from the time she was nine years old through her teen years. Things only got worse after she started to look more like a woman. Ken described some of what her life was like when he was an adolescent girl:

> I had started to develop, my breasts were getting bigger. My father's hands were always on me when no one was looking. I'd be doing the dishes and my father would . . . slip his hands around and he'd fondle my breasts.
> We did a lot of things out in the barn . . . he'd always want me to help him. . . . He'd give me a soda to drink and . . . then he'd give me another one. Of course, I had to go to the bathroom. "Oh no, you don't have to go up to the house. You can go out here." . . . I'd go around to one of the different stalls where the horses were and I'd pull down my pants real quick, and I'd squat, and I'd go to the bathroom.
> All of a sudden my father would be standing there. And . . . he said . . . "Look I told you not to do that" and he probably hit me. And then he wanted to give me a hug and I hadn't pulled my pants up yet. He said, "As long as your pants are down, let me show you what you can do. I might as well show you now because no one else is ever going to." My father would unzip his pants and out comes his penis again. . . . He put both of my hands on his penis. Then he put my mouth on it and he showed me what to do. Meanwhile here's my dad getting stiff, and then

he'd push me up against the side of the stall and he put his penis inside of me vaginally.

You know, today, I really think he was really careful. Son of a bitch was really careful! He never shot off when he was inside me. Just before. I mean it must have been great control. He'd pull that penis out and he'd stuff it down the back of my throat. I mean, I thought I was going to choke. And here it comes. He'd just shoot off. And he says, "Here" and he'd make me lick it. And one time he says, "You know there's other ways we can do this too." . . . I mean son of a bitch! He got me anally once. I was bleeding.

Ken, like Peter, had very little other sexual contact while she was a teenager. It was not until Ken was seventeen years old that she was able to establish a sexual relationship with one of her peers.

Jordie, Simon, and Bruce were all sexually molested by nonfamilial adult men when they were children. While they were in their teens, members of their families also took advantage of them sexually. Jordie's father started to sexually abuse her when she entered her teens. Simon's stepfather molested her when she was twelve years old and visiting at her mother's house. When Simon was fifteen years old she started to live with her mother and stepfather. Simon was ready for him when he came back for a second try:

Having gone through the first time with him when I was twelve I had decided that if he ever tried it again that I would be prepared. I used to sleep with a knife, a little pocket knife. My mother was working a night shift at the time and he came home around 2:00 A.M. after the bars had closed and was drunk. . . . He came over to the bed and he started to touch me and I pulled out the knife. He was drunk and the room was dark, but he had enough sense to know what I had and he got up and went out of the room. I was scared, just totally panicked! I waited until I was absolutely sure that he was asleep and then I snuck out of the house.

Simon later went on to have consensual sexual relations with her peers, but at the time of this incident, sexual exploitation constituted the sum of Simon's sexual experiences.

Bruce came into her teenage years having survived an attempted rape. She had no sexual experience with any of her peers during her adolescence, but she did have multiple sexually exploitative interactions with various people who passed through her home after Bruce's parents divorced when she was eleven years old. While Bruce was living with her mother, three of her mother's boyfriends made sexual advances to Bruce. Two of them fondled Bruce in sexually inappropriate ways and a third man repeatedly cornered Bruce and pressed his erection against her whenever he found himself alone at the house with her. Bruce's older brother also made use of her in a similar fashion.

The experiences which seemed to have done the most damage to Bruce's bodily integrity, however, were those which directly involved her mother. The stories which Bruce told about this time described a woman who seemed to be obsessed with her daughter's developing breasts:

> She would do things like, "I want to see your boobs." And I would say, "What for?" "Well, I just want to see how big you're getting." And so, of course, I felt intimidated, I showed them to her. . . . And she would rub my back . . . like when I was a kid. . . . And then she'd say, "Roll over." And she'd feel like, my chest, "What is she doing? This isn't right." I had little breasts but I could feel that it was more than my chest. It was everything. . . . It didn't feel right. This is wrong. I would not want her to put me to sleep at night. . . . Then she said, "Well, if you don't let me see your boobies, I'm going to come tonight and I'm going to look at you." And so from then on I wore two sets of clothes to bed every night. I wore all my school clothes on top of my underclothes and pajamas on top. . . . And I would sleep in a little ball in a corner of my bed against the wall every night for fear that she would come in and touch me.

As a teenager, Bruce too became concerned with her developing breasts. She tried in several ways to stop their growth. When that proved impossible, she did what she could to conceal them. Around the same time as these incidents occurred, Bruce started to verbalize an interest in securing a sex change. Most of Bruce's stated anxiety in this regard focused on the removal of her breasts.

Alan's father, who had been physically and emotionally abusive to her as a child, also began to sexually abuse her when she became a teenager. When Alan's father abused her "thirteen different times in one night" she left home at the age of seventeen to live with a woman whom Alan described as also physically and emotionally abusive. Alan and three other participants (9 percent) were also the objects of nonconsensual sexuality with persons outside of their families during their adolescence.[7] Each of their encounters was within the context of their heterosexual explorations. I will detail those episodes along with those participants' other heterosexual experiences in a subsequent portion of this discussion.

Aaron was the only other person who had an incestuous sexual encounter during her adolescence. Unlike the others, Aaron placidly remembered having had sexual intercourse with her older brother. Aaron recalled her brother as a very gentle young man who, as an adult, became a gay man. Aaron did not seem at all traumatized by her experience.

In sum, seven participants (16 percent) were sexually used by family members during their teen years.[8] In all seven cases they were sexually used by males. Of the seven, Simon, Aaron, Ken, Jordie, and Alan all became involved in consensual heterosexual relations before the final years of adolescence. Bruce, who was also sexually molested by her mother, had no heterosexual or homosexual contacts during her adolescence. However, all of these participants eventually were able to establish more satisfactory relationships with partners of their choice.

Masturbation and Erotic Fantasies

Masturbation, and the romantic or erotic fantasies which usually accompany the practice, make up many adolescents' first sexual experiences. Young people use their fantasies as a way to explore their sexuality, to discover what works to arouse them sexually. As young people become clearer about what they find sexually stimulating, they often make use of their preferred masturbatory fantasies as a kind of rehearsal or wish list for their hoped-for later enactment.[9] It is not unusual for children and adolescents to engage in such practice sessions for a number of years before they actually engage in sexual activities with other people. When such solo performances become repetitive and enhanced by the physical rewards of orgasm, they are more likely to become securely lodged in individuals' preferred personal sexual scripts.[10]

Thirty-seven participants provided information about the ages at which they began masturbation.[11] Twenty-two of them (59 percent) remembered having begun masturbating either as children[12] or while they were in their teens.[13] A number of those participants who started to masturbate at the earliest ages shared two features in common. Firstly, five of the six participants who reported that they either masturbated by simulating the male role in the missionary position of heterosexual coitus or masturbated with a penis substitute in their trousers began masturbating by the age of eleven years.[14] In addition, five of the eight participants who said that they had masturbated "as often as possible" began their masturbatory practices by the age of thirteen years.[15] The remaining individuals in each of these categories did not provide specific information as to the ages at which they had begun their autoeroticism.[16] It would seem that there may be some correlation among these participants between early onset of masturbation and the desire for frequent male-style autoerotic sexual release.

In addition, most participants who recalled having masturbated as teenagers also recalled imagining themselves performing as heterosexual males in the fantasies which brought them to orgasm. Therefore most participants who made use of masturbation and erotic fantasy as a rehearsal for later sexual interactions were thereby priming themselves to prefer the sexual practices of straight men.

"I Hated My Body! Why Would I Want to Masturbate?"

Fifteen participants (40.5 percent) did not start to masturbate until they were adults.[17] Three overlapping factors seemed to contribute to the delayed initiation of masturbation in these participants. Aaron and Jack said that they were ignorant of the possibility of masturbation. Six participants (16 percent) expressed very negative feelings about their bodies which contributed to their inability to find sexual pleasure in them during their adolescence.[18] In addition, most of those who delayed the onset of their masturbatory practices did not begin masturbation until after they had begun their transitions into men. In other words, their unhappiness with their bodies was such that they refused to touch themselves sexually until they could more realistically imagine themselves sexually performing as men.[19]

Mel succinctly explained why many participants were unable to sexually satisfy themselves until later in their lives. He said, "I hated my body! Why would I want to masturbate? I didn't touch my body at all!" Morgan expressed similar sentiments: "I really didn't like my body. . . . I was cut off from the neck down." Rick and Darren were unable to deal with their bodies at all until they became men's bodies. Rick remembered the way she felt:

> My personal anguish was constant. . . . I was never comfortable or happy with myself, even privately. I never looked at myself in the mirror, or getting out of the shower, or any of those things. I never touched myself sexually. I did reasonably well at disassociating myself from the things that I could not handle.

Darren's memories of her relationship with her body as a teenager also precluded anything as intimate as masturbation. Darren remembered her feelings about her body like this:

> I don't think I ever looked in the mirror except to comb my hair. . . . There was a definite alienation and estrangement . . . It wasn't a part of me. It was there, but it wasn't a part of me. . . . I wouldn't look at myself naked. . . . I didn't masturbate. . . . I guess the hate wasn't there initially, because I didn't even recognize it as part of me. . . . So, I kind of divorced it from myself. But, there was definitely a tremendous feeling of queasiness and uneasiness. And . . . there was feelings of disgust and such. . . . I wasn't even sexually conscious. It was all up here. I didn't even want to touch my body.

Despite their ignorance about masturbation or their alienation from their bodies, all of these participants were attracted to other females during their adolescence. Thus, although they did not have the reinforcement of orgasm to accompany their fantasies, they, like their masturbating counterparts, mentally fashioned images of their desired relationships. As well, all of them but Morgan became involved in consensual sexual relationships with females, males, or both during their adolescence. Thus it would seem that their lack of interest in autoeroticism did not indicate a corresponding lack of interest in interpersonal sexuality.

At a bare minimum, masturbation usually requires physical engagement with one's own body. To do so requires (1) sexual desire, (2) knowledge of how to achieve one's aims, and (3) a willingness to proceed. It would seem that all participants had at least some level of sexual interest, although two of them didn't know that masturbation was a possible option for them. The remaining thirteen participants who did not begin to masturbate until adulthood were delayed by their aversion to touching their own bodies in a sexually intimate way. They were repulsed by precisely those aspects of their physiognomy which were most sexually sensitive. Four of these thirteen people overcame this obstacle while still living as women.[20] Nine participants were able to find autoerotic sexual satisfaction only after their bodies began to look, feel, taste, sound, and smell more like the men whom they had long felt themselves to be.[21]

Masturbatory Fantasies

Well over three-quarters (82 percent) of the twenty-two participants who masturbated as adolescents said that they did so while imagining themselves as men.[22] All of them except Jordie and Grant imagined themselves to be straight men wooing heterosexual females. Jordie and Grant envisioned themselves as gay men. Walter, who had a bisexual identity, also sometimes thought of herself as a gay man. In addition, Robin, who sometimes pictured herself as a straight woman, more often saw herself as a straight man; Stan said that he didn't remember having any view of herself as either male or female when she masturbated; and Keith and Larry didn't say anything either way. Ed seemed to be speaking for most of these people when he recalled about her adolescence: "I spent half my life fantasizing about being a male and being with females."

One common ruse which participants employed was to fantasize themselves as another person altogether. Peter created a male persona who could do what Peter could not do:

> How can I fantasize making love to a woman when I'm not equipped completely to make love to a woman? . . . Okay, in . . . most of my fan-

tasy life . . . I could be . . . this other person who is normal. Now, that person. . . . he can be as normal as possible. Absolutely.

Eli also created many male fantasy characters for herself to be in her masturbatory reveries. Eli started out masturbating with simple scenarios when she was "three or four" years old. As she got older, they became more complex. By the time she was in her teen years, Eli recalled, "I got real good at it. I'm an expert. I could write books about orgasms."

Bruce did not learn to masturbate until she was eighteen years old. He recalled, "I'm sure I heard it was something that boys did, but I didn't know what it was." However, before that time, Bruce had engaged in erotic fantasies about women:

I would read for hours [my dad's] *Playboys*, and I would look at women's bodies. And I remember seeing women's bodies in Sears' magazines. You know, in underwear. But, like, these were beautiful, voluptuous women. And I liked what I saw. . . . I just knew that I liked watching it. I liked looking at it. . . . I didn't want to be that. Then there were some stuff with men too, and that's what I wanted to be. I wanted to be this hard body next to this soft body.

Bill also projected herself into a male self-image in her adolescent masturbation fantasies. Bill remembered that her imagination helped her to counteract the mentally debilitating effects of her pubertal changes:

These changes affected my self-esteem which, by now, was heading rapidly down the old commode. I hated my body, my life, myself. I think I had an increase in libido during this time because I masturbated with greater urgency and climax especially when watching Steve Reeves' Hercules movies. I would watch him carry some scantily clad woman into a cave and be up and in the bathroom getting off. I had an increased interest in romance. I lived it out, as I did so many things, in my fantasies, or via TV.

Other participants were able to transform themselves into men in their erotic fantasies. They were often gratified by fantasizing themselves performing sexually with a full complement of male sexual appurtenances.[23] For example, Sam, Steven, and Howie masturbated in adolescence by humping against something while imagining themselves as fully equipped males engaging in coitus.

When Sam started masturbating at approximately the age of three years, she masturbated entirely for the pleasurable sensations but had no erotic fantasies. Sam recalled that when her mother caught her masturbating as a child, her mother looked at her with "the absolute look of hate, pure, outright hatred . . . just like I was the most disgusting thing in the world." Not to be deterred, Sam carried on. As Sam reached puberty, she began to picture herself as a man in her masturbatory fantasies. She fantasized that she had a penis and stimulated herself by humping a pillow in "a male position . . . any time I had an opportunity."

Steven likewise started to masturbate as a three year old girl. Like Sam, Steven masturbated avidly and in a masculine style. Steven "mounted the couch" so frequently that when Steven was five years old her little sister wanted to know why she played "horsey" on the couch so often. When the nuns at Catholic school preached that masturbation was wrong, Steven rationalized, "If it was a sin, why would God make my arms long enough to reach it?" and continued to give herself pleasure. As a teenager, Steven's thoughts turned to girls. Steven recalled:

> Around twelve, thirteen years old I started becoming very attracted to females, and I thought, "Well, this is par for the course. This is normal. Wouldn't it be a little abnormal to feel like a male and be attracted to men?" . . . I didn't know anything about sex 'til about that time. So, I didn't think of intercourse 'cause I didn't know anything about it other than just kissing and feeling a romantic feeling. . . . I always fantasized myself as a full-grown man.

Later, to further help her to live out her fantasies, Steven developed a "phantom penis" in her mind to counteract her "totally repulsive" and "hated" female body.

Luther, too, always envisioned herself as a properly endowed male. Luther remembered:

> Even though I had these enormous breasts, I had worked it out in my mind that they just had no feeling, and that my genitalia was male. And when it came to a point where I knew it was not, but I knew that I wanted to have sex, then I got a prosthesis.

Grant also always imagined that she had "all the right equipment" to be a man in her mostly sadomasochistic sexual fantasies. However, Grant was not rehearsing to be a straight man but rather to be a gay man. Approximately 30 percent of the time Grant masturbated to images of herself as a heterosexual male. After only a few years, the heterosexual images faded altogether.

Robin was the only participant who reported having had a mixed gender catalogue of sexual fantasies during her adolescence. Robin learned to masturbate at eleven years of age, and her imagery included heterosexual rape scenes. She pictured herself as either a man or a woman in these thoughts, although more often she saw herself playing the male rapist role.

In sum, all but three participants who masturbated as teenagers did so while imagining themselves to be men most or, more commonly, all of the time. By so doing, they were both formulating and enacting their gender, their sex, and their sexual orientation identities. Their masturbatory fantasies helped them to crystallize their identities by providing them with arenas in which to experiment with and develop their masculine propensities free from the judgements of their peers or families. In the privacy of their fantasies they still had to contend with their own internalized version of the social values of the world in which they lived. However, the glory of the creative imagination is that no hurdles are too high and no future impossible to achieve. In their own minds, they could begin to envision themselves as the men whom they one day hoped to become.

Summary and Commentary

Fifty-nine percent of reporting participants said that they had begun to masturbate by the time they reached adulthood.[24] This proportion is similar to what other researchers have found to be the case among girls who came of age in the same decades. The percentage of participants who came to enjoy these practices at an early age[25] was also in line with previous research results for general-population girls.[26] Participants' adolescent masturbatory practices were, however, unusual in two regards. In one instance, there was an unusually large number of particularly avid masturbators. Forty-one percent of participants who masturbated during adolescence reported that they did so twice a week or more.[27] This rate is at least twice that reported elsewhere among other teenaged girls.[28] The other aspect of their autoeroticism which was different from that of most teenaged girls was their almost universal employment of fantasies which featured themselves as men. Eighty-two percent of participants who masturbated at all during their adolescence made use of this type of fantasy to stimulate themselves.[29] In both of these regards, they showed themselves to follow more closely male, rather than female, patterns.

By the time participants had reached adolescence, they had already passed a number of years indulging in nonerotic fantasies about being or becoming boys, men, or males. During that time, they were also frequently playing beside boys in masculine activities. In the course of their formative years, many participants were therefore able to build a well-fortified edifice of masculine aptitudes, attitudes, and beliefs. When they reached adolescence, especially with the advent of puberty, the ground began to shake under the masculine self-structures which they had built. Erotic and romantic fantasies provided many participants with a way to quell some of their growing tremulousness. To imagine themselves becoming properly potent men was not only a salubrious stop-gap measure but also the logical next step in the developmental stream which they thus far had been pursuing. Using such masturbatory fantasies allowed them to subtly subvert some of the chilling effects that puberty might otherwise have had on their fledgling masculine gender and sex identities. The fact that these fantasies usually resulted in orgasm only served to more incisively encode the desirability of masculine gender and sex identities in the habituated response patterns of their bodies, as well as in their minds.

Adolescent Heterosexual Relationships

Most participants felt the social pressure to take part in teenaged heterosexual explorations, and most of them complied to some degree. However most of those who did try out heterosexuality seemed to have done so with some reluctance. They only minimally became involved with boys during their adolescence. For some of them, these brief interludes constituted their entire heterosexual careers. For other participants, their limited engagements with heterosexuality during their adolescence were predominantly stalling tactics used to postpone their later entry into opposite-sex relations. There were also a minority of participants who made good use of their teenaged years to ascertain whether or not heterosexuality was appropriate for them as females. A few participants who began their investigations of heterosexuality in their late teens continued their search for suitable sexual identities into their adulthoods. However, by the end of adolescence, most participants had determined that they were not cut out to be straight women.

Just Looking: Little or No Adolescent Heterosexual Experience

More than two-thirds of participants (70.5 percent)[30] had had little or no voluntary heterosexual experience by the time they had become adults. As adolescent girls, fifteen participants (34 percent) managed to avoid all consensual relations of a romantic or sexual nature with males;[31] nine (20.5 percent) of whom never voluntarily functioned as heterosexual women.[32] The participants in this study were clearly less heterosexually oriented during their adolescence than are most teenaged girls.

Regrettably, their voluntary abstention from heterosexuality did not mean that none of them were coerced into such experiences. In addition to Ed and Peter, whose only adolescent heterosexual experiences were coercive ones, Nathan reported that his only lifetime heterosexual experience was a date rape situation which occurred partly as a result of Nathan's extreme naiveté regarding heterosexuality. The encounter took place when Nathan was a girl of sixteen visiting in a foreign country. Nathan described how it happened:

> We were at this bar with the family I was staying with. We had been drinking some and [my date] started kissing me. I found it very enjoyable to have the affection. Then he asked if he could "sleep" with me. Well, being the naive person I was then, I thought he meant actually sleeping. So I said yes and we went out to a spot in the yard. He pulled his pants down and took my hand to touch his penis. I was afraid and not really sure of what was going on. He felt me after pulling my pants off and then laid me down. He spread my legs and entered me. I screamed and tried to pull him off. He kept trying to reassure me. He went in and out a few times and pulled off. He didn't ejaculate in me and I was apparently very tight. . . . He got rather disgusted, and shook my hand, and left. Not a very pleasant experience. . . . I liked the affection but the sex bothered me a lot. . . . After this experience I figured out I wasn't attracted to men.

Another sixteen participants (36 percent) had limited voluntary heterosexual experience during their teen years.[33] They did some desultory dating, experimented with kissing and various degrees of touching, and perhaps tried heterosexual intercourse a few times. Their level of romantic engagement varied from those who were quite detached and only participated in heterosexuality as a sop to social pressures or out of an otherwise disinterested curiosity, to others who either enjoyed males as buddies or felt strong romantic attractions to them.

Eleven participants (25 percent) dated and may have partaken of adolescent exploratory kissing and fondling but never willingly took the leap into heterosexual intercourse during their teen years.[34] Steven's attitude was typical of that of several participants who began to date when they felt they could no longer resist the social pressure to do so.

> The dating, the things you're supposed to do as a female, I tried to do. Not because I wanted to, but because I didn't want them to know that I was different. And maybe, in a sense, I didn't want to accept that I was different at that stage. That I really wanted to be what other people wanted me to be. And I really tried to be that, and it was not something that I could deal with for very long. . . . And to tell you the truth, most of the time I felt like I was a gay man . . . when I would have to kiss a guy goodbye, and it was like a service I had to perform to make myself look normal.

Eli, Fred, and Morgan were even less enthusiastic about heterosexual dating. Eli and her friends dated boys but, it seemed, mostly as a joke. Eli recalled that when she and her girlfriends dressed up for dates they spoke of it as "repulsive" and thought of their dates in derogatory terms. Eli recalled:

These boys asked us to go out, and we had names for each of them. My so-called boyfriend was the "Squid," one of them was the "Snail," and the other one was "Octopus," or something. Sometimes when they would come around we would sort of hide our bicycles inside and pretend we weren't home and other times we would dress up and go out with them and they'd just sit there with those sweaty hands and kind of stare at us through the movie. . . . They always seemed to be undergoing a terrible sexual desire kind of thing. I thought it was a joke. . . . It was kind of a sense of pity, at least, that I had for these guys and revulsion . . . I kind of enjoyed the dressing up part but then with these sweaty hands and glaring eyes, you know, people touching my hair made me sick.

Both Fred and Morgan felt actual physical revulsion at heterosexual contact of even the most elementary kind. Fred remembered having to date as one of the worst parts of being a teenager.

I was in Junior Achievement . . . and we had to go to a party and a dinner and, of course, you had to have an escort. And I had to go with a guy. And it was very depressing. I felt like I was out with my brother, but yet I knew this guy felt like it was a date. And I remember him giving me a kiss on the cheek when we got home, and I remember going in and throwing up cause I felt like, "God, I've just been kissed by another man." You know, it's disgusting! It was horrifying, really.

Morgan dated from time to time when she was a teenager, but mostly with ill effects. Morgan may have reacted poorly to any hint of heterosexual contact, but her parents reacted violently, as did some of her dates. Morgan remembered her teenaged heterosexual experiences this way:

I was walking through these woods with my girlfriend and two guys, and my brother saw us. He went and told my dad. . . . And this was the worst incident that ever happened. I got in and my mother was saying, "This isn't a goddamn whorehouse!" and she slapped me. And my father came in and beat the shit out of me. They cut my hair way up. . . . They just butchered my hair. . . . And I heard my father say, "Well what did he do to you? Screw you? What a pig!"

And I was so afraid of sex, there's no way, you know. If he only knew how little interest I had in men anyway. . . . Like if someone started kissing me or something. I never let them have like intercourse or anything, and even if they tried to touch the breasts, my stomach would just be vibrating. I couldn't deal with it.

I was almost raped once. This guy, I actually had to let him do oral sex on me or I think he was going to rape me. It was one of those situations. And he sort of forced me to give him a blowjob. And I did it for a little while and I said I can't do it anymore. I couldn't stand it any longer. And then he started to rip my pants. . . . but I didn't do hardly anything he wanted me to. I just couldn't do it. . . . There have been a couple of other times like that.

Grant's few forays into heterosexuality shared some features with both Fred's and Morgan's. During adolescence, Grant only rarely dated, but she had a very active sexual fantasy life. Like Fred, Grant saw herself as a gay man when she imagined herself in sexual liaisons with males. Unlike Fred, Grant was always attracted to the idea of gay men's sexuality. Like Morgan, Grant's only genital heterosexual contact was a date rape when she was seventeen years old. Grant was abducted, brutally bound, beaten, and raped by a man she was supposed to be dating.

Walter's approach exemplified a startlingly different adolescent attitude toward heterosexual contact. Walter was particularly curious about the functioning of male sexual organs and was exceptionally aggressive about satisfying her curiosity. At the time, Walter thought of herself as a bisexual man and therefore felt that her contact with teenaged boys was undertaken as a gay man. Walter remembered relating to approximately six different boys.

> The kid across the street . . . was about three years older than me and was the horniest fucking kid you ever want to encounter in your life. He was incredible. I think he suffered from priapism. The guy had a constant erection. . . . He was very muscular, very athletic. Big. He had a very big penis. I swear it must have been ten inches long. Very developed, at sixteen he was totally a man. . . .
>
> My father . . . had a lot of sexual material and I always used to share this stuff with [this kid], we were buddies. So eventually, after looking at all these dirty magazines, one thing led to another. . . . I basically mostly just did stuff to him. Because I really wasn't into him doing stuff to me. . . .
>
> I enjoyed it a lot. . . . I had given him the material hoping that he would get turned on. . . . I was just feeling like finding things out, I wanted to know what was going on. . . . I never even took my clothes off. . . . I would masturbate later. . . . I was really into it. . . . it was very exciting, very exciting.

Five other participants were also interested in finding out what heterosexuality was all about. They went further than Walter did with her experimentation; they investigated heterosexual intercourse.[35] There was no romance involved; nor was there any reward beyond the satisfaction of their curiosity.

Simon and Tony took advantage of relationships which they already had with men who were their buddies. They each tried to have heterosexual intercourse only one time, but as Simon said, "It didn't work very well." Tony, who drunkenly happened into bed one time with a dear friend, was sorely disappointed with the affair.

> I have never been sexually . . . or romantically attracted to a man. The one experience I did have was with a close friend, somebody I cared about very much. Someone who cared about me. It was kind of not really planned but kind of expected to happen. Got a little drunk and this and that. And, man, was it disappointing! I really felt bad that there was absolutely no excitement in it for me at all. There was no physical excitement, there was no physical pleasure. It . . . was absolutely nothing.

Scott and Stan did their coital experimentation with boys about whom they had no concern. Scott enjoyed the physical aspect of sex with a few young men before abandoning the whole project. Stan remembered making use of a willing fellow known as "horny Hank." Once was enough to satisfy Stan's curiosity. As Stan put it:

> I used him. I mean, I used him because I was curious about what was the deal. And when I found out what the deal was I was done with him. Like, thank you very much. I was nice to him, but I didn't want it to go any further. I didn't want to get involved in regular intercourse. Like, no, I didn't want to do that.

Roger experimented a few times with heterosexual coitus. She started dating when she was in her last year of high school. She dated two boys throughout that last year of school but never felt other than a buddy's fondness for either of them. After high school, Roger became enamored of two traveling men, a trucker and a sailor. Roger was contemplating marriage to the trucker, but when she found that "it came time to get down to the nitty-gritty" and she "couldn't handle it," she jettisoned the idea. Roger finally "went to bed several times" with the sailor, who was on shore leave. Although she did not experience orgasm, Roger recalled enjoying the sex.

The most striking theme to emerge from these stories is that most participants exhibited little interest in heterosexuality during their teen years. Approximately a third of them (34 percent) rejected heterosexuality altogether during their adolescence,[36] although three of them had it forced upon them anyway. Approximately another one-third of participants (36 percent) had only a dilettantish association with heterosexuality during their teen years.[37] Some of those participants who dated boys felt as though they were actually behaving homosexually by doing so. As long as things between themselves and their dates remained simply companionate, they could interpret the state of affairs as male buddy-style relationships. When their dates wanted things to become more sexual, most participants quickly became disaffected with their male friends. Most of those few participants who initiated sexual relations with males quickly satisfied their curiosity and moved on to other concerns.

Loveless Searching:
Serious Heterosexual Involvements during Adolescence

Those few participants who reported that they had made more serious attempts at being heterosexual females did so for a variety of reasons and in a variety of ways. Harry, Darcy, Phil, Ken, and Jordie became involved in relatively long (by teenaged standards) relationships because they were useful to them in some way. Keith and Ron said that their adolescent heterosexuality consisted mostly of a series of exploratory casual sexual encounters. Lee, Dale, and Aaron each married in late adolescence mostly because that was what was expected of them. Sam also married, in flight from possible lesbianism. Both Alan and Jorge became involved with male-bodied transgendered persons as part of their own searches for identity. Alan also became a teenaged street prostitute who serviced a variety of male clients with various tastes.

Harry, Darcy, and Phil got involved in loveless relationships with male peers for utilitarian purposes. Harry was a teenaged musician who found that her musical career was facilitated by having particular young men as her boyfriends. She dated two fellows in succession during her upper-school years. These associations gained her "acceptance" and cost her little in emotional or physical output. Of the first of these boyfriends, Harry said: "He was a very nice guy. He never touched me. And for the first six months of our relationship he was up north in a juvenile camp. . . . So, it was a wonderful relationship." With a similar calculating attitude, Harry decided when it was time to lose her virginity. He told this tale about the incident:

> When I turned eighteen . . . I couldn't decide whether to give blood or get drunk. And I thought, "I'll get drunk." . . . At that point in my life, I became very frightened that I was going to die and never have experienced sex of any kind. . . . So, I went to a bar. . . . I remember going to the washroom, and there was a table of about eight guys, and I winked and I did all that. . . . I came back to my table, and said to my friend, "Come on. We're going to this table." . . . We went back to one of the guys' apartments, and . . . we started to get sexually involved, and I said, "I have a confession" and he said "What?" and I said, "I'm a virgin." He said he was married. I was furious, and I threw him off the bed. And he said he was separated. We ended up having intercourse. I was very drunk. It hurt, but he was very gentleman. I remember thinking that he would be a very good lover for someone.

Darcy was also quite detached about how she became heterosexually involved. Darcy's own description of how, as a teenager, she related to men was that she "had a bit of a nasty streak." Darcy, who started having intercourse with boys when she was about fourteen years old, said that what she would do was "seduce somebody, and then run the relationship, and be serially monogamous." Darcy reported that she "was in control . . . in a very clinical way" of the "really screwed up" boys with whom she had sexual relations. She finally gave up on these bloodless relationships after making use of one young man to facilitate her final departure from her parents' home. Darcy explained that the last young man had made one too many demands, "So, one night I finally got fed up, and I balled him all night until he couldn't even see, and I walked out. And I left, 'cause I'd finally had it. And that's the last time I slept with a guy."

Phil could force herself to date boys only when it would get her closer to a girl whom she liked. During adolescence, Phil tried several different times to date boys, even getting drunk once and trying to have intercourse with a young man. Each time she "just couldn't go through with it." The only time that Phil was able to maintain a heterosexual relationship during her teen years was when she did so because she wanted to be able to double date with another girl to whom she was attracted. That lasted for a full year but ended when Phil "couldn't take it any more."

Ken looked hopefully to her male peers for solace to counteract the misery of the sexual abuse to which her father regularly subjected her. Ken said that as a teen she was romantically attracted to certain young men because it felt good to know that she "was capable to love someone or feel something for someone." Ken also "always dreamed that I really wanted to have sex with them. I wanted to know what it would be like to lie down and actually have sex." When she did finally have intercourse with a young man on several occasions in the back seat of a car, it was because she didn't want people to think that she was lesbian. Ken was "uncomfortable" and "embarrassed" about the experiences and had no more.

Jordie was unusual in that, from a very young age, she was attracted to men at the same time as she maintained an unwavering sense of herself as male. When Jordie was a teenaged girl, she had a one-year sexual relationship with a male peer. The relationship had little emotional content. As Jordie put it, "it was just fast, relieve himself, him on top." It was extremely confusing to her because, on the one hand, she was attracted to the boy, but, on the other hand, it seemed to be a heterosexual relationship at the same time as she felt like a boy. Jordie ended it because she felt guilty about the dishonesty of deceiving her partner into thinking that they were having a straight relationship.

Ron and Keith tested heterosexuality more broadly. Ron had casual sexual encounters with many men starting when she was fourteen. Her first heterosexual intercourse was with a 35 year old man for whom she was posing as an artist's model. Ron recalled "using him to see what the act was like." She went on to try heterosexuality with other types of men in other circumstances to see if she could find any satisfaction in heterosexual relations. In the end, Ron concluded, "I never did like it with men. . . . I couldn't handle the male psyche. . . . I was too competitive. . . . I couldn't respond to men as a heterosexual female." After experimenting with approximately twenty short heterosexual relationships and never achieving an orgasm, Ron abandoned the project.

Keith considered herself a "nice Catholic girl" because she "remained a virgin till well after my eighteenth birthday." But Keith also suffered from low self-esteem as a teenager. She allowed herself to be "taken advantage of" because she was "sexually attractive" and because she "just wanted the physical closeness and being intimate with someone." Keith recalled that she "didn't get anything in return" except "a few drops of romance that I was able to squeeze out of it." Keith remembered her sexual adventures this way:

> I sucked off a lot of guys who didn't give a shit about me. . . . They were men that I liked. I chose to put myself in that position. Usually they were guys I picked up at the beach. This continued not just in my high school years but later teen years also, after high school. Usually I would perform oral sex on them, and they would get off. And I obtained a certain amount of hugging and physical closeness, which is something I thrived on, in the process. And that was the end of it. I never really dated in my teen years. It wasn't until later on I began to understand I had a right to be taken out on a date. Kind of a sick way to look at it. None of these guys ever took me out. Why should they? I was willing to come to their place to give them head and then leave.

When Keith did lose her virginity it was with a much older man about whom she spoke in a detached and unromantic way. Keith remembered him as "a man twice my age who I lived with for several years and he more or less supported me. And that was, I think . . . probably a father image to me. It was a way to get out of my parents' house and still be in a reasonably secure living situation."

Only four participants went so far as to marry near the end of their teen years. Lee's marriage was the shortest, the actual cohabitation lasting only a few months. Dale remained married to her husband for three years. Aaron and Sam made the most profound commitments to marriage. Their marriages lasted ten years. I will discuss their courtships here and present their married lives in more detail in chapter 16 covering participants' adult lives before their transitions into men.

Lee was a virgin in her late teens when she started dating her future husband. They dated for a few months before they had sexual intercourse. Lee said that at the time she thought that she was in love with him because she had an orgasm with him. As Lee put it, "that's how much I knew. I figured that if [you have orgasm] . . . that has to be love. I didn't know any better." Lee also "felt guilty every time" they made love because "in those days, you were either a good girl or a bad girl" and she knew that "it was wrong" to be having sex outside of marriage. After only a couple of months of having sex, Lee discovered that she was pregnant. Lee said, "I was scared. I would have had an abortion, but I really didn't know how to go about that." So at the age of nineteen, Lee, somewhat reluctantly, went to the justice of the peace and they got married. In Lee's words, the marriage "was a disaster."

Dale also married the first man with whom she had sex. Dale had lived a very isolated life up until that point, and therefore she had very little perspective from which to judge her situation. Dale recalled that at the time she "had no idea" what heterosexual intercourse might be like. Her husband-to-be taught her about heterosexual sex and "controlled" their sex life together. Like Lee, Dale thought that since she was having sex with a man then she must also be in love with him. When her future husband asked her to marry him, Dale accepted because "I felt I was doomed. I had to be a woman. It was impossible for me to be a guy." Dale said that going through with the marriage was "a bloody mistake" because "he turned out to be a drinker, and an abuser, and he would run around." The marriage lasted three years and produced one child.

Aaron got married at nineteen because "that's what you do." She married a young man whom she had been seeing whenever he was home on leave from the military. Aaron enjoyed his company and described the relationship as a fraternal one with a sexual component. Aaron still felt a lot of fondness for the man decades later, at the time of his interviews. At the age of nineteen, Aaron felt that she was "making the best choice for the situation," which he described this way:

> As long as I'm stuck being a damn female, I might as well do the one thing that I like about being female, which is make a lot of babies. . . . As long as you've got it and you're stuck with it, find a way to enjoy it. So [it was] a situation that was probably grossly unfair to him . . . because I knew what I was a lot more than he knew who I was . . . because I simply couldn't tell him. There weren't words. I didn't have the vocabulary. . . . . And yet, we enjoyed each other sexually. The sexual part of the marriage wasn't the problem. . . . I didn't enjoy his body in the sense of, like, kissing and that sort of thing. . . . It didn't turn me on like a woman's body. But I enjoyed sex, and I enjoyed making babies, and

enjoyed having kids. And, like I say, he was a hell of a nice man to be with.

Aaron and her husband went on to have a relatively amiable ten-year marriage during which Aaron fulfilled her reproductive desires and had four children.

Sam's first marriage began as an anti-lesbian assertion. Sam remembered that it made her "tremendously angry" when people called her a lesbian, and Sam said flatly, "that's why I got married." Sam married a man sixteen years her senior whom she had known for only three months. His offer to take Sam to faraway and exotic places appealed to Sam because she was keen on the idea of "absolutely running away from everything that had ever hurt." Once they were married, her husband forced her to have sex frequently. Sam ended up having eight pregnancies which resulted in five difficult births. The relationship ended miserably ten years later.

Jorge and Alan had long-term and unusual heterosexual involvements during adolescence. Both had started to consider the idea that they might be transsexual while still in their early teen years, and this influenced their choice of partners. By the time Jorge was eighteen years old she was already engaged in gathering information about how she might accomplish gender and sex reassignment. Her first intimate relationship was with the first transsexual person she met, a pre-operative male-to-female transsexual. At the time when the relationship began, Jorge was "very upset, depressed . . . and on the verge of suicide." Jorge said, "I was so happy to meet a transsexual that I idealized her" and "I became emotionally dependent on her." Jorge felt "manipulated," "taken advantage of," and "disgusted" after allowing herself to be sexually stimulated manually by her transsexual friend. The relationship lasted about one year, and in retrospect Jorge said, "I regret the whole thing and hate that it happened."

Alan, who was also beginning to identify as a transsexual person in her later teens, had extensive adolescent sexual experience throughout her teens. Alan first ran away from home at age fourteen and became a street level sex trade worker. During her time on the streets, she "had a lot of paid and unpaid sex with anyone," which soon resulted in an uncompleted pregnancy. She was also raped at age sixteen. In her work, Alan, who felt that "sex was often a drug" for her, was exposed to a wide variety of sexual proclivities and modes of gender expression. She serviced male, female, sadomasochistic, and transgendered clients. Alan recalled:

As a teenager, I felt ugly, alone, and different. I was grateful if anyone would have sex with me because I felt so undesirable as a human being. Being paid for sex made me feel that I must be worth something.

Concurrently with her prostitution, between the ages of fourteen and seventeen, Alan became involved in a heterosexual relationship with a young adult man who was a crossdresser. Her transgendered lover allowed Alan to further explore her incipient transsexual identity. Upon retiring from prostitution, Alan ceased to relate to men sexually until much later in life, when she briefly returned to heterosexuality in an attempt to become pregnant.

To summarize, only 29.5 percent of participants made a concerted effort to explore heterosexual relations during their adolescence.[38] However, fewer than half of these people did so with any significant emotional involvement.[39] Furthermore, two of the five who did care about the males with whom they became intimate chose transgendered males as their partners.[40] For the most part, those participants who had more than a fleeting flirtation with heterosexuality did so in a detached way. Those few participants who did allow themselves to fall in love with men, with the exception of Aaron and Alan, found that their hopes were unfounded and their affections were spurned.

Summary and Commentary

The unmistakable pattern which stands out from these stories is one of disinterest and alienation from almost any form of heterosexual relations during adolescence. Thirty-four percent of participants never voluntarily dated or otherwise became romantically or sexually engaged with males.[41] Another 36 percent of participants had only cursory heterosexual involvements.[42] Eleven participants were introduced involuntarily to heterosexual relations.[43]

It is noteworthy that almost half of those who did give heterosexuality an extensive try did so either for self-serving utilitarian purposes or entirely within exploitative and loveless relationships.[44] Among the six who had committed relationships with men whom they loved, four retrospectively considered their unions to have been grievous errors. Furthermore, one of the two people who did not regret her lengthy and committed relationship during her adolescence had formed a partnership with another transgendered person in the context of concurrent "compulsive" prostitution.

These trends make sense when considered in light of the gender identities with which participants struggled throughout their teens. Although the unmistakable evidence wrought by puberty forced participants to recognize the facticity of their femaleness, most still clung to the belief that they were, in some intangible ways, male. Many participants therefore evaded heterosexuality altogether, as it contradicted their self-images as males. However, the physical reality of having female bodies was enough to convince some participants to throw their lots in with the overwhelming social expectations that they would explore heterosexuality.

Many of those who followed this path did so in a stereotypically masculine fashion. Some remained emotionally detached, and sexually objectified the men and boys with whom they interacted; it is no wonder that they found little emotional satisfaction in their escapades. Some felt distressed at what seemed to them to be a charade of heterosexuality. They felt male, and all but one of them felt the common adolescent male revulsion at what seemed to them to be falsified male homosexual relations. Two participants approached their heterosexual relations with transgendered persons in ways which allowed them some expression of their gender and sex identities. Clearly the reality of the social expectations placed on straight women was radically in contradiction with the self-images of most participants during their adolescence. This disjuncture worked to seriously undermine the possibilities for participants having successful heterosexual relations during their teen years.

Adolescent Homosexual Relationships

During their adolescence, participants were far more romantically and sexually interested in females than they were in males. However, this is not to say that they were more actively involved in sexual exploration with their female friends than they had been with their male friends. In fact, almost the same number of participants abstained from homosexual involvements during their teen years as abstained from heterosexual ones. The qualitative difference lay in the attractions which participants felt. In the first instance, fifteen of the sixteen who did not become involved in heterosexual relations during their adolescence also said that they had not been interested in doing so. By contrast, fifteen of the sixteen who did not become involved in homosexual liaisons during their adolescence said that they *had* been attracted to girls or women but had not felt able to act upon their attractions.[45]

By the time they had completed adolescence, all but two participants had developed some sexual interest in women. One of the two who was not interested, Jordie, identified as a gay man. The other, Larry, had "never been sexually or romantically attracted to either sex." Most participants did indeed become homosexually involved during their adolescence. A little less than one-quarter of participants (24 percent) had only limited homosexual encounters during their teens.[46] Forty percent of participants became seriously enamored of and sexually involved with other females.[47]

Three of the relationships which participants began during their teen years became lifelong partnerships.[48]

Girls Don't Do That: No Adolescent Homosexual Involvements

One-third of all participants[49] were sexually or romantically attracted to females during their adolescence but did not act upon their feelings during their teen years[50] even though several of them had been interested in girls or women since their childhoods.[51] The reasons they gave for their abstentions, when they gave any explanations at all, were mostly three-fold. One reason which was given by several people was that they were sexually ignorant and had no idea that it was possible for two females to have sexual relations. They were only aware of a heterosexual option at that point in their lives and thus took their attractions to girls as an indicator of their repressed maleness. A second frequent impediment to participants' acting upon their desires was their belief that homosexuality was wrong and that they should therefore deny any such feelings as much as possible. A third explanation for a lack of action was some participants' profound ambivalence toward the whole idea of sexuality.

Aaron was the most articulate of those who, during their adolescence, were ignorant of the existence of lesbianism. Aaron started having "mad crushes" on other girls in 1950, at the age of fifteen, around the time she started to see the effects of her puberty. Although Aaron was clearly aroused by the presence of certain of her girlfriends, she had no idea what one might do about such feelings. Aaron described how she felt then:

> The times were such that girls did hold hands and hug and nobody called them "lezzies" or anything in school. People were innocent. Two girls could not do anything. We did not talk about the little piece of equipment that girls have for entertainment, in fact I didn't even know exactly how that worked. . . .
>
> I was physically aroused and all that with a girlfriend but, you see, you can talk about loving a girlfriend, you could sign a card "love" to a girlfriend and give her gifts and so on, and this was socially acceptable in those days. And so I knew that I loved more intensely than they did but it was innocent. . . .
>
> Hey, I knew I had to wash out underpants after . . . spending a night with a woman that I was madly in love with. . . . I didn't do anything sexual. I didn't know what to do! I was innocent because I was ignorant. But I remember being so terribly horny that I stayed awake until three in the morning. . . . it'd been so much easier if I'd have known, just go into the other room, jerk off, and go to sleep. But I couldn't do this. I didn't have the necessary sex training. Boys were queers, and queer boys were simply boys who not only might be involved with other

boys, but they were effeminate. And one thing I wasn't was effeminate. So there's no way in hell I could have been called queer, right?

Robin similarly recalled that, as a teenager, she "felt that only boys could love women, or that only boys could be [sexual] with girls." The possibility of acting on her attractions for other girls was also beyond Terry's ken. Terry plainly "knew that I could not physically make love to a woman."

As a teenager, Stan also believed that sexual involvements with girls were "out of the question" and so she had to make do with "secret admiration . . . from afar" because she "just couldn't compete" with the boys for her girlfriends' affections. This is how Stan recalled feeling at the time:

> That really embarrassed me. I knew that that was wrong. . . . I fantasized things that I wanted to do—to live with them, and be with them, and date them. . . . I felt that that was wrong . . . for me to do that with girls. . . . So, I didn't tell anybody about that. . . . I didn't know what a lesbian was. I didn't know that was a possible choice. . . . [I thought] I was the only one. . . . Nobody else is doing this. . . . This is very abnormal.

Peter, Sam, Bruce, and Stan all felt themselves wanting to become sexually involved with females while they were still in their teens but couldn't bring themselves to do so because of their fear of the ramifications of breaking such a strong social taboo. Peter thought that her childhood and adolescent attractions to girls meant that she must be "gay," but Peter recalled, "There's always been the social stigma about being gay. . . . that really backed me off. That kept me really under wraps." In fact, Peter was never even willing to consider kissing a female until after beginning to live as a man.

Sam, who also felt very strong romantic and sexual pulls toward women when she was a teenager, said that she felt a lot of "I want, I can't." Like Peter, Sam had a "very limited" understanding of lesbianism and a very low opinion of it. Sam outlined the nature of the predicament in which she felt herself to be at the time:

> At that point, I knew what I wanted, but I wasn't right for it. I wanted to be a male and be with a woman. But I wasn't, my body wasn't right for it. And the idea of two females was just, I mean, like, I got fighting mad when I started getting called a lesbian.

Bruce had very explicitly sexual thoughts about women when she was a teenager, but for reasons similar to Sam's, she did not act on them either. Bruce remembered:

> I used to get out my parents' Sears catalogue and look at the women in their underwear. I got turned on. . . . But I thought, I can't do this the

way I am. I have to be a boy because girls don't like girls. . . . So, I saw men and women together. So, I thought, that's what it's supposed to be, and all the girls liked me because I was a boy. . . . But I used to put those kinds of feelings behind me, I think, because I felt that I couldn't . . . be sexual. . . . It wasn't allowed. It wasn't right. Because, how can women be attracted to women?

During her adolescent search for identity, Bruce, like Sam, got fighting mad when it was intimated that she might be a lesbian. Bruce recounted this tale:

I worked at my dad's . . . agency, and this . . . real dyke . . . invited me to come to her house one night. . . . And I went to this bar with her, but I didn't . . . drink. Then she took me home to her house. . . . and then her lover walked in, and was really upset that I was there. And I remember the feeling that "I need to go home now." And . . . I felt sick to my stomach, for some reason, about being there. And then I remember the next day, she came up to me when I was changing a tire, and she tried to caress me, or touch me, and I just blew my stack. And I just blew it. I lost it all. . . . I couldn't admit that it felt nice to me. It was taboo. It needed to be taboo. Because it was wrong for girls to like girls. . . . It's just not okay. And I heard that she was a lesbian, and she touched me, and I blew off the handle.

Four other participants declined to move on their attractions to women because they were unsure whether they wanted to become involved in sexuality at all. Morgan, for example, thought of herself as a lesbian for a few years but said that she didn't act on her feelings during her teens because "I was too shy and I was so afraid of sex." Nathan and Gary, although both attracted to females, both chose to refrain from initiating or consenting to any kind of sexual relations until after they had made sufficient progress in their quests to become as fully male as possible. Thus neither of them had sexual relations while in their teens.

Brian ended up with a similar outcome, but for different reasons. Brian was largely sexually ignorant until late adolescence because sexuality "involved questions that we forcibly learned not to ask." For a brief time in her teens, Brian was attracted to girls, but that quickly passed and Brian settled into a more long-term antagonism toward sexuality. Brian put it this way:

Sometimes I thought about romantic relationships, like the types one reads in novels. But I felt I should be a boy, and girls were intensely repulsive. Anything related to femininity was a source of oppression that had degraded me. It was hardly easy to feel sexual attraction to either males or females, since either way I was degraded. I could withdraw into the woods and my own private world and avoid as much confrontation as possible. I found it hard to relate to people at all because sexual matters in one form or another was a major interest to most people and I wanted nothing to do with it.

It became clear from these stories that homophobia played a significant role in discouraging these participants from acting upon the attractions which they felt for females. The generalized homophobia of the decades during which they were children and adolescents acted to abort their lesbian activities mainly in two ways. Firstly, information about lesbianism was not readily available. Thus, the only sexual model to which many girls had access was a heterosexual one. Therefore, when they felt sexual desire for other females, the only logical interpretation which they could place on their feelings was that they should be males in order to have such lusts. Furthermore, since they were not males, there was nothing which they could do about their feelings but contain them and bide their time until an opportunity arose to somehow transform themselves into men. Secondly, much of the information that was available was false. Those participants who had heard of lesbianism had only the most negative of angles on the phenomenon. They had absorbed the messages which their society wanted them to believe: that lesbians were sick and dangerous people; that lesbian activity was sorely stigmatized and totally taboo. Thus those individuals who wanted to retain some modicum of self-respect and a decent standing in their society avoided tainting themselves with the stain of lesbianism.

The participants who were acting under the sway of this level of homophobia were left few alternatives. Some simply could not act. Others could only see themselves as males and their attractions as being heterosexual in form, if not in content. Some participants later found the strength to face up to the possibility of social stigma and explore the rocky foundations upon which homophobia has been built. However, even those participants who eventually acted on their desires found that lesbianism was not the answer to their gender, sex, and sexual needs.

Tentative Touching: Limited Adolescent Homosexual Experience

Ten participants (22%) had limited homosexual experiences during their adolescence. They engaged mostly in kissing and touching of their partners' breasts in the context of short-term infatuations.[52] As had those participants who abstained entirely, most of these participants kept their attractions for females in check because of their fear of social stigma. Among them, Steven alone thought of herself as lesbian as a result of her attractions to girls and her sexual contacts with them. However, Steven did so even though she "hated" the word lesbian.

Keith was the most circumspect in her teenaged homosexual encounters. Keith kissed only one girl, one time, when they were both drunk. Colin, Steven, and Lee had several girlfriends, but they kept their sexual activities at the kissing and petting stage. Lee explained why things never became any more sexual:

> I knew that queers existed. . . . Things like that weren't talked about. . . . That was almost like Mafia. They's just dirt road people or something. So, that was a bad word. You didn't want to be that. . . . You knew it wasn't accepted. . . . It makes me sound stupid, but I didn't just sit down and think about things like that. I just did it. You knew that it wasn't right. . . . but it's something you enjoyed.

Along the same lines, Eli said that the whole gay scene "felt very foreign to me" and that "back in the fifties, it was really a pretty dismal scene . . . It was just weird people. . . . It wasn't a nice thing to be around." At that point in her life, Eli "just couldn't imagine why two girls would want to be together" and thought that lesbians "were scary people." However, Eli took great pleasure in enacting dramatic roles as a man during which she felt at liberty to perform as if she were a straight man. To Eli, that was not lesbianism, that was "normal heterosexual attraction." Eli recalled how her only teenaged homosexual contacts took place:

> We were Nelson and E. Hamilton . . . and we did it. We did the real thing. One minute I was lying there, she was touching my hand. The next minute, I grabbed her, you know, Whew! . . . And then we got out of character after that was over and talked about it in the next room like some movie we had seen. . . . I had orgasm and thereafter we would find any opportunity we could. . . . I never did it as two girlfriends, you know. That was a no no. . . . We were pretty hair trigger in those days and it didn't take very much. We did exactly what you do, except I didn't have the proper equipment. . . . It was Whoomph, hot stuff!. . . . It was a no no any other time.

During adolescence, Jorge was also completely unwilling to imagine being lesbian. Jorge said, "I never thought of myself as a lesbian. I was sort of naive about anything other than heterosexual relationships, and for a long time I didn't even understand a homosexual relationship." However, Jorge did get involved with a woman on the understanding that the woman was bisexual and on the assumption that she would relate to Jorge as a man. Jorge recalled, "I stopped the relationship when she wanted to perform lesbian sex acts on me" because "lesbian sex acts tend to disgust me and I want no part of them."

A few other participants also interpreted their roles in their adolescent homosexual explorations to be male-like but they did so with a less homophobic tinge. For example, Harry's adolescent homosexual experience had a similar tone. The girls in Harry's neighborhood were starting to prepare for "the big time" of kissing and petting with their future boyfriends. Some of them practiced together, with one or the other of them taking the role of the boy. Harry found these games very exciting as long as she could play the part of the boy. However, Harry believed that the crushes which she had on other girls were "wrong" and that she was "screwed up" and "fucked up" for feeling the way she did.

Dennis was unusual in this group of participants in that in her late adolescence, during the late 1970s, she identified herself as gay and regularly went to gay bars in a large metropolitan area. Dennis did not think of herself as lesbian because she did not think of herself as a woman. She was attractive in a butch sort of way, and many lesbian women approached her for possible sexual contact. Dennis enjoyed the attention but refused to do more than kiss and fondle with these women because she felt that such relations were inappropriately lesbian until such time as she had procured the hysterectomy which she so ardently desired. At times, the temptations were great. Dennis recounted one such evening:

> It was her idea that we get together, and I remember it was a nice hot summer night. And I picked her up, and I . . . had no idea what she was like, but she's kind of a wild type. Not necessarily my type . . . a little too . . . kind of like cheap . . . for my taste. . . . The bar . . . was fun. . . . [Afterwards], before we got to her apartment, just as we were pulling up, she asked me if I'd like to come and stay. And. . . . So she came over to my side, and reached in the window and grabbed me, and. . . . just pulled me to her, and kissed me. You know, it's like what they write stories about. I really did see stars. And so, this kind of half-assed relationship went on for quite a while.

Clearly, participants who were willing to become involved in minor forms of homosexual relations during their adolescence were neither completely ignorant of lesbianism nor lacking in imagination and adventurousness. Still, it would seem that many of those who took this road did so under constraints similar to those experienced by participants who did not act at all. For the most part, the only acceptable sexual model available to participants was a heterosexual one. Societal images of lesbian women were sufficiently repugnant to make them entirely uninviting. Hence, with few exceptions, those who took only halting steps into female homosexuality during their teen years did so while mentally casting themselves as males in a heterosexual model. Those who took this tack thereby avoided the necessity of considering themselves as lesbian at all. Only Steven reluctantly accepted the label lesbian.

Thus it seems plausible that had more of these participants lived in a time when information about lesbianism was both more readily available and more salutary, most of them would probably have been more homosexually active as teenagers. In a climate more conducive to positive lesbian identities, many of them might well have adopted lesbian identities more avidly and cleaved to them more persistently. Be that as it may, gender and sex identities are not the same as sexual orientation identities. More extensive homosexual experience and lesbian identities will not banish but only obscure underlying identities as men and as males. Experimentation with lesbianism was for most participants a step in the process of clarifying that identities as men and as males were the most suitable ones for them.

True Love and Earnest Lust: Major Adolescent Homosexual Relationships

During their adolescence, nineteen participants (42 percent) became involved in one or more homosexual relationships which included genital sexuality and lasted several months or more.[53] These relationships were the first in what were to become lifelong patterns of preferences for pairings with women.

These homosexual connections evidenced a number of interconnected themes. Most of these unions were undertaken by both partners with the understanding that they were, at least in all apparent aspects, lesbian relationships.[54] In some relationships, participants, but not necessarily their partners, maintained the belief that they were men and that therefore their relationships were de facto straight ones.[55] A few also foreshadowed what was to come, in that both partners agreed that in their own eyes they were in straight relationships.[56] In cases where participants passed through more than one relationship during their adolescence, there was often movement between more lesbian-defined relationships and more straight-defined ones. In some cases, particular relationships became redefined as they progressed and as participants came to have better insights into themselves and into the nature of lesbianism. As they did so, they generally moved more toward the rejection of the label of lesbian and of the womanhood implicit in that title.

When participants did think of themselves as lesbian women during their adolescence, they did so principally for two reasons. Firstly, they were faced with the unmistakable evidence of their own and their lovers' bodies, and they knew that the definition of lesbian therefore technically included them. Secondly, some participants were persuaded by the popular misconception that lesbians are women who want to be men. As that was precisely how participants felt, they uneasily accepted the appellation lesbian despite the fact that it required them to acquiesce to being women.

The sexual expression of participants in their homosexual relations often followed a pattern which set them apart from most homosexual women. Many participants refused to allow their partners access to their own bodies in any explicitly sexual way.[57] Forty-two percent of participants who had major homosexual relationships during their adolescence refused to allow their lovers to make love to them.[58] By so limiting their sexual expression, they were able to circumvent physical contact which would contradict their representation of themselves as men. In all cases, their lesbian relationships helped to clarify for participants that a lesbian existence would not eradicate their growing gender and sex dysphorias.

Only a very few participants easily accepted that their intimate relationships with women fully qualified as lesbian ones. More commonly, participants recognized a superficial similarity between their own relationships and those of lesbian women but retained a sense of themselves as different. Mel was one participant who did accept the label of lesbian as self-descriptive. Mel reasoned her way through things this way:

> You figure that you're gay because you know what that is, or you think you know what that is. But you're not sure because you haven't read anything and you know you better not read anything because someone's gonna' catch 'ya. . . . I thought lesbians were women who wanted to be men . . . until I talked to a lesbian and she just kinda' laughed at me.

Walter not only accepted a lesbian identity but did so in a politically militant way. As a teenager in the 1970s, Walter became a member of a national gay rights organization. Later she was drawn to a lesbian sadomasochists' organization, where she felt that she could better express both her sexuality and her gender. Walter said of herself at the time, "I was a bull dyke. I was just a very macho dyke. . . . I wasn't denying the fact that I was a woman." Walter found that her masculinity was something that she could use to her advantage among lesbian sadomasochists. Walter recalled, "Accepting? Oh, my God! They were totally into it! Oh, man! They loved it!" Walter enjoyed many and varied lesbian sexual partners and practices upon which she seemed to put few restrictions of any kind.

Roger also accepted that her homosexual relations qualified as lesbian ones. Roger's initiation into lesbianism when she was a girl of twelve was with another tomboy. Roger took the boy's part in their early adolescent gropings. Roger remembered the relationship this way:

> This was nonexperimental. This was more like what a boy and a girl would do in the back seat of the car in the drive-in. Heavy necking. . . . We were laying down behind the piano and it's like when two people are laying on a blanket under the sun or something and one rolls over to kiss the other one. I was the one on top, so to speak. . . . We knew that

we were in deep shit if we got caught. . . . I knew what I was doing. I'm not stupid; and being raised in a whorehouse, and being raised in boarding school, you're pretty well educated in what is heterosexual and what isn't.

Roger later became involved in a teenaged affair with a foster sister. Roger again took a boy's role in these interactions. This time Roger was just being helpful:

> It wasn't really a relationship on her part. It was on mine. . . . She was having trouble with her boyfriend so I . . . proceeded to show her . . . how to better make it with her boyfriend. . . . Her boyfriend lived right next door. . . . and my bed was right next to the window, right next to his driveway. And I would know when they were having a fight. So, then I would know when I could make my moves to help her improve things. . . . I can remember masturbating . . . with them in the driveway and me next to the window in bed.

Later on in her late teens, Roger joined the navy. While there, she engaged in a sexual relationship with another woman for the better part of the year during which she was enlisted.

At the other end of the spectrum, Dale was particularly tormented about being homosexual. Dale knew what a homosexual was because she had looked it up in a dictionary, but she was not happy about being such a disreputable person. Dale remembered being "horrified" and "so ashamed" of herself for her "unnatural feelings." Dale described the way she felt as a teenager in the late 1950s:

> I just shivered. Because I didn't want to be called that. Because people spoke of it as a sick thing. . . . We knew we had to hide. . . . We were both afraid of getting caught. Paranoid. . . . I felt really guilty about it. Terrible. . . . I don't think I could have lived if people knew. I was, believe me, really ashamed of how I felt. And I couldn't control it. If I could have, I would have. That's how bad it was. . . . I really felt ashamed of how I felt. . . . It was a sin in those days. Very much. . . . I really, really felt horrible about myself. . . . I really didn't like myself at all.

At the same time as Dale fought with these feelings, she also revelled in the intimacy which she enjoyed with her mate of three years. Dale recalled, "She totally worshipped me. And I just fell in love with her in a way that I didn't even think was possible to love." Yet Dale was so concerned to appear to be heterosexual that she also briefly took up with a young man "to leave an impression on my parents that I wasn't queer." When her girlfriend indignantly left her, Dale was so despondent that she began drinking and tried to slit her wrists with a broken bottle.

Scott also suffered because of her ambivalence about lesbianism. Scott was "obsessed" with other girls and women teachers. Scott was so distressed about her attractions to females and about her unwelcomed puberty that she started drinking heavily at age eleven. She said that the first time she kissed another girl she had to be drunk to do it. Scott recalled, "I knew it wasn't right. That I shouldn't be doing that, being female. And I felt really bad about the whole thing." However, knowing that she had a female body, Scott concluded that she was lesbian. Later, when Scott went off to college, she also went off in search of others like herself. She found a group of homosexual women in the athletics department at her school. Not satisfied, Scott said, "I still felt like I was a man in a crowd of women. I still felt I was somehow different from them."

Persevering, Scott found a woman to be her first lover. Scott told her that she felt like a man and they settled into a seven-year relationship in which they had "real traditional" masculine and feminine roles. Scott was still very conflicted about engaging in homosexuality and recalled how their sex life together suffered from Scott's gender and sex dysphorias:

> That wasn't too good because every time I'd be on top of her, you know I'd be fantasizing that I had a penis and I was inside of her. And I was just about ready to come and I'd go completely numb from my waist down. . . . That went on for . . . about three years. . . . It was . . . probably something to do with not having a penis and not being able to . . . perform. . . . I didn't get to have orgasms all those years. Well, when I masturbated I could. . . . As far as making love, I really probably wasn't very good at it 'til later. But I don't think she ever did have orgasm.

Tony also went hot and cold about being a lesbian. Tony's introduction to sexuality was when she was seduced by one of her girlfriends when they were sixteen years old. The two girls went on to have an eight-year relationship. When they went to college they met other women who seemed to be like themselves. However, Tony discovered that there were some differences:

> A lesbian is a woman that loves women. I'm not a lesbian. I'm not gay. I'm not a woman. I never was, and I never will be. The reason I did get involved was because it was so new to me. Because it was only me and [my girlfriend] and "Wow! There's other people like this. And we can go somewhere. And we can kiss and laugh, and scream, dance, and hug. And all the people around us are doing the same thing." So it was good. It was a good experience.
>
> But this level of gays was such that the butches did not take their clothes off. The butches did not allow their lovers to touch them. One time, we were at a friend's house, there were five couples and we always kind of separated the butches in one place and the femmes in another

and talked about different things kind of deal. And one of the femmes had remarked how she was tired of feeling dungaree against her body. My lover at the time didn't understand and said, "What?" And she said, "she doesn't take her clothes off." She remarked, "Well [my partner] does." And I remember the four butches dragging me off into the kitchen . . . And they said, "You take your clothes off? And you let her touch you?" I said, "Whoa. We're talking about making love here. We're talking about the becoming of one. The experience of pleasure." I said, "You people don't know what you're missing!" This was feminine to them. To them, it was not a man to let a woman touch you. And that was really insane.

However, although Tony enjoyed being naked and being touched by her lover, Tony never allowed her lover to penetrate her vaginally.

Ron went back and forth between identifying herself as a man and as a woman in her numerous adolescent relationships with women. Ron first started relating to women sexually when she was thirteen years old. In her first affair, with a 30 year old woman, she thought of herself as a man, although they did have what Ron called "lesbian sex." In her later teens, after a fair bit of "experimentation," Ron remembered:

When I was about seventeen or so, and I thought [I was a lesbian]. That was the easiest conclusion, you know, like, my brother had gone before me, he had already come out and been disowned, and what not. And I knew his environment, and I knew other lesbians, and it just seemed the path of least resistance.

In her late teens and early adulthood, Ron went on to become active in women's and lesbian rights organizations while still feeling unsettled about her gender identity. Later still, as an adult, Ron went back to identifying as a man in her relationships with women.

As a teenager, Alan was so starved for love that she would do almost anything to get affection, including switching genders according to the preferences of her lovers. Alan's introduction to homosexuality, when she was a girl of nine, came by way of seduction by a cousin. Alan next became involved with two female schoolmates before she first left home and took up prostitution at age fourteen. Both of her girlfriends at school "insisted" that Alan "pretend to be male," which Alan was already adept at from her sexual intimacies with her young cousin. At the age of seventeen, Alan ran away from home for the third and final time and moved in with "an abusive female lover" with whom she lived for the next seven years. The woman was a butch and "heavily into S/M." Alan, with the help of drugs and alcohol, played the femme role for her and submitted to her beatings as part of their sexual life together. Alan recalled, "when I had sex with my girlfriends . . . I believed I got the love and approval I was missing at home."

Some participants knew that they were men even if they lacked the credentials to fully claim that status and even if their sexual partners remained unconvinced. Darren's story of her first love affair illustrates this predicament. Darren started having crushes on females when she was about thirteen years old but kissed someone for the first time at age eighteen. As Darren put it, "I was a late bloomer and repressed."

At that time, two years after the death of both of her parents, Darren had already begun to think of herself as transsexual. While she was hospitalized because of a threatened suicide, Darren met a woman who thought of Darren as a "butch lesbian." Darren tried to explain to her that she was transsexual, but to no avail. Darren described the course of the relationship over the next few months:

> She still, kind of, considered this was a lesbian relationship. And I let her think that, because I was in love with this person. My first love. And I wanted to be close to someone. I had nobody. . . . So, like a dummy, I let her go on believing this premise that wasn't true. . . . It was alien to me. It was not something I could identify with. . . . We moved in together when I got out [of hospital]. . . . I let her touch me . . . but I didn't like it. . . . In fact, when I went to bed first, I had . . . all my clothes on. She started tearing away the clothes, and I was getting more and more anxious, more and more uncomfortable, but I gave in. Probably because, if you've never been close to someone physically, and it's someone you like and are attracted to, and emotionally starved. . . . I didn't really like it, but then I liked the fact that we were physically intimate, and we were close. . . . But it felt awful in another way, because it was a part of my body that I didn't want acknowledged. . . . I guess there was quite a bit of anger, and ambivalence, and disgust, too.

The relationship ended after five months when the woman decided that she couldn't countenance being in a lesbian relationship.

Still other participants were quite clear, within their adolescent relationships, that they were to be given all the rights and privileges of straight men. For example, Luther had a four-year sexual relationship with a female cousin. Luther said that neither of them thought of it as a lesbian relationship. In Luther's memory of it, it was not an issue; Luther was the boyfriend. They each had "very rigid" gender stereotyped roles, about which Luther remembered, "I felt proud of myself because this is what men did." For Luther, that pride "really helped me a great deal because it was something that buttressed me against having to be [a girl] for most of my life."

Although several participants claimed the prerogatives of men in their relationships with women, there was one important difference between their own performances of their roles and the stereotypical enactment of heterosexuality as usually performed by straight men. Whereas straight men are notorious for satiating themselves sexually with little regard for the satisfaction of their female partners,[59] participants often behaved in the reverse fashion. Forty-two percent of those participants who had genitally sexual relationships during their adolescence prided themselves on providing sexual release for their partners but would not allow themselves to be touched in sexually explicit ways. Thus their own sexual satisfaction was gained either vicariously, from serving their partners' pleasure, or not at all.

Fred, who took a masculine role in her first love affairs, had two sexual relationships while a teenager, one lasting three years, the other stretching through four years and into her young adult years. Fred said that she "never felt female . . . always male" in those relationships. One of the ways that Fred defended the sense of herself as male was to adhere to clearly demarcated gender styles. Another was to prohibit her lovers from "doing anything" sexual to her beyond kissing and hugging. Such arrangements supported her fledgling male identity by allowing her to perform as if she were a man and by avoiding the possibility of the exposure of her discrediting female body parts. Fred remembered that her first relationship, and the early years of her second one, made her feel "cocky" because "here's one place in my life that I can be me. And here's one person in my life that understands me. And it was great!"

Rick was also among those who could not allow intimate sexual contact. Rick described the one time she tried to cooperate with a woman who identified as lesbian:

> I never let a partner touch me physically. I just wasn't capable. I did make an effort at one point with a woman that I did care about a lot. . . . And it just was the most uncomfortable experience I've ever had. So I learned very quickly that there was no way that I could adapt to that kind of a situation. It just couldn't work.

Three participants began teenaged relationships in which they were still involved at the times of their interviews. Each of their partners was accepting of participants' evaluations of themselves as men from very early in their relationships and supported them in their later transitions into men. These deeply committed and enduring relationships exhibited some of the same characteristics as found among those of other participants, and also some unique ones.

Simon had three "failed" homosexual relationships before meeting the woman who was eventually to become his wife. All of the women with whom Simon became intimate considered themselves to be heterosexual and accepted Simon's assertions that she was a man on the inside. Simon recalled the difficulty of the sexual aspects of the first relationship, which she had at age eighteen:

> Sex isn't difficult any more. But at that point in life it was very, very difficult because what I wanted when I made love was to have a penis and what I had was a vagina. Mostly I wouldn't let her touch me, which in itself, I'm sure, was frustrating for her, but it was frustrating for me as well. So, I think it's probably like being impotent, you know. You get aroused but you can't ever get it off. . . . I think I did come a few times, but not generally. It was more work than it was pleasure.

When Simon first met his future wife they were both in college. Simon recalled, "She had seen me and was attracted to me. And then she found out, by word of mouth, that I wasn't a man. And that threw her into a loop 'cause she never identified as a lesbian." At the time, Simon "was not attempting to look like a man." A year later, when Simon started to cross-dress as the first step in permanently becoming a man, the relationship started to get serious. Simon's future wife professed her love for Simon. Simon got "totally drunk" and told her that he felt the same way. However, before Simon would make a commitment he needed to clarify a few things. Simon recalled those tense moments:

> I said, "It's really important to me that you never be embarrassed, and that you never be ashamed by what and who I am." And she said that she didn't think that she had any problem with that. And I trusted that, and she never has been. So I guess I trusted the right person.

At the time of this writing, Simon and his wife have been married for approximately twenty-five years.

Howie met his future wife when they were twelve year old schoolmates. Howie and her "soul mate" were "mutually obsessed with one another" from the beginning. Howie reminisced:

> We had a very exclusive relationship. . . . there was never any room for other friends. We spent all our free time together, took long walks, went shopping, to movies, etc. She was (and is) my everything. . . . I don't think I'd have much desire to live if she weren't in my life. . . . She always related to the male inside of me. She knew where I was at and our relationship became a saving grace, as well as a nightmare of lies. We lived in our own little world with no space for others.

Howie reported, "We were romantically involved throughout junior high and high school. We started living together when we were nineteen years old and we married when we were thirty."

For a brief while, Howie said that she had thought of their relationship as a lesbian one because "I knew that I was a female and that I loved a female. So, I assumed that made me a lesbian." However, the ongoing support of her partner's belief in her hidden maleness sustained her until such time as Howie could become a man. At the time of Howie's last interview, they had been together for twenty-five years.

Grant also found his life's partner while still a teenager. Grant described their first encounter as momentous. Grant was fifteen years old at the time.

> I've got it bad over the phone hearing her voice. I know her, I want to meet her, I want to be with her. When we met . . . Cupid caught me between the eyes with a twelve-pound sledge! He'd been doing steroids for six years! Everything! The 1812 Overture, skyrockets, bells, sirens! I was in love! We went back to my place, talked till four in the morning. She left. A month later, she'd moved in.

Their relationship soon took an unusual turn. Not only did Grant want to be a man for her new girlfriend; she also wanted her girlfriend to be a man for her. Apparently they were a perfect match. They immediately became happily embroiled in a sexual relationship which they fashioned as a gay men's bondage-and-discipline arrangement. Grant was thrilled to be the submissive partner. Grant remembered how it evolved:

> The bed collapsed. We wound up in a clinch. We wound up making love, but there was an underlying, "Oh, my god. I'm going to be told to get the hell out." We were paranoid that the other partner was going to react that way, and it didn't happen that way at all. . . . That was my first actual sexual encounter with another human being. . . . We saw it as two men. . . . Put it this way, we each have two hands. That was as far as it went that time. But within a matter of weeks, we had been to the [sex shop], got the proper equipment, including [two dildos and] a full set of restraints. . . . But we have related ever since in an S/M relationship, and a gay man's S/M relationship. And it's worked.

However, at first, Grant had trouble trying to figure out how to think about and name what it was that they were doing together sexually. Grant remembered the confusion:

> I thought I was a lesbian at that time, and that all lesbians wanted to be men and were identified as gay men. And that's not the case. I found that out very quickly. But since I had no way to describe myself, I described myself as male identified, but a lesbian. And it was like I'm male identified and I'm gay, so that I'm not a dyke. But I'm in love ostensibly with another biological female, so I must be a lesbian. . . . Within a year of our relationship we figured that would have to be how we described

ourselves. But we're not gay women. That was the whole thing. It's like, "Not quite."

By the time I met them for the purposes of this research project their relationship had endured, under those same terms, for over twenty years.

In sum, nineteen participants (42 percent) became involved in ongoing genitally sexual relationships with other females during their adolescence.[60] Due to the explicitly sexual and nonfleeting nature of these unions, they could not be dismissed as merely girlish affection or experimentation. Nor could participants distance themselves by claiming innocence. These liaisons forced participants to confront issues of sexual identity and, by extension, issues of gender and sex identity. Almost two-thirds of this subgroup (63 percent) thought of themselves as lesbian for at least part of their adolescence.[61]

On the surface of it, it was clear enough that participants were females in sexual relationships with females. No one was delusional enough to miss that fact. Nonetheless, there were more factors to consider than raw anatomy. Two other aspects of their definitions of lesbianism became important in participants' deliberations about their identities. One concern was about what exactly lesbians do in bed with one another and how they feel about it. The other came back to the question of whether or not participants were, in truth, females.

Eight of the nineteen participants (42 percent) who had major relationships during adolescence did not want their lovers to touch them in an explicitly sexual manner.[62] Some participants, who were more familiar with the 1970s and 1980s lesbian-feminist concept of lesbianism, reasoned that lesbians were women who enjoyed receiving sexual attentions from other women. Because they did not want to be touched in that way but did want to provide that kind of pleasure to women, they concluded that their relationships were more straight than lesbian and that they were more like straight men than like lesbian women. They could not, of course, fully claim to be straight men as long as they were female-bodied. However, they could disclaim membership in the world of lesbianism and inhabit some kind of in-between space until a better explanation for their proclivities came along.

The other tack that some of these, and a few other, participants took was to distance themselves from the woman part of the definition of lesbianism. All but one of the eight participants who thought of themselves as men in their teenaged, same-sex relationships had already begun to adopt transsexual identities during their teen years.[63] Thus they could rationally claim that although they appeared to be women in lesbian relationships, they were really men in the wrong bodies. As such, they could assert that, anatomy aside, their relationships were straight, both in nature and in spirit.

Summary and Commentary

By the time participants had concluded adolescence, almost all of them had evinced some level of sexual attraction to females. However, they varied widely in the degree to which they acted on their attractions. One-third of them had refrained from becoming intimately involved with females.[64] Approximately one-quarter (22 percent) had experimented with adolescent homosexual kissing and petting.[65] Another 42 percent had become involved in genitally sexual relationships of some duration.[66] Thus by the last days of their adolescence, approximately two-thirds of participants (64 percent) had made, at the least, some tentative steps into homosexuality, most of them having made more serious commitments.

These homosexual desires and involvements drove most participants to crises of identity and representation. Many participants entered adolescence holding fast to cherished beliefs that they were boys. When they began to undergo the physically feminizing changes of puberty, their physical femaleness became virtually impossible to ignore. For some participants, the realization that they found females sexually attractive provided them with something of an explanation for the apparent contradiction between the evidence of their bodies and the convictions of their hearts and minds. For others, their feelings for females only compounded the problem.

Participants came through adolescence in different decades and with differing levels of knowledge about lesbianism. Some participants were altogether ignorant about lesbianism. Many of them laboured under the misconception that all lesbian women want to be men. Others conceived of lesbian women as those who love, and want to be loved by women. However, all of them were teenagers during times when homosexuality was still highly stigmatized in popular culture. There were few social incentives for them to think of themselves as lesbian.

Fifteen participants (33 percent) simply avoided the whole issue by not becoming sexually involved with other females at all. However, their feelings for other females helped to buttress their destabilized identities as males because the only explanation which they could imagine for their romantic leanings was that they were really boys in girls' bodies. Those who knew of lesbianism but abstained from acting on their feelings were motivated by morality judgements. They knew lesbianism was "bad" and "wrong" and so they stayed out of it for the time being.

Ten participants (22 percent) tested the waters with adolescent excursions into homosexual kissing and nongenital caressing. They too had to reconcile their limited, often homophobic, knowledge of lesbianism with their bodies and their gender and sex identity issues. Most of these people retreated from the label of lesbian. Most of them imagined themselves to be boys engaging in heterosexual courtship when they were kissing and touching other girls. Thus these participants were also able to use their feelings for girls to bolster their masculine identities when they became besieged by puberty.

Nineteen participants (42 percent) became involved in full-fledged same-sex relationships during their adolescence, most of them beginning during their late teens. The duration and genitality of such involvements negated the possibility of participants' simply ignoring the issue of lesbianism. Each of them had to come to grips with issues of sexual orientation identities. In order to do so, they also had to deal with questions of gender and sex identities. They confronted these issues in three ways. Some participants reluctantly admitted that the category of lesbian seemed to capture what it was that they were about. Other participants challenged their qualifications for membership in that stigmatized group in two often concurrent ways. From one direction, there were those who accepted lesbian-feminist definitions of lesbian women as those who love and want to be loved by women. They figured that they were not lesbian because they were not happy being women and because they did not want their women lovers to make love to the women in them. They claimed that they were not lesbians, but neither were they necessarily men. From another direction, some participants had begun to learn something of female-to-male transsexualism and had begun to think of themselves in those terms. They therefore were able to exempt themselves from lesbianism on the basis of not really being women at all.

Thus approximately two-thirds of participants (64 percent) were able to find support for their precarious identities as men and as males in the ways in which they experienced and interpreted their romantic and sexual feelings for, and involvements with, women. They were able to counterbalance the psychically traumatic physical transformations of puberty by recourse to homophobic, heterosexist, or lesbian-feminist explanations for their feelings. Later in life, many participants learned to recognize the fallacies in what they had believed as children and teenagers. Those people subsequently were able to make sense of their gender, sex, and sexual identities without such large helpings of the added confusion of misogyny, homophobia, or lesbian-feminist oversimplifications. However, as adolescents, few participants were sufficiently sophisticated to make such distinctions. Indeed, at the time, few people at any position in society were highly critical of such forms of discrimination or intolerance.

Summary and Commentary: Adolescent Sexuality

Learning about sexuality is one of the primary tasks of adolescence. All participants entered into this enterprise to one degree or another, although for some participants it was a forced education. Participants learned about sexuality through nonconsensual heterosexual and homosexual relations, through masturbation, and through consensual heterosexual and homosexual involvements.

Four main interlocking elements must come into play in any consideration of participants' experience of adolescent sexuality. Firstly, the contexts in which participants first experienced genital sexuality with other persons are particularly important because they can set foundations upon which subsequent sexual encounters will be judged. Whether consensual or not, the practices of genital sexuality often make more lasting impressions than do other less involved kinds of sexuality. This may be so both because of the level of intimacy involved and because of the social meanings attached to such activities.

Secondly, it is useful to think about the nature of the erotic fantasies and desires which participants used to stimulate themselves. In particular, for many adolescents, masturbatory fantasies and desires are a much more frequent and reliable source of sexual satisfaction than are interpersonal relations. Such fantasies allow adolescents to create, in their own minds, sexual scenarios which are most in keeping with their personalities and preferences. Their predominance in the sexual careers of most teens thereby enhances their value as determinants of later sexual response patterns.

The third and fourth factors which contribute to adolescents' sexual development are their teenaged experiences with heterosexuality and with homosexuality. Obviously, greater social rewards adhere to heterosexuality than to homosexuality. However, individual experiences of physical and psychological needs and desires and the relative satisfaction of them offered by heterosexual, as compared with homosexual, relations can often carry greater weight than more generalized social norms. Despite social disopprobrium, most participants soon abandoned any interest in being straight women which they might have temporarily sustained. Rather, the bulk of the evidence presented by participants points to their use of their teen years as a time to entrench their images of themselves as either lesbian women or as straight men.

Eleven participants (25 percent)[67] were introduced to sexuality in the context of exploitative heterosexual relations.[68] More commonly, participants first experienced genital sexuality through masturbation. In total, eighteen of the twenty-two participants who masturbated during their teen years (82 percent)[69] did so before taking up consensual genital sexual experience with anyone else.[70] Furthermore, all but three of the twenty-two participants (86 percent) who reported that they had engaged in masturbation as teenagers imagined themselves as male during their masturbation.[71] One tentative conclusion which might be drawn from these data is that most participants entered into genital sexuality with other people only after they had begun to establish sexual habits in which their satisfaction was tied to their ability to perform sexually as if they were male. Furthermore, those participants who did not begin interpersonal sexual relations until later in life largely remained unfettered by comparisons between imagined ideal sexual relations and the realities of interactions they were actually able to obtain. Thus they had years in which to uninterruptedly habituate themselves to sexual response patterns in which they could imagine themselves to be as unequivocally male as they wished.

For obvious reasons, those who subsequently entered into heterosexual relations must have found that such a predisposition worked as a substantial impediment to their potential for successful relations. Somewhat different dynamics would have been involved for those participants who became engaged in homosexual relations during adolescence. In those cases, there remained considerably greater latitude for participants either to convince their sexual partners to share in their portrayals of themselves as male or to retain the option of privately envisioning themselves in that fashion. Whereas in heterosexual relations one partner has a monopoly on all the major signifiers of maleness, in homosexual relations noncorporeal or minor physical attributes could be construed as indictors of maleness.

For the most part, participants' experiences in adolescent heterosexual relations did little to encourage them to identitify themselves as straight women. Indeed, it was more common for participants' experiences to drive them away from that identity. Some of their reluctance may be chalked up to social impediments to genital involvements for teenagers of their times and places, but more of it seemed to have been connected to their aversions to making any commitment to actions which would mark them too clearly as female. Among those who did take steps into being straight women, many of the relationships in which they experimented were remembered by participants as exploitative or otherwise devoid of emotional warmth.

Homosexual relations provided more fertile grounds for participants' gender and sex identity needs. These relationships involved more emotional intensity and commitment than did participants' heterosexual ones, and they provided a higher degree of sexual satisfaction. Perhaps more importantly, they offered many participants arenas in which to play out more effectively the intersection of their gender, sex, and sexual self-images. In fact, three of these relationships so successfully satisfied these needs that they have continued for more than twenty years.[72]

The overall picture of participants' adolescent sexuality which can be drawn from the stories which they told was, as with most teenagers, one of exploration and search for identity. Many participants entered adolescence with images of themselves as boys. The logical next step for young teens who identify as boys is to become sexually and romantically attracted to girls. Almost all participants followed this path in fantasy and desire, if not in fact. However, social forces were also exerting pressures on them to make use of their feminizing bodies in heterosexual ways while discouraging them from investigating lesbianism. Some participants did try to conform to the dictates of society and made concerted efforts to find places for themselves as straight women. Almost all participants who did so reported feelings ranging from extreme anxiety to flat alienation. Clearly, heterosexuality did not answer their needs.

In many cases, rampant homophobia was also successful in temporarily derailing participants' interests in pursuing sexual relations with females. Some participants simply didn't know that such things were possible. Others were deterred by fears of becoming social pariahs. In other cases, homophobic misinformation planted the idea in adolescent participants' minds that if they were sexually interested in women, then they either were or should be men. Some participants deferred on such relations until they could become men, others fantasized themselves to be men, and some found partners who accepted their appraisals of their inner identities.

Whatever their actual sexual experiences with others, most participants took up masturbation before or during their adolescence; and almost all of those participants who masturbated as teens did so, in their own minds, as men. Their erotic fantasies and desires were therefore available to them as safe places where they could be who and as they wanted to be. Their fantasies and desires thereby provided both refuge and correction. For those who found that their sexual involvements with others were not precisely as they wished them to be and for those participants who remained virginous throughout their teen years, they also served the purpose of emotionally and physically rewarding rehearsals for what they hoped that they and their sexuality would one day become. Those participants who had happened to become aware during their adolescence that female-to-male transsexualism was available made plans to realize their desires. For the others, their adolescent fantasies and desires had to remain as unobtainable hopes and dreams. They simply had to adapt themselves to what was available until better options presented themselves.

15 | Concluding Adolescence

As HAVE MANY other people, participants reported that they experienced their teen years as difficult ones. As teenagers, they faced all of the same developmental dilemmas which confront other adolescents as they traversed their journeys from children into young adults. As do all teenagers, they wrestled with finding suitable social and sexual identities for themselves. However, unlike most teens, participants were also confronted with the problem of finding gender and sex identities which were satisfactory to them. As gender and sex are so integral to so many other aspects of identity with which teenagers struggle, it seemed as though almost all of participants' adolescent identity development and clarification efforts became somewhat entangled with their gender and sex issues.

As participants' bodies changed from those of androgynous children into those of female adolescents, participants' own gender and sex identities were sorely challenged. Their cherished images of themselves as either boys or "not really girls" were forced to give way to the realities of their maturing female bodies. As participants looked to their peers for companionship and advice in negotiating the treacherous shoals of adolescence, there too they were repeatedly confounded by the gap between the gender and sex attributions which others made about them and their own identities.

As participants turned to their peers in the context of romantic or sexual desire, their own feelings about their genders and sexes were still more pointedly contradicted by the ways in which others perceived them. The boys who were their peers ceased to treat them as if they were "just one of the boys" and increasingly related to them as if they were members of an intrinsically different category of humanity. Boys began to treat them as potential sexual conquests and girls either blithely ignored them as possible romantic interests or acted toward them as if they were lesbian.

Furthermore, participants found that the rules governing their familial relationships shifted as they entered adolescence. Even their siblings and more distant relatives joined in with the chorus of voices loudly proclaiming that society demanded that the time had come for them to cease to be tomboys and to become women. Those relationships which had been difficult before generally remained difficult, but many of those which had offered hope and encouragement to them as masculine girls failed to deliver on their promises during participants' teen years.

On the whole, participants' experiences of family life during their adolescent years seemed, more than anything else, to be lonely. They were especially hurt and angered as the elder males in their lives seemed to abandon them to the world of women by dropping them from their coterie, or by actively demanding femininity of participants who were neither interested in, nor practiced at, its execution. Thus, although several participants were able to hang on to some of the pleasures they had found in their childhood family lives, most remembered feeling misunderstood, alienated, and alone among the families of their adolescences.

These added stresses, over and above those which all teenagers have to endure, tended to make participants' adolescences particularly difficult for them to survive. Although many teenagers report depression, suicidal thoughts, alcohol and drug use and other signs of anxiety, the participants in this study seemed to be atypically burdened with such problems.

One result of these stress-filled years was that participants reported higher-than-average rates of adolescent depression. Whereas approximately 30 percent of adolescents have been found to suffer from depression,[1] approximately half of all participants (51 percent) reported that they had been "miserable" or "depressed" as adolescents.[2] In almost all cases, the source of their distress was either directly or indirectly due to the changes wrought by puberty to their bodies. If they were not directly distraught at the very fact of their physical transformations into adult females, then they were disturbed by the impediment that their femaleness posed to their romantic interests in other females.

Luther's recollections very aptly illustrated how many participants felt as teenagers. Speaking of her teen years starting at her puberty, Luther recalled:

> I hated the changes in my body. . . . I couldn't stand it. . . . It affected my identity. I became very upset and depressed. As a matter of fact, by this time in my life, I spent most of my time in my room. . . . I just became very depressed and isolated. I just felt that life was over. . . . I thought about suicide, but not very seriously. . . . I was just living in depressions, and I was not really moving on anything. . . . It was this gender stuff. . . . When I went away to college, [my girlfriend] went to the same college as I went to, and she decided, at that point, that she was going to have a real man, and left me. So, I kind of went into a great depression.

Many other participants echoed these feelings. Their descriptions of their adolescent depressions ranged from those of Sam, who was "always in a mild depression," to those of Fred, who was so "very depressed and disgusted" about her physical and social maturation that her state of mind deteriorated to the point that she ended up having a stay in a mental hospital.

Participants also reported higher than average rates of adolescent suicide ideation. Whereas 15 percent of teenagers in general have been found to think about taking their own lives,[3] almost twice that many participants (27 percent) reported having considered such action during their adolescent years. Eight of the twenty-two people who recalled having been depressed or miserable, along with another four people, spoke of having felt suicidal or having attempted suicide during their teen years.[4]

Participants' suicidal impulses ran the gamut from those who reported having relatively harmless thoughts in that direction to those who seemed to have made serious attempts to take their own lives. For example, Scott, Morgan, and Darren only briefly considered suicide. Nathan, however, "became extremely depressed, suicidal and being very self-abusive, especially to the breasts." Dennis took her depression still further, almost killing herself by anorexicly starving herself down to a weight of sixty-two pounds in an attempt to stave off her menses. When Dennis started to gain weight again and it looked as though she might resume her menses, she started to plan ways to kill herself more expeditiously. Eventually, her survival instincts prevailed. Similarly, Jorge often was "very upset, miserable, crying" and "very depressed" about her gender quandary. Jorge remembered, "on numerous times I wanted to kill myself." A few participants actually did attempt suicide. Simon tried to kill herself on the occasion of her first menses. Ed, who was "very suicidal and totally depressed" about being female, was hospitalized for her depressions after she made an attempt to take her own life the year she graduated from high school. Jordie, too, "was depressed, felt unlovable and unloving," and attempted suicide "several" times.

Brian described a suicide attempt which she made because of how unhappy she was about unequivocally, and seemingly irreversibly, becoming a woman. Brian recalled:

> When I was fourteen or fifteen I tried to kill myself. I was so intensely depressed for so long, my mother thought I was sick and took me to see a doctor. The doctor prescribed tranquilizers for some reason, but warned me very strongly to follow the directions precisely. He told me that if I took too many, they could kill me. My depression was extreme and neither the doctor nor my parents could really see what was hap-

pening with me. After a couple days with using the pills, I consumed nearly half the bottle. I don't remember how many. When I woke up, my mother said I'd slept more than forty-eight hours. . . . I never told any of my family what I had done.

A number of participants also reported other behaviours which are often taken of indications of unhappiness in youths. More than one-third of participants (36 percent) reported that they had used alcohol[5] or drugs[6] in more than casual ways; most of them remembered that they were heavy users. Six people also reported that they had eating problems during their teen years which they believed to have been related to their gender and sex dysphorias.[7] In addition, Jack suffered from ongoing and disruptive levels of insomnia; Brian, Dale, and Nathan hit or slashed their own bodies in anger over what they had become; and Alan was "sexually compulsive." Thus, by such criteria, these twenty-one participants (47 percent) also could be said in all probability to have been unusually unhappy during their adolescences.

For example, the stories which Alan, Ron, and Scott told suggested that they had severe adolescent substance abuse problems. Alan said that starting at age twelve, she "self-medicated" daily with alcohol, marijuana, hashish, LSD, and amphetamines to "escape from my pain" and "avoid dealing with the androgyny." Alan also ran away from home at ages fourteen, sixteen, and seventeen, during which times she prostituted herself and became "sexually compulsive."

Ron also started trying to escape from her gender troubles at an early age. Ron began drinking and using drugs on a daily basis at age thirteen. Ron recalled how her puberty affected her:

> I spent more time in my mind, and when I had enough of that, I started to just act up, like, live it up. You know, I didn't want to stick around. So, it wasn't like I was directly suicidal, it was just, all the things I was doing were, you know, I was pretty wild. And I was doing a lot of drugs, and I was drinking a lot, and driving like a maniac, and racing motorcycles, and stunt work, and whatever. . . . Because . . . I had to find something where I could prove myself, you know, my masculinity. I always had to prove, always.

Scott's substance abuse also constituted a major coping device for her during her teenaged anguish. Scott drank alcohol on a daily basis throughout her teen years and took up regular drug use later in her teens. Scott described it this way:

> From twelve to eighteen I was basically drinking all during that period. . . . In fact, I remember . . . most of the time I'd drink a couple of shots of vodka before I even walked . . . [to] school. . . . I'd usually drink a

couple shots and smoked a little bit of pot. So basically I was just taking drugs. . . . Boy, probably at least four ounces of hard liquor every day during the week, and then weekends, it would be like probably . . . 'til I pass out, wine and stuff. . . . I really didn't get into pot until I was in college. And then I got into other stuff for a while which wasn't too good. . . . doing drugs. Well, a lot of LSD in college, a lot. Like every weekend, get high at least once a weekend for four years. That's a lot of acid.

These three, however, were by no means the only participants who sorely abused drugs or alcohol. Although other participants generally started their alcohol and drug abuse later in their adolescent years, they too were often unrelenting in their indulgences once they had taken up their habits. Some participants preferred alcohol. For example, Jack began drinking beer while helping her father with farm chores when she was fourteen years old. Jack said that within a few years she reached the point where she "very easily could have been an alcoholic" because she would "drink . . . until I passed out on the sofa." Mel also was a drinker. Mel remembered taking up drinking during her middle teens with a group of her male buddies. Mel recalled drinking a case of beer a day, every day, with her friends.

Other participants chose drugs over alcohol. Morgan remembered the year that she discovered LSD as "the best year of my life." Morgan said that she "did a lot of acid for a few years." In her later teens she also "started to drink a lot of beer." Ed took up drug use at around age eighteen. Ed recalled that she used marijuana "morning, noon, and night. . . . real heavy for a long time" and that she also regularly enjoyed using LSD. Walter also favoured marijuana use. Walter reminisced that from age fourteen onward, she "always smoked pot." Tony, too, was an inveterate marijuana user. Tony, who began smoking around the age of sixteen, described her relationship to the drug in these words:

I'm a pot smoker. I smoked a lot of pot. I went through a lot of years smoking anywhere between ten and fifteen joints a day. Like most people would light up a cigarette, after a meal I would roll a joint. . . . I felt that God grows it so how bad can it be.

A few participants also experienced eating difficulties which they tied into their discomforts with their puberties. Three participants tried to inhibit the feminization of their bodies by remaining "boyishly" slim. Dennis and Morgan both starved themselves, and normal eating made Fred sick to her stomach. Bill, Howie, and Nathan took the opposite approach to their attempts to escape from encroaching femaleness. Bill recalled that "food was my only 'drug' and I continued to balloon to huge proportions. I ate whenever I was extremely anxious, and I was anxious around the clock." Howie described his female teenaged self as "fat, fat, fat, hairy . . . freakish." Nathan perhaps summed up this tack the best when he said, "I had always been obese, and I got worse after puberty. I think it was a way to hide being female. . . . I tried to hide these changes by gaining weight."

In sum, approximately three-quarters (73 percent) of participants reported that as teenagers they had exhibited signs of extreme anxiety,[8] abused alcohol or drugs,[9] suffered from depression,[10] or been suicidal.[11] Clearly, adolescence had been an excessively stressful time for these people. Just as clearly, their difficulties with trying to adjust to social expectations regarding the appropriate styles of gender expression for females were at the base of much of their distress. They seemed to have felt penned in at all sides by the demands for increased femininity placed upon them by their social and familial environments at school, at play, and to a lesser degree in their love lives.

Some participants found pockets of relief from these ubiquitous gender requirements in sexual and romantic relationships with other females. Those few participants whose families were accepting of their masculinity also found some solace there. However, for most of the people in this study, adolescence was a time dominated by feelings of frustration, helplessness, and despair. A few participants concluded their adolescences having already made up their minds as to their appropriate courses of action and had set out in search of gender and sex reassignment for themselves. Others, lacking knowledge of the possibilities of gender and sex reassignment, soldiered on, trying to force themselves to fit molds which were inimical to them. Eventually they too would discover the possibilities of gender and sex reassignment and come to their own conclusions that therein lay the only viable solutions available to them.

PART IV

Pre-Transition Years

Billy Lane

16 | Finding Identities

As PARTICIPANTS CAME into their adult years they were young women faced with many of the same problems as were other young women of their generations. They were engaged in various sorts of quests to find both communities and identities which allowed them to express themselves in fulfilling ways. However, the people who participated in this study differed from most of their female peers in that they generally came into their adulthoods with strong senses of themselves as manly women. They knew that their bodies were female and that such physical evidence was definitive in marking them as women in the eyes of their social comrades. Nonetheless, they also persisted in feeling ill at ease with the unavoidable conclusion that they were women. In their own hearts and minds they persisted in feeling like men and like males. Thus, faced with contradictions between their own self-images as men and as males and their undeniable statuses as women and as females, participants spent much of their pre-transition adult years searching for ways to reconcile themselves to being women and female.

A number of participants took to heart the social expectation that females are supposed to be heterosexually oriented, and they engaged uneasily, with varying degrees of commitment, in relationships with straight men. In these relationships, they simultaneously attempted to find ways to express their masculinity and to integrate themselves into the social fabric of the communities in which they lived. As women in straight relationships, they had available to them the opprobrium of the general public and the possibility of intimacy with one or more men. This approach therefore offered four somewhat tantalizing yet unlikely possibilities.

Firstly, participants might find men for sexual or romantic partners who might privately accept participants as if they were men buddies, thereby allowing participants the emotional satisfaction of having their self-images as men reflected back to them by persons who knew, from the inside, what it meant to be men. Secondly, participants might be able to reap the benefits of sexual satisfaction and the rewards of heterosexual family life. Thirdly, by engaging in heterosexual relations, participants were presumably able to enjoy the advantages of membership in the mainstream and aboveground world of straight couples. Finally, there was always the possibility that having tasted the *bon mots* of heterosexuality, they might abandon their masculine identities in favour of more feminine ones. However, because of participants' strong feelings of masculine identity and their increasingly intense needs to express that masculinity, they were probably doomed from the start to find few reprieves.

Most often, participants turned to lesbian relations and lesbian communities in their searches for ways to more comfortably express their masculinity. Those who did so generally found that lesbian women and lesbian communities afforded them a great deal of freedom to explore their attractions to women and their masculine personas. They were able to find both women lovers and communities of women who appreciated them and joined them in their enjoyment of masculinity. Lesbian relationships and communities thus offered participants the potential to explore their masculinity in supportive environments. Their lovers were attracted to participants' masculinity and thereby gave validation and reinforcement to participants' feelings of being manlike. In addition, lesbian communities have always made room for manly women, although this has been more the case in certain times and places than in others. Those participants who integrated themselves into lesbian communities availed themselves of opportunities to be among both other masculine women and more feminine lesbian women whose attitudes toward masculine women served to socially normalize, to some degree, participants' masculinity.

For the most part, however, the potential benefits which participants might have gained from their involvements in lesbian relationships and communities were tempered by the social stigma which continued to be associated with lesbianism. In addition, more separatist members of lesbian-feminist communities of the 1970s and 1980s were often theoretically inimical to extremely masculine women and denigrated those whom they felt overstepped the line between appropriate feminist rejection of femininity and the adoption of patriarchal masculinity. Thus, although some lesbian relationships and communities had the potential to powerfully validate participants' identities as extremely manly women, most participants felt unable to live their lives as freely and openly in their masculinity as they wished. For those participants who took no pleasure in being either rebels or social outcasts, the comforts which lesbianism offered were also limited.

Doing What's Expected: Heterosexual Relationships

Experimenting with Heterosexuality

Participants were split in terms of their adult experience with heterosexuality. More than half (55 percent)[1] of them made at least some minimal efforts at exploring heterosexual relations while they were living as adult women;[2] the rest declined the opportunity.[3] Although twenty-one participants (55 percent) became involved in some form of relationship with men during their adult years prior to embarking upon their gender and sex transitions, most participants limited their involvements to superficial and short-lived experimentation. Having experimented and found heterosexual relations unsatisfying, they generally abandoned the idea and became more firmly planted in their attractions to women.

Pat, Eli, and Hal were the least enthusiastic among those participants who did explore heterosexuality as adults. None of them went so far as to engage in heterosexual intercourse. Pat's entire heterosexual career consisted of "a couple of dates" when she was in college which were accompanied by "some trying to kiss and things like that." Pat gave it up because she "just couldn't deal with it."

Eli became slightly more involved in heterosexuality. Eli had dated as a teenager but recalled thinking that it was all a big joke. Later, as a young adult, Eli recalled dating a few young men "on a lark."

> You know, I thought this was what you were supposed to do, so I'll try it. And I tried it at a party one night and this guy was feeling me, and I was following him around the room because he was good looking. He looked like I wanted to be. I couldn't *be* him, so I went after him. So I feel that I was being the aggressor. . . . You know my body was responsive to it, but psychologically, emotionally, I was standing out here going, "That's interesting." . . . I wasn't turned on. . . . I wasn't afraid of it, it just made me feel uneasy inside like it was wrong.

Eli's total adult heterosexual experience consisted of two nonsexual dating episodes and two more in which her dates insisted that Eli become more sexually involved than she had intended. Eli seemed to have been quite unperturbed by her dates' sexually aggressive behaviors.

> One guy in college tried to pin me down or something. He invited me over for dinner . . . then really tried to force himself on me a little, but I felt sorry for him. I was stronger than him and I gave him an arm lock and said, "You don't do this to me. I came here for dinner." And one guy wanted me to play chess, he started to, you know. And I had to

wank him, because he was getting so turned on and he was nutty and we were drinking again. . . . I was just kind of going away scratching my head and wondering what the hell these guys want with me in that way, because I could never understand it. I thought they were kind of nuts to be interested in me in that way, because I just assumed that everybody knew that I wasn't like that.

Hal decided to try to have heterosexual intercourse one time but the whole incident turned into a hopeless fiasco which finished off her interest in such activities. Hal told this story about the evening:

> A young man . . . invited me to a party at his parents' house. I went, and his parents were out of town. There were three other couples there, and all they were interested in was getting it on. We were drinking up his father's liquor cabinet, and he got pretty plastered and took me to his parents' bedroom. I was not drunk, so I thought I was in control of the situation, and since I had never seen a penis before (other than my little brother's years ago) I thought I'd see what happened; maybe I'd learn something.
>
> The whole thing was pretty pathetic. We kissed a bunch, and I felt aroused but uninterested. He couldn't get an erection because he was too drunk. I let him touch me however he wanted to because I wanted to see what boys did. Then all of a sudden his parents came home and we had to split. He walked me home and got sick on our front patio. I had to drive him back to his house, and he threw up on the side of my mother's car too. I got him home, said goodnight (no kissing!), went home and hosed down the car and the patio. . . . I never saw him again (thank God!). This confirmed that I was not interested in having sex with men.

Another twelve participants (31 percent) who did try out heterosexual intercourse described their adult heterosexual involvements as having been limited to casual sexual encounters with men for whom they felt little or no affection.[4] Most often, participants reported that they engaged in these encounters because they felt some curiosity about the much-touted heterosexuality which was socially expected of them.

Mel had had relationships with other young girls while in her teens. She turned to men because she felt vaguely guilty about her lesbian relationships and felt she ought to try out heterosexuality because it might cure her of her growing gender and sex dysphorias. Mel recalled:

> I went through a period of denial . . . where, you know, "It's just me, I'm not trying hard enough to be female, it's my fault." And so I did all the things I was supposed to do. I went out and made sure that the guys liked me. Went out on dates. Tried that for a couple of years. That didn't work. . . . [I had sex with a guy] once. It was OK. It didn't do anything

for me. I was there. I was a body. I was not a participating body. I was just there.

Robin and Grant each had a single consensual heterosexual encounter which was motivated by curiosity. Robin recalled:

> I basically wanted to find out if I liked that. He knew that I was a lesbian, or he knew I was with women, and he was a friend of mine that I happened to find him attractive. . . . I wanted to find out what it was like to sleep with a man because I thought that was important to know. And so it happened once and that was it.

Grant, who identified as a gay man and generally found gay men sexually attractive, thought that she might try out sexual relations with a man. Grant's single voluntary investigation of heterosexual intercourse left her entirely unsatisfied. Grant remembered:

> If I was a heterosexual woman it would have been great. It was a total wash out. And I kept thinking—I think about it now, and it's hysterical—"You fool, what do you think my asshole is there for?!" That was a wash out. A complete and total wash out. . . . And it's like, what a waste, what an incredible waste!

Stan's approach to heterosexuality was also inspired by curiosity. Stan never dated but did instigate two experimental ventures into heterosexual coitus. The first occurred when Stan was a teenager, the other took place after Stan had decided "to do something about myself" but before she had taken any initiatives in that direction. Stan engaged in heterosexual intercourse the second time because she felt that once she had become a man, he would find the information useful.

> It was more like an observation. . . . I wanted to know what sex felt like for women, so I'm going to remember. . . . I'm going to do this this one time to see what it feels like; what you're supposed to do. . . . I didn't want to have sex like that. I didn't want to have someone doing that to me. . . . It's like I'm different from my body. It's like I took my body and said, "I'm going to check in and be with my body this one time so I can feel it, so that I'll know, so that I'll remember." I wanted to know how women felt. I, technically, was a woman, but I'm going, "I want to know what it feels like to have sex as a woman" so that when I had a relationship I would know what they were feeling. So I would know what works. . . . I wasn't in love with a man. . . . It was for the sex. I used him.

Only three participants' experimentation with heterosexuality was more prolonged. Ron, Ken, and Alan had extended but emotionally superficial relationships with men during their pre-transition adult years. They each continued patterns of heterosexual involvements which they began during their teen years.

Ron's heterosexual career started when she was fourteen years old. Ron recalled that she had had sexual relations with "under twenty" men during the years before commencing gender and sex reassignment. Ron said that despite her varied experience she had never loved any of the men whom she had bedded; nor had she had an orgasm with any of them. Ron remembered:

> They were buddies. We were friends, but it wasn't a sexual attraction. There was no chemistry, per se. I didn't feel like a heterosexual woman. I [felt] like somebody who was trying to fit in. Or just somebody who was checking it out. . . . I felt very, very odd.

The bulk of Ken's heterosexual experience consisted of the sexual abuse to which her father subjected her for many years. However, Ken did experiment briefly with heterosexual relations as a teenager. Later, as a young adult, she became "very involved" with a single male sexual partner until he asked Ken to marry him. Not only did Ken reject the man's proposal but she also ended the relationship, and, apparently, her heterosexual leanings.

Alan's sexual proclivities were decidedly the most varied of all participants. During periods of Alan's teen and young adult years she worked as a street prostitute, sometimes as a man, other times as a woman. Her work brought her into contact with many sexual partners with disparate sexual tastes. Alan described the range of her sexual experiences thus:

> I had a lot of paid and unpaid sex with anyone from the ages of fourteen to seventeen, and eighteen to twenty-four, and twenty-six to twenty-eight. Sex was often a drug for me. . . . I have been sexually or romantically attracted to females, males, transvestites, and transsexuals. I like pretty people who are feminine. It doesn't matter whether they are male or female, or in-between, as long as they are pretty (not handsome) and sexually submissive. I prefer females because I like the vaginal smell of women but I have had satisfying relationships with gay men or male-to-females.

The overwhelmingly clear pattern evinced by participants was a lack of interest in having sexual relations with men while they themselves were women. Half of all participants abstained from any kind of pre-transition adult heterosexual relations at all; twelve participants (32 percent) never engaged in any kind of consensual heterosexual genitality during their entire lives as women.[5] A further 21 percent of participants had only the most fleeting of either teenage or adult experience with men, having partaken in heterosexual intimate sexual relations less than a handful of times.[6] Thus by the time they had reached the points in their lives when they began to transform themselves into men and into males, twenty-five participants (66 percent) had had either no direct personal experience of consensual heterosexual coitus or very superficial experience gained through casual assignations with men for whom they felt little or no fondness and with whom they had no meaningful relationships to give emotional depth to their contacts. Although another nine participants did report considerably more comprehensive heterosexual experience,[7] three of them also had done so with very little emotional openness or commitment.[8]

Doing the Right Thing: Serious Heterosexual Relationships

The few participants who did become committed to extended heterosexual relationships as adult women were often doing what they felt was expected of them as women. In doing so, they tended to become attracted to men with whom they felt some commonality on the basis of their gender identities. They were attracted to men who seemed to be similar to the men whom they would themselves like to have been or they became involved with men who were somewhat androgynous. Peter and Keith recounted stories about long-term and personally meaningful relationships with men during their pre-transition adult lives. Lee, Dale, Aaron, and Sam each married and bore children with their husbands.

Peter talked about two involvements with men which occurred more than ten years apart and under very different circumstances. The first brief affair took place when Peter was a twenty-year-old college student. According to Peter, she felt neither love nor lust for the young man but rather became engaged in the liaison because "there was a lot of peer pressure." Peter described her rationale in these words:

> I go through periods in my life where I can't do anything about who I am . . . when you figure you're going to give it a big try. It's like the guy in college. . . . I was going to marry this guy. . . . I can't go out and be who I am, I can't be me. I don't have a choice about it. . . . But if you don't want to be alone then you're going to go along with the program, you're going to play this game.

Ten years later, Peter became involved with a man approximately twenty years her senior. In this instance, Peter said of their affiliation, "I think I was looking for a daddy; I found a hero." Although the relationship was a frankly sexual one, Peter was reluctant to see it as having been a heterosexual one. He recalled:

> It was crazy . . . but he taught me to fly an airplane. . . . He was my friend. And I helped him out with stuff. And he initiated something. And I went along with it. . . . I wouldn't turn it down, you know, be-

cause . . . this guy spent a lot of time with me. He taught me everything
he knew . . . and he's one hell of a pilot. . . . He would definitely see it
as male/female. I don't know how I would see that. I really don't know.
I would say we just touched one another. That's another segment of my
life that I would like to take a little Exacto knife and [cut out] that part
of the relationship.

These two relationships were the only consensual sexual or romantic relationships Peter had up to the time of his interviews.

By contrast, Keith had a full heterosexual life as an adult woman.
Keith said:

I had several relationships with men where I lived with them for a couple of years as marriage-type relationships. In between those times, I
dated. But here again [as had been the case in my teens], these relationships were basically based on the men being pleased, usually sexually.

The men with whom Keith became involved tended to be, in Keith's
memories, both macho and sensitive. One was a man whom Keith described as both "a really sweet, sweet person" with "a lot of very suppressed femininity" and "obviously a loser." The man had had "an extremely abused childhood" and had been "a derelict" who had been "in
and out of prisons" for such "extremely masculine" things as "beating
somebody's face in with a shovel." Keith described another of her long-
term lovers as a "lumberjack," "a genuinely masculine man" who was
"strong enough to be gentle," another "sweet man." Keith was particularly articulate about her reasons for taking up with these men:

I tried every partner and I couldn't get along with any of them. . . . No
matter what kind of person I was with, I related as what I felt a female
should be. In other words, my ideal female. And my ideal female . . .
was extremely different from what I really am. . . . I related to them as
something that I was not. And the relationships always fell apart. . . .
    What were my partners like? . . . Mostly a lot of very masculine men
because two reasons. For one thing, I relate to those kind of men because I am like that, we had a lot of similar interests, outdoorsy kind of
things. . . . Also, at the same time, I was with masculine men because by
contrast that made me more feminine. . . . And I had to say a lot of my
men were role models for what I've become today. I got involved with
men who, regardless of the fact that they were unsuitable in various
ways, nevertheless they were men who I wanted to emulate in some way.
Men who I looked up to, although ultimately I ended up not looking up
to them because in most cases I was every bit as masculine, and usually
more masculine, than they and they couldn't be aware of that because I
never let that show. . . . I tried my best to fulfill that role until I simply
could not do it any longer.

Keith's final heterosexual relationship was one in which she and her man-friend in many ways exchanged their gender and sexual roles. However, not even that relationship provided the gender expression of which Keith felt in need. Eventually, Keith came to the conclusion that she could no longer sustain such relationships because they were "a lie because I was putting myself across as something that I was not."

Lee and Dale both married at the age of nineteen years and had children with the first men with whom they ever had sexual relations. Neither their husbands nor their marriages gave Lee or Dale much satisfaction. Their cohabitations with their husbands were stormy and short-lived. However, the children whom they bore brought them both lasting pleasure.

Lee's marriage began after she became pregnant with her first daughter. She married because she knew neither how to procure an abortion nor how to transgress the 1960s social expectations that she should marry the father of her child. Lee and her husband lived together for brief periods off and on over the course of a few years. In between, Lee either lived with her parents or with a woman friend and the woman's husband. Neither living situation was very comfortable for Lee. Lee speculated that perhaps she went back to living with her husband because "I had no other life . . . maybe familiarity. . . . I must have thought I loved him." Lee also thought that sexual need might have had something to do with their reunions.

> I would disguise it then because I didn't look at sex as sex. It had to be romance. . . . I couldn't fathom any other way. In other words, a lot of times, if it were presented to me in a horny situation, I'd be turned right off. 'Cause I just couldn't fathom it. It was just dirty or something. It was just a really mixed up type of thing. . . . I didn't hate sex, except, actually, there were times when I did. . . . I was pretty immature with sex. I wasn't comfortable with it until I was almost thirty. So, he told me a lot about sex that I didn't know.

Lee became pregnant with her second daughter as a result of their reunions and her own ignorance about matters of birth control. Shortly before that birth, Lee became despondent about the future of her marriage and ended it. The combination of the abusiveness of her husband, the demise of her marriage, and Lee's dim prospects as a young, unskilled, single mother of two left Lee feeling suicidal.

> We lived together again. . . . It was worse than the first time. . . . It seemed like whatever I did, it wasn't right. . . . He put me through hell, and . . . I was as close as I've ever come to committing suicide. Well, no, not suicide. I wanted to blow his head off. And then I just wanted to die.

> I can remember thinking after I got out of that with the kids, I said,
> "My life is over. There's nothing left for me. So, I just got to make sure
> I get my kids raised, and then I can die."

Lee did go on to experiment with heterosexuality two more times after
escaping from her marriage. Each was a one-night stand. That proved to
be enough heterosexuality for Lee.

Dale's entire coital experience as a straight woman was with one man.
Dale also got pregnant and married young. Like Lee, Dale was extremely
naive and self-conscious about sexual relations and ended up in a sour
marriage because of her belief that she, as a young woman in the early
1960s, was "supposed to get serious about getting married." Dale's husband turned out to be sexually profligate and physically abusive. Dale described their relationship in these terms:

> I just never had a fucking happy moment. . . . He actually [wanted to]
> move out on me, and I begged him not to go. I didn't tell my family
> what was going on. I was too ashamed. Here I was, a failure. . . . He
> was terrible. He never came home, he partied all the time . . . he fooled
> around with other women. . . . I'd confront him and he'd beat the ever
> living shit out of me. But even then I guess I was afraid of being alone.
> . . . I had busted teeth. I had black eyes when I was pregnant. I was so
> embarrassed going to work. . . . He'd come home drunk, or wouldn't
> show up. . . . I thought I was a good wife. I cooked, I cleaned, I did
> whatever I was supposed to, and then I worked. When I was pregnant,
> I'd go to work, and he would come home drunk. . . . He really abused
> me. And he'd come home and he'd be sick a lot of the times. He'd be
> throwing up, and I hated him. I just really hated him. But . . . I was
> afraid to be alone. . . . [Finally] I decided . . . the only way I could sur-
> vive was to leave, and I moved back home with my daughter—which
> was another terrible time in my life.

With that move Dale closed herself off from heterosexual relations. Dale
made no further forays into sexual relations with men.

Sam, too, first married while still a teenager and probably a virgin.
The marriage soon started to yield both babies and abuse. Sam's first husband was a practicing Catholic who did not allow birth control and often
forced her to have sexual relations with him. Sam gave birth to five children as the result of eight pregnancies over the ten years of their marriage.
He remembered both the sexual relations and the childbirths with bitterness—the sexuality because it was coercive, the childbirths because, Sam
said, "with every pregnancy, I was not normal. I should never have had
kids. It almost killed them and me to have them."

When Sam married her first husband, she had great hopes for their
relationship. A promised trip to a tropical island never materialized and

the man's femininity, to which Sam had been attracted, gave way to life-threatening violence. Sam depicted the course of their relationship thus:

> I think the reason I could marry him, he was so female. . . . He was very, very happy being domestic. Makes a wonderful Grandma now. . . . You see he offered the adventure to me but also he offered this other side of himself that I could accept. . . . I took the responsibilities of the finances, the planning. If something would break down in the house, he would sit down and cry about it. [I would say,] . . . "Don't worry about it, I'll take care of it." And he did a lot of the cooking and a lot of the cleaning too. . . . He was the one who insisted on the clean house and taught me how to do it. . . .
>
> But slowly he progressed into an abusive pattern. And it got to the point where he was even sitting on top of the kids and beating their heads with his fists. He was trying to kill me at times. At other times, he would sit on my lap and cry. . . . Other times, he would jump up and he would hold his hand and arm up and say, "God made me perfect and you will obey me!" . . . And after trying to get him to the psychiatrist. He did go for a while and that doctor recommended that I get away, and get the kids away, as quickly as possible. Priest, same thing. Doctors, for years, had been telling me to get away from him. I finally had to do it.

Sam lived for many years as a single mother of five children while collecting welfare. During those years, Sam began to have severe health difficulties which caused her to be concerned that she might become hospitalized and thereby be forced to hand her children over to their unstable and pernicious father. When her mother became overburdened with other family obligations and was no longer able to offer Sam help with the care of the children, Sam, in desperation, accepted an offer of marriage from another man. Sadly, this man, too, turned out to be unsafe because of his psychological problems and because of his criminal connections. Sam soon realized that their marriage was not legal and dissolved the union. Although they lived together for only a few months, Sam reported that she continued to feel that her own life and those of her loved ones were endangered by this man for many years. These two marriages constituted the sum of Sam's pre-transition heterosexual encounters.

Aaron probably had the most successful and satisfying experience of heterosexuality of all participants, but even that relationship was marred by Aaron's gender and sex confusion. The best part of being married, for Aaron, was having children. Aaron explained that bearing children gave Aaron pleasure in her marital sexual life and a clearer sense of herself as a woman. Aaron elaborated on her feelings about having children:

> I enjoyed it. . . . I told my daughters that if you do it right the sex act can last for eighteen months. It's carrying a baby, delivering a baby. . . .

I liked having babies and nursing, it was a sexual thing. Very stimulating. . . .

And there's more to it than that. When a person has been ambiguous . . . you live in a sense where you never can quite please anybody. . . . Parents, spouses . . . the people you went with, the people you loved, you can't be what they want you to be. . . . When you're carrying a baby you're operating on instincts, things that nobody can argue with. And if you do that easily and well . . . you know damn well you're doing the right thing. People relate to you in a very comfortable way because they see you as a totally normal person during that time. A pregnant woman is obviously a woman and whether she's wearing pants and acting masculine really doesn't matter a damn. And . . . when I was actually delivering children I remember thinking, "Well for once I'm doing exactly what I'm supposed to be doing . . . and there's no conflict". . . . And I remember the satisfaction of being absolutely right and absolutely 100 percent involved in what I was doing. . . . So you see this whole thing of pregnancy and childbirth was an animal-level thing where I was very real, very in touch. . . . Very whole. Very complete. And very satisfied.

Aaron's marriage first floundered after Aaron had what he recalled as a possible fugue episode. Aaron, alone with the children while her husband was traveling for work, became enamoured of a female neighbour. She also "was exhausted a lot," and one day she "beat up the kids." Aaron recalled what happened next:

I didn't hurt them that bad, but I obviously had wanted to kill them or something had crossed my mind enough that I panicked and . . . [I went] running down the street to a neighbour, thinking I'd killed my kids. This panicked me. . . . What do you do? You don't want to be alone with kids you're going to kill if you care about them. So I asked for psychiatric help and the psychiatric evaluation diagnosis [of schizophrenic and possibly homosexual] was incorrect.

Aaron's husband reacted to Aaron's psychiatric diagnosis as a "crazy" homosexual by asking, "What does this make me?" Aaron assuaged her husband's apprehensions with a quick retort.

Our marriage stayed together for five years after that. You know why? Because this terribly distraught, upset, "mentally ill" person came up with the right words at the right time. Thank God for the gift of gab, and what I said to him, I laughed and said, "Honey, don't you realize that you are one of the few men that was so masculine you made me feel feminine by comparison?"

However, both Aaron and her husband continued to have problems with Aaron's emotional state. Aaron became "suicidal after a couple of years from all the guilt," and her husband became peripatetic, only living with the family from time to time. When Aaron became despairing about her ability to have more children, the marriage fatally faltered:

> I lost a baby. He didn't get any sex for about a month because . . . I was very very down from that loss. . . . When I lost that baby I knew I lost any chance at my one female rightness. . . . That is when my female self died. That identity died at that point. . . .
>
> He [came] . . . into the bedroom a day or two . . . after I had lost the baby and said, "Aren't we lucky?" meaning, I'm sure, financially. . . . But I knew that I could not sleep with him again. Because the reason for sex, the excitement of sex with a male had always been the remote possibility that I might get pregnant. . . . To sleep with a man that did not want the children that he was going to possibly conceive was just foreign to my mind. The desire for a male was the desire for babies. He would not make any more babies and I knew it . . . And that was the end of the marriage and I knew it. . . .
>
> He wanted a piece of tail one morning, 5:00 in the morning. I had been up during the night with the little girl that had allergies. . . . And for the first time in over nine years by then in our marriage . . . I just looked at him and said, "No." And he hit me. And that was maybe the second time in almost ten years that he had hit me and the other time he was drunk and it was a mistake and he felt terrible. . . . But I had grounds [for a divorce]. . . . So I thought, well I better file [for divorce] while I've got the grounds. . . . It was a pleasant relief for both of us.

This marriage and a single adolescent sexual encounter with her brother formed the sum of Aaron's heterosexual experience. Aaron's marriage was also her only pre-transition sexual relationship which lasted for a year or more.

In the end, each of the six participants (16 percent) who most seriously probed heterosexuality found that there were both rewarding and stifling aspects to their pre-transition adult heterosexual relationships. Peter found social acceptance among her young peers during her first relationship and placed a high value on the masculine companionship she enjoyed in her second one. Keith likewise appreciated sharing masculine pastimes with her lovers. Keith also benefitted from having opportunities to explore more fully than most participants what she felt like when playing out both feminine and masculine roles in heterosexual contexts. All four of the participants who married did so while they were still in their late adolescence, and each gave birth to children shortly after their marriages. Without a doubt, all four were grateful for the chance to have and to raise children of their own. As well, Lee, Sam, and Aaron periodically took some enjoyment in the sexual aspects of their marriages. Aaron also reaped a lifelong friend in the person of her ex-husband. All probably profited from the kind of female identity confirmation described by

Aaron—if not in their own eyes, at least in those of others, since women who are heterosexually married are credited by most members of society with genuine womanhood and full femaleness.

When participants weighed the benefits of straight relationships against the privations they suffered within their boundaries, however, they seemed to conclude that as long as they were women the deficiencies far outweighed the advantages. They enjoyed companionship but not passionate love. Although they took some sexual satisfaction in heterosexual relations, they also were just as likely either to be emotionally uninvolved or to be sexually used by their partners. Straight marriages also proved, for those participants who married as women, to be sites of multiple forms of abuse. Thus all of those participants who delved most earnestly into heterosexual relations eventually concluded that female heterosexuality required them to repress far too many aspects of themselves.

Summary and Commentary

Several incentives seemed to draw participants into some level of heterosexual involvement. On the simplest level, there were social pressures to conform. Females are supposed to be heterosexually inclined. This factor no doubt influenced all participants to some degree. Carnal desire was also clearly a factor in several instances. Males were widely available, socially approved, and easily accessible sources of sexual stimulation. Many participants reported finding some physical gratification in their sexual relations with males, but few recalled having found much romantic or emotional satisfaction. Apparently participants wanted more out of their intimate relations than fleshly fulfillment.

Masculine camaraderie was also an attraction for several participants. They searched for people with whom they could share their interests. The men to whom they gravitated were the kinds of men they wanted to be. In some cases, participants looked to these men in order to be defined as womanly in their shadows. Other participants were more inclined to prefer men with whom they felt they could function as masculine peers. Still other participants took a slight twist to their relationships by becoming involved with men who were somewhat feminine and would allow participants to feel masculine by comparison, while still retaining the social benefits of appearing to be appropriately heterosexually engaged.

The dominant pattern which emerged from the tales told by participants about their heterosexual exploits as adult females nonetheless was one of disinterest, disappointment, and dissatisfaction. Approximately half of participants were so uninterested in being women in sexual relationships with men that as adults they never gave them a try.[9] Among the 55 percent who did delve into the matter,[10] most of them retreated again after a small number of hasty skirmishes. It almost seemed as though they wished to establish a claim that they had not repudiated heterosexuality on the basis of hearsay alone. Having taken their obligatory tastes of their socially prescribed medicine, they could faultlessly pronounce to themselves and to others that they had tried to do things the correct way and had found that it did not work for them. As such, their nods to conventions may have made it easier for some participants to justify their more wholehearted pursuits of homosexual relations.[11]

Those participants who did make more substantial commitments to heterosexuality as a lifestyle indicated that it served them in two important additional ways. Lee, Dale, Sam, and Aaron gleaned the lifelong pleasures of parenthood from the children whom they bore during their marriages. All were proud to have their own children, at whatever cost. The other major way in which their long-term heterosexual relationships were useful to them was in the assistance they provided in helping to clarify gender, sex, and sexuality issues for them. Both those participants who became involved with a variety of men and those whose associations were more binding were able to use the men they knew as foils against whom to measure themselves as women and as men, as females and as males. Their senses of themselves as failures as women and as females were deepened by their inabilities to respond to men as they believed women should. At the same time, they appeared to make use of the men with whom they were intimate as both positive and negative role models for their own incipient masculine identities.

Thus it would seem that participants either avoided heterosexual relations entirely during their pre-transition adult years or managed to construe such relations in ways which allowed them to continue to move further into their identities as men and as males. Clearly, a number of participants passed many years in heterosexual relationships committed to doing their best to fulfill their roles as women. No doubt they succeeded as well as do many people who never question their own genders, sexes, or sexualities. Nevertheless, the fact remains that all of them not only eventually turned their backs on being heterosexual females but also were able to reinterpret their heterosexual experiences in ways which validated their identities as men and as males. Their heterosexual interludes thus became learning experiences which furthered them on their roads to transsexualism, experiences from which they could profitably draw later in their lives as straight men.

Leading to Love: Homosexual Relationships

During their pre-transition adult years, participants exhibited a clear preference for sexual and romantic relationships with women. Whereas twenty-nine participants (76 percent) had little or no pre-transition adult heterosexual experience,[12] an identical number of participants (71 percent)[13] became involved in homosexual relationships lasting one year or more during the same portion of their lives.[14]

Waiting to Get It Right:
Little or No Pre-Transition Adult Homosexual Experience

Eight participants (19.5 percent) refrained from pre-transition adult homosexual relations altogether.[15] Morgan, Bill, Terry, Gary, and Larry had neither frankly sexual homo- nor heterosexual experience during their entire pre-transition lives. Jordie had minor involvements with men as an adult but abjured relationships with women because of her identity as a gay man. Peter had heterosexual experience but eschewed sexual relations with women until becoming a man. Thus, of the eight, only Peter, Jordie, and Keith, came to their transitions into men with any experience of consensual genital sexuality of any kind.

Brian, Eli, and Aaron were the only participants whose explorations of homosexual relations during their pre-transition adult years remained relatively superficial. Brian, who was uncommonly uninterested in sexuality, said:

> I did not explore sexual experience until I was in my late teens and early twenties when I was very much on my own and trying to learn my way in the world. I had a few experiences with both males and females, based more on the other person's persistence than my desire. These acquaintances fell apart very quickly and I avoided them soon after such experiences. Temporary sensations did not override my sense that my own integrity was jeopardized. I have remained celibate since my early twenties.

As an adult, Eli was seduced by a woman on only one occasion. That single sexual encounter took place after the onset of Eli's delayed emotional adolescence, which Eli said didn't materialize until she was in her fourth decade. As Eli had done the one time she had had sexual relations with a female during her youth, Eli saw herself as a man. Eli recalled how it happened:

> I had consumed a rather intense bottle of whiskey, I was pretty smashed. . . . And she kind of lured me into her bedroom. . . . So, I thought . . . here's a real woman. I don't have to make this up, you know. She dragged me . . . into her bed, and I was giggling and falling around, and then I was really freezing cold. . . . I was like a block of ice. And she just put her arms and legs all around me and held me like that 'til I started to warm up. And after that, as they say, the inevitable happened. . . . I was going at it like a real guy would go at it. Missionary position and all. And this went on and on. Finally she must have had some kind of

gigantic orgasm, 'cause . . . it was incredible. . . . But nothing happened for me. . . . I felt kind of stupid. . . . [But] I felt kind of proud of myself the next day, 'cause I knew that she really got off on it. . . . It made me feel like kind of . . . a stud.

Aaron also postponed her homosexual adventures until she was in her forties. Aaron started to think of herself as "probably gay" around the age of twenty-five when her psychiatrist diagnosed her as homosexual. Aaron accepted that label as descriptive of herself because "the only image I could think of was women that fell in love with women, and women that dressed and wanted to be men and acted masculine. I figured that was what a gay woman was." After her divorce from her husband three years later, Aaron remained celibate and separate from other lesbian women because "frankly, I wouldn't have kept my kids if I wasn't." Nonetheless, during that fifteen-year period, Aaron recalled, "I was living primarily in male clothing. . . . [people] just assumed I was a dyke."

At the end of the 1970s, two days after Aaron's youngest daughter turned eighteen years old, Aaron started having a series of affairs with lesbian women at the university where she was taking courses. A number of brief affairs and one ten-month relationship demonstrated to Aaron that she was not like other lesbian women. Aaron concluded that this meant that she was actually transsexual.

Aaron described two aspects of her process of discovery. On one level, she found herself at odds with the lesbian community in which she was situated.

Let's face it . . . they saw the woman's body, and figured I was a gay woman, and I went along with that. . . . It means sticking up for the female when you get into a discussion with a bunch of women on wife beating, or sticking up for the feminist role when you get with a bunch of women and no men around, or when there's men and women both, preferring the company of the women. . . . I was trying to get along with these women; I was trying to love some of these women . . . but I didn't fit. And the longer I was with them, the more I realized I didn't fit. . . . I hated the word. . . . I never used the label lesbian. Because lesbian throws out anything male. Lesbian is a female word, and I could not handle it. . . . One of the things . . . I learned was that I wasn't too attracted to most gay women . . . for loving relationships. . . . They're more brothers.

Although Aaron did integrate herself into an activist lesbian community, she always felt different from the women around her. Aaron recalled why:

When I got involved with gay women and found out how frigging different I was it was obvious. Up until that point I thought that other gay females were the same as me, they wanted to be male. And when I found out that was not true, no matter how masculine they acted that they had female identities, I realized I don't quite fit in here, but I fit in closer here than I ever have, of course, we had a lot of the same problems, and the same causes. So I worked with them, and dealt with them, and enjoyed them, but . . . I didn't fit in. A room full of gay women is just as bad as a room full of pregnant women as far as I was concerned. I felt the same way. They were still women.

On a more intimate level, Aaron further found that she did not respond to her lesbian lover in the ways which both of them believed were characteristic of lesbians. Aaron drew this picture of the issues involved:

> Basically she wanted a woman. At the nitty-gritty deep level I wasn't a woman. . . . Okay, concrete example. She didn't mind if I went to a party in a male shirt, a male pair of pants, and so on. But she wanted me to wear a chain around my neck that she had bought for me and I said, "No. . . . I'm sorry. I'm not compromising. . . . I can't do it." . . . And our lovemaking. She would resent it when I got too masculine. . . . When I became too aggressive and too demanding, too macho, whatever, it ruined it for her. As long as we were equals, or I was being the passive one and let her be a little bit aggressive, it was alright. But. . . . hey, I want to be on top part of the time . . . figuratively and literally. And it would . . . slow her response down and turn her off right when mine was speeding up. We didn't match.
>
> Out of bed, the same kinds of things. I could get sarcastic and smart enough with the guys just like I do at work or something like that and she would resent it. "Why are you behaving this way? You don't have to act this way with company, you don't have to show off." I wasn't showing off, I was being me. It's the way I learned to be with a gang of guys, we have a good time. But it offended her. . . . It bothered her enough that she knew . . . there was something basically wrong there. And what was basically wrong was my maleness.

Aaron construed these events as evidence that she did not belong among lesbians. With the assistance of her lover she concluded that she was transsexual.

Thus eleven participants (27 percent) either mostly or entirely evaded homosexual relations during their pre-transition adult years.[16] Five of them began their transitions never having experienced consensual sexual relations with partners of either sex.[17]

For the Love of Women: Major Homosexual Relationships

The bulk of participants (68 percent) became involved in significant sexual or romantic relationships with women during their pre-transition adult lives.[18] The reasons which they gave for these liaisons were largely based in romantic explanations; however, participants' intimate relationships with women also served as testing grounds for their gender, sex, and sexual identities. In the process of fully exploring lesbian relationships, participants came to feel that the social and sexual relations of lesbianism did not satisfy their needs for masculine self-expression. Thus, although lesbianism allowed for better articulations of their masculinity and sexual orientation, ultimately they rejected it as not viable for themselves. Having done so, they felt that they were left with few options other than finding ways to live as men.

Exhausting All Possibilities:
Major Adult Homosexual and Heterosexual Relationships

Eight participants (19.5 percent) moved into significant commitments to homosexual relationships after extensively exploring heterosexuality either as adult women or as teenaged girls.[19] For the most part, these individuals initially threw themselves into lesbianism wholeheartedly. They became friends with other lesbian women and participated in social or political activities with them. They were thus exposed to socialization processes which taught them something of what lesbian subcultures expected from their members. That exposure convinced them that lesbianism did not suit them well.

Lee and Ron both had fully engaged with heterosexuality before abandoning that sexual orientation in favour of their attractions to women. Lee discovered a lesbian crowd some years after taking her two daughters and finally separating from her husband. Her first two lesbian relationships were with other women who also had children from previous marriages. Lee had little time for a social life during either her first four-year lesbian relationship or her second two-year lesbian relationship because of the nine children in the first and four children in the second of her blended families. Lee remembered that she was confused about her identity through both of these relationships because "I would always take on the male role, and yet, I knew I wasn't a male." At the same time, Lee recalled, "It's like I wasn't gay enough. Of course, I didn't want to acknowledge gay either. I mean, what the hell am I? . . . You had to think that we were lesbians. . . . I didn't dwell on it a lot."

While in her early thirties, Lee began to enjoy the community life of the gay bars in her city. In that environment, she gradually began to indulge more in her masculine proclivities. Lee remembered one part of her gay bar life this way:

> I felt my best with . . . hair short and combed back, and with men's
> pants on . . . and a flashy shirt with it buttoned down here, and maybe

> with the collar up . . . People know that you're not a guy, but yet, you're certainly more that way than you are the other way. . . . When I looked in the mirror those times when I was dressed up and those times when I was a few years younger, I thought, "Yeah. You're a nice looking young boy". . . . [But] there's absolutely no future in being a very masculine lesbian. . . . It was great, up to, say, five years ago. . . . I'm getting older, and it's showing. Up till then, I got away with [it]. . . . I was young looking. . . . I looked more like a boy.

As time went on, Lee began to realize just how different she was from the other lesbians whom she knew.

> In the lesbian world, from what I've observed . . . is if you're a true lesbian, you're a woman who enjoys being a woman who enjoys being with women. So, I don't fit that. Because I very rarely acknowledge being a woman. It even bothers me to have to say that. . . . I have to feel . . . that I am the aggressor. . . . I don't want to be loved as a woman wants to be loved.

Ron, after extensive explorations of heterosexual relations, became embedded in a lesbian community. Ron came to be extensively committed to lesbian-feminist activities in which she acquired a thorough knowledge of the culture of lesbian feminists. Ron enumerated the extent of her affiliations thus:

> I didn't really take the [lesbian] identity. What I did was I worked off my guilt, and committed hours of community service; guilt about wanting to belong to the other pack, for wanting to be a man. . . . I used it very much to get an education in what women wanted. . . . I participated in and organized a lot of marches and stuff, and I participated in the rape crisis centre. . . . And with a lot of the activities, I could empathize because I was in a female body.

Like Lee, Ron also concluded, on the basis of her knowledge of lesbian social and sexual mores, that she was neither a lesbian nor a woman.

Ron said that she had sexual relations with between twenty and fifty women during her lesbian phase. Among them were three relationships of four years' duration each with women whom Ron described as heterosexual and one noteworthy relationship of six months' length with a "radical lesbian feminist." It was in the sexual aspects of these relationships that it became clear to Ron that she was better suited to being a man and male than to being a woman and female. Ron remembered:

> For one thing, sexual definitely played a big role. . . . I used the sexual avenue to clarify things in a lot of ways. . . . I had to go through and analyze for myself whether I was just a strong female, or whether I was

a male. Whether I just didn't fit into the stereotypical female sexist kind of role, or whether there was something biological. . . .

For instance, being with women . . . the love I got was towards the woman, the physical woman. And for me, that was a conflict sexually. . . . For instance . . . I was not making love as a woman with a woman. From my heart, it was that I was a male. . . . It's a completely different dynamic. . . . There is a different approach from a woman to her man than the approach from one woman to another woman who are lovers. . . . it comes out in power differences. . . . With relating to a masculine female, the areas of allegiance are different ones, that have to do with common experience. . . . there's so many more similarities. And really, a depth of understanding of the psyche, and of the heart, and of the sexuality. And in a heterosexual relationship, you also have depth, but it brings in other unknown factors that kind of demand a stretch, a greater give. . . . There were a lot of needs that I could not express with lesbians, because the lesbians that I was having relationships with were not open to anything that had anything to do with male.

Thus Ron preferred the sexual relations which she had with women whom Ron identified as heterosexual. Ron called them heterosexual because of the prior sexual histories of the women and because it was in relation to those women that Ron felt like a man. These relationships, especially when contrasted with those which Ron construed as truly lesbian ones, felt the most corroborative of Ron's rising identity as a man and as a male.

Darcy likewise found that the sexual aspects of lesbian relationships provided her with little more satisfaction than had her adolescent attempts at heterosexuality. Darcy had always had trouble reconciling herself to the fact of her femaleness. She generally thought of herself as not female, not male. Darcy said that thinking of herself as a lesbian was "the closest I've come to try and think of myself as a female person." Darcy found a niche for herself, for a time, among S/M lesbians, but Darcy usually would not allow her women lovers to touch her in explicitly sexual ways. Darcy gave several reasons for her abstemiousness:

I think I felt dishonest. . . . I don't think I had a right to any sort of satisfaction, frankly, because I don't think I was who I was. I felt guilty, and like there's something wrong.

Darcy went on to become the first female hired to the staff of a gay publication. Her position at the publication provided Darcy with a window into a gay men's community. While working with the men, Darcy began to move from a lesbian identity into a gay one. Darcy, however, was not particularly interested in actually becoming a gay man. As Darcy put it:

> If you don't have the equipment, there's no point in being a gay man. . . .
> I like the attention. I would like to be kept by an older gay man, per-
> haps, for a time. I don't think I'd want to be porked up the butt. I don't
> like giving head. So, I don't think it would work.

Ironically, at the time of her interview, Darcy was living with a woman
whom Darcy described as a "fag hag" and who thought of Darcy as a gay
man even though Darcy had not yet embarked upon living full-time as a
man. Darcy was willing to have intimate sexual relations with this woman
but mostly felt unable to do so as long as she was still physically female.
Darcy explained:

> I feel guilty now. . . . I'm just about seized up at this point, sexually. . . .
> I feel dishonest. And a lot of the situations are very much trust oriented.
> . . . And I cannot do that now, 'cause that's breached that trust. . . . Be-
> cause of the transsexual stuff. Because I finally figured out that I'm not
> going to change on my own . . . and so I'm walking around with a lie. I
> couldn't expect somebody to trust me.

Ken, after a long history of being incestuously heterosexually abused
and a few unfulfilling consensual heterosexual encounters, went on to
have three major homosexual relationships before she began her gender
and sex transitions. The first took place when she was in college and lasted
for three years. Ken said of it, "I guess we were considered lesbians at that
time." During the second, five-year relationship, Ken decided that she was
transsexual. Ken and her female partner "did have everything two female
people could have," including Ken playing "the masculine part of the
role" in their relationship. Ken had "millions of lesbian friends," went to
a gay church and gay bars, and sometimes thought of herself as lesbian.
Yet as soon as Ken found out about the availability of gender and sex reassignment, lesbianism seemed entirely inadequate and Ken "decided
point-blank" to leave it behind. Ken's female partner "walked out, she
couldn't handle it. . . . she rejected me." Ken's third woman lover took up
with Ken with the understanding that Ken was headed into gender and sex
reassignment. When I met Ken, seven years later, he and this woman were
married as a straight couple and had an adopted son.

Harry went through half a dozen relationships with women in the
process of coming to identify as transsexual. In the beginning, Harry was
convinced that her attractions to women were "wrong," but she acted
upon them anyway. Therefore, when Harry first visited a gay bar and met
gay women, she was both excited and uneasy. At the bars, Harry "still felt
there something was wrong . . . something was off." Harry's first sexual
experience with a woman left her cold and confused. Harry recalled:

I didn't orgasm. I didn't feel comfortable. I was basically a dead fish. . . .
It seems to me she was very excited about my femaleness, and that was
the one thing I didn't want her to be excited about. So, that part was a
turn off. . . . I didn't enjoy it, and didn't understand it, and I was confused. Then I thought, "If I don't like this, then what the hell do I like?"

As Harry continued to try out lesbianism in other relationships, she
found that she could not find any sexual enjoyment with women who in
any way wanted to relate to the specifically female aspects of her body.
Therefore, as had many other participants, Harry generally kept her
clothes on throughout her lovemaking sessions. As Harry put it, "It was
a lot better to leave my clothes on because it helped with the illusion."
Harry's lovers, for the most part, were more than willing to cooperate
with the maintenance of this illusion. Harry recalled that both she and her
partners were reluctant to label their relationships as lesbian ones.

When Harry did start to imagine that she might be transsexual, she
spoke with some of the lesbian women whom she knew at a gay bar. Their
reactions served to further alienate Harry from any rapport which she
might have felt with them.

I started having problems with some of the women at the gay bar, when
I started telling them about myself. . . . I remember some of the women
freaking out on me, like, "You're nuts! You're really crazy! You're a traitor! You don't know what you're talking about. You're confused. You're
trying to turncoat on us!" . . . But there were two or three that I could
talk to, and I felt close to.

In sum, these participants found that neither homosexual nor heterosexual relations allowed them to express their identities adequately. Having abandoned heterosexual relations, they entered into homosexual ones.
After some initial delight at the increased tolerance for their masculinity
which they found among lesbian women, participants began to encounter limitations. They found that the social and sexual values of lesbian
women did not align as well with their own as they might have wished.
Eventually the disjunctures between their own self-images and the images
which they held of what lesbian women were like became too disquieting to them. They concluded that they were neither straight nor lesbian
women. Transsexualism offered them a way out of their conundrum.

Following Their Hearts: Major Homosexual Relationships but Little or No Heterosexual Experience

More commonly, participants' major pre-transition sexual experiences were entirely or almost entirely homosexual ones. Twenty (49 per-

cent) of those participants who became involved in major homosexual relationships during their pre-transition adult years did so against a backdrop which included little[20] or no[21] consensual heterosexual coitus during their entire lives as girls or women. However, the concerns with which they embraced homosexuality and those over which they ultimately came to reject it were similar to those which occupied the attentions of participants who had more extensively tested themselves against heterosexuality.

Half of those participants whose pre-transition sexual experience was almost entirely homosexual stayed away from places where homosexual women congregated. They fell in love and built relationships with women, but most of them never fully accepted identities as lesbian women.[22] They cast themselves as lovers of women whom they thought of as strictly heterosexual. They conceived of their partners as being attracted to them for their manly qualities and did what they could to nurture their mutual conceptualizations of their relationships as straight ones. In addition, Dennis, who had been integrated into a lesbian community, also characterized her relationships as straight ones.

Several participants were particularly virulent in their rejection of any hint that they might be lesbian women. For example, Mel was unable to ever become comfortable with the idea that she might be seen as a lesbian. Mel went so far as to tell all of her lovers that if they ever told anyone about their relationships Mel would "do what is necessary to make the biggest liar out of you." Mel concluded that, appearances notwithstanding, she had nothing in common with lesbians:

> [My lover's] sister was gay. Because of her sister I knew I wasn't gay. Her sister lived with us for a couple of months, and another time a friend of her sister who was a gay man also lived with us for a couple of months. And I would talk to them, and I would listen, and I would ask them questions, and I would listen to what they said about how they felt with their partners, and it was just not me at all. . . . The difference between me and lesbians was when I would make love, and when I would think about sex, I always thought of myself as having a penis; that would make it complete.

Stan also refused to be branded as a lesbian. Although Stan remembered always having had "feelings about [women] like guys do," Stan always felt exceptionally guilty about those feelings, even as she was having several years of otherwise satisfying relationships with women. As Stan tried to work through this contradiction, she became so depressed at the thought that she might be lesbian that she ended up spending several months hospitalized for psychological problems. Stan also reported that she later destroyed one of her relationships with the heavy drinking and marijuana which she used to help her cope with her extreme aversion to being thought of as a lesbian woman. Stan explained:

> When I came to grips with I must be a lesbian, I couldn't deal with that. I couldn't handle that. . . . I don't know why. . . . but I couldn't be one. I just could not tolerate being a lesbian. . . . I guess the sin of it all. I couldn't consider myself that bad, that sinful.

As was probably common among many homosexual women of Stan's generation, Stan seemed to have two different views of what it meant to be lesbian. On the one hand, Stan held a more traditional view of lesbian women as sinful and sick. On the other hand, Stan had also been exposed, through the media, to a more feminist vision of lesbianism:

> I knew about lesbians but it just didn't occur to me that's what it was. . . . What I knew about lesbians was that two women can be together and it's okay if you are a lesbian. . . . It was something they did on the coast in the big cities, more liberal people did. I just didn't consider myself that liberal, that open-minded. . . . To get into being a lesbian, like, you have to march for things, and you gotta go to caucuses, you gotta hate men, you gotta dress butch, and you gotta get into all that stuff, and I didn't want to do that.

Having been unable to comfortably adopt a lesbian identity, when Stan discovered transsexualism, she latched onto it with great hopes for its normalizing potential.

> Could I just be a normal? God, what was I? I don't even know what I was. I was not a woman, a girl. I didn't really put a label on it. I was just a person with female parts that the whole world thought was a girl. . . . I thought [gender and sex reassignment] would make it better. That we could be normal. We could be normal. This is what's really been going on anyway, and now we can just act like it. We don't have to pretend that we are lesbians. We don't have to go to gay bars. We don't have to be on the fringes of society. We can be perfectly normal. We could have the horses, and the white picket fence, and we could get married. . . . People could be proud of us. We wouldn't have to slink around. We could just be proud to be in love and be a couple, and pay credit cards back, and barbecues in the back yard, and just all that stuff.

Jack, too, refused ever to picture herself as a lesbian woman. Jack had had only one lover up to the time of his interview. They had met at their place of employment at a time when Jack was a female and her lover (eventually his wife) was a straight married woman. Jack was very naive about sexual matters and became disoriented by the woman's advances.

> We were working on some paperwork standing next to each other and she says, "You know, I love you," and I almost fell over because I

thought, "No, no, this is not for me! I don't know what to do! Get away!" All the warning signs are coming on, and I said, "Okay that's nice." . . . I didn't want people to think I was gay because I'm not, and that's the first thing you're going to think if you have any feelings [for women]. . . . I was so shocked. I thought, "What the hell's the matter with her?" I thought, "Maybe it's like when my mom says it," you know? I was so innocent.

The woman went on to seduce Jack and to leave her husband so that they could establish an ongoing sexual and romantic relationship. Jack provided the woman with sexual gratification, but Jack was unable to find orgasmic satisfaction until after she began to identify as transsexual. Until then, Jack usually "went numb" shortly after becoming sexually aroused.

Significantly, when Jack told her partner that she felt more like a man than a woman, the woman was relieved and encouraged Jack to proceed with gender and sex reassignment.

She was the only person . . . outside my mother that I actually said anything to her about it. And she said, "That's why I feel this way." She was very happy to hear about it, 'cause I think we were both feeling like we were gay for a while.

Jack's partner thereby helped to substantiate Jack's belief that she was more like a straight man than a lesbian woman. Their eight years and ongoing relationship and the fact that Jack's partner stayed with Jack through Jack's transition only serve to underscore the power of having an intimate partner who shares one's hopes and dreams.

Dennis managed to have a very full life among lesbian women while still remaining convinced that bodies and beloveds notwithstanding, she was not lesbian. Dennis frequented gay bars, gay bookstores, lesbian dances and support organizations because "I enjoyed being out and socializing, and having a great time." Dennis was very popular with the women she met, and many of them approached her for sexual relationships. Although Dennis enjoyed a number of sexually active relationships with women whom she met in these environments, Dennis was able to retrospectively interpret these relations as straight ones. Dennis claimed that the women with whom she had been involved were bi women who related to Dennis as a man. When Dennis first connected with the idea of female-to-male transsexualism, she "had no doubts whatsoever. I felt like, you know, where did I miss the boat? How did I not know this was me?"

Howie's comments summed up well the logic of how these participants rebuffed lesbian identities in favor of ones as men. At first Howie thought that she and her lover were lesbian but then:

Later . . . upon closer investigation I realized that lesbians enjoyed their womanhood and didn't want to change their bodies surgically. They were simply women who loved women. I realized I didn't fit that mold at all. . . . A lesbian is a woman, who is glad she's a woman, who happens to relate sexually to other women. She does not wish to be male. In fact, she rejoices in her femaleness and wants to be with other females. . . . I knew that wasn't for me. . . . I often wish I could have accepted myself as gay, or identified as gay, because it is infinitely easier than changing.

These eleven participants were all sexually oriented toward women but resisted seeing themselves as bona fide lesbian women. Nine of them found ways, outside of established lesbian environments, to meet women with whom they could establish sexual or romantic relationships. One result of their making contact with their lovers independently of communities of similarly disposed women was that they had only popular construals of the nature of lesbianism against which to measure themselves. By the time that they were making such comparisons, lesbian-feminist definitions had begun to move definitions of *lesbian* away from the "mannish woman" typology popular before the 1970s and toward a "woman-loving-woman" characterization which has become more dominant since then.[23] As a group, they found the later definition less acceptable than the arguably more stigmatized former one and so rejected the label of lesbian in favour of identifying as men. The situation was, of course, compounded by the deeply entrenched homophobia of the day.

Ten participants among those with extensive homosexual but little or no consensual heterosexual experience (50 percent) did avail themselves of communities of homosexual women during their pre-transition adult years.[24] In some cases, these communities were highly politicized ones whose members espoused lesbian-feminist ideologies concerning the nature of lesbianism. In other instances, they were communities of women who came together at bars or ball games and who were less heavily influenced by feminist political analyses of lesbian identity. Nine of these ten participants accepted, at some time during their adulthoods, the label of lesbian as descriptive of themselves only to later reject it as inadequate.[25] They came to their conclusions after making comparisons between their senses of themselves and their visions of how they believed that lesbians thought and acted. When they reckoned that they were beyond the range of what constituted lesbian thoughts and deeds, they became receptive to the possibilities of transsexualism as a means of realigning themselves with their social worlds.

Robin began her lesbian career at a gay bar. At first, Robin had difficulties assimilating into a lesbian identity. Robin recalled, "I never really felt comfortable with the name lesbian for a long time." Despite this discomfort, Robin wanted to meet other women who were sexually aroused by women and so she found her way to a gay bar. But the women she met there were less than hospitable.

> The first thing out of their mouths was, "You have to change your image if you want to be with women." And I definitely didn't understand that. So my whole experience with that bar was a total negative experience. I went out of there feeling totally I hated it. This wasn't me. I wasn't accepted the way I was. What was wrong with me? I still don't know to this day why they said that.

Robin persevered and found a more accommodating community of women at the local gay centre. From there she went on to have a number of highly committed lesbian relationships through which she became "pretty settled in with" a lesbian identity. Nevertheless, the sexual dynamics of her lesbian relationships came to convince Robin that she would be better off as a man. Robin described her sexual relations with one of her partners as typifying the problem. Robin wanted to perform as a man and her partner wanted to make love to her as a woman.

> My sex with her, it wasn't real good. For one thing, I was used to being in my fantasies, and masturbating I was most of the time a man. And in sex with her . . . she saw me as a woman and . . . the way I wanted to have sex was not the way she wanted to have sex. . . . Well for one thing I was really naive at sex, I didn't know many ways of doing sex . . . and most of the time I wanted to be on top. . . . For lack of words, riding her. And she didn't enjoy that. When I was with her . . . she wanted to touch me and I allowed her to touch me. . . . I didn't like my body, didn't like my breasts, didn't like it when she touched me or made love to me. . . . It became an issue in our relationship. . . . We started having less and less sex. The relationship just dwindled down.

Like Robin, Bruce felt an attraction to lesbianism both as an identity and on a sexual level. Bruce at first believed that it was wrong for her to be sexually attracted to other girls or women: "And then the gay movement came in and I thought, 'there's my out, I'll be a lesbian.'" Soon Bruce became immersed in gay politics.

> I think I really felt compelled to the gay movement. I really wanted to be a part of it because . . . I believed in it. I believed in that people should love people whoever they are. There's so much hate in the world. If two people of the same sex want to love each other, who cares? It's love, right? Who has the right to dictate what the heart does? Heart has no boundaries.

Bruce subsequently went through a series of relationships with women in which she garnered very little sexual satisfaction. Bruce eventually settled into a four-year relationship with a lesbian-feminist woman who seemed supportive of Bruce's identity as a man. Shortly after they had had a child together by donor insemination, Bruce stumbled upon the idea of transsexualism and began to pursue it in earnest. Bruce described how these events unfolded:

> It felt better being a lesbian than before because it felt right that I could love women this way. . . . But I felt the sex part wasn't working. . . . for a long time, I think our relationship was just a relationship . . . but there was no more sex, really . . . [Then] I saw this show [about trans-sexualism] and I called up [a friend], and she gave me a book, and I was glued to this book for . . . two days. . . . And I remember sitting at the table, and I put the book down at the last page, and I just started to cry. I said, "This is me." And I got up and I went to bed, and I just cried and cried. I couldn't stop crying. I just cried. Tears like I had never cried. It was like, "This is me. There's hope."

Luther, who also hopefully threw herself into a lesbian-feminist community, found both conflict and comfort among lesbian feminists. Luther explained:

> If I was going to be a woman, why couldn't I be a normal woman? . . . On my path to normalcy I said to myself, "What you are going to do is you're going to be a lesbian. This is clear. It's the best you can do, so you may as well do it." So, I decided to live as a gay woman, and did so from the time I was about eighteen to thirty. . . .
>
> When I decided to go into the gay life, the first group of women that I met were white women. And at that time, white women were going through this controversy over role playing versus non-role playing. . . . I was always trying to explain my position, and saying that I was not imitating anybody. This is me. This is who I was. This is the real thing. . . . That was not an issue with black women. And so, that was very good for me. Although I didn't feel that there were women there that understood my position, I certainly could be who I was, and not have anyone . . . tell me that I was politically incorrect. . . .
>
> [But] people were still relating to me as a woman, and I just couldn't take it. So it didn't work. And I think that's what really made me decide that I would eventually have surgery. Because . . . I was still the outsider.

In Luther's more intimate relations, this was less of a problem. Luther said, "all of the women that I had relationships with . . . were women who were having their first lesbian relationship and were happy that they could have a heterosexual relationship with me." Luther proudly pointed out that as a woman she never allowed any of her lovers to see or touch her breasts or genitals and that she always pleasured them using a dildo. Thus

Luther found confirmation of her identity as a man and a male in the sexual and emotional practices of these relationships.

Walter's story further illustrated the experiences of some of those participants who became embedded in lesbian feminist communities. Walter recalled how her identity as a man developed as she passed through a lesbian-feminist stage:

> Being newly involved in the lesbian community, I had to de-emphasize certain aspects of myself. . . . I felt that I was male but, because I had decided that really the lesbian community was the only place that I could ever begin to fit in in a sexual context, I felt that I had to. I really felt that I was being dishonest . . . because I was pretending to be female identified, but I really wasn't. . . . After I had been involved with the lesbian community for a while, then I started to assert my own personality, and I just said, "Fuck it." And I started to be [more] masculine. . . . And I actually would be crossdressing, and I would go into lesbian bars with a moustache on. It causes a lot of problems. . . . It wasn't easy. And then, thank God, I discovered transsexuality.

Of all participants, Hal probably made the deepest commitments to lesbianism and lesbian feminism. Hal spent twenty-two years living as a lesbian, during which time she had five major relationships, four of which lasted for a year or two and one of which went on for thirteen years. Hal said that as a lesbian woman she always felt like a man on the inside and believed that her women lovers recognized this facet of her.

> I didn't know what to do with my male energy/persona. Not that I ever tried to hide it . . . but I often tried to ignore it or rationalize it with philosophy or explain it away with words like androgyny and human being. I was confused, and I confused my lovers, too.

Hal felt that all of her pre-transition women lovers related to her as some kind of quasi-man. Hal remembered one lover as saying that being with Hal sexually "was just like being with any of her former husbands (and she had three!)." Another woman told Hal when they first became lovers: "I don't know how to tell you this, but it feels like I was just with a man." Hal and the woman went on to be lovers for fourteen years and to have two children together through donor insemination.

Hal called herself lesbian and functioned well within a lesbian-feminist community. Hal discussed how she handled her co-identities as a male and as a lesbian-feminist:

> When a transsexual goes into the lesbian community it's because they get support there for wearing the clothes they want, relating to women . . . as sex partners. For being strong. . . . You go to a place where you're going to get some support in the world. And it seems like a nurturing

kind of community. . . . What happened was that I thought for a long long time that, although I knew inside that I was male, it was okay for me to identify [as a lesbian]. I never was homophobic. . . . As long as my lover understood that I was male, and some of my friends understood that I was male. . . .

I went along like that for many, many, years. . . . I felt the pressure of the lesbian doctrine. I was trying to be a "strong, handsome woman," and not a man in a woman's body after all. . . . I put off [starting a transition] for at least ten years out of a fear of rejection, fear of the risks, and fear of making a political mistake with respect to my lesbian feminism.

Hal eventually reached a point in her life when despite the critique of gender and sex offered to her by lesbian feminism of the late 1980s, she could no longer find a way to see herself as a woman. Hal recounted how she came to this conclusion:

Two salient incidents that clarified my gender for me were, number one, the birth of my first child (I was the father, not mother!). I had to come to grips with who I was because I realized I could not fool or lie to a child. And, number two, over a period of a couple of years I gradually realized that I could not see myself becoming an old woman. I had this little boy look. I was a corporate vice president. I felt I needed to grow up, and I could not grow up to be a woman. I could look in the mirror. . . . I'd try to imagine myself as a fifty-year-old woman, and there would be nothing there, nothing to see. One day I tried to imagine myself as a fifty-year-old man, and I was amazed to see someone, a man with strong shoulders and graying hair, a neat beard, a handsome face; it was me. And it frightened me. These events meant I should be male because I was male; it was time to make the change, time to grow up.

Phil succinctly summed up the issues which seemed to propel each of these participants out of lesbianism and into transsexualism. Phil said of the women she had loved: "I really loved each of them but I wasn't truly happy. They wanted the perfect woman, and I only wanted to be the perfect man for them."

Thus these ten participants searched for and found both lovers and identities among women who defined themselves as lesbian feminists during the 1970s and 1980s.[26] The definitions of lesbian women which they learned among such women allowed them more room for the expression of their masculinities than was readily available to them in the more conservative social environments from which they had come. However, after varying degrees of exploration, they concluded that they were more different from lesbian women than they were similar to them, and they were left to search in other quarters for labels which more snugly fit their self-images.

Summary and Commentary

Only a small number of participants (27 percent) failed to commit themselves to ongoing homosexual relationships of a year or more during their pre-transition adult years.[27] Five of the nine participants who refrained altogether from such activities also avoided all consensual heterosexual contact and thus came to their transitions with very little direct sexual knowledge[28] The others satisfied themselves either with fleeting or superficial homosexual experiences or with heterosexual knowledge only.

By far the stronger pattern which emerged from the stories provided by participants was one of participants' earnest attempts to fit themselves into the world of women. As participants came to their adulthoods, they followed their hearts and their loins into romantic and sexual relationships with women. More than two-thirds of participants (71 percent) found women with whom they were able to establish relationships of some duration.[29] Drawn as they were to become lovers of women, participants were confronted with difficult-to-deny characterizations of their love as lesbian.

Eighteen participants (44 percent) also found ways to socialize with groups of women who shared with them their attractions for women.[30] Among these groups of women, participants honed their understanding of what it meant to be lesbian women. Originally attracted to making such affiliations because of their awareness of the common social definition of lesbians as mannish women who are sexually interested in other women, fifteen participants (37 percent) initially thought of themselves as gay or lesbian women.[31] However, once they began to move among such women, they came to make more finely sifted distinctions.

Two major issues became important to participants in their process of moving though and out of lesbian identities. Both of the axes on which participants judged themselves to be men rather than lesbian women were products of a particular historical period wherein the definitions of lesbianism constituted contested territory. The 1970s and 1980s were years during which the proponents of lesbian feminism were waging a campaign to supplant the idea that lesbians are mannish women with the image of lesbians as women-identified-women who celebrate their womanhood with other women.[32] These decades were also ones during which transsexualism was becoming more widely understood as a treatable medical condition, similar to but distinct from lesbianism.[33] Thus participants searching for viable words to use to identify themselves were caught up, quite unwittingly, in these shifting meanings.

Participants therefore were often in positions of having been drawn to

lesbian identities on the basis of older definitions of lesbians only to discover that lesbian pride movements of the 1970s and 1980s required that
they reject those characterizations. When participants tried to measure
themselves against the newer images of lesbians promulgated by lesbian
feminists, they found themselves lacking on two accounts. Firstly, they
were ashamed, embarrassed, or disgusted by the specifically female aspects
of their bodies and therefore had little desire to join with their companions in the glorification of their womanhood. Secondly, they were generally not interested in having their sexual partners enjoy their womanliness
or attempt to provide them with pleasures in specifically female ways. In
other words, when participants compared themselves to both generalized
and specific lesbian others, they were struck more by the contrasts than by
the similarities. By comparison, it seemed to participants that they had
more in common with straight men than with lesbian women. Eventually
their discomfort with being included in the lesbian camp was alleviated by
their discovery of the increasingly socially available concept of female-to-
male transsexualism.

Those participants who did not avail themselves of lesbian communities seemed to have been less affected by the politicization of lesbianism in
the 1970s and 1980s.[34] Undoubtedly they had some exposure to lesbian-
feminist ideas through media representations of feminists. However, such
influences seemed to have had little effect on their identities. These participants who were also drawn to love women, tended to reject the label of
lesbian as ill-fitting. They steadfastly persisted in the idea that they were
men who appeared to be women. They saw their relationships as straight
ones and bided their time until they too stumbled upon the egress offered
by transsexualism.

Summary and Commentary: Heterosexual and Homosexual Relations In Pre-Transition Adult Years

Forty-one participants entered their adult years still struggling to find
identities which fit how they felt about themselves, about others, and how
they wanted to move through their social worlds. The crux of their difficulties lay in the mismatch between their personalities and the bodies which society insisted were required for the legitimate expression of
such personalities. Thus it was that issues of gender expression became
wrapped up in issues of sex and sexuality.

Few participants, however, were entirely clear throughout this section
of their lives as to exactly what steps would be required to assuage their
growing distress. They searched among the small assortment of identities
available to them for ones which might give them more solid feelings

of social embeddedness. They recognized that their physical bodies con-
signed them to being women. The task then was to try to find women's
roles within which they could live with a minimum of anxieties.

Participants also needed to find sources of confirmation for their masculine self-images. It was in the contexts of their most intimate relationships that participants were most vulnerable to discreditation or were able
to garner their greatest support. Their lovers were women and men with
whom they bared all. As such, they were best positioned to reflect back to
participants information about how well or how poorly they were performing in the roles which they were attempting to fulfill.

Twenty-one participants (55 percent)[35] experimented with being straight
women while they were adults; almost all of them did so superficially. The
adult flirtations with heterosexuality of fifteen participants (39.5 percent)
went no further than dating or short-term casual sexual relationships.[36]
They reported that these encounters left them cold. They therefore eliminated the possibility of being straight women from their repertoires. Six
participants (16 percent) ventured further into heterosexuality. Peter and
Keith tried out the role of straight woman in long-term relationships with
men. They too concluded that they were unable to play the part with any
acceptable degree of satisfaction. Four participants married and bore children, thereby making full commitments to being straight women.[37] Each
participant found some satisfaction and confirmation of their femaleness
in these arrangements but, in the end, they also had to abandon the project and admit that their experiences with their husbands had permanently
alienated them from the option of living as straight women.

Thus participants' attempts at being straight women helped to clarify
their gender needs to them largely by a process of elimination. However,
their heterosexual relations also taught them important lessons about
straight men and a world of social protocols which would prove useful to
them in their post-transition years. They also learned how straight men
behave in intimate relations with women. Later, when most of these individuals went on to live as straight men themselves, they would be able to
draw on this knowledge to guide them as they learned to become adept at
the minutiae of their performances of those roles.

Thirty-three participants (80.5 percent)[38] were attracted to the possibilities offered by lesbian roles.[39] Not surprisingly, those participants who
became involved in homosexual relations, did so as butch women. However, not all of them accepted the appellation of lesbian as being applicable to themselves. Fifteen participants (37 percent) tried to become settled
with lesbian identities,[40] whereas fourteen participants who engaged in
homosexual relations (34 percent) refused the title,[41] and four made no
comment in this regard.[42] In any event, all eventually found lesbian social

relations unsatisfactory for similar reasons. Roles as lesbian women allowed participants only to partially enact their sexual orientations and their gender and sex identities. The combination of their own alienation from being women-identified and their partners' insistence upon relating to them as women and as females prevented participants from adopting enduring identities as lesbian women.

A handful of participants simply refrained altogether from becoming sexually intimate with anyone during their pre-transition years. Like those participants who refused to name themselves as lesbian women, these participants simply remained undeterred from their youthful beliefs that they were somehow wrong as females. They waited for a solution to appear.

In the end, participants gradually exhausted their possibilities as women. Each probed the roles for women which were known to them. As each alternative was weighed and found wanting, the field of possibilities narrowed to that which was perhaps ultimately the most attractive but also seemingly the most unobtainable: to live as men. Until participants stumbled upon the option called female-to-male transsexualism, they felt relegated to forever being misfits, even among those sexual minorities who already inhabited the fringes of society. It is no wonder that female-to-male transsexualism, when participants discovered it, must have seemed to offer emancipation from the blight of their invalid femaleness.

PART V

Changing Over

Aaron
(This is not the Aaron
whose story appears in this book.)

17 | A Long Road

Changing from life as a woman and a female into life as a man and a male is a prolonged and arduous journey. It is never undertaken lightly. A whole lifetime of preparation must precede any decision to undertake gender and sex reassignments, just as another lifetime must ultimately be dedicated to the actualization of such undertakings. The processes in which participants engaged to change their lives from those of women and females to those of men and males were both lengthy and complicated. The first steps in their journeys necessarily began with their profound discomfort with their lives as girls or women. The next stage consisted of their recognition that they might be more content as men and males. For most participants, however, their dreams of living as men and as males were for many years no more than mere escape fantasies to which they optimistically clung. For the most part, their dreams were stymied because most participants remained ignorant of the possibilities which transsexualism offered to them until they were well into their adult years. With an awareness of the existence of the phenomenon called female-to-male transsexualism came the consciousness that escape from womanhood and femaleness might truly be possible.

However, it was still a long road from possible to actual manhood. When participants felt the need to find out how to accomplish such changes, they often discovered that information about female-to-male transsexualism was hard to locate. Some participants were fortunate enough to stumble upon an item in the media which provided phone numbers or addresses of clinics or self-help groups. For them, reliable information was forthcoming. Other participants were left to browse furtively in their local libraries or to enquire sheepishly among their friends. The information gathered through these means was often harshly judgmental professional or journalistic opinion or cruelly graphic and dated depictions of unsightly surgical outcomes. Either way, the information gathered by participants gave them a clear message that female-to-male transsexualism promised them an incomplete, painful, expensive, and highly stigmatized path to manhood. Only the most dedicated of aspirants could remain undaunted by the difficulties which they discovered most assuredly lay ahead of them.

Once they felt reasonably well informed about the issues involved, participants had to figure out whether or not they themselves were indeed transsexual. This process of coming to identify as transsexual and deciding to pursue a transsexual transition was a deeply disquieting one for many participants. Coming to see themselves as transsexual required them to re-evaluate all of their relationships. They had to examine under a new light the meanings they made of their interactions with lovers, friends, families, and co-workers. They had to face the possibility that many of those relationships would have to be almost entirely recast or abandoned were they to entertain the possibility of future lives as men and as males. Taking on transsexual identities also meant confronting the extreme social stigma attached to being transsexual persons at the same time as such identities offered participants possibilities of attaining lives of which they had long dreamed.

Once they had accepted themselves as transsexual, participants were confronted with questions concerning their best course of action. A few participants continued to deliberate as to whether or not they should engage in major life changes. For the time being, they lived knowing themselves to be transsexual but uninclined to take action to change themselves into readily recognizable men. Some participants involved family, friends, and lovers in their decision making processes. They discussed with their significant others the seriousness of their situations and the implications of the actions which they contemplated. Some participants engaged therapists to help them sort out their gender and sex issues. Others simply forged ahead singlemindedly, certain that the characterizations of female-to-male transsexuals which they had encountered were descriptions of themselves and that no further dalliance was necessary. However they reached their decisions, participants' deciding to embark on transforming their lives into those of men meant that they had to gamble everything that was important to them. As Hal put it, "It was a hard decision to make because I realized that I risked losing the love and support of a large number of people. I would be risking my life, my sexual functioning, my professional reputation, everything." Few people are ever faced with such difficult decisions as these.

Those participants who made their decisions to proceed were then confronted with the business of accomplishing their desired level of transition. Depending on the degree of transformation which they desired and the specifics of their particular body types, participants followed a number of courses. A few participants were temporarily satisfied to simply change their appearances in a number of nonmedical ways which would allow them to move through their everyday worlds as presentable men. Most often, however, participants soon wanted some combination of hormone treatments, breast removal or reduction, and hysterectomy. Only a few participants were able to procure some approximation of male genitalia, although most participants did express some interest in such procedures.

Those participants who wished only to change their social personas and not their bodies could do so on their own through a process of trial and error. Participants who wished more complete alterations had to find professional assistance. Physicians and therapists who were skilled in dealing with the issues of transsexualism were, and still are, scarce. One route taken by participants was to approach university-based gender dysphoria clinics. Since 1979, such clinics usually have been guided by the Harry Benjamin International Gender Dysphoria Association's *Standards of Care*.[1] Gender clinics offer a relatively comprehensive staff of trained specialists who guide transsexual persons through their transformation processes. Participants who took this option were required to undergo a period of psychological evaluation before the commencement of sex reassignment procedures. All such clinics provide hormone treatments, but they vary as to the levels of in-house surgical services which they provide. Thus, even some of those participants who made use of gender clinics were forced to join the ranks of those who managed their own physiological transformations.

Many participants, however, declined to submit themselves to the authority of gender clinics and chose instead to piece together their own patchwork of service providers. Genuine or ingenuous stories told by some participants to general medical practitioners or endocrinologists eventuated in prescriptions for testosterone treatment. Breast reductions or mastectomies were purchased by some participants under similar circumstances. Hysterectomies were relatively easy for participants to obtain after the full effects of hormone treatments, mastectomies, and cross-living were manifest and their external physical and social gender presentations had become manly. Surgeries to build malelike genitalia were available for those who chose to pursue them, once they had passed successfully through the earlier stages of transition and if they had the sizable sums of money required to finance the operations.

The differing courses and degrees of transition opted for by various participants in combination with their differing genetic endowments resulted in a variety of outcomes. Some participants seemed to become men virtually overnight with little more than the adoption of a different set of clothing and a new name. Others waited until the effects of hormone treatments were extensive enough to make their continued presentation as women problematic. For still others, breast surgeries were necessary, either with or without hormone treatments, before they could take their places in society as men.

This variance in participants' approaches to accomplishing their transitions highlights two central questions: When do female-to-male transsexuals cease to function in society as women and begin to move through life as men? When do they bid adieu to their femaleness and welcome maleness into their lives? The stories told by participants illustrated that there was no clear-cut transition point which can generally be applied to female-to-male transsexuals as a group. Their social transitions from women into men could happen virtually overnight or could be years in the making; however, their physical transformations from femaleness to maleness could only be accomplished over a series of stages. Thus there was no simple way to determine when such metamorphoses actually transpired. At the very least, the first physical changes wrought by hormone therapies rarely appeared in less than a few months, while long-term effects often took years to materialize. Surgical interventions were undertaken either before or after starting hormone therapies, but for most participants, health and financial considerations required them to be spread over the course of a number of years following the commencement of hormone therapy. When asked, participants gave a variety of interpretations as to when they moved into their new lives.

Similarly, participants' families, friends, lovers, and co-workers made differing degrees of adjustment to the new men in their lives. Some people were willing to accept participants as men as soon as they were asked to do so. Others slowly and incrementally cooperated with participants' transitions. A few people steadfastly refused to admit that participants could ever be men. The unevenness of other people's responses to participants' manhood was an ongoing source of difficulty for some participants, while for others the reactions of other people could be more easily sidestepped. For many participants, however, other people's reactions to their transformations were supportive, even congratulatory.

Whatever the reactions of other people to participants' transitions, they were meaningful to participants' senses of themselves as men and as males. Most participants had seen manliness and maleness in themselves for large portions of their lives. Their central task during their transition years was to bring these qualities unmistakably to the attention of the people around them. Because it was primarily in the attributions made by others that participants could gauge the completeness of their transformations, participants often finally felt that they had fully become men (although perhaps not yet males) only when they ceased to be regarded by others as women. As Darren remarked, "there has to be a perception from others. . . . because I didn't have to convince myself."

18 | Making the Decision

Finding Transsexualism

BEFORE PARTICIPANTS COULD embark upon remaking themselves as socially recognizable men, they had to become convinced that this was indeed possible to do. Therefore participants' first step on the road to transforming themselves into men necessarily began with the acquisition of an
awareness that such a metamorphosis was technologically possible. Most
participants grew up having a vague knowledge of male-to-female transsexualism, but few were aware until later in their lives that female-to-male
transsexualism was also possible. More than three quarters (76.5 percent)[1]
of participants reported that they had encountered some kind of information about the existence of transsexual persons during their childhood or
teen years.[2] Participants' information came largely from three phases of
media attention to the topic of transsexualism. The remaining eight participants (23.5 percent) did not remember hearing about transsexualism
until they were adults.[3]

Many participants' first contact with the concept of transsexualism
came in the 1950s in the form of news items about Christine Jorgensen. A
few slightly younger participants seemed to have missed that media blitz
but happened upon one or more articles in a small spate of accounts of
transsexualism published in popular magazines of the late 1960s. Most of
the youngest participants first heard about transsexualism from television
talk and news magazine shows in the late 1970s and the 1980s which featured transsexual guests or stories. Those participants who were first exposed to transsexualism as adults most often also heard of it through such
television programs. Only a few participants' first exposure to transsexualism came in the person of a transsexual acquaintance or friend. Whatever their sources of information, most participants expressed relief and
excitement at the possibilities which they felt open up before them when
they first came to know about female-to-male transsexualism.

Transsexualism first hit public consciousness in North America on December 1, 1952, when the news media blared out the message that a young
U.S. citizen named George Jorgensen had gone to Sweden as a man and

had returned home as an attractive young woman named Christine.[4] More than half of participants (53 percent) specifically recalled having heard of Christine Jorgensen and her astonishing transformation.[5] Some of them disregarded the Christine Jorgensen story as something which had happened in a faraway time or place. They thought of it as no more than a curiosity with little relevance to their own situations. Others did not initially extrapolate from Jorgensen's gender and sex transformations to the ones which they desired for themselves. Jorgensen had been a man and a male who had become a woman and a female. They dared not imagine that the reverse could be done for them.[6]

For example, Aaron remembered her initial reaction to the news:

> About the same time I graduated from high school was when Christine Jorgensen came back over and made the papers. But you see, I'd never heard of anybody going the other direction. . . . It was a gut level reaction. God, it would be great if it worked my way, and if it was possible, and if, if, if. But I didn't expect it to be a thing of possibility. . . . Down inside it was just another twinge of jealousy. One more thing that a guy could do that a female couldn't.

As a youngster, Grant had also heard about Jorgensen. Grant, too, remembered regretting that there was no similar option for her. At the time, she thought, "They can make George into Christine, but what the hell can they do for Christine? It's easier to slice something off than to put it on! It can't be done. . . . They can't do anything for me."

More commonly, participants made some connection between their own feelings of discomfort with their femaleness and what they had heard about in the news.[7] A few participants recognized a commonality between themselves and Jorgensen but did not immediately assume that they would follow in her footsteps. Others never had a doubt.

As a teenaged girl, Steven was one of those participants who was unsure of what her future would hold. Steven recalled her insecurities about the possibility of a gender and sex change.

> I think Christine Jorgenson was maybe the first thing I had heard about. . . . I was I'd say maybe sixteen, seventeen. . . . I wasn't sure how this was done. I didn't know if they could do it for me, but I had always hoped that someday this would be possible. It was always in my mind.

Howie assumed that what could be done for Jorgensen could also be done for her, but like Steven, she harboured doubts about whether she could accomplish her goal.

> I heard about Christine Jorgenson when I was about ten or eleven. I was elated that it was possible. . . . I was so relieved to discover there were

others like me in the world. That made it less freakish somehow. . . . It was a dream. But I felt I'd probably never have the guts to do it. . . . I intentionally put it on the "back burner."

Rick was one of those participants who, as a girl, knew immediately that what had happened for Christine Jorgensen was also good news for her. Rick recalled:

I was about twelve . . . at the time of Christine Jorgensen's change. That was in the headlines of every magazine and newspaper in the entire country and I read it in a Sunday paper, word for word, and studied every picture, and realized that she and I had an immense amount in common. The lights went off like a penny arcade. There was someone with at least a parallel situation. Obviously there was help for her, so, hopefully, I would be able to do something about my problem at some point. So, that was the first inkling I had that there was anyone like me and that there was some sort of resource that, at some age in my life, I could pursue.

Similarly, when Jack heard about Christine Jorgensen she decided on the spot that a sex change was what she needed. Jack said:

When I was ten my dad got one of these smut magazines like *Enquirer*, and there was a big article, and it was . . . Christine Jorgensen. . . . And I was, "That's me! That's me!". . . . Boy, from then on, I knew exactly.

By the late 1960s Christine Jorgensen was no longer news. Participants who were born in the 1950s were therefore less likely to have been exposed to her story as it was not the kind of thing about which most adults talked with children. However, by the time these younger participants were old enough to have become sensitive to media reports or community talk about transsexualism, a new round of public discourse on the topic had begun.

Simon and Bill both recalled first learning what to call the way they felt by reading a particular magazine article which appeared in approximately 1968. Simon remembered it like this:

When I was sixteen I was in a waiting room kind of place and there was a magazine article about seven transsexuals. I still cannot remember if it was *Life* or *Look*. It was this big several page spread and one of the people was a female-to-male. . . . And it caught my eye and I read the whole article and they had kept the female-to-male to the last one. It was like . . . "Oh, ho! That's what I am!" And the light bulb came on.

Bill, who probably saw the same article, was less sanguine than Simon about the possibility of a satisfactory gender and sex change after reading the report. Bill summed up how she reacted to the news this way:

By my early teens, I had discovered an article in one of those large for-mat magazines, either *Look* or *Life*, about sex changes. I read it under my bed and didn't know then why I was so thrilled and anxious upon discovering it. What I recall reading was not very heartening because the tone of the article made it sound truly bizarre. The photos of the male-to-females looked clownish and the story of the one female-to-male did not make his life sound very good. There was no discussion of surgery for the female-to-male and although I didn't know why then, the article depressed me. . . . It portrayed the whole business as being . . . relatively hopeless, especially for the female-to-males.

Darren happened upon a media report about transsexualism when she was a sixteen year old girl around the same time. Darren recalled how the news item gave direction to her feelings about her gender:

We had these three-day work things, where you sort of apprentice. . . . I was interested in journalism, so I went to a radio station. . . . So, on the Teletype, this wire came out about the Seattle Gender Clinic, and it mentioned the word "transsexuals." It was the first time I had ever heard that word, and I guess it explained it. So I figured out, "I'm not the only one in the world like this." Up to that time, I thought I was the only living person on the planet. . . . and that sort of got me thinking.

Younger participants, who were children in the 1960s, became gender inquisitive teenagers in a decade when daytime television began to discover that the public had a seemingly infinite fascination with transsexualism. Talk shows featured a steady stream of transsexual guests beginning in the late 1970s and continuing through the 1980s. News magazine pro-grams also began to feature reports about the mysteries of gender and sex reassignment around the same time. Some participants first heard about female-to-male transsexualism though these outlets. Some older partici-pants were also prompted by such television programs to move from their earlier passive curiosity about transsexualism to a more active pursuit of information about gender and sex reassignment.[8]

Jorge first learned about female-to-male transsexualism from childish schoolyard banter but thought nothing of it. A year or two later, watching a talk show in approximately 1978, Jorge began to envision herself chang-ing her gender and sex:

I didn't know anything about sex changes until fourth or fifth grade. Some kids were making jokes about [a person] who had a sex change. I didn't really realize I was a transsexual then though. Later, I saw [twin female-to-male transsexuals] on a Phil Donahue show. I admired how good they looked. I then fully understood I was a transsexual, and I knew surgery was possible. From that point on I've always planned to have the surgery.

Bill remembered seeing the same television show and finding it particularly useful. It prompted Bill to seek out a therapist who specialized in gender issues and who could help her to decide whether or not she was transsexual.

> The Donahue show . . . dealt with the topic in an informative way, stressing the significance of therapy, the greater success of surgeries, and showed twin F-to-Ms who seemed sane and coherent to me. It also gave me the address of the Janus people in California who provided a referral list of therapists. . . . Therefore, I found out that I was not alone in my feelings and beliefs and that I could get help from someone familiar with this.

Mel, Gary, Dennis, and Steven also mentioned having been enlightened as to the feasibility of female-to-male sex reassignment by watching similar television programs which aired in the late 1970s and early 1980s. When Mel came upon the possibility of transsexualism, Mel immediately "knew" that she was transsexual:

> Everything fit for the first time in my life! I had a label for myself that fit instead of one that I was squeezed into. I thought it was great! . . . I thought, "I'm not so strange after all because they have a title for this." I remember the thought that "Damn, I got to earn some money because this is too fucking expensive!"

Other television talk shows which were specifically mentioned by Jack, Eli, and Bruce as having been informational and inspirational were ones on which a female-to-male transsexual activist, Jason Cromwell, appeared in the late 1980s. Jack's partner was the one who actually saw Cromwell's appearance on television. She knew how Jack felt and leapt at the opportunity to get help. Jack recalled:

> Jason was on a show and [my partner] was watching it at her work. . . . [She] saw him on there, knew what I wanted all this time (we just didn't know where to look for it) and wrote the number down quick. And without telling me about it or saying anything to me wrote to them, sent them pictures and that's how things got moving.

Bruce also happened upon one of Cromwell's talk show appearances. Bruce told her lesbian partner about the show and the two of them embarked upon an active investigation of female-to-male transsexualism. Bruce told this story about how it happened:

> I was sitting at home watching the Geraldo show, and Jason showed up on the show about transsexuals. And I thought, "Oh, my God. That's me!" . . . [My partner] was the one that made the move. She wrote

Jason. . . . Jason talked to me for like an hour on the phone, and sent me all this information.

However, Cromwell was far from the first transsexual whom Bruce had met. Bruce's initial discovery of transsexualism, like Eli's, Stan's, and Harry's, was somewhat unusual in that her first contact was with a transsexual person. Bruce, as a sixteen year old girl in the 1970s, had a neighbour who was a transsexual man. Upon finding out about her neighbour's status, Bruce was immediately mesmerized by him and cast him as her "idol." Bruce recounted this story of what that time was like for her:

> There was a guy who lived on my mom's block, just down from us. . . . And he was a female-to-male . . . and he used to come out Saturday mornings and cut his grass and I would get up early in the morning, come out and sit on my grass and watch him and try to figure out what was so different about this guy. . . . And I wanted to run over to him and hug him. I wanted to say, "Take me with you wherever you've been." . . . And I never could do that. . . . [He] was the first one I'd ever heard about . . . but nobody talked about it. It was like hush hush.

Eli's first meeting with transsexual people partially lifted her out of a severe depression when, in her early forties, she met two transsexual people who talked freely with her about gender and sex issues. Eli came away from that conversation thinking, "Well, now, maybe this is after all what is happening here with me." However, it wasn't until Eli saw Cromwell on a television broadcast several years later that she made any concrete moves toward affirming the accuracy of a transsexual identity for herself.

Stan had never given any thought to transsexualism when she first met a female-to-male transsexual who was a patient in the hospital where she was working as a nurse. Stan was immediately "fascinated" and made it her business to get to know the man. What she found out from him galvanized her to action on her own gender and sex issues. Stan conveyed this story about the meeting:

> I was working at the hospital, my first job out of nursing school, and we had one of them on our floor . . . going female-to-male. And he was in there for a revision of the phalloplasty. . . . And of course everybody had to go by there and . . . see this guy. And I'm thinking, "I do not want to make a freak show out of this . . . just so I can get a gawk at him." But I was still fascinated. . . . And I went by there and made some time to talk to [him] and it was like immediate. It was immediate. We hit it off, and he started telling me his story, and . . . it just clicked. It just clicked. "That is it, that is it." And it's like immediately I started making plans.

Harry's introduction to transsexualism came in the person of a cousin of one of her women lovers. It came as quite a shock to Harry that such a thing was possible. Harry remembered being "very much interested" but was emotionally unprepared to make any irreversible moves at that point in her life.

> [My girlfriend] had a cousin . . . [who] was a transsexual. And it was like, "What is a transsexual?" . . . And I was told she had a sex change . . . and it just blew me away. It's like, "What do you mean, sex change? What the hell is that all about? I can't do this kind of stuff." So I met [her]. [She] was very aggressive, a very terrible ambassador to the trans-sexual world. . . . [She] started pumping horror stories into me. . . . And [she] was male-to-female. . . . So, I think, at some point back then, I said, "Nothing can be done. . . . That doesn't apply to me."

Walter found out about transsexualism through still other channels. Walter chanced upon information about transsexualism through her involvement with lesbian life, after having been a committed lesbian cross-dresser for several years. Walter recalled getting "tremendously excited" at the "idea that I could be more than just a crossdresser" but "still was very skeptical that a woman could really become a man." Nevertheless, Walter soon became attached to the idea of trying.

In sum, participants came across information about the existence of a condition called transsexualism at different points in their own lives and at times when treatment options for transsexuals were at various stages of development. The earliest media attention to transsexualism was narrowly focused on the story of one individual, Christine Jorgensen, who changed from a man into a woman. For many participants, the facts of Jorgensen's transition did not seem generalizable to their own circumstances. By contrast, news reports of the 1960s in which transsexualism was treated as a subject rather than being about the personal story of a particular transsexual person were more likely to evoke empathy in participants because they included mention of female-to-male transsexualism.

Those accounts which appeared to have the greatest impact were those which came in the late 1970s and in the 1980s. This was probably the case for two main reasons. Firstly, by then all participants had reached sufficient age that their gender and sex discomfort was becoming acute. Secondly, by that time, many reports about transsexualism had begun to take a slightly more sympathetic human-interest slant. More importantly, key female-to-male transsexual individuals had begun to appear publicly as advocates for popular tolerance and acceptance of transsexuals. It was after participants' exposure to these transsexual community leaders via television and print media that participants were most likely to be moved to actively pursue gender and sex reassignment. Participants saw remarkable similarities between their own stories and these individuals' official accounts of their lives before their transitions. Such media personalities also demonstrated by their self-assured manhood that women could become men. Thus they and their stories provided participants with tangible proof that there was a well-marked escape route from their unhappiness with living as women and as females. Not insignificantly, they also provided phone numbers and addresses to contact for further information.

Becoming Knowledgeable on the Subject

A little more than one-third of participants (36 percent)[9] explained that they began to identify themselves as transsexual as soon as they heard the term and understood its meaning.[10] Most participants, however, passed through a period during which they were interested in transsexualism but not yet fully committed to it as the best option for themselves. Before coming to the decision that they were indeed transsexual, these other two-thirds of participants (64 percent) generally sought out further information to help them with their self-evaluations.[11] Participants who knew immediately that they were transsexual engaged in a similar quest for information about transsexualism. The knowledge which they gained in the exercise proved to be invaluable to those participants who later decided to take concrete steps toward becoming men and males. They became more effective managers of their transitions as a result of the greater insights which they gained into the procedures and processes involved in gender and sex reassignment.

Several main sources of information were tapped by participants. Half of participants (51.5 percent) said that they made use of university and public libraries[12] in which they were able to peruse many of the major books and professional journals which featured articles about transsexualism. Any participant who happened across popular media accounts of transsexualism eagerly paid attention to them. Twenty participants (61 percent) also made mail, telephone, or personal contact with one or more of the handful of transsexual support groups which were then extant.[13] The information which participants gathered in these various ways helped them to conclude that they were transsexual.

Rick's recollections of her exploratory steps were typical of those of many other participants. Rick stored away the news about Christine Jorgensen until a later time when she was ready to find out more. When that time came, Rick was not yet living as a man but was often mistaken for one by other people. Rick wanted to know if she were transsexual.

> I was eighteen or nineteen when I finally moved out of the house . . . and I started looking into what I could do for myself. . . . I finally took books out of the library and could do some reading. . . . It put me more in touch with my problem, although I have to say that the material was extremely negative and very sparse . . . very lacking, but at least something. . . . I stumbled across some female-to-male photos. . . . The photographs were close-ups in black and white, very grisly. The surgeries were extremely experimental twenty to twenty-five years ago, and limited in what they could accomplish.
>
> So it was sort of another monstrous choice. "Do I stay the strange that I am with these feelings and try to muddle through for a while longer? Or do I do something about it now?" And I decided, at that time, that I would not do anything because the results were not satisfactory at all. I didn't like my body . . . at all at that time, and looking at the pictures of what I would get in the trade-off was almost equally as unpleasant because the scarring was massive. The results were mediocre, at best, and non-functional. So it didn't seem like a real good trade-off. It was one kind of suicide for another.

Almost twenty years later, after having kept in touch with surgical progress in the area, Rick finally decided that what medical science had to offer would have to do.

Aaron, unaware that transsexual people could come in the female-to-male variety, happened upon the topic in a psychology textbook when she attended university after her children had grown up. Aaron was intrigued, but when she proceeded to gather more information, she was not encouraged by what she found. She took no immediate decision on the issue.

> My response to [the textbook] was one of . . . definitely marking the page and going back and looking at it more than once, several times. Not selling the book back at the end of the year when I was broke and sold a lot of books back. . . . Here again the response was an inward smile. Didn't know whether I would do it, didn't know whether I would be accepted, still had a lot of doubts from what I read. I went and got books right away . . . and found out more about it. But the books were several years out of date, had so many strong criteria. And, of course, one of them is that you are oriented sexually in the appropriate way. And one of them is that you don't have children. And . . . I didn't know whether I would be accepted into a program.

Some participants felt that what they read described them perfectly. When that happened, it was not unusual for the person to experience a kind of epiphany. Grant, who was a crossdresser at the time, described one such fortuity which occurred while she was reading about transvestism:

> I found out reading Feinbloom's book, *Transvestites and Transsexuals*,[14] there was the definition of transsexual. I'm sitting on the living room couch in Colorado, and I'm crying like Niagara Falls. [My partner] says, "What's the matter?" I said, "I found myself. I found out what's wrong. . . . I've been selling myself out. I really screwed myself worrying about what all our friends thought." She said, "What do you mean?" and I said, "I'm a transsexual."

Some participants found that when the reading which they did was guided by recommendations from other transsexual people, the results were salubrious. For example, after Bruce saw female-to-male transsexual activist Jason Cromwell on television she wanted more information. Bruce sought help from a local support group and from a friend.

> I wrote the [support group at the] Ingersoll Center[15] and I started to do research. . . . And I have a very good friend who's a male-to-female lesbian transsexual. And she started giving me all this information. I saw that [video]tape *What Sex Am I?*[16] . . . And I said, "There's people out there. I'm not alone." And I started getting help. . . . So then I went to [my transsexual friend] and she gave me this book by Mario Martino called *Emergence*.[17] . . . I got through it in about two and a half days. . . . I'll never forget it. I just finished the last page, I put the book down and I just started to cry. And I mean the tears wouldn't stop. I just said, "I'm a transsexual." And I got up and I went to my room and I buried my head in my pillow and I must have cried for two hours. And I thought, "I've never felt this good in my life". . . . And that's where I made the connection.

Ken wrote letters to transsexual spokespersons and support groups. They steered her reading and provided moral support. Ken remembered a few pioneering individuals as having been particularly helpful.

> *A Handbook for Transsexuals*[18] by Paula Grossman. I corresponded with Miss Grossman several times. . . . and we talked on the phone once. *Emergence*, by Mario Martino. . . . That book is the best book. He sent me a copy. He signed the inside, and it means a lot. There were female-to-male transsexuals out there, and I was in my glory. There was a book by Lothstein, I think, *Female-to-Male Transsexualism*.[19] There was one, *Transvestites and Transsexuals* . . . by Feinbloom. I ran into a *Journal of a Transsexual*[20] by Leslie Feinberg. . . . There were a lot of journals that I read from FACT.[21] . . . And then I have to throw in there Rupert Raj and his . . . magazine.[22] He's the best information source there's ever been. Rupert and I wrote . . . and he opened my eyes to so

much. I could ask him a question, and it might take a month, but he always came through. . . . .Outstanding man.

A few participants felt the need for very little information beyond a definition of female-to-male transsexualism. However, most participants were careful consumers. They studied their options assiduously. They recognized the momentousness of what they were considering and wanted to make fully informed decisions. Generally they were aggressive and thorough investigators who became knowledgeable about the life changes which they were entertaining. When they were prepared to take action, most participants undertook it armed with as much understanding of female-to-male transsexualism as their resourcefulness and their intellects would allow.

What's Love Got to Do with It?

Once participants had become aware of transsexualism and had some understanding of what its parameters were, they were able to better determine whether they qualified as transsexual. One central point of delineation for many participants had to do with their sexual attractions and activities. All but two[23] of those participants who dealt with this issue did so in a context of attractions to women. They needed to sort out whether their sexual attractions typified them as straight men or as lesbian women. At the same time, they grappled with the significance of their preferred sexual practices, practices which were bound up with questions of body image. They were forced to question what, to their minds, constituted the limits of sexual expression for lesbian women and what practices and desires marked them as men.

Half of participants[24] worked through these issues while they were actually engaged in relationships with women. Ten participants (24 percent) had women partners with whom they had begun relationships before their transitions and with whom they continued to be lovers afterward.[25] Their relationships lasted between three and twenty-five years, with an average duration of eleven years. The continuity of their love offered wholehearted support for participants' identities as men and an intimate form of confirmation of their manhood. Another eleven participants' (26 percent) relationships with their women partners collapsed under the weight of their transsexual issues near the beginnings of their transitions.[26] In some of these cases, participants' partners lovingly encouraged them to make their transitions only to discover, often to their own dismay, that they themselves wished to remain as lesbian women even as participants began to live as men.

Eight participants who were attracted to women (19 percent) had either only the most minimal or no pre-transition sexual involvements with women.[27] Thus they came to their transsexual identities without the measure of a sexual partner's opinions to guide them. However, several of these participants took their feelings toward women as indications of their manhood. An additional eleven participants (26 percent) engaged in short sexual affairs with women while they were coming to terms with their transsexualism.[28] These individuals did not emphasize the roles that any particular women played in their deliberations. Keith and Jordie measured themselves against the feelings which they had for men.

Typically, those partners of participants who stayed with them through their transitions were women who were comfortable with lives as straight women. Most of them had been entirely or largely heterosexual in their prior attractions and relationships and seemed to have been attracted to participants precisely because they were so much like men in their everyday and romantic lives. In addition, these women were comfortable with or preferred having participants sexually approach them in ways reminiscent of their previous heterosexual experience. In harmony with many participants' own desires, they welcomed the use of penis substitutes and their associated sexual positions in their lovemaking. These factors combined to make them receptive to and facilitative of participants' desires by reinforcing participants' images of themselves as performing sexually and socially as if they were straight men.

Jack's case illustrates some of these points. Jack had had only one relationship with a woman. Jack met this partner and began the relationship while Jack was still a woman and Jack's future wife was still married to her first husband. When Jack first told her partner that she wanted to become a man, the woman was relieved because it meshed with how she felt about Jack and alleviated some of her own confusion at having been attracted to a woman. At first, Jack's new girlfriend was worried that her own straight sexual orientation had somehow influenced Jack to be interested in sex reassignment, but Jack reassured her, "If I'd never met you, I'd still be doing it." She in turn assured him that he was "a natural" as a man in bed and went on to find Jack the information which Jack needed to actually start her transition. After Jack began living as a man, they married. At the time of Jack's interviews, they had been together for approximately nine years.

Simon had a similar experience with the woman who was later to become his wife. They met just as Simon was taking the first steps into living as a man. The woman was immediately attracted to Simon but disconcerted by her feelings. Simon recalled what she had said of her feelings at the time:

> Unbeknownst to me, [she] had seen me, and was attracted to me. And then she found out, by word of mouth, that I wasn't a man, and that threw her into a loop, 'cause she never identified as a lesbian. She was confused because when she saw me, she thought I was a man. . . . She didn't have any problem with [my plans] at all. She was quite relieved that that was what was going on.

For Simon, it was an issue of body image which clarified her transsexualism. As Simon put it:

> It probably would have been easier to have been a lesbian than it was to go through what I've gone through. If nothing else . . . surgically it would have been a whole lot easier to have been a lesbian. I still could've loved women, but that wasn't the issue. The issue had more to do with my body and it not being the image that I wanted it to be than it had to do with loving women.

At the time of this writing, Simon and his wife had been together for approximately twenty-five years.

Howie and his wife had been in love the longest of all the couples. They met as twelve year old schoolgirls, stayed together through Howie's gender and sex reassigments, and now "are as close as a family can be." The strength of Howie's affection for his wife and daughter was touching and of a magnitude which a great many people might envy. Howie said of his wife: "She reads my thoughts telepathically. We are very dependent on each other and very deeply in love. She is my blessing in this life."

Some participants found that their partners' support of their changes was not as profound as they had hoped. Ken and Ed, like several other participants, had both positive and negative feedback about transsexualism from the women in their lives. Ken, after having studied female-to-male transsexualism thoroughly, decided that she was transsexual. When Ken told her partner about what she had decided, "She walked out. She couldn't handle it. She hasn't talked to me since." Ken soon met another woman who was "100 percent behind" Ken's plans and they soon married. At the time of Ken's interviews, they had been together for eight years.

When Ed was just entering into her transition years she began a relationship with a woman who had been married when they first met. Although the relationship lasted five years and saw Ed through most of the transition, Ed "never felt that she was 100 percent" in support of it because Ed "knew that she had a real strong attraction towards males and towards the penis." In the end, it was that attraction which broke them up. Ed recalled the miserable ending to that relationship:

> She ended up having an affair with her best friend's boyfriend. Which I found out kind of by mistake . . . when I came to pick her up one day and found them in bed together. And he was a fairly large guy and my trying to beat his head in didn't really work too well. . . . I ended up in the psychiatric ward trying to commit suicide . . . just basically from the disgust of being dumped for somebody that I felt was more the scum of the earth. . . . He won. That was pretty much how I viewed it. Because there was nothing in the world I could see this guy had over me besides that. He was fat, long scruffy hair, you know. Type to pick his nose in public and think it was great. But he had a penis. . . . That's all I could see. There might have been more, but I'm afraid my viewpoint was a little bit narrow.

Ed was not the only participant to tell tales of errant wives or girlfriends who took their pleasures with men who had fully functioning penises. On the one hand, such behavior fed into participants' insecurities about their own bodies and their abilities as lovers. On the other hand, the fact that their partners turned to other men rather than to women might have served as a kind of oblique, however bittersweet, confirmation of their own manhood. Thus, although no relationship is guaranteed to last forever, those relationships which spanned the years of participants' transitions provided both stability and validation. The support of having the affections and arousing the passions of women who were exclusively romantically and sexually interested in men must have been invaluable to the development of participants' confidence in the rightness of their identities as men.

Approximately another one-fourth of participants (24 percent) were involved in relationships with women which dissolved around the time that they embarked upon their changes.[29] In some cases, their partners had strong lesbian identities which prevented them from being able to sustain intimate relationships with participants as they became increasingly virilized. In other situations, participants or their partners broke off their relationships because of internal stressors which may or may not have been directly related to participants' transsexualism. However, it is hard to imagine that pre-existing or independent points of conflict would not have been aggravated by the heightened emotional, physical, and financial burdens of such major life changes. In seven (70 percent) of these ten cases, participants credited their partners with providing the impetus for them to decide that they were transsexual or that they needed to act on their transsexualism, even though those partners did not stay with participants for their metamorphoses.[30]

For example, Rick credited two of her relationships with moving her along toward making the leap into being a man, the first, because of the woman's demands and the second, because of her sympathies. Rick explained:

> In the course of that twenty years I had two long-term relationships. One lasting nine years with a very nice woman. And we had a very good relationship. And she really did understand. She reached a point where she wanted a family and things that I just didn't want and could not deal with in the form that I was. So that was why we actually parted company. And then after that I had a three and a half year relationship with a woman . . . who also seemed to understand the situation and didn't put a whole lot of pressures on me but it was a difficult relationship for her and . . . the demise of that relationship finally freed me up. That was the straw that broke the camel's back. It was very clear to me that my life was never going to be any better if I didn't take some control and do something.

Aaron also felt as though a woman with whom she had been temporarily partnered gave her the shove that she needed to realize that she was transsexual. Aaron described the woman as "a gay woman who was . . . bisexual. She had been married for a while, could relate to me as either male or female, and went back and forth." They lived together for almost one year and then became good friends because "when it got down to the nitty-gritty she wanted a woman and I couldn't be a woman for her any more than I could for my husband. It broke my heart that I couldn't, but I simply could not give her that." However, this woman gave Aaron the rationale she needed to begin to see herself as transsexual. Aaron told about it in these words:

> We talked about the transsexual thing and then I just couldn't do it. See I was . . . involved up to my ears with gay people and everything. I said that would be disowning all these people that I feel are like family. . . . I felt like it would be a terribly selfish thing to do. But you see I had always lived for other people because I didn't have an identity of my own. . . . She took hold of both my shoulders and stood there and looked me straight in the eye and just said simply, "Isn't it about time you did something for yourself?" And those words were a key. . . . Sometimes people cannot give themselves permission to do certain things. . . . And some person they trust . . . can give them permission to do something. They can be life changing. Okay, this particular person was in a position to give me this gift. She did. Within a day I had started writing letters. Within weeks I was making phone calls.

The story which Bruce told about the demise of her last lesbian relationship was also poignant. The relationship started out as an avowedly lesbian-feminist liaison. About two years into the relationship, the couple had a baby together via donor insemination. A year and a half later, Bruce began to think that she might be transsexual. Although it was Bruce's partner who gave her the push that she needed to delve into the possibilities offered by transsexualism, the woman identified too strongly as a lesbian to accompany Bruce on his journey. Bruce outlined her dilemma:

> She's a therapist. . . . And she's known for a long time, I think, that something was awry. So [she] started the process . . . and I said, "I'm doing this. I have to do this." And also that meant the loss of my relationship. . . . I knew that. And she knew that, and she said . . . "I love you now, and I'll always love you, but that we'll be together, I don't know, because I'm a lesbian." And I understood that full and clear, and I knew that I would be giving up this partner . . . to find myself. . . . The relationship you have with yourself is far more important than anything you could establish. And she knew that, and I knew that, and she encouraged me to find out who I was, because she knew I was unhappy.

Once Bruce started into transition, Bruce's partner remained true to her identity as a lesbian. At the time of Bruce's last interview, they were living near one another and remained dear friends and amicable co-parents.

Dale also had a woman partner who at first encouraged her to think of herself as transsexual. Dale's first exposure to the idea of transsexualism was when her partner gave her an article to read on the subject. Prior to that time Dale "didn't know the difference between homosexual and gender change. . . . I was homosexual and I guess I thought all homosexuals wanted to be the opposite sex." When Dale read the article provided by her lover, Dale felt "like a thousand pounds was off me" and set out to find out more about it. Dale started with a visit to their family doctor.

> I wanted to just go right now and get it done. . . . He said that they weren't very successful with anything they were doing. It was just a hunk of skin that was hanging down, and I just felt I was just never going to be able to get it done. I knew I wouldn't have the money. . . . I think I felt at peace for quite some time that I finally knew who I really was. . . . at least there was a name for what I felt, or what I was. And I felt really relieved to know that.

It was five or six years before Dale was able to save enough money to take any tangible steps toward her goal. Those years of waiting and saving were difficult ones.

> [My] feelings and desires . . . intensified in a lot of ways, 'cause . . . I still had to go on the way I was, and it was even more painful, because I knew I could be the other person. Like a whole person. . . . I just was very unhappy. I had to put on an act. I didn't even tell [my partner]

about a lot of how I was feeling. It wasn't long after that that basically I think our relationship started to deteriorate, and I felt, "If I could only be a man, I know she'd stay with me." My father accused me, and so did a lot of other people. They felt that I went through the change just to keep [her]. That was their firm belief. . . . 'Cause I really loved her.

Despite Dale's expectations to the contrary, the woman was not in any way reassured by Dale's move in the direction of "normal." Dale believed that her partner was willing enough to live a closeted lesbian existence and that she would have happily lived with him as a man. Dale's partner apparently could not face the public exposure of their homosexual relationship which would have ensued had they stayed together in their community while Dale became a man. As Dale began to remake herself as a man, the woman was unable to remain by Dale's side and their relationship ended.

Hal also told a long and complicated story full of pathos and despair about the breakup of what must have seemed to any observer to be a near-perfect fourteen-year lesbian-feminist union. Within two years of the start of their relationship, Hal started to refer to herself as transsexual with her partner and among a few select friends. Hal said that her partner was generally supportive of the idea.

[She] thought it was fine as long as I considered myself nonsurgical. She related to me as if I was a man, told her friends I was "really a guy," and generally encouraged me to actualize myself in every way.

Approximately eight years into their relationship, they decided to start a family. They went to a sperm bank and picked out a donor who resembled Hal as closely as possible. They bought a house together and Hal fell deeply in love with the baby when she was born. A year or so later the relationship was starting to show strains. They were planning to try for a second child, and Hal started to feel that her life as a woman was increasingly untenable. Hal highlighted these issues in his account of those years:

It was during this time . . . that I began to feel the pressure of the need to do something about being a transsexual. [Our daughter] was talking then, and she kept trying to call me Daddy, and we had to explain to her that only men could be daddies, and [Hal] was not a man, even though she looked like it and acted like it and did all the things that daddies do. [Our daughter] thought we were crazy. I felt like a daddy, and it was killing me.

I would look at myself in the mirror and think something was wrong, my shoulders weren't thick enough, my neck was too thin. I would worry about how I was going to appear professionally at forty-five and fifty years old as a dyke in men's clothing. . . . My image was that of a little boy, and I was feeling like I needed to grow up, and I couldn't imagine becoming an adult woman. I could only see myself as an adult man. I sought out a transsexual support system and began to gather as much information about the process and about myself as I could. [My partner] was very supportive, going to meetings with me, defending me to her friends, telling me she loved me.

About a year later, Hal's partner became pregnant again and Hal entered a gender program at a local medical center. It was then that Hal started to have a glimpse of what was to come between them.

I was about to start hormones. The night before I was to see the doctor, I asked [my partner] if she was sure this was all right with her. She said, "If you don't go through with this now, I'll leave you for sure." I thought something was wrong, but I assumed she was just tired of hearing about my decision process and my fears. I knew she didn't like it when I was indecisive or weak. So I thought I'd best keep my fears to myself.

After the birth of their second child, Hal's partner withdrew from him. When Hal asked her what the problem was, he walked headlong into the denouement of their relationship.

She shouted, "I'll tell you what's going on with me. This relationship is over!!!" I cried all night. I knew there was no arguing with her. I was so scared she would take the kids away from me. She assured me she would never do that. She wanted to stay with me while I had my mastectomy; she wanted to take care of me (it was six weeks away). I still hoped she would change her mind, but I knew it was over.

I became one of the walking wounded. I'm amazed that I kept my act together at work. There was nothing for me to look forward to except my surgery. And after that, I was damned lucky that a nurse friend came and stayed with me for the first two days, because [my partner] completely ignored me. She later told me she was completely appalled by the process and that she almost drove us off a bridge on the way home from the surgery. She was actually ready to kill herself, me, and our new baby.

It's been over a year now since she moved out . . . and she still treats me as though I am the most despicable person on earth. She allows me to see [our daughter], but she does not allow me to see [our son]. She has changed his name and is trying to have my name removed from his birth certificate.

It must have been especially hard for those participants who survived such painfully ill-timed dissolutions of their relationships. Most of them initially felt the vital encouragement and support of their lovers. The endorsements which these women gave to participants' quests for manhood provided essential validations at critical moments in their passages. Their backing provided both catalyst and ballast to participants in the days when indecision was a major obstacle to participants' advancements toward their eventual goals. When participants' relationships ruptured, they were not left to face the immensity of their decisions entirely alone. By then, they had the knowledge that others had gone before them and had left markers to help them to find their ways. Whereas some participants suffered badly at their losses, others rebounded admirably. Those who initiated new relationships with women did so with partners who began intimacies already aware of participants' transsexualism. Either way, participants had the benefit of having overcome inertia and having begun to move while still harboured by their prior relationships. Once that momentum had begun, participants could go on knowing that they were no longer alone with their transsexualism.

Six participants (14 percent) stood out from the rest in terms of how their sexual or romantic relationships and attractions factored into the development of their transsexual identities.[31] Although they represent minority approaches to female-to-male transsexualism, their stories are important in that they illustrate some of the more subtle complexities of the issues involved.

Jordie and Grant both identified themselves as gay men. Although Jordie never had a relationship with a gay man, Jordie had identified as a gay man since she was in her teens. The only time she "had sex with a lesbian friend . . . it confirmed for [my friend] that I was male . . . and confirmed for me I'm gay." However, Jordie said, "it was not until I turned thirty years old and met some nice gay men that I accepted who I am. It wasn't until I was thirty that I talked about being transsexual." Apparently, for Jordie, the two types of conversations were closely connected.

Grant met his partner of over twenty years while they were both still in their teens. Ostensibly, they started out as a lesbian couple. Soon, however, they discovered that they shared a penchant for sexual identities as S/M gay men and for the corresponding sexual activities. By the time that Grant discovered transsexualism, he had been living as a man for some time. To become physiologically transformed into a man seemed to Grant and his partner both an obvious and a logical step. Curiously, Grant's partner seemed to have no interest in living as a man despite her own stated identity as a gay man and her intimate awareness of transsexualism.

Darcy's story added still another twist. At the time that Darcy began to accept a transsexual identity, she was in a relationship with a woman whom she described as a "fag hag." Although Darcy didn't identify as a gay man, she still felt like their relationship made sense. Darcy explained:

> All her associations are with gay men. She'd never slept with a woman before, and she slept with a man . . . once. . . . She does see me as a gay

man. . . . We're not having a lesbian relationship. So there's no dishonesty there. . . . She can't have a fag, and I can't be a real man. So, we're pretty close in some ways. . . . She's being very supportive, and I think she knows it's the right thing for me to do.

Still another variation was demonstrated in Jorge's brief love life. Jorge had an affair with a male-to-female transsexual after she identified as a female-to-male transsexual but before she began her own transition. This was Jorge's only sexual relationship before transition. Contrary to what one might expect, this experience almost turned an already committed Jorge away from transsexualism. A subsequent friendship with another male-to-female transsexual, rehabilitated Jorge's attitude. Jorge recalled:

> I knew two male-to-female transsexuals, the first one I met by accident. She was pre-op. . . . She was very negative, because she hadn't had any luck getting surgery. She told me it was impossible to get surgery in the U.S., and a person had to answer all psychological questions in a specific way to be accepted. She told me lies (which she believed, I think), like a person has to have had sex with both a man and a woman or they won't be accepted.
>
> I became very depressed from hearing all of this negative talk. It sounded hopeless to get surgery. On numerous times I wanted to kill myself. Through this male-to-female transsexual, I met another one. She was post-op. I sort of began idealizing her. She gave me the "real" info—after all, she had just had surgery. But I was so messed up from the previous lady, that it took about a year for me to believe in the post-op enough to start therapy. It took me about a year and a half to get over a lot of the emotional head trips I got from the first woman.

Alan had a complicated experience of transsexualism. Alan had identified as transsexual since sometime in her teens and had gone back and forth between living as a woman and as a man, partly in response to the wishes of her lovers. In her teens and early twenties, Alan had friendships and sexual relations with male-to-female transsexuals and male transvestites. At age sixteen, Alan first lived as a man while working as a street prostitute. Alan again lived as a man for two years in his early twenties. This second stint as a man was interleaved with a seven-year S/M lesbian relationship with an older woman. Alan made a gender adjustment to suit this partner but refused the favour for other persons with whom s/he became involved. Alan explained:

> [My] lesbian S/M lover objected when I was twenty-one so I left the area and crossdressed and passed full time. When I returned to her, I gave up the crossdressing. But the desire never really went away. When I started crossdressing and passing the next time at age twenty-seven, I

was rejected by a lesbian lover who does not speak to me to this day. . . .
At age twenty-seven, I went on male hormones for the first time. . . . I
stopped prostituting and started dating heterosexual women. I would
tell them I was transsexual before I had sex with them. It felt better to
me than living in a female identity and relating to lesbians or bisexuals.
At twenty-eight to thirty-three, I married (not legally) a straight woman
and it was the best experience of my life.

Alan's transsexual identity proved to be the undoing of even this "perfect" relationship.

I had a perfect mate from 1982–1987. . . . She was classically beautiful
with large blue eyes, long blonde hair, and a shapely figure. We lived
together and passed well as man and wife for five years. I still have not
recovered from her leaving me. She left because she wanted to get legally
married and I chose not to have transsexual surgery. I wanted to have
more sobriety and to earn a Ph.D. before I completed the change. She
has married and we have had no contact since we broke up in 1987.
She was my "showpiece," the best-looking woman wherever we went,
and we also had a peaceful, sexual, and meaningful relationship. It was
the best time of my life. I am still trying to move on with my life. . . . I
was devastated. . . . She brought out the best in me. I have never been so
happy and satisfied.

After the demise of this relationship Alan once again returned to being a woman because "I wanted to see if I could cope with being a sober
female. . . . [but] I still long to be male and I only have sexual relationships
with partners who agree to treat me as male." At the time of her interviews, Alan was "hoping to meet a pre-op male-to-female in order to parent, and then we can both complete our changes." Alan said that she feels
"beyond gender."

By contrast, Keith was in some ways very conventional: while Keith
was a woman, she worked out her gender identity in relationships with
men; when Keith became a man, he became a straight man. It was Keith's
final relationship with a man which really illuminated the matter for her.
Keith saw it this way in retrospect:

Another thing that really clarified it to me, and was sort of the catalyst
in my turning point, was that just before my change, I met up, completely by accident, with a male who became my lover. And he had a
very strong aspect in him that was female, and he carried a lot of guilt
about it. . . . worrying that he might be gay. . . .

When I became involved with him, our sex life quickly developed into
intense role playing, where he was the female and I was the male. And
in a short time, that spread to our entire relationship, whenever we saw
each other. In each other's eyes, and in our own eyes, I was the male and
he was the female. And this was a really big catalyst to me in the sense

that . . . once I experienced having somebody accept me as a male, I never wanted to go back. . . . for him, that meant a lot of guilt, and he eventually ran away from the relationship in fear of what he was seeing in himself. But for me, it completely opened up my ability to be male. It was shortly after that that I cut my hair very short into a male style, began buying male's clothes. . . . I changed my name to a male name . . . and just naturally progressed into a gender change.

These few brief vignettes graphically display how gender, sex, and sexual orientation can be distinctly separate, yet socially linked. It becomes clear when contemplating the stories of these few unusual individuals that being female-bodied convinced them to see neither their gender, nor their sexual orientations, as dictated by their sex status. Similarly, while these participants and their sexual partners were fully aware of their femaleness and their pre-transition womanhood, they were nevertheless able to sustain sexual orientations which belied both facts. Finally, however, their lives would be greatly simplified and readily intelligible for one and all if these three central markers of status and identity could be aligned in a more usual fashion. Thus, although they might conceivably have carried on as they were, their options to do so were extremely limited.

Thus in answer to the question, "What's love got to do with it?" I suggest that love and sexuality were for many participants the crucibles in which their gender identities were tempered. It is in love that we are stripped bare. It is in love that we most expect to be seen as we really are, unadorned by assumed roles, camouflaging costumes, and false facades. Indeed, to be truly known in this way is one of the greatest joys of love. Thus, when participants found lovers who gave them this gift, for many of them, it allowed the last piece of the puzzle to fall into place. When they found their rudimentary identities as men reflected back to them in such exquisitely intimate ways, they felt more free to demand that the rest of their lives begin to provide them with similar confirmation of their manhood. To elicit that level of affirmation from more distant others required that participants present understandable evidence of manliness. The technologies of transsexualism offered participants the tools with which to do so.

Other Contributing Factors

Clearly, no one undertakes such a major life transformation as sex or gender reassignment without dramatically compelling reasons. More than half of all participants (62 percent)[32] spontaneously talked about feelings and behaviours which normally belie acute unhappiness of a most tenacious kind. They spoke of having been severely depressed,[33] having considered[34] or attempted[35] suicide, having escaped into daily drug[36] or alcohol[37] use, or having developed eating disorders[38] during their pre-transition adult years. In all but a handful of cases, participants directly related these problems to their gender issues. When participants had alternate interpretations, they generally linked their emotional disturbances to upsets in their sexual and romantic lives. As already noted, participants' relationship difficulties almost always articulated with and were aggravated by their gender and sex discomforts. Whatever explanations for their emotional states were put forward by participants, Aaron's cautions seem useful to keep in mind:

> I'm talking about a transsexual before they change. Like any other handicapped person, they carry a stress load, like a person who is partially sighted, like a person who is mentally retarded, a person that's deaf. . . . they've got a stress load that adds to everything else. . . . If you're in a situation where you're about to go over the edge, it's going to shove you.

In addition, the timing of the decisions of eight participants (18 percent) to embrace transsexualism may have been connected in some way to the death of a parent.[39]

Typically, by the time that participants decided that they were transsexual and that they had to take action on their transexualism, they saw such moves as last options. They felt that they had exhausted all known ways to live in the world as women. Many of them came to points in their lives where they conceived of their choices as being to live as men, or to not live at all. Jordie simply said, "The real decision was not to live as a man, but rather would I live as a man or die." Similarly, Sam stated that the "fantasy" of one day having sex reassignment surgery "was the only thing that kept me alive" for many years. Steven, who had a history of deep emotional problems which had previously caused her to be hospitalized, became suicidal after being turned down for sex reassignment the first time she requested it. As well, Morgan, Darren, Ed, Howie, and Dale all reported having been suicidal around the time of their decisions to start their transitions.

Scott and Mel flirted with suicidal thoughts in their depressions over being confined as women and as females. Scott articulated these feelings in this way:

> In the last five years . . . I was getting to a point where I was feeling so bad about myself. . . . when somebody called me "she," it just pissed me off, you know, maximum. Because I just didn't want to play the game anymore. I didn't want to have to sit with my legs crossed. . . . I didn't

want to have to wear a bra. . . . I felt awkward going out in public with my lover. People stare. . . . I didn't want to be identified as a lesbian. And it's like it just finally came to a point where I was just really depressed and didn't want to go out of the house. . . . So I was just getting really to a point of getting desperate. . . . I thought about it but there's a little tiny part of me that probably would never kill myself.

Mel echoed Scott's revulsion at conforming to other people's expectations when he said:

I turned thirty-six in December and it kind of was like, "I got do something about this, I can't deal with it any more, I'm going to kill myself." . . . I decided, "I can't live this way any longer. I can't trade off for the money, for what society expects of me, for what my parents expect of me. I have got to start living for myself."

Luther, too, tried to fit in however she could. After trying to be a butch lesbian and a feminist, Luther was at her wits' end:

I was getting to be more and more depressed . . . and I was thinking about suicide. Every time I got to that point, I said, "There must be something else." . . . I knew what the something else was, and so I just had to do it. . . . "Do you want to live or do you want to die?" That's what it had come to. . . . I was dying. I was just dying inside.

Keith suggested that, although she was not contemplating actual suicide, her depression and debilitation were such that she would have come to a similar end:

If I had remained living as a female . . . in that role and trying to fulfill the expectations people had of me to be a woman, I'm sure that I would have slowly killed myself. Which is what I was doing up to that point in time, with drugs and drinking and just general self-hatred and self-loathing.

The testimony of these participants would seem to indicate that the taking on of transsexual identities was not so much a choice between various life options as it was a recognition and acceptance of the only viable life which they saw open to them. It also seems possible that those participants who considered or attempted suicide at earlier points in their lives might have done so precisely because at those junctures they had not yet realized that transsexualism might offer them relief from what seemed to be insurmountable problems. One can only speculate as to how many "successful" female suicides might have been motivated by similar inabilities to uncover this particular route of egress from what felt like an unendurable bondage to femininity.

In addition, eight participants noted with sorrow the passing of one or both of their parents a few years prior to their commencement of their transitions.[40] It seemed to a few participants that the death of their parent(s) in some ways acted as catalysts. Others denied any connection. However, several people's comments mirrored those of Steven, who said, "I thought that everyone in my family would have to die before I could do this," or of Mel who explained in the context of coming to her decision about her transsexualism, "there's two things that I can't deal with, my religion and my family." It would seem that facing their parents with such a momentous announcement may have been a terrifying prospect for many participants. Therefore, it would also seem likely that the passing of their parent(s) might have given some participants a melancholy kind of freedom to become more precisely who they wanted to be.[41]

Walter's case is suggestive of this last point. Walter's decision to move from crossdressing into a hormone treatment program coincided with the death of her mother. Walter pointed out that until her beloved mother's death, she had not been able to be a fully independent person who could autonomously chart the course of her own life. Although her mother's demise was a tremendous blow to Walter, it freed her to make more permanent changes to her gender presentation. Walter recalled:

> That was my ultimate fear, losing my mother. . . . And in fact, within the six-month period before she died I started having premonitions that she was going to die. . . . I started going to therapy because I started feeling so much stress trying to deny these feelings. . . . I thought for sure when my mother died, I would die. Or I would end up in an insane asylum. . . .
>
> I survived my worst fear. I actually survived it and I actually realize now that I actually can see the benefit in it. That now I'm an independent person and that I couldn't be while [my mother] was around. Because I was so attached, you know, now I'm really realizing my own individuality.

Hal, who had been close with her father before he died, also seemed to have independence issues with her parent. Hal had been identifying as transsexual for many years and finally took the decision to start gender and sex reassignment procedures in the year after her father died. Hal did not say how she responded to her father's death, but she did look for his advice and approval when she was making her decision: "I went through all these exercises of writing down imagined conversations with him. How he would react and how he would fight me and how he would accept me."

Both of Darren's parents died when Darren was sixteen years old, just as Darren began to identify as transsexual. Darren, who had "hero-worshipped" her father but who had felt no warmth from or to her abusive mother, felt that the deaths of her parents were unrelated to her desire for sex reassignment surgery. Certainly Darren had been showing signs of manliness for several years before their deaths. As soon as Darren graduated from high school and was free of her legal guardians, she checked herself into a psychiatric hospital, stating that she was feeling suicidal and hoping that her doctors would start her on a transition. As an orphan, Darren had no familial restraints on her pursuit of sex reassignment. She was free to act as independently as the medical profession would allow.

Eli's response to the death of her father seemed to reflect Eli's need to recoup her loss. When Eli's father died, she "went into a tailspin," which was eventually resolved when Eli realized that she could live as a man if she adopted a transsexual identity. Eli, who had thought of her father as "like God," took a long time to recover from the shock of his death. Eli elaborated the stages she went through in coming to a solution to her panic at her loss of her father:

> I've been . . . coming out of the deepest, most destructive depression imaginable anyone could ever go through and live . . . during which all this stuff really came to the surface. . . . Little by little I began to be able to talk to people, but not without totally freaking out and crying and shaking and feeling really weak and drained. . . . I just fell apart at the drop of a hat. . . .
> I realized suddenly that everybody saw me as . . . a middle-aged female . . . and I started getting terrified. I thought, "Nobody knows who I am. Nobody knows what I am." . . . And then I just flipped out.
> I think I was probably clinically depressed. I used to sleep fifteen hours a day and have the television on all the time. I would never go out. I went through that for several years. . . . so I have to turn my wrath on myself. . . . I loathed myself for a time. . . . So, I just went back into my fantasies [of being a man] again. Bigger than ever. Then I finally found out about transsexualism.

Perhaps Eli's return to equanimity was motivated by forces similar to those which Bruce theorized might have been at play in her case. Bruce, who idolized her father, was the participant who most clearly tied her father's death to her decision to become a man. Bruce explained:

> My dad's death triggered something in me. And I lost a very positive male role model. And . . . maybe I'm creating that for myself. . . . I think so because . . . I don't know if I could do this [if my dad was still alive] . . . say to my dad, "Dad, I'm your son."

Alan, whose story was unusual in so many respects, gave an interesting account of the impact which his mother's death had on him. At the time, he had been on hormone therapy and living as a man for about four years. Having felt cast as her mother's protector and surrogate husband as a youth, Alan responded dramatically to his mother's passing.

My mother and I were very emotionally involved. She died when I was thirty-one. She had been invested in me not having children. She loved children but she had remained in an abusive marriage because she was a mother and she saw no other options for survival. She never wanted me to have children and I wanted to please her, so I didn't. Now, since I've been sober for 4 1/2 years, and she's been dead for 4 1/2 years, I want children. . . . This is the main reason I went back into the female role ten months ago. I'm sober and I want to parent. I'm still exploring these surfacing feelings. I may never parent but I want to allow myself to have parental feelings.

Clearly, the death of a parent is always a deeply moving experience. One need not be transsexual to feel that such a loss provides impetus for more independent thought or action. Likewise, it is not unique to transsexuals to want to embody in one's own life some of the cherished characteristics of a lost loved one. Similarly, many people feel moved by the death of a parent to take bold steps in their lives. Realizing one's own mortality at the death of a parent has a way of catapulting people into the kinds of changes prefaced by "Life is too short . . . " Participants seemed to have been affected in some or all of these ways. They were not unique in that regard. What was unique to these people was that the leap that they were emboldened to take was into transsexualism.

In sum, it seems clear that the entry into transsexualism of at least half of the participants was accompanied by pain and desperation. In some cases (31 percent), participants were agonizingly depressed.[42] A few (16 percent) were hospitalized and medicated for their malady.[43] Some (22 percent) tried to hide from their pain in drug abuse or alcoholism;[44] others (9 percent) starved or ate themselves into oblivion.[45] Fully 40 percent of participants were so unhappy during their pre-transition adult years that they considered[46] or attempted suicide.[47] All of the 18 percent of participants whose parent(s) died around the time that they commenced their transitions also suffered from one or more of these complaints.[48] Other participants who were more reticent on these topics may have experienced similar distress.

Summary and Commentary

Making the decision to call oneself a female-to-male transsexual and deciding to change one's life accordingly must be one of the most profound redirections of one's life that a person can make. Participants could not and did not take such steps frivolously. They came to them after lifelong feelings of embarrassment and failure at femininity, at womanhood, and at femaleness. They carried within them a sense that there must be some way for them to fit better with the expectations of those among whom they lived. When they learned of the phenomenon called female-to-male transsexualism, approximately one-third (36 percent) of participants immediately recognized it as the solution for which they had been hoping. Others needed to know more.

Most of those participants who immediately embraced the idea of transsexualism, as well as most of those who were more cautious in their approaches, went in search of more information against which to test their newfound fascination with the subject. They made use of four main levels of expertise: popular media accounts, professional literature written mostly by medically trained researchers, reports from transsexuals who had gone before them, and the physical and emotional feedback of their lovers.

Popular media accounts of transsexualism provided the least detailed but most readily available information on the subject. Therefore this was where most participants first learned about transsexualism. Most participants went on to educate themselves in more detail while they continued to be eager consumers of any popular media coverage given to transsexualism in general or to female-to-male transsexualism in particular. As participants found more information in professional literature or from other transsexual people, participants continually held themselves up to measure against what they had learned about transsexualism. The better the fit, according to each individual's own idiosyncratic standards of necessary congruence, the more firmly participants became wedded to thinking of themselves as transsexual.

The professional literature was sometimes helpful, sometimes horrifying. It was helpful in that it gave participants insights into what profiles of female-to-male transsexualism were recognized by gender clinics and other medical service providers. Those participants who fit the picture were reassured; those who did not were forewarned as to how to represent themselves if and when they wished to secure the cooperation of such professionals. The professional literature was just as often horrifying in its descriptions of surgical procedures and outcomes of phalloplastic techniques. Some participants were understandably put off by the dim prospects of complete corporeal transformation. Others were daunted by the high financial costs involved. Still others could not be deterred by anything.

Accounts provided by other transsexual people proved to be highly influential sources of information. The fact that these reports were provided by persons who had successfully crossed over the invisible line which separates men from women, males from females, provided extra heft to their testimonials and guidance. They were also able to provide invaluable insider knowledge which helped participants to gain better perspectives on what lay ahead of them. Not the least of the services which they provided were the compelling examples of their apparently satisfying lives. If they had become men, then so too could participants.

The final arena in which participants played out their explorations was in that of love and sexuality. It was in the safety and privacy of their intimate sexual relationships with others that they made test runs of their manhood before launching it into the wider world. If they were to think of themselves as men and as males, if they were to become such, they had to be able successfully to do so in the mundane minutiae of their domestic lives and in the unabashed physicality of sexuality. In some cases, participants had partners who reflected back to them the images which they craved, that is, they saw them as performing in ways consistent with manhood. Those participants who enjoyed this level of confirmation took confidence from it. Some participants' sexual partners most decidedly saw them as women in their interactions, albeit very masculine ones. They could not or would not authenticate participants' manhood. Eventually, even these participants were able to find substantiation of their rightness as men despite these "lesbian" relations. On the one hand, they construed their own inability to find peace within the expectations of their lovers as proof that they were simply unable to be successful as (lesbian) women. On the other hand, many of them then went on to find partners who would mirror them as they wished to be seen, as men. Thus, having proven to themselves that they were not (lesbian) women, they found partners who would validate them as straight men. For some participants, this level of acceptance gave them the confidence to demand that more distant others also begin to recognize their manhoods.

A great many participants, no matter how well informed and well loved they might have been, were still unable to face with equanimity the monumental implications of accepting and acting upon their transsexualism. For them, it was only after they had reached a point of quiet desperation in their lives that they could come to a peace with the idea. Some participants became sorely depressed, at times to the point of psychiatric hospitalization. For some participants this despair took the form of suicidal thoughts or attempts. Some participants overate, drank, starved, or drugged themselves before they could face their transsexualism. For a few participants, it was the death of a parent which provided the impetus to recognize what needed to be done to bring them to a more integrated wholeness. In the end, what it typically came to for many participants was a process of elimination. Step by step, participants did everything that they could imagine, and in which they could bring themselves to partake, which might have allowed them both to remain as women and to remain alive and functional. When they had exhausted all the possible forms of womanhood of which they could conceive, their only known path to survival lay open ahead of them. With terror, apprehension, and exhilaration they were ready to take their first steps on the road to more fully becoming men.

19 | Making the Changes

THE COURAGE INVOLVED in taking on a stigmatized identity in the privacy of one's own mind or in the relative comfort and safety of an intimate relationship represents quite a different kind of challenge than actually stepping out in the world wearing that identity. In order to live as men and to transform their bodies, participants had to be able to say to a sundry collection of people that they were transsexual. At the very least, they had to present themselves to those who would assist them in their physical transformations. Beyond that, there lay a world of others to whom participants might speak about their transsexualism.

The decisions which participants made about when and how to undertake their changes were varied. Although twelve participants said that they began to think of themselves as transsexual while they were still in their teens,[1] only Simon, Ed, Darren, Jorge, and Phil made their decisions to pursue sex reassignment before they became adults. The other thirty-four participants who had embarked upon their gender shifts did so as adults,[2] sometimes after considerable delays between their acceptance of themselves as transsexual, and their actions on those identities. In addition, at the time of their interviews, Morgan, Eli, Robin, Terry, Darcy, and Pat thought of themselves as transsexual but had not made any firm decisions about when they would begin their journeys into manhoods which could be easily recognized by other people.

How participants inaugurated their new lives also varied. Some began by contacting established gender clinics and then following their protocols. Some people made use of the services of counsellors, therapists, or psychiatrists to help them to work out the details of what exactly they did and did not want to do. In some cases, participants' only interest in psychological therapy involved the referrals for hormone therapy which such practitioners could provide. Other participants leapt directly into cross-dressing and living full time as men. However, most participants felt that they would be unable to live successfully as men without the aid of medical interventions and therefore underwent periods of hormone therapy and/or breast reduction or removal before they began to present themselves in public as men.

Because of these many variations in the steps taken by participants to eventuate their transitions and because not every participant did take or intended to take all of the same measures, there is no single point after which all participants can be said to have completed their transformations. I have therefore chosen to use the approximate time when participants began to "pass"[3] full time as men as a rough marker of participants' moves from living as women into living as men. If participants did not provide this information, I have assumed that participants were successfully living as men within a few months of commencing to crossdress[4] or to take hormone therapy, whichever came first.

At the times of their last interviews, six participants had not yet begun physiological changes.[5] All other participants had begun hormone therapy.[6] The thirty-eight participants who gave information ranged in age from nineteen to forty-seven years at the time that they began taking testosterone injections. Their average age at the outset was 30.2 years. As a group they averaged 6.5 years of hormone therapy, ranging from a minimum of three months on androgens to a maximum of nineteen years. Six participants (15 percent) had had breast reduction surgery,[7] and thirty participants (77 percent)[8] had received mastectomies and chest reconstruction.[9] Of the thirty-four participants who had breast reductions and/or mastectomies, twenty-eight specified how old they were at the time. They ranged in age from twenty to fifty years. Their average age at the time of their most radical breast surgeries was 33.7 years, or approximately 3.5 years after the average age at which participants began hormone therapy. Twenty-three participants (59 percent) had had hysterectomies,[10] two of which were done for medical reasons other than sex reassignment.[11] Of the twenty-one participants who had hysterectomies performed for reasons connected with their transsexualism, sixteen reported how old they were when they had them done. They ranged in age from twenty-one to forty-three, with an average age of thirty-four years. Howie and Hal had undergone "genital free-up" operations[12] at age twenty-three and forty-one respectively. Simon, Scott, Rick, and Dale had had phalloplastic surgeries.[13] Simon was twenty-seven and Scott was thirty-seven when they had theirs done; Rick's and Dale's were done when they were in their forties.

Approximately half (52 percent)[14] of participants said that they had made use of gender clinics for some or all of their transitions.[15] All participants who used clinics, except Ed and Luther, initiated their transitions after 1979, the year in which North American gender clinics generally adopted the Harry Benjamin International Gender Dysphoria Association's *Standards of Care*.[16] They specified, among other things, that hormonal or surgical sex reassignment should be allowed to patients only on the recommendation of "clinical behavioural scientists" and that it was considered to be "professional misconduct" for clinicians to recommend people for such procedures "on demand."[17] In addition, the *Standards of Care* required that any clinician who would refer a person for hormone therapy must have known that person "in a psychotherapeutic relationship for at least three months prior to making said recommendation."[18] Furthermore, if a clinician who abided by the *Standards of Care* wished to recommend a transsexual person for breast or genital surgeries, the clinician must have known the person "in a psychotherapeutic relationship for at least six months prior to making said recommendation" and get a second opinion from another properly accredited professional. Furthermore, the transsexual person was required to have lived "full-time in the social role of the genetically other sex" for at least one year before becoming eligible to be recommended for breast or genital surgery.[19]

In other words, participants who used the services of gender clinics or of professionals who followed the *Standards of Care* during this period were supposed to submit themselves to a minimum of three months of psychotherapy before they could get a prescription for hormone therapy. In addition, they were to undergo another three months of therapy with the same therapist, plus at least one other evaluation with another clinician, and live full time as a man for a full year before they could be referred for breast or genital surgery. In practice, mastectomies almost always preceded genital surgeries and some individuals had hysterectomies without genital reconstruction, while others had both procedures done together.

Both those who used gender clinics, and the other half of participants who did not, managed some or all of their own medical services. Most often they convinced general medical practitioners to prescribe testosterone for them. They bought breast reductions as cosmetic surgeries or made use of the services of surgeons who would perform mastectomies on recommendations from psychotherapists. Hysterectomies were similarly obtained. It was only in the area of the surgical production of masculine genitalia that the services of doctors associated with gender clinics were unavoidable.

Wanting and Waiting: Not Yet Living as Men

Six participants had come to the point where they identified themselves as transsexual but had not yet begun to live as men.[20] Eli, for example, did not want to make any physiological alterations to her body; Terry "would like to start hormonal and psychological treatments sometime in the near future" but was afraid she might lose contact with her family if she did; Robin was "in therapy right now to receive hormones"; Darcy was "looking for someone who will start hormone therapy [for me]."

Eli, although clear about her transsexual identity, was perhaps the most ambivalent of all participants about the necessity of undergoing any body-altering procedures in order to be taken as a man. Eli said that other people perceived her to be a woman "about 80 percent of the time." Although this was often deeply disturbing to Eli, she had reasons for eschewing any actions more radical than presenting herself in her preferred appearance as an Edwardian period man. When Eli explained why she didn't want to take any more complicated steps, she made use of the same kinds of reasons given by other participants in justifying why they had taken some measures and not others.

> I'm kind of lazy. I just want things to be simple. . . . I don't like messing around with hormones and stuff, or messing with my body's chemical balance. It's working OK. I'm never going to be a real physical guy . . . so I'd just like to look and feel more like I feel inside by doing weight training. . . . If I was shaped differently, real big boobs and stuff that was hanging off me and giving me a bad time and driving me nuts . . . then I might decide to do more. . . . When I look at my self in mirror with no clothes on, I see a guy. . . .
>
> If there was a safe way of doing all this stuff, so that it didn't injure me, and . . . if I won the lottery . . . I'd do it. . . . I'm happy to acknowledge that I am in a transsexual condition. . . . And I'm proud of the fact that I'm a guy. I feel happy about that, even though my body doesn't express it as fully as I would like it to.

Morgan seemed to be the participant most mired in confusion and insecurity. She had a history of a series of psychological problems which may or may not have been related to her gender and sex issues and was feeling suicidal at the time of her interview. Morgan had been identifying herself as transsexual for five years but had already been refused entry into a gender program because of the instability of her psychological profile. Morgan both "hated" her body and was "afraid of having a sex change" at the same time as she identified herself as transsexual.

Pat was still in the planning stages about her gender and sex reassignment. She said that she was more comfortable thinking of herself as a man than as a woman, but she clearly was not entirely alienated from her female body. Pat had already borne one child via donor insemination and was intending to bear another. At the time of the birth of her first child, Pat had already begun to think of herself as a man. She described an intriguing way of dealing with the apparent dissonance:

> I really was concerned about how I would feel about being pregnant. . . .
> I felt myself to be a pregnant man. I would look at men, especially men

with big bellies, and marvel at how they could get their pants to stay up under their belly, because I certainly was having trouble doing that. And in many ways, I really identified it as just me, who I am, having a baby. And of course men can do it, because I'm doing it. And I know that sounds delusional . . . It really was just my way of coping with what other people would think would be totally absurd and out to lunch. . . . By the way, I nursed my son until he was almost three years old. I think that I did this primarily to have my breasts be functional. Since I have stopped nursing, my breasts are again more problematic.

Pat, like both Eli and Morgan, expressed some ambivalence about becoming a man.

If we didn't deal with gender at all, I'd be the most happy. . . . I struggle with this. Like, I know that if I make some physiological changes that I may appear to the world more consistent with how I am, but I don't know that it really solves the underlying problem of having a mismatch between my body and my sense of myself. . . . A lot of the time I just see myself as myself, without affixing any gender label. I am more comfortable with the male label than with the female, but would mostly like to avoid the whole thing. . . . I feel that I don't want to change genders but that I want to be perceived as male or as genderless. I feel that there is something wrong in the process of gender reassignment. I am already male, why do I have to do anything about it?

In sum, three of the six participants who had not yet begun transition stated that they were ready to begin as soon as they could make the necessary arrangements.[21] Three were unsure about when or if they would become engaged in the technologies of gender and sex reassignment.[22]

Getting Started on Hormones and Crossdressing

For most participants, stepping across the line that separates women from men, females from males, was a long awaited and deeply desired process. Slightly more than one-third of participants (37 percent)[23] began by crossdressing without the assistance of the usually dramatic effects of hormone therapy,[24] which allowed them to begin their "real-life test"[25] to determine their satisfaction with living as men. After a while, all of them found their way to hormone therapy.

A few participants began to crossdress because they felt like men and knew no other way to externalize their feelings. Walter, for example, said that she had been "very much intensely a crossdresser" for the better part of ten years before he discovered transsexualism, "that was like the best I could come up with because I didn't think there was any alternative."

Grant also took up men's attire because it was the only way she could figure out to look like the man she felt herself to be. When Grant first started crossdressing, at age eighteen, she did so part time when she was working in a gay men's bar. Grant said that she was only "read occasionally,"[26] despite the fact that her bound breasts were "somewhere between 44 and 45 DD in size." Grant later went on to crossdress full time for approximately another two years before discovering transsexualism.

Once Grant knew about transsexualism, he immediately went to a psychiatrist to see what could be done, while thinking, "The doctor's going to throw me out of the office. She's going to tell me I'm sick." That doctor didn't, but the next one did. Nonetheless, Grant's psychiatrist made sure that he got the hormone treatments that he wanted.

> And I'm in there [at my psychiatrist's office], "Oh, my God. I think I know what my problem is. I'm a transsexual." And she goes, "What do you want to do about it?" And I fell out of the chair.
> She put me in touch with an endocrinologist, and he didn't like it one bit. But I went through whatever tests he . . . felt were necessary. . . . I had to get a second opinion. And I went in, and the first words out of this male doctor was, "How dare you want balls?" And I looked at him and I said, "How dare you claim to understand what yours are for, if you have them." And he looked at me, and I said, "Do I threaten your masculinity that much?" And I started putting him on the defensive. . . . I mean, I struck a nerve. And I walked out. And I went back to the first doctor, and I said, "I'm having a problem finding a second opinion." . . . The psychiatrist had to put the screws to him, because he . . . approved of the procedure. . . . I started the shots. And I used to be terrified of needles, and I'm used to them now.

At about the age of twenty-seven, Harry just "slipped into" fully crossdressing. Harry had for years been a masculine looking woman who was sometimes mistaken for a man.[27] At some point, she realized that she was more often attributed by others with being a man than with being a woman. Harry decided to simply go along with the convenience of the situation.

> I was going to [a local college]. And it seemed like half the students thought I was male, and the other half thought I was female, which was quite awkward. . . . It's amazing what people will live with and deal with in a conversation and not know what's happening. Like one person will say "she," the other person will say "he," and there won't be a conflict for either one 'cause they're not really listening to each other. So, it really is amazing how much you can get away with. But sometimes . . . somebody would say to me, "Do you know she's calling you a he?" or "She's calling you she." . . . I'd really try to throw them off somehow. . . . Redirect their focus, which I became very good at doing. Now, I left

[that school] after a couple of semesters, and went to [another] college. And most of the students there saw me as "he." So, I went with it.

After living as a man for five years, Harry entered a program at a gender clinic and began psychotherapy as part of the evaluation process. Harry felt that "I didn't get much backing from them," so he dropped out of the program and found a physician who "doesn't know a lot" about transsexualism but who was willing to start Harry on a hormone regime.

A number of participants deliberately crossdressed as a precursor to sex reassignment. Simon knew that she was transsexual from the age of sixteen. She made the transition into living as a man in the early 1970s, when most public and professional attitudes about transsexualism were still quite unsophisticated. Simon decided that, from what she knew about what was available for her from professional sources, she would be better off taking matters into her own hands. Simon explained her logic:

> At that point in the writing there was a whole lot of talk about pathology and deviancy. . . . the whole attitude that anybody who even thought that was sick. And I didn't feel like I was sick. I felt like I had finally figured out what was going on with me and why I always felt the way I had. But because of the attitude in the literature and stuff I made a very strong decision that I would just do it. That when I was ready, I would start living as a man and that I wouldn't go to therapists. I had a real strong fear that if I did, they'd lock me up. I think that considering where I lived and everything, that was a possibility at the time.

When Simon was eighteen years old and away from home at college, she decided that the time was ripe for her move. She made some minor adjustments to her appearance and started to tell people to think of her as a man now. It was not easy.

> At that point I just started telling people my new name and losing friends right and left. . . . People would walk across the campus purposefully, like they would see me coming and they would cross over so that they didn't have to walk past me and possibly have to look at me and say hello or something. . . . and the whole struggle around my gender and stuff was really interfering with what I was doing at school, and I was going to quit. And I went to the dean and told her that I was going to leave and the reason that I was going to leave was that I couldn't handle going to school and going through the transition. . . . And she advised me to stay.

Within a year, Simon had found his way to a group of transsexual people at a local mental health clinic. There he met a transsexual man who taught him how to bind his breasts. Also at that group, Simon made

friends with transsexual people who knew a doctor who would give them
hormones on demand.

> We used to make these monthly trips to [a neighbouring city] because
> there was a doctor, no questions asked, who would give you shots. We
> could only afford to come over once a month. . . . Sort of a field trip . . .
> to get a shot. I quit going to see after maybe five or six times because
> how much does 100 mg once a month really do you? . . .
>
> But this doctor—the last time I went to see him—the testosterone is
> clear, it's in an oil base. And he gave me this shot and it was kind of
> milky looking. And I had seen the M-to-F's get this and so I said, "Did
> you just give me estrogen?" And he said, "Yeah, isn't that what you're
> supposed to have?" And I said, "No, I'm supposed to have testoster-
> one." And he said, "Oh, okay" and turned around and gave me testos-
> terone in the other arm. . . . .Incompetent, and not only that, his whole
> attitude was, "Well, how in the hell do you expect me to tell if you don't
> tell me?" And here I am sprouting chin hairs at this point.
>
> What that did to me physically was just incredible. I already had . . .
> 100 mg of estrogen and then to turn around and get 100 mg of testos-
> terone on top of the estrogen I was already getting. I had one of the
> worst weeks of my life. It was like up and down, up and down. I'd be
> real moody. I felt almost schizophrenic, or manic depressive. It was just
> like they were bouncing off of each other and it was like push, pull. You
> know, one was making me kind of on the sedate side and the other one
> was going "Rah, rah, rah let's get out there and kill." . . . So, after that
> I quit going to see him and I did without hormones.

About six months after that Simon convinced another doctor whom he
had known for a number of years to prescribe testosterone for him regularly. Simon learned to self-inject and continued to do so off and on for
approximately the next ten years.

Ed also told a series of stories about her experiences trying to get help
in the 1970s. When Ed began to identify as transsexual and became suicidal about it at the age of eighteen, she told her parents why she felt so despondent. Ed's mother was "very supportive" and helped her in her transition.

> She, first of all, got a psychiatrist. . . . So I . . . told him . . . "Well, I need
> a psychiatric recommendation before I can be considered for a sex
> change." And he sat there and stared at me for about ten minutes,
> picked up the phone and called up the psychiatric ward and said, "I
> have another one for you." Then he said, "I'm going to have you put in
> the hospital for a while." . . . And I just got up and said, "No way,
> you're wrong." . . .
>
> And there was this guy that [my mother] worked with, he was a Mor-
> mon bishop . . . and he had a friend that worked up at the mental health
> clinic. . . . And when I went in there he was this 60 year old shrivelled-

up guy and I'm going, "Oh, this is really going to be great, he's really going to be understanding about my situation, I can tell." . . . So I went in there and . . . I said, "Well I'm here because I need a psychiatric recommendation to have a sex change." . . . And he says, "Well, we'll help you out then." And I'm sure my jaw fell to the floor when he said that. . . . So we talked for a while and he got me set up.

Ed's experience with a gender clinic in pre-*Standards* days was not a smooth one. The clinic required her to crossdress before allowing her to start on hormones. Ed, however, found crossdressing without hormones or surgery to be too difficult and found a way to persuade the clinic to do as she wished. Ed described some of the difficulties she encountered.

There's a clinic up at the university. . . . I went up there . . . trying to get recommended for hormones. . . . And they dragged me out for about a year and a half saying, "No, you're too young. We don't want to start you on anything we can't reverse." . . . They expect you to live as a male for the entire time. And which is really frustrating when you have to do it all on your own and you don't have help of hormones or anything like that. . . .

So I had a family doctor that I'd been going to for like fifteen years, and I went and talked to him, and my mother had also talked to him about what I was doing, and I asked him if there was any way he could start me on the hormones. . . . And he said, "Bend over." So started me on the hormones and a few weeks later . . . I told [the doctor at the clinic] that my doctor had started me on the hormones, and three weeks later they sent me a notice saying, "Well, we now approve you for hormones."

Ed was extremely pleased with just being on hormone therapy after such a long struggle to begin a transition.

Just having male hormones in me made me feel better about myself. And I felt at least I had accomplished something and was taking a step in the direction I finally wanted to go after so many years of wanting to do this. And it also made me impatient to be able to complete what I had started. . . . I was flying on top of the world.

Steven and Darren began to crossdress shortly before they started hormone therapy. For them, the two activities formed a unit. Steven was instructed to crossdress by her therapist at the clinic she was attending. Her crossdressing constituted the first part of the real-life test. Steven began hormones three months later.

Darren started crossdressing publicly while making arrangements to get on a hormone program; she had been secretly crossdressing in her bedroom for years.

Just before starting classes [at university] . . . I disposed of all my female clothes and bought an all-male wardrobe. . . . Underneath my undershirt, I wore a breast binder . . . to flatten my chest. To further enhance my masculine image, I purchased a pair of men's glasses. Revelling in my new maleness, I would splash Aqua Velva on my face and rub Vitalis into my hair. At home, I wore t-shirts, jeans, and sneakers. To class, I donned a tie and put on a suit, and lugged a heavy briefcase to boot. In this get-up, therefore, I was usually either mistaken for a professor or for a "nerd." . . .

Exalting in my new male persona, I dared to meet the gaze of former high school classmates, eye-to-eye. Would you believe it? They didn't even know me! I "passed" with flying colours. . . . I was treated like a "regular guy." It was great! For the first time in my life I began to feel more natural, more comfortable — as if, after all these years, I truly belonged.

In sum, more than one-third (37 percent) of participants embarked upon their lives as men with the help of no medical technology at all.[28] Some started out this way before they even knew themselves to be transsexual and only later entered into that world and its associated medical procedures. Some participants had already come to think of themselves as transsexual at the time when they began to crossdress but had not yet found access to hormone treatments. Still others started out in this way because they were making use of a gender clinic which followed the *Standards of Care* requirements. All of them proceeded to hormone therapy as rapidly as they were able to do so.

For more than half of the participants (60 percent) who had begun their transitions into men, the first tangible step which they took in their transformations was to start testosterone treatments.[29] They were convinced, without the confirmation of a real-life test, that they were ready to start to become physiologically male. Some participants were able to convince doctors to start them on hormones without recommendations from psychotherapists; others came to their doctors armed with official validation of their transsexual status or went to gender clinics. Some participants began to crossdress immediately upon their commencement of hormone therapy. Others felt the need to allow some of the effects of the hormone injections to begin to show before they had confidence that they could successfully pass as men when they began to crossdress.

Keith probably spoke for several other participants when he stated what her reasons had been for being convinced that she could not live as a man without hormone therapy:

I knew myself inwardly to be a male, and it was a source of lifelong frustration to me that I seemed to be wearing a mask that I could never tear away from my face. That is, no matter what I did, or how I tried to be perceived as a male. . . . I was not perceived as a male . . . even after I changed my name, cut my hair, and began trying to get people to relate to me as a male. When I was still a female, it was impossible to do.

Rick, like several other participants, began crossdressing concurrently with having received authorization for her hormone treatments through a well known gender clinic. Rick remembered the evaluation process as being gruelling. His description of it detailed what other clients of gender clinics also went through, although perhaps not with the alacrity which Rick enjoyed.

> I was put through a two-hour evaluation with this individual who is considered one of the leading authorities on the subject. We did my interview and he said, "I don't know how you managed to stay alive and have done as well as long as you have." . . . I had never been through anything like it before. I had been told by my psychiatrist that I was going to be asked every possible personal question that could be even imagined and that I needed to be prepared for a lot of mind bending intrusion. . . . and it is very intrusive, mentally and emotionally. . . . When I left there I felt that my brain had been finely dissected and diced. . . . I was exhausted.
>
> He then decided that my case was serious, and was critical. I was entering a crisis again at that time. I think that suicide would have been the next step, and I think that he was aware of that. . . . So he made a call for me to the surgeon . . . and they sent me some material right away. . . . It's a very involved questionnaire. It's about your entire life, and family dynamics, and sexual experiences, and things. . . . It was a most intense thing. . . . So I did that, and then they phoned me. . . .
>
> About three weeks later I went down and. . . . the following day I went for a four-hour evaluation with their clinical psychologist and the surgeon, and had pictures taken, and went through a kind of a quick check-up, and some written tests. I was overwhelmed with the intensity of it. Things moved very quickly. . . .
>
> They did tell me before I left that there was no question . . . they had made the decision that they would help me. So . . . it was the greatest sense of relief I had ever felt in my life. I walked out of there just beat. . . . Then I got a letter from them assigning me a doctor here to look after me and start me on hormones. I started that almost right away.

By contrast to this orderly and thorough set of procedures, Dale's transition was somewhat haphazard. Dale started her hormone treatments with a family doctor who "knew very little about" transsexualism and who "openly admitted" that he "was experimenting" as he managed Dale's medical transformation. The doctor started Dale on hormones and surgeries "to take my mind off" a failed relationship which had led to suicidal thoughts. The doctor's inexperience and Dale's fears combined to create an unusual course of events. Dale started hormones in November of that year; two months later, in the following January, she received a hysterectomy; six weeks later, she underwent mastectomy. Through all of it Dale avoided crossdressing. Dale recalled, "I would have loved to have, but I didn't have the guts to. I didn't want anybody to think I was queer." By August of that same year, Dale's body had undergone so many changes that she finally had to plunge into crossdressing and start living as a man. Because he made the transition among people who had known him as a woman, Dale had both some very good and some very bad experiences with it.

Aaron also preferred to see and hear some physical effects from her hormone program before she started to live as a man. Aaron began taking hormones when she was a 47 year old graduate student and teacher at a college. She was well known as a gay activist and was open with her close friends about her transsexualism. When acquaintances asked her about her husky voice or the hair she was starting to sprout on her upper lip, she amused herself by telling them that she was "going through the change," thinking that they would assume that she was referring to menopause. Then, when Aaron found that people stopped seeing her as a "dyke" and started to relate to her as a man, she left school and started a new life. Aaron recalled how much she liked what testosterone did to her body: "It was the first damn time in forty-seven years that glancing at my body pleased me. . . . just the image of it pleased me." But there were a few things about what testosterone did that Aaron noted with ambivalence:

> I can't cry now hardly at all. . . . You can say what you like, but "men don't cry because they're taught not to" is horse pukey. It's a function of hormones more than it is anything else, because I'm the same human being. But I can't cry at a funeral . . . nearly as easily as I used to be able to. . . . Babies, like, they don't respond to me the way they used to, and I don't respond to them the way I used to. I don't have that strong urge to steal anything under six months and run away with it that I used to. That's pure emotional, based on hormones. . . . It's just pure physical urges that aren't there.

As pointed out by Aaron, as necessary and beneficial as testosterone treatment proved to be to the gender needs of participants, there were also drawbacks. Several participants suffered physical side effects which caused some of them to cease their testosterone treatments for years at a time.[30] Others were displeased with some of the emotional side effects. For instance, Howie had some misgivings:

> Regrets have occurred. I never regretted changing, but there are regrets involved, just not significant enough for me to regret the whole thing.

My main regret is about the damage the hormones have caused me. I wish I could change without the testosterone. It's such a powerful drug. . . . In the beginning I found it difficult to deal with the increase in aggression. It made me nervous, gave me higher blood pressure and severe mood swings. In short, it altered my personality.

I was always very sensitive and quick to cry before hormones. After, I couldn't cry even when I wanted/needed to. I even got violent on a few occasions, which was totally unlike me. People don't realize how powerful a drug testosterone is. . . . I stopped hormones altogether for almost two years. During those two years I was much more mellow and less hyper. I cried real easily again, like at a sad movie. Less moodiness, more even-tempered. . . . But I lost most of the facial and body hair the hormones had given me. . . . it all went back to the way it was before hormones. I went back on hormones.

Overall, participants were exceptionally pleased with the main effects of their testosterone injections. A few found some of the side effects to their joints or connective tissues to be noxious. Some were disconcerted at the increases to their aggressiveness or libidos. A few were disturbed at going bald. However, for the most part, these were petty annoyances. Participants took this "powerful drug" precisely because they wanted to be radically transformed. They wanted not only to look like men but also to feel and act and sound male. Testosterone admirably performed these minor miracles.

However much participants were thrilled with some or all of the results of their hormone-induced transformations, they were also motivated by them to proceed further. Having become masculine in their clothing and voices, skin texture, facial, head and body hair distributions, muscle mass, and many of their emotions, participants became more exquisitely aware of the discrepancies between their new personas and their breasts and genitalia. The drive to bring these parts of their bodies into line with their increasingly obvious manliness became ever more compelling. Surgeries were indicated.

Men Don't Have Breasts

Most participants had been disaffected with their breasts since they first grew them as adolescents. As long as they moved through the world as women, however, their breasts served some useful purposes. A few participants found that they could take sexual pleasure in having their breasts touched. As Peter put it, "I'm a normal human. I like having buttons pushed. . . . I have normal nerves. They work." Probably more widely benefitted from, if rarely mentioned, was their breasts' usefulness in marking them as females in those times and places where that was socially convenient. Having breasts gave participants the appearance of being physically normal females. Such appearances gave them opportunities to have socially comprehensible relationships with other members of society, to whom they could optionally explain their gender identities if and when they wanted to do so. As Dennis understatedly pointed out, "they maybe helped me a little to get through using a public bathroom."

Once participants had entered into crossdressing and hormone therapy, their breasts symbolized something quite different for them. They still marked them as women and, as such, they worked in opposition to the effects produced by hormone treatments and crossdressing. If participants allowed their breasts to be conspicuous, they became socially unintelligibly intersexed individuals. Thus, in order to function as men in public life, crossdressing and hormone therapies had to be accompanied by awkward and often stultifying breast binding until such time as breast reduction or removal surgeries could be obtained. Participants also had to avoid being naked in front of other people unless they were prepared to provide explanations which were often both bewildering for others and embarrassing for participants. As Rick said of the time immediately following the commencement of hormone treatments but before surgeries, "I became terrified to get [sexually] involved with anyone. For some reason, it became a lot more difficult to explain than it had been previously."

At the time of their last interviews, thirty-four participants (87 percent)[31] had obtained either double mastectomies[32] or sufficient breast reduction[33] to accomplish satisfactory effects. All other participants who had begun their transitions fully intended to follow the same course as soon as financial or other restrictions allowed them to do so.

For most participants, getting these surgeries done was a relatively uncomplicated process. They had gone far enough into their real-life tests to know that they wanted to live as men, and adequate surgical expertise was available. They were generally satisfied with the results of their surgeries even though extensive scarring, which occasionally necessitated follow-up corrective surgeries, was common. Participants' relief at finally being rid of the uninvited and unwelcomed "growths" on their chests far outweighed the inconvenience of any surgical discomforts or complications. In fact, their attitudes toward their breasts had become so derisive that Darren spoke of them as "those hated hills of flesh" and Aaron recalled "having a couple of warts removed from your chest."

Only three participants, Stan, Luther, and Ron, arranged to have breast reduction surgeries as their first steps to assist them when they actually began to live full time as men. Both Stan and Ron later went on to get full mastectomies. Luther and his partner of thirteen years were both sufficiently satisfied with his chest after breast reduction that he did not request any further surgical attention to that area of his body.

Stan's whole approach to accomplishing sex reassignment was unorthodox. Stan was a registered nurse when she decided to start living as a man. After a brief attempt at doing things according to official procedures, Stan became impatient and decided that she was going to manage things herself. Stan started out by contacting a psychiatrist to whom she had been recommended by a transsexual man:

> This guy was a . . . weirdo but . . . I needed him to get what I needed done. And what I needed done was hormones. . . . I didn't need counselling. . . . It didn't occur to me what an incredibly involved process this is. . . . I knew exactly what to do. I needed to change the clothes I was wearing. . . . Cut my hair, get a different watch. . . . I need to be related to as male. . . . And hormones and the surgery were really . . . just props.
>
> So I went to him over the four or five different interviews and answered the questions. . . . It really was a joke. "I know exactly what I need . . . but I've got to jump through your hoops." . . . So I manipulated things probably a bit. . . . And then I waited and waited. . . . And four or five months later . . . I get this letter saying, "Yes we concur that you're gender dysphoric . . . but you're also manic depressive so you're going to have to crossdress or live in your desired gender role for a year and then we'll talk hormones."
>
> I'm going, "That doesn't help. That is not why I paid you $400. I could have done that without you. I don't need you to tell me that." So that's when I started clicking, "Well, it's not going to work, I may have to do something with the tits." . . . It never occurred to me that I could bind forever.

Stan set to work getting testosterone shots and a breast reduction for herself. He recalled that it was only "when patients that came into the emergency room started mistaking me for a man that I knew I was going to make it. So I quit this job and moved 125 miles away and started all new." Stan described how she reached that point:

> I started doing it myself. . . . I stole a prescription pad, and I forged a prescription for testosterone, and started injecting myself. . . . I was a registered nurse. I put my license on the line. Big chance. I thought, "I'm insane. This was really scary. What the hell am I doing? If I get caught on this, I will lose everything that I know how to do." But I just kept doing it. . . . I didn't know how much to inject myself. . . . I didn't realize how hormones worked. I didn't have anybody to tell me. I had no idea . . . what the normal dosage was. . . .
>
> While I was on the hormones, I went in for an interview for a breast

reduction. Just plastic surgery. Went in as a girl. Didn't tell them anything. Just tried to make the best case I could that I wanted a breast
reduction. . . . You know, the doctor probably had no business—I was
not that big. . . . It was . . . "Please make them as small as possible."
And I went in on a Monday, and he made an appointment to do it on
Wednesday. . . . So, I just walked off the job, and went in and had surgery on Wednesday, and . . . recuperated at home by myself for a month.

Six years later, Stan finally got a complete mastectomy, which he characterized as "completely, totally, magnificently, wonderfully successful!"
Stan's sentiments were similar to those of many other participants when
he said, "The big thing was getting the tits off. Now that they're gone, I'm
not so desperate, I can breathe now."

When Ron was in her early twenties, she, like Stan, manipulated a
psychiatrist into recommending her for a breast reduction to ease her efforts at passing as a man. Although the breast reduction allowed Ron to
pass as a man with ease, Ron had a double mastectomy ten years later. He
felt that despite "some scarring" which necessitated corrective surgery, the
later surgery made a significant difference to the quality of his life.

There's so many things that fall away with the surgery. For instance, I
can walk straight because I don't have to cover up my chest. Which, of
course, has a neurological impact: walking straight, walking tall. . . .
And all those things I don't have to think about any more. Like the way
I dress. I can dress whichever way I want to. I can just be.

All but one other participant who had had mastectomies did so after
they had begun their hormone treatments and crossdressing. Dale was exceptional in that she did not begin to crossdress until after she had had her
breasts removed. All participants were very pleased to have their breasts
be permanently gone from their lives even though some people were less
than completely satisfied with the quality of their surgical results.

Bruce was particularly eager to be rid of her breasts. In fact, the focus
of Bruce's transsexualism seemed to be more on separating her from her
breasts than any other aspect of becoming a man and a male. Bruce made
a number of telling comments in this regard:

The idea of never having tits again was the greatest idea. I wasn't even
so wrapped up in having a dick, but not to have these growths on my
chest. That should have been optional to begin with. . . . And I remember the night before my surgery, sitting on the bathroom floor . . . and
[my partner] came in, sat down with me, and she said, "We need to talk.
It's tomorrow, and just tell me once again this is what you really want
to do." And I remember saying, "I'm not sure. I don't want these
breasts. I'm not sure that I want to be a man, but I don't want these
breasts. . . . .They're foreign. They're not mine." . . . And then when I

woke up after surgery, and I realized they were gone, I said, "Yeah. That was right to get rid of my breasts." . . .

It's easier to live as a man because of that, but it feels somehow . . . I'm just more woman-identified, although I feel male. You know, it's so hard to explain. . . . It's very hard for me. I don't want to be a man. . . . But I like parts of being a man. I don't like the tits and I want the hair on the chest and I want the male body but . . .

As an added bonus, participants occasionally were able to find some humour in the incongruities which arose for them while between phases of transition. For example, Grant was unable to raise the money to purchase his mastectomy for close to ten years after he began taking testosterone. In the interim, Grant found ways to amuse himself. Grant reminisced:

When the hormones started, and I started growing hair, I referred to myself with very intimate friends as "Queen Kong." [The surgeon] removed 2.2 kilos, which is just about five pounds. Talk about getting a lot off your chest. You can't take yourself too seriously.

Grant also garnered a good story to tell about his first consultation with a plastic surgeon who had never done a mastectomy and chest reconstruction on a female-to-male transsexual:

When I went in to see the doctor . . . I explained I needed to have some surgical revision done to my chest. I'm there with a full beard. And I opened my shirt and the doctor kind of gasped. It was great. It was one of those things you would expect from a cartoon character. And he just said, "Alright." . . .

After that surgery . . . I was walking around like someone had done a low-cost spay and neuter [on me]. I was on tiptoes just like my terrier had been when he was castrated. I couldn't balance. But emotionally it was a relief. I'd look down and there were bandages. And it's flat. And it feels so damn good. "They're gone! Oh, thank God!" . . . I stood in front of the mirror and did a profile and looked. And it was the most wonderful feeling. They were gone!

Not everyone's experience was so joyous. Ed had his mastectomy done privately after about three years on hormones. Like many other participants' surgeries, Ed's resulted in complications. Even though Ed never did get a satisfactory revision done, he was still happier with his botched mastectomy than without one. Ed told this horror story about what went wrong:

It was like an assembly line, there were so many transsexuals there it was scary. . . . I waited around for about an hour and a half and this nurse comes out and says, "Well, he's in the middle of some other surgery right now. He's going to be a while. . . . Come back in about an hour and a half." So I did that. And then she says, "Well, I'm sorry but he's really tired right now. If you really want him to do the surgery he can do it today, but like I said he's really tired and he might not do his best work, you know. But otherwise he's going to be out of town for about a week. So if you don't want to do it now you're going to have to reschedule it for about a week." So that's what I ended up doing. Having to go through the whole trauma again. . . .

He did it in his office, you know, on the table, and both of my friends were in the office watching him doing it. It couldn't be any more slap and dash. . . . I remember he gave me this sedation . . . and you're half conscious when they're doing it. I remember laying on the table and you could feel and hear the scissors cutting away at you, and you could feel this dripping. I'm sure it was blood going down my side and, you know, then an hour and I was awake and he threw me in the car. . . . I was too young to know the difference between a butcher or anything else. . . .

The results. . . . were pretty shabby . . . It's very saggy, you know. And the nipples actually fold over themselves. . . . When you put your arm down your whole side sags here. So, like I say, the doctor butchered many people . . . a lot of them took their lives. He was really bad. . . . [But] as far as I'm concerned he did a better job than I could have done, and that's the point that I was at, you know. It's like, "Give me a knife I'll do it myself."

Of all the medical procedures which participants employed in their achievement of manhood, breast removal seemed to have been the most unequivocally satisfying. This seemed to be true regardless of the fact that many participants experienced disappointments at the quality of the skill with which their surgeons performed. The important point for participants was that once this surgery had been performed, no matter how poorly, they were much more able to move through their everyday lives as men.

The significance of breasts as markers of gender should not be underestimated. When asked, most people say that genitalia are the ultimate arbiters of both sex and gender.[34] However, in the routine activities which fill everyday lives there are few times or places where genitals must unavoidably be displayed.[35] In the normal course of events, sex characteristics are assumed to match the genders displayed by normally clothed human beings. Thus what was of paramount importance to these individuals who were striving to become credible men was to look and act the part.

Hormone effects appropriately shifted some secondary sex characteristics, but they stopped short of making any appreciable differences to participants' breasts. Their breasts then became the major stumbling blocks preventing them from moving easily through their daily lives as men. Men don't have breasts. Furthermore, men often go bare chested or wear clothing which does not thoroughly cover their upper bodies. In addition, other people frequently touch men's upper bodies in a casual fashion. Bound breasts, therefore, could only be, at best, partial solutions which were always in jeopardy of being uncovered. Thus participants generally concluded that hormone treatments, crossdressing, and breast removal were all necessary conditions for them to function effectively as men in their normal social worlds. Once participants achieved this level of manhood, they seemed to reach a plateau on which they could feel temporarily more comfortable. Their remaining female genitalia could remain a private issue between themselves, their lovers, and their doctors as long as they wished, whereas male genitalia could be simulated in almost all circumstances with some well formed stuffing. However, because most participants were eager to have intimate sexual relations and because some participants found any reminder of their female origins intolerable, many participants were interested in securing further corrective surgeries as soon as possible.

Bringing the Bottom into Line: The Inside Story

With four exceptions,[36] it was only after participants had been on hormone therapy, had been crossdressing, and had had breast surgeries that they followed up with making physical adjustments to their more private body parts. In other words, it was only after participants were satisfied that they were able to live in the public arena as men that they became more highly motivated to attend to their inner spaces or to reconstruct their genitalia beyond what testosterone had already done for them.

All but three participants[37] who had begun hormone treatments and crossdressing at the time of their last interviews either had already had hysterectomies[38] or were desirous of doing so.[39] Generally, those who had not yet proceeded were either those participants who had only recently begun their transitions and had not yet reached this stage or those whose financial situations had prevented them from acting on their intentions. Those participants who had had hysterectomies were generally satisfied with their surgeries. Participants mentioned no complications and had few problems in procuring their surgeries.

When participants explained their reasoning for having their internal reproductive organs removed, they made recourse to arguments concerning both health and identity issues. More frequently, participants emphasized that uteri and ovaries were simply incompatible with being male. Even if no one else knew what was inside of them, they knew, and it grated on their self-images. A few participants also made recourse to legal definitions of sex. In some jurisdictions, persons could legally change sex only after they had permanently lost the capacity to reproduce in their originally assigned sex.

Almost all of those participants who had not yet procurred hysterectomies stated that they were interested in undergoing them. However, many of them appeared to feel little urgency about obtaining these operations. They wanted to have them but they could wait relatively calmly while they saved money and found the appropriate times in their lives to devote to surgery and recuperation. For example, Jack's feelings about the significance of having a hysterectomy were typical of those of several other participant. Jack said that as long as he had not yet had a hysterectomy he still felt "a little bit female," but that he was not going to rush into having one unless his health required it.

> At times I still feel I'm in no man's land, because I still feel like, physically, I'm not one or the other . . . and I don't like it. . . . Because I haven't had a hysterectomy or anything. I know that in here, regardless of if I see it every day or not, I know it. . . . I am a realist. . . . You cannot ignore it.

Walter, who was "scared shitless" of surgery, believed that female reproductive organs constituted inexplicably female marks on a virilized body. Walter, however, seemed more concerned with the external than with the internal manifestations of femaleness. Walter made reference to health concerns as a reason for wanting a hysterectomy but then went on to espouse other reasons:

> I want to have the hysterectomy too. . . . I feel that I can't keep being female now. . . . I want to do as much as I can. I don't want to have a vagina. . . . I feel it is important. I feel that I should not have those organs, because they are contributing to a sense of confusion that I don't need to have, because I don't have gender confusion. The only thing that confuses me is the fact that I have these female body parts.

A few participants had their hysterectomies done at atypical points in their transitions. Brian had a hysterectomy after many years of life as a man because he suffered from an extremely rare form of cervical cancer. Dale started on hormones, then had her hysterectomy and a mastectomy in rapid succession, all before she began to live as a man, because neither she nor her doctor was aware of usual procedures. Dennis started her transition with a hysterectomy, even before she called herself transsexual, because of her dread of menstruation. As a teenager, Dennis almost died from anorexia trying to permanently expunge menstruation from her life. As soon as she reached legal adulthood, a doctor authorized the removal of her internal reproductive organs. It would be another four years before Dennis began cross-living and taking hormone shots.

Lee also wanted to be rid of her internal reproductive organs even though she was not living as a man. Lee had started taking hormone treatments a few years earlier but had stopped them after only a few months because she had to leave the area in which she was living. Before Lee was able to take up the therapy again, she began to enter menopause. When her doctor suggested that she go on estrogen therapy for her menopausal symptoms, Lee balked.

> After taking the shots, and then going off them, my body started falling apart, and the doctor says, "Okay, if you're going to be a female, you're in menopause, so you should take these hormone pills to maintain your bones." So, you take that stuff, and that means you get the period back. . . . And the only way you get away from that is to get a hysterectomy. And I hadn't had [my period] for about three years. . . . And I thought, "Oh, Jesus, I don't want this." So, I went to my doctor. . . . and so he sent me to a gynecologist. I said I wanted it and he said, "Is so and so wrong?" And I said, "No, there's nothing wrong." And he says, "I'm not going to do it." So, I stormed out of there, and I stormed back to my doctor, and I said, "He said he's not going to do it." And he said, "Just leave it with me, and I'll talk to him." . . . Whatever he said to him, I don't know, but he did it.

Sam had a hysterectomy because of reproductive difficulties which she experienced many years before she began to think of herself as transsexual. Sam was married at the time and often pregnant. Sam recalled the circumstances surrounding her hysterectomy:

> We ended up having five kids with a lot of problems . . . with every pregnancy. I was not normal, I should never have had kids. It almost killed them and me to have them. . . . I was all male-formed inside. . . . I had a lot of difficulty, because I would try to abort all the time, I mean . . . I did lose three. . . . I just wasn't right. I wouldn't dilate in labour and I'd hemorrhage. And out of the five kids, two have brain damage and one was born without any hip joints and a few other medical problems.

Bruce, who had not yet had a hysterectomy, also told a story about odd goings on in her reproductive tract. Bruce's complaint, several years before deciding to live as a man, was about a rare form of ovarian cysts which might also have been described as a version of "all male-formed inside."[40] Bruce elucidated her condition to the best of his recollection:

> Well my periods got more painful. They got so bad and I eventually had surgery. . . . I started to have . . . really really painful periods, like what it might feel like if someone stuck a broom up your butt. I would bend

over, I couldn't get up. And I'd be down for like two hours. Just pain. I sometimes could hardly breathe. . . .

So one day . . . I had flu or something and I went to the doctor and . . . she checked my stomach area and she hit my ovaries and I about kicked her teeth out. And so she said, "Right now, you need to get in for an ultrasound." So . . . the next day I went in and they found three large cysts had grown on my ovaries. . . . And the doctor went in. It was so big he couldn't retrieve it from my belly button without cutting it out. . . . The one in particular was branched off of the ovary and it was large, the size of a tennis ball. . . .

And what was happening was, it was what was left over from a male. It's hard to explain this but it's the way he explained it to me. When I was in utero, I probably had a male twin or something . . . but with a lot of women it dissolves into the system, into the body. . . . What happened is the male continued to grow in me in the form of this sack. And it continued to grow and grow and grow. And it was alive all this time because it was being fed off the ovary. And so what would cause the pain is that . . . when it would twist it would cut off the blood supply to it which would throw me into these cramps. . . . [The doctor] said there was hair and it looked like testes tissue.

Darren raised another complicating factor in the question of hysterectomies for female-to-male transsexuals. When Darren was ready to have his hysterectomy done through the auspices of a gender clinic, he was sexually involved with another female-to-male transsexual. Darren did receive the surgery which he wanted, but he had to lie in order to get through the screening process.

When we went to the clinic, they found out we were lovers together, so they asked us about it. So, I knew I couldn't lie, 'cause they . . . must have heard it from somebody. So, I said, "We were for a while, but we're no longer now." Of course, we were. Because his surgery would have gone, and my surgery would have gone, and that would have been that. . . . I don't like lying, but if you gotta lie, you gotta lie. You just have to know how to do it right. Tell them what they want to hear. There's no way they would accept that [we were lovers].[41]

Steven talked about still another kind of peril associated with having a hysterectomy as a transsexual man. Steven had his performed twelve years after he started taking testosterone shots. By that time, Steven looked like any other bearded and balding middle-aged man. Nevertheless, his medical chart clearly stated the reason for his hospital stay and several doctors and nurses used it as an excuse to gawk and to refer to Steven as "she." Steven, ever the gentleman, managed to stay good humoured despite the slights.

In sum, although there were clearly a few exceptions, the general pattern among participants was one of a calm and orderly unfolding of events. Participants first attended to establishing themselves as men in their everyday lives. That is, they enjoyed the virilizing effects of testosterone treatments and chest reconstruction before they concerned themselves with markers of femaleness which were invisible to them once testosterone had caused ovulation and menstruation to cease. As time and money became available, they attended to hysterectomies, largely, it would seem, for an abstract sense of completeness rather than any more compelling body image or interpersonal needs. Because hysterectomies are widely practiced for a variety of medical reasons, participants had no trouble finding reliable and skilled surgeons to accommodate them. Those who had not yet had hysterectomies were moving toward them in an unhurried fashion. They seemed, with good reasons, to assume that when they were ready there would be easily accessible, reasonably priced, and efficient services available to them. Thus the evidence suggests that having hysterectomies constituted one of the least problematic aspects of the entire transition process for participants.

Two cases, however, deserve special review. Sam and Bruce both said that their surgeons had described their internal reproductive organs as having appeared to be not only malformed but also "male-formed." The stories of the circumstances surrounding Sam's and Bruce's hysterectomies raise important questions about the limitations of the definition of the term *female-to-male transsexual*. Most working definitions include the concept that, within current medical knowledge, female-to-male transsexuals are biologically "normal" females. The stories told by Sam and Bruce seem to indicate that something about part of what defined them as female was far from normal. An assumption that their representations of their medical conditions were tolerably accurate must lead to a question as to whether the highly stigmatized label of female-to-male transsexual is appropriate to apply in such cases. Perhaps they and others like them would be better served by a more finely graded sex system which included more sex statuses than female, male, hermaphrodite, and transsexual.

Bringing the Bottom into Line: The Outside Story

The ultimate signifier of manhood is, of course, the penis. Participants were clear that they would have preferred to have been born with penises. They also agreed that they would like to acquire them and that as long as they were without penises they were incomplete as men and as males. However, few participants seemed to believe that a penis represented a sine qua non of manhood. In other words, they believed that they were men and that they were males, with or without that particular piece of flesh.

Thus, although only six of the thirty-nine participants who had begun their transitions (15 percent) had undergone any genital reconstruction,[42] most expressed at least some qualified interest in some day having such surgeries performed on themselves. Their interest in proceeding was qualified by three main factors. Firstly, their understanding of and concerns about the health risks associated with the various procedures made many participants hesitate. Secondly, their inability to meet the sizable financial costs involved prevented a number of participants from even considering the possibility.[43] Thirdly, their willingness to deal with the first two obstacles was often mediated by the impacts that they believed their genital status would have on their future sexual possibilities. That is, if they had partners who accepted them as the penisless men they were, they were less interested in genital reconstruction than if they imagined having to approach new partners as physically "incomplete" males. Some participants wanted to get either genital free-up surgeries or phalloplasties as soon as they could. Others would not have taken a phalloplasty at any price under the then-current levels of surgical expertise.

Approximately half of the thirty-three participants who had begun transition but not yet had genital surgery (51.5 percent) expressed little or no faith in the claims of surgeons who offered their services in the construction of neophalluses.[44] These participants had done research into the surgical outcomes available to them. They had seen articles in professional books and journals or spoken with other transsexual men who had gone before them. They learned that phalloplasties were extremely costly, involved multiple surgeries spanning a number of years, and produced phalluses which were cosmetically questionable, generally oversized, awkward for intercourse, and probably unusable for urination. As Roger put it, "I can stand up to pee down my leg just fine right now without spending $20,000 and having medical problems for years to come."

Peter felt very badly that he could not be "normal" and have a penis but he, too, was not interested in having what the medical profession could offer him. Until such time as Peter could have a phallus that looked and acted like a real one, he felt "stuck in between, not feeling like you're much of anything," and preferred to refrain from having any sexual relationships. As a result, Peter felt that it "could be ten years before I start my life." Peter described his disillusionment with phalloplasty in these caustic words:

> If you've got the bucks for it, there's still a problem. . . . The problem is
> . . . a normal flaccid penis is what, three inches, maybe. . . . they're not

huge. And because . . . they can't transplant corpus cavernosa tissue. . . . what they're doing if you have a phalloplasty . . . you're walking around every day, twenty-four hours a day, with a six-inch dick. I'm sorry, I don't want to be rude, but it's true. . . . Now this is kind of tough to hide in your pants all the time. . . . You're carrying extra weight. . . . Basically what you're packing is a somewhat flaccid penis that is the same size as an erect penis. That's kind of difficult.

Aaron, too, was reluctant to put his body through phalloplasty. He highlighted a different set of problems than those with which Peter was concerned:

The question is, do you want this to function as plumbing, do you want to function sexually, or do you want decoration? . . . Well, I'm a little leery of the plumbing thing. Like any other guy, I like to stand up and pee. Let's face it. But is it worth $20,000 plus the risk? Well, look under your sink. You've got a dip in a pipe and what happens? It collects things. And when you put this kind of plumbing in a female anatomy, essentially that's what you got. You got a dip in a pipe which collects things, which makes about a 50 percent chance in any given year that you'll have some sort of urinary tract irritation or infection. Hey, I like being healthy. I've been healthy most of my life, I kind of enjoy it, okay? So I'd think twice. I'd want maybe a little better odds, but maybe by the time I'm ready I'll have better odds. Who knows? . . .

I live alone at this point and I'm not sexually involved. I would like to marry and I want a straight woman. If I find someone that's happy with my body the way it is . . . and if she can relate to me without diminishing my manhood, I think it would probably be that I would rather spend the $20,000 on her.

Stan reiterated the same kinds of hesitations as Aaron about the feasibility of getting a good quality phalloplasty.

I'm not a desperate individual any more. I'm a consumer. I'm not going to have my body mutilated just to look right and tell the folks, "The plumbing may not be perfect but the electricity works." . . . I really don't need it right now. A factor in that is my partner that I have right now. We have a good physical relationship without that.

Keith was definitely not planning on having any genital surgery done. He plainly stated:

I wish I was born with something different but I'm pretty happy with my genitals such as they are. They do the job, which is urinating and giving me sexual gratification. So I don't really plan to mess with them too much. I figure I can live with them.

Darren, too, decided against having a phalloplasty. At first Darren was very interested. He went to a surgeon who discouraged him from proceeding. When Darren persisted, the surgeon suggested that he look at some of the work that he had already done. What he saw convinced Darren to wait. Darren concluded:

> You realize that you're not going to be able to have a real penis. . . . I know that sounds very harsh and very hard, but that's the actual fact. It's a phallus, it's not a penis, and there's a hell of a difference. And you can't ejaculate, and you can't get it voluntarily erect. . . . And there's no erotic sensation. . . . And I'm almost forty now. I don't want to spend all my life in a bloody hospital. . . . And I don't want to spend $50,000 U.S. on something that's not even a workable sexual organ. My wife's happy, and I'm reasonably happy. . . . If I was going to go through hell, I want something more to show for it than a piece of insensate salami dangling there . . . So, for a while yet, penis envy still reigns!

Like any other men, these transsexual men wanted to have healthy, attractive, and well functioning penises. However, not having been born with any such equipment, they were forced to become medical consumers. When they did some consumer research, many were repulsed by the poor value they were offered at very high prices. Many found that their cost-benefit analysis convinced them that they should wait until a better product became available.

Those participants who did think that they might want phalloplasties fell into three overlapping types. Firstly, all of them felt that having a surgically constructed phallus would improve their masculine body images. They would feel more complete as men and as males. The major obstacle stopping these people (33 percent) from proceeding was cost.[45] Secondly, some participants (15 percent) were just starting out on their transitions and had done little research into the pros and cons of various genital options. They seemed to assume that surgical expertise could provide them with what they wanted and therefore also assumed that they probably would be proceeding when they had made other sufficient changes and saved the necessary monies.[46] Thirdly, Howie and Dennis were considering having further surgery done because they felt it was incumbent upon them to have penises if they were to sexually function as males.

Ed wanted a phallus because he thought it would help him be more of a man, but he held out little hope of being able to save the cash needed to pay for the operations. He talked about the way he felt:

> I haven't had any reconstructive surgery and I'm not even sure that's something that's existent in my life because the prices that they want are just so outrageous. . . . I think it would probably improve my attitude about myself because . . . I'm sure that most people see me as a full male you know, and as I view myself without the equipment, you know . . . I feel a little bit lacking.

Dennis, who was a competitive body builder, seemed ambivalent about the advisability of having a phalloplasty done, but he seemed to be leaning toward the affirmative.

> I'm sure I will. I just don't know when. After building my body up to this point . . . I hate the thought of tearing a part of it down. . . . 'Cause I don't believe that a penis can bring me that much joy in and of itself. But all that I have to risk to have it, what I have to sacrifice. . . . The thing it keeps me from the most is relationships. . . . I don't want to see . . . my disability as I am now. And I certainly don't want the woman that I'm with to see that either. So, I have self-imposed limitations. Whether she would accept everything the way I am, I don't accept it. . . . I think I really am a complete man with limitations. I could also say that that would make me feel more complete.

Steven was entirely sure of what he wanted. He not only felt a very strong need to crown his manhood with a phallus of his own, but he was also entirely uncomfortable with the state of his genitalia as they were. At the time of his last interview, Steven's words were vehement.

> It's very, very difficult for me to confront my genitalia. And even with that I had a phantom penis, and a microphallus, that I have to use to survive. . . . If I related to my genitalia as female genitalia, it is revolting! It is uncomfortable! It produces anxiety and distaste and disgust! I guess it's hard for someone who isn't going through this to understand these feelings, but they're very strong feelings.

Howie was unusual in that he had had a genital free-up operation but still wanted to have a phalloplasty. His reasons for wanting more surgery were similar to but more pronounced than those of other participants. Howie explained:

> I wish I had been able to get phalloplasty so I could feel whole and complete and be able to make love to my wife like any other man can to his wife. . . . I have testicle implants, but no penis. So, I feel more incomplete than ever. I feel kind of trapped between the two sexes. I'm not female appearing in the crotch area, but not male appearing either. I feel I look freakish "down there." There is some appreciation for not looking female, but more pain than ever for not being totally male.

The metoidioplasties, or genital free-up operations such as Howie and Hal had received were considerably more attractive to a few participants than were phalloplasties. Jorge, Keith, and Stan, who had all rejected phalloplasty as an option, each expressed interest in finding out more about this surgery. Jorge, who scorned phalloplasty because of the insensitivity of the resulting phallus, instead wanted to have a metoidioplasty because "a penis . . . is important . . . so I can please my girlfriend." Stan also explained why he wanted a metoidioplasty and described in some detail what he saw as some of the advantages of it.

> I want one that works. I want a penis that does everything it's supposed to, and I can't have that. And I don't want these . . . shitty substitutes. . . . The surgery that I have seen that I'm interested in is called the clitoral free-up. It more or less just takes some of the fat that's around the clitoris, and it frees up the clitoris from the tiedown. . . . And they do some liposuction around it. . . . It's more or less accentuating the enlarged clitoris, the mini phallus that you do have. . . . And then you can get testicular implants that they put in the labia that are pretty realistic. . . . You have a mini penis that's probably not going to be long enough to penetrate, but at least you can feel with it. . . . If you had small testicles to go with this ultra small dick, then people just have to feel sorry for you. It's not something that you're going to flaunt, but there's a whole range of sizes out there, and this is just one of those at the far end of the bell shaped curve. This poor guy who really had some problems. But this poor *guy*.

In sum, participants were interested in having surgically constructed or augmented phalluses so that they could look and feel more authentically male. Those who wanted phalloplasties were either less informed or less disturbed about the inherent dangers and failings of that set of operations. Those who wanted metoidioplasties were willing to accept the multiple compromises which came with that option. As Stan pointed out, they would become poorly endowed men, but probably healthier and less scarred ones than their brothers who sported phalloplasties.

Only six of the thirty-nine participants who had begun any of their gender and sex changes (15 percent) had undergone any kind of genital reconstruction. Scott was just beginning to go through the multiple procedures involved in phalloplasty at the time of his last interview. He was understandably enthusiastic. Simon had regrets about having had a phalloplasty owing to the insensate and unsightly nature of the results, which he described as "lifeless" and "worthless." Both Rick and Dale had gone for as many phalloplastic updates and improvements as were available. Although their experiences were not without difficulties, both were happy with the outcome. Howie and Hal each had genital free-up surgeries. Howie wanted more. Hal was more than happy.

Dale provided a detailed description of some of what was involved in the creation of his phallus. The entire process spanned approximately five years and involved numerous visits to the operating theatre. His poignant words conveyed some of the fortitude and perseverance which these procedures require of those who undergo them.

I had two surgeries . . . where they do the phalloplasty and the testicles. . . . I'm just in the middle of [getting] the urinary tract connections. . . . And [they] removed my vagina at the same time. . . . They use part of the skin from the vagina to reconstruct your urethra, because it's a very tough skin. . . .

Well, functionally, I've only had one relationship, and it seems okay to me. . . . For the first time in my life, after I had my surgeries I could look at myself and not be dissatisfied with my body. The actual penis has no feeling. . . . They leave the clitoris in between your testicles, and that's where you get your sensation from. . . . You use an implant as a stiffener. . . . It's a little rod. And it's sort of like a T-bar. You insert it through the middle of your penis, and the T-bar . . . stimulates your clitoris. . . . I've done it by hand and got it down, but to work with a person, it would take quite a while. So, to me, that's the best I can be.

I had a severe setback with my second surgery. The head of the penis [is] attached three months up here [on the stomach] like a handle, and then they release it. . . . And then they roll the skin back. Well, the whole top of my penis turned into a gangrene, and it had to slough off. And that was a severe setback for me. . . . I had to let it rot off. I had to walk around like that for I think it was six weeks before it actually came right off. But, now, the end results. . . . It just looks like I haven't been circumcised, that's all. So it's really no big deal. And there's scarring and that, but the scars don't bother me at all. Not at all. It's these scars inside that are important. I have a lot of scarring, because they take skin from the thigh for skin grafts. . . .

I just came through a tough surgery. I ended up spending fifteen days in the hospital instead of the planned five to seven days. This surgery was to be the completing of the rerouting of the urethra. I was devastated after having the catheter in for fourteen days. I compare it to someone who has had eye surgery. You remove the bandage expecting to see. They removed the catheter and I walked to the washroom (holding my breath) expecting to have my first pee standing up as any other male. To my horror the urine came from the bottom, not the top, of the penis. It appears that there is a hole in the grafting of the tube, which now I have to heal completely and then go back to hospital for repairs. I hope this time it will work. I feel confident, after having come this far, that I will make it. I just want all this to be over and done with so I can get on with my life.

Both Dale and Rick reported that they were happy with the ultimate results of their multiple surgeries. However, both pointed out that their phalluses had no feeling, required mechanical stiffeners, and were larger than most; both said that they would not have the confidence to be fully naked in front of other men.

Hal explained that at first he didn't see any great need to have a penis.

He had the genital free-up surgery largely because he felt that it would make sense for a straight man who was looking for sexual partners to have a penis to offer the women in whom he was interested. Hal put it this way:

> A penis is not necessary to my sexuality, although now I have a very short one and it is fairly exciting to me. If my former partner (of fourteen years) were still with me, I might not have had the genitoplasty because I was satisfied with my genitals and our sexual activities. I felt I had a penis that just didn't stick out, and my masculinity did not (still does not) depend on having a big thing to wave around. But now that I am "unattached" and less likely to end up with another lesbian, I thought it advisable to go ahead with the surgery so that my genitals would be at least similar to what a woman interested in a man would expect to find.

Later, after a woman gave him his first experience of fellatio, Hal was thrilled to have made the decision to develop his own phallus. Hal also recalled that when he first went to arrange to get his surgery done, he spent quite a lot of time thinking about whether or not he wanted to have "balls" because he figured that he'd "just gone to a lot of trouble to get two other 'balls' cut off of my chest." However, when the surgeon told him that it was only another $500 to have them put in, Hal decided to have it done. Hal found, also to his great surprise, that having testicles to go with his microphallus gave him satisfaction far beyond what he would ever have predicted.

In sum, the few participants who had acquired their own phalluses were of mixed opinions about the final results; four were happy, two were disappointed that their phalluses did not resemble congenital penises more exactly. Participants' levels of satisfaction did not seem to be correlated to the degree of surgical hardship or expense involved. Rather, their satisfaction seemed to be more related to their expectations of exact similitude between their own genital equipment and that carried by genetic men. Those who were most prepared to accept the limitations of surgical expertise were probably also those who were least frustrated with the limited penile facsimiles which became part of their virilized bodies.

Participants who had not had genital reconstructive surgeries expressed a wide spectrum of attitudes and opinions about the probability that they might undergo such proceedures. On the one hand, all participants were interested in having penises because of their ability to definitively and unequivocally designate them as authentically male. Participants recognized that as long as they remained without phalluses, their claims to manhood needed to be fortified by recourse to social, psychological, and philosophical rationales which were more easily refuted or undermined than was physical evidence.

However, half of those participants who had begun their changes were wary of what surgical science could offer them in the area of penis facsimiles.[47] Almost all of those participants who researched the subject concluded that what was available would give them little respite from having to make explanations for that physical aspect of their manhood and that such surgeries could leave them sorely depleted both financially and physiologically. Thus they were inclined to wait for better options to appear.

Among the other half of participants were those who had already embarked on either phalloplasty or genital free-up operations[48] and those who looked forward to undergoing one or the other type of operation.[49] Some of the participants who were awaiting such surgeries were aware of the costs involved and were prepared to live with them. Others had only vague notions of the hazards before them and shining visions of the possible rewards. Those who had already proceeded were also divided among the ever-hopeful and enthusiastic, the stoically realistic, and the regretful—none of whom, however, could, without explanation, walk naked as men.

Evaluating the Process

The processes and procedures with which participants transformed themselves from females into men and males were terrifically demanding. Participants threw themselves into the hands of medical professionals as they embarked on hormonal and surgical journeys which they had often studied assiduously but for which no amount of textual learning could adequately prepare them.

Participants differed as to their level of satisfaction with the services provided to them in their physiological transmogrifications. Some felt "thrilled" at what medical technologies had wrought in their bodies, regardless of scarring or their awareness of possible future side effects. Others were less entranced with the ways in which they had been treated but were still more than happy to have come through to the other side with adequately masculinized bodies and lives. A few felt bitterly stranded by the incapacities of medical arts and sciences to make them more truly male. But even those who were the most disappointed were glad to have been able to obtain the extent of masculinization from which they had benefitted. In the end, the overall mood among participants seemed to be one of enormous relief at having been released so far from the shackles which bound them to femaleness and womanhood.

Most participants reported unabashed satisfaction with the effects which testosterone treatments had wrought on their bodies. They described their pleasure in terms such as "I was on cloud nine, it felt so great"; "The hormones have given me a serenity that I didn't have before"; and "I felt more calm and centered. . . . I felt so free and real in my body for the first time." The two major complaints raised by participants about their experiences with hormone therapy had to do with the sometimes annoying quality of their elevated libidos and the irritations to bones, muscles, or joints with which a few participants were plagued. However, it seemed as though all of those participants who experienced these difficulties shared Keith's attitude when he said, "The way I look at it is I would rather live a shortened happy life than . . . a long *healthy* miserable one."

The feelings which participants expressed about their surgical experiences were of a similar nature. In these instances, too, participants' attitudes were almost entirely positive, despite the less-than-perfect outcomes with which they were left to continue their lives. Participants seemed to have relatively realistic expectations when they entered into surgical procedures and therefore were not unduly outraged at the approximate character of their masculinized body parts. Their high degree of satisfaction with their surgical effects must, however, be seen in light of the fact that almost all participants restricted their surgical involvements to breast surgeries and hysterectomies, i.e., procedures which are well established and widely available from practiced surgeons. Those participants who availed themselves of genital reconstruction were less uniformly pleased with the results of their operations.

Some of the more positive comments about surgical outcomes included the following: "It was the most wonderful feeling." "I just felt great. . . . I was just really happy. I didn't care how much pain I had." "Since my surgery I feel more excited about my body, more self-accepting, more appreciative of myself, more comfortable in the world, more self-confident." "I feel more in tune with my body even though it's not perfect. . . . with each surgical procedure it brings me closer to my finale. So I'm very, very happy with all the surgeries I've had, even if they're not perfect. I adjust to the imperfections because life is full of imperfections." "Surgeries simply help put the period at the end."

Several participants commented on their reasons for not being angry about the lack of availability of good phalloplastic surgeries. The gist of their statements was that although they waited eagerly for their chance to have fully functioning penises, even without them they felt like men. Their comments on this subject were remarkably similar: "I definitely do not feel phalloplasty is necessary for one to be a male." "I don't have to have a penis to get through life." "A man doesn't have to have a penis. It makes a complete man. In saying this, I'm saying I'm incomplete, but I can function as a man." "You don't have to have one to be a man."

When participants talked more generally about their perspectives on what they had to go through in order to become more male, their opinions again were largely positive. They spoke with palpable relief at the release they felt to be able to express their personalities using socially consistent bodies. They used words such as these: "This is the first time in my life I feel like a real person." "I feel more confident because my body is more the way I want it to be. I feel more free. . . . I am finally at peace with myself." "I don't have to pretend to be something I'm not. . . . I can just be myself." "It was like being released from my cage." "Now my presentation is totally normal." "I could never go back to the pain, misery, sadness, and loneliness I had being female."

Hal's comments nicely summed up many of these sentiments:

> In spite of the risks and the difficulties, this was the best possible thing I could do for myself. . . . I would love to have had society accept me as a male without having to have surgery. But society would not. And you have to not misinterpret that as saying that I've done this for society. When I look at myself in the mirror now, and I look at my shoulders, and my chest, and the thicker aspect of my neck, and I hear my voice now, and I know this is who I was, who I am, who I was meant to grow up to be. . . . I may be in transition the rest of my life, but I know that I'm male and I knew I was male before I started this process.

Steven's experiences with transition were more draining for him than were Hal's, but Steven was no less enthusiastic about the benefits which he derived from his somewhat trying experiences.

> I have never changed my mind to go back, no matter how much I have suffered, and believe me, I have done a lot of suffering. I don't know that it's all been because of the sex change, but yes, the sex change has given me quite a bit of suffering, and I have surmounted that. . . . have never felt so whole in doing what I've done. And I don't think there's anything that would have given me a stronger identity had I not made these decisions. . . . So whatever sacrifices I've made, I've more than made up for in the things I've gotten in exchange.

Despite these glowing endorsements by most participants, a few people voiced misgivings and complaints about the whole process. Peter in particular was angry because he felt he was in limbo between being male and female because of his inability to obtain a phallus which would function like a normal penis. Peter lamented:

> I feel like I want the chains off. I want to have a normal life. I want to be able to go out and have a normal relationship. . . . I do not want another woman relating to me and seeing a woman. . . . And there may not be any answer. And in some respects sometimes I feel like I'm just . . . hanging on and hoping they find an answer. Because this is not

life. . . . this is not living and anybody who tells you it is is lying through their teeth. . . .

But I tell you, you get some real fears going on right now. You bet. I'm going to be that lonely old guy who's sitting there gumming it on the park bench and doesn't have anything else to do, because I don't. . . . My Saturday nights consist of (and this is pretty sick, this is sad) going up to the store and renting a couple of movies. And it's pretty bad when I know a couple of these checkers so well they know me by name. And that store's only been open for two months. . . . Well, I'm ending up a lonely guy that . . . you think of a reason to go up and buy a carton of milk so that you can go through the line and say, "Hi Tracy." Even though Tracy is married, she's nice, and at least smiles at you. I mean that is getting pretty sad. . . . This is not fun. . . . Being in the middle.

Another area of discontent had to do with the gatekeeping function which many service providers performed. Some participants felt that the *Standards of Care* were an unnecessary impediment and that they should be able to procure the services which they wanted whenever they became able to pay for their costs. Other participants were concerned that too few safeguards were in place.

Keith was of a mixed opinion about the *Standards of Care*. When Keith was going through his changes, he believed that the guidelines were good for other people but need not apply to him:

When I found out the information that I needed to go forward with the sex change, I went forward immediately. In fact, not only did I not put it off, but I railed against the restrictions that are placed on a transsexual by the medical and psychiatric professions. I understand why they have those restrictions. Those are for the good of the transsexual, to weed out the people who really should not go forward with the change. However, I was, and I am, a true transsexual, and I knew that within myself, and I put up with the restrictions as much as I had to, but I pushed against them as much as I could.

By contrast, Luther's experience at a well known gender clinic in the late 1970s left him an ardent supporter of the *Standards of Care*. When Luther was about thirty years old, she hurt her back and went to a hospital, which also housed a gender clinic, for breast reduction surgery to remove some of the strain to her back caused by her "very, very large" breasts. Luther recalled:

I had been thinking about [transsexualism], and I was in the hospital, and I got up, and I didn't have any breasts, and I said, "Jesus Christ, what's the difference?" And I said, "Well, it's obvious to me that this is not all there is, so I better go on." So, I did.

Luther elaborated upon what it was about her experience with the gender clinic which he felt was less than appropriate:

It's good that now the standards are such that everyone needs to have at least a year's therapy. Because I had very little. I had therapy on my own, but in terms of my transsexuality, none. And I could see that there were a lot of issues that. . . . I thought would be reconciled with reassignment, but they haven't been . . . I went into a depression for three or four years . . . until I got back into therapy. Very depressed . . . because I had higher expectations. . . .

I think that the way it was handled [at the clinic] was really neglectful. I think that one of the reasons why [they] had a lot of suicides—if the way they treated me was any indication—was just that they just do not . . . expose people to the kinds of therapy that they need to have. I was in the hospital, and I know it was very hard to get in touch with . . . the gender clinic. And so, I said to myself, "Well, I'll write them a very impressive letter." So, I sat down and got my freshman abnormal psych books and looked up nice little words and wrote them this letter, and they called me in forty-eight hours and said, "Come in." And I came in, and we spoke for about . . . forty-five minutes. She gave me the Minnesota Multiphasic. I went home. She called me in a month. I came down. I got hormones. That was it. You see what I mean? . . .

And I'm fortunate. I'm a strong person. . . . When I heard that [that clinic] wasn't doing them anymore, I said, "I'm so glad." . . . Because when I did it, I was thirty-one; had I been nineteen, I don't think I'd be here. By the time you're thirty-one, you're stronger; you've got life experiences. I could bounce in and out of my depressions.

The participants in this study all defined themselves as female-to-male transsexuals. As such, they all had abiding interests in becoming men and males. Thus most participants judged the various stages in their physical transitions on the basis of how well they enabled them to live as men and as males. For most participants, all other considerations were secondary. Many participants saw themselves as boxed into untenable positions before embarking upon their changes. They therefore were willing to pay any price to achieve their aims and were largely unperturbed by inconveniences such as extensive scarring, monthly injections of powerful drugs with unknown long-term side effects, or the high costs of treatments. In the end, then, most participants were thoroughly pleased with their transformations. They got what they wanted. They were able to live their everyday lives as unremarkable men.

Finally, participants' happiness with the process of which they availed themselves hinged on two matters. One was the competence of the various practitioners with whom they came into contact. Those who were less than fully satisfied were disappointed that they had not been treated to the

highest quality or most expeditious care. The other, a more profound issue, had to do with how badly participants needed to be able to put their
transsexualism behind them and become simply men, simply male. Those
participants who most wanted to get beyond being transsexual were
bound to feel short-changed. Every time they needed or wanted to present
their genital area to any other persons it would become obvious that there
was something abnormal about that part of their bodies. In other words,
no matter what price participants were willing and able to pay, they absolutely could not have bodies which, upon close inspection, would pass
as male without explanation. They could, of course, falsify the origins of
their abnormalities, but most participants were not so inclined. The truth
of the matter, however, remained. Participants were bound by the limitations of medical technology to remain in their intimate lives, and for the
foreseeable future, men who were once female.

Summary and Commentary

Changing oneself from a woman into a man, from a female into a
male, is a transformation which must take place on many levels. Most participants had lived with feelings that they were men on a psychic level for
much of their lives. Some found that other people, in selected situations,
would share their self-appraisals. However, when participants wanted to
be able to live their lives fully as men, they had to start to alter the ways
in which they presented themselves to others. Depending on whether they
expected or wanted to be able to pass cursory or detailed inspections, they
had to transform themselves in more, or less, far-reaching ways.

Simply crossdressing could allow successful actors to be taken as men
in situations which involved neither physical contact with critical body
areas nor exposure of those same regions. These limitations, however,
eliminated many types of common human activities such as many sports,
the use of some public toilets, many physical expressions of affection, and
sexual intimacies, to name a few.

Hormone treatments were used by all participants to provide more
extensive, long-lasting, and seemingly internally produced physical manifestations of maleness. The changes wrought in the bodies of participants
by testosterone added more indelible and more legible layers of legitimiza-
tion to participants' manliness then sartorial shifts could ever accomplish.
Facial and body hair, deep voices, and bulky muscles combined with masculine attire and mannerisms to maneuver participants well into the world
of men. However, as long as participants continued to have breasts ob-
scured beneath their clothes, all their other signs of manhood could become undone by the disclosure of their hidden assets.

Thus participants precariously traded in two different currencies at the same time. They made use of gender markers, such as clothing and mannerisms, backed up by secondary sex characteristics, such as beards and deep voices, to convey the message to others that they were male. That is to say, they looked and acted like men on the outside so that people would assume that they had correspondingly entirely male bodies to match. At the same time, the assumptions which they manipulated could also lead to their defrocking. Physical markers of sex generally hold considerably greater power in attributions made by others than do social ones, and breasts carry greater weight than do beards and voices. Thus if participants' breasts were to be discovered, they could override all other cues of participants' manhood.

For these reasons, all participants decided that they would remove their breasts and remake their chests to look more like those of other men. Once participants had taken these steps, there remained few areas in which their manhood might be questioned by any but their most intimate acquaintances. For all intents and purposes of everyday life, participants became securely entrenched as men once they had achieved this level of transformation.

Participants' identities, however, encompassed more than smoothly passing through their everyday lives as men. Most of them wanted to become more fully virilized. For some participants, this necessitated the removal of their female reproductive organs. For some participants, this also meant the acquisition of phalluses made of their own flesh, although medical technology could offer them only rough approximations of that with which other men were born. Most of those participants who were fully aware of the limitations of what was possible for them in this area therefore chose to remain phallusless men until better surgeries became available.

By choosing to be men without phalluses, they left themselves in a kind of sex limbo. However, even those participants who purchased genital reconstruction were not exempt from insecurities about their sex. Either way, participants' bodies were different from those of other men. In any circumstances which demanded genital exposure, participants' appearances necessitated explanations. Furthermore, because the evidence of primary sex characteristics is the most persuasive in sex attributions, as long as participants were truthful about the origins of their genitalia they were unable to finally dissociate themselves from their female beginnings.

After all of their physical transformations were completed, participants could enjoy the full benefits of being men only so long as those perquisites were not dependent on the possession of verifiably male genitalia. They could be men in every social way and they could be male in many physiological ways. They could obliterate most signs of their female past, but they, like other members of society, continued to carry their pasts with them in their most intimate of places. They therefore were stranded as transsexual men. Although they had indeed ceased to bear the bodies of females, neither were their bodies exact replicas of those of men who were born male.

20 | Coming Out Stories

ONCE PARTICIPANTS BEGAN to actually look like men and to pass as men, they were faced with new challenges. The people with whom they were in frequent or ongoing contact needed to be informed as to the nature of the transformations which they were witnessing or participants needed to remove themselves from contact with such people. Thus participants' next step was to choose, often person by person, to whom they were going to come out and from whom they were going to go away. In some cases, participants found that once they had done the former, they wanted to do the latter. Most participants, however, reported that they generally received positive responses from people who knew them to be transsexual.

Family Members

Participants had little choice about whether to tell their family members about their transitions. They could, up to a point, orchestrate the timing of their disclosures, but avoiding such revelations altogether was virtually impossible in most cases. Family relations, by their very nature, are rarely entirely severed by anything less final than death. Thus for those participants who had living parents, siblings, children, and other kin, simply slipping away and starting their lives over again was not an option.

Some participants went to their family members with news of their transsexualism almost as soon as they themselves were aware of it. Others held back from talking about it until the changes to their bodies and mannerisms were so pronounced that the issue begged to be raised. Some participants approached family members seeking and assuming their support. Others came to the subject prepared to inspire and receive outrage and condemnation. Few participants reported being disappointed by the responses which they received from their family members.

Parents Struggle to Understand

Thirty-six participants (80 percent)[1] still had both parents alive around the time that they began to live as men. Forty-one participants (91 percent) had mothers who were still alive,[2] and thirty-seven participants

(82 percent) had fathers who were still alive.[3] In addition, eleven participants (24 percent) had children in their lives.[4] Participants also mentioned miscellaneous other family members' responses, but they seemed for the most part to be of secondary importance to them.

As might be expected, participants approached telling their parents about their intentions to live as men with some trepidation. It was obvious to them that no parent would be likely to easily accept that their daughter was to become their son. Many participants accurately anticipated that their parents would be unable to readily accommodate themselves to the shifts of consciousness which their children needed to demand of them. In a few cases, participants' only recourse was to cut themselves off as much as possible from contacts with parents who would not or could not adjust to a degree which participants needed for their own mental equilibria. Most often, parents initially reacted with bewilderment and fear, but with time they were able to come to a peace with their new sons. Thus most participants correctly assumed that their parents would support them in their new lives once they had a chance to understand how profoundly their daughters needed to transform themselves. The validation and succor which participants gleaned from such parents were invaluable in anchoring participants in their new lives.

Typically, even those parents who were willing to try to understand and support their transsexual children went through a phase of awkwardness. They had borne and begotten, named and raised their children as females and had fully expected that they would remain that way for the rest of their lives. When participants asked their parents to begin to think of them as men and to speak of them in masculine terms, they were asking their parents to retool anywhere from twenty to fifty years of habituation to referring to them in the feminine. Unlike participants, their parents had not spent significant portions of their lifetimes preparing themselves for the time when participants would remake themselves as men. Thus participants' parents' real reorientations usually had to occur largely after the fact, once participants had begun their lives as men. Fortunately, most participants were sympathetic to the enormity of the demands which they placed upon their parents and were forgiving of their parents' numerous inadvertent references to them as women.

Of the six participants who had not yet begun their transitions, only Eli had discussed her transsexualism with her mother. Morgan, Robin, Lee, Terry, Darcy, and Pat gave no indication that they had discussed their transsexualism with family members. Terry expected that when she did say something about it, she would "lose them . . . since we are all Catholics." Pat also anticipated that her parents would not be supportive. Nine

participants (20 percent) gave no indication of how their parents had reacted to their transsexualism.[5]

Two-thirds (67 percent) of the twenty-seven participants who did provide information about their parents' responses to their transsexualism
considered one or both of their parents' reactions to their changes to have
been generally positive ones.[6] A few participants even thought that remaking themselves as men had produced improvements in their relationships
with one or both of their parents. For example, Sam said of his mother, "I
think she's more comfortable with me now that I've made this change. I
think she can accept who I am better than she could in the female role."
Steven said, "My family has got very close to me in the last, I'd say, five
years . . . because I'm more consistent in who I am and I think I'm more
reliable in presenting myself consistently."

The responses of Ed's and Mel's mothers and of Phil's father were exceptionally positive. Ed's mother arranged for Ed to get hormone therapy.
Ed's father was less actively supportive, but he too was helpful in small
ways. Phil's father helped her to contact a gender clinic. Mel's mother
struggled hard to understand what Mel wanted and went so far as to accompany Mel when she went to get her first hormone injection to start her
on her way into maleness. Mel recounted how her mother adjusted:

> [I sent] a newsy letter. There was a few sentences in there about, "I have
> a problem that I need to look into and get more information about. . . .
> It's called gender dysphoria and it has to do with problems I've been
> having with my sex and my gender." And . . . I filled in with some more
> news. . . .
>
> She called me a couple of days later and said, "I got your letter" . . .
> and she didn't mention it and I didn't either. A couple days after that she
> called at seven in the morning. . . . And we talked for two hours. She
> was real supportive about the whole thing. . . . Her response to it was,
> "This isn't the first century this has happened. I'm sure people just
> learned to live with it." I said . . . "We're in a different era now where
> things can be done, and I think it's important for me to be happy with
> myself. And if this is what it takes, then this is what I need to do." She
> said, "I think you're right. I don't live with you any more and you don't
> live with me any more and I can't live your life. You're the one that has
> to be happy, and who am I to judge? By the way, you know that skirt
> that I gave you five years ago, you know the one . . . that still has the
> tags on it? . . . Can I have that back?" . . .
>
> Since we don't see each other on a daily basis it's hard for her. . . . She
> does say "she" constantly. In fact I said, "I'm not goin' any place with
> you while you're out here." And she said, "Why not?" I said, "Because
> you keep calling me [Sissy]." She said, "Did I do that?" I said, "Non-
> stop." It's tough. People can't just change over night.

Aaron's parents were quite elderly when she told them what she was about to do. To her astonishment, they were neither surprised nor shocked and were in fact quite encouraging.

> I was fascinated with my parents' reaction, because they were so old. They're . . . eighty-five and eighty-seven now. And basically, people in that age bracket remember more from many years ago than they do from the recent. So they remembered me as a child more than they did as an adult. And my mother's reaction was just, "I'm surprised you waited so long."
>
> My father . . . had no problem at all relating. . . . His reaction on the phone within minutes of me telling him was to ask, "Could we go fishing again sometime?" In other words, he remembered the boy, and how close we'd been, and how we never could be close while he was trying to treat me as a woman. . . . It wasn't hard for either one of them to acknowledge that this was right or appropriate, because they remembered.

Jack was surprised at the entirely accepting responses which she got from her parents, especially her father, of whom she had always been afraid. Jack's father called him by her previous androgynous name but was otherwise accepting. Jack recounted the anxiety of telling her father about her intentions:

> My dad, he's a redneck. And with him, things are either black or white. If it's gray, shoot it. Really. And I thought, "God, if I make it off the place alive, I'm lucky." That's the way I felt about it. I was very shocked, 'cause when I sat down and said, "Dad, I need to talk to you," I'd already talked to my mom. And she was kind of wringing her hands, 'cause she didn't know what to expect either. He said, "You know, I understand. You have a great uncle that killed himself when he was twenty years old from the same thing." . . . So he says, "I do understand that. It doesn't bother me none. I always knew you were different."

The reaction of Simon's parents was more typical of the ways in which most parents reacted to the news. They were willing to adjust, but it took time.

> I finally went to my mother and told her, and then she went home and told the family. [My dad] didn't have any problem with it at all. He had a little hard time getting used to a new name and he ended up calling me "son" for about two years before he finally got [my] name.

Luther's parents were mixed in their acceptance. Luther's mother didn't want anything to do with him after he became a man, whereas Luther's father stood by him in his own unique way. Luther explained:

My father wasn't very articulate at all. He was a very, very bright man, but he lived in the South and Blacks just weren't educated. He made a lot of money, but, you know, he didn't have many words. And he said to me, "It doesn't matter that you're a freak. Every family has a freak. And I love you, and I don't care if you're a freak." Now, I could have spun out and got very crazy on that, because he called me a freak, but . . . if you expect the person to take you where you are, you've got to take the person where they are.

Dale's father was also more encouraging than was Dale's mother. Dale summarized his parents' attitudes:

Mom and Dad, when I first told them, they cried and put their arms around me, and said I should have come to them sooner. . . . Dad and I are close. My dad likes me, and I like him. . . . I'm honest with him, and I think he respects me for it. I showed him parts of my surgery as I went along. . . .
My mother has not got the ability to understand or whatever. She calls me Dale, but she calls me "she." She's off in another world type of thing. My mother . . . she says some dumb things. . . . And yet when my first program came on TV, she got her friends together and they watched it, and my dad didn't watch it . . . [but he] is accepting of me today. I knew that a year or so ago when he was in the hospital and he introduced me to his doctor as his son, but the one that had the gender change.

These participants' lives were enriched by being able to enjoy the backing of at least one of their parents as they faced one of the most difficult passages of their lives. No matter what had gone on between them before, the value of their parents' approval at this juncture in their lives would be hard to underestimate.

Eleven of the twenty-seven participants who reported on this subject (41 percent) were less than pleased with the ways in which one or both of their parents reacted to their disclosures that they were transsexual.[7] Some parents were fairly mild in their disapproval, but participants' tolerance for parental negativity was also minimal in those cases. A few people's parents were more seriously damning.

Peter's and Howie's parents' reactions were on the more benign end of the spectrum. They resorted to trying to inspire guilt in their children—a technique which proved ineffective. When Peter told her mother what she was planning, her mother said, "I'm just glad that your grandmother isn't alive because this would kill her. Because you were her favourite. . . . She'd just be rolling over in her grave." Howie's parents were more dramatic. They threatened that they would have heart attacks if Howie had the nerve to go ahead with her transition. Howie did, and they did not.

A few participants' parents withdrew from them as they proceeded into their new lives. Hal said that his mother "went into denial regarding my change, but I persisted in seeing her and she has slowly been adjusting." Brian's relations with his parents continued to be as "strained" after his change as they had been before it. Luther's mother cut him off entirely after he began to live as a man.

Among the most extreme reactions were those suffered by Bruce and Grant, who had openly hostile confrontations with their mothers. Their mothers simply refused to accept them as men. After lifetimes of alienation from their mothers, this was enough to destroy all hope for reconciliations between them. Although Bruce did credit his mother with "doing what she can . . . in bits and pieces," overall he had an antagonistic attitude toward her.

> She still refers to me as "she". . . . And I ignore her. . . . See, my mother's always discounted me. . . . She doesn't get it. And I want to shoot her! I get so mad. Like, "Wake up mom!" And I don't talk to her. And I said to my brother today, "If she died today, I would go 'Oh, well.' " That's what I'd say. . . . I wouldn't miss her.

Grant fought bitterly with his parents, especially his mother, about becoming a man.

> When I told them I was going through the procedure . . . my mother started, "You listen to me young lady." I said, "Mom, God damn it, shut up for the first time in your life and listen to what somebody else has to say. You can write me out of your will, you can condemn me, you can curse me, whatever. But you're going to listen." . . . It was the first time I showed backbone to the woman. My father gets on the phone afterwards and tells me, "You'll be a freak. All women will find you repulsive." . . . And then they tried to take legal steps to stop the treatment. I was over twenty-one . . . [but] they made it very difficult for me. It turns out that . . . they bled out whatever trust funds I had. Thoughtful.
> [My dad] dies. I'm not told about it. I hear about it through [my partner's] sister who read it in the newspaper. I confront my mother over the phone. I'm 1,800 miles away from this lady. "Oh, I didn't want you to come. . . . You'd have shown up with your moustache, and you'd have embarrassed your father." I said, "First of all, Mom, it's moustache and beard. Secondly, I would have embarrassed you. You can't embarrass a dead man. . . . And third, and most importantly, where was I going to get the money?" And there's been a lot of bad blood still. . . . She figures I've probably forgiven by now. I have not. That was underhanded. If she had told me "Please don't show up," I would have considered not showing up. I even would have gone as far as to show up in drag, if that

would have made things better. . . . I decided at that point, since she was going to shit on me like that, I wasn't going to pull any punches with my family now.

In sum, most of those participants who managed to muster the courage to face their parents with honest disclosures about their transsexualism were able to find acceptance from them. Often, however, that opprobrium came in a piecemeal fashion and participants' parents were far from flawless in their references to participants in masculine terms. Those participants who could tolerate their parents' blundering progress through their own transitions were those who were also most likely to report satisfaction with their parents' responses to their new identities.

Infrequently, participants' parents behaved in ways which made it seem unlikely that they would ever come to terms with their children's transsexualism no matter how much patience and perseverance participants demonstrated. The children of these parents thus had little choice but to carry on without the comfort of their parents' acceptance. A depleting disappointment, no doubt, but one which countless other people have had to live with over a myriad of other matters.

Other Family Members Come to Terms

In general, when participants mentioned the reactions of other family members to their transitions, they told positive stories. It is unclear from what participants actually said whether the untold stories were ones of sadness and rejection, were a manifestation of minimal contacts for reasons unrelated to participants' transsexualism, or would have been more of the same had they been recounted. Be that as it may, the tales which participants related were reassuring ones.

Fourteen of the thirty-one participants who had sisters made brief comments about how their sisters acted around them after they began to live as men. Eleven (79 percent) of them indicated an encouraging degree of acceptance from their sisters.[8] When participants described their sisters, they were usually quite terse but enthusiastic. They used terms such as "very supportive," "wonderful," "more accepting and closer." Only Walter's sister seemed ambivalent, and only Sam and Phil had sisters who reacted badly. At their sisters' preference, Sam rarely saw his sister and Phil had not seen his sister for seven years after she told him, "You're sick and I don't ever want you to come over and see me or my kids ever again."

Dale was "extremely close" with one of his four sisters and felt good about his relationships with the rest of them. He elaborated:

My sisters all think the world of me. I'm not really close to the very youngest. Actually, the one that was going to university . . . she was in some kind of a . . . class. She had me come down for the day so the class could ask me questions. So, you know, she wasn't ashamed of me. But now that she's a schoolteacher, she doesn't particularly want the school to know. See, there again, they're very accepting of me.

Walter's sister displayed ambivalence combined with filial loyalty. Although she could not quite accept Walter as a man, in several respects she indicated that she no longer thought of Walter as a woman either. To some degree, she indicated her acceptance of Walter in that they lived together, sharing a large apartment. Walter described how she responded to him:

It's funny because my sister, even now . . . I'd say she probably sees me more of as an androgyne type of individual, or like a hermaphroditic individual. . . . She can't accept me just as a man. And I can almost understand it because, I mean, anyone who's realistic, anyone who's objective, you can't deny the fact that I was born biologically female. . . .

And she wants me to be her sister as well as her brother. . . . I know for a fact that my sister liked . . . the fact that I was not a man or a woman, and that I was a little bit of both. . . . And this is why she calls me by my female name . . . she feels that she has accepted me as a woman who's different. . . . she's already accepted my masculinity in my feminine me. And she considers it a loss for her to lose her sister. . . . She always felt that she had a sister who was also like a brother. Now she has to accept the brother and give up the sister, and she really doesn't want that. . . . And she really considers that a loss. And it's a very hard thing for her to deal with.

As Walter perceptively noted, sisters of participants had a particular set of issues to come to grips with in finding ways to accept participants' transitions. In adjusting to the loss of a sister and the acquisition of a brother, they had to reconcile themselves to having one fewer sibling with whom they nominally shared those familial duties which often fall to adult daughters. In addition, participants' sisters also had to adapt to the increase in status and privileges which participants amassed as they grew into men.

In a sense, participants were leaving their sisters marooned in a socially lesser valued status which they once had shared with them, while they themselves socially stepped up to lives as men. However, because participants' sisters knew them to have been women for much of their lives and knew something of the pain involved in participants' paths to manhood, perhaps their sororal sympathies were stronger then any intergender sibling resentment they might have felt.

Eleven of the thirty participants who had brothers mentioned something about how their brothers took to them as men. As was the case with participants' sisters, most brothers who were mentioned had been accepting of participants' transsexualism. Participants' comments about their brothers were succinct. Eight of the eleven (73 percent) said that they had responded positively.⁹ Tony's brother's behaviour was a mixture of friendly and treacherous. Only Jordie's and Dale's brothers were markedly hostile.

Mel's relationship with his brother was typical. Like many participants' family members, Mel's brother needed time to adjust to the idea of his sister turning into a man. However, after Mel answered some of his brother's questions and guided him through his initial confusion, he became acclimatized to the new situation.

> I talked to [my brother] the same day that I initially talked to my mom. . . . I actually thought that [my brother] would do better with it than my mom. Didn't work out that way. His thing was, "Well, why don't you just be gay?" . . . I said . . . "It doesn't have anything to do with this." So he said, "Well, I can't even think about this. Give me some books to read." So I gave him the names of some books. . . .
>
> And we talked kind of off and on about it. And then I moved up here and then he came up. I showed him an interview tape from a Geraldo TV show and it took us three hours to get through that interview tape because he kept saying, "stop," and then he'd ask a question. He spent the weekend and we talked about a lot of things. . . . He's done real well.

A few participants who had good relationships with their adult brothers felt free enough to turn to them for help in the one area of their lives as men in which they were the most deficient; they asked their brothers for access to their penises. Bruce and Stan wanted to learn firsthand about how natural penises looked, felt, and acted. Tony's and Nathan's brothers both agreed to be sperm donors so that they and their wives could have children who were genetically related to their legal fathers.

Bruce talked unabashedly and with some excitement about his "incredible" relationship with his brother after they were both men. In telling this story, Bruce seemed to indicate that both he and his brother made some kind of connection between an incident which they had shared as teenagers and some of what they could share as adult brothers.

> I saw him for the first time since the change in April . . . and we talked a long time. . . . And I had told him that more than anything in the world I wanted to be able to jack off a guy; stand behind him and know what it's like to feel that dick get hard in my hand, and to shoot, and . . . sort of by osmosis, to feel what was happening.
>
> And my brother said to me . . . "I want to apologize for sexually coming up against you when we were kids." And I totally blanked this out of my mind. . . . He said, "You know, I often wondered how that affected your life, and I'm so sorry today." And, really, what he did was

> he . . . was fourteen or something, and I was thirteen, and he attacked me and . . . what he was trying to do was to sort of hump me. . . . He said to me, "All this time I felt guilty, and never said anything. But I want to apologize now, and hope that it's not taken away from you anything." . . . And he also said to me, "You know, I feel more comfortable with you as my brother than I ever did as my sister."
>
> And on the way home, he took out his dick on the freeway, hard as a rock, and he said, "Here, I want you to know what it feels like." And I said, "Oh, my God." This great looking dick, you know. He said, "Just take it. And if you want to jack it off, go ahead, and I'll just keep driving. Whatever I can do to make you feel and know what it's like, I will." He didn't come on to me. He didn't overpower me. He said, "Here, take it." Like taking a gear shift knob. And I did. I wrapped my hands around it, and I thought, "Wow!" And I said, "I think you better put it back in your pants. That's about all I need on the freeway." And he said, "Well, if ever you need to know, and you want to see me do this, I will be more than willing to do this. But this can only be between you and I." And I said, "Okay." . . .
>
> The experience I had was the intimacy with my brother that I had never had, and the bonding that took place because we were men now. It was okay. My brother has a brother.

Stan, who also had an abiding interest in seeing another man's erections and ejaculations was considering asking his brother similarly to oblige him but had not yet worked up the nerve to do so.

Tony's relationship with his brother displayed a different kind of push and pull. On the one hand, Tony's brother did not in any way reject him when he became a man. On the other hand, Tony's brother was deceitful with him.

> I found out a lot of things about [my wife] after she left. How she wasn't faithful to me. . . . There was even a situation with my brother. I really don't know if I can blame him because he was donating the sperm for our inseminations without anyone else knowing, his wife included. And the way I understand it, we were going for an insemination, and we had gone through a whole bunch already and they weren't working, and he . . . was in love with her. He was very jealous of our relationship. He was envious of me, and I think that, in his mind, he told himself he was doing me a favour. . . .
>
> She denied everything, of course. And he didn't tell me everything, of course. . . . No doubt . . . she picked up the phone and called him up and said something like, "Why don't you come here? We're going for insemination tomorrow, why don't you come here and see if I can get pregnant today?" And he ran.

Ironically, despite his brother's duplicity, Tony characterized him as a "caring" and "sensitive" man.

Jordie and Dale reported the most negative reactions from their brothers. Jordie's brother cut him out of his life completely when he made his change. Jordie was blasé about it. He said of his brother, "He is uncomfortable and will not talk to me. He is an old stuffed shirt. His loss."

Dale had long had a difficult relationship with her older brother. When Dale became a man his brother responded with derision. In return, Dale decided that he didn't need him in his life.

> My brother mocked me, belittled me, and said I'd never be a man. To him, a man is a big guy, 'cause he's a huge son of a bitch . . . and he made fun of me. And I remember it was Mom and Dad's . . . anniversary and we all went and took them out for dinner. And by then I had to use the men's washroom. And he came in after me, and he said, "What the fuck are you doing in here? You don't belong in here." . . .
>
> I haven't actually talked to him now in about four years. I don't have nothing to do with him. . . . He's just a very self-centered person. So it doesn't matter to me that he accepts me or doesn't.

The stories told by Bruce and Dale about how their brothers dealt with their transitions brought to the surface what were probably the two main issues which most complicated participants' brothers' acceptance of them as men. From one direction, participants' brothers were challenged to cease seeing participants in the sexualized terms in which most men view most women. From another perspective, if participants' brothers were to acquiesce to affording participants the status of men, then issues of masculine competition and hierarchy arose. Participants' brothers had been accustomed to enjoying certain prerogatives which came to them as men and as sons. Accepting a new brother into the family probably meant that the familial masculine dominance hierarchy had to be reorganized. Most likely, participants' appearances as men were usually sufficient to dissipate the first source of tension. As for the second issue, the degree to which it was a problem at all was one indicator that participants' brothers were indeed forced to deal with participants as men.

Four participants talked about how their children had adjusted to them as men. Aaron, Sam, Lee, Dale, and Pat had children whom they had borne themselves while they were living as women. Bruce, Howie and Hal had children whom they had fathered via donor insemination. Ed, Jack, and Roger lived with children from their female partners' previous marriages. Neither Sam nor Lee commented on their grown children's attitudes toward their mothers' lives as men. Pat had not told her son of her intentions. Bruce's daughter had always known Bruce as her father. Ed, Jack, and Roger did not discuss the children with whom they lived.

Aaron had four children and eight grandchildren at the time of his last interview. Three of his offspring were entirely accepting of his new life. One daughter was unable to resolve her feelings of betrayal.

> My oldest girl still does not accept. . . . She's the one that likes things black and white. . . . And she's also the one that spent most of her years with me when I was in the female role. But she's also the one who happens to inherit from the other side of the family more bullheadedness than I have (if you can imagine). And she's just damn stubborn, and she decided she didn't want to deal with it, so she's not dealing with it.
>
> But the other three, they have no problem . . . seeing me as more comfortable and more appropriate since then, and no problem letting me into their lives as Uncle Aaron. . . . They accepted the new name without any problem. It's a lot harder to stop hollering "Mom" to somebody that you always hollered "Mom" at, or to switch pronouns. . . .
>
> Grandchildren [are] no problem. Kids don't mind things like this. . . . I'm just Aaron to most of them, so it's no biggie. . . . My kids have a little trouble . . . but the grandkids don't. . . . The point is, I'm in the grandparent role, and they know it.

Dale had only one daughter, who was twelve years old when Dale first told her that she was going to live as a man. Dale recalled with compassion how hard it was for her daughter to understand that her mother was changing into a man. To ease the way for both of them, Dale sent her daughter to live with one of Dale's sisters while she went through her changes. When they reunited, Dale's daughter was more acclimatized. Dale remembered some of what transpired.

> I wish she could have been a little bit older. . . . I just told her that I was going to be a man. That I was going to be her dad. And it was really tough, and I knew she didn't understand. . . . she said she was worried what was going to happen to her. . . . I can't imagine, when I look back, what it must have been like for her. . . . I had a lot of guilt then. But, you know, I never ever wanted to hurt anybody, but I had to do it. . . .
>
> She spent four years with my sister and her husband when I was actually going through all the surgery. . . . But in those years where she was a teenager, it wouldn't have been fair to keep her with me. Because she would be picked on. You know what people are like. . . . and to this day, in a sense, I wish she had been with me all along, and yet in another sense, she had an opportunity to be with a real family. . . . So, I mean, she doesn't hold anything against me for it today at all. . . . And she came back to live with me when she was eighteen and a bit. We got to know each other then. . . .
>
> [My daughter's] been having some troubles recently. . . . Now she's more aware of what other people think and say. They are cruel. . . . She doesn't want any of her friends to know. It's not that she's ashamed of me. It's what society's going to say that is what upsets her, is what other people are thinking. . . . Like she doesn't want anybody at her work to

know. For instance, I went there about a month ago . . . and this guy is coming around the corner, and my daughter wanted me to disappear into a crack. And I really felt humiliated. But . . . I know she loves and respects me. She thinks I'm the greatest dad in the world.

Howie's only son was four years old at the time of his last interview. Howie was his father by donor insemination. Howie was undecided about when and what to tell him about his transsexualism. Howie wasn't sure if he would ever tell his son that he was born female, but if he did tell him, it probably wouldn't be until the child was grown.

Hal's daughter was three and a half years old when Hal decided to live fully as a man. Hal explained to her what was going to happen. At first the little girl was confused by it all, but she soon adjusted.

My daughter's first reaction was that she didn't want me to change. . . . She was afraid I was going to die. Then she was afraid I was going to grow real tall and she wouldn't recognize me. I assured her those things wouldn't happen. Then she asked, "Do mommy and I have to become men, also?" I told her, "Absolutely not." After that she seemed to be okay about it. Now that the change is complete (and she is six), she is very comfortable with it. I think she likes having a dad. . . .

The actual transition has been easy for her. Sometimes she relates to me as if I were always male ("Dad, when you were a little boy, did you . . . "), and sometimes she acknowledges the change ("Dad, when you were a woman, did you . . . ", or, "So, Dad, do you have a penis now?"). I hope she's as accepting when she hits adolescence.

These few stories about participants' children suggest that there was variety among participants' relationships with their children. When participants came to think of themselves as transsexual, their children ranged from preschool age to adult. Lee and Pat were still living as women at the time of their last interviews; Aaron, Sam, Bruce, Dale, and Hal became men as their children looked on. Howie's, Ed's, Jack's, and Roger's children had always known them as men. Some children remained innocent of their parent's transsexualism; others knew of it and accepted it; only Aaron reported a single daughter, his eldest, who would not accept her mother's transformation into "Uncle Aaron." Perhaps youthfulness made participants' children's adjustments proceed a bit more smoothly.

Stan, Howie, and Luther told stories about less immediate family members whose responses to their transitions into men were meaningful for them. Stan's grandparents, who raised her when she was a girl, had never seen him as a man. Stan told them what she was doing over the telephone. Their only query was "Oh, Honey, are you sure?" Stan said, "Not bad for 80 year old grandparents. . . . 'Cause I think they made the effort, they tried. . . . they were pretty good. They'd forget, but Grandma forgot her daughter's name too." Howie's story was a proud one about an uncle who "was going to give me money for surgery and try to collect a contribution from other family members until he knew my insurance would pay for it." Howie understandably stated, "He'll have my love and loyalty for the rest of his life because of that kindness."

Luther's comments about his mother-in-law nicely conveyed the role which family can play for transsexual persons as they negotiate their ways into their new lives.

> It was an important relationship because she met me as I was just beginning my transition. So she knew me as both [a woman] and as Luther, and treated me just like, "OK, this is who you say you are and either I'm going to like you or I'm not going to like you." And it was just wonderful. I think it helped me not to fall into some of the depressions people fall into at the time that they're undergoing a transition. It certainly gave me a sense of family which is important for anyone.

Summary and Commentary

Participants asked their family members to do a fantastic thing. They asked them to disregard lifetimes of direct knowledge and experience of participants as girls and as women. They did not ask them to forget all of those years but rather to discount them as some kind of grand mistake or to reinterpret them in an entirely new way. They also asked of their families that they rupture, at least temporarily, the usually foundational relationship of gender to sex.

In order for their families to be able to make sense of participants' transitions and new lives, they had to be able to believe it possible for persons to be men without having been born and raised in male bodies. Thus the loyalty and approval which participants sought from their families was not simply about trust, love, devotion, and faithfulness but also about the meanings of bodies in the casting of gender. Participants and their families had to be able to believe that participants' bodies were wrong but that their minds were right, and that participants' mental states were more definitive arbiters of gender than were their bodies. This understanding of the relationship between gender and sex makes sense of transsexualism but runs counterintuitively to the everyday beliefs of most people. As such, it presented a major hurdle.

Almost all participants authoritatively told their family members that transsexualism is caused by unobservable biological mechanisms which are impervious to family dynamics. As well, they most frequently presented their cases to their family members with the promise that they were going to do whatever was medically possible to bring their bodies into line with social expectations. With such assurances, they eased the stress they had placed on their families' understandings of the "correct" relationship between gender and sex. In other words, they made the case that although their bodies may have looked female for much of their lives, there was some hidden critical mechanism that meant that they should have been male all along. Their transsexualism was simply a recognition of this biological imperative and their transitions were their inevitable surrender to it.

Fortified with such biological rationale, it would seem that most participants' families had remarkably little trouble believing that participants should be men. After all, participants' families had known them all of their lives and had in most cases acquiesced to if not encouraged their masculinity many years before. Recall that most participants had either been very masculine as women or had been stunningly unhappy in their rendition of femininity. Add to this that participants' family members remembered participants' happier days as youthful tomboys. Armed with such lengthy and acute hindsight, assuaged by guilt-free biological explanations, and driven by compassion and love for participants, it seems more than logical that participants' families would be more willing than not to struggle to accept participants' transsexualism. They did so admirably.

Friends, Acquaintances, People at School and Work

Friends are the people, other than our families and lovers, to whom we feel the closest; the people with whom we feel that we can share the most. Men's friendships tend to be based more on the sharing of activities, whereas women's friendships more commonly are measured in terms of emotional intimacy.[10] Most participants who talked about how their friends responded to their transitions seemed to be judging their friendships on the criterion of intimacy. In a few cases, participants seemed to use the term *friend* to refer to anyone whom they knew socially.

Most participants who talked about the reactions of their friends remembered them as generally being supportive. However, participants also appeared to take the attitude that those who merited the title of friend were those with whom they could share the truth about their gender identities and still retain their loyalty. Thus, although a few people talked about losing friends, participants more often retroactively discounted the friendship of people who failed them in this way. They often worked from the axiom that those who counted as friends were those who could be supportive of their changes. Steven's comments illustrated this attitude:

My friends have been very supportive, those people that I call friends, extremely supportive. And the so-called friends that weren't supportive weren't really even friends. They have drifted out of my life and, you know, I can't really say that I lost many friends. . . . And I thank God for that, because I think it's important to have someone in your corner when you're going through this.

Thirteen of the twenty participants (65 percent) who spoke of their closest friends' reactions said that most of them had been their allies during their transitions.[11] A number of participants simply stated that their friends had been "supportive" or "very supportive" and said little else. More often, participants remembered their friends as having provided them with the encouragement which they wanted. However, some of participants' friends behaved in ways which were less to their liking.

One common theme in participants' stories was an appreciation of friends who told them that they were not at all surprised at participants' transsexualism because they had long perceived their manliness. At the same time, most participants recalled friends who were disturbed by their transitions. As Simon recalled, "a number of people said that that explained a lot about their inability to relate to me as being female and my being incongruent as a female." However, Simon also recalled, "I started telling people my new name and losing friends right and left." Aaron similarly recounted, "most of my close friends, it didn't offend, because they felt that way all along. . . . And for those people who were probably wrapped up in feminist things or too busy dealing with their own [things], for some of them it was upsetting."

Rick severed her relationships with all but a few best friends.

I kept a few good friends that I had had over the years. They all knew about me anyway. It was no big deal. They were just waiting to see how long it would take me to do something about myself. And I still have those friendships. . . . I cut off more distant people. I basically went out for a pack of cigarettes and never came back. I closed down 99 percent of my life. Most of the people who stayed were people I had known for twenty years. There was no question of whether they would cope or not.

Unlike Rick, Hal did not just disappear from her friends' lives as she began to live as a man. Hal reported that he had mixed but mostly good reactions from his friends.

Most people I know have easily accepted me as male, although some people who did not know me as well have had difficulty. I think the ones who had the most problems . . . had those problems because they didn't know me well enough to really talk about it and break down the barriers and the prejudices they had. . . .
My friends have mostly been supportive; a few were tolerant at first, and have grown to be supportive. My "best" friend . . . was supportive

until she stopped speaking to me because she was dating my lover. . . . I guess the two best responses from friends were one lesbian who said she thought it was wonderful because it seemed I was more grounded, more real, more present as a man than as a woman; and one guy who looked me in the eye and said he was really happy for me that I was so together and knew what I wanted and what was right for me, and he was proud of me.

A handful of participants told stories which ran the gamut from excellent responses to horrible ones,[12] but only Ken and Grant recalled predominantly difficult times with their friends. Bruce's memories illustrated most of the questions which arose for other participants whose experiences with their friends were not always the best.

I was sort of in the lesbian community. . . . And so when I was going through the change . . . we went to the bar. . . . I had not been to the bars since I went through this. And I ran into a woman who was watching me the whole time. I was the only man in the bar . . . and she knew the story, and I went up to her, and I said, "Hi. Do you remember me? I used to be. . . . Now I'm Bruce." And she looks at me and she goes, "Oh, yeah." And she pushed me away from her, just total like, "Get out of my way." I was like, "I'm leaving now. Fuck these dykes!" You know, because I've gotten more oppression from them than from anybody. It's like, "I used to be one of you." . . .
    It has been . . . varied. . . . And there's some lesbians that are so loving. . . . So there's been this really warm reception, and then there's been these women that I really feel have difficulty with their own sexuality. . . . So, generally, it's just really been good. . . . I have no problem with any of the men that I knew before. They just love me and I love them.

Most of Keith's friends were straight men, and because of an active past as a heterosexual woman, Keith had conflicts with her friends.

Have my friends been supportive? For the most part, yes. I was rather disappointed in that many . . . people who I thought were my friends . . . apparently only wanted me because I was a pretty woman, an attractive woman, and that was an ego stroke to a lot of my male friends. . . . But, for the most part, my true friends, they tried to understand it. . . . They all pretty much accepted it, because they could see what a difference it made to me once I actually started becoming serious in my progression through the change. Then my friends became much more supportive.
    One of the worst responses was someone . . . I thought that he was a true friend, and I was opening my feelings and concerns about my gender to him. . . . And he was very . . . insulting about my feelings. . . . And he has since totally avoided me. . . . The other probably worst response was from a very close friend who still is a close friend, and he

has grudgingly accepted my change, but for a long time, even after I was totally passable, he ridiculed me. He still makes references to the fact that we ought to sue my psychiatrist for referring me for a gender change.

Participants tended to report that their social acquaintances were less understanding than were their friends. Four participants said that their acquaintances were mostly easygoing about their transition,[13] an equal number reported a roughly equal mix of responses,[14] and two people remembered having more trouble than support.[15]

One major source of derision about which participants complained was the assumption made by acquaintances that people who wanted to change their sex and gender were necessarily delusional. As Mel put it, "Acquaintances don't know you that well to know that you're not nuts." Keith, for example, suffered from the gossiping of people who lived in the small town where she had made her transition. Keith explained:

> I'm running into the situation more and more often where when new people come to the area, and I can tell if they've been told about me. . . . I've even had situations where . . . people meet me and they assume I'm a male, and they start out using the pronoun "he." And after being in this little town for a while, where a lot of people have resisted my change, pretty soon they'll switch to "she," which really bothers me, because I'm completely passable.

The people who refused to accept Ken's right to live as a man were probably morally offended. Ken complained that the "friends" she had made at school all shunned him after she became a he.

> I've lost a lot of friends. I went to a Christian college for four years, and none of the 107 people that I graduated with talked to me. And we were close. It was a Bible college. It hurts. It's like I don't even exist.

Several participants pointed out that they felt condemned by another kind of moralism. Transsexualism was considered to be "totally politically incorrect" among many lesbian women in the 1970s and 1980s when participants were starting their transitions. Seven participants complained of lesbian-feminist friends or acquaintances who considered them to be traitors to womanhood who were capitulating to manhood because they had been seduced by the social rewards attached to that status.[16] For instance, Luther remembered a lot of discussion on the topic among her circle of acquaintances, all of it "negative." He commented, "I find it very surprising how intolerant gay people can be of transsexuals and transvestites. It's just really outrageous." Luther kept quiet about her transsexual leanings until her change and then "lost lots of friends." Walter, however, found a way around the taboo on being male-identified among the lesbian women she knew.

> What I did was I sought out the more enlightened and . . . more flexible lesbians, and that's how I got involved with . . . [a group called] Lesbian Sado-Masochists. . . . Because what the group really is, is women with alternative sexuality; women who are politically incorrect sexually. . . . And they are totally open. . . . And they were accepting of the transsexuality.

Harry also received mixed reactions among the lesbian women she knew.

> There were a few, maybe three or four, that I could actually talk to and tell them about myself, and they didn't freak out. I started having problems with some of the women at the gay bar, when I started telling them about myself. . . . I remember some of the women freaking out on me, like, "You're nuts. You're really crazy. You're a traitor. You don't know what you're talking about. You're confused. You're trying to turncoat on us." And all this stuff. There were some that I couldn't talk to.

Simon found that although some lesbian women were hostile to her because of her transsexualism, not all were. Simon had a "friend of a friend . . . who was a very radical lesbian." The woman "accused" Simon of being "a traitor and betraying womanhood." Other lesbian friends defended Simon.

> I think it had a lot to do with how radical they were. The more radical were really into me betraying womanhood. And I kept trying to explain to them, "how could I betray something that I had never been." But, you know, it doesn't compute for them.

To summarize, participants' friends and acquaintances reacted to participants' transsexualism with varying degrees of equanimity. Those who were better established, more intimate and longer standing friends seemed to be the most likely to be accepting or encouraging of participants' transitions. However, those people who believed that transsexualism represented a mental, moral, or political failure were forced to choose between their beliefs and their loyalty to participants. Participants suffered from the barbs of those who opted to believe in transsexualism as a manifestation of weakness, but were buoyed by those friends and acquaintances who went on treating them like normal human beings.

The other places where participants hoped to be able to pass freely as men were their workplaces or schools. Some people made their transitions while remaining with a single workplace or school. There were both difficulties and rewards associated with this approach. More frequently, participants changed jobs or schools when they felt that they could move full-time into living as men. However, there were often reasons why employers and administrators, co-workers and other students might come to know of participants' transsexuality either at old or new locations. More often than not, employers and school administrators were sympathetic and helpful to them. Participants' co-workers and student peers could be kindly or cruel.

All eleven participants who talked about how their employers or school administrators handled them around the times of their transitions reported accommodating treatment.[17] They assuaged the fears of participants' co-workers or schoolmates and made adjustments to participants' records so that they could move on in their new identities without losing the benefit of the years that they had spent amassing qualifications in their previous personas.

Simon and Jack chose to remain where they were. But after Simon began her transition while at college, she found the ostracization of her schoolmates to be so demoralizing that she considered dropping out of school. When Simon went to her dean to tell her that she was leaving school, the Dean gave Simon some very sound advice.

> She advised me to stay. She felt that if I couldn't go through the transition there that I couldn't very well go through it, period, if I couldn't go through the adversity that was going to happen around that. I decided that she was right and that I should stay.

Jack stayed with the same employer while she made her transition. People at Jack's workplace were generally understanding and respectful of Jack. Jack's boss and co-workers seemed to accept him fully in his new life as a man. However, there were some amusing incidents.

> The people at work weren't shocked and I've stayed with the same job. I happen to have a boss . . . that nothing bothers him, you know. It's like water off a duck. It's live and let live. And he told me . . . "I'll try to help you financially any way I can." I'm very lucky that way. . . .
> I thought this whole thing would scare me to death, but there's been so many times I've gotten such a laugh out of it. I never thought I'd have fun with it. There was one time . . . I was about six months into this, and I was on a forklift, and a guy, a little guy like me (little guys have big mouths, and he was real cocky) he comes over. He doesn't know anything about it. My voice is starting to change. I sound like I have a cold. He jumps up on the forklift, puts his arm around me. I thought, "Man, this jerk must be desperate." You know what I'm saying? He puts his arm around me and says, "How've you been doing?" I said, "I don't know. I'm tired. Burning the candle at both ends." He says, "How

would you like to burn the candle with me?" I said "Well, you leave me no choice but to tell you what I'm doing."

This guy jumped off that forklift. He had a cup of coffee sitting on his truck . . . he drove out of there. We never saw him again. . . . He quit his job. He wouldn't come in there again. The guy up front said, "What happened to this guy?" I was just laughing my butt off. "What happened to this guy?" I said, "Man, you know, he'll never make another pass at a woman in his life." . . . Oh, boy. Tears were running down our faces . . . 'cause that was just hilarious.

Ken and Rick both decided to try starting over with new jobs as they began their lives as men. When Ken started her changes she stayed with the same employer but moved to another division. Ken's boss was obliging but his co-workers made his life miserable.

When I was ready for the whole nine yards, I was working . . . for a lab at the university. . . . And what I did was I transferred. . . . I talked to my boss and said, "I need a week off. I'm going to grow a beard, and I'm going to come back as a man. What do you think?" And he was like, "Okay. Let me check this out." It took him two days to answer me, and he said, "Hey, there's no problem there. Keep yourself clean." I talked it over with one or two supposed friends, and they were very negative about it. Rumors started to fly . . . the ridicule, laughing. No one would even sit beside me in the lunchroom.

Rick decided to avoid trouble at work by starting a new life. One of the drawbacks of this approach was that when Rick took on a new identity he lost access to the job history he had amassed while living as a woman. Luckily, Rick had some friends who were able to help him to start over.

I was self-employed. I sold my business, so I had some income from that. And I just took part-time jobs here and there as I could get them because I did change my name and I did not have any history really that I could call upon. So I suddenly became a new arrival in the state even though I had lived here twenty-some years. You learn to fabricate a history. . . . What happened was that I had two or three very close friends over the years in the same industry who gave me jobs with my new name and were very respectful of my situation. So I could create a new history with them. So I had a safety zone there. But it was very difficult financially. It was an enormous come-down and hardship.

Keith, who also was self-employed, did not change jobs and start anew but wished that he had. Keith was happy that his friends accepted him as a man but found that his clients and "the majority of the people" in his community did not, even after three years.

Only a few participants told stories about despicable treatment at the hands of their co-workers. However, those few stories displayed the baseness and fear with which some people react to those whom they do not understand. Ron worked at construction jobs after he began to live as a man. His co-workers purposefully placed Ron in life-threatening situations more than once when they discovered his transsexualism. Ron came through these incidents physically unscathed and remarkably philosophical about the incidents.

> I was thrown off the scaffolding twice, and I was run over with a forklift once. . . . And they were pretty good with me before. They appreciated me before and so they felt really betrayed. . . .
>
> It was in the winter, and I always had to wear a lot of stuff like pullovers and overalls and whatnot. And all we had was outhouses. . . . And while I was in one of those outhouses, I was really sweating, so I took off a T-shirt. But I hadn't latched the door, and the forklift driver walked in. . . . It was just like, "Ahh!" 'cause there I was. . . . He slammed the door, got in his truck, and tipped the whole thing over. . . .
>
> I didn't go back . . . but news travels fast, and this one guy . . . threw me off the scaffolding at another job. . . . He felt really betrayed because the day before he was trying to get me together with his sister. . . . I was lucky because there was a vent sticking out of the side of the wall, and when I fell off, the vent hit my back so it knocked me on a lower floor. . . . It was just three floors, but I only fell down one story. . . . Well, it's just like, "Die like a man, bitch." . . .
>
> And then somebody else. . . . I went across from one corner scaffolding and there was a piece missing, so we put planks across. So when he saw me coming, he just moved the stuff over so when I stepped on the plank there was no support and I went "Whoosh." It was only about a story and a half. . . .
>
> I felt [emotionally] hurt more than anything because usually the people I work with I get very close with, and . . . I'm always very openminded about their stuff. Like, I don't judge them about whatever they're doing. . . . So I felt hurt because I felt I didn't get the same credit.

Dale stayed at the same warehousing job during the transition and for approximately the next fifteen years. When Dale was ready to switch to living as a man she approached management personnel with the news. They were accommodating, and while Dale was on two weeks' holidays, one of Dale's supervisors informed her co-workers that when Dale returned it would be as a man. When Dale returned, he was well received by some co-workers but brutally harassed by others.

> That first morning, our assistant manager at the time, he really was kind. He took the guys aside before the store opened . . . and told them. So just before the store opened, I went into the washroom and put on

my tie, and my name badge. . . . I never have used the men's washroom.
A lot of guys couldn't have dealt with it, so I have a washroom down
by our snack bar, and that's the one I've always used. It's my washroom. . . .

A lot of the guys came to me and shook my hand, and said, "If you
want to know anything about being a guy or whatever." . . . Some
people couldn't deal with it, okay. The hardest thing, I think, for them
was really to call me Dale, and "he." It was "she" all the time, and
they'd make a mistake . . . and they'd feel bad about it. . . . But like I
said, after a time it just all disappeared. But it was very tough. I mean,
I knew, like I said, people were looking at me, they were watching me.
Some of the staff were bringing in relatives. . . . I wouldn't look at anybody. I just did my job. And I could just feel people watching me. I
didn't want to be looked at, okay. I didn't want to be stared at. But God,
that was a tough day. I'm telling you, it was just brutal. . . . It went on
for a couple years. . . . I mean, I would leave work just drained.

Some of the men with whom Dale worked never did adjust. They became
viciously sadistic. Dale gave this rendition of how he was hounded for
years by a pack of co-workers:

I had a problem with some of the guys. . . . One of the first guys . . . was
a big guy, and I always liked him 'cause he kind of reminded me of
my brother. . . . After I went into the change, he became a buddy of
mine. . . . But all he talked about was women. How many women he'd
had and everything else. So, anyway, we had a disagreement at work one
day . . . and I wouldn't allow myself to be shoved around anymore. . . .
But he was a guy. He turned out to be horrible. He's always talking
about killing. And he would take mice, spray them with hairspray, and
put a match to them. He was kind of a sick kind of a guy. He's still there
today. He's a great big ugly, fat son of a bitch today. I haven't talked to
him in eight years.

Anyway, what happened is I was working two jobs, and I'd met [my
girlfriend] at 7-Eleven. And . . . I stopped at a restaurant to have a hamburger, and he walked in, and he came and sat beside me. I didn't really
want to talk to him, so all I talked about was [my girlfriend]. . . . The
very next day someone came into 7-Eleven where [she] was working,
and said something to the effect, "Do you know that this girl is living
with a guy-girl?" . . . and really embarrassed her. . . .

Well . . . they harassed her. . . . for about a year and a half. They
threatened her life. Two of the other guys in the store joined in on her.
. . . I think in his own sick mind he didn't feel that I should have a
woman, 'cause he had a terrible time ever keeping one, and he still
doesn't have one. . . . They said filthy things to her. I was paranoid
that they were going to rape her. . . . They insisted she leave me, or else
. . . and this was my first relationship as Dale, even though I didn't
have my sexual parts. . . . So we were afraid that they were going to get
hold of her mother and tell her, so [my girlfriend] went and told her

mother about it. . . . Her mother accepted me, but it was never the same. But these guys just never let up. . . . There were three, four guys phoning her. Two different women phoning. And then they finally laid off.

And I hadn't seen [my previous lover] in about six years. She came into 7-Eleven one day and thanked me for the Christmas card. I hadn't sent her one. They had sent it to her from me. And her husband hated my guts. And they also sent a filthy picture to her mother of two women in bed. . . . That was the worst of the worst.

Clearly, there were advantages and disadvantages to the various ways in which participants chose to handle their work and school situations. Co-workers and schoolmates could become boons or banes to participants once their transsexualism became known. Starting new jobs or school careers as men could avoid many of the problems associated with more sedentary approaches. However, even when participants chose to start anew, they ran the risk of their secret leaking out anyway and they were dependent upon the generosity of others to provide them with coherent job histories or school records in their new names. The stories told by participants on this point were consistent and hopeful. In all cases described by participants, employers and school administrators co-operated with participants entirely and graciously.

Most of the people around participants were supportive, accepting, and tolerant. There were, of course, a number of instances where participants experienced rejection or pronounced hostility from other people. However, even those people who told of such lamentable treatments usually had counterbalancing stories about other people who were more humane in their attitudes and actions.

Some of those people who reacted poorly to the revelation that participants were transsexual may have believed that transsexualism violated a religious principle in which they believed. Other people who treated participants poorly seemed to be acting on the assumption that participants were perverts who were either mentally ill or morally depraved. The people who held such opinions seemed to feel that participants did not deserve the respect and courtesy merited by persons whom they considered to be more normal. Some lesbian women said that they considered transsexualism to be politically incorrect and therefore treated participants as traitors to feminism and defectors in the battle for the betterment of women. Finally, some people undoubtedly found that participants' transsexualism brought up some of their own gender instabilities and wanted to disown any such possibilities for themselves by denying them to others.

People who helped and supported participants during their transition years fell roughly into three camps. In the first place, there were those

people who were longstanding close friends to participants. Love and loyalty seemed to propel them to tolerance and empathy. In many cases, they
had long been witness to participants' trials at being women and thus were
cognizant of participants' motivations for deciding that transsexualism
offered them the answers which they needed. Acquaintances did not have
such background information on which to judge participants as individual
cases. If they were free of the kinds of credos mentioned above, and if they
had no personal reasons for feeling insecure in their own gender identities,
it would seem that they had every reason to exhibit tolerance as well. Finally, persons in positions of authority in participants' work and school
lives seemed to have been simply doing their jobs with compassion.

The fact that the overall picture given by participants was one of understanding and approbation should be taken as an indication that public
prejudice against differently gendered people is far from ubiquitous. However, a note of caution must also be observed. Participants, to their credit,
appeared to favour memories of their successes over more unpleasant ones.
Such optimism must be very helpful in overcoming the many obstacles
which transsexual persons must surmount. However, abuse and harassment were also part of their reality. Participants rose above them, as have
countless other victims of stigma and bigotry, but such persecution often
leaves scars behind. Some participants wore their scars proudly, others
learned to burrow deeper into their hiding places, but no one seriously
considered turning back because of them.

Summary and Commentary

Announcing oneself to families, friends, schoolmates, co-workers and
acquaintances as members of a highly stigmatized and usually invisible
minority must by definition be anxiety-producing. However, as anyone
who has ever faced the acknowledgment of such an identity in themselves
will know, once the stage of telling others has been reached, the hardest
part is probably past. I say probably because in some cases the results of
disclosure can be far reaching and devastating. However, participants reported very few cases wherein their coming out culminated in catastro-
phes for them. Rather, participants noted predominantly positive responses from the people in their lives.

Family members may initially have been mystified, outraged, hurt, or
astounded by participants' announcements of their transsexualism, but
most were able to find it within their hearts to acknowledge participants
as men and to go on. Once they had had opportunities to assimilate the
new perspective which participants asked of them, most family members
began to see the coherence of it. They, like participants, were able to look

back and piece together participants' histories in such ways as to make their futures as men appear consistent with their pasts as women and girls. The theoretical information about transsexualism which participants provided to them gave them some of the tools with which they built bridges between their older perceptions and their newer understandings. As well, family members realized that no matter what they might do, the women kin whom they had known were gone. Either they learned to accept participants as men or they lost them in their lives. A few of participants' family members chose to sever relations rather than capitulate, but most participants were able to report that their families eventually regrouped and moved on to other family crises.

People with less tenacious ties to participants were much more open to the possibility that if they didn't like what participants were doing, they could distance themselves from participants. In some cases, their attachments to a particular set of values took precedence over any loyalty which they might have felt toward participants. In some people's minds, what participants were doing set them apart from others so much that the usual norms of human decency were no longer applicable. Participants suffered from the loathsome behaviours of only a few such people.

More often than not, friends and acquaintances at school and at work displayed compassion and decency toward participants around the times of their transitions. Surely, having a person change gender before their eyes must have been an unsettling and unaccustomed feeling for these people. To their credit, most took responsibility for their own adjustments and learned with time to see participants as men. Special credit must also be given to those participants who, through choice or necessity, remained present in the lives of their friends and acquaintances. Their stalwart perseverance in the face of both benign and abusive ignorance not only served themselves and their colleagues but also paved the way for those who might come after them. By forcing open some minds and hearts to make more space for themselves to live their day-to-day lives in peace, participants also made room for untold others whose gender presentations were somehow anomalous. By their inability or refusal to quietly start their lives over as men, they may have forfeited some of their recourse to unmarked manhood, but they also earned places as unsung local heroes. Their small skirmishes helped to advance the struggle for greater tolerance, understanding, and acceptance of all transgendered people.

21 | Are We There Yet?

Despite media reports which might imply otherwise, female-to-male sex reassignment has never been an in today, out tomorrow kind of affair. Not only do hormone treatments usually take months to produce noticeable changes, but surgical transformations are, of necessity, piecemeal and spread over many months or years. Moreover, most participants in this study declined to purchase genital reconstructive surgeries. Those who did acquire the latest surgically produced approximation of penises found themselves in possession of organs which left much to be desired. They could not be exposed at urinals, in locker rooms or hot tubs, at doctor's offices, or in sexual encounters without explanations. Thus even those participants who grasped every method of virilizing themselves which was within their reach still had to accept that they were unlikely to ever be men whose maleness was self-evident beyond the shadow of doubt. Unlike other men, they could not simply rely on the possession of a penis as the marker of manhood. Nor could they be satisfied with facile abstractions about postmodern symbolic phalluses. They were men, but they were men either without penises or with phalluses purchased from plastic surgeons.

Nevertheless, few participants appeared to be uncertain about their own status as men or as males. When so proclaiming themselves, most participants used the terms for sex statuses (male and female) interchangeably with those for gender statuses (men and women), as is commonly done by most members of society at large. Moreover, with the exception of those participants who were not living as men, only eight participants qualified their claims to manhood in any way.[1] Those who did either specified a difference between their sexes and their genders or laid claim to a third sex called transsexual. Simon and Fred both made the distinction that they were female sexed but "male gendered." Fred explained this position:

> From my perspective, I have always been male. I can't say that I've ever seen myself as anything other than male. From the physical standpoint, I'm female. From everyone else's viewpoint, other than intimate relationships I've had with women, they have seen me as female. Of course, the women that I've dated did not see me as female. As far as I'm con-

cerned, yes, I've always been male. The reality of it is, physically, I'm female.

Ed, Walter, and Peter saw themselves as belonging to an intermediate sex called transsexual. Ed and Walter seemed to feel alright about that status, whereas Peter was resentful. Ed's comment was "I see myself as male but I'll always see myself as transsexual too because it's just an experience that's always with you. . . . And, you know, I don't see it as a negative. If anything, I see it as more of a plus." From a slightly different viewpoint, Walter announced, "I'm biologically female, I mean, there's no escaping that. But, you know, I'm a female-to-male transsexual." Walter also made a distinction between femaleness and womanhood when he said, "No matter what genitals I have, I'm not a woman." Peter, like many other participants, denied ever having been female, but he did not see himself as male:

> I don't know that I ever thought that I truly was [female] but, at some point in time, I said you're not even going to get to call me this. . . . I'm getting to the point where I hate the word "transsexual." It's a label, and I don't like it. I also don't like "F-to-M." It implies that there really was something else that I don't really feel, I've never been comfortable with. . . . There's a real bitter pill to swallow.

Bruce appeared to have very mixed feelings about within which gender boundaries he wanted to live. He retained both a strong attachment to his lesbian past and a profound uncertainty about joining the ranks of men. As did Ed and Walter, Bruce would have preferred to have found a niche somewhere between genders and between sexes. Bruce identified the issues which were prominent for him:

> I'm a lesbian man. . . . I'm very committed to the lesbian movement. I'm very committed to women. And to their struggle in this life. I just happened to be born with tits. And I feel like, and I'll be real honest with you, I feel like a third gender. I feel like I don't have to have a penis to get through life. But I can't have tits. . . . I never used to look in the mirror. Now I shave every other day. . . . I look in the mirror at myself, I'm proud of myself. I have something to do with my face besides put mascara on.
>
> So I feel like I'm a third gender. And I think that twenty years from now they will discover the third gender. There will be somebody that says, "Yes, it's okay to have both sets of genitals, or to function normally in life or to have both identities." . . . But for right now, I have to be a transsexual man because there is no place for me as a third gender. . . .
>
> I would like to be able to not have to be a man. I would like to be able to be a lesbian without tits. But I can't. . . . I would like not to be on hormones because they're harmful to my body. I would like not to have

lower surgery. I would like to keep my libido. I would like not to have tits which is what I don't have. I would like to be able to shave. Although I can't without the hormones. So it's like I want the best of all these different worlds. It's very difficult. So I sort of have to pick what is available to make it acceptable. I can't be to my child her daddy and her mommy at the same time. I don't want to be her mother. I want to be her father. But I take a shower with her and I don't have a penis. . . . I feel like I have two people inside of me fighting to be one and I'm saying, "Do I have to compromise one for the other? Do I have to give up being one for the other?" I have to.

Bruce's dilemma raised two interesting sets of questions. The first set queried when female-to-male transsexuals actually become men. Is it a matter of outward appearances in the social world? Do they cross over when they begin to show the effects of hormones? What surgeries are definitive? Or is the dividing line more properly located somewhere in the psyches of the individuals involved? The other set pointed to by Bruce's quandary is whether female-to-male transsexuals are, can be, or might want to be neither, or both, females/women and males/men. I broached both of these topics with a majority of participants.[2]

Although most participants who were living as men agreed that they were males, when asked how they determined their own gender and sex statuses and those of other female-to-male transsexuals, they drew various lines of demarcation between being female and being male. Ten participants denied ever having been truly women or females. They did so even though their bodies may have displayed all the usual indicators of femaleness and they had lived as women.[3] Aaron and Jordie exemplified this position. Both retroactively discounted the significance of their female bodies in favour of using their mental states as the deciding factor in determining their maleness. Calling his sex "ambiguous," Aaron denied that female-to-male transsexuals ever have been female:

How can they stop being female if they've never been? They can stop looking female. They can stop acting female. They can stop trying to play the games as a female, and all this shit. But they can't stop being something they've never been.

In a similar vein, Jordie remarked, "I was never a woman. At one time I looked different, bulged in different places, but I was never a woman."

Most other participants readily admitted that they had been born female, no matter how unsuitable that had felt to them through most of their lives. But when asked to elaborate on when they thought that the transition from one sex to the other actually transpired, several participants seemed to hesitate, recognizing that the processes of female-to-male sex reassignment were far from perfectly aligned with the classifications within which society demanded that they function.

Darren, after initial difficulty with the question, ultimately voted for hormone treatments as being the crucial step. But he hedged his answer by pointing out the limitations of the language available for discussing these topics.

> Talking about the physiological level, I think when I started male hormones and the first effects were coming through. That was sort of the goodbye to the old and come in the new. 'Cause the male hormones are very dramatic and very visible. . . . There can be an overlap from a physiological point of view. . . .
>
> I'd also like to say that I think we're getting into semantical traps here, and I don't know what the way out of it is. . . . Words and labels are sometimes meaningless, or don't convey the appropriate meaning. They're not always useful tools, although they're the only tools we have. . . . This stuff transcends this so-called semantical and rational level. That's why a lot of . . . the stuff I'm saying is totally meaningless, because it can't really be conveyed. . . . I can't even understand this on an intellectual or rational level. . . . That's why I guess I find it so fascinating. Because it's totally inexplicable to me. Even though I've lived through it.

Keith was able to credit that there were socially meaningful differences between men and women, but he argued that the only real differences between men and women were in the attributions made by others. According to his views, the only reason for sex reassignment was that it was the only way for females to live their lives legitimately in those ways which society reserves for people who are deemed to be men:

> The acceptance of other people of me as a male rather than as a female is the argument in favour which made me go through with it. . . . That's really the only reason for a sex change because if a person was biologically a female and had not gone through the sex change, and they were able to be completely accepted by society as a male, then there would be no reason for them to go through any physical changes to be accepted as a male. I'm talking about in every way: by their lover, by their friends, by business associates, just by society in general. . . . The thing that makes a person a man is the perception that they have of themselves as well as the perceptions of other people, and if this female-to-male transsexual is perceiving himself to be a man, and also is passable, and others are perceiving him to be a man, then he is a man.

Stan and Luther agreed that society would not allow female-to-male transsexuals or anyone else to live openly as men with female bodies. According to Stan,

That's a society rule. In society we're forced to pick. And if it weren't for . . . society . . . they could be a person that "some days . . . I feel more feminine, some days I feel more masculine. I feel like doing things the men are doing. I feel like taking care of children with the women." . . . You've got to make up your mind and decide. . . . The people around you . . . need consistencies. . . .

Actually, I've been neither. I really don't feel a part of either camp. Even now. I'm different. . . . I was never a woman. Being female. That's a little bit trickier there. . . . Boy, it's a shame that it comes back to this feedback issue, but it does. When you're constantly reminded that you're female, it's real hard to not be female. . . . And it is a process. . . . It took me a while to let go of the female stuff. . . . It's just like any phase of growth . . . it's a percentage thing that the percentage just gets higher and higher. . . . As a person becomes more mature, can they maintain their femaleness and then grow in maleness. I think that just takes a bigger person, a bigger heart. But you could keep both.

Luther railed against the simplistic dualistic division of humanity into only two genders or two sexes that was forcing people to make choices which went against their inner dispositions.

This gender stuff is just outrageous. Why must it be? Why must it really be? There are some of us, like myself, who are going to have to make that change, but some people are being forced into the change because no one has a place for them. They just can't be. And so, they're forced either to be transsexual or homosexual or heterosexual. They can't just be "sexual." . . . We just have to let folks alone to be what they want to be. . . .

People are upset and miserable and lonely all the time . . . because people are "You have to be this, and you have to be that." If you comb your hair in a certain way . . . just a slight part of the hair, and the whole world changes. That's it. Boy. Girl. Life is set. Amen. It's stupid. . . . I don't want to hear all this madness. There's something deeper here than what somebody looks like.

Ron also seemed angry that society demanded that humanity be halved by gender and by sex. He complained of gender as a disruptive force in social relations.

So, basically, the way I feel about gender is, to me, there are no differences. . . . For me, it's just an emotional . . . and physical thing that I have to do. . . . My feelings are, or my politics, are more androgynous. . . . It was part of the change too. There's just a realization that it doesn't mean dick whether you're a woman or a man. You know, it doesn't mean anything to what's in here. . . .

If society were a different place, we could be both at the same time. Like, just people. Like that's my idea. . . . When I relate to people, I usually don't relate to their gender at all. And even with the change . . .

sometimes, it annoys me even when somebody calls me "sir." . . . Just not make a mention of gender, because it's divisive. . . . I like both. It's just that a lot of the qualities that I'm living, like for this society, they're male. . . . It's just the body feeling that I have. . . . In this society . . . physically, I need my body to be male instead of female. Psychologically, I wish we'd all honour both our aspects, and then there'd be a lot less hardships, a lot less denial.

Brian argued that gender is entirely a social construction with which members of society have to live, then made a plea for the separation of gender and sex in everyday life.

There is no universally accepted, absolute definitions of man, woman, or transsexual. These are all achieved by manipulation of definitions. The person is quite free to choose to impose whatever arbitrary rule one wishes, then define that as a limitation to justify the behaviour one attributes to oneself. As one becomes a more self-realized, self-confident, experienced, and mature individual, the definitions of male and female will fall more outside oneself and have to be dealt with as a part of the current historical sociocultural milieu in which we find ourselves.

We have to take these attitudes and beliefs seriously, and according to what is in our best self-interest, while recognizing that they are changeable and changing over time. If we choose, we can actively try to define and influence the growth of new cultural values that will bring about historical changes. Such proselytizing isn't required of us, but we should critically acknowledge the factors influencing our beliefs about ourselves and others. . . .

Gonadal function doesn't define true manhood. . . . I wish there was a well-defined gender that was entirely free of gonadal sex and the biochemical oppressions that accompany sexes and genders in the interest of animal reproduction.

A strong undercurrent runs through the emotionally charged words of this small group of participants. The point seems to be that they resented having to mark their genders or sexes in an either/or fashion. They seem to have felt cheated by dualistic notions of gender and sex which were imposed upon them by the social worlds in which they lived. They wanted to be able to mix and blend genders and sexes in creative ways which would more accurately reflect their own unique dispositions. Instead, they each had felt compelled to choose to live in the gendered social slots which most closely approximated the lives which they really would preferred to have led. Thus, although they may not have whole-heartedly wanted to do so, they marched across the gender divide.

Those participants who were able to specify points of transition from female to male gave answers which referred both to issues of self-perception and identity[4] and to distinctions based on physiognomy.[5] Walter made use of the distinction between sex and gender to build his case for man-hood being a state of mind. He used one criterion for social gender and another for physical sex. He explained how he thought it worked:

> I never had the desperate feeling that I had to change my body as soon as possible. . . . I'm a man and that's it. . . . When you decide you're a man, you're a man. When you're committed to being a man, you're a man. When you're living as a man, you're a man. You don't have to compromise. Because the fact is that you don't have to be physically male to be a man. . . . I feel strongly that no matter what your body is, you are a man. Even though I'm legally still female, I'm a man, and that's it. And if anybody tries to argue with me, woe unto them. . . .
>
> Strictly on a physical basis, it would have to be after you've had the minimum of surgery. After you've removed your uterus, the feminine breast. . . . In other words, once you've done something physically to get yourself in line. . . . It depends on the individual. There's plenty of women who have hysterectomies who are not male. But for a transsexual, I think that hysterectomy is the big one. Like, you could say after the hysterectomy that yes, that person is male. Physically and legally.

Ron and Terry agreed with Walter on the psychic aspects of sex changes. Ron claimed that all it takes to be a man is "saying, 'I'm a man.'" Terry's opinion was that "a female-to-male transsexual stops being a female and starts being a male when your inner self tells you that you are male. It does not matter what your body tells you." Grant likewise claimed that female-to-male transsexuals stop being female and become male "whenever you feel you have stopped."

Although Hal agreed that self-identity was sufficient to qualify a person as a man, he also made interesting connections between the personal identity concerns of female-to-male transsexuals and the contingencies of living among other people.

> I don't know what makes a person a man. I think if a person feels that they're a man, then they can be a man . . . for themselves. For everyone else, I think you need to give them a lot of clues. The body is a clue. I think that if people are born with certain bodies, that they get treated in certain ways and they adapt in certain ways. . . . I think you can be a man without that body. Now, whether or not you're going to get perceived that way is another matter. . . . I think you can be perceived that way without the right body. Because as far as genitalia go, it's very rare that you see someone else's genitalia. So, yes, I think a person, if they want to be perceived as a man can do so.

Those participants who considered the division between female and male to rest more firmly in the body fell roughly into two camps. Only two participants believed that the overall look of the body was the salient factor;[6] the majority counted reproductive capacities as the essential marker of sex.[7] Only Dale stated that female-to-male transsexuals were not male until they had completed masculinizing genital reconstruction surgery. Participants' comments on this subject were sparse and provided little explanation as to why they chose their positions.

Ron and Luther were among the few who elaborated. Ron credited hormone therapy with being the key step because "there's no way back. . . . that cancels any kind of cop-out . . . because after hormones everything is different than you ever thought it was." Speaking from the other position, Luther discounted the effects of hormone treatments and mastectomies as "window dressings." He suggested quite strongly that reproductive capacities were the deciding factor ending femaleness and allowing female-to-male transsexuals to claim their maleness.

When participants argued that the states of their minds were more important than the states of their bodies, they were more loquacious. The idea that bodies determine sexes and genders is so taken-for-granted that it needs no justification, whereas any suggestion to the contrary must be well fortified if it is to stand up against criticism. Furthermore, it is worthy of note that those participants who commented on this question were almost evenly split between the two points of view. That is to say, their stances mirrored both those of specialized medical analysts of transsexualism and those of society at large. From one side, they insisted that they were men if, in their minds, they otherwise could find no peace. From the other direction came the categorical demand that men must have identifiably male bodies. The two approaches intersected at the issue of when participants felt able to say, "Today, I am a man."

Conventional wisdom said that they had to have male bodies in order to be men, whereas the best of medical wisdom told them that for the foreseeable future that was to remain beyond their reach. Thus some participants compromised by staking their manhoods on their identities while doing what they could, post haste, to bolster their assertions with physical transformations. Other participants settled for thinking, "I should be a male, but I'm not one yet," until they no longer felt female and then compromised on the issue of having fully male bodies. They accepted partially masculinized bodies which had been stripped of their femaleness as adequate to make them men.

Some participants made another kind of compromise. They believed that it was possible for one person to be both a man and a woman. One-third of the twenty-four participants who gave their opinion on this issue[8] denied that anyone but intersexual people could be men and women at the same time. However, they were willing to concede that they were men who had once lived as females, women, or girls.[9] Another one-third felt that being a man and a woman at the same time was a stage through which some female-to-male transsexuals pass while they are in transition.[10] Still other participants (12.5 percent) thought that being both genders was a more or less permanent condition of their own lives and the lives of their fellow female-to-male transsexuals.[11] A few participants (12.5 percent) thought of themselves as neither gender.[12]

Dale's position typified that of the eight participants who proposed that only intersexual people can be both men and women at the same time. However, Dale did grant that he had been a woman before and a man after sex reassignment. Dale explained how and when he had been sequentially both a woman and a man:

> [A man and a woman] are two different people. Their anatomy is the difference. . . . [I was] a man and a woman at different times by sex reassignment. . . . Here, you receive a birth certificate stating you are a male after final completion of the male penis and testicles. . . . Once you receive your certificate, you are a recognized male. Some places will not issue this birth certificate but that does not mean you are not a male.

Harry experienced his transition period as one during which he oscillated between being a man and being a woman. He seemed to accept this "difficult" condition with equilibrium and as a simple matter of fact. Harry never felt himself to be a man and a woman in the same instant, but neither did he remember his transition as steadily incremental. In fact, most participants went through similar stages during which they only intermittently passed as men. However, not all of them interpreted those periods of their lives in the same light as did Harry. Harry described what it was like for him:

> I'm thinking in the strictly social sense, and, for me, no, I have not been both at the same time. I am constantly bouncing back and forth between the two. . . . I'm not the female . . . that I was before. She's gone. I am male now. . . . It was gradual. . . . I mean, for a while I was living here in [one city], surrounding myself completely with people who saw me strictly as male. Then I'd go to [another city], and I was surrounded strictly by people who saw me as female. . . . And it was a difficult thing. . . . The point at which I stopped being female is related to how other people see me. . . . I know it happened when people would say "she" and I didn't react . . . or I didn't even know that they were talking about me. . . . Then I knew that the integration was more complete.

Grant talked about how he thought that everyone had the potential to enact aspects of two genders:

> There is androgyny. It's like there is male and female in everyone. There is someone we know . . . [who] is both male and female at the same

time. And I don't understand how it is, but that's the way that she reso-
nates to me. . . . It is a possibility. . . . I think somewhere inside [of me]
there's a Suzie Homemaker dying to get out, but it's not going to
happen!

At one time I was very confused. I, in sexual fantasy, had to, for a
while, perceive myself as female to be "normal." And it's a matter of
when I came to terms with who I am, it stopped. . . . I've always been
male, but I was trying to fit in. . . . And it was confusing as hell to me.
It was not pleasant. But . . . this happened quite a while before the hormone shots and the whole understanding of transsexualism.

Eight (33 percent) of the twenty-four participants who commented on
the subject said that they thought that they or other transsexual people
went through an intermediate stage wherein they were both genders and
sexes at once. To these participants, it was almost paradigmatic that transsexual people must spend large portions of their lives being both women
and men in the body of one person.

Walter explained, with impeccable logic, that persons who are transsexual have to be able to acclimatize themselves to the cognitive dissonance of believing themselves to be members of one gender and sex while
living in bodies which usually designate the other gender and sex. According to him, it was a natural condition of transsexualism to be able to sustain this apparent contradiction.

That's what being a transsexual is, is knowing that you can be a man
and have those other body parts. So I believe that one can adjust to it, if
you're healthy. . . . But, in the meantime, there's still that vestige there.
And it would undoubtedly make one feel more complete to go as far as
one can.

Phil, Alan, and Ken made recourse to the classic definition of transsexualism in their reasoning. They said that they had been men trapped in
women's bodies, hence both genders at the same time. Ken elaborated:

Can a person be both a man and a woman . . . at the same time? I want
to say no, but during the transition, especially for a transsexual, as the
physical changes are taking place, mental changes take place too. And I
think it's hard to separate those two. At different times in one lifetime?
Yes, before [and after] surgery. There's a lot of people that stop in the
middle of surgery. . . . And then where are you?

Have I been both a man and a woman? Yes. I was a man trapped in
a woman's body for a long time. My thoughts were male. My chest was
female. . . . I lived as a male for some time, but I still had those female
organs, and I knew that. There was just something there. They were
hanging on to me. I think the surgery does make the difference.

Bill also emphasized that being both a man and a woman at the same time was a normal part of the transsexual transition process.

> One can be both a man and a woman. I think most transsexuals experience this state in some part of transition. . . . I think it is accomplished through an acceptance of ambiguity, or role flexibility. . . . But I still believe that beneath it all there must be a core sense of gender identity which constantly struggles to find a means of expression. Once that is successfully accomplished, then, and only then, can one be comfortable in expressing oneself as both a man and a woman. . . . I have been and still am both. . . . [But] I am only comfortable with myself as having female components since I have fully lived and expressed myself as a male. . . . S/he stops being female when she chooses to. . . . He becomes male when he can say to himself with full awareness that he is male and knows it in his heart to be at the core of his truth in being.

Although all participants would probably agree that they had felt more or less as these participants described, they did not all concur that they *were* men until they could either successfully pass or, more likely, until their bodies had been extensively altered. Once again, the question comes to the issue of how much corporal evidence is required to merit the title of man or of male.

As Bill's comments implied, several participants recognized that they retained female or womanly remnants even after they became men. Bruce's point of view on this issue was that female-to-male transsexuals never actually stop being women even though they may also become men. Thus, to Bruce, transsexual men remain both women and men even after their transitions. Bruce, however, felt that his opinion was a renegade one which he could not articulate in the presence of other female-to-male transsexuals for fear of raising their ire. Bruce put forth his perspectives this way:

> I've been growing into becoming a man. I just didn't all of a sudden decide to be one, and I am. It's been a process of growing to become this other person. And I thought . . . hormones, and I'm a man. But no, it doesn't work that way. There's a whole personality change that takes place. There's a bonding that takes place with men. There's a whole thing that you have to learn. There's manners. There's ways that men talk and move, and it's learning all over again all these different ways to do things. . . . It's a misconception that one shot of hormones is going to make you a man. . . .
>
> An F-to-M stops being a woman when they deny who they are. See, I think the reality is, you are born physically a woman. You come into the world as a woman . . . and I think that you need to come to terms with that part of you, and then move on. . . . I don't think I'll ever stop being a woman. I could never say this in my support group. . . . But I don't think you ever stop becoming a woman. Physically you might, but I

think that there's these imprints in your character and your personality that carry over from being this person after thirty years of being that way. . . . You're always becoming a man. It's a process. . . . You never make it. . . . Not for me. But I'd never say that in my support group. . . . Or to any other men, I'd never say that. I've told you more than I've told anybody.

Gary, like Bruce, postulated that female-to-male transsexuals always retain some of their womanhood within them.

All of us have both inside of us even though most try to keep it in the background. . . . I think you are both all your life. . . . I may look more male, physically, but I still keep my femininity with me because if I didn't I wouldn't be myself. What I mean is that both are in me and I don't want to lose either one. Physically, [female-to-male transsexuals stop being female and become male] when most of the operations are done; but emotionally, never. . . . But you do start to be more male to try to fit in.

Aaron, who resolutely maintained that he had never been female, took the position that all people's personalities are made up of a blend of gender characteristics.

I think everybody is both male and female in their personality, and their likes and dislikes, and roles, and everything. I think anybody who is totally one or the other is probably very unhappy, and rather sick. Very limited. I don't know if I could be happy just being a man. . . . And I don't think you can be both. . . . When it comes to identity, you can only be one or the other. That's black and white. . . . I see myself as a gentle man with an awful lot of female characteristics.

Hal took a similar position, though more abstractly:

You can do it physically because there are people who have very physical characteristics of both. . . . I also think that . . . there's a continuum. You may manifest closer to one side than the other, but that doesn't mean you don't have qualities, or even that you don't understand what the other is, so that you can move in between to choose to accentuate certain psychological characteristics.

The feelings and beliefs communicated by the thirty-one participants who commented on their shifting gender and sex statuses conveyed a less-than-perfect congruence between the apparent trajectories of their lives as female-to-male transsexuals and their stances vis-à-vis the meanings of gender and sex in their worlds. Twenty-seven of the thirty-one were living as men at the times of their interviews, but only a little more than half of them (56 percent) unequivocally pronounced themselves to be men or males.[13] Another one-third of participants identified themselves in ways which recognized that they were men or males who retained some of their womanhood or femaleness.[14] In addition, Peter, Aaron, and Stan said that they felt like they were neither men nor women, males nor females. Thus 41 percent of the participants who discussed these questions indicated some ambivalence about the thoroughness of the transsexual process. For some participants, this seemed like an advantage; for others, it was a drawback.

These widespread observations by participants about the inconclusiveness of their transitions may have been simply reflections of the realities and limitations of medical technologies. They may also capture dissatisfactions which participants felt about their progress through the stages of their own transitions. However, because this group of twenty-seven participants averaged 6.4 years past the commencement of hormone therapy, it would seem safe to assume that many of them had at least had sufficient time to have become fully integrated into their everyday worlds as men. In order to probe this issue further, I asked most of these participants how satisfied they were with their lives as men, whether being a man was a perfect fit, and whether they might prefer some gender other than the ones that they knew.

A sizable majority (68 percent)[15] of the twenty-five participants who made their opinions known said that they were happy being men and that they had little or no interest in any other gender configuration for themselves.[16] Despite misgivings, being men was a more rewarding enterprise for them than not. Phil summed up these sentiments: "I wouldn't want to be something else if there were more than two genders. And it's not that I wanted to be male; it's that I am male, and I always was."

Most participants didn't need to dig any deeper. As Ken said,

> If there were more genders, what would I be? I'd be male. There's no ifs, ands, or buts. . . . There's no question of that. Yes, being a man is a perfect fit for me. It's something that I've always wanted. It's natural now. Sometimes I have some self-doubts. Not about being male, but how to go about it.

Steven did not even want to consider any other possibilities.

> I hope to God there's no more genders. I like being a man. I wouldn't choose being anything but. . . . I don't know that I would even want to have to deal with any more genders, because that just makes the world even more confusing, and more trying to understand things that I can't even understand of what we have in this world. So, I'm perfectly content being a man. I think being a man is a perfect fit for me. I feel comfortable about myself. I like the way I'm related to. I like the opportunities I'm afforded. And I like the responsibilities I have. . . . The only limita-

tions I really feel at this point in my life are the intimacies that I can't enjoy. And the part of me that I can't truly divulge. That's where I feel my limitation.

Bill thought that being a man was a perfect fit but had a little different perspective on why. He asserted that his manhood was enriched by his past as a woman.

> Being the man I am is a perfect fit for me. It's a perfect fit because I let myself be a man who was once a woman and that makes me a better person because it has helped me find integration.

A number of participants had complaints about what kinds of men they had become. What they complained about most frequently were the ways in which their reconstructed bodies were less than perfect but as Hal realistically quipped, "It's a perfect fit in an imperfect world."

Howie listed ways that living as a man was a "perfect fit" except for the fact that he had not been born to it:

> Being a man is a much better fit than being a woman, It's hard to say if it's perfect, though. If I had been raised male, it would have been perfect. But being female for twenty-seven years and then becoming male, it doesn't feel like a "perfect fit" because there's a boyhood I was cheated out of, and I missed a lot of experiences that would have made me a more confident, self-assured man today. Adolescence and teen years are so different for boys and girls. I didn't fit into either category. Because there's so much I can't relate to with guys my age, that makes the fit less than perfect and at times it makes it quite lacking.
>
> I'd be a man with working genitals and be able to father children. And I wouldn't have any bitterness, resentment, or sadness about being born the wrong gender. I could live in my old hometown (or anywhere) without worrying about who I'm going to bump into who knew me before. I'd be just a "regular guy" without surgeries hanging over my head. The children I have with my wife would be mine biologically, not from some stranger.

Brian objected to the entire sex/gender social system. He definitely thought that living as a man was the best option available to him, but he also looked forward to a society less concerned with sex as a defining feature of gender.

> Living as a man is the best way for me to survive in this world, to minimize the crippling effects of sexual discrimination. I can better get on with a truer expression of life, free my time and resources to more rewarding interests and creative goals, unburdened of a constant struggle with social condemnation for not behaving according to their rules about body definition. In a better world, sociocultural values would

promote positive human potentials, would be free of any form of prejudice that imposed discriminatory limitation of psychological, social, legal support to any subgroup based on factors of birth over which an individual can have no self-determining free choice or control.

A sizable minority (32%) of the twenty-five participants responded that they would have preferred some other gender options or that they were unhappy with the fit between their personalities and their gender statuses as men.[17] When participants noted that they were less than happy with being men it was not because they wanted to return to living as women. They lived as men because it was the best option available to them under their life conditions. Participants who expressed wavering satisfaction with their manhood only did so in the context of wishing that there were other genders for them to explore. For example, Stan said that living as a man was a "better fit" than living as a woman, but he allowed that if there were an intermediate gender available, "I think I could try something in between."

Darren was one of several participants who were attracted to the idea of a multiplicity of genders. He would have liked to have been more than just a straight man if he could have done so without becoming a "freak."

> I wanted to have clones so I could be a gay male, a lesbian woman, a straight man—never a straight woman, for some reason that didn't quite click. . . . So, I would like to be all those things. . . . From an intellectual point of view, I'd probably want to be an androgyne. That would probably combine the two. But I only want to be that if there was a social niche. Because I don't want to be an outcast. If there was like these shamans. Like a shaman is sort of both. That's probably what I'd want to be. As long as I was comfortable physically and psychologically.

Harry was eagerly looking forward to the day when there would be more gender and sex choices than just two of each. He used science fiction models to help him to imagine what such a future might be like.

> I think something else would suit me better. . . . I think that the male and female biological states are a choice—I was going to say a bad choice, but it's just a . . . creative choice that was made, that I think will soon outrun its time. I don't know what the new one would be. I'd be just as interested to find out myself. . . .
>
> I don't like to limit myself, and I haven't come up with any specific ideas . . . in what the alternatives are . . . As an example . . . one of my favorite writers, Samuel Delany, he does a lot of science fiction fooling around with the sexes. He'll have multiple sexes and some with no sex. . . . I don't know specifics, but . . . I think this . . . male and female is running out. And I'd be glad to see that happen.

Bruce explained that he already felt like a third gender, even though he could not live that way. He wished that he could remain as a lesbian, but he also felt the need to live as a man because of the therapeutic value he derived from remaking his gender.

> I like the way I look. I like the way my body's changing. Today. I don't say that's for everyone. But for me, I don't think I would be here [otherwise]. [Being a man] . . . fits fine. It's a nice fit. But I have no problem with being seen as someone who was a woman in the past.

Gary and Ron were also less than totally at peace with living as men. Both remarked that they were perfectly happy living in the bodies of men but, as Gary put it, "not so much emotional, because I still like my feminine qualities." Ron explained his frustration:

> Q: Is male a perfect fit? A: Physically, I couldn't imagine another one. . . . I think I'm a fairly balanced person, and that I'm very much a person who appreciates qualities of both genders, and recognizes shortfalls of both genders. Psychologically I just don't buy into a lot of the things. I just don't feed into a lot of the things. Because I don't consider them male, I consider them patriarchy. Patriarchy rules . . . every area of your life, and everything that comes out of me has to be so calculated.

In sum, participants were not without critical perspective on the scope of their gender and sex changes. They were fully cognizant of the inevitability of imperfections in their transitions which resulted from technological and personal limitations, and limitations in social systems predicated on binary divisions of gender and sex. Some participants embraced the inconsistencies in their gendered lives as sources of inspiration and strength. They recognized that all the years which they had lived as women or girls were far from lost to them. Rather, they were able to call upon those years as resources with which to enrich themselves as men. Having been girls, women, and transsexual seemed for some participants to act as a hidden well of insight and fortitude.

Summary and Commentary

Participants came to their lives as men having survived some of the greatest personal identity challenges possible. They looked into their hearts and souls and found that how they experienced themselves did not match the bodies to which they were born. After years of doing what they could to live in ways which were socially condoned for persons with female bodies, they exhausted both themselves and their possibilities. Sometimes in despair, sometimes in desperation, sometimes with great hope, and always with a dash of serendipity, participants found out that there was a name for, and a promise of release from, the discomfort which they felt within their own skins.

Once they realized that they might be transsexual, participants searched libraries, the popular media, and their own intimate lives in the course of concluding that they were, indeed, transsexual. A few participants, at the times of their last interviews, were working out what to do about their transsexual identities. However, most participants did enter into transforming themselves into men.

As they left behind their lives as women, they could step away from some people and entanglements, but not all. Family and close friends were not easily abandoned. Co-workers, schoolmates, and other acquaintances of necessity were observers during some parts of participants' transitions. Bureaucracies of various orders needed to be informed and relied upon for cooperation. Fortunately, most participants found that few people dedicated themselves to making participants' lives any more difficult than they already were. In most cases, participants could either absent themselves from people who were so disposed, or the actions of their detractors were more than balanced by those of sympathetic and kindly others.

Overall, participants reported general satisfaction with the lives they came to lead as men and with the bodies in which they lived them. They readily discussed the hardships through which they had come and the deficiencies in the transformations wrought by medical technologies. Furthermore, they were often quite candid about their retention of many characteristics from their lives as women. Some participants seemed chagrined that they were not indistinguishable from men who were born and raised in male bodies. Other participants appeared to think that their prior sojourns as females in the worlds of women had made them better men than most.

The consensus among those participants who had lived as men seemed to be that whatever the drawbacks of who they had become, no better option was available for them. Some yearned for social statuses as yet unformed, for niches in an altogether revamped social order, but none wanted to live again as women. They may have loved, respected, and admired women more than many men who had never lived as women, but they felt those emotions as men. There was no going back.

PART VI

Life after Transition

Michael Hernandez

22 | Nature's Calls
Toilet Traumas and
Medical Necessities

At the time that they were interviewed, thirty-seven participants were living as men.[1] Four participants lived as men but had not undergone any form of breast surgery.[2] Twelve participants still retained their female internal reproductive organs.[3] Six participants had undergone virilizing genital surgeries.[4]

Whatever their differences, all thirty-seven participants who were living as men could move more or less freely through their everyday worlds. Those people who had not undergone breast surgeries could take special care to disguise their breasts and to prevent people from casually touching them in ways which might arouse suspicions. When successful at such subterfuge, they could live as completely as men in their public lives as did their less encumbered brothers. Under such conditions, participants were free to move through many aspects of their lives as men without having to make explanations for the states of their bodies. The greater the degree of their masculinization, the larger became their zones of freedom from their past lives as women and as females, but none were all-encompassing.

Thus participants had little to say about their everyday lives as men beyond the period during which they were first learning to live as men. For most participants, their days of passing were numbered in months rather than years. Once they had learned the tricks of living day to day as men, they simply proceeded with the lives they had planned for themselves. Within the spheres of their everyday lives, they ceased being transsexual and became simply men. As women, most of them had been unusually masculine women who did not fit well within their assigned genders. As men, they became remarkable or unremarkable on the merits of their personalities and accomplishments rather than on the basis of their gender presentations. They held down jobs, socialized with friends, did community work, practiced their religions, took lovers. Some of them married; a few became fathers through donor insemination to their partners or stepfathers through liaisons with women who already had children. In all of these everyday ways, they were simply men.

There were, however, three main areas in which all participants who lived as men were reminded of their transsexualism no matter what their stage of physical transition: in public toilets, in doctors' examination rooms, and in sexual intimacies. These were areas of their lives wherein they were required to expose those parts of their bodies which proclaimed them to be other than physiologically average males. With a certain amount of ingenuity or discipline, any or all of these situations could be avoided. However, the sidestepping of these three areas could come at some cost to participants' short- or long-term comfort, health, or happiness. Sooner or later, all participants who lived as men had to confront these rends in the fabric of their lives as men.

Toilet Traumas

The most superficial but persistent arena to manage was the somewhat messy issue of public toilets. Public toilets had long posed problems for participants for several reasons. When they were living as women, many participants found that their rights to use women's public toilets were challenged by other users. Many participants were then already so masculine as women that Bruce's experience was a common one: "I used to go into the women's bathroom and they would scream and call for the guard. It was so embarrassing." These participants therefore began their explorations of men's lavatories already feeling disenfranchised.

When participants began to live as men and entered into men's public toilets, they encountered a different set of problems. In the first place, participants entered men's public toilets with little or no knowledge of how to behave. There were no manuals from which to study men's toilet habits. Participants were required to enter one of the few places in their worlds where women were forbidden to go, and once they were there, they needed to know how to go about their business quickly and without drawing attention to themselves. Commonly, participants were initially fearful that if they behaved inappropriately, they would expose themselves as impostors and be subjected to swift and violent retribution for their hubris.

Moreover, participants rapidly discovered to their dismay that men's public lavatory facilities usually consist of a combination of exposed urinals and a few stalls, which are often doorless. Thus participants were presented with the dilemma of whether to sit to urinate, often in full view of others, or to stand to urinate, without the usual equipment and always in full view of others. Of course, participants could alternatively arrange their comings and goings so that they only entered public lavatories which they had previously explored and found to provide satisfactory facilities. In that way, they could make use of only those facilities which they knew to have private stalls with doors which closed. They would thereby be able to avoid the anxiety producing exercise of attempting to urinate at a public urinal without exposing the true condition of their genitals. However, few people's lives are so predictable that such arrangements could become routine.

Participants had to resolve their "toilet trauma." Some participants sat in stalls when they needed to urinate. However, rightly or wrongly, many participants concluded that it would be considered abnormal by their fellows to urinate while seated in a stall, and they therefore refrained from using stalls unless their bodily functions left them no alternative. Those who determined that they would urinate standing like other men purchased or fashioned urinary assist devices which they could have ready-to-hand when they needed them. Most often these devices allowed participants to stand with other men but did not give the appearance of penises. Participants who sat in doorless stalls and those participants who stood and used such devices therefore relied, for the protection of their secrets, on the men's toilet etiquette which they had learned. That is, widespread homophobia and privacy concerns among men combine to dictate that men no more than casually glance at one another's genitals while standing at urinals unless they are cruising for sexual adventure. Thus if participants stayed out of toilets used by men for making sexual contacts and if they went about their urination quickly and unceremoniously, they found that they could relieve themselves in peace.

However, not all participants were able to subdue their anxieties completely. Ken, who had been living as a man for fourteen years and had been on masculinizing hormones for six years, said that "the restroom is still the only place I worry I may not pass."

Ed, who had been living as a man for sixteen years at the time of his last interview, also still felt uncomfortable in public toilets for men. His movements in public spaces had continued to be circumscribed by the size of his bladder and the architecture of men's lavatories. His comments were typical of those made by several other participants:

> And I think I do feel threatened by most males in, you know, in restroom situations. . . . It limits me a lot from going out in public and doing things because a lot of the men's restrooms like they don't have the doors on the stalls. And you know there are situations in places where you could get yourself killed if the wrong person walked by. So it's kind of hard. . . .
>
> I don't frequent any male-only places just because . . . if it's a male-only, then you know there's not going to be any stalls with doors or anything like that. And you know, you go into a restroom and you have the choice of a urinal or this toilet sitting out in the middle of everywhere, and it's kind of like, "Well, I really didn't have to go that bad." My bladder's bursting but, you know. You check out a lot of alleys. You

become real proficient at going behind dumpsters and that. It's amazing how desperate you can be to go to the bathroom and not be able to go. . . . Don't men have modesty? It really makes me wonder. I mean, it's like, "Give me a paper bag at least to put over my head."

Bruce, who had been living as a man for only one year, was considerably less tense about public toilets. He felt that he knew what to do in a variety of circumstances which might arise in men's lavatories. He provided these words of advice:

So, if you go into a bathroom, and you think that it's a questionable situation, you go in, and you start to go like you're going to take a shit. You sort of grunt, 'cause men do that when they go take a shit. . . . And you sort of mumble to yourself. And the thing is, that if you are in a place where there is one urinal, and a stall, that man is going to be out of that bathroom like fast if he knows you're taking a shit, 'cause he doesn't want to have to encounter the smell. So, this is a safeguard that I've learned. And it works every time. You just kind of go, "Oh, man. This diarrhea. You know what it's like, don't you?" . . . And he's out the door. Just the sort of thing you can't do in the women's room. . . .

They always have a newspaper in there. And . . . they're in there for fifteen minutes. Men get into taking a shit. And it's acceptable. Women, it's not. And they make all kinds of noises, and they smell up the bathroom, and they're talking to each other across the wall. They don't know who they're talking to. It's just this thing that men do. . . . And most men pee before they take a shit, so if they hear you peeing, it's just normal. . . .

Standing up and peeing, I use my little funnel. And nobody questions me. . . . You gotta go, and so you go and you leave. Most men don't wash their hands either. That's another thing you should know. Men rarely wash their hands. . . . But I want to tell you that not all men are that gross.

Walter had been living as a man for approximately ten years and had been on hormone therapy for the last four of those years. He too had carefully studied men's toilet habits as part of his self-education into the ways of men. He concluded that there is a wide range of toilet behaviours among men and that he need not feel shy or self-conscious about his own technique.

There's this one bathroom out at the mall. . . . And on the first stall, there's a peephole. This is so amazing. I've learned so much from just observing men. Like observing them going to the bathroom, observing them masturbating, just watching how they hold their penises, what they do with their penises. In the first stall, you can sit on the toilet, and then . . . there's about ten urinals. . . . And you can watch the urinals, and the hole is placed so that there could be ten guys pissing at once, and you would be able to see them all, because of the perspective involved. It's amazing. I've really observed a lot. I really am into watching because I learn so much.

For a few participants, using public men's toilets presented no problem at all. For them, in fact, it was easier than using women's public toilets had ever been. Hal's comments captured the feeling well:

> The first time I used the men's washroom was a tremendous relief. I was anxious about it, but I realized that I wasn't any more anxious than when I had to use the women's room (women would often tell me I was in the wrong room, or they would scream). Once I actually walked in and went in the stall, I was relieved. And no one noticed me or talked to me or screamed. It was bliss.

Clearly, all participants who lived as men needed to confront their apprehensions about using men's public toilets. Fears about first entering such men-only spaces, where men freely exposed their penises, were understandably widespread among participants who could not do likewise. Participants were concerned that they would be seen as women masquerading as men because of their lack of masculine toilet habits and equipment. Although their expressed fears focussed on their anxieties about possible assaults, there may have been other ways in which participants' anxieties were aroused.

On a very basic level, if participants were routinely unable to make use of men's public toilets, their freedoms to move throughout their public daily lives would become sorely restricted. Their access to women's lavatories had evaporated. If they could not use men's toilets, they could never be away from known facilities for more than a few hours at a time. However, on a more symbolic level, participants' abilities to pass unchallenged through exclusively men-only spaces represented an important achievement of manhood. It was only in such places that participants could be absolutely certain that they were not being perceived as some sort of hybrid sex. It was there that they were accepted as males by a representative and random sampling of experts intimately knowledgeable about the parameters of manhood. Thus it was that participants' lingering insecurities about the effectiveness of their presentations as men might be periodically piqued or appeased by their passage through such public spaces reserved exclusively for males.

Getting Proper Medical Care

Another area of participants' lives as men which occasionally presented problems for them were visits to physicians. Participants usually had established relationships with general practitioners who sufficed for their routine medical care. Their family doctors were familiar with their medically induced hermaphroditism and knew how to care for their needs. However, when participants needed a new doctor or had medical requirements which necessitated the services of specialists, participants had to tell a new set of people that they were transsexual men. The doctors with whom this was most likely to occur were those whose practices were concerned specifically with female anatomical features. When participants' breasts, female genitalia, or female reproductive organs needed attention, they needed to proclaim themselves to be transsexual men and to discuss their conditions with their newly attending physicians. The doctors with whom they dealt were not always well prepared to treat such anomalous patients.

After living as a man for many years, Ken developed a number of health problems and found that it was very difficult for him to get proper medical care as a transsexual man. He bitterly recounted some of what he went through trying to get appropriate attention for his medical needs.

> I didn't have a family physician. I started to have a vaginal discharge. Who do you go and see? The gynecologist that did my hysterectomy then is done doing this. How does a male go into a gynecologist's office and want a pelvic? . . . We have some of the finest doctors in the world here. And do you know that I can't find a physician to treat me?
>
> I did find one physician because I needed to take care of my blood pressure. I was having some hot flashes. I was concerned about my testosterone level. I hadn't been checked for some time. . . . When it came time to tell him that I was having a discharge from both of my nipples and on one side I had a little lump. He said, "It's natural." You know, he never put his hand on my chest to feel. I went every three months to get my scripts filled, but you know, he never felt my chest. I never had a pelvic. And my testosterone level was checked, and just sat there on my chart. He didn't know what to do with it. I called him one day, and my blood pressure was on the ceiling. I was real anxious about something. He ended up giving me some Valium and some Librium. Stress.
>
> Three days later I had surgery by the surgeon that did my mastectomy, and he found a lump in my chest. . . . and we had cancer. . . . I went back and had a partial mastectomy again. He took all of the breast tissue out. I was out of work for six weeks. Not because of the surgery, but complications. I lost my job. . . . I'm a social worker. . . . In a certain situation I couldn't get a proper therapeutic hold on a client because of all the stitches, the torn muscles, and stuff in my chest. I pulled her hair for ten seconds. I was charged with assault. I will never be able to work in the field again. Why did it happen? There's got to be someone out there that is willing to take care of a transsexual. . . .

I guess what I'm trying to say is the . . . Harry Benjamin guidelines for gender change are very definite standards. They need to be followed. Gender reassignment surgery is very expensive both in time and cost, wear and tear on an individual, and their family and their loved ones. But once we approve someone for surgery, basically we let them go. I have seen so many male-to-female transsexuals that have had their surgery and not had electrolysis, voice training, etiquette, or anything. They are laughed at, they are assaulted, and basically they commit suicide.

Not all participants had wholly unpleasant experiences when introducing new doctors to their transsexualism. For example, beyond the discomfort of having to disclose his status as a transsexual man, Brian discovered that his physicians and other health care workers were entirely satisfactory in all their conduct with him when he had to be treated for a rare form of cervical cancer.

Dennis, who had been living as a man for two years, and Steven, who was thirteen years into his life as a man, actually enjoyed the ignorance which they encountered when they went to a cosmetic surgeon to enquire about liposuction. Dennis reported with some amusement about the confusion in the consultation chambers.

It was for love handles. . . . We both went to him and we said, "We're not going to say nothin' until we absolutely have to." So we're both in the examining room together, and he says, "Let me take a look." And I took off my shirt, and . . . he looks and he says, "Yeah. I know what they did." And I figured I didn't have to tell him. He thought that I had been very, very heavy and that they did some work on my chest. And then he said, "Let me see the rest, get a full look." . . .

Before I took my pants off I said, "Look, this is the situation. We're transsexual." And he said, "Okay, that's cool." So, I take my pants down, and I'm standing there, and I said, "We wear something, you know." And we're standing there and he says to me . . . "Wouldn't you like to keep a little fat to keep . . . to give you a feminine appearance?" And I said, "What?" And he thought I was going the opposite way!

Participants' health care needs demanded that they be able to build relationships with doctors who were unafraid of the special challenges involved in treating transsexual patients and who were knowledgeable enough to meet those challenges successfully. Considering that the long-term effects of the medical interventions used in female-to-male transition processes are presently almost entirely unknown, the paucity of well-trained doctors could have grave consequences for participants and for all transsexual men. It would seem as though transsexual men would do well to be careful and demanding consumers of medical services.

Summary and Commentary

These few stories underline the open-ended nature of participants' transsexualism. Although participants generally could live their daily lives as if they had always lived as men, they could never completely leave behind their transsexualism. As long as their bodies retained vestiges of their female pasts, they always would remain, in some areas of their lives, transsexual men. Until medical technology evolved sufficiently so that they could acquire cosmetically acceptable phalluses which could pass urine in the usual fashion, participants would remain vulnerable to uneasiness with the use of public lavatories where their transsexualism might become exposed. Furthermore, it is hard to imagine medical developments ever becoming so sophisticated that the female origins of transsexual men might become medically moot. Be that as it may, participants in this study ignored the female aspects of their anatomy and physiology at their peril. Their continued physical health required attention to the short- and long-term effects of their various sex reassignment treatments and to those parts of their female anatomy which they retained. One prerequisite to participants' receipt of proper medical care of necessity was their announcement of their transsexualism. Thus it might be said that after their transitions, participants lived segmented lives. So long as they could remain entirely clothed, they could live entirely as men. However, when the more private parts of their bodies became pertinent, participants were subject once again to becoming men and males who used to be women and females.

23 | The Naked Truth about Sexuality

T HE PLACE IN participants' lives where the incomplete masculinization of their bodies was most acutely a presence was in the practice of their sexuality. As men, they lacked the usual complement of sexual parts and many of the sexual socialization experiences which help to shape men's sexual performances. Nonetheless, if they were to enjoy sexual relations, they wanted to do so as men. They therefore had to figure out how to sexually perform as men despite their foreshortened practical experience in the role and, furthermore, they had to be able to explain why their bodies were different from those of other males.

A few participants were spared the angst of dealing with interpersonal sexuality by their lack of sexual contact. Peter, Aaron, and Brian were not ready to start using their new bodies in sexual relationships with other people. Gary and Larry were virgins at the times of their interviews. Larry was satisfied with that condition. Gary was interested in moving on. Mel, Sam, Bruce, Keith, Fred, and Jordie were also interested to know what they could do sexually as men but had not had opportunities to find out.

More than half (53 percent) of the participants who were living as men[1] became involved in sexual activities with new sexual partners after they began to live as men.[2] Those participants who started new relationships needed to confront a number of awkwardnesses. They needed either to concoct ways to disguise their shortage of typical male genitalia or develop methods of explaining what they did have between their legs (and in some cases, between their shoulders). Furthermore, they had to figure out, in situ, how to sexually behave in ways consistent with whatever accounts they gave of the reasons for their unusual bodily configurations.

A further seven participants (19 percent) were involved in long-term relationships with women which had spanned their transitions.[3] They were therefore spared the necessity of explaining to their partners why their bodies looked the ways that they did. However, their sexuality was also affected by their transitions. They, too, reported changes in their arousal patterns and in the sexual practices which they enjoyed.

Off the Market

Those participants who had declined to become sexually involved with other people since they had begun living as men held themselves back either because they did not feel adequate to the task as long as they remained as penisless men or because they had little or no sexual interest. Peter was a strong example of the first reason for noninvolvement. Peter stated that he refused to engage in sexual relations with anyone else until he could do so as a man with a penis. At his last interview, he was still smarting from being rejected for exactly that lack by a male-to-female transsexual whom he had been dating. Peter swore that no matter how interested in a woman he might become, "It's not going to get physical. It's not going to come down to that."

Aaron was holding back from becoming involved in any sexual relationships because he was saving money and considering the possibility of purchasing a phalloplasty. Aaron elucidated the connection between the two concerns:

> Hey, if I love somebody, I spend money on them. . . . But I'm staying clear of relationships. I don't like sex just overnight and forget it. I like to be involved with people. I like loving people. . . . I'm not out looking for relationships because I'm trying to save money, primarily. . . . It doesn't mean I don't think about it. Sometimes very strongly. But I work long enough hours, and I'm tired enough. I don't think about it too long at a stretch. Here again, I think being fifty-five is an asset in dealing with this.

Larry and Brian were simply not interested in sexuality at all. Larry had never been moved to sexual arousal by another human being. Brian seemed to consider sexuality to be no more than a somewhat annoying bodily function which needed to be attended to from time to time:

> I see sexual arousal as a largely biochemical reaction. Since I can alleviate it with masturbation, there is no reason to involve another person. These arousals have come and gone in spells over the years. It has never really been that strong a "need" for me as it seems to be for most people. And often I think people are really sexually preoccupied due to mental programming rather than self-awareness of their real physical and emotional needs. I see too, too many people in frequently miserable emotional states because of the ins and outs of sexual relationships, most of them more related to alleviating physical sexual irritations than out of any depth of emotional attachment to another human being.
>
> I am still not at all comfortable about my own body at the sexual level to be comfortable with someone else's, male or female. Also I don't

want to feel like a freak. I wouldn't want to have someone else interested in me because I am odd. I wouldn't trust their mentality.

These few participants were exceptional among those transsexual persons who volunteered for this study. They not only had not yet tried out their new bodies in interpersonal sexual ways, but they did not express any particular desires to do so. Of the four of them, only Peter seemed unhappy about the state of their affairs.

For the Love of Women

Ready and Waiting

Five participants (14 percent) who had become men were interested in having sexual liaisons with women but had not yet been able to negotiate relationships for themselves.[4] Mel and Fred had only very recently become men. Both had been involved with women, but their relationships had ended as they were making their transitions and they had not yet started new ones. Sam, Keith, and Gary were open to new relationships. Gary, who had never had a sexual encounter but was willing to do so, assumed that he would have a long wait.

> I will probably wait to have a relationship until I'm done with most of the surgery. I think it would be difficult to find someone who would be comfortable and open enough to deal with a transsexual. They would have to be a special kind of person. . . . I would like a relationship right now but it's hard.

Fred's eagerness for sampling experiences in his new persona was probably a common feeling among newly transsexual men. He was not ready to settle down into a committed relationship with any one woman.

> I feel like I've been hindered all my life, and I haven't really got to live. And no, I don't feel like I'm going to go out and get wild and pick up people and things like that. . . . I just want to be able to experience new things, and learn more about myself. Really get to know me.

Keith was unusual in that his sexual interest in women only began with his life as a man. He was the only participant who explicitly talked about maintaining a sexual orientation identity as a straight person both before and after his transformation. In other words, when Keith was a woman, she enjoyed being a straight woman, and when Keith became a man, he was anxious to live as a straight man. Keith explained:

> I always have enjoyed that heterosexual interplay even when I had to play the female side of it. . . . not because I wanted to be a female with

men. . . . I'm enjoying it even more now with a woman as myself being a man, the true me. . . .

I have to say that I enjoyed male lovers in many ways, and I'm sure that I would enjoy female lovers. To this day I have never had a female lover, although I've flirted with them, and I've even dated them. I feel like a fifteen-year-old kid who's afraid to make the first move, because of his lack of experience. That's where it stands at this point. I hope to change that soon.

It is interesting to note that two of the six participants who wanted straight relationships with women but had not been successful at starting them had never had sexual encounters with women. Not only were they faced with uncertainties as to how to approach women as transsexual men, but they were also altogether inexperienced as to how to initiate relationships with women at all.

Foretalk: Telling Potential Sexual Partners about Transsexualism

Half of the thirty-six participants who were living as men and who provided information on the subject said that they had become involved in new sexual liaisons with women after their transitions.[5] Of the eighteen participants in this group, only Ed, Tony, and Steven started their lives as men while involved in relationships with women who had known them as women. After those relationships ended, they, too, went on to form new ones.

When participants were hoping to start new sexual relationships with women, one of the first hurdles which they had to surmount was to decide when and what to explain to their prospective sexual partners about the conditions of their bodies. In a handful of cases (14 percent), the women with whom participants became involved knew them to be transsexual men close to the time of their first acquaintances.[6] Participants were thus spared from having to make that basic revelation. They could also enter into their sexual encounters secure in the assumption that due to the prior knowledge of their partners, the women were unlikely to feel either shocked or duped by participants' physiques.

Bill's first sexual relationship of his lifetime came in the years immediately following his transition. During those years Bill spoke out publicly about being transsexual and thus became known to many people in that capacity. Bill's first lover had been a student in a human sexuality class before which Bill had appeared at a local university. Bill recalled that the relationship was initiated by the young woman and lasted one year. In the beginning, their sexual relations had been "hot," but they had "dwindled to nothing" by the end of their year together. According to Bill, although the woman was nine years younger than he, she "was better able to see that our relationship was going nowhere. . . . I think I was clinging to her despite my own dissatisfaction."

Bill's second relationship was also with a younger woman, fourteen years younger than Bill, who also already knew him to be transsexual. This woman, too, pursued Bill. Bill astutely observed that his sexual inexperience and his newness at being a man set him at par with these two younger and open-minded women:

> [My second lover] was twenty-two when I met her. She apparently had read an article about me that appeared in the newspaper and was curious. . . . This woman brought [her] to a human sexuality class I was speaking to. Afterward she, two friends, and I went out for a few beers. . . . I numbed myself to any real attraction. . . . A week or two later I received a nice letter from her in which she told me how much she enjoyed meeting me and confessed that she had wanted me to hug her. . . . Her risk in this honesty got me and I wrote her back. So we wrote one another for two and a half months and when she went home . . . for Christmas, I sent her a [present]. She called to thank me and I told her that I really wanted to take her out. When she got back . . . she and I had a romantic dinner at a cozy French restaurant, walked along the canal, and went back to her room where she read me a letter, after which we made love all night long. This relationship lasted five–six months. . . . Our sex, which had been so passionate and wonderful, dwindled to zero.
>
> Both these women were very much younger than myself in years but about my equal emotionally. I believe that I have had to go back and recover a few essential developmental steps and they both were a part of that. . . . Both were interested in me before I approached them, which made things somewhat easier for me. I didn't have to tell them I was transsexual. They both knew. Both had been sexually active prior to my meeting them. . . . I got along well with both and enjoyed learning from them as well as sharing with them.

Harry also began his first relationship as a man with a much younger woman (fifteen years younger) who came to him knowing that he was a transsexual man. The woman was researching an essay about transsexualism for a school assignment when she met Harry at a transsexual support group meeting. Harry's partner was very forthcoming about what she wanted. This young woman's sexual demands helped Harry to become more at ease with his body. Harry learned to have a two-way sexual relationship and to be able to enjoy sexual relations while fully naked for the first time ever.

> With [her], the sex goes both ways. . . . because . . . she was very insistent from the beginning. . . . It's taken some adjustment, but yes, [I like it]. Because, before . . . I was afraid when someone made love to me,

they would make love to me as a female. And sometimes I would say after they made love . . . "I can't handle this." . . . That's not an issue for [her]. She says, "Fine, then you can't touch me." If I walk around with my clothes on all the time, then so does she. . . .

When we make love to each other, it's like we really want to. Not like we read a book. . . . Books mean you have to identify gender, and books mean you have to follow procedure. There's an enthusiasm there. . . . nobody has to tell me. . . . I penetrate [her], and she doesn't penetrate me. . . . And I let her touch me everywhere. . . . [She] is the first one that I've gotten absolutely naked with. . . . I have used a prosthesis; it was satisfying to a point. But I really now yearn for the contact of a penis with the vagina. I don't have that right now. Because I am becoming more and more aware of that, it's like I go half and half. I like to think there's one there, and then the other half is, I know there's not.

Hal, like Bill, met the first woman with whom he became sexually involved as a man as a result of his willingness to speak to the media about his transsexualism. Thus he too was relieved of the obligation of revealing his transsexual status to a woman in whom he was sexually interested. Both Hal and his new partner were happy with what they discovered about his sexual abilities in his revamped body.

Now that I've had surgery, my body feels much more erotic. Even though I don't have feeling in my nipples, the muscles of my chest are more prominent and I like the hardness of my body; and I like to see my erection when before I could only feel it. Needless to say, I would certainly permit a lover to touch me all over now, though I am still uninterested in anal sex, and I would not want vaginal penetration if my vagina were discovered. . . .

The first time I dated as a man, I was pretty nervous. I wasn't (I'm still not, really) sure what a woman expects from a man. And I'm not going to come on like gangbusters, so I have fears that women will think I'm weird, or wimpy, or gay because I don't try to kiss them or go to bed with them right away. Anyway, the first date turned out to be fun. . . .

The first time I had sexual contact as a man it was with a woman who knew my story, but had only known me for a few weeks. She wanted to have sex with me, but she was worried that she wouldn't be satisfied because my penis is only one and a half inches long. But she found out that I know a bit more about making love to a woman than most men, and she's quite pleased with me as a lover.

I was surprised how good sex felt with my "new" genitals. I was very excited by the fact that I identify very much with the male apparatus, when as a woman I withheld a lot because I did not identify with my genitals. In a way, it made me sad that I waited so long to discover this. But if I had not waited, my children would not have been born to me and my ex-"wife," so I feel it was worth the wait.

Darren's love life during his approximately twenty years of life as a man was complex. Darren was very flexible in his attitudes about gender and correspondingly eclectic in his sexual attractions. Darren said, "What I prefer is a physical and anatomical female, but who has some masculine qualities psychologically and/or physically." Darren had casual affairs and serious relationships with several other transsexual people who were at various stages of change going in either direction and with a handful of gay men. All of Darren's sexual involvements with women since he had begun to live as a man had been with male-to-female transsexuals. They all knew Darren to be transsexual when they met him, either from remarks made by mutual friends or as a result of the extensive transsexual activism in which Darren engaged. Darren said that his involvements with other transgendered people had been "not totally by design." He explained why he thought that things had worked out the way that they had:

> It's because I lived in an insulated situation. . . . It's by default, although not totally, because obviously it would be harder for someone else to accept me the way I am now. So, partly, I guess there is that extra incentive. . . . I'm not really radical, but I tend to like someone who has an androgynous approach. . . . I think there's more chance to find that in someone who's going through this, or having gone through this.

In addition to "a couple of times" when Darren had casual sexual encounters with both "pre-op" and "post-op male-to-females," Darren had two long-term relationships with transsexual women. Darren explained the casual affairs by saying, "I guess we were lonely and trying to be close, but I kind of regretted it the next morning."

Darren's first long-term relationship, with a transsexual woman "almost twice my age," began when Darren was in his late twenties and while the woman was cross-living but had not yet undergone surgery. They lived together for three years, during which time Darren financed her surgery. Their sexual contacts, however, were minimal both before and after the woman's surgery. Before the surgery, both partners felt very ambivalent about using the woman's penis, and subsequently, sex reassignment surgery destroyed the woman's erotic sensations. Darren also reported that the woman had never expressed much interest in touching Darren in explicitly sexual ways. In addition, their sexual life was further stymied by the woman's traditional views of how sexuality should transpire. Darren said:

> She was from a different generation, too, she'd say, "I want you to do it to me the proper way." . . . Plus, she was a Catholic. . . . Well, she

wanted me to have the penis, and have the missionary position. . . . I guess she had hang-ups about it.

Darren's second relationship with a transsexual woman followed soon after the first one. When they first began to live together, this woman, like the last one, was cross-living but had not had surgery. She, too, went on to have sex reassignment surgery, and soon afterward, they married. Darren described this woman as "my life partner . . . we want to be together for life. I'm not interested in anybody else." Their marriage continues to thrive.

Their sexual relationship was more satisfying for Darren than the prior one had been. Darren remarked, "We're very comfortable with each other, in terms of dressing, undressing, touching, sex, and all that." He also explained that unlike his previous transsexual woman partner, this woman did not want him to acquire or simulate a penis for their lovemaking sessions because she saw him entirely as a man without one and she knew the dangers of genital surgery.

As Darren had done on a few occasions, Ron also had a casual affair with a pre-operative cross-living male-to-female transsexual whom he met through a transsexual friendship network. They dated and had casual sexual relations a few times. Ron put a stop to their affair because, as he remembered it, "She put the clamps on right away. It started out being fun, and then it turned into counselling very quickly. I was counselling. And then it was getting problematic."

In sum, three of these few participants who did not have to inform their prospective sexual partners about their transsexualism were relieved of having to make such anxious announcements by another sort of bravery. Bill, Hal, and Darren were all transsexual activists who presented themselves publicly as transsexual men. One way in which they were rewarded for their willingness to campaign for the rights of transsexual people was by being released from having to personally tell other people about their transsexualism. Their public statements carried that news for them. Three participants also benefitted from their integration into transsexual support and social networks. Darren and Ron found transsexual women lovers through such connections. Harry met a young non-transsexual woman lover at a transsexual support group meeting.

Thus, all five of these participants found themselves in the relatively luxurious positions of beginning new sexual relationships with women whose original attractions to them were formulated with full knowledge of participants' transsexual status. On the one hand, having relationships which were couched in such terms must have eased participants' minds about the potential for pernicious effects from partners' ambivalences

about participants' unusual bodies. However, on the other hand, participants whose partners were initially attracted to them as transsexual might
also have been subject to lingering doubts about their partners' sexual proclivities and how they might, by implication, reflect upon their own. Perhaps not surprisingly all five of these participants were willing to see themselves as somewhat androgynous men and were thus also less than totally
adamant about completely committing themselves to identities as straight
men. As Hal's remarks illustate, sexual orientation identities can be problematic for transsexual persons:[7]

> My relationship with my girlfriend makes me a straight man, but I don't
> feel like a straight man, and I don't feel like I have a lot in common with
> straight people. I feel culturally and politically like a lesbian, or actu-
> ally I'm a man now, I guess I must be gay. But then, I'm not a gay man
> sexually.

Twelve participants (33 percent) also started new relationships with
women wherein they chose to tell the women with whom they became
involved that they were transsexual men.[8] Their announcements were always made with some trepidation. A few participants outlined the highlights of their more successful pronouncements.

Stan had had occasion to explain himself to two different women lovers since he had begun to live as a man. Both of the women were able to
accept his explanations and have full loving and sexual relationships with
him. His first story began when a woman whom he met at his church became enamoured of him. At the time, Stan had some "light and fine" facial hair, surgically reduced breasts, and female genitalia.

> She was attracted to me immediately like the man that she thought that
> she was with, and then it got to where . . . there is a definite sexual pos-
> sibility here, and that terrified me. "What am I going to tell her?" . . . I
> was playing the role I always wanted to play. I could take her out, I
> could open her door. . . . She was very feminine, and allowed me to be
> as masculine and gentlemanly as I'd always dreamed to be. . . . I got
> scared of her rejecting me, of course. "Oh, you're weird, you fooled me.
> That's it. You lied to me. You led me on, and you're not really who you
> say you are, you're just this thing." And that really terrified me. . . . And
> so, I had to set it up. . . .
> I was still an alcoholic. . . . The alcoholic took care of me. "Feel sorry
> for me. There's something I need to tell you that's very close to my heart
> that I'm very scared." It brings out all their mothering. . . . So I . . .
> finally told her . . . I was a transsexual. . . . And then explained it imme-
> diately. . . . And true to form, she responded, "That's okay. I love you
> anyway. There's so many wonderful things about you. I don't care.
> You're wonderful." . . .
> That's before she touched me. She didn't find out by accident. I kissed

her and I'm sure she touched me around the waist, but I avoided people touching my chest, because it had these lumps, and I was afraid they'd find out. . . . I was so paranoid, just so nervous. . . . And then we proceeded to have a sexual relationship. And it scared me to absolute death, but she reassured me, and reassured me.

Stan also had some explaining to do in his more recent relationship. By the time Stan met the second woman he had had a mastectomy and become more fully virilized by the ongoing effects of testosterone treatments. They were living together at the time of Stan's last interview and he was thinking about marriage. Stan summarized his feelings about her by saying, "This is a woman who I could fulfill some of my serious marriage fantasies with." As it turned out, Stan was the embodiment of some of the woman's greatest fantasies as well. However, Stan first had to reveal his secret to her before she told him hers.

It was the greatest performance of my life. . . . I planned out an evening that, "I've got to tell you something about myself. The Stan story." So she knew it was big. I had made such a big deal about it. . . . I wrote it out. I knew I couldn't tell her without fudging. . . . So I spent two nights and . . . wrote out about a twenty-page little thing that just tells the story. And I spent that evening setting it up. . . . I practiced reading it out loud. I brought in a tape of a song . . . that's just kind of, "All I can be is who I am." So I played it . . . and then I read the story, and then I had another song. . . .

I just told her that when I was little, I was different. I don't think I used the word transsexual 'til later on. . . . And just kind of told the story. . . . Afterwards, I just kind of looked up, and. . . . then we hugged, and we were dancing. . . . we get to the end of the song, and she wouldn't let go. I thought, "She's in shock. She doesn't know what to do. Rigor mortis has set in." . . .

I was ready to go, and she was pretty quiet. . . . "I need to process this." Okay. I expected that. . . . So I left that with her, and drove home. . . . And I got home, and it couldn't have been a few minutes later before she called me, and just wanted to reassure me that "Stan, I'm processing this. I just want you to know that I haven't gone anywhere, I haven't left, I'm still processing this. I can't say either way. Can we just talk for a few minutes? Not about it. . . . Just talk normal?" So we chatted a little while just normal. . . .

[Afterwards] I could not believe that someone could actually listen to this story and still accept me and love me. It was a fantasy of unheard of proportions coming true right before my very eyes! I was flying incredibly high! The love thing, and just, "She knows. She knows and she likes me anyway! She knows and it's okay! She's so neat and she knows."

Once Stan had recovered from his shock at not being rejected for being transsexual, he discovered just how fine a match the two of them were for one another.

> She has an interesting view on sex that we were made for each other. She had fantasized about making love to a woman with a penis, and didn't know the word for it. And when she discovered me, she said, "I cannot believe this. I cannot believe this. This is my most deepest, darkest, never told anybody kind of fantasy, and I cannot believe it. My fantasy person is a little more feminine than you are, so it's not perfect, but it's pretty dang close." So that's interesting. She has helped me come to terms with my female parts. They're not as bad as I made them out to be. That they are not, "If anybody knew I had these parts they wouldn't have anything to do with me."

Stan's partner's full sexual appreciation of the mixing of sex characteristics in Stan's body helped Stan to overcome a long-standing and deep-seated alienation from his female body parts. Because of the freedom of their lovemaking, Stan acquired still another secret to add to his collection: the secret of how much he had come to love himself. Stan learned with this lover that he could sexually enjoy all of his body:

> I was pretty slow about [sexuality]. At night and in the dark. I was pretty scared and none of this daytime stuff. . . . Her pace was definitely, "I want you to know that I'm having a relationship with you, and I do know you, and I do see you. This is not a sneaky, secrety, we'll only do it at night, and the next morning we don't acknowledge what happened. But this is something that I want to acknowledge, that yes, I am having sex with you. With these parts right here." And I wasn't ready for that. That took me a while to get into. But I did get into it. And it's been so free. It's been a wonderful, beautiful thing. I've learned a lot. It is truly a dream fantasy come true.

Tony's stormy ten year relationship with his wife began before he started to live as a man and spanned the subsequent nine years between his commencement of hormone therapy and the completion of his mastectomy and hysterectomy. According to Tony, it ended because of his wife's violence, infidelity, fanatical religiosity, and general capriciousness. Tony was deeply disturbed when, after steadfastly suffering through so many of his wife's vacillations, she left him: "The last time she came for her stuff, I flipped out. I almost ran her over with my car. I was screaming and yelling. . . . I tried to kill her [male companion] with a rake."

As Tony was on the rebound from his ex-wife, he briefly became involved with a woman nine years his junior. Tony said that "she gave me back a confidence that had been crushed. . . . I really had tremendous feel-

ings for her," but that their sexual relationship was short-lived because she
had to take a new job which forced them to live more than 100 miles
apart. Tony described how it started:

> My most recent sexual romantic relationship was with a woman that I
> had met on the bus. . . . She started talking to me. She's strikingly beau-
> tiful. It got to a point where I would make sure I would make the bus
> she was on just to look at her. . . . We talked for about two years. . . .
>
> I invited her here for dinner. I threw her all my "Feel sorry for Tony"
> that I could. . . . Everything was really beautiful. The fire burned beau-
> tifully. The jacuzzi was great. Even the stars came out. What I never
> expected to happen was for her to make a pass at me. She did. I pushed
> her off. She knew me only as a genetic man, but she knew I wasn't the
> kind of man that just would sleep with anybody because we had spoken
> about this. She eased off. . . . She made another pass at me . . . and I
> said, "Listen, I don't take advantage of drunk women," and I pushed
> her off. Well, luckily she got so drunk, I threw her in bed . . . and she
> fell asleep.
>
> Well, to make a long story short, we were talking the next day and
> she told me she wanted to tell me something about herself. . . . She said,
> "Well, I was a lesbian once." And I leapt up and said, "Well, I have a
> secret too! I'm not a genetic man! . . . I was not born a man." So we
> talked about it for a while and it just worked out fine. . . .
>
> She was there when I needed it. She's very popular. I never expected
> anything to happen, any future, but we were together a few times. . . .
> And, sexually, we had a fantastic time. And I have some great memories
> that I'll take to my death. Again she's strikingly beautiful and just the
> fact that she gave me some of her time and some of her pleasures is just
> something I will never forget.

Bob dated and proposed marriage to a woman shortly after he began
to live as a man. Bob didn't immediately tell her that he was transsexual.
However, after some initial distress at Bob's dishonesty, the woman proclaimed her love to Bob and accepted his marriage proposal. Bob summarized the course of events this way:

> I was introduced to her through the Japanese friendship society. . . .
> And I didn't take much notice of her at first. I thought she was very, very
> attractive to look at, and she was very . . . quiet. . . . And then we met
> again at another function. . . . And we found that we started to enjoy
> one another's company. . . .
>
> She's in Japan now. I tried to end it . . . because . . . she would not
> admit to her parents who or what I was. . . . And this hurt me, and
> made it very hard for us. And at one time, [she] asked me things about
> myself which I wasn't truthful about. I lied to her. And, of course, cer-
> tain . . . so-called friends of mine informed her of the true facts. . . . She

was very hurt and said that I'd lied to her. After which, the relationship then broke down a lot, and I felt that she no longer loved me, trusted me, or felt that she wanted to marry me, and she was only going through a farce with me.

So, to save face for both of us, I wrote to her, and offered to cancel the engagement. . . . And she wouldn't have it. "No way," was the word I got from her. "No way this side of the black swamp. I'd sooner kill myself." And she told me she did love me, and she could not marry a Japanese man, or any other man. That she wanted to marry me. That she wanted to be my wife, and she loved me, and she only wanted to be with me. . . .

I showed her myself, which is something I would never do with anybody else. I physically showed her what I looked like, and asked her what she saw in me. And she said she saw a man. And she trusted that I would get to where I was going, and my physical appearance didn't disgust her in the least. Which I thought it might have done.

These stories told by participants who revealed their transsexual status to potential women lovers were, on the whole, encouraging ones. It must be borne in mind, however, that these accounts are only those which were antecedent to successful sexual encounters. Participants were neither asked, nor did they offer, to retell tales of their rejections by women who might have been unwilling to countenance their ambiguous bodies and bifurcated gender histories. Be that as it may, the fact remains that participants were able to find women with whom they could establish compatible sexual relationships as men, even though their bodies were less than perfectly complete in their approximations of anatomical maleness. Thus it would seem that participants' acknowledgments of their transsexualism to the women whom they desired as lovers was not necessarily an impediment to the establishment of viable sexual and romantic relationships with women who expected their partners to be physically normal straight men.

Only Steven and Walter chose not to tell their sexual partners that they were transsexual men. Both preferred to describe their condition as intersexed. Steven, who was thirty years old at the time, had a three year relationship with a woman eleven years his junior which began after he'd been living as a man for a couple of years. When it came time for Steven to expose his body to her he told her that he "had a hermaphroditic condition" but did not advise her as to how he had come to be that way.

Walter, who used the same ruse, proclaimed that he considered his approach to be perfectly honest. In fact, he derided those transsexual men who did otherwise. Walter explained the rationale inherent in his methods in these terms:

I don't really feel it's being dishonest not to disclose the fact that you're a transsexual. In fact, I think it's kind of dishonest to disclose the fact that you're a transsexual. . . . When you're involved in a significant relationship, obviously, you're going to have to broach the subject. But, in general . . . to me that indicates that they have a problem with their own identity. . . . It's like they can't give up their femininity. In other words, if you are insisting that you're a transsexual, then what you really are is a man in a woman's body. . . . By doing that, you're really giving up your own life as a male.

And what I do is, in a sexual situation, I tell people that I'm a hermaphrodite. Initially. Eventually, when and if I get involved with someone, I tell them the whole truth. But, in a sexual situation. . . . I just totally act like any other guy. . . . And I ignore the fact that I don't have a penis. . . . Usually, I would have a woman in bed, undressed, preferably having at least one orgasm before I even take all my clothes off. So, at that point, you're not talking about rejection anymore. . . . They've already accepted you. So, if they try to touch me, I just say, "No, no. Don't do that. I'm too excited. I'm too turned on. You'll make me come too quick. I want to make you happy." . . . I always wear a prosthetic, of course. It feels natural . . . if they grab me. . . .

So then, what happens is, after . . . it comes time when they actually have to find out what I have inside my pants, then I would say my standard line. . . . "Look, I just want you to know I'm a little bit different from other guys . . . physically. Do you know what a hermaphrodite is?" . . . And I've never been rejected for that reason. I've been rejected, but not for that reason. . . . If a woman initially sees you as male, it's sort of like initializing the disk on the computer. It's like once that's the thing that's set, they're always going to see you that way.

Steven and Walter, who chose to use euphemism to inform their sexual partners about the reasons why their bodies did not look like most men's bodies, ran the risk of later undermining the faith which their lovers might hold in their truthfulness. However, Walter seemed prepared to accept that risk and confront his partners with the truth when he believed that a brief affair might become a more enduring relationship. It was unclear from his comments whether or not Steven had similar plans.

Things Are Different Now: Changing Sexual Patterns

Seven participants (19 percent) never had to encounter the awkwardness of explaining to new sexual partners about their bodies. They began long-term relationships with women before or around the time of their transitions, and all of them but Scott remained still involved with those women as of their most recent communications. Their relationships ranged in duration from three years to twenty-five years. At last report, Scott's relationship had lasted three years, both Jack and Ken had been with their wives for eight years, Luther and his partner had been together for thirteen years, Grant and his lover had enjoyed twenty-two years of union,[9] Simon had been with his wife for approximately twenty-four years, and Howie and his wife had the pleasure of twenty-five very loving years between them. These men therefore enjoyed the solace of knowing that their partners fully knew their gender and sex backgrounds and loved them for who they were.

They did, however, report that they shared with other participants the experience of feeling differently in their bodies and in their sexuality as they went through their transitions. In some cases, participants attributed the changes in their sexuality directly to the physiological impact of having male-typical quantities of testosterone circulating in their bloodstreams. In other instances, they considered the changes in their sexual desires and responses to be more sociopsychological in nature. That is to say that as they were able to live more fully as men, they were less willing to engage in sexual activities which they saw as incompatible with being men. Furthermore, as they became more secure in their manly identities and bodies, a number of participants began to feel that they were entitled to ask for pleasures which they thought of as prerogatives which were normally only available to men.

Numerous areas of change were cited by participants as possible correlates with testosterone therapy. Almost all participants commented on the enhancement effects of testosterone on their libidos. However, a few participants said that the reverse had been true for them, and a few people lamented that these effects were confounded by a corresponding decrease in their ability to have multiple orgasms. Also frequently mentioned was an observation that testosterone seemed to make participants feel more sexually aggressive. A few participants further noticed that they seemed to have become more visually oriented in their sexual arousal patterns and attributed those changes to their regular hormone injections.

Bill's comments on the effect of testosterone on his libido were typical of those made by almost all participants who said anything at all about the effects of hormone therapy.

> The male hormones have substantially increased my sex drive so that I am almost insatiable unless I am really tired or emotionally drained. So I guess I would say I could have sex daily which . . . has given me an empathy for adolescent boys.

Several participants also suggested a causal relationship between testosterone treatments and the kinds of sexual interests and activities which became exciting to them. For example, Hal felt that the quality of his lovemaking had been affected by being on testosterone therapy.

My sex life has changed vis-à-vis my sexual expression, which is more intense and more aggressive than before, though the aggressive behaviour is the expressed preference of my current sex partner. I don't think I would have been capable of sustaining the level of sexual intensity and aggressiveness in my female body.

Walter also believed that his sexuality had been altered along with his hormonal balance. In Walter's view, his sexuality had become more crude.

The thing that's been different since the hormones is the libido aspect. . . . I have become more sexual, and it's . . . not just that I have more sex drive . . . my tastes have changed. Like, I never ever enjoyed oral sex with a woman. . . . I was really turned off to it. . . . when I was a lesbian, I never did that. . . . But now, I love it. . . . It's a qualitative change in my libido. . . . It was really just the wetness that was a real turn off to me. And that's the difference. You see, as a man . . . you're into grosser stuff. I hate to say it that way, 'cause I hate to make a woman's wet vagina sound like it's gross, but to a certain degree, that's effluvia. . . .
    But sexually, that has definitely changed. I've gotten into urine, which I never was into before. Just grosser things. . . . It's like a visceral change. It's just more gutsy somehow, sexually. And that, I think, is a male characteristic. I mean, not that women can't have that. . . . But, for me anyway, it seems like that's a male thing.

Ron and Keith both reported that they looked at women differently since they had been taking testosterone injections. Both men found themselves taking pleasure in sexually objectifying women in ways that they had previously found offensive when they were themselves passing through society as women. Ron made sense of his new perspective this way:

It seems like I'm more visual sexually also. Where before I was never attracted to physical features. . . . Whereas now, I see bodies differently. I felt guilty about that in the beginning. I was wondering where this was coming from, and this is wrong. And now I know it's of no consequence really. And there is not malice. And I do attribute it to the hormones.

Keith also saw women differently. He observed that his views on the sexual objectification of women reversed themselves along with his sexual orientation.

My view of sexual exploitation completely changed when I became a man. Whereas as a female I was very indignant about sexual exploitation, as a man I find it rather fascinating and somewhat appalling that my viewpoint has very much changed. And I now see sexual exploitation of women as a very enjoyable thing, and I feel that they should enjoy it too. I don't consciously and rationally feel that, because . . . I certainly understand better than most men why women don't enjoy sexual exploitation, but yet my emotional feelings . . . seems like, "Well, gee, it's so much fun. Why don't they enjoy it too?"

Many participants also noted that as their bodies became more masculinized, they felt more comfortable in them. Several people reported that it was only after they had manly bodies that they were first able to enjoy looking at themselves in mirrors when naked, allowing others to look at them naked, permitting others to touch their bodies freely, and taking pleasure in solo sexuality. For a few participants, their first orgasms arrived in their lives only after they began to live as men.

Furthermore, as they began to see their bodies as those of men, a number of participants began to refuse to partake in activities which they construed as lesbian ones and began to demand those which fit with their expectations of men's sexuality. Some people stopped permitting vaginal penetration to be performed on them; however, other participants were able to begin such activities only after they started to enjoy the look and feel of their bodies. Concomitantly, quite a few participants moved more determinedly into the use of strap-on dildos, or penile prostheses, to better simulate the sexual activities which they envisioned and desired for themselves and their partners. Conversely, a few participants felt unable to use such prosthetic devices because their rubberiness and removability only reinforced in their own minds their lack of possession of that important piece of flesh.

Thirteen of the nineteen participants for whom it was a relevant issue (69 percent)[10] stated that they refused to allow their sexual partners to penetrate them vaginally.[11] However, Darren, Ken, Stan, and Nathan stated that they had no problem with such activities.

Walter explained how his feelings about the way he wanted to be sexually touched had changed as he began to see himself turn into a man:

See, there's been developmental stages in my sexuality because of my lack of knowledge of being able to do anything about it. Before I realized there was something I could do about it, I resigned myself to it, and I was not about to deny myself sexuality because of it. So what I did was I was mostly involved in a lesbian community. I mostly got involved with bisexual women, and I let them interact with my body. Now that I've discovered that I can do something about it and I can be completely male, which I never thought I could be before, now I am very loath to let my partners interact with my body because now I have a different image in my head. Like I can actually achieve what I want to achieve, so I don't have to accept that feminine thing anymore.

Fred said that he could not imagine being able to countenance any penetration of his vagina since he had realized his manhood.

> Now I will allow a lover to touch my private parts. I definitely will. Not penetration. I honestly believe that would make me feel female. It would make me feel really strange. . . . If I did that, I would lose all the arousal; I would lose everything that I need to make me feel like who I know I am. It would just be devastating. I don't think I could deal with that.

Tony took the attitude that vaginal penetration was totally incompatible with his manhood. He did not seem to have any doubts about what such contact symbolized.

> I do not in any way, shape, or form allow any kind of penetration, I don't. I don't like it. It means woman to me. I will not have it. . . . I don't like it, it's not exciting to me. It's not pleasurable to me. It's nothing, and I just won't be bothered with it.

Not all participants interpreted vaginal penetration as definitive of their gender or even of their sex. Some participants were able to take pleasure in vaginal penetration without losing their grips on their identities as men. Nathan explained how he was able to incorporate it into his love life:

> At first it was very difficult to allow a lover to touch my private parts, but after, I found it very important to be a receiver. . . . I've discovered the day before I take hormones my vagina needs to be "filled" and sometimes I'll let the girl put a finger or two in there, but not very long.

Stan not only allowed vaginal penetration, but he became an enthusiast of it at the hands of a lover who wanted to have sexual relations with his entire body. Stan elaborated:

> I allow myself to be touched differently big time. Before, no female partners had ever touched the female part. It wasn't there. . . . They knew I wouldn't allow it. . . . And that is a part now that we play with. We play and it's fun. It's an extra play toy. So I allow penetration and enjoy it. . . . It's just very weird. It sets me apart even from the transsexual community, 'cause I don't think they would understand that. . . . [But] we enjoy it. . . . It's not where sex is focussed, but it's just another part of the repertoire. . . .
> We use silicon dildo toys. Both ways. . . . I wanted [her] to experience as mirrored to real sex as I could muster up. And of course that's what she wanted. . . . So I had this thing fitted up, and I was anxious to use it. I'd never done that before. I'd . . . never put one on and tried to make it a part of me, to fit and everything. I felt like a kid. . . . .I got some lessons [from a friend], and I went home, and kind of felt stupid jockeying the thing around. But it did seem to work out okay. . . .
> She also uses the dildo with me. . . . That was kind of a fantasy that she wanted to try. . . . I was excited. I was elated that we're sexual. . . .

[She] has a much more comfortable feeling with her body that I am envious of. . . . I've always been shy. . . . And she is just, "My body is wonderful, I love my body. I am sexual. I am sensuous." And I am learning that from her . . . and that was a way I could show her that I'm sexual and I'm sensuous too by allowing you to do something kind of scary with me.

These stories illustrate some of the variety in the symbolic meanings attached by participants to the incorporation of their vaginas into their sexuality as men. Few participants had a problem with having their hormonally enlarged clitorises manipulated by their partners because they saw them as analogous or equivalent to penises. However, there was no easy homologue for them to equate with their vaginas. Thus for most participants, vaginal penetration represented the quintessential act of female sexuality.

A minority of participants refused to be denied access to a source of sexual pleasure as long as they and their partners had a private agreement as to its symbolic value. For them, it represented a way to feel closer and more connected to their lovers, not a statement of their femaleness. Furthermore, it seems as though, for those few participants who accepted it, vaginal penetration may have resonated at another level of symbolic meaning. That is, vaginal penetration may have forged exceptionally tight bonds between these lovers because, on the one hand, participants entrusted themselves to their lovers in deepest intimacy while, on the other hand, their lovers were able to accept the gift of that residual femaleness without doubting participants' manhoods. Such exchanges of trust must have formed powerful links between them.

Considering their sexuality from another angle, twelve participants (63 percent) reported that they made use of penile prostheses in their sexual contacts with women,[12] whereas another four participants said that they avoided such devices. Howie was unwilling to use one because "that's a powerful reminder that I don't have what I should." Darren and Phil refrained from using dildos because their partners had no interest in such activities, and Bob expressed a dislike of any sexual "things with toys . . . that are not part of the human body."

Those participants who did use prostheses in their sexual activities with women did so because they wanted their sexual activities to be commensurate with their lives as straight men. For example, Tony was especially fond of using his "apparatus" against his hormonally enlarged clitoris in intercourse with his women partners. His biggest delight was when they could have simultaneous orgasms together in missionary position intercourse.

Alan also used a dildo in his relationships with women, both when he was living as a man and when he was living as a butch lesbian woman. Alan explained in more detail how it worked:

> I best find sexual satisfaction through tribadism, preferably when I am penetrating a woman with a dildo while the base of the dildo presses against my naturally large clitoris. . . . I prefer tribadism with me on top or, if on the bottom, totally in control of the movements, approach, or mood. . . . I wear a dildo to bed at night, especially if I live with a lover. I do not have sex with people who do not accept my maleness. I discuss my transsexuality before I become involved with anyone. I like to use a dildo. It is part of me so I refer to it as my dick or my cock. I do not call it a dildo except in the nonsexual dating stage of a relationship or to explain my sexual preferences. . . . I like blowjobs with or without the dildo, but mostly with the dildo because the dildo is larger than my clitoris and makes me feel more masculine and in control.

Luther also enjoyed using a prosthetic device. He said, "The best way I find sexual satisfaction is by having my prosthetic manipulated in some way, preferably orally." Steven, who also used a dildo, was a little less enthusiastic because he said that he would prefer "to have my own body part to do that with, because it's more psychological gratification."

Those participants who offered their perspectives on the use of artificial phalluses appeared to have been of two minds on this question. There were those people who saw them as prosthetic devices substituting for a lacking organ. As men, they should have penises. If technology could fill in where nature had failed them, so be it. They availed themselves of what was accessible to them to make them as whole as possible. Other participants seemed unable to see or disinterested in seeing manufactured phalluses as anything more than dildos. As such they represented only sex toys, not prostheses, to these participants. They or their partners were not enthused about "playing" at participants having penises and thus declined to make use of their imaginations in that way. They instead made love using what nature and medical technologies had provided.

Summary and Commentary

Thirty-three of the thirty-eight participants who had lived as men (87 percent) expressed some interest in establishing sexual relationships with women. Twenty-four of those thirty-three participants who were attracted to women (73 percent) told stories about their successes which ranged from brief affairs to relationships lasting more than twenty years. Clearly their transsexualism did not constitute a major obstacle in participants' pursuit of the love of women.

A number of noteworthy points can be taken from the stories told by participants. Firstly, participants seemed to have gained a high degree of reward for being honest about their transsexualism with their women partners. Presumably, participants deliberated carefully about which women were likely to be receptive to such news and about how and when to communicate it. Nonetheless, the point remains to be made that there seemed to have been an adequate supply of compatible women for participants' needs.

Secondly, it seemed from participants' accounts that those women who were amenable to intimacies with participants were frequently significantly older or younger than the transsexual men with whom they became involved. Eight of the nineteen participants who started new relationships with women after their transitions (42 percent) became involved with women who were nine or more years divergent in age from themselves. As it is the case that transsexual men often look younger than their chronological years, especially in the early years of their lives as men, perhaps young women were attracted to participants erroneously thinking them to be their age peers. Perhaps older women were charmed by participants' boyishness. Perhaps participants felt safest with women with whom they either savoured an advantage by virtue of their superior age, or with women who conveyed the comfort of a motherly authority.

A third point to be noted is that a few participants found compatible women partners while being activists for transsexual causes. These participants were publicly known as transsexual men and therefore any women who showed an interest in them must have found their transsexualism at least acceptable, if not titillating. As well, women who became sexually partnered with politically active participants were clearly women who were prepared to have themselves known as the girlfriends or wives of transsexual men. In addition to Darren, Bill, and Hal whose activism has already been noted, Simon and Walter also publicly made themselves known as transsexual men in the service of transsexual advocacy.

A last noteworthy point is that participants came to both their new and their pre-existing relationships with some new sexual expectations. Regular testosterone injections and daily doses of masculine socialization transformed many participants' sexual desires. They often came to their women lovers randier and more demanding. In addition, most participants ceased to allow any sexual practices to be done to them which could not be construed as possible to perform on male bodies. Furthermore, many participants became more committed to the routine use of penile prostheses in their lovemaking as temporary alternatives to phalloplasties. They spoke of using their prostheses in both intercourse and fellatio, and receiving great sexual and body image satisfaction thereby.

In sum, participants' reports indicated that although they were still transsexual in their sexual lives, they were transsexual *men*. They orchestrated their intimacies so that their love lives contributed to their comfort in their skins, which for some participants meant a seamless fit between their public lives as men and their more private ones in their homes and in their bedrooms. However, other participants took greater solace in being able to let down their everyday lives' vigilance when they were with their loved ones. The reality was that they were men who had been born as females and lived as women, and who retained some aspects of both their femaleness and their womanhood. As such, having lovers who could see them and love them as they truly were must have been a most profound relief from the unrelenting burden of concealment which consumed such vast expanses of the rest of their lives.

A Fascination with the Unknown: Attractions to Men

As participants grew into their lives as men, many of them found themselves in an odd position. They were finally realizing what for most of them had been a lifelong dream, yet many of them knew very little about some of the most central aspects of being men. Fifteen of the participants who had lived as men (40.5 percent)[13] had either never had any genital heterosexual experience at all[14] or had seen penises in action only while they were being heterosexually abused by them.[15] Furthermore, another twelve people (32 percent) had only the most cursory of genital heterosexual experiences from which to build their own repertoire of phallic behaviours in their everyday lives and sexual relations.[16] Thus, at the time of their transitions, a scant ten participants (27 percent) reasonably could be said to have had a good working knowledge of the functioning of penises.[17] Be that as it may, men are supposed to be entirely conversant with all aspects of, at the very least, one penis: their own. Most participants, however, lacked phalluses and knew little or nothing about anyone else's. Understandably, they were curious. As Jack, who had never seen or touched a penis, said:

> Even now, I have very much of a curiosity. I would just like to see how it works once, and see what it feels like . . . Not because I lust for it or anything, but because of my curiosity.

Many of the participants who had had the least sexual contact with men prior to their transitions were among those participants who became the most intrigued by penises once they lived as men. They expected themselves to be able to perform sexually as men, but they were not certain about precisely how to go about their rites. By studying various forms of pornographic representations, they could fill in some of the gaps in their knowledge, but even the most graphic words and pictures are no substitute for hands-on experiences. There was only one way for participants who wanted such information to obtain it: to have sexual contact with men.

Furthermore, it would probably be safe to say that few persons born to the female sex ever become so preoccupied with men and masculinity as do female-to-male transsexuals. For most participants, much of their lives consisted of both unconsciously and consciously acquiring the ways of men. Their quest to understand how to be men, from the inside out, was a life's work. As participants moved through their transitions and became settled into their lives as men, they continued to watch and to learn how better to be men, both from their own experiences and from what they saw of the men around them. As their knowledge of men deepened and as their immersion in society as men consolidated, many participants came to appreciate and love men more than they had ever been able to do while they had lived as women. Once participants began to become secure that their affections for men would not mark them as straight women, those who were so inclined were freed to admit to their hunger for intimacies with men.

Thus it was that most of the fifteen participants (40.5 percent) who were sexually interested in men came to be so disposed.[18] Few participants' interests, however, became translated into actual sexual contact owing largely to participants' concerns about their missing penises or the threat of HIV infection.

Thought Experiments: Attractions without Actions

A handful of participants reported unrequited attractions to men which ranged from mild curiosity to lustful fantasies. These participants freely admitted that they were unlikely ever to move to realize their fantasies in this regard. The most dispassionate of this group of participants was Brian, who had very little interest in sexuality as such but did express desire for emotional intimacies. Brian said, "I wish I could find someone who I could develop a mutual life partnership with. I probably would be inclined toward a male, but someone who was gender-free. I have a poor tolerance of 'sociocultural female' behaviours and accoutrements."

Although sexual relations with men still held allure for Aaron and Keith after their years of sexual relations as straight women, neither of them expected ever again to become sexually involved with a man. As a man, Aaron retained some of his appreciation for men but was more sensitive to the potential drawbacks which he saw as inherent in any liaisons which he might have with gay men. He allowed that he probably could still take pleasure in sexual relations with men but didn't feel motivated to deal with the risks involved.

> I've stepped back and looked hard at everything . . . and wondered if I would be interested in a gay relationship. . . . And the point is no, because of two things: One with the AIDS thing, why gamble? Why play around and try to find out if that's what I want? And two, because I don't think I could ever be with a gay man without him thinking of me as female in some way. . . . I probably have the capacity to enjoy a man at this point but I have no desire to do so. I mean, hell, if I was going to make it with a man and live with a man, I would have stayed the other way.

Keith, who had a wide-ranging history as a straight woman, considered himself to be entirely a straight man after his transition. He noted that as long as he lacked a penis he expected that neither he nor any potential male sexual partner could be persuaded to construe sexual relations between them as anything other than heterosexual ones. Therefore Keith did not plan on pursuing sexual relations with gay men despite some responsiveness to their appeal.

> I have nothing against gay sex. In fact I have a small tendency towards gay men. I have some gay male friends and I see gay men that attract me from time to time. But I don't think I'd feel comfortable with one sexually because I don't have the penis to give a gay man what he wants. I guess that's putting it in a simplistic way. So I avoid gay sex, or if you want to consider the fact that I do have female genitals, I avoid heterosexual sex actually. . . . See technically that would be heterosexual, because I have a vagina, but in my mind that would be gay. Well, it wouldn't be gay, because the male would not be thinking as gay.

Harry expressed a similar level of mild interest in sexual relations with gay men but, like many other participants, assumed that his lack of a penis precluded any such activities. Harry remarked, "I've thought about it. I've often thought, if and when I had the male parts, I could have a male lover. Maybe."

Jordie was the only participant who consistently identified himself as a gay man both before and after his gender conversion. Jordie said of himself, "I'm a queen and proud of it!" Jordie also explained that he was very visibly active in his local gay political and service organizations. However, Jordie had not had any sexual relations with men since his transition nine years before his interviews and held out little hope for any in the near future. As Jordie put it, "It's hard to find a gay lover with no cock! I have a social place in town, but not sexual."

In sum, these participants were mildly interested in experimenting with gay relationships but considered them to be untenable as long as they did not have well-functioning penises. They seemed to be of the opinion that gay men would not be able to see them as suitable objects of gay desire so long as they lacked definitively male sexual organs. Some participants also assumed that they would be perceived as heterosexual females—clearly, an undesirable outcome for participants to invite.

Putting Women First:
Commitments to Women Lovers Preclude Gay Relations

The extent of some participants' sexual adventures with gay men were largely circumscribed by their overriding loyalties to the women who were already their loved ones. For example, Ken, like a number of other participants, expressed interest in having sexual relations with men as a man. However, as was also the case with several other participants, Ken's preexisting relationship with his wife and his concerns about contracting AIDS deterred him from taking any action on his attractions. Ken said, "For some reason, it's something that does attract me, but I know it's something that I will never do. It took a lot to become a man, and it was in order to be with a woman."

Before Stan became involved with the woman to whom he was committed at the time of his last interview, he had a few experimental tastes of sexual relations with gay men. Stan recounted how he went about relieving some of his inquisitiveness:

> I was curious about how the penis worked. A live one. . . . [I tried] just casual one-night-stand experiences with men that I picked up in a bar, where they . . . didn't touch me. They thought it was a gay kind of relationship. I might have been coming on to them, but it was more a use thing. I wanted to see the equipment work, and, okay, if I've gotta put it in my mouth, or if there's certain things that I've gotta do in order to get this information, I was willing to do that. But I wanted to see one in action. Like what's it look like? How does it feel? How does it work? And unfortunately, in order to get a partner to do that, I was fairly drunk and high, so the information is distorted. . . .
>
> I did to them. I got to see their equipment. They didn't see nothing of mine, but I got to see theirs. Limited under my fuzzy condition, and even now that is an issue that grates on me now. . . . I want to see one during the daytime instead of just sneaky at night, late in a bar. . . . And I don't know how to do that. How to get permission. . . . I think that in gay relationships is where I could possibly get permission. I've been trying to think . . . like what if I could take an ad out? "I just want to look at yours. I just want to see." . . . I would like to just be straightforward about it, so that I don't have to look back. . . .
>
> Something that I want to pick up too is that pride. That pride which I don't have. It's all fake. I play along with the jokes, but I don't have that real pride with what I've got that I can play with.

Although Stan was in a satisfying relationship with a woman, it did not preclude his having fantasies about gay men while having sexual relations with his partner and at other times. Stan explained that one of the ways in which he put these two aspects of his sexuality together was to imagine that he and his woman lover were engaged as gay men when she used a dildo to penetrate him vaginally.

> To me, I feel very much like this is a gay relationship, or a gay scene, at that time. In general, I mean [she] is . . . very, very feminine. . . . But in my mind it's a gay relationship. . . . We don't do anal intercourse. . . . [But] I'm a man, and I happen to have this extra part. I'm an uniquity of nature, and we're using this special part. . . . She's actually kind of a boy . . . and it's kind of the mutual use. . . . But during the time of sex, the twenty minutes or so when we're engaged in it, it's more of a homosexual encounter in my mind. . . . I'll say things like, "Fuck me, fuck me." Something I've heard in videos and movies of what it would be like.

Stan also said that because of his very satisfying relationship, he was willing to forestall his interest in gay men and their penises.

> In general, I'm not gay. I've gay fantasies . . . I have this fascination with gay men and the penis. . . . [But] there's a complication with . . . the fidelity issue now. I would probably pursue it more actively if I weren't in a relationship. But now it's not just me. I'm sure [my partner] finds that very threatening.

Scott was similarly intrigued by men and their bodies, but he was unclear about whether or not he wanted to live as a gay man partly because of his predominantly straight sexual orientation.

> I still am attracted to some men's bodies but there's no emotional stuff there. See, with the AIDS thing now, I'm hesitating to pursue any activity, bisexual or homosexual stuff. Plus not being finished [surgically]. . . . Now I'm finding as I'm a male that I can see where it would be easy for me to be a gay man. Whereas being a female, I could not have been a female being with a male, but being a male, I could be with a male. I don't know if I could be in love. . . . I'm probably a repressed homosexual male in a lot of ways.

Despite his ambivalence, Scott did experiment one time with picking up a gay man for a casual sexual encounter before he'd begun his phalloplasty surgeries. Scott explained how he felt about it:

> My wife was out of town and I just thought I would go. . . . have a drink. So I stopped at one of the men's bars and there was a guy and he was really giving me. . . . this heavy staring. . . . And finally he asked me if I wanted to sit by him. . . . So I'm sitting by him, you know, and I

can feel his leg against my leg and I'm, like, really getting excited. And so I put my hand on his leg and I just started rubbing his leg, you know. And we're sitting there talking. And so then I start playing with his penis under his pants and he gets an erection. And I'm really getting excited, and he's getting excited. . . .

So he invites me to his apartment. . . . I'm really turned on by the guy and he's asking me what my story is. So I'm telling him that I'm married and I've never been with a man before, which I hadn't really as a man. . . . But anyway . . . like I don't have a whole lot of time, but I really want to jack him off really bad . . . And so I'm, like, rubbing him, and he wants to rub me. And it's like, hey, I'm giving him this line about how, "I really feel uncomfortable, I've never been with a man before but I'm really curious but I really feel uncomfortable about you, like, touching me and stuff."

And at this point, I've sort of talked him into, like, pulling his pants off, pulling his shorts off, and he's sitting there with this erection you know, and I'm playing with him and stuff. And he wants to do something to me but he can't because. . . . I'm giving him this line about how I can't be touched. . . . And then it's like it's getting late, so I got to split. . . . I got to play with him a little bit but it's like it got to the point where there was too much talking going on and so we lost . . . the sexual. . . .

I'd probably need to find out if that's what I want to do. . . . See I'm sort of stuck right now because I feel not having a penis, or at least a reasonable facsimile. . . . I feel there's going to have to be too much explaining. . . . But now with the surgery coming up and new equipment, it's like I want to be out and test it to a degree. I'm totally going to be into safe sex but I definitely want to be with some women and I definitely want to see how I feel being with men too.

These few participants attributed their limited sexual experiences with gay men not to deficiencies in their own motivations but rather to their greater desire for relationships with women. Although these participants wanted to know more about the sexualities of men, they put women first in their lives and were unwilling to jeopardize their then-current relationships with women for the sake of curiosity and ongoing experimentation with gay men. It did seem, however, that should they find themselves unattached, they might well follow their inquisitiveness to its logical conclusions.

A Rainbow of Men: Man-to-Man Sexuality

Several participants expressed unabashed interest in having sexual relations with other men. Their tastes and enthusiasms were varied, as were their sexual activities. Their stories illustrate the enormous flexibility and adaptability of human sexuality. Bruce was curious and ready to explore. Walter, Simon, and Darren translated their curiosity about men's sexuality into sexual encounters with gay men. Walter also had anonymous sex with ostensibly straight men. Simon and Darren expanded their sexual horizons to include other transsexual persons.

Bruce, whose entire sexual experience with men consisted of several experiences of exploitation and one quick feel of his brother's erect penis, was eager to know more about how penises perform. Bruce had been sexually active with women up until the time of starting transition, but he became more diversified in his sexual interests as he began to live as a man. It remained to be seen whether he would translate his desires into action.

> As I go through the change, I've been really attracted to men. . . . When I think about having sex with a woman, it just sort of grosses me out. I don't know why. It just grosses me out. . . . But I would like to be with a man, because I like the company of men, and I like the camaraderie and the buddiness that goes on with being men. . . .
>
> I think about it all the time. . . . I'm sort of fascinated by the whole thing. I'm fascinated by the jacking off. . . . My fantasy is to be with a man, to take a man's dick in my hand and jack him off, or suck him off or something like that. And to experience that. I've never done that before. . . . I don't want a relationship with a man, I don't feel attracted to men in that way. I don't feel that kind of bond. But sexually I feel like I want to grab that dick. Give me that thing. I want to see how it works. And it's part of my own identity, finding out who I am and how it all works for me. . . . It's so fascinating. . . . It intrigues me. I'm curious about it. . . .
>
> Like I go to the peep shows down here and I've seen men do it. . . . It's like all these men standing around grabbing each other's dicks, yanking on them and jacking off. And it's kind of fascinating. It's much more fascinating than watching a man and a woman doing it. It seems like it's more high energy. . . . It's different with men. It's like they both want it and they want it hard. It seems more equal to me than with a man and a woman. I wish I could get into one of these jack off nights down here. . . . It's like I see that and I want to experience that. I want to know what that's like.

Walter, who was also sexually active with women, had acquired extensive knowledge of the casual sexual habits of both straight and gay men during the six months directly preceding his interviews. He frequented both heterosexually oriented pornography cinemas and locations where gay men indulged in semipublic casual sexual encounters. While there, he observed what went on and made himself obliging. Walter said, "I've had more sexual encounters with men in the past six months than I had in all the rest of my life!"

Walter took great pleasure in fellating men and observing men masturbating themselves. He talked about his observations at "tearooms," places where this sort of thing happened, and about creating a "glory hole" in a public toilet stall wall through which men placed their penises to be anonymously fellated.

> There are certain bathrooms that are tearooms. . . . from an observer's point of view, it's just incredible. You can sit in a stall and there's peepholes, and you can watch everything that's going on. . . . Generally what happens is the guy goes in the stall first, and pretends to be going to the bathroom, and then he starts masturbating. So, if you see him masturbating through a hole, then you know that he's into doing something. And guys go in stalls with each other. It's mostly just sucking cock. It's not too much fucking. . . . .I usually just watch. Occasionally, when I've been in places where there are glory holes, I will engage. . . .
>
> There's a bathroom in a park nearby. . . . I've taken up a new hobby, which is making glory holes. Now, it requires a lot of brute strength, let me tell you, to cut through a metal wall, okay. And there's this one bathroom where I did it. I made this great big . . . really nice [one] and what I do is I take toilet paper and I pad the sharp edges, and then I take gaffers' tape and I upholster the hole. So it's a real inviting little man trap there. Because that's nearby, very often I will go there, and it depends. Sometimes I'll go there two or three days in a row, but then I won't go for a week or two weeks. It's a very active spot now. I created a scene, is what happened. Now it's incredible. It's like every time you go there there's guys there.

Walter's descriptions of some of his experiences fellating ostensibly straight men were also quite ribald:

> [At] heterosexual porn theatres, guys generally are jerking off in their seats, and they'll come over . . . and sit next to you. One of the big things is to go like this . . . [on] the knee. But this one kills me when they go like this. Why not just turn to the guy, and say, "Hey, you want me to jerk you off?" . . . So, it's pretty wild.
>
> In fact, just last night . . . this friend of mine was going to this new place. . . . and I went and checked it out. . . . And it's these two little video screening rooms with large screen TVs and then there's this packed room that's almost pitch black. And I could not believe it. It was a constant sex. Constant sex. And I actually did engage a little bit.
>
> And it's funny, because I always use condoms, and the thing is, I have a good method. What I do is if I think I'm going to get in a sexual situation within a few minutes, I have the condom handy in my pocket, and I put it in my mouth. So, I put it on with my mouth so that usually they're not even aware of it. It's amazing. A lot of times they'll look down and they'll say, "Oh, wow. How did you do that?" In fact, last night. . . . what happened was this one guy, I was giving him a blow job with a condom and . . . some management guy walked by. Anyway, he got nervous, so he walked away. And then he came back about ten minutes later and he didn't have the condom on anymore. So, he wanted me

to do it again. So I put the condom on him again. . . . and I put it on with my mouth, and he goes, "Boy, how do you do that so fast?" And I looked up and I said, "Magic." And he said, "Oh, you're a pro." But the thing is, if he only knew, I'm really not. It's like I'm really very inexperienced for this scene.

Walter may have been a novice at man-to-man sexual encounters but his stories certainly made him sound skilled at turning his assignations to his advantage. Consider this example and recall that Walter still had small breasts at the time:

This is wild. I was with this guy. It was here in the house, and. . . . I didn't want to get undressed, and I was touching him, and he was very turned on. So . . . he was basically straight, and he was having problems. He was saying, "Gee, this isn't right. This is wrong." . . . So, I wanted to give him some added stimulation, so I let him put his hand inside my shirt. And he unbuttoned my shirt, and he saw my breasts. . . . And I'm uptight about it. I said, "I know they're really big. I'm really shy about it," and stuff like that. And he looks at them, and he touches them, and he goes, "Yeah. But still. It's not like a woman's." Now, my breasts are feminine. . . . They're not big as breasts go, but as men's breasts go, they're huge. And I have really feminine nipples. To me, I can't see how he could possible see it as anything else. They're hairy now, granted, but he actually said that. I tell you, that made my year. I will never stop thinking about that. But, "They're not like a woman's?" God. What a fulfillment that was!

Although all of the post-transition sexual contacts with men about which Walter related stories were "strictly anonymous," he argued that they were very beneficial to his development as a man and suggested that other transsexual men might similarly profit from such experiences.

It's such an education. . . . First of all, it's like a very intense male bonding thing. I cannot describe it. When straight FTMs say to me, "I don't understand how a woman can become a man to be gay," I don't understand how they could not at least explore that. Because it's the ultimate in masculinity. People think faggots are queers; they're fairies. No way. They're more men than anybody, 'cause they're totally homoerotic. How much more masculine can you get? They're not even interested in women. They're just interested in men. It's incredible. I love it. And, of course, it's risky and it's a real adventure.

Simon revealed that he, too, had long been attracted to men but had felt unable to act upon his fantasies for a variety of reasons both personal and sociopolitical.

Ideally, if I could have an arrangement, what I would have would be [my wife] and [my son] and a man living all under the same roof. And I think that that's been probably true for a long, long time. . . . Up till seven years ago . . . I suppressed my bisexual feelings because trans-sexuals weren't supposed to have that. And so you put that away, and you pretend that it's not there. And for a long time it was very easy to do that, because my whole world was surrounded by women. I didn't have men friends. I didn't feel comfortable with most straight men. They were wanting to swagger and talk about sports and go out and work on the car, and all that shit that I could care less about. . . .

And then, how things sort of expanded out . . . was I started meeting transsexuals and transvestites. Well, they weren't men, but they weren't women either. And then when . . . I'd done a number of talks [about being a transsexual] I met some men who . . . would come up and talk to me, and they seemed more interested in just what I was there to talk about. They also seemed interested in me. So that told me that maybe gay men would be cool with the fact that I'm transsexual, and that I'm out about it, and that I don't have a problem with that. So I started going to this gay bar, by myself. . . . I wanted to meet some men, and I wanted to be friends.

Simon had casual sexual relations with four males over a seven year period starting more than ten years into both his marriage and his life as a man. He described two of the people with whom he had affairs as "male-to-female who identified very strongly as female, pre-op, male body." Another man identified as a gay man, and the fourth was bisexual. Simon declared that his affairs had been "all with men, because I don't mess with women. . . . I have a wonderful woman in my life." Simon also explained that he was attracted to men's bodies and considered himself to be "pansexual." He further added that he had no hesitations about any sexual practices as long as he was "a top, the person in charge" and there was no vaginal penetration of himself because "it's physically painful . . . even though . . . intellectually I find it erotic."

Darren's total sexual experimentation with gay men amounted to a couple of drunken casual encounters. In both instances, the men knew Darren to be transsexual. Darren engaged in receptive anal intercourse with the men but recalled that it was psychologically unrewarding to him. Darren elaborated on why his interest in gay men never really materialized into any significant involvements.

If he was a genetic male, then I wouldn't feel comfortable. Because he'd have a penis, and I wouldn't. And that would make me feel "less of a man." Which is probably another reason I never got involved with ge-netic males. Even though I prefer women anyway. . . . I'd always think they would think, "This is just a dyke or a masculine woman." I would think that that would always be at the back of their mind. . . . I can't really blame them, I guess.

Darren did, however, live with another female-to-male transsexual in a three year relationship in which they saw themselves as two gay men. Neither of them had penises, and so Darren felt relieved of his self-consciousness about his own anatomy. It was in this relationship that Darren was naked with a lover for the first time. It was also with this lover that Darren first started having orgasms. As well, it was this lover whom Darren attributed with teaching him to appreciate androgyny in other human beings and to be sexually experimental.

> This was a gay male relationship. That's the way we perceived it. . . . This person had had no surgery, and was not on hormones. Initially. . . . we mostly did oral sex. We used a dildo for a while for anal penetration, but then we didn't keep up with that. So, it was mostly oral sex. And some digital. . . . It was the first time for me that I could be physically close with someone, where I didn't mind if they saw my body. I could undress or dress, and I didn't mind if they touched me. . . . Probably because we were both . . . in the same boat, you know. And because this person saw me the way I perceived myself, as a male, despite the anatomical difference or deficiency. And I perceived this person as a male. So, we were both perceiving each other as we wanted to see each other. . . . We did not address the vagina in either case. . . . That person gave me my first orgasm. And I've never stopped since. . . .
>
> I learned androgyny from this person, and I guess he probably learned it from me. This person . . . liked fantasizing . . . liked wearing female panties. . . . And I got into a bit of that, so we'd do that fantasy. So, in a sense, we were like male crossdressers. . . . When we were together, sometimes I would pretend . . . to be the girl. It was a fantasy we'd do. He'd be the father, and I'd be the girl, and . . . weird stuff like that. . . . I don't think the researchers would be able to understand that, or the shrinks. . . .
>
> We moved to [another city] for the sexuality clinic there, and I gave this person some money to start the program, which he frittered away on something else . . . Then a male-to-female came in to live with us as a roommate, and those two got it on one time . . . so that was that. There was a big fight, and I attempted suicide twice, and all that stuff. Then I moved away.

Grant's single long-term relationship was also unusual. Like Darren's female-to-male transsexual lover, Grant and his partner began their relationship as a couple of teenage girls. Over the more than twenty years of their exceptionally close relationship Grant became first a female crossdresser, then a female-to-male transsexual, and finally a transsexual man while Grant's partner continued to live as a woman in all non sexual aspects of her life. Almost from the very beginning of their relationship, these two lovers saw themselves and their relationship as a gay men's S/M relationship in which Grant happily took the submissive, or bottom, position in both anal intercourse and in bondage-and-discipline S/M sexual play.

> We went out and got our restraints. And . . . a couple of dildos . . . We had full leather gear. . . . .We were going into the gay leather bars, in with the guys. There was never any problem. . . . at all. We were accepted. I was seen as male. . . . They accepted that we had a master/slave relationship, that it worked, and that they didn't mess with [my partner] . . .
>
> [Now] I'm trying to learn to stand on my own two feet a little more. We got out of the master/slave relationship briefly, at the insistence of some well meaning friends, and it really screwed me up. . . . because this was long before I was ready to stand on my own two feet . . . I'm trying to get a little more backbone. I'm working on it. I'm getting there.

In addition to Grant's life partner, his fantasy life also revolved around gay men and S/M themes. Grant concluded that although his sexual orientation and his relationship with his partner gave him both security and excitement, his sexuality was unspeakable in any therapeutic context. After talking freely in his interview about his love life and sexual fantasies, Grant emphatically announced, "I couldn't mention that to the therapist!"

Ed was the only participant who had sustained a long-term emotionally engaged relationship with a male-bodied gay man. It started approximately eight years after Ed had begun to live as a man. The two men met at Ed's place of employment and lived together as lovers for approximately one year. Ed had some interesting things to say about what the relationship meant to him as a transsexual man.

> You know, I was amazed that I could ever get into that type of relationship where I was comfortable with a male because on a female level there is no way I ever wanted to be with a male. But male to male, for some reason, I find that acceptable. . . .
>
> It was kind of difficult. I mean I was thoroughly amazed that a gay male would want to have anything to do with me in the first place because most gay males I know the word penis is the first thing on their minds. And you know I was thoroughly amazed that he could really love me and be sexually happy with me when I didn't have a penis. And he was very satisfied in the relationship.
>
> Even though I loved [him] . . . I feel like transsexuals, at least I, have a fascination for penises just because they don't have one. And I'm real curious to know how this thing works. And it was very hard because as much as I enjoyed it. . . . whenever I'd get a lot of satisfaction out of it, it just made me feel very bad that it wasn't something that I could do with a female and make her feel that good. And I think that pretty much broke up the relationship. . . . I felt like I was doing it as a man but it was with some pretty divided emotions. . . . It was real hard for me. . . .

Because when I am with a male, the presence of his penis and the lack of mine just makes it that much stronger in my head that I'm missing something. I feel very inadequate, and I don't want to see myself as female. And when I'm with a male, it's very hard not to. . . . It's hard to see this physical and get past that.

Each of these people appeared to find various combinations of sexes and genders to be sexually alluring. They seemed unwilling simply to go from living as women to living as men and abide by social norms which prescribed that they should be straight men. These participants wanted to know more about love, lust, and sexuality. Their sexual desires and behaviours were as transgressive as were their gender and sex identities. Moreover, perhaps the most weighty measures of their transgressiveness was in the fluidity of their sexual desires, behaviours, and identities, and in their reluctance to wholly embed their gendered sexualities in the signifiers of their ambiguously sexed bodies.

Summary and Commentary

Fifteen participants (40.5 percent) expressed some interest in exploring sexual relations with men after they themselves had begun to live as men.[19] Although only seven of them actually followed through on their interests,[20] there are several reasons why it seems likely that other participants might have had or will have similar desires and experiences.

In the first place, participants were predominantly orientated toward sexual relations with women. In order to perform convincingly as straight men, participants needed to understand how men typically behaved in sexual and romantic encounters. Participants who wanted such information might have acquired it while they were still living as women, and a few participants purposefully did precisely that. More commonly, participants only incidentally knew something about how men conducted themselves because of their prior experiences as straight women. However, most participants' daliances were brief and superficial ones from which they retained little useful information. Indeed, few other groups of adults could be so innocent of the sexuality of men as were these participants.

Participants were men who knew precious little about how penises sexually function. Thus, most participants were doubly disadvantaged as men. They had only limited knowledge about how men characteristically feel and enact their sexual desires, and they were further limited by their possession of relatively inexact phallic approximations, none of which worked in sexual situations as did other men's. Nonetheless, they had substantial investments in being able to fully claim their places in society as men. To do so, they needed to claim intimate understanding of those most central symbolic signifiers of manhood: penises.

Lacking fully operational models of their own, and having very little observational data left over from their lives as women, many participants became fascinated with the penises of other men. Moreover, participants who were desirous of conducting their own fieldwork were vulnerable to feeling that their interests in the sexualities of men marked them as straight women. Interestingly, those participants who desired sexual encounters with men tended to be well established in their lives as men. They were, on average, seven years into their lives as men when they started wanting to engage with men on sexual levels, and they averaged eleven years into their lives as men at the times of their last interviews. Thus most participants who spoke about their post-transition attractions for men were probably well enough grounded in their identities as men that they could confidently feel that their sexual interests were from one man to another.

Participants could not, however, consistently assume that other men would share their liberal interpretations of the parameters of manhood. Thus it was that those participants who had actually engaged in sexual relations with gay men, did so under one of two conditions. A few participants came to their gay men lovers as transsexual men asking that their bodies be taken by their lovers as those of men, however they might be equipped. Although participants had some success with their partners on this tack, participants themselves seemed to have difficulty maintaining this stance. Alternatively, some participants refused to grant their gay men sexual partners full access to their bodies, thereby effectively eliminating the threat of exposure of their transsexualism. This technique, only viable in casual sexual encounters, allowed participants to observe and manipulate their partners' penises without having their own bodies or identities disturbed. They thereby achieved their proximate goals of acquiring familiarity with erections and ejaculations without undermining the credibility of their own manhoods. With that knowledge in hand, they further consolidated the thoroughness of their claims to possession of authentic understandings of what it means to be men.

Finally, there may also have been still another level of yearning which drove these desires: fraternal love. Participants long had wanted and awaited acceptance into the brotherhood of men. As Walter suggested, casual sexual relations between men can be experienced as an enactment of an elemental kind of male bonding, as ritualistic initiation rites into the arcane secrets of an entirely masculine kind of sexuality. Those participants who passed this test could confidently assert that in the embrace of their male sexual partners they had earned both the love and the visceral acceptance of their adopted peers.

Summary and Commentary: Post-Transition Sexuality

Overwhelmingly, participants' sexual preferences pointed them toward women partners. All but three participants who were living as men[21] expressed sentiments which indicated that they expected that it would be women to whom they would turn throughout their lives as men for romance, sexual satisfaction, and emotional sustenance. Indeed, seven participants had maintained such relationships for extended periods of time stretching from their lives as women into their lives as men.[22] Another eighteen participants began new relationships with women after they began to live as men[23] and another ten participants hoped that they, too, would one day enjoy loving relationships with women.[24] Thus thirty-four of the thirty-eight participants who had lived as men (89.5 percent) leaned toward women partners for the combined satisfaction of their sexual, romantic, and emotional longings.

However strongly participants might have been inclined toward taking women as their long-term lovers, they were not exclusively so orientated. In fact, participants exhibited a remarkable flexibility in their sexual responsiveness to other human beings. Four participants had sexual relationships with other transgendered persons,[25] two of whom[26] made commitments to their transgendered partners which they intended to last for the remainder of their lives. Additionally, thirteen of those participants who preferred women lovers and another two participants found men to be sexually alluring.[27] Six participants had sexual encounters with men while living as men.[28]

It would seem a mistake, however, to presume that only those participants who expressed an interest in sexuality which included men and/or other transgendered people were unconventional in their sexuality. Indeed, in some ways, the erotic choices of almost all participants and most of their sexual partners could be seen to demonstrate the lability of categories of desire. Bearing in mind that many participants retained some vestiges of their past lives as women and that almost all of them continued to be marked as originally female by their genitalia, the question of how to understand even the apparently most conservative of sexual attractions becomes complex.

Although it may be true that participants could lead their everyday lives entirely and unquestionably as men, sexuality requires the introduction of another level of communication and understanding. Initial sexual attractions and seductions or courtships usually begin in the everyday world where interactions are generally transacted using the medium of gender. However, as soon as things begin to become explicitly sexual, sexed bodies enter into the picture. Participants who may have been perfectly conventional men were certainly highly unusual in their bodies as males. Thus it was that participants who wished to have sexual relations could only engage with partners under one of two conditions. Either their sexual partners had to be informed as to why their bodies looked as they did or participants had to remain sufficiently clothed so as to disguise the tell-tale female parts of their bodies.

Therefore participants who wished to have any more than the most cursory of sexual affairs could only do so with partners who had a higher than average tolerance for physical, and often also emotional and psychological, androgyny. A handful of participants turned to other people who were themselves transsexually identified to find this kind of tolerance, but most participants found their partners among women and men who had never before knowingly dealt with transsexual persons.

Most participants who became sexually involved with women were fond of pointing out that their partners had always been entirely heterosexual in their prior relationships. I have no reason to doubt this. Nevertheless, those women, and the women whose sexual histories were more varied, might more appropriately be referred to as heterogenderal in orientation[29] so as to underscore that the primary consistency in their sexuality was in their attractions to men rather than to male bodies per se. Indeed, it may have been the case that many of participants' sexual partners were relatively unconcerned about the actual physical attributes of participants so long as they behaved in accordance with their gender preferences. Furthermore, it may have also been the case, as was stated in a few instances, that either or both, participants and their partners, actually preferred some blending of gender and sex characteristics in their lovers.

Another element of participants' sexuality, and that of their partners, which they probably share with many of the rest of us was their ability to selectively attend to more attractive features of their relationships and to collectively and imaginatively supply desired but missing components. This capacity can be most strikingly observed in Darren's and Grant's gay men's relationships with female-bodied persons or in Stan's gay imaginings as his female partner vaginally penetrated him with a dildo. However, any relationship in which participants allowed their bodies to be fully viewed required either an appreciation of physiological androgyny or similar kinds of mental gymnastics.

Thus it can be seen that although participants came through incredible journeys to become men, and although their bodies told the stories of both where they had been and how far they yet had to go, they were able to engage in sexual relations which in many qualitative ways made use of the same kinds of conceits and compromises as do most other people in their own love lives. In other words, participants and their partners, like the rest of us, took their sexual and body image fantasies to bed with them. They, like almost everyone else, imagined themselves and their lovers to have far more perfectly formed bodies than they actually did. They projected onto their lovers images of the people they wished them to be while secretly hoping that their partners would obligingly do the same to them. They joined their bodies together in enactments of sexual dramas which they found mutually titillating and employed whatever props were effective in helping them to live out their sexuality, however they found it most satisfactory. In all of these ways, they were, indeed, no different from other members of society who have the courage to follow their sexual yearnings to fulfillment.

24 | Visions of Genders

THOSE PARTICIPANTS WHO had become men had traveled a most uncommon path. Having lived the earlier parts of their lives first as girls, and later as women, they had opportunities to observe and participate in the social and emotional worlds of women, as apparently full members of those societies, for prolonged periods of many years. They therefore had access to the "backstage"[1] areas of women's lives as other men rarely if ever achieve. They thus learned more about the ways in which women are socialized than is normally available to men. Furthermore, as they became men and moved further into their lives as men, they gained a similar kind of entree into the details of the social pressures, impediments and perquisites of men's lives. Participants were therefore better equipped than most members of society to comment, as insiders, on the nature of the lives of both women and men in their social environments.

Moreover, because participants were positioned to make observations from vantage points afforded to few members of society, they had the potential to see women and men differently than do those of us who have never lived as anything but either women or men. In some ways, their binary vision probably sharpened the acuity of their reflections on both genders' trials and tribulations. Perhaps even more intriguingly, many participants seemed to have a heightened sensitivity to the differences and similarities between the social expectations placed on women and on men, and to the many ways in which women and men react to and enact the prescriptions and proscriptions of their socially mandated gender roles.

Little of what participants had to say on these subjects was unprecedented in the voluminous literature which has been produced about gender roles over the years. Be that as it may, the insights offered by participants pointed up particular aspects about social role expectations, and about the ways in which adult women and men socialize one another, which are worthy of consideration both for their more general interest and for the window which they provide into participants' ongoing development as men. Many of the remarks which participants made on these subjects underscored some of the ways in which the insights, beliefs, and attitudes of transsexual men tend to differ from those of men who have never lived as women. At the same time, they also emphasized how and why it was that participants tended to retain many of the more socially beneficent aspects of what they had learned from their years of training as women, even as they became more adept at the ways of men. It is also laudable that as participants acclimatized to living as men, many of them also resisted masculine socialization which was offensive to their more "womanly" sensitivities. Thus it was that participants' comments on the gender roles of women and men had the potential to be explanatory both of their own unique positions vis-à-vis gender, and to chart a course for a "kinder, gentler" kind of masculinity.

Women Are Different

I Can See Clearly Now: Understanding Women Well

When participants spoke about women from their more recent vantage points as men, they did so as outsiders who had once been insiders. Approximately three-quarters of participants (73 percent)[2] said that they were of the opinion that their sojourns among women had provided them with better insights into women than they believed that other men held.[3] Only four participants (15 percent) stated that they felt that they had no advantage over other men in this regard.[4] Scott, Jorge, and Brian were mute on the subject.

Steven was one of the few participants who proclaimed no extraordinary ability to understand women once he had become a man. In fact, Steven seemed to have been quite befuddled by women. He explained where his difficulties lay:

> No matter what you do, you really don't ever get to please a woman, because you're always in a state of confusion as to what it is they want. So, I don't feel I really understand women at all. As much as I've really tried to. . . . .
>
> I don't think any man understands a woman, and I don't care if they went through transsexual or they're genetic. . . . it's difficult to understand women because they give you so many mixed messages. They say, "No." They say, "Stop." They say, "Don't." And then before you know it, they're saying, "Don't stop." Or they're saying they want certain things, and yet they go after other things. And you do what you think they want, and it's not the right thing. . . . And I just don't understand them at all. And it's just so frustrating.

Most participants did not share Steven's outlook. Rather, they felt that, having lived intimately among women, they garnered a life long advantage over other men. Ken succinctly came to the point that was made by all participants who claimed any special insight into women. He said, "I'm sensitive. I think being a woman, and then becoming a man, the sensitivity is unreal. You understand. You've been there." Gary made almost the same claims when he said, "I've been there. . . . I was raised as one and I know what their thoughts are and how the world sees them. . . . In a way I understand them more than I do men."

A number of participants made recourse to their previous biological commonalities with women in explaining why it was that they had greater insights into women than did most men. For example, Bruce forcefully claimed that he understood women better than most men because, as a woman, she had had the experiences of menstruation and sexual objectification by men. He said, "I understand PMS. I understand sore breasts and chocolate cravings. And I understand what it's like to be preyed upon or to be discounted in the way men do it."

Phil similarly made reference to menstruation and further pointed up his sensitivity to women's emotional volatility.

> I understand women better than other men because, since I was one, I know what it was like to go through menstruation, to be emotional and cry. And to do a man's job and be underpaid. Until a man goes through all that, he really can't understand the emotional roller coaster a woman goes through.

Jack was of a mixed mind about his perspicacity when it came to women. On the one hand, he stated that he had never understood the "extreme sensitivity" of his wife of eight years. However, in a more general sense, Jack did argue that he had reason to have a special kind of insight which was not available to other men. Jack was especially aware of some of the many ways in which men regularly discount the intelligence of women.

> I think I'm more understanding of women, because I know how they feel . . . when some idiot walks up to them and says, "Oh, now, honey. Everything will be okay. We'll get your car fixed." And you just want to smack them 'cause he's just so patronizing it just chokes you. . . . And I think women hate that, unless they cannot absolutely do anything for themselves. Then I imagine those kind appreciate it.

Aaron, who had been a wife for ten years and a mother of four children, also thought that all her years as a woman gave him some advantageous and some disadvantageous insights into the ways of women.

> I feel that I understand women better than other men. And in a sense, that might be a hangup and a handicap in relating to them if you wanted to date and so on. Because, hey, they can't twist me around their

little fingers as easily as they could a normal male. I'm wise to their tricks. And I just excuse it in a relationship or with people I work with or something . . . simply by, "Hey. I raised three daughters. You can't pull that shit on me."

Stan explained that although she had often felt like an interloper among women when she was living as a woman, once Stan took up his life as a man, he was grateful for the insights that he had gained from her years among women.

I have had the opportunity to live in the other camp for a fair amount of time, and have some insights, some understanding of tenderness and gentleness that women are. . . . I got to be around them while their guard was down. And I always felt guilty about that before. "They really shouldn't be saying this in front of me." But now I'm real grateful for that.

A few participants considered their lives as women to have been excellent training grounds which helped them to understand women's attitudes toward sexuality better than do most men. Walter felt that as a man he "definitely" had a special insight into women's thoughts and feelings from his previous life as a woman. The focus of his comments was mostly on the vulnerability of women to sexual abuse from men.

I lived as a woman. I had that experience in society. I was oppressed as a woman. . . . I know still what it's like to be vulnerable, to be able to be raped. . . . The idea of being raped as a woman totally blows my mind. So that's definitely something. That feeling of vulnerability . . . And I'm just much more understanding, because women are more understanding than men, and I have been a woman.

Keith argued that he understood women better than most men because he had an insider's knowledge of what women prefer in their sexual encounters with men.

I have very much advantages with women in that I understand women very much. That helps me relate to women; it helps me attract women. I also feel that I have an advantage over other men in pleasing a woman sexually. . . . I know beyond a shadow of a doubt that the first time I'm sexually involved with a woman I will be able to please her, probably better than 99 percent of most men. Why? Because I have those sex organs myself, and I know exactly what they feel like; where, and how much, and how hard, and for how long.

Dale had a similar perspective on his abilities as a lover of women. However, unlike Keith, Dale had had an opportunity to test out his theories.

I think maybe I'm more sensitive. And I have the advantage, I know what parts of a woman need to be caressed, or whatever. A lot of men don't. . . . And in all my relationships, especially the last one as a full male, this lady just thought I was the greatest lover. I take a lot of time. I'm an artist at it, I think.

In sum, most participants who commented on their abilities to understand women said that they believed themselves to be more likely to correctly interpret women's actions, thoughts, feelings, and desires than would be other men. They based their confident assertions on their own histories of living as women. Having lived within the bodies of women, and within the social body as women, participants presumed that they had a kind of empathy for, and intuitive understanding of, women which was not available to other men.

The Many Faces of Eve: What Women Are Like

When participants described women, most of them (61.5 percent) noted that women are generally socially disadvantaged, relative to men, in terms of sexual objectification and abuse, earning power, and interpersonal authority.[5] Half of participants also typified women by their social vulnerability to various other dangers, whereas some spoke of women's psychological vulnerability as a laudable attribute which makes women more sensitive to the feelings and needs of other people.[6] Several participants (42 percent) seemed to regard the capacities for supplying nurturing, caring, or warmth as distinctively womanly traits.[7] For a few participants (15 percent), these and other feminine features meant that women were unfairly able to take refuge in such stereotypes and use them to their advantage in their dealings with men.[8] Some participants (23 percent) seemed to feel that such qualities amounted to an awesome womanly strength.[9]

A few participants, however, were reluctant to make any generalizations about women or men. Howie said:

Stereotypes have been assigned to both genders, but there are billions of exceptions. You are what you feel and how you live. . . . Any straightforward answer you get on these questions is merely a reflection of the prejudices of the person answering. . . . There is no specific emotional or spiritual makeup that is just male or female. Human beings run the gamut of all qualities. . . . Anyone can possess any quality regardless of their gender.

Brian similarly noted the arbitrariness of gender role expectations.

I have come to believe that the innate biological differences between male and female are functionally very limited and neutral in respect to what is universally and innately truly human. It is cultural programming that has created the perceived radical differences. They are entirely artificial, and often crippling in effect. . . . The majority of males and females are just culturally programmed automata. . . . They bore me, if they don't disgust me.

Despite his strong words, Brian did comment that becoming a man had relieved him from being subjected to "sexual innuendos" and alleviated his feelings of being "endangered by those who victimize women in the workplace and other environments." Thus it would seem that even if Brian had little regard for the philosophical usefulness of gender, he did recognize detriments in life as a woman and advantages in living as a man.

Other participants emphasized vulnerability as characterizing women. Keith listed what he saw as major drawbacks to being a woman, all of which suggested feminine susceptibility to violation or domination.

I certainly don't miss the demeaning and degrading sexual innuendos that men give to attractive women. And I don't miss the fact that I had to be aware, when I was . . . by myself . . . of possible danger to a single woman. . . . A female is conditioned to always take a back seat to a man. She's actually expected to admit that she can't do something . . . and I definitely learned that pattern. . . . Women are supposed to be more content with less ambition.

Ken also thought of women in terms of their vulnerabilities, but from a somewhat different angle.

They're fragile. . . . A woman needs to care. She needs to care about the way she looks. She needs to care about other people. A woman, to me, should be a fragile, soft, tender person. But they have to be able to receive.

Several participants focused on women's wifely or motherly qualities.[10] They thought about what women could provide for them. When they spoke of women they referred to women's inclusiveness and emotionality more than anything else. For instance, Luther's point of view on the social and emotional aspects of women centered on women's propensities for emotional caretaking behaviours.

I think that women need to feel more than just liked, but depended upon. Not so much for support, but depended upon to listen, depended upon to be the soul mate. Let your emotions flow from you to that person. I think it's important for women to make things pleasant about their environment . . . pleasant and functional. . . . I think women define themselves in terms of their ability to be intimate with people in a way that men don't. And I think that women—I'm trying to find a better word for this—women have a need to be very seductive, and I don't mean necessarily sexually seductive, but they need to have this ability to draw people into themselves.

Gary similarly characterized women as "loving, caring, supportive. . . . emotional and very sharing with their feelings. They want to talk." Darren used words such as "maternal," "sensitive," "compassionate," "accommodating," "courteous," and said, "I value those very highly."

Although it was not unusual for participants to hold idealized images of women as a group, a few participants seemed resentful about the ways in which women used their social skills and roles. Steven cautiously stated that there were no absolutes when discussing men and women, then remarked that his experiences with womanhood left him with the feeling that women were routinely sexually objectified by men and that they were "looked down upon as second-class citizens." Steven also described women as tending to be "more emotional," and he said that "they want to be understood" and are "family driven."

> They don't get the same kind of respect. . . . I don't think [a woman's] going to be trusted in a man's eyes as quickly as another man would be. Or if she knows something about cars and she goes to buy a car, she's really going to have to prove that she has some knowledge before she's going to get a good deal on a car. When someone sees a woman coming, they figure, "Here comes a dumb blonde." . . .
>
> Although I don't think they have as much violence perpetuated upon them in general, the types of violence they have I think are probably worse. . . . I think being raped is probably a horrible thing.

Steven then went on to lament women's use of the techniques of persuasion commonly resorted to by disadvantaged people to obtain security in an admittedly imbalanced power structure.

> Women can allow themselves to be crybabies. . . . they tend to get little advantages in some ways. . . . I don't particularly envy women at all. . . . They tend to get away with a little more. I'm sure that if you're a man and . . . you get stopped for a speeding ticket, it's going to be a lot harder for a man to get out of the ticket. Whereas a woman could cry or bat her eyelashes, and more often than not she's going to get out of the ticket. . . . Women tend to be coddled or expected not to have to perform a job as well, or have as much knowledge, or have as much command. . . .
>
> The women also get taken out a lot. . . . I know myself, if it's a woman, even if I'm not dating her, I have a tendency to pay her way or to do favours for her that I might not necessarily do for a male. . . . They

seem to know how to work men to their advantage and work situations to their advantage.

Howie, Phil, and Mel perceived women as being able to get men to take on onerous responsibilities which allowed women to enjoy freer, more comfortable lives. Howie and Phil both agreed that "women have the advantage of not having to work if they don't want to," and that those who were not employed for pay were under "less stress/pressure" than were men. Mel also seemed to find men disadvantaged relative to women.

> [My friend] says, "It's a different ball game. It's two different worlds."
> And it really is. When you're a woman you can get away with the I don't
> knows. You can get away with, "Can you do this for me?" Even though
> you're totally capable and totally competent. It's OK if you don't know
> something and you're honest about it. It's also OK if you do know some-
> thing and you want to be helpless, so that strokes the man's ego. All
> those little things are OK.

After noting that women seemed to suffer no major negative consequences for appearing to be helpless, Mel stated that he believed that women could be very powerful and controlling. Specifically, Mel thought that women had total control over romantic relations between women and men, and that he had not been able to perceive this point until he had entered into a relationship with a woman where he fully felt himself to be a man.

> I've sure learned a lot. All these things that I thought I knew, I found
> out I don't know anything. I used to think I understood love. I was al-
> ways in control of it. I knew exactly what was goin' on and I'm finding
> out, hey, women have a whole different perception of what love is than
> men do. And my perception of what love is is NOT what their percep-
> tion of love is. And I have no idea. I'm still tryin' to figure out what
> theirs is. And I don't think I'll ever know. . . .
> I've also realized that women have total control over relationships.
> Men don't have anything to say about it. . . . They figure out who they
> want to have a relationship with. They figure out when they want to end
> it. If they don't want to end it, what they want to do about it. And we
> just kinda' sit back and try to feed it and perpetuate it and keep it going,
> or whatever, but we really don't have a hell of a lot to say about it.

In striking contrast were those participants who had learned to love, admire, and respect the power and wisdom which they saw in women. These transsexual men held women in the highest regard without being blind to women's less endearing habits. For example, Hal proclaimed that he had trouble making any definitive statements about what human fea-tures were particular to women. He was able, however, to discuss what he felt were some of the traits which are more typical of women than of men.

Despite his statement that women "are allowed to abdicate responsibility now and then," in Hal's mind, women held a particular kind of "incredible" power.

> Those things [which are typical of women] are the desire to be penetrated sexually, breasts, softness, physical softness, a tendency to see the world as a place of being rather than of doing. These things don't belong to all women either. But these are my answers. I perceive in women a kind of a strength that is just sort of an incredible—I don't know, I hate to say these words, they are so stereotypical—an incredible earthiness that just is a solidity that's different from male strength.

Walter not only respected women for their special gifts, but he also indicated that he thought that women were smarter and better social citizens than were men.

> I think women have a better type of intelligence. It's a more well rounded type of intelligence. I think women are much more open, even though there are plenty of castrating bitches who will screw you every time, and just give everybody the runaround. But, in general, I think women are more open, they're more understanding, they're not violent like men are. I mean look at the sex crimes. They are all done by men. In that way, I think women are superior. From a societal standpoint of interpersonal relationships, I think women are superior.

Grant went even further along the same lines. He argued that women, in general, were a more advanced form of life than were men.

> Women are nurturing. They are the creative force. . . . There is a theory, which is one that I'm willing to back, which is if you get into reincarnation regression, you will find that every woman has at one time been a man, but most men have not been women. And as far as I'm concerned it's a step up on the evolutionary scale.

In sum, participants pointed out women's socially disadvantaged positions in terms of vulnerabilities to sexual objectification, harassment or assault, and in terms of women being typecast as incompetent in many areas of endeavour. They also seemed generally to appreciate women for their sensitivity to, and concern for, the well-being of other people. Participants, however, were split as to their appraisals of how women made use of their social positions. Some participants spoke of women as if they were overindulged and cosseted recipients of misguided men's largess. Other participants saw women as powerful and somewhat superior human beings who were sorely underrated in society. Nonetheless, the single message that most clearly came through participants' evaluations of women was that most participants viewed women as different from themselves. While many participants accepted women as kin, participants were no longer in the sisterhood. Women had become "other."

No Longer One of the Girls: Changes in Women's Behaviours

Participants who were living as men discovered, sometimes to their dismay and sometimes to their delight, that women often behaved differently around them in three main areas after their transitions. One difference involved the increased level of competence which both men and women seemed to attribute to men. Another difference was that women did not trust them as men and refused them the kinds of easy nonsexual intimacies which participants previously had enjoyed when in women's company. A final difference was in the sexualized ways in which women interpreted participants' motivations and appeared to project their own.

Many participants commented on women's expectations that they, as men, should be willing and able to be dominant. Most participants (61.5 percent) commented on this as part of general statements about their lives as men.[11] A few participants spoke of the expectations which they, as men, felt emanating specifically from women. Participants noted that they were received with greater respect, that they were assumed to know what they were talking about when they spoke, that they were assumed to be able to handle difficulties with panache, and that they were afforded preferential treatment as a result of their presumed superior abilities. For example, Grant observed that many women treat men with an unwarranted amount of deference and respect. He said, "A lot of them seemed to have this attitude that we're demigods or something. And we're certainly not!"

Keith said that he liked the way women acted with him as a man. Keith had never felt any particular closeness with women and so did not consider himself deprived when women would be no more open with him than to flatter him with flirtations. Furthermore, Keith stated that he was more than happy to carry more responsibilities than the women around him. He said that he had felt artificially diminished when, as a woman, she had curbed her "natural" strengths.

> I have more friendships with women now, I feel more comfortable with them, and I like women much better. And I'm sure that's not just my way of viewing them, it's also their way of viewing me. It seems to me that as an attractive female, women treated me in a more catty manner, because they saw me as competition, whereas now I'm an attractive man, and women are much more friendly to me. . . .
> It's easier to be with women in the sense that women expect me to be strong, which is my natural inclination. As a female I often felt that I had to act weaker than I was to bring myself down to the other women's

level, so that they wouldn't feel threatened by how rough and tough I was.

Ron was not pleased by the way women related to him; rather, he was shocked and dismayed. Ron's lesbian-feminist background and social circle had perhaps insulated him from the more common realities of women's routine deferrals to men. Ron therefore was distressed when he encountered some women's complicity in the systematic devaluing of women to the benefit of men.

> I'm just surprised at how heterosexual the world still is. How women respond to men, the privilege they give away with open hands. Where I'll get treated real friendly by a woman, and then another woman has to stand behind me and wait for ages. I ask for information and I get it, and another woman asks and she gets snapped at. And things like that. I find them surprising. Because I thought there would be more of a change. That there was more awareness among women. But there's not. It's really scary.

These participants' remarks pointed up two of the many ways in which women contribute to the socialization of adult men. By both demanding of men that they take control of situations in which there are women present and by deferring to men whether they expect it or not, women help to mold men's behaviours and presumptions. Women who support men's dominance in these ways help to train men not only to actively dominate women but to believe that they are doing so at women's behest. Fortunately, many participants were feminist enough men to have some insight into how women themselves are trained by patriarchal socialization to be complicit in the perpetuation of their own subjugation.

It was also the observation of more than half of those participants who commented on the matter (58 percent) that women simply would not open their emotional lives to men under any circumstances which they had thus far encountered.[12] In eight cases (31 percent), participants also expressed regrets at having lost their privileged access to the warmth and emotional openness of women's friendships.[13] As men, they felt that they were denied such intimacies entirely on the basis of their gender. They had discovered that many women were highly distrustful of men.

For example, Stan recognized that he no longer had rights to the intimate friendship of women on the same terms as she had when living as a woman. Although Stan still enjoyed some closeness with a few women friends, his new vantage point as a man allowed him to see women in a somewhat different, less flattering light. According to Stan, women regularly and purposefully misled men about any number of issues. However,

Stan did recognize that men just as often treated women with a similar level of distrust.

> Women aren't honest with men. There's no way a man can really get to know a woman if she won't let him. And most of the time they don't. On the superficial level, the game playing is terrible. It's just horrible. And men don't stand a chance. . . . I don't think I was aware of it before. . . . I didn't notice it. It was probably there, but . . . I was in the female camp, and so I didn't realize . . . because they shared with me. They told me. And now I feel . . . real excluded that they have girl things and girl secrets that I don't know. . . . They don't want me to know the tricks, and the secrets, and the sneaky stuff. . . .
>
> It's a shame they have to do that. Why can't you just be honest? Why do you have to go through all these manipulations just to get the guy to ask you out when you really want to spend time with him? . . . But guys do the same thing.

Stan explained that although women seemed to assume the worst about men, he enjoyed the challenge of working to break through the barriers which women erected in front of him. Stan described how he saw the "battle" between the genders.

> In some ways, I miss the close relationship I felt I had . . . with women. As a woman, they trusted me. As a man, I have to overcome that barrier . . . because they treat [me like] I'm an adversary. I'm the opponent. In the enemy camp. And inside I'm just chuckling, "If you only knew." . . .
>
> My behaviour can be misinterpreted. That they expect me to be an asshole. . . . They say, "Just like a man." . . . They're looking for trouble. They'll put a real negative connotation on something that I'm doing when, as a woman, they wouldn't have done that. . . . "Like, what a jerk. What a self-centred, conceited asshole." . . . I think women love to fight with men. They're an automatic adversary. . . . It's more a friendly kind of joust. And I think they enjoy it. I think, as a man, I enjoy jousting with women too. . . .
>
> And what is so funny is that, before, I would have given anything for a woman to say, "That's just like a man." That would have been primo, the perfect response. And now, it's not so perfect now, because . . . I'm not just a man, I'm Stan. And Stan is not always "just like a man." Stan does some female things.

Keith spoke in almost identical terms:

> Many women tend to put me down, or put down what they perceive as my masculine tendencies, simply because I am a male. Which I guess is the other side of the coin, because in the past I was put down by men simply for being female. . . . What I mean by that is that women who tend to have a somewhat bitter attitude towards men and say, "All men are alike." And so I am automatically lumped into that category, which,

in a way, somewhat amuses me, because I think to myself, "Oh, if they only knew."

Gary too, felt that women treated him like a foreigner in whose presence they needed to practice vigilance, but he was aware of the sexual interests which sometimes motivated such behaviours.

> [Women are different] in almost every way. They don't talk to you as a friend, but as a potential partner. . . . I found out that when I walked up to a group of women they would sort of change the subject and switch to something else. . . . You can't talk to women in a group anymore because when they see a man coming they clam up. But now you're kind of shut out of the female world.

Hal and Ron, who had both been long-term and highly committed lesbian feminists, seemed sensitized to the wariness which many women entertain with regard to men. Perhaps due to a heightened awareness among radical lesbian feminists of the many ways in which men can be dangerous to women and children, both of these men deeply felt women's fears of them as sexual predators. Hal commented:

> I don't like feeling like I'm suspected as a rapist, or child abuser, or misogynist, or potential threat, just because I'm male. . . . I really don't like being perceived as a threat to women, but I understand. But it makes me really really sad when that happens. Like when there's a woman on the street and I'm on the street and she gets scared. I want to say that I am the last person in the world that you should be afraid of, but sure she's going to believe me. So that's sad. It's sad that . . . some people, if you smile at their child, they get uptight, they think you're some kind of child molester.

Ron, too, made observations which displayed his acute consciousness of women's fears of men's unenviable record of sexual assaults on women and children.

> It's harder [to be around women now]. Because of the way things are changing, and the push towards equality. And a lot of women being kind of coached to be more assertive, and also aware of the abuse that's going on everywhere. There is a gender suspicion that I really find hard. I find it hurts my feelings sometimes.
>   But last year I was working looking after different farms. And it could be that kids would come into the barn with me when I was feeding the horses. And their mothers would come in and check up whether they were okay, and those kind of things. That hurt my feelings. At the same time, I understand it.
>   And when women withdraw, I understand why they withdraw. And I don't try to push myself as a goody goody guy who has to be accepted right now, because I understand where they are coming from. . . . So,

that's a big change, being on that end. And also . . . I like children. I used to always spend a lot of time with kids, which I don't do now because of the gender suspicion. Just being aware of it. . . . The only thing I do miss is the closeness. The only thing that's kind of a sadness is the gender suspicion, that I have to participate in that. . . . The hostility is fierce.

The irony in these participants' observations was poignant. On the one hand, these transsexual men had waited for many years to have other people see them as typical men. Sadly, many women have learned to see all but their own favourite "exceptional men" as potent with the dangers of violence and sexual abuse. Thus, when women treated participants as typical men, they related to them as if they could erupt into violence at any time if not handled with extreme caution. Participants, having lived as women themselves, were probably more aware than were most men that they were being kept at a distance. Thus it was that participants found themselves in a most ironic of positions. They found themselves held guilty of being members of a gender which regularly perpetrated crimes against women, but as several participants pointed out, women had very little to fear from participants in this regard. Participants' own histories as women, and often as feminist and lesbian women, combined with their own anatomical limitations to all but eliminate any possibilities that these men would carelessly perpetrate violence against women. However, so long as participants maintained their images as men, rather than as *transsexual* men, there was very little for them to do but to accept the inevitable stereotyping to which they were subjected.

While living as women, many participants had been unhappy at the ways in which men related to them as sexual objects when they themselves had no such interests. After their transitions, some participants found that women seemed to treat them in kind; ten participants (38.5 percent) talked about women's propensity to see as sexualized anything which they, as men, said or did.[14] Some participants were happy to have women be flirtatious with them. Some participants felt unfairly misjudged. Other participants recognized this behaviour on the part of women as being a reflection of the ways women had become accustomed to being treated by men.

Despite misgivings, Howie preferred the way women related to him as a man.

I learned that women often expect sexuality to enter into a relationship. For example, if I try to be just friends with women at work and talk with them, they think I'm either flirting, or I don't fit in. People aren't just people. It always comes down to male or female, or black and white, or whatever. The stereotyping doesn't fit me, and I try to show that. Consequently, I think my coworkers regard me as being real different.

Before, women would see me as lesbian, or very masculine, and would fear me or shun me. Now, women act cutesy, etc. And I can see all the games they play much clearer now that I've been on both sides. It's easier to be myself.

Bruce was not entirely happy with his new and more sexualized relationships with women, but he did find them more often pleasurable than not.

I find that women are more coy with me . . . straight women. They're more, "You do this, Bruce. Can you move this for me Bruce?" It's like you know they can do it, but it's like a stroke that they want to give men. . . . It's just something women have been taught to do. It's not that these women can't move that desk. . . . And it's sort of expected of you to go, "Yeah, sure. I'll get that." And you do it. It's sort of a game that men and women play. . . . It's sick. But . . . what I do often times is . . . I feel sort of flattered that they would think that I could do this. . . . And then I say, "Well, why don't we do this together?" And then they feel flattered, and then we do it together. We look at each other's eyes, and they're kind of coy with me, and . . . I get goosey, and then I put it down, and I go away. I feel embarrassed. . . .

It's kind of fun. It's a game. And it's with women that you never intend to have anything with, but it's just sort of this thing that men and women do . . . it's the hunt.

Steven seemed to think that women who thought that men were always interested in women for sexual pleasure were often correct in their assumptions.

[Women] seem more demanding to me, and they seem to have such a bunch of criteria you have to meet before they fall in love with you, or they think of you seriously. . . . I just want to have fun and enjoy my life and not have a lot of head hassles which I had in the past with women. . . .

It is probably harder to be with women as a man because they are always thinking that you have one thing on your mind, and that's to get them into bed. And generally they're right. But I guess that's very typical of the way women think. That if a man does something, there must be something he's trying to do to get them into bed.

Scott and several other participants were less than totally thrilled at the ways in which straight women began to sexually objectify them when they lived as men. Scott explained that he felt more alienated from many women as a result.

Women see you now, and it blew me away, they really start seeing you as . . . a sex object in ways. You know, straight women do. They really flirt, and they don't even really care if you're married a lot of them, which was really a surprise to me. And in a way you feel more distant from women and you feel closer to men and so it's, like, because they have changed their whole behaviour toward you.

Brian cynically observed that some women appeared to participate willingly in their own subjugation. He seemed to appreciate that patriarchal social structures encourage such behaviours in women when he said, "I'll never miss the levels of oppression and imposed limitation I experienced before." However, Brian had little patience for either feminists who were angry about such oppression, or with those women who co-operate with it. Brian somewhat sourly noted:

Many women tend to indiscriminately project the same sets of oppressions on me as they have experienced from other men. It is very hard to associate with "feminist" types. I dislike associating with effeminate types [of women]. So I tend to associate with moderate, more intellectual types with whom I can have average levels of conversation, without sexual overtones. . . . There are a large number of women whose major interest in life really is only sexuality, and really are interested in men only as sex partners. They reinforce the degrading stereotypes that men traditionally project on all women. They reject the efforts of other women to become human beings, and consciously encourage men to believe that it is their animal values that really define females.

Several participants seemed surprised that straight women approached them in sexualized ways. Perhaps because they, as women, had found men's sexual innuendos unappealing and unwelcomed, they assumed that sexualized gender banter was always initiated by men. When they lived as men, they discovered that many straight women were willing players, and often initiated sexually flirtatious exchanges.

Thus it was that participants discovered some of the pluses and minuses of living as men among women. On the negative side, more than half (58 percent) of those participants who commented on how women were different around them after their transitions noted that women were more distant or treated them with suspicion.[15] Few participants enjoyed being seen in such a light. In addition, several participants (38 percent) objected to some women's apparent assumptions that all men enjoy women whose behaviours exude sexual connotations.[16] However, on the plus side, most participants (61.5 percent) enjoyed the esteem, respect, or obeisance with which they were treated by women,[17] and several participants regarded women's flirtations as a benefit of their status as men. No matter how participants interpreted the changes in women's postures toward them, one thing was clear: women's deportment demonstrated that participants had crossed over the gender divide and forfeited their entitlement to the sisterhood of women.

Summary and Commentary

Participants' accounts of their experiences as men among women displayed a number of apparently contradictory themes. To begin with, most participants claimed that their lives as women provided them with unique and advantageous preparations for their lives as men. They were convinced that they could draw upon the lessons of their previous lives in order to help them to understand women better than do most men. In many ways this appeared to be true.

Participants, however, seemed ill-prepared to understand certain aspects of women's behaviours toward them. Some participants seemed to have had difficulty comprehending why some women would actively encourage men to see them as seductresses or potential sexual conquests. Participants' own backgrounds as homosexual females whose philosophies were often tinged with feminism, may be explanatory. For the most part, when participants lived as women they had felt the sexual attentions of men to be unwelcomed intrusions, if not outright revolting. Thus, those who were surprised at women's initiation and support of their own sexual objectification probably had generalized their own experience beyond the collectivity of women to whom it suitably applied.

Furthermore, it seems entirely possible that participants' often youthful appearances as men combined with their circumspect politeness around women to make them seem to be naive and shy young men. Having had little prior experience with the interpersonal dynamics of flirtation and seduction in sexually straight environments, participants may have been unaware how many straight women find such a combination irresistible. As cute, bashful, and polite young men they epitomized a kind of man around whom many women feel entitled to flirt unabashedly. The women who aggressively flirted with participants probably correctly perceived them to be men who would not become sexual predators. They were, therefore, men with whom such women could safely enjoy some of the thrill of the direct sexual chase in which it was usually too dangerous for them to indulge.

However participants may have calculated the relative values of their relations with women, they were committed to being the finest men that they could be. Their backgrounds as women, no doubt, contributed heavily to their success both in terms of what they had learned from living as women, and in the judiciousness with which they selectively accepted the masculine socialization which was directed at them.

A Lonely Brotherhood

Men Are Hard to Get: Trying to Understand Men

Most participants said that they had no special insights into what characterizes men as men. Whereas only six participants (23 percent)[18] claimed any special understanding of men on the basis of their positions as men who had lived as women, more than twice as many participants (50 percent) said that having lived as women had not given them any advantageous acumen beyond that of their fellows.[19] Another seven people (27 percent) did not comment.[20]

Commonly, those participants who felt lacking in their understanding of men pointed out that they had missed a lot of important years of socialization during which men and boys learn the basic elements of masculinity. As well, a number of participants noted that as long as they did not have fully functioning penises, they would never fully comprehend some of the most central experiences of manhood. Thus they would always remain, to that degree, outsiders among men. Howie's straightforward comment about why he didn't feel at par with other men was typical of those participants who claimed no special knowledge of men: "Not growing up male, never bonding with boys or men, never into sports, etc. I don't think I know men as well as other men might."

Stan, too, was aware of how much masculine socialization he had missed during the years that she was living as a woman. However, Stan's prior socialization as a woman also contributed to his resistance to pressures which he felt were imposed upon him in his life as a man. After living as a man for seven years, Stan had this to say about the conflicts which he felt:

> I think I understand [men] worse. I just got a late start on it. I don't know what it's like to grow up to where I was forced to be a guy. 'Cause a lot of the things that men do now, they do because they were forced to. . . . When really you . . . do have a choice. But you've just been fed this, "I have to do it." . . .
>
> I feel those pressures on me now a little bit. Not real bad. I still go against them, and people make comments about that. [My girlfriend] and I will go out to something, and I'll pay for mine, and she'll pay for hers, and everybody will kind of go, "What's the matter. Can't you buy that? . . . A man would pay the woman's way." . . . There are a lot of expectations. . . .
>
> I've been thinking lately my problem is in maturity. I'm real immature and my vision of maturity is doing all the things that the guys are being pressured into doing. I need to work harder. I need to make

more money. I need to be more responsible. I need to be the head of the family. . . . All the stuff that's going to lead me to a heart attack and ulcers. . . . but I don't want to do all of that stuff, but I want to be mature. And I don't know how I'm going to resolve that yet.

Those participants who did believe that they had learned some things about men from their years as women most frequently argued that the source of their knowledge of men lay in their having been exposed to a side of men which men usually withhold from the view of other men. Keith, for example, suggested that part of his deep understanding of men came from an adulthood in which she was a straight woman.

I think that I . . . understand men very well, not only because of being one now, but because, as a female, having always had male friends and growing up with boys, male buddies, I understand the male way of thinking. And then also as an adult, in the extensive sexual relationships I had with men, I was able to observe men very closely and understand the way that they think. . . . Yes, I understand men better than other men.

Ron concurred:

I think . . . it's a real benefit to go through the change. Because I've experienced [men] as a biological female and I experienced them as a male. So I understand what they're . . . putting out on an intimate level.

Participants were aware that they had missed many central masculine socialization experiences of childhood, youth, and earlier adulthood. Even though any number of them had been close with boys as children and many had played the parts of men in their pre-transition relationships with women, their experiences were not, in their own minds, truly equivalent to those of their male peers. In addition, participants were also exquisitely mindful of the fact that they would probably never experience erections, ejaculations, or intromissions after the fashion of men. Thus more of those participants who made any statements one way or the other considered themselves to be no better equipped to understand men than were other men.[21] They assumed that any edge which their bifurcated experience of gender might have given to them was either cancelled out or deluged by all that they had never had the opportunity to experience.

Another half-dozen participants (23 percent) saw things differently.[22] Rather than privileging all that they lacked, they counted the wealth of their past experiences as women. They reckoned that they had greater insight and sensitivity than most men from having been trained as women. Furthermore, those participants who had been sexually active as straight women certainly knew a side of men that men never show to other men.

Battling and Bonding: What Men Do Together

Whether or not participants thought that they had any better understanding of the inner workings of men than did other men, they certainly
had studied men carefully. Participants had been catapulted into living as
men virtually overnight, but they had been scrutinizing men as carefully
as they could for years before actually joining them, and they continued
their research after their transitions. Hence it should come as no surprise
that participants had much to say about men.

What many had to say was remarkable in that they seemed not to like
men very much. They often empathized with men and were sympathetic
to the pressures under which they had come to be how they were. Nevertheless, as happy as participants were to be members of their new gender,
most of them found men to be less noble creatures than those from whence
they had sprung.

Several themes were nearly ubiquitous in participants' characterizations of men. Many participants found that their relationships as men
with other men were more distant than those which they had enjoyed as
women with women. Many hypothesized that men kept other men at a
distance owing to socialization which trained them to be territorial, to assume that other men were their competitors, and to respond with apparently fearless aggression when their rivals crowded their domains. They
noted that men were expected to carry heavy burdens of responsibility
without complaint, never admitting to insecurities, inabilities, or pain. Ac-
companying all of this, participants universally perceived men to be automatically conferred with various forms of power and respect simply by
virtue of the fact that they were men.

Fourteen participants (54 percent) seemed to think that men put these
traits together in largely unattractive or irresponsible ways.[23] They described men in sometimes quite harsh and unflattering terms: they used
words such as "obnoxious," "jerks," "ridiculous," "stupid," and "Nean-
derthal" to characterize their chosen brethren. Other participants were
less condemning but still clearly disapproving of much of what they saw
in men's enactments of their masculinities.

Keith was among the sharpest critics of men. According to him, men
were pack animals who could be callous and cruel to one another.

> I've learned a lot of information about male hormones; what they do
> physically and mentally. And also in my understanding of animal behav-
> iour, particularly male dogs which are very extremely similar to human
> social behaviour among males, gives me a real deep understanding of
> the ways men operate. Not just socially and emotionally, but also on a

level dictated by their hormones, which is far, far more extensive than most people assume, or would like to admit to.

Males in a group are very hard on each other. . . . Men take the attitude of "Well, buck up, tough guy. You can take it." . . . not necessarily in a literal sense, although sometimes they do that too. But emotionally and mentally they tend to push on each other and beat on each other as a way of toughening themselves and each other. . . .

It's difficult for most men to admit that they don't understand something . . . or that they physically can't do something because of the pressure on them as males to always be in charge, and to know what to do, and to be physically able to do things. . . . A man doesn't snivel and show weakness a lot. He's expected to carry a burden on his shoulders without complaining. . . . They are conditioned to suppress their emotions, to suppress their fears and insecurities . . . They are expected to be more aggressive and stronger.

Gary didn't seem to think any better of the men he had known.

Men are a strange breed. . . . I always knew they were, in general, a bunch of jerks, except the very few. . . . I'm glad I was not raised that way or I would probably be a jerk. . . . Men are stupid about life. . . . But they are human, even though sometimes you wouldn't think so."

Harry, Mel, Bill, and Steven all indicated that they were unimpressed by what they called men's propensity for "bullshit." For example, one of the many areas in which Harry noticed men's tendency to "bullshit" was in discussions about their penises. He noted that men were "incredibly sensitive about their genitals. They'd rather be killed than for you to laugh at their penis."

Mel found it most irritating when he saw men's "bullshit" involve their common habit of refusing ever to admit any weaknesses.

If I don't know how to do something, I will tell someone I don't know how to do something. But I know that most guys won't do that if it kills 'em. They'll say that they know how to do it, and they'll do whatever it takes to try and fake it; and maybe screw it up entirely, which I think is such a waste of time. I can't see myself playing those games. . . . I don't see myself fakin' it. I've spent my whole life fakin' part of it.

According to Bill, men engaged in "a lot of bullshit" because they "are not granted the freedom to express affection in public . . . and must therefore suppress feelings . . . [Men] are permitted to be competitive and assertive." Bill related that he'd "learned that being a man can all too often mean hiding what one feels and wearing an armour of maleness that says to the world, 'I feel no pain. I am invincible!' " However, Bill also thought that "men are actually more dependent on women than women are on men," but that they would rarely acknowledge it.

Steven, who had lived as a man for approximately fourteen years at the time of his last interview, declared that he was becoming increasingly frustrated with other men.

> A lot of men play games. The more you live as a male, the more you see how many men try to bullshit their way through life, rather than try to detract from their masculinity by saying, "I don't know" or "I am afraid." . . . Men are expected to know so much, and be shown something once and be experts at it. It's almost like a man is competent, whether he's done something or not. . . .
>
> Some men are very, very competitive. . . . Men seem to be more goal oriented and success driven. . . . A man is expected to know a lot more, to be able to handle a lot more. That he's got to be tough, he's got to be able to bear up under the pressures. . . . There's a lot of responsibilities that a man has. . . . I think our society is harder on men in measuring up and in fulfilling not being a wimp.

Walter, who called himself a female supremacist, dismissed men as "dumb" and "inflexible" when it came to handling interpersonal relationships.

> In general . . . men are not sensitive and understanding. . . . Men tend to be . . . dumb, nonverbal. . . . in general, men, supposedly are smart, but . . . men are dumb in general. But it has nothing to do with intelligence. It's a dumbness that doesn't really relate to other types of intelligence. It's like it has to do with interpersonal relationships and being understanding and being able to communicate. They're just dumb in that respect.

Bruce expressed sympathy for why men acted like "jerks" so much of the time.

> Men prey on women. . . . It's like a hole. They don't care what hole it is, whether it's a keyhole or a bowling ball hole. It's a hole. And it's prey for them; it's meat. . . . men just sort of think through their dicks. . . . They take everything through their dicks personally. Like if a woman doesn't want to screw . . . it's his dick. It's not that she's tired and exhausted, or just annoyed with him, but "It's got to be my penis." They think with their dicks. . . . I really think that the bigger men's dicks are, the smaller brains they have. The less they think. Because there's power in their penis. And a man will never admit how small his dick is, but he'll always admit how big it is. . . .
>
> Well, I think there are a lot more men out there that are more sensitive, but there's this peer pressure, and just when you think a guy is not going to buckle, he does. And you really want to think good of this person, but you know the difficulty is in what he's doing, because you

fall for it too. . . . And they come away kicking themselves going, "Why the fuck did I do that? That wasn't right."

Grant wryly quipped:

It was very strange when people figured it's that funny little piece of meat that makes you intelligent. It's not. As a matter of fact, I think it can be a definite detriment, because the majority of men I've dealt with in my life think with the head, but it's not the one on the shoulders. . . . That's the frightening part.

Luther said that men were "not allowed to be multidimensional" and that they were "always having to be the doer, that aggressive asshole who's out there ripping up the world and being king of the mountain." However, despite his somewhat negative attitude toward men, Luther had interesting perspectives not only on what behaviours and attitudes distinguish men from women, but also on what motivates men to act in the ways in which they do.

Men are scared most of the time. . . . Going out on a date . . . the man is cowering at the table. . . . Men spend most of the time believing that she is judging him against every man that she has seen, will see, for the rest of her life. . . . Because that's what men do to one another. So they think that women are doing that to them. . . .

Men have a very difficult relationship with women because . . . they have a relationship that women never have to go through. . . . Men are in a bond with their mother, so that when they become emotionally and sexually active with women they have to disregard or break this bond with their mother that's always in their head. What happens is that men feel themselves in a situation where if they treat a woman very, very well . . . they're doing what they did as a young boy for their mother, and not being the man that they should be. And not understanding. . . . you don't have to be a cad not to be a mama's boy. . . .

But it's always in your head. You're always carrying it around, and it's a burden. And I think most women . . . think that men are doing it just out of some sort of obnoxious dislike of women, but it's not. It's just trying to keep that identity. Men's identity is . . . a very fragile thing, and in order to keep this fragile thing together, you bind it up . . . so that it holds.

Luther also had some observations about men's sexuality.

I believe that what you do has a lot to do with not only what you feel about yourself, but your body image. Just look at a male body. . . . I think it's a very powerful thing for males to realize at some level that they have not a lot of control over their genitalia. . . . Not only do you have lack of control, but there's no privacy about your genitalia. Women's genitalia is private . . . in the positioning of it [and] in terms of the clothes they wear. . . . Men's bathroom habits are not private. There is nothing private about male genitalia. You have sex with genitalia. There is nothing private about sex. . . .

And women don't understand that they have to teach men the intimacy of sex. It's not that they don't want it to be intimate. . . . You've got to understand that you're talking about a species who has no idea that there's intimacy involved in sex. . . . No one teaches men about sex except other little boys. Women don't teach men about sex, so men know what makes them sexually satisfied, which is not the same thing for women. So what they learn that brings them to orgasm is not what helps bring a woman to orgasm. . . . And the man has to still be up here, king of the mountain, so he can't ask.

Although Jorge and Darren didn't have many kind words for men, they were more equivocal than some of their fellow participants. Jorge was happy to have become "one of the guys" even if he didn't find "the guys" to be very decent to him or to anyone else.

I've learned that men can be cruel, and there is definitely a need to be a big shot, even if it means putting other guys down. Men say a lot of cruel things and sexual innuendo about women. . . . Men talk about conquests, sports, and being big shots. . . . I've found out how mean men can be towards others, and towards women. I've been treated sort of bad by other men, because I'm small and not too assertive.

Darren, who had been living as a man for approximately two decades, was more hopeful. He had seen some change. He found most men's behaviours to be "obnoxious . . . hype." However, he said that it was "gratifying" to him that in recent years men were "widening up and becoming more human . . . talking about stuff that men wouldn't dream of talking about years ago."

In sum, more than half (54 percent) of those participants who were living as men and offered their appraisals of men were extraordinarily damning in their evaluations.[24] In the first place, they remembered with resentment the sexist or otherwise insensitive treatment to which they and other women had been subjected. Once participants had lived as men and observed men from a different vantage point, they were less than favourably impressed. Not only did they observe men's sexism toward women uncensored by attempts at flirtation and flattery, but they also became privy to the callousness with which many men treat other men. Participants discovered, to their dismay, that in many ways men were kinder to women than they were to other men. Considering participants' general dissatisfaction with their relations with men when they were women, this must have been a shattering disillusionment.

Eight participants (31 percent) seemed more neutral in their appraisals of men.[25] Four participants (15 percent) appeared to enjoy the way men acted in the company of other men.[26] The participants who felt either neutral or warmly toward men raised many of the same kinds of issues in their descriptions of men as had their more disconcerted fellows. However, they were less judgemental and more sympathetic in their opinions. For example, Ken noted without rancour that men have more pressures placed upon them to be persevering and successful.

> A lot is expected of you. There are a lot of responsibilities . . . I think men feel failure more. It's a stereotype thing, I guess, that the man is the power of the family, he's the breadwinner, etc. And when a man fails. . . . I think failure hits really hard to home. Men need to succeed.

Stan, who stated plainly that he liked women better than men, was also able to discuss men's foibles without making them sound foolish.

> I'm afraid of men. I'm afraid they're not going to understand me. . . . I don't like to play a lot of games. I like to try to. . . . be real with them, and that's harder with men. It's harder to be real, because real involves a lot of the fear, and a lot of the vulnerability and the giving out information that could be used against me. . . . Men, I don't trust as much. I think they would use that information more against me. . . .
> They keep their guard up all the time. And they keep their guard up even more with men than they do with women. I think that's why my relationships with them aren't as satisfying. They think I'm out to get them, as a guy. . . . Guys are just so afraid. They're just scared to death. . . . They're scared of being soft and that that's not going to match up with the way they're supposed to be. They're supposed to be tough. . . . You need the armour. . . . But then if you're soft. . . . then you've given away the fort. You've given away the key to the front gate. And now. . . . I know now that you can hurt. When the image is . . . I'm unhurtable; if you let people know that you do hurt, then they're going to find a way to hurt you.

Dennis seemed to both ridicule and appreciate men when he remarked, "Before, I felt more jealousy than I do now. Most the time I'm not really jealous of any of them for anything. . . . I don't have to be centred on my dick and nothing else. . . . But I have great male bonding with some of the Spanish guys at work. . . . I just feel like one of the guys."

Howie and Scott both discovered that once they lived as men, other men started to treat them in ways which did not make them feel defensive. Consequently, they were able to start to like men for the first time in their lives. Howie explained:

Sexual innuendos are no longer a problem. It's totally different. There's a male bonding, a brotherhood, that's present that is missing between a man/woman relationship. I don't feel the resentment and jealousy of men to the extent that I used to when I wasn't seen as one of them.

Scott likewise recalled:

I think the reason I didn't like men is because of probably the sexism that was directed directly at me. And once that stops it's like. . . . the change in behaviour around you is so dramatic in every way. . . . You know, men treat you with respect for a change. And, of course, they don't see you as a sex object, so sex stops immediately. And they see you as a buddy, or a pal, you know. And you actually feel, if you didn't like men in the first place, you'll begin to like them as a male because they're closer to you. . . . All the game shit tends to disappear. They tell you more of their feelings. And they're more physical with you actually than they are in female to male relationships. They'll touch you more. . . . You actually feel closer to men.

Ron similarly remarked that his "love for men had come back. . . . because the treatment I get from them is different." He went on to explain:

There's more openness. There's not the tension that they have as soon as a woman walks in. Usually when women are around, they might be friendly, but it's either in a sexually repressed friendly way, or it's in a patronizing friendly way. But there is always this fear of opening up to their own femininity. So, with another male they don't see it reflected, so it's okay. And if they see a male who's soft, then it's still okay. It feels comfortable.

Even those participants whose assessments of men were either neutral or positive were clearly cognizant of some of men's less cordial behaviours. They were, however, willing to ignore the sexism which they knew continued to exist so long as it was not directed at them. Once they had been befriended with brotherhood and bestowed with the privileges of men, they were able to appreciate the remoteness of men's affections and accept their shortcomings with equanimity.

Thus, in the aggregate, participants were predominantly dissatisfied with what they had learned of men. Unlike the boys they had known as children, they did not particularly find men to be enjoyable companions. Be that as it may, participants did not become men so that they could form close relationships with other men. It would seem that to be men who do not have intimate relationships with other men is only to be typical men, disappointing as that may have been to these transsexual men who had once known a more fulfilling kind of intragender camaraderie.

Summary and Commentary

Most participants who commented on their insights into the natures of men assumed that they had certain advantageous viewpoints from having been able to experience men while they themselves were women. However, participants were split two to one on the question of whether or not they thought that they had understandings of men superior to those of other men. Twice as many participants thought themselves to be no more perceptive than other men. They presumed that their advantages were neutralized or subsumed by their genital deficiencies and by their abbreviated years of masculine socialization. Whether or not participants believed themselves to have excellent knowledge of men, they were certainly keenly motivated and assiduous observers of men. As such, they had garnered much information about what makes men recognizably men.

A number of major themes arose in participants' descriptions of what they had learned about men after first living as women and later living as men. Participants often observed that men were automatically offered greater respect in almost all situations, and that they were assumed by other people to be competent at whatever they undertook, until proven otherwise. Participants also frequently observed that men tended to refuse either to feel or to express any sentiments which might represent less than complete self-confidence. However, many participants also unhappily noted that men commonly lack sensitivity not only to their own and other men's emotions but also to those of women. Thus most participants believed that men often have little finesse in their dealings with women.

Moreover, they observed that men regularly approached other men with either distant caution or thinly veiled competitive rancour backed by overinflated estimations of their own abilities. Furthermore, participants noted that men often compete harshly with one another, presumably for positions of dominance in whatever hierarchy of rewards may be at stake, and that they do so with little regard for any pain which they might inflict upon themselves or their supposedly invulnerable fellows.

Finally, participants observed that the price which men are required to pay for the respect and privileges which they accrue is in the level of responsibility which they are expected to bear without complaint. According to several participants, men carry wearisome responsibilities for the care and support of women and children.

To their regret, few participants could boast that they had had the pleasure of personal experiences of "male bonding" or of the "brotherhood of men." Although participants did feel that they were fully accepted as men in their everyday lives, most of them seemed to have been sorely disappointed at the men who had become their putative fraternal siblings. As is the case in so many other areas of life, the reality did not live up to the ideal.

Double Vision

Comparisons: Who Has It Better?

Having lived as both women and men during their adult lives, participants were well positioned to make comparisons concerning the relative merits of various aspects of how women and men live their lives. More often than not, participants concluded that men had many material and status advantages over women but that women were better outfitted to deal with the vagaries of the ongoing human drama. Although most participants were willing to make judgements as to which gender held preeminence over the other, they maintained that both genders had their strengths and weaknesses. Whether particular abilities were counted as advantageous or disadvantageous seemed to have been idiosyncratic to the individuals evaluating their relative worth. Thus it was that there appeared to be little correlation between the ways in which participants characterized men and women and their opinions about how well placed each gender was to contend with the social worlds in which they moved.

Twelve participants (46 percent) proposed that men's advantages outweighed those of women.[27] For example, Brian had no doubts at all about whether women or men prevailed in society. To his mind, men clearly were more advantaged in every way.

> Men have a wider range of condoned behaviours and opportunities permitted them. Women are more apt to be deprived of the basic childhood skills and support to allow them to develop their capabilities for self-awareness and realization of their unique individual potentials as a human being. If they are lucky enough to grow up under environments that do nourish their skills and intellects, they still face a larger society where such human potentials in women are not recognized or not willingly accepted by the dominant cultural system. They are required to exert more effort to achieve similar levels of recognition as men might, and this drains them of the energy to go even further, which it would for anyone. The world is gradually changing, but it is going to take more than a few generations. In most parts of the planet, cultures still devalue females, almost below the level of value they place on livestock.

Alan shared Brian's perspective on the issue. He, too, thought that "women have no advantages over men unless she is young and beautiful" and "there are no ways that men have it worse than women." Alan ex-

plained where some of the differences upon which he had based his estimation lay.

> Men are more personally bound by society's rigid roles. Women are
> more socially bound by society's rigid roles. Men have to be men be-
> cause they don't want to be perceived as women or "less than." Women
> have to be women because there is no other role open to them (other
> than sex change). . . . Women are sometimes less socially direct than
> men because they receive less direct stimulation than men during
> sex. Women have to learn to like indirect stimulation. Men don't have
> that problem. . . . Women are lazier in groups. Men are lazier by them-
> selves. . . . Women have it worse than men because of the fear of rape,
> lower salaries and not being left alone. . . . Men have the advantage of
> freedom of movement.

Phil maintained that "even today, men still have it better" and enumerated a brief set of advantages and disadvantages associated with each
way of life.

> Employers put more pressure on men than women. Being a man is easier
> I think. . . . .Women have the advantage of not having to work if they
> don't want to and can show their emotions without being labeled.
> Women have it worse than men because they go through menstruation
> each month. They have to settle for less sometimes because of society.
> Men have it worse than women because, even today, boys are taught to
> be the stronger one, not show their emotions and to be more dominant.
> Men have it better than women because they don't have to be on an
> emotional roller coaster each month.

Steven was explicit about the disadvantages under which most women
labour relative to men. He spoke about the difficulties involved for women
trying to garner respect for their capabilities, their vulnerability to sexual
assault, and the travails of menstruation and childbirth. Furthermore, he
stated that men get more respect and "more opportunity in this world."
However, Steven hedged his answer as follows:

> Basically, from what I've researched lately, the white male has it worse
> than anybody in society. The women, the minorities, and whatever else
> is out there seems to get the opportunities before the average white
> male. So maybe they don't have as many advantages as we've come to
> believe with the advent of women's lib and the minority movements.

Keith saw that both genders had their areas of expertise in which they
outshone the other. However, in Keith's estimation, any man "has it easier
over any woman."

> Women can use their sexuality to control men, and that is, I suppose,
> one of their few advantages over men. . . . Whereas men control women

with physical force, women control men with emotional force, or manipulation might be a better term for it. . . . Women, for the most part,
control the children, and if a woman is controlling the children that a
particular man has fathered, then she has an advantage over him. . . .

[Women] are certainly far less valued in our society, which is manifested in pay scales. . . . Women are physically the victims of men since
they are, generally speaking, smaller and weaker than men. . . . They are
sexually exploited. . . . In their suppression of their emotions, men have
it worse than women. They are conditioned to suppress their emotions,
to suppress their fears and their insecurities much more than women
have. . . . Men are expected to be able to support themselves, whereas
women traditionally have been expected to rely on the support of someone else. . . . The three best advantages men have over women is their
earning power, their physical capabilities, and . . . they certainly get far
more respect.

Although Aaron recognized that men's extra economic earning powers placed them at an overall advantage relative to women, he shared
Steven's concern that "the white male" was an endangered species. He
stated, "Yeah, men have advantages in most situations, but some of these
have been reversed, so they're discriminated against terribly right now."
On the other side of the balance sheet, Aaron saw women's childbearing
capacities as women's one tremendous advantage over men.

The only good thing, the only positive thing about being a female is
being able to have babies. And I feel that to this day. I feel like that's the
one thing I've had that a lot of men that are very caring good parents,
hey, they missed something. I feel like, "Sorry sucker, I had something
you didn't have." And I look back at it and I don't know if I would
voluntarily have traded that off. . . . It still excites me when somebody
has a new baby and they're proud of it and all this. And that's the one
thing I did get completely involved in in the female role, and I can't do
that now. It's not appropriate now.

Ron also believed that men had more advantages than women, but,
like Aaron, he also saw women as having their own special strengths. Ron,
who had been an active feminist before his transition, said that he "definitely" thought that men have more "power and . . . economic and emotional privilege" than women. Along with the acquisition of that power
and privilege, Ron said that he felt a "big responsibility . . . to always be
accountable to myself as far as privilege in concerned." By contrast, Ron
declared that women "are a lot wiser" than men because "they're a lot
more clued in to the world." However, he thought that most men had a
very limited sense of responsibility and little awareness of the depth of
their privilege. Most men, according to Ron, acted like "they're on their
little patch [of life], and the rest can go to hell."

In sum, close to half (46 percent) of those participants who had experienced life both as men and women felt that men were the more privileged of the two genders because men were more respected, better paid, and more physically and socially powerful. Furthermore, they argued that women's relative disadvantages were largely based in their sexual and reproductive vulnerabilities and obligations.

Participants did, however, qualify their contentions in two ways. On the one hand, a few participants bemoaned that affirmative action initiatives were undermining some of men's long-standing preferential treatment in employment. On the other hand, a few participants indirectly argued that although patriarchal control of social structures was sufficiently strong to limit the material rewards which might accrue to women by virtue of their childbearing capacities or emotional sensitivities, there were intangible intrinsic benefits which women enjoyed and from which men were largely excluded.

Only Bruce and Stan thought that women's advantages outweighed those of men. They measured relative advantages using a different scale than the one used by other participants. Bruce saw women's morality as being based in women's life-giving capacities and as superior to that of men. However, Bruce recognized that his was not a dominant opinion in the wider social world.

> There is a sense of justice about men and women just in general. But achieving that justice is very different for men and women. The difference is that men will try to achieve their justice by not very honest means, and women will try to by honest means. Men will buy and steal, rob, take. And women, not that much. . . .
>
> I think emotionally and spiritually I am bonded with what is a woman, but I think physically and psychologically I am bonded with what is a man. There's a way that a woman is in the world that is very different than a man, and it's hard to explain in just a few words. It's like women are all encompassing; women speak from the womb. . . . Men . . . direct with their penises. . . . And women are coming from . . . the womb. Because this is creation, this is where it begins, this is where all of it happens, right here. And men will never know that. Never. . . . But I know that. Because I have the ability to do that, today. . . . When they cut that out, I will not stop knowing that . . . because that's imprinted in my spirit, my emotions. . . .
>
> Women have it easier because they don't have so much stuff to fit into. It's like women don't start wars. . . . The amount of corruption in things that are women operated, are minimal, but for men . . . it's just . . . bred into you to get ahead. So, I really think men are at a disadvantage, although the idea is to make women feel disadvantaged. And they are, and they're oppressed, so unfortunately, women are more oppressed than men, but I think it's very oppressive, it's a disadvantage to be a man.

Stan also evaluated "quality of life" concerns when he proposed that women are better off than men in contemporary society. He argued that women had more options for self-expression because of the gains won by feminists. However, Stan seemed to have missed the fact that just as feminism had increased a few women's economic options, so too had it made it more possible for some men to be more emotionally expressive.

> I think women have more choice, believe it or not. . . . At least in . . . the world as I know it. . . . I think women have it better. Because they have the choice of being breadwinners and company presidents and all that stuff, and really playing their masculine side to the hilt. And they can still get soft and feminine and cry and be close and loving and girl-friends. And men, it's just real hard for men to be soft. The homophobia comes up. . . . Do men really have close friends? Like, they don't. . . . We can't get too close 'cause it won't look right. And it's not allowed. It's that that soft side is just not allowed in this society to grow. It's "you faggot, you wuss, you wimp."

Nine participants (35 percent) saw significant ways in which each gender alternatively suffered and prevailed. Thus they were unable or unwilling to pass judgement on which gender had more advantages.[28] For example, Gary could see merits in the positions of both women and men, but he would not declare either to be more advantaged than the other. He enumerated a short list of benefits and deficits associated with each gender:

> [Women] can share and be open with one another without being looked at funny. They can let loose where men still don't seem to be able to. Women may still have it tough in the job market. They are still looked at as sex objects. Still, some people think they are not as smart, which they are just as, or more so. Men don't seem to be allowed to show emotions or to really say how they are feeling. Plus they are expected to always be in control and get ahead. I think most men are afraid of failure. They have better pay at jobs.

Howie stated, "life is what you make it. Each gender has its advantages and disadvantages." He then listed good and bad parts of life on both sides of the gender divide.

> Women menstruate (cramps, mood swings, etc.). . . . Women can have babies even if they're gay or unmarried. Artificial insemination can help them achieve what they want easily. Men can't unless they're wealthy and can pay a surrogate. Women often don't have to work for a living. Women tend to have less stress/pressure, especially if they're not employed.
> I have to support a family, which often entails doing a job that is horrible. Men die of heart attack, etc. earlier (I know this is starting to

change). And in today's competitive job market, it's harder for men to get jobs because so many women want them too. . . . Unless they're feminist and assertive, women have to wait till a man asks them out. . . . I think there are more lonely women than lonely men. Men can almost always find a woman to date, but the reverse is not true. Men can be rejected a lot because it's primarily men that ask women out and you have to have a strong ego to deal with the rejection. . . . Men get listened to more, and respected more automatically. Women's views are often discounted or ignored. Men are accepted more for who they are. . . . They're not judged as much by appearance as women are.

Grant similarly stated that he believed that "in different areas, each has the edge."

Men have the advantage in being able to be completely outrageous, blustering fools. We can make complete assholes of ourselves and be respected. I guess that's the closest I can understand the male privilege. Women, however, have the advantage in being able to stay in touch with themselves, be true to themselves, and not have to worry necessarily about fitting into . . . the stiff upper lip, you can't cry. . . . Men are unfortunately restricted in what we are permitted to feel and permitted to do. We get locked into the gray suit mentality a lot of times. The disadvantage for women is, often, you're not taken seriously. You're considered very expendable. A disadvantage of being male is who goes to the front lines first to get some old tiger's war fought. Some young man who basically doesn't have a say in the matter. . . . That's a disadvantage.

Similarly, both Bill and Walter plainly saw an imbalance between men's and women's statuses in society, but each of them claimed that women had certain compensations available to them. Bill began by acknowledging, "I know what it's like to live in a society that has viewed women as being a step down on the ladder" and told a story to illustrate his point.

I learned that in certain situations what a man says seems to hold more weight than what a woman says. Right before I began living as a man full-time I went to buy a new tire for my van. I told the service man exactly what I wanted and he wrote the ticket up, calling me "sir" all the time. Then I gave him my credit card with [my old] name on it and he said he'd better check the van out to make sure I was getting the right tire. As a man, I knew what I was talking about; as a woman, I did not.

Despite his clear example of the higher status afforded to men in certain situations, Bill refused to take sides on the issue of which gender is more generally advantaged in society. He said, "both and neither," and went on to point out that "right now each still has some advantage over the other in different areas and yet both pay a price for these advantages."

> Women are allowed to cry and express affection for other women in public while men are not granted this freedom. . . . Men quietly envy women their particular kind of closeness and affection in friendships but also are terrified of it. . . . Men are permitted to be competitive and assertive while such behaviour in women is open to suspect, viewed as "bitchy." Men, since permitted to be more direct, are less likely to back-stab, to talk about other men behind their backs. Women, being encouraged to be indirect or passive, are more likely to engage in such behaviour. . . . Woman are more flexible in looking at the world than are men because women seem to be generally less fearful of the unknown while men feel more secure in looking at the world through black-and-white glasses, in seeing a linearity with an anticipated outcome.

Walter plainly preferred women's company to that of men, and seemed to like women better than men. However, even after acknowledging "rampant" sexism and "male privilege," Walter couldn't make up his mind whether or not men's advantages were stronger than women's.

> There's definitely male privilege. Definitely. . . . Societally, men have an advantage, but does that mean that they have it better? . . . Can you say that somebody has it better just because they're not as oppressed, when we're really all oppressed by the system anyway? So, one could say that women are more oppressed. But on the other hand, there's women who . . . work inside the sexist system, and they use their sex appeal to get what they want, and they wrap guys around their finger or whatever. So, I think it's. . . . what the individual gets for themself. It's not a matter of gender, it's how you use the society to get what you want.

These nine participants who refused to count either men or women as more advantaged in society observed women's disadvantaged economic position and sexual objectification, noted the differences between women's and men's participation in reproduction, remarked on the differences in quantity and quality between men's and women's emotional lives, and pointed at men's greater responsibilities for family support. However, according to these participants, there was a rough justice among these many conditions.

Thus it would seem that there was both much upon which participants agreed, and very little. Not surprisingly, one of the points of highest concurrence was that if either gender sustained an overall advantage, it certainly was not women. Beyond this point, there was also a general accord on a few other major points. Having lived as women, these transsexual men seemed to feel quite poignantly men's collective ineptitude at emotional intimacy. They were, therefore, in agreement that this was an important way in which women were more advantaged than men. Furthermore, they were unified in their enjoyment of greater respect as men. However, participants were far from consistent in their evaluations of the relative importance of other differences which they cited between women and men. Thus although participants' common experience of their transsexual passage might have given them an extra sensitivity to the drawbacks of being women in a patriarchal society, exactly what participants were happy to have left behind as women and what they welcomed into their lives as men shared few commonalties. The one shared belief among them was that they saw few compelling reasons to prefer to be women.

Feminist Men

As might be expected from participants' appraisals of the patterns which define the lives of women and men, participants were generally sympathetic to the goals of feminism. They had not only experienced the systematic and individualized sexism under which women struggle, but they had also found out how their lives differed upon their release from it. Participants' own lives thus acted as a kind of controlled experiment in which the main variable was their own gender. What participants consistently observed was that by living as men they increased their status, power, and freedom of movement. Not surprisingly, all of those participants who answered a question as to whether or not they considered themselves to be feminist sympathizers answered in some kind of affirmative.[29] Certainly this represents a higher degree of feminist support than is usually found among men. The reasons which participants gave for their support were instructive.

Some participants denied the label of feminist but said that they agreed with axiomatic feminist beliefs. For example, Jorge said, "I'm not a feminist, but I believe that women should have all the rights men do." Similarly, Ron, who had been active as a lesbian feminist before becoming a man, said, "I wouldn't call myself a feminist man because a feminist man is, in many circles . . . a politically incorrect expression. I'm nonsexist. Put it that way, or adhering to feminist principles."

Brian seemed to find feminism not radical enough in that he wanted to do away with gender distinctions entirely and found feminism to be too tightly linked to gender concerns. However, his comments to the effect that "feminist values and goals are only baby steps in that direction" seemed to indicate that he was supportive of feminism because it was proceeding in the right direction.

A few participants preferred to call themselves humanists or some other more gender-neutral term because once they had lived as men they believed that any word connoting female was inappropriate for them. Bill,

Harry, Dennis, and Darren all took this position. Harry defined his feminism by saying that women had a "God given right . . . to do whatever it is they bloody well want to do. . . . And the same with men." Darren explained his reasoning in these words:

> Labels are good to an extent, but they're limiting. . . . At one time I did [call myself a feminist], and then I didn't, 'cause I thought that was elitist and exclusive and discriminatory. But then I kind of thought about it some more, and now I realize that no matter what the semanticists say, and the philosophers, you can be all things. And I'm a humanist, and I'm also a feminist and a masculinist.

Steven and Aaron were the kind of men who said, "I'm a feminist, but." Steven said that he knew that he might sound "chauvinist."

> I don't like a woman who hates men or is condescending to men. I enjoy a woman who has a mind of her own, but not to the point that my opinion is second to hers. I think women should be given equal pay for equal work and equal opportunity. And in some respects you can say I'm a feminist, but I would still like to think that the male has a slight edge over the female in certain situations, and that a woman's going to look up to me and respect me for being a man and being a good man to her. And I think I am sympathetic.

Aaron was happy that his three daughters could benefit from feminist inspired improvements in opportunities for women and agreed with feminist principles so long as they didn't devolve into what he considered to be anti-male sentiments.

> I can approve and agree with most of the feminist cause. I have three daughters . . . and I'm very glad for most of the changes, for their sake. . . . You see, I'm a feminist in the sense that I want everybody to have the options to be all that they can be. . . . That's their basic goal, is to get women an opportunity to be all they can be. But whenever they became anti-male, I became very angry. . . . you're attacking me, so lay off.

Howie and Jack seemed to have become more convinced of the necessity and value of feminism since becoming men. Howie explained his intensified feminism by saying, "I see how often I am listened to more and taken more seriously as a male. I am sympathetic to women's issues." Jack's observations only redoubled his commitments to feminism.

> I'll always be a feminist. Always. My whole life. The way men, society, even women, treat women. . . . They treat them like they're a bunch of twits. It just drives me nuts. . . . It's just like I gained 50 percent more brains . . . overnight. I was the same person, basically, but just a different name, and pronoun, and the same income. And all these companies that wouldn't even look at me before for a credit card, and now fifteen

of them are sending me things. . . . Because they saw "Mr." on there. It's stupid. . . . I don't know how anybody could be a female and not be a feminist.

Keith couldn't imagine how anyone who had lived as a woman could not be a feminist.

I am a feminist man. As a female I used to get very indignant about the way that women are treated, and as a male I still do. If anything, more so, because now that I am a man, I know that there is no reason in the world why men have to treat women in an inferior way. So, yes I'm a feminist man. . . . The obvious reason is because I've experienced it firsthand, and anybody that has experienced any sort of bigotry or unfair prejudice, of course they're going to be sympathetic. They know what that feels like.

Bruce, who associated with lesbian feminists before becoming a man, had retained his attachment to lesbianism and to feminism. He said:

I guess to everyone I'm a man. . . . inside, I'm woman-identified. And I identify with the struggles of women. . . . There's so much that I can appreciate about being a woman that I could never appreciate before. Just the good stuff about how women are that you don't see in men generally.

Stan's feminism also took the form of believing that in many ways women are superior to men and that they are underrated in society. Stan illustrated the basis for his opinions:

I think I am . . . feminist, by my own version. . . . I think that women can do it, if you just let them. I think women are basically emotionally stronger than men. I see hospital cases that, I mean we're talking real strength here. We're not talking just physical strength, but the real strength to carry on after a devastating illness or a lengthy, chronic illness. I find women are much stronger in holding together the family and holding themselves together. Making loving decisions and staying there while painful things are taking place, while the guy can't handle it. . . . So I see women as being much stronger than we give them credit for. . . . And I feel that that's to my advantage that I learned how to develop some of that. . . . I think women can handle positions of power and in government kind of thing. . . . Keep their heads about them when things are all falling apart around them.

Grant and Walter went still further. They took the unusual position of being men who called themselves "female supremacists." Grant explained:

I would say I am a feminist, because my attitude has been for a long time that you're doing the same work, get the same money. You are a human being. You have the same rights. What you have or do not have between your legs has nothing to do with anything other than reproduction. . . . I call myself a female supremacist. I think women have it over men in more ways than one. . . . I'm relieved [to no longer be a woman]. I don't want the responsibility. I don't want the headache.

Walter similarly enthused: "I can really understand female supremacy. . . . I think that's good, the idea of women being dominant. . . . I believe in that. . . . I believe the patriarchy is pretty fucked up. So I guess that's a feminist attitude."

In sum, all participants who said anything at all about how they as men felt about feminism were inclined to be supportive. A few participants seemed to have mouthed support for feminism almost as a kind of voguish platitude. However, most participants' support seemed genuine, even if qualified to some degree. Participants who had been active feminists when they were women,[30] or had socialized with women who espoused lesbian feminist ideas,[31] were especially likely to be sympathetic to the concerns of feminism. In addition, a few participants seem to have been galvanized into greater feminist support by the contrasts between their own lives as women and as men. Probably few people who shared their dual experience of gender could have felt otherwise.

Summary and Commentary

Each participant who had lived first as a woman and later as a man could claim a kind of double vision unavailable to any but transsexual men and a few hermaphroditic individuals. As such, they belonged to a very exclusive group. What particular participants made of their special circumstance varied with their own social positions, personal predispositions, and philosophical leanings. However, for all participants, their double vision enabled them to see two sides of gender in a way that is simply unavailable to all but the rarest of individuals. It seemed as though many participants' grasp of gender may have become considerably more astute as a result of their enlarged scope and the immediacy of their gender experiences.

Be that as it may, participants' views must also be considered with an eye to how their special circumstance might also have blinkered their vision. It is therefore important to bear in mind that although participants were ostensibly raised as girls and lived as women, most of them never fully cleaved to their positions as girls and women. They lived within, but close to, the perimeters of lives as girls and women. Few participants ever reported having enjoyed many aspects of being female or of living as females are expected to live. When and wherever possible, they made themselves over to be as much like boys and men as they could until, eventually, female-to-male transsexualism enabled them to fully take up their lives as men.

Furthermore, during their lives as women, most participants greatly yearned to be men. They observed men as carefully as they might from the distances at which they had placed themselves. For a few participants who were heterosexually active, their placement was close enough to intimately observe one or more men. However, most participants shunned intimacies with men. Until they themselves became men, most of their information about the lives of men came from casual or workplace contacts with men, from familial relations, or from their mostly fond memories of childhood friendships with boys who had not yet begun to treat them explicitly as girls. Thus it was probably the case that most participants entered into their lives as men with more speculations and abstractions about men than solid data.

As many participants pointed out, having been socialized to be women, they had developed a high degree of sensitivity to interpersonal dynamics and were adept at reading emotional cues. Armed with such skills as they became totally immersed in living as men, participants quickly learned how to present themselves as credible men in their everyday lives. However, some of the sensibilities which they had acquired among women also inoculated many participants against some of the more virulent aspects of masculinity. Thus it was that participants' sensitivity to sexism largely prevented them from succumbing to masculine, or feminine, peer pressure to act in sexist ways toward women. Participants' prior experiences with the intimacies of women's friendships also made them less tolerant of men's intragender aggression, competitiveness, and callousness. Finally, participants came to their lives as men well versed in the techniques of self-examination. Consequently, they were largely appalled at men's general lack of sensitivity to the nuances of their own or of their companions' emotional lives. Participants thus also largely rejected masculine socialization which favoured the suppression of all emotions save anger and acquisitional desires.

Looking at participants' impressions of women and men from another angle suggests that there were areas of the lives of both genders about which participants were particularly ill prepared to perspicaciously perceive. In the first place, few participants had extensive heterosexual experience. This gap in their life experience impinged on participants' lives as men in several ways. On a casual level, it made them probably less aware than most men of the myriad ways in which a running sexual banter provides ongoing pleasurable entertainment for many straight women and men. As well, for those participants who wished to become sexually involved with women, their own backgrounds left them somewhat deficient in knowledge of dating and courtship practices among straight people. Lack of heterosexual experience also meant that participants had little knowledge of the daily care and keeping of penises. Thus they were also naive in the details of the sexual performance rituals of straight men and of the relationships which men have with their generative organs. Finally, very few participants had ever mothered children, and so they seemed, as a group, to have less empathy for the position of mothers in patriarchal society than would most other people who had lived as women.

From another perspective, the price of the power and respect which participants so enjoyed as men seemed to have come as something of a shock to them. What had appeared from the outside to be the shining privileges of men seemed less gleaming to many participants once they had lived as men. What they somewhat dejectedly discovered was that men are expected to carry a wearisome burden of responsibilities. In the first place, they are supposed to be entirely self-sufficient, never needing or asking for assistance in any endeavour, always competent and capable. In addition, participants reported that they felt the burden of a yoke of responsibility for any women, children, or less capable men with whom they might come into contact. Furthermore, participants were probably more aware than are most men of the thinness of the vaulted brotherhood of men. It was participants' observation that men were more likely to compete aggressively with one another than to band together to help one another shoulder their collective and individual responsibilities.

Participants' dismay at the silence and solitude with which they felt obliged to carry their responsibilities must have been amplified in several ways. Firstly, participants were aware that women could share their anxieties with other women and expect to receive both sympathies and practical suggestions in return. Secondly, participants seemed to have little empathy for the profound responsibilities for children, the aged, and the infirm which women carry. Participants' lack of deep appreciation of this last point perhaps made their own responsibilities as men seem that much more onerous. Finally, several participants noted that what camaraderie men did share was often centered around activities in which participants had little or no interest. To participants' eyes, men seemed to bond best around shared enthusiasms for automobiles, spectator sports, and the sexual objectification or disparagement of women. Participants' backgrounds as women did not incline them toward the enjoyment of the former and made the latter loathsome to them.

Thus participants were veterans of two "real-life tests." They had first lived the real lives of women for eighteen to forty-seven years. While doing so they had learned to appreciate and incorporate many values and skills which typify women. After deciding that they were not well suited to women's lives, participants moved into lives as men. At the times of their last interviews, they had lived as men for periods ranging from several months to twenty years. As they lived their real lives as men, participants continued to broaden and deepen their recognition of the worth of the ways of men. Having brought with them particular skills, insights, and sensitivities from their lives as women, certainly, they were not just "average guys." Probably they were far better than average.

25 | Lessons from the Journey

THOSE PARTICIPANTS WHO had traversed the gender divide had clearly learned many lessons from their voyages. In order to effect their transformations they had to engage in far-reaching self-examinations of a magnitude not often required of more average people and they had to accept themselves as members of a category of human beings who are woefully misunderstood and commonly believed to be misbegotten. Having acknowledged their transsexualism, participants then had to learn how to accomplish their sex reassignment. They had to become veritable detectives, in the 1970s and 1980s, to discover what treatments were available, to discern which were best for them, to ferret out acceptable sources of those treatments, and to secure them for themselves. Finally, they had to learn how to live among their families, friends, loved ones, co-workers and acquaintances as transsexual men. Surely, participants looked more closely at the minutiae of female-to-male gender and sex reassignment than do those of us who have had occasion to consider these issues from a greater distance.

Among all of the details which participants needed to learn, there were many occasions for them to ruminate on the causes and consequences of female-to-male transsexualism. Thus I asked those participants who were living as men to comment on what they thought causes female-to-male transsexualism; on what they saw as some of the advantages and disadvantages of their lives as transsexual men; and to provide their fellows who were coming after them with the benefit of some of their wisdom.

Why Me?: Causes of Transsexualism

Certainly all persons who vary significantly from the established norms of their society have occasion to ask themselves how it was that they came to be different from so many of the people around them. Participants were no different in this regard. They, too, were curious as to why they had become transsexual. By far the most popular explanation, given by 89 percent[1] of participants, was that they had been born that

554

way.[2] In some cases, participants stated or implied that they meant that they had been born with some kind of error of the body which required repair, whereas other participants meant something more abstract by their assertions that they were born transsexual. Furthermore, most of those persons who attributed the source of their transsexualism to something with which they had been born also entertained the possibility that any number of other factors might have contributed to the development of their transsexualism.

Seven participants (26 percent) stated that they believed that their transsexualism had been caused by some kind of error of the body which required repair.[3] Jack said that he had "always learned it was a biological defect" and that he had never questioned that explanation because it seemed right when he measured it against his own experiences.

> I certainly didn't ask for this. I didn't learn it anyplace. . . . You know some things are learned, and there are some things that are just born in you. . . . Those things that are born in you, I don't think you can change them. . . . This is one of them. It's born there, and you can't get rid of it.

Aaron, like several other participants, called his transsexualism a "handicap": "I assume we're born this way. . . . I didn't have anything to do with it." He suggested that it might "be a genetic thing" that ran in his family. He backed up his contention with some family history.

> Well, my family, there are a lot of in-betweens in one form or another. . . . I do have one brother and he's gay. . . . I have my father who is primarily asexual in his behaviour and appearance. . . . He has one brother who is gay and who is a drag queen. . . . And my father had one sister . . . who was happy in the female role, but was very domineering in her family, very aggressive, ran anything she got into. . . . .
> Of my four kids, none of them happen to be cross-sexual in appearance. . . . none of them happen to be attracted to the same sex physically. . . . But my son is very artistic and doesn't have much aggression in him at all. My second girl was very aggressive, very competitive, and when she chased men, she chased men. I told her once she should have been a gay man. She had a different boyfriend every day. She went for the physical appearance; she had nudie male posters all over her walls . . . and yet she's very female looking. . . .
> So, for me, it's probably genetic. I assume it's something I was born with. Perhaps I could have gone either way. Perhaps the first two or three years and things that happen can affect you that way. . . . But by the time I was three . . . it's obvious it was settled.

Fourteen participants (52 percent) suggested that female-to-male transsexualism probably had some amount of biological basis but qualified their opinions by including other possible contributing factors in their speculations.[4] Most of them considered their family dynamics to have been relevant. For example, Howie put most of the responsibility for his own transsexualism on biological causes, saying that he believed he was "just correcting a mistake of nature. . . . a birth defect." However, he also suggested that family dynamics, in the form of his admiration for his brother whom he used as a "role model," might also have "played a minor role."

Darren hypothesized that, in general, biological, psychological, and social factors can all come into play in the development of female-to-male transsexualism. However, in his case, he thought that biological causes were paramount.

> I think there's probably a biological determinant there, but obviously the socialization and the identification that goes on post-natally is also a strong factor. . . . Definitely a combination. I think that social and psychological experiences could bring on a transsexual life, even without a biological basis. . . .
>
> I guess there's what they call a primary and a secondary [transsexual]. . . . I think they really are two quite distinct groups. I think I fall into the primary . . . I think with the primary transsexuals it's just so driving and so constant, and started from way back when, and it never relented. No gender confusion, no ambivalence. . . . I think there is some indication that there is a biological thing there. Perhaps in the prenatal stage.

Luther similarly stated:

> I don't know exactly what happens, but I think that probably everybody is essentially female at first, and . . . the hormones come into the brain . . . and ours just got whacked out. Got crossed. . . .
>
> I think that family dynamics probably accounts more for if you try to do the ages at which people decide. I think people who decide later in life are probably people who lived in families where they were very rigid in sex roles and it took a long time to break out. Those that did it earlier probably lived in families where they were not so rigidly brought up, so they were allowed to kind of live freely. But I think essentially . . . people who are transsexual are transsexual. . . . I don't think it's caused by environment or psychological makeup. . . . I certainly don't think it has anything to do with . . . homosexuality. I would have stayed a lesbian if I had thought that. I was having a pretty decent time.

Several participants cast still more widely in search of reasons for their transsexualism. They, too, made reference to being born transsexual but were less firmly wedded to the idea that an inborn physical substrate was responsible for their transsexualism. Keith considered a possible biological explanation but was willing to consider the relevance of social experiences as well.

I suspect there may be a biological predisposition. For example, my two sisters were raised in exactly the same childhood environment that I was, and both of them are quite comfortable and happy with being women. So what is it that caused me to go differently than they were, even though we were raised exactly the same? It seems that there must be some biological predisposition there.

But I do believe it is also because of family dynamics. I also believe that it is because of bad experiences. For myself, like I mentioned earlier, my very, very early experiences as a baby and a toddler being mistaken for a boy. I suspect that that planted a subconscious seed in my mind that it was far more desirable to be a boy than a girl. And that psychological seed was reinforced by almost all of my later experiences in society, in the Catholic church in which I was raised, and also in my family in the sense that my personality was directly in conflict with what all these influences expected me to be like. . . . And then also there were bad sexual experiences being exploited as a female by men. And that also reinforced the belief that I should be male rather than female, because obviously men have it better than women.

Bill similarly seemed to find psychological explanations for his transsexualism to be the most cogent ones. He provided a catalogue of possible causes.

I don't know the reasons in my case, though I certainly have thought about it. . . . Did I want to be "special," the only boy among five children? Did I identify with my persecutor, my father? Did I perceive women as weak and ineffective victims of male aggression and domination and identify with my father in order to survive? Did I simply hate the thought of growing up and see this as a means of escape from the responsibilities and craziness of the adult world? Did I see myself as my mother's rescuer and need to be male to fill that role? Perhaps the answer to these and others is "yes" with a little of the 'ole biological predis' thrown in. Or perhaps none of these questions fit the bill. I will never know unless God indeed provides answers some day.

Like Bill's, Pat's point of view included a biological element but was heavily weighted by psychological reasoning.

I don't know whether there was a little girl that, like, fairly early on, through some abuse, like, disappeared. And I don't know that. But I do know that even if that happened, and I were to try to identify that and work it through, it just seems like the way I've lived my life to this point for forty-one years says there's something to be said for that identity, whatever it might be. . . . I am also aware that I have issues that are unresolved about intimacy and about early childhood trauma (the content of which remains unclear) and I wonder to what extent there is an interaction effect between my gender issues and these childhood traumas.

A number of participants conjectured that transsexual persons are born with spirits or souls which rightfully belong in bodies of another type. It was their contention that a more ephemeral body was what animated their physical ones. At one point in his discussion, Walter favoured a biological explanation for the source of female-to-male transsexualism, saying, "I think it's something physical. . . . It just makes so much sense." However, Walter also equally as strongly suggested that gender identity has "psychic" causes.

> What your body is has nothing to do with what gender you are. . . . Maybe it's the soul. . . . Absolutely definitely I was born with it. I don't think it's a socialized thing at all. . . . It must be on a spiritual level. . . . I guess it just must be that inner thing, that core identity, that psychic thing inside you that makes you know that you're male or female.

Furthermore, Walter also added some compelling social benefits to his medley of motivations.

> By virtue of the fact that I'm a transsexual, I'm buying into the patriarchy. . . . from a feminist standpoint. But the fact is . . . I have no choice. I am a man, and I have to be like this. It's not because I'm supportive of the patriarchy. . . . I think even though people wouldn't admit it, I think, in a way, one does want to become a man because of the privileges involved. And so, you are buying into the patriarchy in that way.

Hal, too, favoured a metaphysical approach.

> I think there are probably some individuals who have more biological justification than others. I think there can be tests made and biological rationalizations found but I don't think ultimately that that's where it's at. . . . I think it's both spiritual and psychological. And probably physical as well. . . . I would say it's something that you come into the world with, that may not have anything to do with your physical body. . . . I really think that there is some kind of spirit thing going on in people that moves them.

Stan similarly suggested that "it's very deep internal. Maybe something they are born with. . . . It's in the essence of them." Dennis's idea was that "the heart . . . and maybe even the brain . . . the soul . . . are all lined up" but the body doesn't match. Eli, a follower of an Indian guru, thought that people were born transsexual because of some kind of mishap in their reincarnation process.

> I do have a kind of past life belief that people do tend to have a favourite sex. And I've been told that 75 percent of all my past lives were male, and that made me feel better. And I think some people just have a favourite sex, and when they're not that, they're uncomfortable with it,

and so they just backpaddle like crazy to be what they were before. . . .
I think that's probably the best explanation that I've ever heard.

Only three participants thought that their transsexualism was something which they had acquired since birth. None of them saw their gender and sex identities as any more of their own choosing than did those participants who argued that their transsexualism was innate. Rather, they pointed to irreversible formative influences in their early years as having set them onto transsexual trajectories.

Ken leaned toward a social environment explanation, but only obliquely so.

> What makes a person want to change gender? I wanted to be in control. Macho. Accepted. I didn't want to live a lie anymore. . . . I didn't like my breasts. And I didn't like having periods. . . . It was a preoccupation. I wanted to be male. I wanted to take my shirt off and go to the beach. I wanted to get sun on my chest. . . . I wanted to shave. Not my legs. My chin.
>
> I don't think family dynamics really had something to do with it. Is it because of some bad experiences? In part one I told you about some experiences. Basically the emotional, mental, physical, and sexual abuse by my father. But I'm a firm believer that if a male did that to me, why would I ever want to be a male? I don't think bad experiences have anything to do with it. . . .
>
> I think it's a mix of a lot of reasons. Upbringing. I was close to my mother. She taught me a lot. My father was there, but there was an absence of a male role model. Outside of my circle of family friends, there were a lot of males I looked up to a lot. I liked the way they acted and what they did. Maybe that made a difference.

Brian and Bruce placed the basis of their own transsexualism firmly in their family dynamics. Both spoke about feeling as though the treatment which they had received as children had scarred them irreparably and turned them forever away from their femaleness. Brian evoked the notion of transsexuals having spirits which are mismatched to their bodies, but seemed to count human social factors as the crucial determinants. He blamed his parents and their upbringing of her within a sexist society for making him transsexual.

> There is surely no one recipe of experiences and environments that promote the transsexual response to self-identity. . . .
>
> A person has a certain predisposition of spirit that is hypersensitive to the limitations that society imposes based on body form. If society did not place the stringent rules of bodily form and function on how a human spirit can express itself, self-identity would be less clearly connected with the clay physical body.
>
> Family is the most immediate and most powerful initial represen-

tative of society, culture, tradition. The parents who see their children according to limitations, actively punish and suppress unique and creative human development in their children. A child can learn social values by being terrorized by them. That kind of trauma sticks for life, however actively and consciously one may strive to neutralize the pain of it. . . . Positive experiences provide a lifetime of inner strengths, a foundation upon which to grow and express a maximum of the greatness of human potential. Negative experiences require a lifetime of struggle and compensation to neutralize the crippling effects, even for a successfully creative person. One's very core of being has been shattered and scarred in a way that can never be healed to the extent it could be forgotten. . . .

I believe a very different parental interpretation of my childhood character could have changed how I defined myself. If my early creativity and expression had been reinforced for what they were, independent and undefined by traditional notions about body significance, I might not have found reason to despise my physical form so intensely. . . . Some emotional scars are too deep to be overcome by pragmatic logic or psychoanalytic games. . . .

Bruce mentioned biological and social components so as to provide a context for his main contention, which was that it was her childhood home life which had made her transsexual.

I have this theory about transsexuality. Seventy-five percent of it, or close to that, is an emotional, psychological mending of something broken. . . . And 25 percent is genetics. And part of that 25 percent is also environment.

So you see, I really believe if, as a girl, I was given a real positive self-image by my mother . . . if my mother had let me explore myself, come to terms with whoever I was as a child . . . I may not be a transsexual today. . . . I may have a more positive outlook about my breasts had my mother not created such an oppressive thing for me. . . . Or the stuff around your period or things like that. And I think my environment, the separation, where I was thrown into this role of being more male. . . .

It's a mending of the ways for the emotional and psychological pain that I endured as a child. And that I think that . . . when I started to go through this . . . that was thirty years of my life of pain. That was long enough. That, obviously, no amount of therapy at this point was going to help me recover the loss experienced as a child over the loss of my body. That I needed to find a new vessel. I needed to create a new vessel. I needed to be, do, something different.

And so this has allowed me to create a new vessel that I can look in the mirror and go, "Oh. I love that person." . . . And I'm working through now my loss and grieving . . . the person I could have been, and accepting this person that I am today. And the wholeness that I found about myself. . . .

The little girl is healed, because she's found her place. But not as a girl, and not as a man, but as a person that is accepting of whoever she or he is. Like I feel like that little girl will heal in time, and it's this other stronger person that's come out of this that will bring that little girl in and go, "It's okay now. You're home. It's okay." It's like my dad embracing me. . . . I'm grieving at the loss of [the woman I was]. I miss her. Sometimes I wish she were never gone.

I think, as I look across the board at all the different transsexuals that I know, there is a disturbance that takes place in their environment at a very young age. . . . I'd say at age five, something traumatic happens. . . . And then they gravitate towards an image that is positive, because there is so much negative in the other direction. And the gravitational pull just gets more and more and more, because it's positive. . . . And I'm not saying some of it is not genetics. Some of it might be that in the womb, something happens that makes you more susceptible to this, and maybe that happened to me too, and I was just prone or more susceptible to this. And so, here we are. We have to make the best of it.

Summary and Commentary

Participants were nearly unanimous in their assertions that, whatever other influences later came to bear, they were born as females who were destined to become men. They were somewhat less uniform, however, in their theorizations about precisely why. The most commonly proffered explanations were biologically based ones about misdirected fetal developmental pathways. Alternate proposals supposed that participants were born with souls or spirits which were unable to find satisfactory expression within the limitations intrinsic to, and imposed upon, female bodies.

Another class of etiological hypotheses favoured by participants concerned childhood family dynamics. Although very few participants were willing to give psychological factors full explanatory power, many participants said that they could see how their relationships with their parents and/or siblings may have been influential in their own cases. Indeed, participants noted many of the same family psychodynamics which have been proposed by less personally involved students of transsexualism. Participants' opinions differed from official ones mostly in the prominence which they gave to their rearing. According to most participants' reckonings, psychological factors were of secondary importance and provided no justification for refusing their transsexualism. They took the tack that whatever psychological damage might have been done, it was both permanent and irreversible.

One last consideration, which only peripherally came into participants' theories was the role of the social organization of gender and sex. However, participants' focus was more upon their parents as enforcers of social roles than on the limitations of social structures which provided insufficient space for participants to grow up to be females who could express, in the words of Brian, their "unique and creative human[ity]."

Thus it was that participants were unable to find social niches for themselves as female persons. From earliest memory, most participants had felt wrong trying to live as females were expected to live. If living as women and as females did not suit them, their only other option was to live as men and as males. Whether participants were born different or became different, in the end, was immaterial. The fact remained that participants could neither fit, nor be made to fit, within the identities which their society had made available to them as female-bodied persons. They had no other choice but to abandon their lives as women and as females and to heal the rift between their inner and outer selves by creating "new vessels" to more comfortably contain the people whom they were, and were becoming.

The Good and the Bad: Appraising Life as Transsexual Men

Those participants who had lived as men saw both advantages and disadvantages to their lives as transsexual men. In some ways, they felt that both their previous lives as women and their transition experiences put them ahead of other men and women. In other ways, they lamented that there were certain central life experiences which they had missed as a result of having changed from living as women and females to living as men and males. To their regret, participants generally maintained that they would never be able to recoup such losses. However, whatever they had missed, participants clearly felt that what they had gained was far more valuable to them than what they had lost. Furthermore, most participants also stated that they felt that the obstacles which they had had to overcome had strengthened and sensitized them in beneficial ways. Thus, not only did participants count themselves bettered for having come to live as men and as males, but they also felt permanently enriched by the process of having negotiated their passages.

The Missing Pieces: Disadvantages to Being Transsexual Men

Participants rarely felt disadvantaged by their transsexualism once they made their transitions into their lives as men.[5] Most were happy to be living as men and were more than willing to accept whatever limitations came along with that status. The drawbacks which participants noted in relation to being *transsexual* men were few. Some missed the easy intimacy of women's friendships, others complained about deficiencies in the virilization of their bodies,[6] and some were sorry they had missed out on the socialization experiences which they presumed that other men had shared when young.[7]

Brian made some general observations which were certainly applicable to all participants and which recognized the tremendous toll which making a transsexual transformation takes on any individual who goes through it.

> The transsexual must sacrifice a great deal of life energy to discovering a workable self-identity, seeking out information, support, and medical help to bring body in line with mental and spiritual self-identity. This is a tremendous psychological, financial, and time-consuming burden. It drains off resources that might have been used to further one's more creative dreams, goals, skills, education, etc.

Walter also made reference to how much of a drain the transition process had been for him. Like Brian, he also felt that he would have been further ahead in his life had he not had to go through so much in order to live as a man and he envied men who were born to their physical, psychological, and social manhoods.

> Well, they got penises. . . . There's a lot of great hunks out there, and I'm not one of them. But just the basic advantage of having been born genetic males and not having to have gone through what I went through. They're much luckier than they even know. . . . They just had it all come to them. That makes a big difference. It's like the difference between rich and poor.

Although Howie's comments included a passing reference to social awkwardness, he too focussed more specifically on how he felt himself to be physically disadvantaged by being a transsexual man.

> Problems relating to others arise when you're socialized as one gender and you change to another. Other disadvantages [include] the necessity for surgeries and other medical problems. And for me, the hormone testosterone has caused a great deal of problems. . . . When you have to inject your hormone, you have to deal with the emotional peaks and valleys it forces upon you. . . . I'd be a lot taller, have more hair, and have a penis and scrotum that work properly. I'd be able to father children biologically.

Bill harboured an ongoing "fear that I don't 'live up' to being male, don't satisfactorily meet the requirements of the role." He listed the disadvantages that he still felt approximately five years into his life as a man:

> The biggest disadvantage over other males involves, I think, the inability to ever completely understand and identify with the male experience, what it fully means to have grown up as a male in society. Another dis-

advantage is to never really know what it is like to have a penis and all that goes with that including the embarrassment of unanticipated adolescent erections, first wet dream, and what it feels like to ejaculate. I often wonder what all that must be like, how it must feel to know this as a part of your body that you discovered with great awe too long ago to remember. Phalloplasty will never give me such feelings and memories. Another disadvantage for me, though not perhaps for all female-to-male transsexuals, is height. The majority of men are taller than I.

Aaron similarly cited his stature and lack of masculine socialization as disadvantages. He also added his lack of sexual experience as a straight man as a distinct and obvious gap in the life history of a man over age fifty.

> I just lost too much life. I never served in the armed services, and I'm sure I would have. It was universal military training when I was a kid, so I've missed a whole range of experiences that most men my age experienced. . . . A lot of my experiences with cars and mechanical things and so on would have been a lot bigger. . . . As a father of children. . . . I can't experience as a male. It's too late, and there's no use worrying about it. . . . The biggest advantage most men my age have over me is the simple fact of long years of sexual relationships and experience that I haven't had. . . . I have never slept with a straight woman. So I'm still that thirteen year old boy in that sense. And so their confidence. And all those fights I didn't have. . . . They're not there. The confidence isn't the same.

Hal was less perturbed by the holes in his history:

> If other men have advantages over me, they are physical ones like size, strength, fertility; or the shared experience of boyhood and youth, such as scouts or military service or fraternity hazing. I'm not sure that any of these things are advantages, they are really just differences.

Stan had found a way to capitalize on his abridged manhood. Although he sorely felt his lack of a penis, he claimed that he was a better lover to the women in his life for not having had one.

> It's real hard for me to know what [men have] got, and they've always had. . . . But I don't think they do know how to use it. I think they've really missed out on exploring plans B, C, D, E, F, and G, because they stick with plan A because it works, or it's supposed to work. I was denied plan A, and so I had to develop . . . those plans B and C and oral and manual and visual and talking and those kind of skills. I wonder if I would have just fallen back on plan A. . . . That's all they do, get it up, stick it in, and it's over. And I can't do that, so I gotta do something else. Which I think is to my advantage there. But I sure do miss plan A. I miss not having plan A.

Keith, three years after beginning to live full time as a man, had learned not to be concerned about what he had missed.

> Having come from a position of total weakness in proving my masculinity, I proved it to myself beyond a shadow of a doubt. I had to earn my right to call myself a man. So I feel that I'm more masculine than most men . . . because I no longer have to prove that I'm masculine. It has been proven to me 100 percent to my satisfaction, and I'm comfortable. I'm masculine enough now that I don't fear my femininity. I've always interpreted masculinity as being strong enough to be gentle, and I am that now that I have become a male. I'm able to drop all those ways that I was subconsciously and consciously trying to prove what a real man I was.

In sum, participants' comments about how they felt disadvantaged by their transsexualism were few. In keeping with the generally positive and hopeful outlooks which they had exhibited when discussing other topics, participants did not voice many complaints about their lives as transsexual men. Several participants noted that the very process of becoming transsexual men was time consuming, expensive, and extremely demanding of all their faculties. Most participants were disappointed at their physical limitations as men; many expressed a general regret about the seemingly significant gaps in their masculine socialization experiences and their loss of women's friendships. However, participants seemed ready to face these challenges with fortitude and good humour.

Coming Out Ahead: Advantages to Being Transsexual Men

On the whole, participants were more positive than negative in their appraisals of the legacies which transsexualism had left in their lives as men. More than two-thirds (68 percent) of participants who commented on this issue were pleased at the opportunities to understand both women and men which their transsexualism had afforded to them.[8] More than half of them (52 percent) noted that the intensity of the soul searching which they had undergone in their transitional processes had taught them much about themselves and about tolerance for other nonconforming members of society.[9] Ten participants (44 percent) felt that in having found their way through the maze of gender which they had been required to navigate, they were able to gain sufficient perspective to become more relaxed about their own gender presentations.[10] Thus it was that participants tended to be the kinds of men who were conscious of, and responsive to, the sensibilities of women; who had faced and developed some appreciation of the womanly aspects of themselves; and who were unafraid to integrate their feminine aspect within their masculine personas. As such, they could be men who incorporated many of the better aspects of both genders.

Several participants claimed that their bifurcated gender histories had taught them to recognize and understand a wider range of gender vocabulary than they would have otherwise known. For example, Keith believed that transsexual people have more finely honed senses of both men and women as a result of their transsexualism. He said, "I think absolutely . . . they very much have an advantage in the sense that they understand women from the inside out, they understand men from the inside out because they've experienced life coming from both of these sides." Ken saw himself as similarly advantaged by his gender development. He explained:

> You know how the other side feels, the other sex. There's a sensitivity there. . . . An emotional limbo that lets you have foresight into what's going on and you know what a woman wants to hear, because you wanted to hear it. You've heard it.

Hal likewise saw himself as having a better overview of society from having surveyed it from so many different angles. It was his opinion that all transsexual people necessarily have better perspective because of their unusual positions in society.

> It's sort of like being an eagle. . . . I do have a view that encompasses more than what most people's view is, and I think that's an advantage. A view of the world, a view of social relationships, a view of society . . . actually a view of cause and effect too.

From a slightly different slant, Brian argued that transsexual men, by virtue of their own explorations of gender, are more adept than most people at seeing not only the specifics but also the arbitrariness of gender.

> They can more clearly recognize that the physical body is the least real or defining aspect of one's self-identity as a living entity. They can see that male values are not intrinsic to born sex of body. They can see that being born male doesn't justify the unearned privilege society bestows on boys. Gonadal function doesn't define true manhood. . . . The transsexual finds a way to escape the trauma and degradation of having a female body. He realizes that he is far more than that body and should not accept injust degradation because of these traditionalized sexual oppressions. He proves that the female body does not define and limit the human spirit.

Thus these participants claimed for themselves, and by extension for other transsexual persons, privileged positions vis-à-vis gender. They each had experienced gender both looking out from the inside and looking in from the outside, as women and as men. What they absorbed, of course, was a function of the astuteness of their powers of observation. Be that as it may, each individual's opportunities to observe and absorb nevertheless had been doubled.

Another common claim of several participants was that they had become more compassionate human beings as a product of their own transitional trials. Aaron felt that he had learned to know himself in the process of his transsexual transformation better than most people ever do. He located the benefit which he derived as being "in understanding and accepting myself and other people."

> I probably have an extreme advantage over most human beings walking the face of the earth, simply because . . . of our digging deep, and because of our own shortcomings, because of our own lack of success. . . . It's harder to see things black and white and be judgemental about society when you're not black or white, and when you've fallen in the cracks and walked out a few times. . . . I don't like a lot of other people, but still I can forgive and understand a heck of a lot easier than somebody who hasn't dug in themselves and dealt. . . . I feel proud of the fact that I'm a survivor.

Bill likewise said that he felt that he had been able to come to a much deeper and more serene acceptance of himself as a result of self-examination.

> I think that those who even explore their gender identity have an advantage over those who have never taken the pilgrimage of self-unfolding. . . . These involve a sense of empowerment that comes from learning to identify what motivates an individual to feel, think, and behave in the ways that s/he has in the past and continues to in the present. It is this self-awareness that sets a person free, allows him/her to choose in the light of knowledge. It involves the acceptance of oneself with one's foibles, peccadillos, such that one is then in a better position to understand and accept those of others. All of this comes, hopefully, from the experience transsexuals have in the therapy that is required of them. . . . I am proud that I've had the courage to risk so much, to go against the odds in order to be who I am.

Ron similarly believed he had become more empathetic to others' difficulties.

> I've matured a lot, and I've stretched a lot, and basically I've gotten rid of judgements. . . . All the changes I had to make to accommodate this, all the different lifestyles I had to pick, everything. That's part of transsexual life, change every twenty minutes. There's always something new. And for me, the change was enriching that way, that I have an understanding of people, and I have a greater sense of love. And that's wonderful.

Steven expressed pride that after being "traumatized" and having his "brains picked" as part of his transition odyssey, he had developed "a perseverance and a strength that . . . is beyond just the average person," and had become a more empathetic person as a result.

> I have grown more, I have learned more, I have gone through tremendous situations of embarrassment, harassment, and hardship, and it has taught me something, because I've extracted things that were positive. . . . But, all in all, I choose to see everything I went through, even the negative, to find a positive end in that. And I have grown from it. . . . Also I feel that I've developed more of an empathy towards others in their plight to discover who they are, and be who they are, and not be judged for who they are. So, I think, all in all, my life has had a positive effect on me by changing. . . . And I seem to have more insight, because I've gone through more types of problems and most people haven't gone through. So I have a great reserve of life experience.

It would seem as though, having learned both an appreciation for the spectrum of gender and a greater tolerance for human diversity, many participants were able to permit themselves to be more multifaceted. Harry contended that after living eight years as a man he had become better able to accept and incorporate his feminine side.

> The funny thing is, in sinking myself more into the male role, I've actually come to better terms with the femaleness in me. . . . I don't know how to explain it, other than it's like I was overly male before because I needed people to recognize that. Once they did, I'm not a macho person, I'm not a chauvinist. I already understood, a long time ago, the social attachments. And it's crap. . . . The things that people attach to being male and female . . . that's a crock of shit. . . . No, it's actually helped more the femaleness.

Stan, eight years after his transition, noted that he was more comfortable with his feminine aspects than he had ever been as a woman.

> I accept my feminine side. I think in those early days I rejected it all. Completely. . . . I didn't want to be gentle and tender. . . . I didn't want to be known for that. And I think I was a little rougher and a little tougher, and less gentle and wouldn't talk about it.
> I'm gaining more. . . . It's okay to be soft. It's okay to care about people. I'm taking that part back. That that's okay. I feel comfortable enough with my masculinity to accept the feminine part of me. . . . It's always been part of me, and now that I can accept it, it's okay. I'm the one that had problems accepting it before, not other people. . . . I can remember when I wasn't comfortable with my masculinity, and I needed every bit of pseudo-masculinity I could possibly generate. I don't need that so much any more.

Walter said that he was relieved to feel that he could display some of his more feminine side without having to be concerned that it would undermine his claim to manhood.

> That's one thing I really am happy about being a transsexual, because . . . now . . . that I have a beard and my voice is deeper, it's so wonderful. I feel like now I can relax. Like, if I want to wear a fucking earring, for instance. . . . Now, I could do it and just be. And I really like that . . . because when I was crossdressing, I went to extremes . . . because my voice was high. And as soon as I opened my mouth, I had a problem. So I had to go to extremes. And now it's so nice to be able to relax.

Bill shared a similar sense of relief.

> These days I believe I am a bit more integrated, so the issue of maleness versus femaleness ceases to be as relevant. I did not so much abandon it as it simply ceases to be the main focus of my life. Maybe this is because now that I have a beard, I no longer have to prove to society that I am male in order to obtain a validating mirror. . . .
>
> I have improved the way I live as a man by simply stopping my ridiculous early efforts to take on the bullshit, to live down to the stereotypes. The best way for me to be a man is for me to embrace the feminine aspects to my being and to value the unique individual that I am, faults and all. I've stopped participating in the sexist ways too many men talk about women. I've stopped trying to walk with a long lope. I've stopped pretending to have some sort of Gary Cooper silent strength. . . . I think that I am more feminine than masculine.

After thirteen years of being a man, Steven's perspective on how to best live his gender had also become less rigid.

> I think I've allowed myself to get away from the stereotypes of what's male and female, and be able to be freer in choosing things that initially I might not have done because that's female things, and I don't want to have anyone think I'm a faggot, or a female, or whatever. So I think I've come to be my own person and not to label my interests or my behaviours or my style as a female or as a male, although I would hope that the way I do things is a male-oriented way. And I think it's important for me to feel very male in everything I do, but I think I've become less difficult with myself on avoiding things that may be construed as society's construction of it as female.

Darren, too, was of the opinion that he had a better incorporation of the more desirable qualities of both genders than did most people.

> I think my past has given me an advantage. I think it would be foolhardy to say not. It's sort of given me a perspective, and some experiential background that other men have not had. . . . Perhaps having access to those social qualities that women, in the old days, were supposed to

have more than men, or did have more than men, such as the maternal, the sensitivity, all that stuff. Compassion and all that. . . . I was conditioned to be accommodating and courteous and sensitive and all that stuff. And I like that. . . . I value those very highly. Some of the so-called male qualities are very obnoxious.

Bruce was even more definitive about the desirability of the mixing of genders. He strove not to lose the benefits of the lessons he had learned during his life as a woman.

I feel like I'm more in the middle. I feel like I have the best of both worlds. Because I know the struggle that women have and I know the disadvantages of being a man. I know what men are going through and I know what women are going through, and I feel comfortable in the middle of knowing both. And you're the only one that I've told. . . .

But I'm much more comfortable with who I am today. . . . I really think it's important to take the most you can from both sides. . . . And it's like there's not one role model out there for me as a man. . . . You sort of find your own identification through looking at both sides and finding the best in both. . . . In myself, I am not a man, and I'm not a woman. . . . In the world, I am a man because I move easily through life as a man. In my spirit, I am part woman, because I was born a woman, and I know what comes with being a woman. . . . And it's made me a better person, because I have both experiences.

Thus, a sizeable minority of participants definitively stated that they were happy to retain some of the femininity which they had picked up during their years living among women. They noted with both relief and consternation that behaviours which would have been anathema to them as women felt like enhancements in their lives as men. Rather than, in Stan's words, thinking that "their feminine parts are the bastard child," participants seemed to have been able, as men, to readopt some of their once rejected kin, and they did so with pride.

Summary and Commentary

Having braved the protracted and undeniably difficult efforts necessary to reach their lives as men, participants had invested heavily in their futures as men. As with most people's experiences of moving to a new and foreign culture, entry is often bumpy and involves many missteps and initiations. As does any immigrant who assimilates into a new culture, participants' lives as men were lacking in a number of the attributes and history which are commonly shared by those people who are native to their adopted culture. As do any persons who leave behind the places in which they were born and raised, no matter how willing their departure, participants missed feeling close to and accepted by those among whom they once lived. With calm rationality participants accepted that these were the inevitable prices of their moves into their new worlds.

Most of the advantages which participants felt that they had accrued as *transsexual* men were founded specifically in their transsexualism rather than those which came to them simply by virtue of their being men. In the first place, they assumed that they had better understandings of both women and men due to their dual perspectives as both insiders and outsiders of each gender. In addition, many participants noted that the ways in which they had been forced to examine themselves so deeply during their transitions had taught them a greater tolerance for nonconformity, inconsistency, and change. Furthermore, having learned to see each gender with greater empathy and clarity than do most people, many participants were able to choose more selectively from among admirable gender traits and to reject those which were not to their liking.

These qualities surely made participants into exceptional men. Having traversed a wider gender terrain than do most human beings, they brought to their manhood a broader humanity and greater generosity of spirit than is commonly found in men who have never had to question and earn their rights to call themselves men.

Words from the Wise: Advice to Fellow Travellers

The transsexual men who participated in this research had lived through processes about which only an elite fraternity can claim first hand knowledge. As such, they had a specialized expertise which can be found through no other source. Twenty participants who were living as men took the opportunity to offer advice to other persons who might be considering making the kinds of far-reaching changes which participants had undertaken.[11]

One message upon which all participants agreed was that anyone considering such a path should be absolutely sure that it was the correct thing for them to do. Participants came to this point from several directions. Some made the point directly; others counselled their prospective brothers to search for their most authentic selves, unfettered by the needs, desires, or demands of others; still others stressed the paramount importance of psychotherapy in clarifying the root issues for would-be transsexuals.

Participants also made observations about the intensity and difficulty of effecting such changes. They reiterated numerous ways in which the transition from living as women to living as men demanded almost more of them than they thought that they were capable. They saw the processes involved in transforming themselves as excellent opportunities for personal growth. Thus, participants reported that, as hard as the road may be, for the right persons, there were no others which could provide greater personal satisfactions.

Several participants exhorted others to enter into the transsexual process only after all other options had been fully considered and found untenable. For example, Bruce's advice was that first and foremost they had to know themselves before deciding to alter their lives so drastically.

> I would say that the most important thing is not becoming a man or a woman, but finding peace within yourself. Becoming the whole person, whoever you are. And try not to do battles with both sides, but try to allow Camp David to take place between both of them. You know what I mean? It's like, let something peaceful happen, because in that peace, you'll find out who you are, and what you are meant to be.

Jack also stressed that anyone who would consider gender and sex reassignment had to be entirely sure of their decision.

> Know damn well what you want. And you better be sure. Because it's a hassle enough to go through it once, but if you find out later you don't like it, and you have to go back the other way, people are really going to think you're a nut. . . . So, hey, you better know which end is up before you do it. Because it's a serious business. It's your whole life.

Grant's advice was similar:

> Follow your dreams. Make sure it's what you want to do. . . . Be true to yourself. . . . And if you can be happy by not doing anything, fine. . . . It's not a cure-all. If you go into it really screwed up, you're going to come out of it really screwed up.

Steven spoke from the perspective of almost fourteen years' involvement in transsexual transition. He felt that much profound soul-searching should precede any transsexual decisions.

> Anyone that is planning to take this road less travelled, I suggest they really soul-search their reasons. That they do not be idealistic. That they become aware that this process is a very long, sometimes drawn out, filled with disappointment, frustration, heartache, anger, bitterness, tears, joy. It encompasses every type of emotion, and it can bring you to the brink of practically wanting to shoot yourself, and it can also bring you to the brink of feeling that you're in heaven. . . .
> I would also like to say that if you have some type of problem, you're not going to cure it just with changing your sex. You've got to work on you, and you probably should do that before you even start undergoing any type of reassignment. . . . You can't just go into this and say, "Well, I'm going to change sex, and my life is going to be rosy." Because you're going to be basically the same person. . . . if you've got other underlying problems, you have to work on them. . . . Nothing is a miracle cure. . . .

And I think that it's important to realize, that if you're not a true transsexual, this can be an absolute disaster for you, because there is so much you may have to sacrifice to do this. Your life isn't always going to be easy, but then again, there's so many positive things to it. I'm glad I did it, and for the right candidate, I'm sure they would be glad too. I think a person that has considerable determination and perseverance can make it in the transition.

Mel, who was near the beginning of his transition, spoke with a catch in his throat about the importance of being absolutely sure before proceeding.

Make sure that this is what you want to do! Make sure that there is no other option because this is truly the hardest thing I have ever done in my life! You put everything that you are in jeopardy. Everything that you have, you will probably lose, any material thing. Talk to as many people as you can that are goin' through it because you're goin' to be able to pull somethin' from each of them that'll apply to you but don't take the word of one person for any of it, 'cause it works differently for everyone. But everyone will tell you it's the hardest thing they've ever gone through. Be sure!

Many other participants strongly advocated that the experience of those who had already traversed the terrain should be garnered and carefully considered. As Aaron said,

Live. Explore. And live. And experience. And be sure. Because nobody else can tell you. And to open themselves to all possibilities. Read everything you can read. Meet all the people you can meet. Find groups or write letters to people and so on. And just basically bounce yourself off as many walls as you can to find out where you fit and where you don't fit, and how. You'll never be just like anybody else. Nobody is.
But to find out where you fit, and to be relatively sure, because you're going to have to defend it to a lot of people, professionals, so you better think it through first. Even if you're sure at gut level, it's good to be sure verbally, because a lot of people, have had to do an awful lot of defending and fighting.

Howie entreated anyone who could avoid gender and sex reassignment to do so, adding that "it was the hardest decision of my life." Howie counselled:

Make sure beyond the shadow of any doubt that this is what you want and need to be happy. Explore the lifestyle fully. Talk to old timers and even people who have changed and then changed back to their original gender. Take the real life test seriously and don't rush into surgery. . . . Get a support network of other transsexuals, especially initially.
If you think you could possibly be happy without changing, try to be

it. People don't know what the problems will be 'til they do it (e.g., rejection by family, friends, employers, religious leaders, etc.). Do whatever it takes to be true to yourself. Talk to an experienced, non-judgemental therapist who has worked with transsexuals. Explore alternatives. Some transsexuals I've met seemed to be gay and just couldn't accept it. For some it was easier to try to be transsexual and say they had a medical birth defect. . . . Genetic women who become men have many permanent changes from testosterone and their lives can be sheer hell if they try to change back. . . . .

The bottom line is, make absolutely certain that this is the only answer for you. You have to want it more than anything else in the world. Most transsexuals say suicide was their only option. You have to have courage, a lot of inner strength, a support network, a strong will, and be ready for a lot of pain and anguish which seems insurmountable (but isn't).

Most participants considered the assistance of properly trained psychotherapists to have the potential to offer invaluable assistance in self-discovery. However, as Walter pointed out, in order for psychotherapists to be helpful, their clients must be fully forthcoming with them. Walter admonished people contemplating sex reassignment not to deceive their therapists.

Really take your time. Because you can always start something, but a lot of times you can't stop something. And people go into this in haste.

And not to lie to the people who are screening you, because you're cutting your own throat. . . . Not only do a lot of people do it, I think it's the standard. . . . How can you have meaningful therapy with someone who holds your future in their hands by what you say to them? There's no way. There's no way anybody is going to be truthful. . . . They say what they think the therapist wants to hear so that they will be certified. That's the problem. It's like they're cutting off their nose to spite their own face. . . . People get confused . . . and they try to manipulate, and they get something in their mind that . . . they know they want. . . . But the fact is, sometimes what you want is not what you should have. And what you need to find out is what you need, not what you want. And the people are so worried about what they want, that they don't be honest, and then sometimes they don't get what they need. Which is honesty, and to understand the real situation.

Darren, who had devoted many of his approximately 20 post-transition years to serving the transsexual community, had ofttimes advised other transsexual people. Hence, Darren had much well thought out advice to offer to his peers. He, too, advised persons considering transition to engage in honest and earnest psychotherapy.

Really, really get in touch with your own feelings. Seek out good professional therapists or counsellors, and not be frightened by them. But don't proceed with them if you're not working, if you're not addressing the things that are important to you, or you don't feel comfortable with them. But if you can find someone . . . that you can really talk about things, that may or may not be related to the gender dysphoria, for God's sake, do it. 'Cause that can change your whole life.

Bill underscored that transsexualism represents a life-long personal growth process.

Seek out a therapist with experience and especially compassion in/for this area. Go slowly, however frustrating that may be. Leave no stone unturned in your search for you. There is no shame in exploring this path only to find you are where you were meant to be. This is not about a finished product. This is about an ongoing process. Take it one step at a time. Learn to love yourself wherever you go. Being transsexual is not about external changes as much as it is about inner growth.

Ron, in addition to his advice that "counseling is definitely essential," talked about his personal growth goals.

Just go and clean up the emotional stuff, because there's a lot of healing that needs to happen. . . . When I make a change I want to make a clean change. I don't want to drag what I had before with me . . . any of the bitterness, or whatever. I just want to hang on to this euphoria of being myself and not having to lie, and all these good things that just put an end to all the denial. And then not only deal with the transsexual stuff, but with therapy, with the whole personal stuff. And let go of the fears of self-expression at the risk of somebody else's judgement of whether what comes out is male or female. Also to let go of the judgements of what is male and female. And you decide for yourself that you're male and that's what you want to do.

Phil also emphasized therapy as a route to genuine self-knowledge, and that the process of changing gender and sex can be a long and lonely one. His advice included taking solace in the company of people who can offer love and understanding.

I would advise others to find a good counsellor and a good doctor who specialized in this field. Join a good support group to help you through the rough spots. Be honest with your family, some might not approve, but you need the support of those who truly love you for yourself and not what they think you should be. Try and go through all the surgery at a young age, the younger you are the better your body will heal, and it will be easier to start a new life. Don't be worried about finding someone to love, once you find the right person you'll know it. And don't

rush into anything, most relationships don't last while you're going
through the surgery, but some do. And most of all, be true to yourself
and your own feelings. Don't live your life for other people and put off
surgery just because they don't want you to.

Luther advocated therapy and also wanted to get across to other
people considering transsexual transitions that it was crucial that they
make their decisions based only upon their own needs, that they not be
influenced by other people's wants and desires.

> I always ask this question . . . "If you were shipwrecked on an island
> and there was no possibility of ever getting off that island, would you
> still want to have reassignment?" And that to me is the bottom line be-
> cause if you say, "No," to me, it has to do with other people and
> not you. And I would say that you really have to ask yourself that ques-
> tion. . . . If it has anything to do with anybody else, then I'd say, "Stop
> now." Because it's not a true decision. . . . I would advise people to
> think about that. And I would advise people to get into therapy and stay
> with it. And to think about those issues that they feel will be helped by
> reassignment. And then look at those same issues and see whether or
> not you can deal with those issues and get them resolved before you ever
> start reassignment. And then, after that, go for it.

Gary likewise cautioned against making any final decisions until having
reached an absolute clarity of purpose arrived at independently of other
people's opinions.

> Be prepared for a long road, and do not take the decision lightly. It
> doesn't happen overnight and it takes years. And if you aren't sure, don't
> do it. And most of all, don't worry about what other people think. It is
> your life and only you can live it.

Brian advocated a different kind of independent thought. He suggested that any persons who think that they might be transsexual should
examine their thoughts in the context of social definitions of gender. Furthermore, Brian counselled turning a critical eye on professional assistance.

> Define your own self-identity independent of the body's sexual physiol-
> ogy. Contemplate hard and critically what is really imposed by biology
> and what is imposed by culture. How are the social and cultural beliefs
> and influences changing?
> Be critical of the doctors and therapists you deal with. Why are they
> interested in working with transsexuals? What are their personal beliefs
> about sex and gender and how is your awareness of their values com-
> promising your real personal beliefs about yourself. If you are telling
> them what "they want to hear," are you telling yourself their values or
> your own?

The risks and rewards of changing over may be worth it. The trauma and struggle of continuing to deal with trying to overcome or compensate against the emotional and cultural oppression of a gender role you don't accept can drain a person's life energy. If it can really free you to leave those traumas behind and get on with living as a fuller, healthier, more creative human being, then the change is justifiable. . . . If you chose to live as a man, live even more as a human being. Don't lock yourself into the false cultural definitions which make a great number of born males one-dimensional, pre-programmed and unaware of themselves beyond their gonadal functions.

Several other participants also directed their attention to the question of choosing their medical treatments wisely. For example, Walter thought that no one should enter into hormone therapy without fully understanding the long-term implications.

They must realize that hormone therapy is a very serious, long-term thing. People tend to take it much too lightly. . . . Before you commit to the hormone therapy, you have to commit to at least having a hysterectomy. And a lot of people don't think in those terms. They just go for it, and they're not thinking about it in a long term. That's so important . . . because once you get those effects, you can't reverse them. You're going to be in the same boat as a male-to-female transsexual if you want to reverse. You have to go to electrolysis. It's really a problem. . . . Hormone therapy should not be entered into lightly. And . . . one has got to come to terms with one's own gender identity without any regard to what surgery you're going to have. If someone feels like it will all be okay once they get the hysterectomy or phalloplasty, there's no way it's all going to be okay. It's so important. And again, not to be hasty.

Keith suggested that therapy was an essential part of self-exploration and counselled, "If there's any doubt in your mind, don't go through with it." In addition, he suggested that once persons are certain of their transsexualism, they should go through accredited offices to ensure that they receive proper care.

I suggest they go through all the proper channels, all the legal and ethical medical treatments, because the restrictions and the limitations and the guidelines that the [Harry Benjamin International Gender Dysphoria Association] sets out for people considering a sex change . . . are there for a reason. And if you are truly a transsexual, then you will have no trouble whatsoever being channelled through the system. Other than the fact that it's somewhat expensive. But I think that going through the proper medical channels is important. If nothing else, it gives the person a legitimacy, not only to themselves, but to society, that yes, they have been diagnosed as a transsexual, and that this is the proper treatment for them to have.

Steven also addressed himself to the issue of choosing medical practitioners and procedures carefully.

> I suggest that someone have a very strong support group that can understand their problems. Especially a therapist who has extensive experience in dealing with the problems and the situations that they will personally face. . . .
> They're going to go through complete scrutiny by the medical profession before they go through any surgical procedures, even hormones in a lot of instances. Sometimes the psychotherapy will be years for them. . . . Look at this as a positive growth period, and be patient. . . . It's really important going through this process that you're not used by quacks. I think a lot of people will put themselves into the hands of a doctor and not know much about his background. Make sure they're Board certified. Make sure that this isn't the first surgery they've ever done. . . . Go to medical libraries, or find someone that can explain to you what types of surgeries are out there. The pros, the cons. You've got to be well informed, or you're going to somehow, somewhere, face some type of disappointment in some aspect of this transition.

Stan, in his own transition, had rebelled against abiding by the *Standards of Care*. In hindsight, he thought that he better understood why he couldn't simply procure the medical services he desired on a "demand" basis.

> There's a reason that it's so difficult. I didn't understand. "Why won't people help me? . . . I know what I want to do." . . . And coming from the other side of it, I can see why that is. No, we don't need help. If you really do want this, you'll get it. . . . You will find a way. And by it being so difficult, it weeds out the folks that think . . . being a man will fix these other problems, but they really just need other therapy for self-esteem problems. And for those folks, they . . . don't need to go through this. . . . If it's too hard to do this . . . then they'll find other ways to live with what they've got. They could stay in their female body and indulge their masculine traits. Do it. Because there is plenty of help out there for those of us who really want it. There is more than enough help.

Several participants sounded warnings and submitted suggestions about what female-to-male transsexuals might reasonably expect to encounter as they undergo physiological changes. Darren suggested that it was essential that female-to-male transsexuals have realistic expectations about what can and cannot be accomplished through medical technology.

> About the sex reassignment surgery itself, I think some of these people have very unrealistic expectations about the surgeons. They aren't gods or miracle workers. They're human beings, they're technicians, they're artists. . . . And I think if a transsexual expects sexual functionability, or even, for the phalloplasty, urinary functionability, they're being un-

realistic and naive in some cases. It's not to say it's not possible, but they really have to do research and homework and get their expectations very realistic and really find out exactly what they want.

And also talk it over with their lover or their partner. That is, in terms of the female-to-male transsexual having the phalloplasty. . . . Because it does really affect both people involved. It's such a major thing, time-wise, expense-wise. And the fact of having a sexual organ that the partner may or may not want. So it should be a thing that's discussed, even if the decision is ultimately up to the individual.

Dennis's advice was concerned with the adjustments he had to make during his transition. He warned others:

Prepare yourself for a long battle, because it's a constant battle. . . . The unfortunate thing is that . . . you have a lot of anxiety . . . about trying to . . . be the perfect guy. . . . There's going to be so much for you to deal with on nearly an everyday basis that it's not easy. You're more relieved your body is in line with your spirit and your inner man, for the most part. But there's still a lot more. . . . Who has the resiliency to go through all the changes that we have to, just the physical operations that we have to go through? How can anyone do it in a short period of time? . . . You have to figure at least ten years of your life devoted just to that. And even then you're still going to have to deal with the changes that you've chosen to make. I thought it would be a lot easier than it is. And I consider myself one of the luckier ones!

Hal, too, was surprised at how hard his transition turned out to be. He offered these words of warning:

Others considering a change need to be aware that this is a long and difficult process, the particulars of which will be unique to each man who undertakes it. It costs more than you expect, it takes longer, and you never know what you're going to end up with when you go into an operating room. You have to be willing to let go of everything you know, and your expectations for yourself, and for others. You have to be willing to start all over again. It solves some problems, and it raises new ones. It doesn't make everything better all at once.

Ken, as had many other participants, cautioned, "Make sure that that's what you want. It's not easy, but if you want it bad enough, do it, and follow whatever your particular gender clinic says to do." Ken then warned his would-be fellows that once they reached a satisfactory plateau in their physical transitions, they would be wise to remain near enough to their doctors so as to secure adequate ongoing medical care.

Once you have surgery, don't move away. Find a physician, and have regular follow-ups. The testosterone level needs to be checked frequently. I'd like to say once a year. It's a very expensive test . . . but it's

important. There's inside and internal things that testosterone can do to
you, and your health is important. As a female-to-male transsexual, you
need to remember that there's still menopause. I still have hot flashes
right now. Ask for help. I've known some transsexuals that have committed suicide. People need to know that. Be honest with your family.
Have someone to go through it with you. Don't do it alone.

By contrast, Keith advised transsexual men to leave the areas in which
they made their transitions so as to avoid the employment difficulties
which he had encountered.

Myself, having stayed in the same community, and having stayed in the
same line of work . . . I can see now . . . why transsexual people relocate
after their change and form a new identity. Because . . . I would say the
majority of people in my community still do not, after three years . . .
accept the change. Many of them don't accept it simply because they're
confused, and they don't understand it. Many of them don't accept it
because they refuse to accept it. The people that are confused, eventually they will forget that I was ever a female, and eventually they will
come around. But the people who refuse to accept it, those people can
make your life miserable.

Steven spoke of the difficulties of interacting with people on a daily
basis.

Not everyone is going to understand you. You are going to face hardships, and I think the people that don't face these hardships are extremely lucky indeed. There's a possibility of losing friends, family, jobs,
housing, embarrassing, harassing types of situations. I don't want to
play on the negative, but I think a person should be aware that there's
got to be a flexibility about themselves, and that things are not going to
happen just because they want them. . . .
    People that are on power trips are going to use their power to hurt
you at times. So you've got to take care of yourself. You've got to know
what type of personalities you're dealing with when you divulge anything that other people are ignorant of, and then are also having stereotypes or fears about. So they're going to try and strike out at you because of their own insecurities.

Darren reminded transsexual men to be gentle with the people who
know them and love them and who have their own emotional responses
to the gender transformations which they watch take place.

And the other thing is to not be so egotistical that you forget your significant others. And these may even be your lesser significant others such
as your lesser friends, or your employer, or your teachers, or your minister, whoever. And it's hard for them. Be patient with them. And if they
are supportive, express your gratitude and try to not let them down.

And try to be more flexible with them, and more patient, and not so selfish, and address their needs too. Unfortunately this happens with transsexuals, especially with family members or spouses. They forget their spouses or their family members' needs. And it's hard for these people, and sometimes, especially the spouses, they have no one else to talk to. A lot of wives have told me this.

Darren also admonished transsexual men not to become mired in feeling sorry for themselves.

Don't use the transsexual thing as a crutch or a handicap. It's only a handicap if you think it is. . . . Everybody's got their cross to bear, for God's sake. Of course, it's like the uninvited dilemma, it's not something a person wishes on themself. But you've got it, you're stuck with it, so you've got to rectify it. But there's people out there to help you, if you're lucky. . . . But, I hate that kind of whining, moocher type mentality that some transsexuals fall into. And this constantly falling back on this as a crutch.

And also, the other thing is, never letting it go. . . . You've got to sometimes move on to new things. 'Cause you get too insulated and too wrapped up in this thing, and you miss that whole world out there. And also, focusing your whole life around this is very limiting. It's psychologically unhealthy. And it's also very egotistical. . . . I think transsexuals have to learn this is . . . both integral and incidental in the sense that you can transcend. You can't totally forget it, but you can go on and see the rest of the world and relate to other people and let some of that go. Or put it in its proper perspective. . . . It's like, there's got to be life after surgery. . . . You can still have transsexual friends and that, but there's other people out there, another world and other things to do.

As a collectivity, participants were entirely lucid about the many potentialities for pitfalls in the transsexual path. Their advice drove home the importance of ruthless self-examination, of caution, and of self-care throughout the entire process. In addition, participants sent another communiqué to their would-be transsexual brethren. On the surface, they almost seemed to be trying to discourage anyone else from confronting the enormous obstacles which they had overcome, however, the fact of their own successes acts to subvert their apparent focus on all that can be troublesome along the way. Participants' lives and words combine together to say that gender and sex reassignments are among the most profound human transformations possible. They are not for the faint of heart, nor for those of limited conviction. However, for those individuals who are sure enough to persevere through the innumerable impediments which must be surmounted, gender and sex reassignments can mean tremendous personal growth and renewal.

Summary and Commentary

In the end, most participants concluded that they really had no other option but to start their lives as females, girls, and women and to complete them as men and as males. Whatever else may have transpired in their lives, no matter how difficult their journeys, whatever kinds of men they might become, most participants concluded that they had been born destined to traverse a lonely course. Fortunately for them, most participants were able to look back on what they had been through and find more for which to be thankful than not. They were largely able to put behind them the torments through which most of them had come. Instead, participants chose to look at their lives as more than survivors: they had faced their most difficult moments with courage and dignity and had emerged victorious.

Participants came through their transitions and into their lives as men and as males bearing many scars. They remembered well from whence they came and sounded warnings for others who might face similar hazards. In addition, they were well aware of all they had missed in their circuitous routes to manhood. However, these were forward-looking men. They counted the benefits of their pasts more heavily then they weighed their losses and lacks. Instead of bemoaning the hardships which they had survived, they demonstrated how their travails had tempered and strengthened them. Rather than focussing in a maudlin fashion on all which they lacked as men, participants profited from the sensitivity and sense of proportion which they had gained during their years living among women. Participants thus looked back on their lives and gained wisdom from them even as they looked forward with hope and vision for all that they were yet to become.

PART VII

Concluding

Patric Magee

26 | Conclusions and Questions

THE FIRST THING which most people want to know about transsexualism is what causes it. That is a perfectly reasonable question. Rather than answering it directly, I offer observations as to what factors seem to me to make transsexualism possible. I start my discussion by stating a number of my assumptions which should help to put my comments in proper perspective.

Firstly, I recognize that something akin to modern-day female-to-male transsexualism appears to have existed throughout the ages and in a tremendous variety of cultural environments. Secondly, I assume that transsexualism is a solution to a problem to which people come from a variety of directions and for a variety of reasons. That is to say that there is no single pattern which could be predictive of a transsexual outcome. Likewise, I assume that persons with similar life histories might come to differing conclusions as to how to deal with their gender and sex dissatisfactions. Therefore I also assume that although any number of people may report similar backgrounds, some may come to think of themselves as transsexual whereas other people may find different and equally satisfactory ways to live their lives. Thirdly, I assume that becoming transsexual is a process comprised of a series of steps, none of which ensures any particular subsequent progression of events, none of which ensures a transsexual outcome. I assume that persons who identify themselves as transsexual conditionally accept that this socially defined category captures their subjective experience of their positions in their social environments. Furthermore, I assume that to do so requires of such persons that they develop certain understandings both about themselves and about the socially agreed upon meanings which inhere in the terms *male, female, man, woman,* and *transsexual.* Fourthly, I assume that, ultimately, the causes of transsexualism in individual person's lives are beside the point. I take this position because it seems to me that most people who would ask to understand the sources of transsexualism do so in order to seek either the prevention or the cure of transsexualism. I believe that a far superior use of our energies as a society would be to apply them to creating an environment in which persons may live in whatever modes of gender or sex expression they wish. Rather than trying to eliminate transsexualism from our midst, I vote for trying to make room for all people to fully express the tremendous diversity of gender and sex which people experience as their own. It is my firm belief that we would all be richer and happier as a result. Finally, I assume that whatever I think today represents only a very partial understanding of these phenomena. I therefore ask you to grant me leave to continue to search for greater comprehension.

Transsexualism as a Developmental Process

Although it may one day be proven that transsexual persons are born biologically preordained to demand gender and sex reassignments, such assertions remain highly controversial. Differences between various parts of the brains and chemical-processing pathways among transsexual persons and among non-transsexual persons may have been established with varying degrees of certainty, but it remains unclear as to whether such differences are causes of, results of, or incidental to the unusual life histories of transsexual persons.[1] What is clear is that all transsexual persons go through developmental processes wherein they come to think of themselves as transsexual and seek to alter their lives to bring them into more comfortable alignment with their subjective feelings about their genders and their sexes.

Thus, as suggested by Baumbach and Turner, in order for persons to qualify as transsexual they must pass through three broad developmental stages. In the first place, they must feel a sense of dissatisfaction, or dysphoria, with their assigned genders and sexes. In the second instance, they must conclude that their discomfort would be alleviated were they to change their genders and sexes. Finally, they must identify themselves as transsexual and pursue gender and sex reassignments.

In the pages which follow, I will attempt to flesh out Baumbach and Turner's sketchy outline. However, before I do so, I will simply state that there may be some transsexual persons in whom a biological impetus toward transsexualism is so compelling that their social contexts, their family dynamics, their individual psychologies, and their various personal choices are of negligible import in the etiology of their transsexualism. However, if such persons do exist, I believe that they are exceedingly rare. It seems infinitely more likely to me that transsexual persons' gender and sex dysphorias are products of the intersection of all of the above factors, wherein any one factor may or may not predominate over others.

A Social Context

In the broadest sense, the phenomena which we today call transsexualism make sense only within social contexts which are predicated upon a number of assumptions. In order for those characteristics which delineate transsexualism to be intelligible, social values must be such that clearly divided categories of gender and sex are believed to exist independently of social will. Furthermore, it must be accepted as truth that those genders and sexes are ultimately verifiable only on the basis of particular bodily features. Such presumptions, however, are themselves social products of particular cultures under particular historical conditions.[2]

Thus transsexualism makes sense only within the context of a socially dominant gender schema which teaches members of society to function as if the following ideological presumptions were elemental truths rather than the products of a particular set of social arrangements.[3]

1. Sex is an intrinsic biological characteristic. There are two and only two sexes: male and female. Sex is usually determined from visual inspection of genitalia, sometimes on the basis of genetics.

2. Normally, all persons are either one sex or the other. No person can be neither. Normally, no person can be both. No person can change sexes without major medical intervention.

3. Genders are social manifestations of sexes. Normally, there are two and only two genders: men (boys) and women (girls). All males are boys or men. All females are girls or women.

4. All persons are either one gender or the other. No person can be neither. No person can be both. No person can change genders without also changing sexes.

5. Gender styles are culturally defined expressions of sexes and genders. There are two main gender styles: masculinity and femininity. Males are naturally inclined to display masculinity. Females are naturally inclined to display femininity. Most males are masculine men. Most females are feminine women.

6. Many persons do not exactly perform their expected gender styles. This is due to imperfect socialization or to pathological conditions.

7. Those persons who are males, boys, men, or masculine naturally deserve greater social status, authority, and power than those who are females, girls, women, or feminine.

Sexes are presumed, in this formulation, to be biologically given properties which members of society merely recognize on the basis of sound scientific criteria. Genders are presumed to be the naturally occurring social expressions of sexes. The distinctions between genders and sexes are, in popular parlance, therefore usually treated as semantic ones. Genders and sexes are treated as innate human features. Moreover, because of the biologically deterministic leanings of this ideological system, it is further presumed that the basic attitudes and behaviours of gender and sex will "come naturally" to most people, but that practice is required in order to improve the grace with which people execute their pre-ordained gender styles.

However, in everyday life, sexes are rarely directly displayed or discussed. Rather, genders and gender styles are the media of most social exchange. As such, genders and gender styles act as markers of sexes in that persons who seamlessly perform particular gender styles are attributed by others with being the corresponding genders and sexes. Thus, although the dominant gender schema ideology claims that gender styles and genders are the results of sexes, people functionally read gender styles, genders, and sexes in the reverse order. That is to say that in everyday life, we actually read gender on the basis of gender styles, not on the basis of sexes. In the gender attribution process:

1. All people are assumed to be either male or female, men or women.
2. Physical characteristics, mannerisms, and personality traits are interpreted as masculine or feminine on the basis of the dominant gender schema.
3. Observed gender styles are instantaneously and unconsciously weighed and a gender status is attributed: predominantly feminine people are seen as women, predominantly masculine people are seen as men.
4. Once a gender status has been attributed to a person, the corresponding sex is attributed: men are males, women are females.

Attributions made by others can either reinforce or undermine persons' identities and can be entirely unseated by the disclosure of inappropriate physical characteristics. Therefore, no matter how effective persons' performances of their genders may be, in order to legitimately claim to be (wo)men, persons ultimately must have (fe)male bodies.

Furthermore, female-to-male transsexualism is provided especially fertile social ground in which to thrive by the sociopolitical realities of the patriarchal organization of society. Not only are gender and sex rigidly and inalterably linked in social vocabularies, but each set of gender/sex statuses are also afforded vastly different rights, responsibilities, and prerogatives. Thus it is that any persons who wish to maximize their freedoms in certain areas of their lives will find that their abilities to do so will be restrained by social restrictions on the permissible use of particular kinds of bodies. However, transsexualism can provide a parsimonious solution to social problems which arise when individual personalities are mismatched to the social limitations placed on the legitimate usage of particular types of bodies. Social order can be maintained by realigning bodies with social expectations rather than by creating a society which recognizes the greater value which could be realized by a diversification of social options. Finally, of course, transsexualism only became a socially meaningful idea within the context of a biologically based model of gender and sex which justifies the medical alteration of bodies for psychological reasons and which has developed the technologies necessary to do so.[4]

However, social order is an aggregate which is both created and maintained in untold numbers of individual and small group interactions between real people who may or may not have any concern for the theoretical underpinnings of the rules and values which govern their lives. Thus it is that although the lives of individual members of society may be taken as illustrative of larger phenomena, individuals may run their own lives on the basis of entirely other concerns than the maintenance or overthrow of the social order which shapes them.

Be that as it may, people are most assuredly products of their social conditions. Just as assuredly, persons are also social actors who make choices about how to interpret the circumstances of their lives. However, the meanings which are available for use in such endeavours are limited in number. As social actors, all members of society must force themselves to fit within the dominant gender schema of their society if they wish to function as credible social actors. Furthermore, even those members of society with the most well developed creativity will, of necessity, only be able to imagine and perform gender and sex possibilities which are variations on those within which they already live.

Therefore, when I try to understand the phenomena of female-to-male transsexualism, I take the approach that transsexualism is, at best, "a perfect fit in an imperfect world." I assume that the persons who spoke with me came to understand themselves to be transsexual as a result of the interpretations which they made of the realities of their lives within the context of the dominant gender schemas of the societies within which they lived. I assume that participants had both as much free will and as many limited choices as do other persons who never entertain the possibility that they may be transsexual. I also assume that they might have made other choices at any step of the way, branched off onto other paths, and never have become transsexual. Moreover, I credit participants with having done the best they could with the materials with which they worked. That is to say that they were dealt particular lives at particular historical moments and that they made sense of their life experiences within those contexts.

Coming to Gender: Finding One's Self

Driving participants through all of the identity-development stages which culminated in their lives as men were their feelings of being ill suited to being females, girls, and women. As I describe some of the forces which helped to shape participants' subjective experiences of themselves as gendered and sexed human beings, I am unable to say with any certainty that any one or another of these factors is necessary or how many of them in concert might be sufficient to qualify as predictive of a subsequent transsexual outcome. I do, however, feel confident enough to assert that the meanings which persons attach to their experiences are more central to the question at hand than are the existence of such experiences in persons' lives per se.

In keeping with many other theorists of gender and of transsexualism, I point first to participants' early childhoods as important periods in the development of their gender identities.[5] However, I emphasize that I also assume that although such childhood experiences may be necessary to explain transsexual identities, they are insufficient to the task. It seems to me that any number of childhood experiences, coupled with particular interpretations of them, only set the stage for later developments which may accrete to transsexual identities. I therefore also note adolescence as a period during which participants took important turns in their developmental paths which pointed them more in the direction of their eventual transsexualism.[6] Finally, I maintain that the experiences of adulthood were no less significant than those of other periods of participants' lives.[7] Throughout all of these periods of participants' lives, their interactions with significant other persons helped to shape their identities and provided them with the templates for the identity comparisons which contributed to their gender and sex identity development.

The participants in this study were born into families located within social worlds which gave meanings to their births and their lives. They may have come into the world with some predisposition toward preferring those traits which their social norms assigned to the male sex. They may have been born with physical characteristics which were more typical of those people whom we designate as males. I have no way to know whether such was true for any or all participants. However, I would point to some of the sketchy medical histories supplied by participants as suggestive that at least a few participants may have been physiologically somewhat atypical as females. Regardless, it is my contention that there must have been many subsequent events, interpretations, and decisions made by participants and the people around them without which few, if any, participants would have become transsexual.

As do all children, participants initially looked to their parents and other elder relatives for love and guidance and as exemplars of their genders and sexes. They therefore learned their first lessons about the meanings of gender and sex in the crucibles of their families. The lessons which participants learned inclined them away from imitation of feminine patterns and toward those more commonly found among boys and men. The circumstances of their young lives seemed to conspire to make participants denigrate or revere femininity, but not to emulate it. Rather, participants seemed propelled toward the adoption of masculinity as sword and shield with which to make themselves strong enough to protect themselves, and their loved ones, against feminine inferiority, violation, and abuse.

However, to say that participants did not use their mothers as role models is not to say that they were not deeply emotionally involved with their mothers. On the contrary, an important element in the development of the masculine identities of many participants seemed to have been quite an intense emotional connection with their mothers in ways which cast their mothers as "other" and highlighted the differences between themselves and their mothers. Four patterns which began in childhood appeared to have continued, in more mature forms, throughout much of participants', and their mothers', lives. In a few cases, participants' grandmothers and aunts filled analogous roles in participants' young lives.

In the first and the simplest of such situations, some participants' mothers were employed at jobs which took them away from their family homes much of the day or were inattentive to their daughters because of their own physical or emotional problems. Their mothers were thus unavailable for participants to use as role models. In several such cases, participants' fathers served as primary caretakers during participants' earliest years.

In a second pattern, some participants did not want to be like their mothers but felt protective of them. They remembered feeling that way because their mothers had been physically frail or emotionally ill during important parts of participants' childhood or adolescent years, or because their mothers had been regularly subjected to abuse at the hands of participants' fathers. Thus, participants whose younger lives were dominated by such situations learned not only that their mothers were ineffectual but that they were innocently helpless or downtrodden women. Participants were not tempted to emulate such women. Rather, they felt that it fell to them to be their mothers' protectors.[8]

In a third pattern, when participants remembered that they had pointedly not wanted to be anything like their mothers, they cited their mothers as shrewish people with whom they wanted nothing to do. Several participants did not want to be anything like their mothers because they felt unfairly treated by them. They remembered their mothers as having been abusive to them, or as irritatingly intrusive people with whom they continually fought about issues of gender styles. They developed aversive feelings about their mothers and turned away from them where ever they could. Thus they failed to be drawn into feminine behaviour patterns by their mothers.

Finally, there were a few participants who remembered their mothers especially fondly from their childhoods. They romanticized their mothers as perfectly feminine women of a type with whom they might one day fall into passionate love. They placed them on pedestals and admired them as "other" than themselves. They too declined to imitate their mothers, rather, they related to them as delightful and lovely women who needed to be gallantly loved and protected.

At the same time as participants seemed to see their mothers as fragile, diminished, repulsive, or romanticized others, they remembered their fathers as larger-than-life figures. They were therefore far more inclined to see their fathers either as admirable role models or as immensely powerful but morally bankrupt masculine competitors. In some instances, participants' grandfathers or uncles played similar parts in participants' upbringings. Participants tended to take one or more of three main attitudes toward their fathers and masculinity during their early childhood years.

Firstly, when participants' fathers were absent or remote but not violent, many participants seemed to have idealized their fathers as heroes. Participants wanted the approval of such grand men and did what they could to gain their fathers' attentions and praise. It seemed from the stories relayed by participants that most such fathers were more inclined to appreciate masculine rather than feminine behaviours from their daughters. Therefore, in many cases, participants responded by acting more like sons than like daughters, both in imitation of their admired fathers and in efforts to garner their fathers' elusive attentions.

Secondly, a number of participants' fathers spent a great deal of time around participants when they were young girls. This may have happened for a variety of reasons. Some participants' mothers were unable to care for them. Some participants' mothers favoured their sons and left their daughters to search for love where they might. Some families lacked a son who satisfied their expectations and recruited a daughter to do the job. Whatever the reason, one outcome of participants' having spent a lot of time doing masculine things while in their fathers' company was that such participants ended up with an abundant appreciation for masculine ways. At the same time, they were also subjected to masculine socialization which encouraged participants to have very low estimations and little knowledge or incorporation of femininity into their own values and behaviours.

Thirdly, in those instances where participants' fathers were angry and violent men, it was not uncommon for participants, their siblings, and their mothers to be recipients of abuse. In such cases, participants recalled that they did not want to be like their fathers. Instead, participants tended to respond to such situations by wanting to fill the masculine provider and protector roles which they saw their fathers as having abdicated. They imagined themselves as growing up to be powerful adults who could neither abuse nor be abused. In the minds of such children, that seemed to have meant that they envisioned themselves as growing up not only to be men, but to be better men than their fathers.

These family dynamics were often fortified by the contributions of sibling and peer relations which mirrored those between participants and their parents. Sisters and female peers were accepted by participants only when they were tomboys like themselves. Most often, participants thought of their sisters and other girls as being preoccupied with nonsensical concerns or as delightfully alien creatures who were suitable grist for romantic fantasies. Brothers and male peers were most often seen by participants as buddies when they accepted participants as equals, and as rivals when they did not. In any event, participants shared little time with feminine peers during their childhoods, and much time with masculine ones. Their tendencies toward acceptance of masculine socialization and rejection of femininity were therefore compounded by their relationships with their siblings and childhood friends.

Adolescence was a further critical period for participants in four main areas of their lives. In the first place, participants experienced crises in relation to the developments in their own bodies at puberty. Secondly, participants' gender and sex anxieties increased as their family relationships shifted in ways which were inimical to them. Thirdly, participants were dismayed at the changes which transpired between themselves and their peers. Fourthly, sexuality issues impinged heavily on participants' increasingly imposing identity concerns.[9]

Puberty was a nightmare for almost all participants. As their bodies matured in undeniably female ways, any hopes which participants had secretly harboured that one day they would become males, or that they would never become adult females, were dashed. Thus, at puberty, most participants who had not already done so began to dissociate from their maturing female bodies. Furthermore, their obvious pubertal development clearly signalled their femaleness to other people who proceeded to treat them accordingly. Their days of carefree tomboyism were over.

Within their families, patterns similar to those of their childhoods continued to prevail in participants' relationships with their mothers and sisters. There were, however, significant changes in their relationships with their fathers and brothers. In the first place, once puberty started to clearly mark participants' bodies as female, their fathers ceased to share their masculine pursuits with them. Many fathers instead began to insist that participants should behave according to their cultural images of proper young women, or they began to treat participants as sex objects or toys. Such withdrawals or changed socialization demands from participants' fathers seemed to many participants to be betrayals of their earlier masculine intimacies. At the same time, some participants also began to see their fathers more as men who were out of control than as the awesome godlike personages whom they had often seemed to be when participants were younger. Furthermore, many participants also observed that their parents encouraged their teenaged sons to take risks and explore larger portions of their worlds while participants concurrently felt themselves become more tightly curtailed and controlled.

Further compounding their distress was the fact that most participants found, to their chagrin, that the boys with whom they had been friends as children would no longer associate with them except in sexualized ways. Many participants also watched in desolation as their tomboy female friends deserted them to become heterosexual and feminine young women. When participants found themselves no longer able to move as boys among teenaged boys, and unwilling to be girls among teenaged girls, they tended to turn inward. Thus it was that loneliness and depression were extremely common among participants during their adolescent years. They felt angry, alienated, and deserted, and their abiding gender and sex anxieties deepened. For many participants, adolescence marked a time when their identity confusion reached crisis proportions as their comparisons with their own earlier freedoms and the new freedoms of their brothers and male peers left them feeling profoundly misplaced as females.

However, it seemed as though participants were not idle in their loneliness. They ruminated long and hard, in their isolation, on the reasons for their situations. In addition to all that I have already mentioned, participants also counted their sexual fantasies, desires, and experiences in their speculations. Two sexuality issues therefore became central during participants' adolescent years and continued to be of importance in their adult lives. Firstly, most participants were sexually attracted to females. Secondly, most participants became habituated to imagining themselves to be men and male in their masturbatory fantasies. Thus, isolated from their peers, alienated from their families, and angry at the development of their bodies, many participants consoled themselves with sexual and romantic fantasies which featured them as fully endowed men wooing or conquering women. Furthermore, with almost no recourse to alternative explanations for their plight, many participants concluded that most of what was making them unhappy would not have transpired had they been boys or men and male. Their bodies' development having convinced them that they were not and would not be boys, many participants began to draw the conclusion that they *should* be exactly that.

Sexuality issues continued to bear upon participants' identity development during their pre-transition adult years. Most participants who entered into sexual and romantic relationships with either men or women, as teenagers or as adults, entered into those relationships while experiencing abiding gender and sex anxieties and gender and sex identity confusions. They used their sexual relationships as arenas for gender and sex identity comparisons in which they knew themselves to be female but were inclined to imagine themselves as boys or men and as males. They were therefore drawn to sexual relationships wherein they could play out their masculine tendencies while still inhabiting their female bodies.

Several participants experimented with heterosexuality. Some did so only superficially and departed from it. Some participants sampled men sexually but remained aloof romantically. A few threw themselves fully into their relationships with men. None, however, found that they were able to express their masculine personalities and sexual fantasies to their satisfaction in relationships with men. Most participants therefore concentrated on relationships with women, hoping that they could be happy as lesbian women.

It was largely in their relationships with women that participants became most firmly entrenched in the idea that their inability to live in ways which felt honest and whole would be cured if they could live as men and as males. As a few had done in their relationships with men, most participants interpreted both their successful and their unsuccessful relationships with women as confirmatory of their inner manhood and maleness. Many participants interpreted those relationships which failed as having failed because participants were unable to function in them as women and as females. When participants counted relationships as successful, it was because they were ones wherein participants were able to express themselves as men and as males. However, participants' successes in their private lives, rather than satisfying their gender needs, only spurred them on to more ardently desire that they could also live as men in their public lives.

Thus an important pattern which seems to have served participants throughout much of their pre-transition teenaged and adult lives was one wherein participants incrementally came to refuse or reject the evidence of any comparisons which might have contradicted the appropriateness of their masculinity. Living as they were in social circumstances which dictated that the only persons who may legitimately lay claim to such well-developed masculinities are men, and that the only persons who may legitimately be men are those who have what are socially defined as male bodies, participants concluded that they were supposed to be men and were supposed to have male bodies. Participants were ripe for the discovery and acceptance of female-to-male transsexualism and the egress from their anxieties and confusion which it promised.

Finding the Way: Going Female-to-Male

Some participants leapt eagerly from their first discovery of female-to-male transsexualism directly into acceptance of that label, then moved as quickly as they could into their transitions. More often, participants went through another set of identity development stages to reach the conclusion that they were indeed transsexual. Throughout the months or years during which participants sorted through their transsexual identity issues, they resorted to many of the same kinds of comparison and analysis techniques which they had used to conclude that they did not belong in the world as women and as females. As had previously been the case, participants' self-images and identities were affected by the ways in which other people responded to them. However, at no time were participants entirely passive recipients of the influences of others. Participants, as adults, were not exceptionally malleable. They were already decidedly masculine in their outlooks and needed only to decide how best to live out their masculinity.

When participants first realized that female-to-male transsexualism was a possibility, most of them immediately were moved to ask themselves if that was the basis of their abiding gender and sex anxieties. Having already come so far into gender and sex dysphoria as they had, participants who asked such questions of themselves readily replied in the affirmative and moved rapidly into making comparisons between themselves and what they knew of female-to-male transsexuals. On the basis of those comparisons, most participants were quick to conclude that they probably were transsexual.

Having come to tolerate the possibility that they might be transsexual, most participants began to research female-to-male transsexualism during that period of delay between transsexual identity tolerance and transsexual identity acceptance. Moreover, participants' research generally continued past their acceptance of transsexual identities and through the next stage of delay as they prepared themselves for their transitions. Participants looked mainly in two areas for confirmations both that they were transsexual and that they should proceed with gender and sex changing transformations. On the one hand, they searched for support and encouragement among those persons who were closest to them. Participants needed and wanted to know that those people with the most intimate knowledge of them agreed with their analyses of their situations and would stand by them throughout their transitions and in their new lives. When participants' intimates were less than entirely supportive, participants either tarried longer in their stage of delay or jettisoned those persons from positions of prominence within their lives. Eventually participants found the level of support which they needed to move on.

A few participants also personally knew other transsexual persons; however, most participants' contacts with other transsexual persons came in the form of correspondence with representatives from transsexual self-help and advocacy organizations. No matter how close or distant were those transsexual others against whom participants compared themselves, the reinforcement value of the validation which they supplied should not be underestimated. Participants trusted no one more than transsexual men to know accurately how to gauge the appropriateness of their candidacy for transsexual transitions. Thus autobiographical information and the written and spoken advice of transsexual men often proved decisive in participants' quests to make sense of their masculinity. Furthermore, the wisdom of their predecessors proved to be of inestimable value to participants during the multitudinous quandaries and quagmires of their transitions. Participants' identities as female-to-male transsexuals were therefore reinforced by those people who were best positioned to influence participants' identities and their choices in relation to those identities.

Coming to Manhood: Integration and Pride

The processes through which participants passed in the accomplishment of their gender and sex reassignments were prolonged and complicated. Although all participants were clear that they would have preferred to have been born as physically complete males, few participants ever achieved the maximum approximation of physical maleness which medical technology could supply. Rather, most participants understood themselves to have embarked on a multifaceted process of sex alteration which would, at minimum, take years to complete and which many participants freely acknowledged that, for a variety of reasons, they might never fully actualize.

Nevertheless, whatever their state of iatrogenic hermaphroditism, participants were nearly unanimous as to the authenticity of their manhood. Thus, although participants were fully mindful of the social requirement that if they were to be men then they had to have male bodies, their own lives belied that dictum. The reality of the limitations of what medical technology could do for participants' bodies left them as men whose ultimate claim to their manhood was founded more solidly on the basis of their social and psychological attributes than on their physical ones.

For many participants, this was initially the source of further gender and sex anxieties. However, participants soon learned that the distinction between gender and sex was as meaningful in their lives as men as it had been while they were living as women and seeking to justify their transsexualism. In other words, they could fully be men in their everyday social interactions irrespective of the fullness of their male sex status. Furthermore, participants learned that many of their lovers were more concerned about participants' gender styles than about the sex features with which they came equipped. Thus even the most wholehearted supporter of the ideological anchoring of gender and sexuality in sex characteristics came to see that whereas gender is a matter of public note, and whereas sexuality begins in gender attractions, sex is a largely private matter. As such, generally its significance can be, and only need be, negotiated with selected others under controlled circumstances. Eventually most participants came to an easy acceptance of themselves as men despite any remaining deficiencies in their physical maleness.

With time, participants also came to learn some important lessons about women, men, and transsexualism. Many participants learned that as out of place, lonely, and isolated as they had felt when living as women, their loneliness and isolation did not cease when they began living as men. It was not until they had the benefit of hindsight that many participants came to realize that women, as a group, have more highly developed emotional lives than do most men. It was only after they had been integrated for some time into society as men that many participants came to understand that in forfeiting their womanhood they had also cut themselves off from the warmth and emotional vitality of women's companionship. They instead found that they had to satisfy themselves with men's rough and competitive camaraderie, which, more often than not, left them painfully cold.

Thus it was that many participants came to value and to take pride in the gifts of their transsexual passages, to appreciate and reembrace many of the skills which they had learned while living among women. Thus it was that many participants came to be sensitive and considerate men who were unafraid to acknowledge and nurture their femininity. Thus it was that many participants came to be precisely the kinds of men whom so many women yearn for in their lives: men who respect and love women for their strengths; men who are emotional, gentle, and considerate; men who shoulder their responsibilities with pride; men who strive to embody the finest features of all of humanity.

Coming to Transsexualism: Placing Oneself in Society

I offer here an overview of how participants struggled to fit themselves into the social categories known to them. I describe only possibilities and choices, not causes and inevitabilities. In so doing, I rework theoretical formulations developed by a number of authors who have discussed relevant issues as they concerned somewhat different groups of people. Just as I have adapted the work of other theorists to my purposes, the propositions which I make here may be profitably generalized to the development of many other types of identities in a variety of social contexts. (See table 1 for a summary of these identity development stages.)

In the first place, all participants experienced an increasing sense of dissatisfaction with their gender and sex over the course of their pre-transition lives. Usually such feelings began in their early childhoods and took many years to crystallize into transsexual identities. Along the way, participants typically went through a variety of stages of self-doubt, questioning, and searching before arriving at decisions that their best option was to live as men and to go through sex reassignment.

In some cases, participants recalled that they felt no discomfort at being girls when they were young children because they were tomboys whose masculine ways were accepted by most of the significant people in their lives. Some participants reported that they were of school age before they realized that they were *not* boys, and so they were spared any feelings of gender discomfort until that time. Even those participants who were uncomfortable enough with their gender to express the wish that they could be boys, or the conviction that they were boys, were not necessarily stigmatized for such expressions because such statements are relatively commonly made by young girls who later abandon such ideas.[10] Thus some participants were able to pass through the earlier segments of their childhoods without feeling any particular anxiety about being girls or about not being boys.

However, at some point during participants' younger years, certainly by the time they reached adolescence, they all began to perceive that there were differences between themselves and other girls and boys. They felt that they were somehow not right either as girls or as boys. In so doing, they entered the first stage on a path which can lead to transsexualism. They began to experience a sense of *abiding anxiety*[11] which was not yet well focussed but was clearly related to gender in some unspecified ways.

As they matured as children, especially as they faced the challenges of puberty and adolescence, most participants' abiding anxiety became more focussed and they entered into a stage of *identity confusion*.[12] At that stage of their lives, participants began to experience "first doubts"[13] about whether they were well suited to being females, girls, or young women. During that stage, participants either continued in their masculine ways or attempted to allay their identity confusion by immersing themselves in identity confirming situations and behaviours. A few participants tried to

Table 1   Identity Development Stages: Female-to-Male Transsexualism

Developmental Stage	Some Characteristics	Some Actions Taken
Abiding Anxiety	Unfocussed gender and sex discomfort.	Preference for masculine activities and companionship.
Identity Confusion	First doubts about suitability of assigned gender and sex.	Reactive gender and sex conforming activities or preference for masculine activities and companionship.
Identity Comparison	Seeking and weighing alternative female identities.	Adoption of mannish lesbian identity. Secret identity as a man and a male.
Discovery	Learning that female-to-male transsexualism exists.	Accidental contact with information about transsexualism.
Identity Confusion	First doubts about the authenticity of own transsexualism.	Seeking more information about transsexualism.
Identity Comparison	Testing transsexual identity using transsexual reference group.	Start to disidentify as women and females. Start to identify as transsexual.
Identity Tolerance	Identify as probably transsexual.	Increasingly disidentify as women and females.
Delay	Waiting for changed circumstances. Looking for confirmation of transsexual identity.	Seeking more information about transsexualism. Reality testing in intimate relationships and against further information about transsexualism.
Identity Acceptance	Transsexual identity established.	Tell others about transsexual identity.
Delay	Transsexual identity deepens. Final disidentity as women and females. Anticipatory socialization as men.	Learning how to do gender and sex reassignments. Saving money. Organizing support system.
Transition	Changing genders, between sexes.	Gender and sex reassignments.
Identity Acceptance	Identities established as transsexual men.	Successful "passing" as men and as males.
Integration	Transsexuality mostly invisible.	Stigma management.
Identity Pride	Publicly transsexual.	Transsexual advocacy and activism.

become more appropriately feminine in dress and demeanour in order to reconstitute their femaleness and their womanhood. Some older participants plunged into heterosexual affairs and relationships for similar reasons.

Subsequently, either directly or after some efforts at conformity, participants began to seriously entertain the idea that they were different from other females, girls, and women. When they did so, they entered into a stage of *identity comparison*[14] wherein they considered the extent of their differences from, and similarities with, other females, girls, and women. In the process of seeking and weighing alternatives,[15] many participants looked to lesbian women as a reference group.

Many participants temporarily took refuge in the stereotypes of lesbian women as manly women or as women who wished to become men. By attempting to find like-minded females among lesbian women, participants looked to locate a comparison group which would permit them to forestall the conclusion that they were unlike any other females, unlike any other women. Once they had eliminated other more feminine reference groups and were no longer able to find sufficient commonalties between themselves and their comparison group of butch lesbian women, participants were faced with the conclusion that if they were not like other females, girls, or women, then they must be some kind of "freaks." They felt neither female nor male; they felt stuck as women who should have been men. Such a conclusion, however, offered participants little or no solace until such time as they became aware of the possibilities offered by the concept of female-to-male transsexualism.

Thus, although participants may have developed relatively high degrees of gender and sex dysphorias and although they may have felt themselves to be more suited to inhabit the only other gender and sex possibilities of which they were aware, it was not a simple step from gender and sex dysphorias to transsexualism. Participants who had experienced *abiding anxiety*, *identity confusion*, and *identity comparison* concerning their femaleness and womanhood also went through a series of stages of identity development, consolidation, and integration in the process of coming to see themselves first as female-to-male transsexuals and later as transsexual men.

In the first stage of transsexual identity development, *discovery*,[16] participants found a name which had the potential to make sense of the constellation of feelings which they were experiencing. When they discovered that there was a condition called female-to-male transsexualism, it opened up the way for them to explain logically how it could be that they appeared to be members of one gender and sex while feeling themselves to be otherwise.[17]

A few participants embraced transsexual identities as soon as they became aware of the possibility. However, most participants went through a number of intermediate stages before they accepted transsexual identities as their own. Having discovered female-to-male transsexualism, many participants once again went through a period of *identity confusion* which, at this stage, was focussed more specifically on first doubts about the authenticity of their transsexualism rather than the correctness of their femaleness or womanhood. During this stage, participants began to gather more information about female-to-male transsexualism.

As participants moved into a second stage of *identity comparison*, they tested themselves using female-to-male transsexuals as a reference group rather than females and women as they previously had done. As they found greater areas of convergence between themselves and what they knew about female-to-male transsexuals, they began simultaneously to move toward transsexual identities and to disidentify with women and with females.[18] In so doing, participants entered a stage of *identity tolerance*[19] wherein they began to increasingly identify themselves as probably transsexual and as probably not women or females.

Once participants had begun to live with the possibility that they probably were transsexual, many of them entered into a period of *delay*.[20] Although many participants went through such a stage, they did not all use their time in similar ways. Some participants realized that it was a possibility that they were transsexual but for a variety of reasons were unable to face the implications attendant upon such an identity. They simply bided their time until something in their circumstances changed sufficiently to allow them to proceed.

Other participants made use of this stage to engage in further "reality testing."[21] In particular, many participants tested their fledgling identities in their intimate relationships and against available information from and about female-to-male transsexuals. They scrutinized their love lives for clues as to whether their own behaviours, and their lovers' responses to them, bore telltale signs that participants were more like men than women, more like males than females. As participants tried, and failed, to fit themselves to each of the models of womanhood and femaleness with which they were familiar, they moved further toward fully accepting themselves as transsexual.

In the next stage, *identity acceptance*,[22] participants began to think of themselves as transsexual and to be willing to claim that identity with selected other persons. Many participants, once they had accepted transsexual identities, began to feel anxious to do something to transform themselves from females to males.[23] However, few participants immediately knew how to proceed. Therefore they once again entered into a stage of *delay.*

During this second stage of delay, participants accomplished a number of important tasks. First of all, they had to find out more precisely how gender and sex reassignments could be accomplished. Secondly, they had to save a least some of the sizeable amounts of money which were required to finance most sex transformational procedures. Thirdly, they had both to work up their own courage and to fortify their various support systems as much as possible in order more effectively to face the hardships of the transitional processes which lay before them. Finally, most participants also made use of the time to embark upon anticipatory socialization as men and as males.[24] In other words, even though they were still ostensibly living as women and as females during this stage, most participants began more assiduously to study the ways of men and to provisionally perfect their own renditions of masculinity. Moreover, as participants further disengaged themselves from their remaining identities as women and as females, they often found themselves to be the objects of angry rejections by women who sensed participants' growing alienation from femaleness and womanhood and felt it as a betrayal of their kind.[25] Additionally, as participants prepared themselves for their transitions and became more knowledgeable about female-to-male transsexualism, they intensified their commitments to their transsexual identities. Thus, during this phase of delay, participants further distanced themselves from identities as women and as females and deepened their commitments to transsexual identities, to identities as men and as males, and to the pursuit of gender and sex reassignment.

Transition was a lengthy and mostly open-ended stage for participants. It usually began with a period during which participants felt as though they were in a "vacuum"[26] wherein they had not yet become men but they were no longer women. During this stage, only a few participants took comfort in their transsexual identities because most participants were eager to move beyond the transition stage and into their lives as men and as males. Due to the high cost and underdevelopment of medical services for female-to-male transsexuals, no participants felt that they had yet completely passed out of the transition stage in all aspects of their lives as males.

Although the physical transitions of most participants may not have been complete, their social transformations into men were usually entirely satisfactory to them in most regards. Thus, at some point, most participants entered a second *identity acceptance* stage wherein they ceased living as women and began to conduct their lives accepting themselves, and accepted by others, as men. However, because of their incomplete physical transformations and because of their previous lives as females, girls, and women, participants acknowledged that they were different from other men who had lived their whole lives in their preferred genders and sexes. They carried their pasts with them in their bodies and in their psyches. As such, they were a particular kind of man with a particular kind of past;[27] they were transsexual men: men who were born as females and had lived for many years as girls and as women.

As transsexual men, they had two more stages open to them: *integration*[28] and *identity pride*.[29] Some participants chose to pass more of their post-transition lives in one stage than the other, but participants more often exhibited each type of behaviour in different circumstances.

In myriad ways, most participants who lived as men were well *integrated* into their social fabrics as men. They lived their lives as unremarkable men whose transsexuality remained invisible except to specifically chosen other people.[30] They treated the information that they once had been female and had lived as girls and as women as potentially discrediting information which needed to be managed with care.[31] However, in situations where it was relevant, such as with lovers, doctors, close friends, and other differently gendered persons, most participants were open about their transsexualism. Thus most participants neither conscientiously hid nor disclosed their transsexual backgrounds. If there were reasons to speak of it, they did. Otherwise it was a part of their pasts which remained quiescent.

A smaller number of participants took a different tack. They made their transsexualism a point of *pride*. By so doing, they preempted the possibility that other persons might call the authenticity of their manhood into question by pointing out that they had come to it later in life. Thus, rather than treating the fact of their transsexualism as a potentially stigmatizing piece of information which needed to be managed with care, they fully and publicly claimed their bifurcated histories. Such participants were those people who were active in transsexual organizations and in efforts to educate the public about female-to-male transsexualism. They proudly posed themselves and their lives as challenges to the restrictive binarisms of the dominant gender schema.[32]

Recommendations and Ruminations

Persons who experience extreme gender and sex dysphorias clearly follow arduous journeys. I suspect that those people who survive and find their ways to satisfying lives as transsexual men may be in the minority. Many others are lost along the way to suicide, drugs, alcohol, and myriad other self-destructive behaviours. For the benefit of those people who discover and pursue gender and sex reassignment, I offer a few recommendations.

Firstly, access to accurate information concerning transsexualism and gender and sex reassignment is difficult for most people to obtain. This could be remedied through a number of avenues. Most people first learn of transsexualism through the media. Generally, libraries, doctors, or therapists are their next stops. I therefore recommend that all public libraries maintain up-to-date and clearly labeled holdings on the subject. I also recommend that all therapists, medical general practitioners, and relevant medical specialists consider it to be their obligation to become well informed about transsexualism *before* they receive their first enquiries on the subject. I recommend that schools which train such service providers include an overview of transsexualism in their regular curriculum and that professional associations make updated information packages available to their members. However, I hasten to add that personnel who are not highly skilled in this area should refer gender and sex dysphoric clients to other practitioners who are more experienced.

Secondly, I recommend that the Harry Benjamin International Gender Dysphoria Association's *Standards of Care* be reviewed approximately every five years by a panel of experts made up of medical and therapeutic personnel, senior researchers, and transsexual activists. I further recommend that one-year real-life tests be retained as important milestones but that the success of those tests be determined by the persons who have lived them rather than by helping professionals unless pathological psychological or medical conditions contraindicate. That is to say that I do not consider transsexualism to be, a priori, a pathological condition. Nor do I recommend that the identification of psychological etiological pathways form a basis for the refusal of access to gender and sex reassignment technologies. Furthermore, because of the power of breasts as markers of the female sex and because of the negative health consequences of prolonged breast binding, I recommend that breast reduction surgeries be made available to large-breasted females early in the real-life test period.

Thirdly, I make recommendations concerning the medical care of female-to-male transsexuals. It has been my observation that testosterone therapy often is not closely enough tailored to individuals' metabolisms. The long-term effects of exogenous testosterone therapy are also unknown at this time. I therefore recommend that careful monitoring and gradual incremental testosterone dosages become the norm so that transsexual men receive no more treatment than is necessary to achieve their desired results. Furthermore, the option of discontinuation of testosterone therapy after a number of years should be made known to all transsexual men.

At this time, few surgeons are skilled at female-to-male chest reconstruction, and although many surgeons are competent to perform hysterectomies and salpingo-oopherectomies, few are fully aware of the special caveats needed when performing those operations on persons who may later undergo genital reconstruction surgeries. I therefore recommend that information and training on these issues be included in surgical education and that practicing surgeons be made aware of the necessity for specialized training before accepting such patients.

The situation for female-to-male genital reconstruction is abysmal. Only a small minority of transsexual men opt for genital reconstruction surgeries. Some people simply are not interested in what they consider to be unnecessary surgeries. However, most people who live as men would like to have phalluses if health and financial costs to them were not excessive. I therefore recommend that increased funding be made available both to support research into improved surgical techniques and to underwrite more of the costs of that which is available. I further recommend that transsexual men research and consult thoroughly before contracting for any surgical services.

Fourthly, I am concerned at the paucity of follow-up psychological or medical care for transsexual men. Many men who were born male have ongoing difficulties with their masculinities. This is no less so for transsexual men, but their issues are sometimes unique. I therefore see a need for voluntary periodic follow-up visits to knowledgeable therapists in the years following transition. Furthermore, the medical needs of transsexual men are different in many ways from those of other men. Far too few doctors are aware of these needs, and far too few transsexual men receive proper medical care. Thus doctors should receive more training, and those who are knowledgeable should make this fact known to their colleagues so that transsexual patients may be referred to them. More funding is needed for research into the ongoing medical needs of transsexual men; and transsexual men must more actively demand attentive health care.

Not every gender and sex dysphoric female-born person procures, or is interested in, as complete physical transformation as is medically possible. Not all female-to-male transsexual persons are equally gender and sex dysphoric. Indeed, many female-to-male transsexuals value many of the aspects of the gender and sex to which they were originally assigned and endeavour to retain them even as they otherwise transform themselves. Thus few transsexual men ever completely leave behind all of their womanness, all of their femaleness. Yet they live their everyday lives as men. Several important points follow from these facts.

In the first instance, the lives of female-to-male transsexual persons graphically illustrate that genders are only loosely linked to sexes. Certainly it is true that people who live as men are supposed to have male bodies. Just as certainly the bodies of transsexual men are hermaphroditic. A few bear approximations of the ultimate signifier of maleness, but most do not. Furthermore, many people who live their daily lives as men carry with them wombs, ovaries, and breasts. Some people live as men without the aid of virilizing hormones. Nonetheless, they live as men. The possession of gender confirming sex characteristics enlarges the sphere in which such persons may move uncontested as men, but the lack of them does not eliminate such individuals from the ranks of men. Thus it is that the lives of transsexual men demonstrate that genders are socially negotiated statuses which can be occupied by persons of any sex if they are sufficiently adept at the associated gender styles.

Secondly, the circumstances of female-to-male transsexuals also make obvious the socially constructed nature of the determination of sexes. Clearly, which criteria are definitive of maleness is a matter which is open to negotiation. The fact that the basis for the alteration of legal sex status varies by jurisdictions and by agencies within jurisdictions underscores that sexes are sociological statuses which are based partially upon physiological attributes and partially upon social and political wrangling.

My third point concerns questions of sexual orientations. An important lesson to be gleaned from the stories of female-to-male transsexuals is that sexual orientations involve both genders and sexes. Before their transitions, many female-to-male transsexuals become involved in relationships with persons who are attracted to their manliness even though it inhabits the female bodies of persons who live as women. It is not unusual for the people involved in such situations to proceed as if the transsexual partner is both a man and a male. After their transitions, most transsexual men become involved in relationships with persons who initially know them only as men. However, when sexual attractions give way to sexual activities, the hermaphroditic conditions of the bodies of most transsexual men must be taken into account—and there seems to be an adequate supply of people, of all genders and sexes, who are happy to do so.

Sexual attractions thus appear to be activated on the basis of genders which persons usually presume will later be substantiated by appropriately sexed bodies. However, if the expected body types do not materialize, many people are able to incorporate sex incongruities via fantasies and other forms of sexual creativity. Thus, although sexual orientations are ultimately about sexuality, it is my contention that they are first and foremost about genders; for most people, sexes, specific sex characteristics, and the sexual practices in which they engage are of secondary import to gender and can be construed so as to appear to follow gender when the need arises.

What my contact with transsexual people has taught me is that the time is upon us to reevaluate how we think about gender, sex, and sexuality. It now seems perfectly clear to me that we live in a world which is far more diverse than any number of simplistic dichotomies can describe. I have learned that we diminish ourselves as a society by failing to avail ourselves of the special gifts and lessons we can receive from the differently gendered and sexed people among us.

Whereas it is heartening that most members of European and North American societies are beginning to come to an awareness of the profound importance of biodiversity for the survival of our planet, it is unfortunate that we have been very slow to generalize this concept to our understandings of gender, sex, and sexuality. We tend to continue to think of people whose genders, sexes, or sexualities fall at a distance from statistical, social, or moral norms as "mistakes" of nature or of nurture. Our dogged insistence on framing our thoughts on the basis of dualistic categorizations of man/woman, male/female, heterosexual/homosexual, either/or, right/wrong, serves to blinker our vision. It is time that we begin to recognize that there are far more "mistakes of society" than there are "mistakes of nature."

It is not only transsexual persons but all of us who labour under the limitations of binary norms of gender, sex, and sexuality. No one fits perfectly the abstract gender, sex, or sexuality ideals to which each member of society is exhorted to strive. Yet, each of us tries. Yet, each of us, in ways large and small, fails. Each of us, transsexual or not, must search for our places within the gender schemas of the societies in which we live. Indeed, who among us have never wondered if they weren't somehow different from all the rest? Who among us have always felt so secure that they have never altered themselves to try better to live up to society's gender, sex, and sexual ideals? Clothing, coiffures, and cosmetics, body building, hormones, hair transplants, and surgeries have all been used by transsexual and non-transsexual members of society alike to make themselves more perfectly fit society's gender, sex, and sexual ideals. Perhaps, in the end, the biggest differences between transsexual people and other members of society lie not so much in the nature of the identity developmental and identity supporting processes through which they must pass, but in the anguish and consciousness with which they must negotiate them.

All of these lessons ultimately lead to a very astigmatic vision of gender, sex, and sexuality. What remains clear is only that the idea that all persons can be neatly classified within the available gender, sex, and sexual categories is an untenable one. We humans may find binarisms easy to understand but nature is not so simple-minded. Many people live openly beyond dualities, albeit often at a high personal price. Many more people yearn to creatively coin more genders, sexes, and sexualities, but they cannot afford the costs to their social standings, family members, or self-esteems. It is time that we, as a society, move toward greater recognition and appreciation of diversity in genders, sexes, and sexual orientation, that we begin to envision and enable a future in which a multiplicity of genders, sexes, and sexualities might be safely imagined and easily enacted by those persons who feel so inclined. When it comes to genders, sexes, and sexualities it is time that we learn to count higher than two, that we learn to multiply and divide, and that we endeavour to expand our options exponentially.

Appendix

INTERVIEW QUESTIONS PART I

INSTRUCTIONS: Thank you for taking the time to answer these questions. Please do not write your answers on these question sheets. Please write your answers on paper or computer disk or speak them into a tape recorder. If you write your answers using a computer, please use Microsoft Word, WordPerfect or send your file in ASCII (text only, with no formatting commands). If you use audio tapes or computer disks, let me know what they cost and I will reimburse you for your expenses. Please allow yourself lots of time. There is no reason why you need to do all the questions in one sitting. Can you return them to me in about two weeks? If not, please let me know when I can expect to see them. Thanks again.

Introductory questions:

1. How old are you?

2. Where were you born?
    (a) Where do you live now?
    (b) Where else have you lived and for how long in each place?

3. What are your racial or ethnic origins?

4. What kind of work do you normally do?
    (a) What is your usual income level?
    (b) What is the highest educational level you have reached?

5. What kind of work did your parents do when you were growing up?
    (a) How would you describe your family's income level?
    (b) What were your parents' education levels?

6. Did you have any brothers or sisters?
    (a) What are their ages?
    (b) Did you live with any other adults or children as a child?
    (c) Who were they? What were their ages and relations to you?

7. What sex are you?
    (a) Have you always been that sex?
    (b) Have you made any changes to get you to where you are now?
    (c) What are they?

(d) What changes to your sex/gender do you intend to make?
(e) What changes are you considering but not yet committed to?

Pre-school years:

8. What are your earliest memories of anything at all?
   (a) Describe two or three of them to me.

9. What do you remember most vividly about your pre-school years?
   (a) Tell me about the two or three best parts of these years.
   (b) Why were they the best?
   (c) Tell me about the two or three worst parts of these years.
   (d) Why were they the worst?

10. Tell me about your mother. What was she like?
    (a) What did you like best about her? Why was that the best?
    (b) What did you dislike the most about her? Why?
    (c) What were the things you did together the most?
    (d) What kinds of things would you never do with your mother?
    (e) Did you fight with your mother? About what?
    (f) Did other people like your mother?
    (g) What do you remember other people saying about her?
    (h) Were you close with your mother?
    (i) How are some of the ways you are like your mother?
    (j) How are some of the ways you are different from your mother?

11. Tell me about your father. What was he like?
    (a) What did you like best about him? Why was that the best?
    (b) What did you dislike the most about him? Why?
    (c) What were the things you did together the most?
    (d) What kinds of things would you never do with your father?
    (e) Did you fight with your father? About what?
    (f) Did other people like your father?
    (g) What do you remember other people saying about him?
    (h) Were you close with your father?
    (i) How are some of the ways you are like your father?
    (j) How are some of the ways you are different from your father?

12. Tell me about your brothers and sisters. What were they like?
    (a) Were you especially close with any of them?
    (b) Did you have a hard relationship with any of them?
    (c) Who did you like best? Why was s/he the best?
    (d) Who did you dislike the most? Why?

13. What were the things you did with your brothers?
    (a) What were two or three of your favourite activities?
    (b) What did your brothers do that you weren't allowed to do?
    (c) What did you do that your brothers weren't allowed to do?

(d) What did your brothers have to do you didn't have to do?
(e) What did you have to do your brothers didn't have to do?
(f) How are some of the ways you are like your brothers?
(g) In what ways you are different from your brothers?

14. What were the things you did with your sisters?
(a) What were two or three of your favourite activities?
(b) What did your sisters do that you weren't allowed to do?
(c) What did you do that your sisters weren't allowed to do?
(d) What did your sisters have to do that you didn't have to do?
(e) What did you have to do that your sisters didn't have to do?
(f) How are some of the ways you are like your sisters?
(g) How are some of the ways you are different from your sisters?

15. Did you have important relationships with any other adults?
(a) What were they like?
(b) What kinds of things did you do together?
(c) Why were they important to you?

16. Do you recall anything like sexual, emotional, or physical abuse?
(a) What people were involved?
(b) What do you remember happening?
(c) Describe two or three incidents.
(d) Do you suspect that there might have been more?
(e) Are there time periods that you can't remember at all?

17. Who were your best friends?
(a) What did you do together?
(b) What were your most favourite activities? Why?
(c) What were your least favourite activities? Why?
(d) Was there anyone you particularly looked up to? Why?
(e) Was there anyone you especially disliked? Why?

18. Did you ever think that you were a boy?
(a) Did you ever think that you would grow up to be a man?
(b) Did you ever want to be a boy? Why?
(c) Were you ever a boy in your play activities? How?
(d) Were you ever a boy in your fantasy life? How?

Grade school years:

19. What do you remember most vividly about your grade school years?
(a) Tell me about the two or three best parts of these years.
(b) Why were they the best?
(c) Tell me about the two or three worst parts of these years.
(d) Why were they the worst?

20. Tell me about your relationship with your mother during this time.
(a) Were you close to your mother?

  (b) Did you fight with your mother? About what?
  (c) Had things changed between you two since you were younger?
  (d) When? Was there an event that changed things?
  (e) How was your mother different?
  (f) How were you different?
  (g) Why do you suppose things changed?

21. Tell me about your relationship with your father during this time.
  (a) Were you close to your father?
  (b) Did you fight with your father? About what?
  (c) Had things changed between you two since you were younger?
  (d) When? Was there an event that changed things?
  (e) How was your father different?
  (f) How were you different?
  (g) Why do you suppose things changed?

22. Describe your relationships with your brothers during this time.
  (a) Were you close to your brothers?
  (b) Did you fight with your brothers? About what?
  (c) What did your brothers do that you weren't allowed to do?
  (d) What did you do that your brothers weren't allowed to do?
  (e) What did your brothers have to do that you didn't have to do?
  (f) What did you have to do that your brothers didn't have to do?
  (g) Had things changed between you since you were younger?
  (h) When? Was there an event that changed things?
  (i) How were your brothers different?
  (j) How were you different?
  (k) Why do you suppose things changed?

23. Describe your relationships with your sisters during this time.
  (a) Were you close to your sisters?
  (b) Did you fight with your sisters? About what?
  (c) What did your sisters do that you weren't allowed to do?
  (d) What did you do that your sisters weren't allowed to do?
  (e) What did your sisters have to do that you didn't have to do?
  (f) Did you have to do things your sisters didn't have to do?
  (g) Had things changed between you since you were younger?
  (h) When? Was there an event that changed things?
  (i) How were your sisters different?
  (j) How were you different?
  (k) Why do you suppose things changed?

24. Do you recall anything like sexual, emotional, or physical abuse?
  (a) Describe two or three incidents.

25. Was there anyone you particularly looked up to? Who? Why?

26. Was there anyone you especially disliked? Who? Why?

27. Who were your best friends, what did you do together?

   (a) What were your most favourite activities?
   (b) What were your least favourite activities?

28. Did you ever think that you were a boy?
   (a) Did you ever think that you would grow up to be a man?
   (b) Did you ever want to be a boy? Why?
   (c) Were you ever a boy in your play activities? How?
   (d) Were you ever a boy in your fantasy life? How?

29. What kind of student were you?
   (a) What did you like best about school?
   (b) What did you dislike the most about school?
   (c) What did you do before and after school?

30. Did you use drugs or alcohol? Under what circumstances?

Teen years:

31. What was best, worst about this time?
   (a) Tell me about the two or three best parts of these years.
   (b) Why were they the best?
   (c) Tell me about the two or three worst parts of these years.
   (d) Why were they the worst?

32. Tell me about your relationship with your mother during this time.
   (a) Were you close to your mother?
   (b) Did you fight with your mother? About what?
   (c) Had things changed between you two since you were younger?
   (d) When? Was there an event that changed things?
   (e) How was your mother different?
   (f) How were you different?
   (g) Why do you suppose things changed?

33. Tell me about your relationship with your father during this time.
   (a) Were you close to your father?
   (b) Did you fight with your father? About what?
   (c) Had things changed between you two since you were younger?
   (d) When? Was there an event that changed things?
   (e) How was your father different?
   (f) How were you different?
   (g) Why do you suppose things changed?

34. Describe your relationships with your brothers during this time.
   (a) Were you close to your brothers?
   (b) Did you fight with your brothers? About what?
   (c) What did your brothers do that you weren't allowed to do?
   (d) What did you do that your brothers weren't allowed to do?
   (e) What did your brothers have to do that you didn't have to do?
   (f) What did you have to do that your brothers didn't have to do?
   (g) Had things changed between you since you were younger?

    (h) When? Was there an event that changed things?
    (i) How were your brothers different?
    (j) How were you different?
    (k) Why do you suppose things changed?

35. Describe your relationships with your sisters during this time.
    (a) Were you close to your sisters?
    (b) Did you fight with your sisters? About what?
    (c) What did your sisters do that you weren't allowed to do?
    (d) What did you do that your sisters weren't allowed to do?
    (e) What did your sisters have to do that you didn't have to do?
    (f) Did you have to do things your sisters didn't have to do?
    (g) Had things changed between you since you were younger?
    (h) When? Was there an event that changed things?
    (i) How were your sisters different?
    (j) How were you different?
    (k) Why do you suppose things changed?

36. Do you recall anything like sexual, emotional, or physical abuse?
    (a) Describe two or three incidents.

37. Was there anyone you particularly looked up to? Who? Why?

38. Was there anyone you especially disliked? Who? Why?

39. Who were your best friends, what did you do together?
    (a) What were your most favourite activities?
    (b) What were your least favourite activities?

40. Did you ever think that you were a boy?
    (a) Did you ever think that you would grow up to be a man?
    (b) Did you ever want to be a boy? Why?
    (c) Were you ever a boy in your play activities? How?
    (d) Were you ever a boy in your fantasy life? How?

41. What kind of student were you?
    (a) What did you like best about school?
    (b) What did you dislike the most about school?
    (c) What did you do before and after school?

42. Did you use drugs or alcohol? Under what circumstances?

Sexuality:

43. What is your earliest memory of sexual activity or exploration?
    (a) Describe what happened.
    (b) Was it your idea in the first place?
    (c) Was it a pleasurable experience? Did you want to do it again?
    (d) Did you feel proud of yourself? Why?
    (e) Did you feel guilty? Why?

44. What was your puberty like?
    (a) At what age did your body start to change? How?
    (b) Were you well informed about menstruation? Who told you what?
    (c) Were you pleased with the changes to your body? Why? Why not?
    (d) Was your puberty normal? If not, how?
    (e) Describe how your body looked after your puberty.
    (f) Did these changes affect your identity? How?
    (g) Did you try to hide the changes to your body? How?
    (h) Did you experience an increased interest in sexuality? How?
    (i) Did you experience an increased interest in romance? How?

45. Describe two or three other early sexual/romantic experiences.
    (a) Who were they with?
    (b) What did you do? What did the other person(s) do?
    (c) Did you feel proud of yourself? Why?
    (d) Did you feel guilty? Why?
    (e) Did these feelings/experience affect your identity? How?

46. Must you be in love to enjoy sex?
    (a) Have you had casual sex? With women? With men? How often?
    (b) How important is love?
    (c) Are you happy when you are not in love?
    (d) How often do you want to have sex with someone you love?
    (e) Is a love relationship OK with you if there is no sex in it?
    (f) Is a sexual relationship OK with you if you feel no love?

47. How do you best find sexual satisfaction?
    (a) Do you have orgasms? How often?
    (b) Describe the two first times. The two best times.
    (c) Are there certain sexual practices you prefer? What? Why?
    (d) Is a penis necessary to your sexuality?
    (e) Are there certain sexual practices you avoid? What? Why?
    (f) Will you allow a lover to touch your private sexual parts?
    (g) Will you/did you allow a lover to penetrate you sexually?
    (h) Do you practice or fantasize S/M sexuality? How?
    (i) Do you masturbate? How?
    (j) Are clothing, fantasies a part of your sexuality? How?

48. What sex(es) have you been sexually/romantically attracted to?
    (a) What do you find sexually attractive in a person?
    (b) What personality traits do you find attractive in a person?
    (c) Describe your perfect mate.
    (d) Describe what the perfect relationship for you would be like.
    (e) Have you married? Would you like to marry?
    (f) If yes, why is marriage important to you?

49. Tell me about some of your relationships/affairs.
    (a) Tell me about two of your first relationships.

(b) How did they begin? How long did they last? How did they end?
(c) What were your partners like? How did you relate together?
(d) Tell me about some of your later relationships/affairs.
(e) How did they begin? How long did they last? How did they end?
(f) What were your partners like? How did you relate together?
(g) If you have married, describe your mate(s).
(h) If you have married, describe your relationship(s).
(i) If no longer married, describe how & why your marriage ended.
(j) Have you had children? When? How many? Where are they now?
(k) Describe your relationships with your children.
(l) Tell me about your most recent sexual/romantic relationships.
(m) How did they begin? How long did they last? How did they end?
(n) What were your partners like? How did you relate together?

Any further comments? (use back of page for more space)

This is the end of part I.
Thank you for your co-operation.

INTERVIEW QUESTIONS PART II

INSTRUCTIONS: Thank you for taking the time to answer these questions. Please do not write your answers on these question sheets. Please write your answers on paper or computer disk or speak them into a tape recorder. If you write your answers using a computer, please use Microsoft Word, WordPerfect or send your file in ASCII (text only, with no formatting commands). If you use audio tapes or computer disks, let me know what they cost and I will reimburse you for your expenses. Please allow yourself lots of time. There is no reason why you need to do all the questions in one sitting. Can you return them to me in about two weeks? If not, please let me know when I can expect to see them. Thanks again.

Health:

50. Describe anything unusual about your body as a female.

51. Describe any chromosomal or hormonal abnormalities you have had.

52. Have you ever suffered from temporal lobe problems or seizures?

53. Did your mother take D.E.S. when she was carrying you?

Childhood Gender Identity:

54. How old were you when you first felt that you wanted to be male?
    (a) Describe three of your earliest memories of this.
    (b) Was it a constant feeling or did it come and go?
    (c) Under what circumstances was the feeling the strongest?

(d) Did you tell others about your feelings then?
(e) If yes, how did they react? If no, why not?

55. Did the idea stay with you all the time?
    (a) If no, what made you abandon it when you did?
    (b) When did you again begin to want to be a male? Why?
    (c) What happened if you talked about your desire to be male?

56. Describe two or three incidents that clarified your gender to you.
    (a) What happened that convinced you that you should be male?
    (b) Why did these events mean that you should be male?

57. Did you live as a boy at all during your childhood?
    (a) If no, why not?
    (b) If yes, describe how you did it.
    (c) Did others accept you as a boy? How did you know?
    (d) Were your parents supportive? Tolerant? Opposed?
    (e) Were your friends supportive? Tolerant? Opposed?

58. As a child, did you know anything about sex changes?
    (a) What did you know? How did you find out?
    (b) Did you plan to have one later?

59. How would you describe yourself as a child?
    (a) What were your three best features?
    (b) What were your three worst features?
    (c) What were the two most masculine things about you?
    (d) What were the two most feminine things about you?
    (e) Were you a religious person? Did you believe in a god?
    (f) Did you like to blend in or stand out in a crowd?
    (g) How important was family and religious community to you?

Teenage Gender Identity:

60. Did you feel that you should be male when you were a teenager?
    (a) Describe three examples of these feelings.
    (b) Was it a constant feeling or did it come and go?
    (c) Under what circumstances was the feeling the strongest?
    (d) Did you tell others about your feelings?
    (e) If yes, how did they react? If no, why not?

61. Did the idea stay with you all the time?
    (a) If no, what made you abandon it when you did?
    (b) When did you again want to be a male? Why?
    (c) What happened if you spoke about your desire to be male?

62. Describe two or three incidents that clarified your gender to you.
    (a) What happened that convinced you that you should be male?
    (b) Why did these events mean that you should be male?

63. Did you live as a male at all during your teen years?
    (a) If no, why not?

    (b) If yes, describe how you did it.
    (c) Did others accept you as a male? How did you know?
    (d) Were your parents supportive? Tolerant? Opposed?
    (e) Were your friends supportive? Tolerant? Opposed?

64. As a teen, did you know anything about sex changes?
    (a) What did you know? How did you find out?
    (b) Did you plan to have one later?

65. Were you sexually attracted to females in your teen years?
    (a) Did you have any sexual relationships in your teen years?
    (b) Did you think of yourself as a lesbian?
    (c) Did you have any lesbian friends?
    (d) Were your female lovers lesbians?
    (e) What is a lesbian?
    (f) Does God approve of lesbians?
    (g) Did you read any books or articles on lesbianism? Which ones?
    (h) Did you ever go to any gay bars? What happened?
    (i) Did you ever go to any gay organizations? What happened?

66. Did you take any steps toward getting a sex change in your teens?
    (a) Did you read or see television about transsexualism? What?
    (b) Did you talk to people about transsexualism? Who?
    (c) Did you see any doctors or therapists about your gender?
    (d) Describe what you found out about transsexualism and you.
    (e) Describe any progress you made toward a sex change.

67. How would you describe yourself as a teen?
    (a) What were your three best features?
    (b) What were your three worst features?
    (c) What were the two most masculine things about you?
    (d) What were the two most feminine things about you?
    (e) Were you a religious person? Did you believe in a god?
    (f) Did you like to blend in or stand out in a crowd?
    (g) How important was family and religious community to you?

Adult Gender Identity

68. Do you always feel that you should be male?
    (a) Describe three examples of these feelings.
    (b) Is it a constant feeling or does it come and go?
    (c) If it's not constant, what makes you abandon it when you do?
    (d) Under what circumstances are the feelings the strongest?
    (e) Do you tell others about your feelings?
    (f) If yes, describe two or three typical reactions.
    (g) If no, why not?

69. Describe two or three incidents that clarified your gender to you.
    (a) What happened that convinced you that you should be male?
    (b) Why did these events mean that you should be male?

70. Have you lived as a male at all during your adult years?
    (a) If no, why not?
    (b) If yes, describe how you have done it.
    (c) Have others accepted you as a male? How do you know?
    (d) Have your lovers/partners been supportive? Tolerant? Opposed?
    (e) Describe each of their responses to your gender choices.
    (f) Have your friends been supportive? Tolerant? Opposed?
    (g) Describe the two best and two worst responses from friends.
    (h) If you have children, how have they reacted to your gender?

71. Have you been sexually attracted to females as an adult?
    (a) Have you had any sexual relationships with women?
    (b) Do you think of yourself as a lesbian?
    (c) Do you have any lesbian friends?
    (d) Are/were your female lovers lesbians?
    (e) Do you read any books or articles on lesbianism? Which ones?
    (f) Do you ever go to any gay bars? Do you feel comfortable?
    (g) Do you ever go to any gay organizations? Do you fit in?

72. How did you find out what you now know about sex changes?
    (a) Have you read books or articles? Which ones?
    (b) Have you gone to doctors or therapists for help?
    (c) Have you asked in the gay community?
    (d) Have you asked in the transsexual community?
    (e) How helpful and informative have each of these been?
    (f) Describe what you found out about transsexualism and you.
    (g) Describe any progress you have made toward a sex change.
    (h) Do you intend to go further? What will you do?

73. How would you describe yourself as a person?
    (a) What are your three best features?
    (b) What are your three worst features?
    (c) What are the two most masculine things about you?
    (d) What are the two most feminine things about you?
    (e) Are you a religious person? Do you believe in a god?
    (f) Do you like to blend in or stand out in a crowd?
    (g) How important is family and religious community to you?

Changing Over

(If you haven't lived as a man yet, please say so and then answer only questions 80–86 in this section based on your expectations of what you think it would be like if you were living as a man.)

74. How did you decide to start publicly living as a man?
    (a) When did you make the decision?
    (b) Did you talk it over with others? Who?
    (c) Did you take advice from others? Who? What?
    (d) Was it a hard decision to make? Why? How?

(e) What were the arguments in favour? Against?
(f) Did you put it off for any reason? How long? Why?
(g) Have you had any doubts since you started? What?
(h) Have you ever changed your mind? When? Why?

75. What were the first steps you took?
    (a) Describe the three most important changes to how you dress.
    (b) Describe the three most important changes to how you move.
    (c) Describe the three most important changes to how you talk.
    (d) Were you able to pass right away? Why? Why not?

76. What else have you done?
    (a) Have you had a name change? Other documents?
    (b) Have you taken hormones? How much? How long? By prescription?
    (c) If yes, how have the hormones changed you?
    (d) Have you had any surgery? What? When?
    (e) What further steps do you intend to take?

77. What did you first learn about living as a man?
    (a) Describe the first time you were sure it really worked.
    (b) Describe the first time you used the men's washroom.
    (c) Describe the first time you flirted as a man.
    (d) Describe the first time you dated as a man.
    (e) Describe the first time you had sexual contact as a man.

78. How do you handle problem situations in public places?
    (a) What do you do when you meet people who knew you as a woman?
    (b) What do you do when people make pronoun mistakes?
    (c) What do you do when people read you as a female?
    (d) Are there places that you worry you won't "pass"? Why?
    (e) Are there things that you must never do? Name three. Why those?
    (f) Can you always tell how people read you? How do you know?

79. How have you improved on the way you live as a man?
    (a) Describe any things you used to do that you have stopped now.
    (b) Describe three things you've learned about being a man.

80. How have your relationships with women changed since your change?
    (a) Are there ways it's easier to be with women as a man? How?
    (b) Are there ways it's harder to be with women as a man? How?
    (c) Has your love life changed? Describe how.
    (d) Has your sex life changed? Describe how.
    (e) Were there any surprises in being a man among women? What?
    (f) Do you understand women better than other men? Why? How?

81. How have your relationships with men changed since your change?
    (a) Are there ways it's easier to be with men as a man? How?

    (b) Are there ways it's harder to be with men as a man? How?
    (c) Has your love life changed? Describe how.
    (d) Has your sex life changed? Describe how.
    (e) Were there any surprises in being a man among men? What?
    (f) Do you understand men better than other men? Why? How?

82. How have your relationships with family and friends changed?
    (a) Describe ways that it's easier for you as a man.
    (b) Describe ways that it's harder for you as a man.

83. Are there things you can't do since your change?
    (a) Describe three things that you'll miss. Why?
    (b) Describe three things that you'll never miss. Why?

84. Are there things that you do now that you couldn't do before?
    (a) Describe the three best things. Why do you like them?
    (b) Describe the three worst things. Why don't you like them?

85. Are there ways that your life has been unaffected by your change?
    (a) Describe three ways you are glad were not affected.
    (b) Describe three ways you wish had been more affected.

86. What kind of man are you?
    (a) Are you the man you always wanted to be? Why? Why not?
    (b) Do you have advantages over other men? What? Why?
    (c) Do other men have any advantages over you? What? Why?
    (d) Are you a feminist man? Are you sympathetic? Why? Why not?
    (e) Describe how masculine you are compared to other men.
    (f) If you could make yourself perfect, what would you change?

87. If you feel different since taking male hormones, describe how.

88. If you feel different since your surgery, describe how.

89. What advice do you have for others considering a change?

Philosophical Questions:

90. What makes a person a man?
    (a) What physical characteristics are absolutely necessary?
    (b) What mental characteristics are absolutely necessary?
    (c) What emotional characteristics are absolutely necessary?
    (d) What spiritual characteristics are absolutely necessary?
    (e) What other characteristics are important? Why?

91. What makes a person a woman?
    (a) What physical characteristics are absolutely necessary?
    (b) What mental characteristics are absolutely necessary?
    (c) What emotional characteristics are absolutely necessary?
    (d) What spiritual characteristics are absolutely necessary?
    (e) What other characteristics are important? Why?

92. What ways are women and men similar?
    (a) Describe the three most important ways.
    (b) Describe three ways that most people wouldn't think of.

93. What ways are women and men different?
    (a) Describe the three most important ways.
    (b) Describe three ways that most people wouldn't think of.

94. Can a person be both a man and a woman?
    (a) At the same time? If yes, how? If no, why not?
    (b) At different times in one lifetime? How? or Why not?
    (c) Have you been both a man and a woman? How? When?
    (d) At what point does a f-to-m transsexual stop being female?
    (e) At what point does a f-to-m transsexual become a male?

95. Who has it better in the world, women or men?
    (a) Describe the three best advantages women have over men.
    (b) Describe three worst ways that women have it worse than men.
    (c) Describe three worst ways that men have it worse than women.
    (d) Describe the three best advantages men have over women.

96. What's the difference between a lesbian and a f-to-m transsexual?
    (a) Are lesbians more socially acceptable than f-to-m TS's? Why?
    (b) Does God approve of transsexuals? How do you know?
    (c) Do lesbians have it easier than f-to-m TS's? How? Why?
    (d) Do f-to-m TS's sometimes think they are lesbians? Why?
    (e) Do lesbians sometimes think they are f-to-m TS's? Why?

97. Can a f-to-m transsexual be a gay man?
    (a) Are gay men more socially acceptable than f-to-m TS's?
    (b) Does God approve of gay men? How do you know?
    (c) Do gay men have it easier than f-to-m TS's? How? Why?

98. Do gender changers have advantages over other males and females?
    (a) Describe the three biggest advantages over other males.
    (b) Describe three worst disadvantages compared to other males.
    (c) Describe the three biggest advantages over other females.
    (d) Describe three worst disadvantages compared to other females.

99. What makes a person want to change gender?
    (a) Is it physical? How does that happen?
    (b) Is it because of family dynamics? How does that happen?
    (c) Is it because of some bad experiences? What kind?
    (d) Does homosexuality have anything to do with it? How?
    (e) Is it a mix of many reasons? Which ones?
    (f) What are the reasons in your case?
    (g) Are you proud of wanting to change genders? Ashamed? Why?

100. If there were more genders, what would you be?
    (a) Is being a man a perfect fit for you? How? How not?
    (b) Describe how you would be in a perfect world.

    (c) Are you doing your bit to change the world for the better?
    (d) What remains to be done?

101. Please take a few minutes to make comments about your experience with this research project.
    (a) What was most useful to you? Why?
    (b) What was least useful to you? Why?
    (c) How would you improve on this project?
    (d) What should future research concentrate on? Why?

102. Any additional comments? (Use the back for more space)

This ends part II.
Thank you again for your generous cooperation.

Notes

Introduction

1. Holly Devor, *Gender Blending: Confronting the Limits of Duality* (Bloomington: Indiana University, 1989).

2. One respondent, Fred, didn't say how he came to volunteer for this project; therefore these percentages are out of forty-four participants. Also, because some participants heard of this project from more than one source, the total exceeds 100 percent.

3. Simon, Rick, Ed, Peter, Aaron, Scott, Jack, Mel, Roger, Sam, Morgan, Eli, Darren, Walter, Bruce, Robin, Stan, Lee, Ron, Harry, Darcy, Dennis, Grant.

4. Keith, Ken, Bill, Jorge, Jordie, Terry, Tony, Howie, Brian, Fred, Bob, Alan, Colin, Gary, Nathan, Phil, Larry, Pat.

5. Luther, Dale, Steven, Hal.

6. International Foundation for Gender Education, P.O. Box 229, Waltham, MA 02254-0229; phone: (617) 899-2212; fax: (617) 899-5703; E-mail: IFGE@world.std.com; Web site: http://www.tiac.net/users/dba/ifge/ifge.htm.

7. California, Colorado, Guam, Hawaii, Indiana, Kansas, Michigan, Montana, North Carolina, New Jersey, Nevada, New York, Ohio, Oregon, Pennsylvania, Texas, Utah, Washington.

8. Alberta, British Columbia, Ontario, Quebec.

9. Median annual income for U.S. men in 1989 was $20,968. Median annual income for U.S. women in 1989 was $10,144. United States Bureau of the Census, *Statistical Abstract of the United States: 1992*, 112th ed. (Washington, D.C.: Government Printing Office, 1992), p. 453.

10. Simon, Rick, Morgan, Colin, Nathan, and Larry gave no information about their religious affiliations.

11. Roger, Darren, Keith, Ken, Luther, Terry, Tony, Phil, Dennis, Steven.

12. Ed, Peter, Aaron, Scott, Jack, Mel, Sam, Eli, Walter, Bruce, Robin, Stan, Bill, Lee, Ron, Brian, Fred, Bob, Harry, Darcy, Dale, Alan, Gary.

13. Howie, Grant, Pat.

14. Jorge, Jordie, Hal.

15. Among those who spoke of their religious upbringing, the following people said nothing about their adult religious leanings: Ed, Peter, Roger, Luther, Lee, Fred, Bob, Darcy.

16. Aaron, Scott, Jack, Sam, Eli, Walter, Bruce, Robin, Keith, Bill, Ron, Brian, Harry, Alan, Steven, Grant.

17. Aaron, Darren, Luther.

18. Mel, Ken, Stan, Jorge, Jordie, Terry, Dale, Gary, Phil, Dennis, Pat, Hal.

19. Morgan, Eli, Robin, Terry, Darcy, Alan, Pat.

20. Alan.

21. Simon, Rick, Ed, Peter, Aaron, Scott, Jack, Mel, Roger, Sam, Darren, Bruce,

Keith, Ken, Stan, Luther, Bill, Ron, Jordie, Tony, Howie, Brian, Bob, Dale, Alan, Colin, Gary, Nathan, Phil, Larry, Dennis, Steven, Grant, Hal.

22. Simon, Rick, Ed, Scott, Roger, Sam, Darren, Ken, Luther, Bill, Lee, Jordie, Tony, Howie, Brian, Bob, Dale, Nathan, Phil, Larry, Dennis, Steven, Hal.

23. Sam, Brian.

24. Howie, Hal.

25. Simon, Rick, Scott, Dale.

26. Simon, Darren, Walter, Bill, Dale, Hal.

27. I have developed these concepts in more detail in "Toward a Taxonomy of Gendered Sexuality," *Journal of Psychology and Human Sexuality* 6, no. 1 (1993), pp. 23–55, and in "Female Gender Dysphoria in Context: Social Problem or Personal Problem?" *Annual Review of Sex Research* 7 (1997), pp. 44–89.

28. Michael Shively and John De Cecco, "Components of Sexual Identity," *Journal of Homosexuality* 3 (1977), pp. 41–48.

29. I inquired as to the chromosomal status of participants but none of them had been tested. Therefore I remain ignorant of the actual genetic statuses of participants.

30. The word *dysphoria* comes from the Greek δυσφοροσ meaning "hard to bear," and is defined by the *Oxford English Dictionary* (2d ed.) as "a state or condition marked by feelings of unease or (mental) discomfort."

31. The term transgendered also has been used to mean persons who cross-live full time but who do not identify as transsexual and have no desire to substantially alter their genitalia.

1. Have Female-to-Male Transsexuals Always Existed?

1. Gerda Lerner, "Reconceptualizing Differences among Women," in *Feminist Frameworks: Alternative Theoretical Accounts of the Relations between Women and Men*, 3d ed., ed. Alison M. Jagger and Paula S. Rothenberg (New York: McGraw Hill, 1993), pp. 237–248.

2. Richard Hoffman, "Vices, Gods, and Virtues: Cosmology as a Mediating Factor in Attitudes toward Male Homosexuality," in *Origins of Sexuality and Homosexuality*, ed. John P. De Cecco and Michael Shively (New York: Harrington, 1985), pp. 27–44.

3. Thomas Laqueur, *Making Sex: Body and Gender from the Greeks to Freud* (Cambridge: Harvard University Press, 1990).

4. This provides an interesting perspective on the procedures commonly used today to transform women into men and men into women. Today, modern science tells us that all human life is essentially female and only becomes male upon the addition of masculinizing hormonal stimulation. Medicine turns females into males partially by the addition of hormonal "heat," whereas in male-to-female sex reassignment surgery, the testicles are removed and the skin of the penis is inverted to form the lining of the neovagina. Thus the modern conception retains a mirror image of the original premise in that we now think of all humans as variations on the one sex, female. Females can still become males by the addition of "heat" (hormones) and males can become females by the removal of their source of "heat" (testicles) and the inversion of their sex organs to make them into a good semblance of their original female form.

5. Vern L. Bullough and Bonnie Bullough, *Cross Dressing, Sex, and Gender* (Philadelphia: University of Pennsylvania Press, 1993); Laqueur.

6. Bonnie S. Anderson and Judith P. Zinsser, *A History of Their Own: Women in Europe from Prehistory to the Present* (New York: Harper & Row, 1988), vol. 1, p. 27.

7. Sarah B. Pomeroy, *Goddesses, Whores, Wives, and Slaves* (New York: Shocken, 1975).

8. Anderson and Zinsser, vol 1; Pomeroy.

9. Vern L. Bullough, *Sexual Variance in Society and History* (New York: John Wiley & Sons, 1976).

10. John Boswell, *Christianity, Social Tolerance, and Homosexuality: Gay People in Western Europe from the Beginning of the Christian Era to the Fourteenth Century* (Chicago: University of Chicago Press, 1980), p. 77.

11. Bullough, *Sexual Variance*, p. 147.

12. Hoffman.

13. Elizabeth Castelli, " 'I Will Make Mary Male': Pieties of the Body and Gender Transformation of Christian Women in Late Antiquity," in *Body Guards: The Cultural Politics of Gender Ambiguity*, ed. Julia Epstein and Kristina Straub (New York: Routledge, 1991), pp. 29–49.

14. Bullough and Bullough, p. 50.

15. Bullough and Bullough; Castelli.

16. Bullough and Bullough.

17. I have chosen to respect the gender choices of individuals wherever possible. Hence I use masculine pronouns and names to indicate individuals who are living as men and feminine pronouns when referring to persons' unaltered female bodies and to persons who are living as women. See the introduction for further discussion of pronoun usage.

18. The term *marriage resister* was used by Sankar to describe an organized movement of Chinese women who refused to marry in the Pearl River delta approximately between 1865 and 1935. See Andrea Sankar, "Sister and Brothers, Lovers and Enemies: Marriage Resistance in Southern Kwangtung," in *The Many Faces of Homosexuality: Anthropological Approaches to Homosexual Behavior*, ed. Evelyn Blackwood (New York: Harrington Park, 1986), pp. 69–81.

19. Bullough and Bullough.

20. Anderson and Zinsser, vol 1.

21. Bullough and Bullough.

22. Bullough and Bullough.

23. Bullough and Bullough.

24. Martha Vicinus, " 'They Wonder to Which Sex I Belong': The Historical Roots of the Modern Lesbian Identity," in *Homosexuality, Which Homosexuality? International Conference on Gay and Lesbian Studies*, ed. Dennis Altman et al. (London: GMP, 1987), pp. 171–198.

25. Julia Epstein, "Either/Or—Neither/Both: Sexual Ambiguity and the Ideology of Gender," *Genders* 7 (1990), pp. 99–142; Randolph Trumbach, "London's Sapphists: From Three Sexes to Four Genders in the Making of Modern Culture," in *Body Guards: The Cultural Politics of Gender Ambiguity*, ed. Julia Epstein and Kristina Straub (New York: Routledge, 1991), pp. 112–141.

26. Lillian Faderman, *Surpassing the Love of Men: Romantic Friendship and Love between Women from the Renaissance to the Present* (New York: William Morrow, 1981).

27. Judith Brown, "Lesbian Sexuality in Medieval and Early Modern Europe," in *Hidden from History: Reclaiming Gay and Lesbian Past*, ed. Martin Bauml Duberman, Martha Vicinus, and George Chauncey, Jr. (New York: Penguin, 1989), pp. 67–75; Havelock Ellis, *Studies in the Psychology of Sex*, vol. 2: *Sexual Inversion* (Philadelphia: F. A. Davis, 1918); Faderman, *Surpassing the Love.*

28. Rudolf M. Dekker and Lotte van de Pol, *The Tradition of Female Transvestism in Early Modern Europe* (London: Macmillan, 1989).

29. Ann Rosalind Jones and Peter Stallybrass, "Fetishizing Gender: Constructing the Hermaphrodite in Renaissance Europe," in *Body Guards: The Cultural Politics of Gender Ambiguity*, ed. Julia Epstein and Kristina Straub (New York: Routledge, 1991), pp. 80-111.

30. Peter Ackroyd, *Dressing Up: Transvestism and Drag: The History of an Obsession* (London: Thames & Hudson, 1979); Bullough and Bullough; Ellis.

31. Gene Damon and Lee Stuart, "The Tragedy: Queen Christine of Sweden and Ebba Sparre," in *Lesbian Lives: Biographies of Women from The Ladder*, ed. Barbara Grier and Coletta Reid (Baltimore: Diana, 1976), pp. 217-222.

32. Oscar Paul Gilbert, *Women in Men's Guise*, trans. J. Lewis (London: John Lane the Bodley Head, 1932).

33. Bullough and Bullough.

34. Bullough and Bullough; Gilbert.

35. Dekker and van de Pol.

36. Dekker and van de Pol.

37. Lynne Friedli, " 'Passing Women' — A Study of Gender Boundaries in the Eighteenth Century," in *Sexual Underworlds of the Enlightenment*, ed. G. S Rousseau and Roy Porter (Manchester: Manchester University Press, 1987), pp. 234-260; Carole Shamas, "A New Definition of Home Sweet Home," in *The Other Side of Western Civilization: Readings in Everyday Life*, vol. 2: *The Sixteenth Century to the Present*, 3d ed., ed. Peter N. Stearns (San Diego: Harcourt Brace Jovanovich, 1984), pp. 102-109; Edward Shorter, *The Making of the Modern Family* (New York: Basic Books, 1975); Lawrence Stone, *The Family, Sex and Marriage in England 1500-1800* (London: Weidenfeld & Nicolson, 1978); Randolph Trumbach, *The Rise of the Egalitarian Family: Aristocratic Kinship and Domestic Relations in Eighteenth Century England* (New York: Academic, 1978).

38. Laqueur.

39. Bonnie S. Anderson and Judith P. Zinsser, *A History of Their Own: Women in Europe from Prehistory to the Present*, vol. 2 (New York: Harper and Row, 1988).

40. Trumbach, "London's Sapphists."

41. Dekker and van de Pol.

42. Dekker and van de Pol.

43. Trumbach, "London's Sapphists."

44. Epstein; Gilbert.

45. Brigitte Eriksson, "A Lesbian Execution in Germany, 1721: The Trial Records," *Journal of Homosexuality* 6, no. 1/2 (1981), pp. 27-40.

46. Julie Wheelwright, *Amazons and Military Maids: Women Who Dressed as Men in the Pursuit of Life, Liberty and Happiness* (London: Pandora, 1989).

47. Trumbach, "London's Sapphists."

48. Breeches roles were theatre roles in which actresses performed men's roles while known by audiences to be women. They were especially popular in eighteenth-century England. See Kristina Straub, "The Guilty Pleasures of Female Theatrical Cross-Dressing and the Autobiography of Charlotte Charke," in *Body Guards: The Cultural Politics of Gender Ambiguity*, ed. Julia Epstein and Kristina Straub (New York: Routledge, 1991), pp. 142-166.

49. Bram Stoker, *Famous Imposters* (New York: Sturgis and Walton, 1910).

50. Faderman; Straub; Trumbach, "London's Sapphists."

51. Eriksson.

52. Terry Castle, "The Culture of Travesty: Sexuality and Masquerade in Eigh-

teenth Century England," in *Sexual Underworlds of the Enlightenment*, ed. G. S. Rousseau and Roy Porter (Manchester: Manchester University Press, 1987), pp. 156–180.

53. George Chauncey, Jr., "From Sexual Inversion to Homosexuality: The Changing Medical Conceptualization of Female 'Deviance'," in *Passion and Power: Sexuality in History*, ed. Kathy Preiss and Christina Simmons (Philadelphia: Temple University Press, 1989), pp. 87–117; Carroll Smith-Rosenberg, "Discourses of Sexuality and Subjectivity: The New Woman, 1870–1936," in *Hidden From History: Reclaiming Gay and Lesbian Past*, ed. Martin Bauml Duberman et al. (New York: Penguin, 1989), pp. 264–280; Bullough and Bullough.

54. Jeffrey Weeks, *Sex, Politics and Society: The Regulation of Sexuality since 1800*, 2d ed. (London: Longman, 1989).

55. Laqueur.

56. Bullough and Bullough; Weeks.

57. MaryLynn McDougall, "Working-Class Women during the Industrial Revolution, 1780–1914," in *Becoming Visible: Women in European History*, ed. Renate Bridenthal and Claudia Koonz (Boston: Houghton Mifflin, 1977), pp. 255–279; Weeks.

58. Kathy Preiss, " 'Charity Girls' and City Pleasures: Historical Notes on Working-Class Sexuality, 1880–1920," in *Passion and Power: Sexuality in History*, ed. Kathy Preiss and Christina Simmons (Philadelphia: Temple University Press, 1989), pp. 57–69.

59. Richard von Krafft-Ebing, *Psychopathia Sexualis with Especial Reference to the Antipathic Sexual Instinct: A Medico-Forensic Study*, trans. F. J. Rebman (Brooklyn: Physicians and Surgeons Book Company, 1906; reprint ed., 1931).

60. Krafft-Ebing, p. 430.

61. Krafft-Ebing, p. 438.

62. Percival R. Kirby, "Dr. James Barry, Controversial South African Medical Figure: A Recent Evaluation of His Life and Sex," *South African Medical Journal*, April 25 1970, pp. 506–516.

63. Vern Niven, "First British Woman Doctor: James Barry," in *Lesbian Lives: Biographies of Women from The Ladder*, ed. Barbara Grier and Coletta Reid (Baltimore: Diana, 1976), pp. 107–113; Ackroyd; Bullough & Bullough; Kirby.

64. Bullough and Bullough.

65. Lennox Strang, "To Be a Man . . . The Story of 'Franklin Thompson,' " *The Ladder*, 8, no. 1 (1963), pp. 7–9.

66. Bullough and Bullough.

67. "He Was a Woman," *Milwaukee Daily News*, July 13, 1894, p. 1.

68. Jonathan Katz, *Gay American History: Lesbians and Gay Men in the USA: A Documentary* (New York: Thomas Y. Crowell, 1976).

69. "Has No Love for Petticoats," *San Francisco Examiner*, Feb. 7, 1895, p. 16; "Miss Wilson Talks," *San Francisco Chronicle*, Jan. 28, 1895, p. 3; "She Has Been a Man of the World for over Twenty-Six Years," *San Francisco Examiner*, Feb. 10, 1895, p. 26.

70. Katz, *Gay American History*.

71. Katz, *Gay American History*.

72. Jonathan Katz, *Gay/Lesbian Almanac* (New York: Harper and Row, 1983).

73. Lou Sullivan, *From Female to Male: The Life of Jack Bee Garland* (Boston: Alyson, 1990).

74. Sullivan.

75. "Charlie Parkhurst: The Stagecoach Driver with a Secret," *PG&E Progress*, December 1979, p. 8.

76. Ellis; Katz, *Gay American History*.

77. Katz, *Gay American History*.
78. Walter Williams, *The Spirit and the Flesh: Sexual Diversity in American Indian Culture* (Boston: Beacon, 1986).
79. Each Native society has had its own name for the persons who filled cross-gender roles, and each society has its own particular version of these roles. The term *berdache*, widely used by non-Native people to describe these roles, comes from the Arabic term *bardaj* referring to a young anal receptive male homosexual. Clearly this term leaves a great deal to be desired under any circumstances, especially when discussing female-to-male persons. See Evelyn Blackwood, "Sexuality and Gender in Certain Native American Tribes: The Case of Cross-Gender Females," *Signs: Journal of Women in Culture and Society* 10 (1984), pp. 27–42; Charles Callender and Lee M. Kochems, "The North American Berdache," in *Culture and Human Sexuality: A Reader*, ed. David N. Suggs and Andrew W. Miracle (Pacific Grove: Brooks/Cole, 1993), pp. 367–397.
80. Ellis; Williams.
81. Callender and Kochems.
82. Reports of cross-gendered females exist for the following North American tribes: Achumawi, Atsugewi, Bella Coola, Blackfoot, Carrier, Cocopa, Crow, Haisla, Ingalik, Kaska, Klamath, Kutenai, Lillooet, Maricopa, Mohave, Navaho, Northern Paiute, Nootka, Okanagan, Papago, Pima, Queets, Quinault, Shasta, Shoshoni, Southern Paiute, Southern Ute, Tipai, Ute, Washo, Wintu, Western Apache, Wiyot, Yukuts, Yuki, Yuma.
83. Katz, *Gay American History*.
84. Ellis.
85. Judith Shapiro, "Transsexualism: Reflections on the Persistence of Gender and the Mutability of Sex," in *Body Guards: The Cultural Politics of Gender Ambiguity*, ed. Julia Epstein and Kristina Straub (New York: Routledge, 1991), pp. 248–279.
86. Dekker and van de Pol.
87. Ifi Amadiume, *Male Daughters, Female Husbands: Gender and Sex in an African Society* (London: Zed, 1987).
88. Amadiume.
89. Graham Lowe, "Women, Work and the Office: The Feminization of Clerical Occupations in Canada, 1901–1931," *Canadian Journal of Sociology* 5 (1980), pp. 361–381.
90. Anderson and Zinsser, vol 2.
91. Chauncey.
92. Radclyffe Hall, *The Well of Loneliness* (London: Hutchinson, 1928, reprint, 1986).
93. Esther Newton, "The Mythic Mannish Lesbian: Radclyffe Hall and the New Woman," in *Hidden from History: Reclaiming Gay and Lesbian Past*, ed. Martin Bauml Duberman et al. (New York: New American Library, 1989).
94. Radclyffe Hall, p. 204.
95. Edward Carpenter, *The Intermediate Sex: A Study of Some Transitional Types of Men and Women* (London: George Allen & Unwin, 1908).
96. Ellis.
97. Magnus Hirschfeld, *Transvestites: The Erotic Urge to Cross Dress*, trans. Michael A. Lombardi-Nash (New York: Prometheus, 1910; reprint, 1991).
98. The *Oxford English Dictionary* dates the verb *to transvest* to 1652.
99. Hirschfeld, p. 154.
100. Harry Benjamin, *The Transsexual Phenomenon* (New York: Julian Press, 1966).

101. Katz, *Gay American History*, p. 256.

102. Katz, *Gay American History*, p. 257.

103. Sullivan.

104. Katz, *Gay/Lesbian Almanac*, p. 516.

105. Bullough and Bullough; Wheelwright.

106. Diana Souhami, *Gluck, 1895–1978: Her Biography* (London: Pandora, 1988), p. 9.

107. Souhami, pp. 126, 128.

108. Liz Hodgekinson, *Michael, née Laura* (London: Columbus, 1989).

109. Leslie Martin Lothstein, *Female-to-Male Transsexualism: Historical, Clinical and Theoretical Issues* (Boston: Routledge & Kegan Paul, 1983).

110. "She Was Fooled for 8 Years, Then . . . Wife Discovers Hubby Is a Woman," *Sun*, Oct. 23, 1990, p. 27; Andrew Benson, "Woman Clings to Second Self: 'I am who I am. I am Matt,' " *Cleveland Plain Dealer*, Aug. 24, 1992, pp. 1-A, 6-A; Donna Minkowitz, "Love Hurts," *Village Voice*, April 19, 1994, pp. 24–30.

111. Epstein.

2. Theories about Transsexualism

1. See chap. 1 for a more detailed account of Laqueur's theories.

2. Amaduime; Callender and Kochems; Serena Nanda, *Neither Man nor Woman: The Hijras of India* (Belmont: Wadsworth, 1990); Williams.

3. Bernice L. Hausman, *Changing Sex: Transsexualism, Technology, and the Idea of Gender* (Durham: Duke University Press, 1995).

4. Bernice L. Hausman, "Demanding Subjectivity: Transsexualism, Medicine, and the Technologies of Gender," *Journal of the History of Sexuality* 3 (1992), p. 284.

5. Hausman, "Demanding Subjectivity."

6. Virginia Prince, *Understanding Cross Dressing* (Los Angeles: Chevelier, 1976).

7. Janice Raymond, *The Transsexual Empire: The Making of the She-Male* (Boston: Beacon, 1979).

8. Raymond, 1979, p. xviii.

9. Raymond, 1979, p. 178.

10. Raymond, 1979, p. 129.

11. Raymond, 1979, p. 5.

12. Janice Raymond, *The Transsexual Empire: The Making of the She-Male*, 2d ed. (New York: Teachers College Press, 1994), p. xxiii.

13. Raymond, 1979, p. xxiii.

14. Olivia Records, 4400 Market St., Oakland, CA 94608, USA.

15. Davina Anne Gabriel, "Interview with the Transsexual Vampire: Sandy Stone's Dark Gift," *TransSisters: The Journal of Transsexual Feminism*, Spring 1995, pp. 15–27; Sandy Stone, "A Posttranssexual Manifesto," in *Body Guards: The Cultural Politics of Ambiguity*, ed. Judith Epstein and Kristina Straub (New York: Routledge, 1991), pp. 280–304.

16. This trend is implicitly demonstrated in the spate of guest lectures given in university and college classrooms by transsexuals and in the frequent appearances on television talk shows by people agitating for increased acceptance of known transsexual persons. It is explicity demonstrated in the work of organizations such as the following: *American Educational Gender Information Service (AEGIS)*. Postal address: P.O. Box 33724, Decatur, GA 30033, USA. E-mail address: aegis@mindspring.com. Phone: (404) 939-0244. Fax: (404) 939-1770. *The Transsexual Menace*. Internet site:

http://www.echonyc.com/~degrey/TSMenace/who.html. *FTM International.* Postal address: 5337 College Ave., #142, Oakland, CA 94618, USA. E-mail address: FTMNews@aol.com. Internet site: http://www.ftm_intl.org. *International Conference on Transgender Law and Employment Policy (ICTLEP).* Postal address: P.O. Drawer 35477, Houston, TX 77235-5477, USA. E-mail address: ICTLEP@aol.com. Phone: (713) 777-8452. Fax: (713) 777-0909. *International Foundation for Gender Education (IFGE).* Postal address: P.O. Box 229, Waltham, MA 02154-0229, USA. E-mail address: IFGE@world.std.com. Phone: (617) 899-2212. Fax: (617) 899-5703.

17. Sherry B. Ortner, "Is Female to Male as Nature Is to Culture?" in *Women and Values: Readings in Recent Feminist Philosophy*, ed. Marilyn Pearsall (Belmont: Wadsworth, 1986), pp. 62–75.

18. Vivienne Cass, "Homosexual Identity Development: A Theoretical Model," *Journal of Homosexuality* 4, no. 3 (1979), pp. 219–235.

19. Frank Lewins, *Transsexualism in Society: A Sociology of Male-to-Female Transsexuals* (Melbourne: Macmillan, 1995).

20. Brian Tully, *Accounting for Transsexualism and Transhomosexuality* (London: Whiting & Birch, 1992).

21. Jeremy Baumbach and Louisa A. Turner, "Female Gender Disorder: A New Model and Clinical Applications," *Journal of Psychology and Human Sexuality* 5, no. 4 (1992), pp. 107–129.

22. Helen Rose Fuchs Ebaugh, *Becoming an Ex: The Process of Role Exit* (Chicago: University of Chicago Press, 1988).

23. Anne Bolin, *In Search of Eve: Transsexual Rites of Passage* (South Hadley: Bergin and Harvey, 1988).

24. Erving Goffman, *Stigma: Notes on Management of a Spoiled Identity* (Englewood Cliffs: Prentice Hall, 1963).

25. Lewins, p. 71.

26. Tully, p. 256.

27. A master status is one "which tends to overpower, in most crucial situations, any other characteristics." See Everett Hughes, "Dilemmas and Contradictions of Status," *American Journal of Sociology* 50 (1945), p. 357.

28. Ebaugh, p. 1.

29. Ebaugh, p. 4.

30. I have found a change of citizenship analogy useful in this regard; one can cease to be a citizen of one's prior country and become a citizen of a new country. In between, new arrivals are required to live in their new country as more than visitors but not yet as citizens. Immediately, with new citizenship, come full rights and obligations but perhaps not full acceptance by those who were born to their citizenship in the new country. When one is still a recently naturalized citizen, it is often obvious to others because there are many nuances of local language and custom which have not yet become fully assimilated. With time, most naturalized citizens come to be able to pass undetected among other citizens, but they will always be naturalized citizens; they will never become citizens by birth. In a similar way, after a "real-life test" residency requirement, transsexual people can change their gender and sex statuses, but they will always remain persons who were not born to their second gender and sex status. With time, their origins will become less obvious; but, although they may become fully members of their new genders and sexes, they will never cease to be transsexual. Some people may be able to conceal this fact, but when they do so, what they are doing is managing potentially discrediting information, i.e., engaging in stigma management, not ceasing to be transsexual.

31. Ebaugh, p. 143.

32. Ronald E. Hellman et al., "Childhood Sexual Identity, Childhood Religiosity, and 'Homophobia' as Influences in the Development of Transsexualism, Homosexuality, and Heterosexuality," *Archives of General Psychiatry* 38 (1981), pp. 910–915.

33. Michael Ross, "Gender Identity Male, Female or a Third Gender?" in *Transsexualism and Sex Reassignment*, ed. W. A. W. Walters and M. W. Ross (Oxford: Oxford University Press, 1986), pp. 1–8, and "Causes of Gender Dysphoria: How Does Transsexualism Develop and Why?" in *Transsexualism and Sex Reassignment*, pp. 16–25.

34. There is an odd tension to be seen in these theories. Harry Benjamin, in the first major work published on the subject of transsexualism, *The Transsexual Phenomenon* (1966), concluded that psychotherapy was ineffective in deterring transsexuals from their desire for gender and sex reassignment. Ever since that time, this attitude has prevailed, with accepted definitions of transsexualism resting on that premise. When persons present themselves to gender clinics requesting gender and sex reassignment, they are psychologically scrutinized. If it seems possible to use psychotherapy to dissuade them from their desire for gender and sex reassignment, then they are deemed to be suffering from some problem other than transsexualism. This logical tautology leaves psychologically oriented theorists in a bit of a conundrum. If they were to be sufficiently clever to uncover the psychological bases for transsexualism, this would imply that transsexualism might be responsive to psychotherapy. If the phenomenon is responsive to psychotherapy, then it may not truly be transsexualism!

35. Robert Stoller, *Presentations of Gender*; *Sex and Gender*, vol. 2: *The Transsexual Experiment* (New York: Jason Aronson, 1975); *Sex and Gender: The Development of Masculinity and Femininity* (New York: Jason Aronson, 1968); "Etiological Factors in Female Transsexualism: A First Approximation," *Archives of Sexual Behavior* 2 (1972), pp. 47–63.

36. Stoller, *Sex and Gender*, vol. 2.

37. Richard Green, *The Sissy Boy Syndrome and the Development of Homosexuality* (New Haven: Yale University Press, 1987).

38. Richard Green, *Sexual Identity Conflict* (New York: Basic Books, 1974), p. 296.

39. Lothstein, p. xiii.

40. Lothstein, p. 264.

41. Lothstein, p. 9.

42. Lothstein, p. 86.

43. Lothstein, p. 94.

44. Lothstein, p. 143.

45. Lothstein, p. 238.

46. Lothstein, p. 198.

47. Lothstein, p. 246.

48. Susan J. Bradley, "Gender Disorders in Childhood: A Formulation," in *Gender Dysphoria: Development, Research, Management*, ed. Betty Steiner (New York: Plenum, 1985), p. 178.

49. Bradley, "Gender Disorders"; Susan J. Bradley, "Female Transsexualism: A Child and Adolescent Perspective," *Child Psychiatry and Human Development* 11 (1980), pp. 12–18; Kenneth J. Zucker and Susan J. Bradley, *Gender Identity Development and Psychosexual Problems in Children and Adolescents* (New York: Guilford, 1995).

50. Alan Beitel, "The Spectrum of Gender Identity Disturbance: An Intrapsychic

Model," in *Gender Dysphoria: Development, Research, Management*, ed. Betty Steiner (New York: Plenum, 1985), pp. 189–206; Vamik D. Volkan and As'Ad Masri, "The Development of Female Transsexualism," *American Journal of Psychotherapy* 93 (1989), pp. 92–107.

51. John Money, *Lovemaps: Clinical Concepts of Sexual and Erotic Health and Pathology, Paraphilia and Gender Transposition in Childhood, Adolescence and Maturity* (New York: Irvington, 1986).

52. John Money, *Gay Straight and In-Between: The Sexology of Erotic Orientation* (New York: Oxford University Press, 1988).

53. John Hoenig, "Etiology of Transsexualism," in *Gender Dysphoria: Development, Research, Management*, ed. Betty Steiner (New York: Plenum, 1985) pp. 33–73; Peter R. Joyce and Les Ding, "Transsexual Sisters," *Australian and New Zealand Journal of Psychiatry* 19 (1985), pp. 188–189; Robert F. Sabalis et al., "The Three Sisters: Transsexual Male Siblings," *American Journal of Psychiatry* 131 (1974), pp. 907–909.

54. Dean Hamer et al., "A Linkage between DNA Markers and the X Chromosome and Male Sexual Orientation," *Science* 261 (July 16, 1993), pp. 321–327; Stella Hu et al., "Linkage between Sexual Orientation and Chromosome Xq28 in Males but Not in Females," *Nature Genetics* 2 (Nov. 1, 1995), pp. 248–256; Angela Pattatucci and Dean Hamer, "Development and Familiality of Sexual Orientation in Females," *Behavior Genetics*, 25 (1995), pp. 407–420.

55. J. Michael Bailey, Richard C. Pillard, Michael C. Neale, and Yvonne Agyei, "Heritable Factors Influence Sexual Orientation in Women," *Archives of Sexual Behavior* 50 (1993), pp. 217–223.

56. Hamer et al. cite 2 percent of the population at large as being homosexual. They acknowledge that this statistic is lower than the more usual 4–10 percent but suggest that it is due to their more stringent definition of homosexual orientation. Robert E. Fay et al., "Prevalence and Patterns of Same-Gender Sexual Contact among Men," *Science* 243 (1989), pp. 338–348, also cite low figures for homosexuality in the male population. They report that 1.4 percent of men had adult homosexual contacts whose frequency was characterized as being "fairly often" and an additional 1.9 percent whose frequency was characterized as "occasionally." They total these numbers to arrive at 3.3 percent of the adult male population as being homosexual, but they caution that most men in their 3.3 percent could not be classified as "exclusively homosexual" throughout their lives.

57. Heino Meyer-Bahlberg, "Hormones and Psychosexual Differentiation: Implications for the Management of Intersexuality, Homosexuality and Transsexuality," *Clinics in Endocrinology and Metabolism* 11 (1982), pp. 681–701; John Hoenig, "Etiological Research in Transsexualism," *Psychiatric Journal of the University of Ottawa* 6 (1981), pp. 184–189; Hoenig, "Etiology of Transsexualism."

58. Arthur Arnold & Marc Breedlove, "Organizational and Activational Effects of Sex Steroids on Brain and Behaviour: A Reanalysis," *Hormones and Behaviour*, 19 (1985) pp. 469–498.

59. The hypothalamus is thought to control moods, emotions, and complex behavioural patterns. It contains centres concerned with the regulation of appetite, sexual drive, sleep, and pleasure. It is a collection of several related groups of neurons lying just below the thalamus. It connects with the pituitary, certain regions of the brain stem, and with the lymbic system. The pituitary regulates the production of many key hormones and forms the link between nervous and hormonal systems.

60. Hoenig, "Etiology of Transsexualism."

61. Simon LeVay, "A Difference in Hypothalamic Structure between Heterosexual and Homosexual Men," *Science* 235 (Aug. 30, 1991), pp. 1034–1037.

62. Jiang-Ning Zhou, Michael Hoffman, Louis Gooren, and Dick Swaab, "A Sex Difference in the Human Brain and Its Relation to Transsexuality," *Nature* 378 (Nov. 2, 1995), pp. 68–70.

63. Laura S. Allen & Roger A. Gorski, "Sexual Orientation and the Size of the Anterior Commissure in the Human Brain," *Proceedings: National Academy of Sciences* 89 (1992), pp. 7199–7202.

64. Lee Emory et al., "Anatomic Variation of the Corpus Callosum in Persons with Gender Dysphoria," *Archives of Sexual Behavior* 20 (1991), pp. 409–417.

65. Walter Futterweit et al., "Endocrine Evaluation of Forty Female-to-Male Transsexuals: Increased Frequency of Polycystic Ovarian Disease in Female Transsexualism," *Archives of Sexual Behavior* 15 (1985), pp. 69–78.

66. Gunter Dörner, "Neuroendocrine Response to Estrogen and Brain Differentiation in Heterosexuals, Homosexuals, and Transsexuals," *Archives of Sexual Behavior* 17 (1988), pp. 57–75.

67. Lloyd E. Seyler, Jr., et al., "Abnormal Gonadotropin Secretory Response to LRH in Transsexual Women after Diethylstilbestrol Priming," *Journal of Clinical Endocrinology and Metabolism* 47 (1978), pp. 176–183.

68. Dörner.

69. Volkmar Sigusch et al., "Official Statement by German Society for Sex Research on the Research of Professor Gunter Dörner on the Subject of Homosexuality," *Archives of Sexual Behavior* 11 (1982), pp. 445–449.

70. Meyer-Bahlburg.

71. Eli Coleman et al., "Theories of Gender Transposition: A Critique and Suggestions for Further Research," *Journal of Sex Research* 26 (1990), pp. 525–538.

72. Richard C. Pillard and James D. Weinrich, "Periodic Table Model of Gender Transpositions: Part I. A Theory Based on Masculinzation and Defeminization of the Brain," *Journal of Sex Research* 23 (1987), pp. 425–454.

73. Pillard and Weinrich were presented with the 1987 Hugo Beigel award by the Society for the Scientific Study of Sex for the most important contribution to sex research published in the *Journal of Sex Research* in 1987.

74. Coleman et al.

75. Pillard and Weinrich, p. 441.

76. Pillard and Weinrich, p. 447.

77. Adrienne Rich, "Compulsory Heterosexuality and Lesbian Existence," in *Feminist Frontiers II: Rethinking Sex, Gender and Society*, ed. L. Richardson and V. Taylor (New York: McGraw Hill, 1989), pp. 120–141.

78. Research has shown that biological structures can "learn" to function in new or different ways as a result of the impingement of continual experiences in a particular direction. See Arnold and Breedlove.

3. Finding Out about Gender: Theories of Childhood Gender Acquisition

1. My formulation of the ideology of the dominant gender schema further develops the work of Harold Garfinkle, *Studies in Ethnomethodology* (Englewood Cliffs: Prentice-Hall, 1967); Sandra L. Bem, "Gender Schema Theory: A Cognitive Account

of Sex Typing," *Psychological Review* 88 (1981), pp. 155–62; Sandra L. Bem, "Gender Schematic Theory and Its Implications for Child Development: Raising Gender-Aschematic Children in a Gender-Schematic Society," *Signs: Journal of Women in Culture and Society* 8 (1983), pp. 598–616; and Suzanne Kessler and Wendy McKenna, *Gender: An Ethnomethodological Approach* (New York: John Wiley & Sons, 1978).

    2. William Shakespeare, *As You Like It*, ed. Horace H. Furness (New York: American Scholar, 1965), p. 121.

    3. Erving Goffman, *The Presentation of Self in Everyday Life* (New York: Doubleday, 1959).

    4. Nancy Chodorow, *The Reproduction of Mothering: Psychoanalysis and the Sociology of Gender* (Berkeley: University of California Press, 1978).

    5. Arthur Brittan, *Masculinity and Power* (Oxford: Basil Blackwell, 1989).

    6. For a discussion along similar lines, see Carol Gilligan, *In a Different Voice: Psychological Theory and Women's Development* (Cambridge: Harvard University Press, 1982).

    7. Erving Goffman, *Gender Advertisements* (London: Macmillan, 1978); Judith A. Hall, *Non-Verbal Sex Differences: Communication Accuracy and Expressive Style* (Baltimore: Johns Hopkins University Press, 1984); Nancy M. Henley, *Body Politics: Power, Sex and Non-Verbal Communication* (Englewood Cliffs: Prentice-Hall, 1979); Marianne Wex, *'Let's Take Back Our Space': "Female" and "Male" Body Language as a Result of Patriarchal Structures* (Berlin: Frauenliteraturverlag Hermine Fees, 1979).

    8. Karen L. Adams, "Sexism and the English Language: The Linguistic Implications of Being a Woman," in *Women: A Feminist Perspective*, ed. Jo Freeman, 3d ed. (Palo Alto: Mayfield, 1984), pp. 478–491; Peter Kollock et al., "Sex and Power in Interaction: Conversational Privileges and Duties," *American Sociological Review* 50 (1985), pp. 34–46; Judith Hall.

    9. Susan Brownmiller, *Femininity* (New York: Linden Press, 1984).

    10. Joseph Pleck, *The Myth of Masculinity* (Cambridge: MIT Press, 1981).

    11. Goffman, *Gender Advertisements*; Judith Hall; Henley; Wex.

    12. Adams; Judith Hall.

    13. Judith Hall; Mark L. Knapp, *Essentials of Nonverbal Communication* (New York: Holt, Rinehart, & Winston, 1980).

    14. Judith Howard et al., "Sex, Power, and Influence Tactics in Intimate Relationships," *Journal of Personality and Social Psychology* 51 (1986), pp. 102–109; Kollock et al.

    15. Donald H. Baucom and Bahr Weiss, "Peers' Granting of Control to Women with Different Sex-Role Identities," *Journal of Personality and Social Psychology* 51 (1986), pp. 1075–1080; Jacob L. Orlofsky and Connie A. O'Heron, "Stereotypic and Nonstereotypic Sex Role Trait and Behavior Orientations: Implications for Personal Adjustment," *Journal of Personality and Social Psychology* 52 (1987), pp. 1034–1042; Warren Jones et al., "The Enigma of Androgyny: Differential Implications for Males and Females?" *Journal of Consulting and Clinical Psychology* 46 (1978), pp. 298–313; Janet Spence et al., "Ratings of Peers on Sex-Role Attributes and Their Relation to Self-Esteem and Conceptions of Masculinity and Femininity," *Journal of Personality and Social Psychology* 32 (1975), pp. 29–39.

    16. The theories of Stoller as outlined in chap. 2 provide an example of this approach.

    17. Chodorow, p. 59.

    18. Margaret Mead, "On Freud's View of Female Psychology," in *Women and*

Analysis: Dialogues on Psychoanalytic Views of Femininity, ed. Jean Strouse (New York: Grossman, 1974), pp. 95–106.

19. Albert Bandura, *Social Learning Theory* (Englewood Cliffs: Prentice-Hall, 1977).

20. Gilligan; Lawrence Kolberg, *Essays on Moral Development* (San Francisco: Harper & Row, 1981).

21. Bem, "Gender Schema Theory: A Cognitive Account"; Bem, "Gender Schematic Theory and Its Implications"; Robin A. Fleischer & Jerome Chertkoff, "Effects of Dominance and Sex on Leader Selection in Dyadic Work Groups," *Journal of Personality and Social Psychology* 50 (1986), pp. 94–99; Deborrah Frable, "Sex-Typed Execution and Perception of Expressive Movement," *Journal of Personality and Social Psychology* 54 (1987), pp. 391–396; Linda Nyquist and Janet Spence, "Effects of Dispositional Dominance and Sex Role Expectation on Leadership and Behavior," *Journal of Personality and Social Psychology* 50 (1986), pp. 87–93.

22. Money, *Lovemaps*; Money, *Gay, Straight and In-Between*.

23. Human brains continue to grow and develop well into life. Growth is 90 percent complete by the age of six years, with 60 percent of growth being completed by age two years. See Steven Rose, *The Conscious Brain* (New York: Vintage Books, 1978); J. M. Tanner, *Foetus into Man: Physical Growth from Conception to Maturity* (Cambridge: Harvard University Press, 1978); Donald G. Stein and Ronald G. Dawson, "The Dynamics and Growth, Organization and Adaptability of the Central Nervous System," in *Constancy and Change in Human Development*, ed. O. G. Brim, Jr., and J. Kagan (Cambridge: Harvard University Press, 1980), pp. 174–177.

24. Dennis M. Parker, "Determinate and Plastic Principles in Neuropsychological Development" in *Brain and Behavioral Development: Interdisciplinary Perspectives on Structure and Function*, ed. John W. T. Dickerson and Harry McGurk (London: Surrey University Press, 1982), pp. 203–232.

25. Michael E. Lamb, "The Development of Father-Infant Relationships," in *The Role of the Father in Child Development*, ed. Michael Lamb (New York: John Wiley & Sons, 1981), pp. 459–488; Michael E. Lamb et al., "The Father-Daughter Relationship: Past, Present and Future," in *Becoming Female: Perspectives on Development*, ed. Clair B. Kopp and Martha Kirkpatrick (New York: Plenum, 1979), pp. 84–112; Judith Langlois and A. Chris Downs, "Mothers, Fathers and Peers as Socialization Agents of Sex-Typed Play Behaviors in Young Children," *Child Development* 51 (1980), pp. 1237–1247; Eleanor Maccoby, *Social Development: Psychological Growth and the Parent-Child Relationship* (New York: Harcourt, Brace, Jovanovich, 1980), p. 255; Jacqueline McGuire, "Gender Specific Differences in Early Childhood: The Impact of the Father," in *Fathers: Psychological Perspectives*, ed. Nigel Beail and Jacqueline McGuire (London: Junction Books, 1982), pp. 95–125.

26. Jacqueline McGuire; Nancy E. Williamson, *Sons or Daughters: A Cross-Cultural Survey of Prenatal Preferences* (Beverly Hills: Sage, 1976), pp. 29–66.

27. Hakan Stattin and Ingrid Klackenberg-Larsson, "The Short- and Long-Term Implications for Parent-Child Relations of Parents' Prenatal Preferences for Their Child's Gender," *Developmental Psychology* 27 (1991), pp. 141–147.

28. Lamb et al.; Carol Seavey et al., R. Zalk, "Baby X: The Effects of Gender Labels on Adult Responses to Infants," *Sex Roles* 2 (1977), pp. 477–81.

29. Anne Wollett et al., "Observations of Fathers at Birth," in *Fathers: Psychological Perspectives*, Eds. Nigel Beail and Jacqueline McGuire (London: Junction Books, 1982), pp. 71–91.

30. Jacqueline McGuire.

31. David White et al., "Fathers' Involvement with Their Infants: The Relevance of Holding," in *Fathers: Psychological Perspectives*, ed. Nigel Beail and Jacqueline McGuire (London: Junction Books, 1982), pp. 126–143.

32. Michael E. Lamb, "Father-Infant and Mother-Infant Interaction in the First Year of Life," *Child Development* 48 (1977), pp. 167–181.

33. Michael Lewis and Marsha Weinraub, "Sex of Parent X, Sex of Child: Socioemotional Development," in *Sex Differences in Behavior*, eds. Richard Friedman et al. (New York: John Wiley & Sons, 1974), pp. 165–189; Howard Moss, "Early Sex Differences in Mother-Infant Interaction," in *Sex Differences in Behavior*, ed. Friedman et al., pp. 149–163; Ross D. Parke and Barbara R. Tinsley, "The Father's Role in Infancy: Determinants of Involvement in Caregiving and Play," in *The Role of the Father in Child Development*, ed. M. E. Lamb (New York: John Wiley and Sons, 1981), 429–457; Brian K. Barber and Darwin L. Thomas, "Dimensions of Fathers' and Mothers' Supportive Behavior: The Case for Physical Affection," *Journal of Marriage and the Family* 48 (1986), pp. 783–794.

34. Phyllis R. McGrab, "Mothers and Daughters," in *Becoming Female: Perspectives on Development*, ed. Claire Kopp and Martha Kirkpatrick (New York: Plenum, 1979), pp. 113–129; Parke and Tinsley; Jacqueline McGuire, pp. 103–104, 118; Beverly I. Fagot, "The Influences of Sex of Child on Parental Reaction to Toddler Children," *Child Development* 49 (1978), pp. 459–465.

35. Jacqueline McGuire.

36. Alfred B. Heilbrun, Jr., *Human Sex Role Behavior* (New York: Pergamon, 1981) pp. 161–162.

37. Jacqueline McGuire; Lamb, "The Development of Father-Infant Relationships."

38. Lamb et al.

39. Such a schedule of aperiodic reinforcement has been shown to produce stronger and more persistent behavioural effects than a consistent one. See Norma Radin, "The Role of the Father in Cognitive, Academic, and Intellectual Development," in *The Role of the Father in Child Development*, ed. Michael Lamb (New York: John Wiley & Sons, 1981), pp. 379–427.

40. Miriam M. Johnson, *Strong Mothers, Weak Wives: The Search for Gender Equality* (Berkeley: University of California Press, 1983).

41. Henry Biller, "The Father and Sex Role Development," in *The Role of the Father in Child Development*, ed. Michael Lamb (New York: John Wiley and Sons, 1981), pp. 319–358.

42. Alfred Adler, *The Individual Psychology of Alfred Adler: A Systematic Presentation in Selections from His Writings*, ed. H. L. Ansbacher and R. R. Ansbacher (New York: Basic Books, 1956).

43. Cecilie Ernst and Jules Angst, *Birth Order: Its Influence on Personality* (Berlin: Springer-Verlag, 1983).

44. Ernst and Angst; Warren R. Rule, "Birth Order and Sex as Related to Memory of Parental Strictness-Permissiveness," *Psychological Reports* 68 (1991), pp. 908–910.

45. Leonard S. Newman et al., "Self-Guide Strength and Emotional Vulnerability: Birth Order as a Moderator of Self-Affect Relations," *Personality and Social Psychology Bulletin* 18 (1992), pp. 402–411.

46. Judy Dunn, *Sisters and Brothers* (London: Fontana, 1984).

47. Adler; Dunn; Joan Pulakos, "The Effects of Birth Order on Perceived Family Roles," *Individual Psychology* 43 (1987), pp. 319–328.

48. Pulakos.
49. Rule.
50. David Lester et al., "Birth Order and Psychological Health: A Sex Difference," *Personal Individual Differences* 13 (1992), 379–380.
51. Kimberly A. Harris and K. Brent Morrow, "Differential Effects of Birth Order and Gender Perceptions of Responsibility and Dominance," *Individual Psychology* 48 (1992), pp. 109–118.
52. Antoinette S. Philips et al., "Type A Status: Birth Order and Gender Effects," *Individual Psychology* 46 (1990), pp. 365–373.
53. Newman et al.
54. Adler.
55. Pulakos.
56. Gregory E. Kennedy, "Middleborns' Perceptions of Family Relationships," *Psychological Reports* 64 (1989), pp. 755–760.
57. Pulakos.
58. Kennedy.
59. Dunn.
60. Harris and Morrow; Lester et al.
61. Newman et al.
62. Zolinda Stoneman et al., "Same-Sex and Cross-Sex Siblings: Activity Choices, Roles, Behavior, and Gender Stereotypes," *Sex Roles* 15 (1986), pp. 495–511.
63. Dunn; William Arkin, "Prolegomenon to the Study of 'Brother' as a Male Family Role," *Family Coordinator* 28 (October 1979), pp. 630–636.
64. Dunn; Arkin.
65. M. Ebrahim Fakouri and James L. Hafner, "Early Recollections of First-Borns," *Journal of Clinical Psychology* 40 (1984), pp. 209–213.
66. The loss of a parent through death can intensify feelings of gender dysphoria in young people; see Stephen M. Bernstein et al., "Changes in Patients with Gender Identity Problems after Parental Death," *American Journal of Psychiatry* 138 (1981), pp. 41–45.
67. Thomas S. Parish, "Ratings of Self and Parents by Youth: Are They Affected by Family Status, Gender, and Birth Order?" *Adolescence* 26 (1991), pp. 105–112.
68. Martha Minow, "Adjudicating Differences: Conflicts among Feminist Lawyers," in *Conflicts in Feminism*, ed. Marianne Hirsch and Evelyn Fox Keller (New York: Routledge, 1990), pp. 149–163.
69. William R. Beer, *Strangers in the House: The World of Stepsiblings and Half-Siblings* (New Brunswick: Transaction, 1989), 127–139.

4. Family Scenes

1. I have used the age of eleven years as the beginning of adolescence.
2. To elaborate, Thomas said (in another context): "There may be, and is, doubt as to the objectivity and veracity of the record, but even the highly subjective record has a value for behaviour study. . . . The subject's view of the situation, how he regards it, may be the most important element for interpretation. For his immediate behaviour is closely related to his definition of the situation, which may be in terms of objective reality, or in terms of a subjective appreciation—'as if' it were so. Very often it is the wide discrepancy between the situation as it seems to others and the situation as it seems to the individual that brings about the overt behaviour difficulty. To take an ex-

treme example, the warden of Dannemora Prison recently refused to honor the order of the Court to send an inmate outside the prison walls for some specific purpose. He excused himself on the ground that the man was too dangerous. He had killed several persons who had the unfortunate habit of talking to themselves on the street. From the movement of their lips he imagined that they were calling him vile names and he behaved as if this were true. If men [sic] define situations as real, they are real in their consequences." W. I. Thomas and Dorothy S. Thomas, *The Child in America* (New York: Knopf, 1928), pp. 571–572.

3. All information about family size is in reference to forty-four participants. One person, Rick, supplied no information about his family.

4. Simon, Ed, Jack, Darren, Bruce, Luther, Bill, Jordie, Terry, Tony, Brian, Fred, Bob, Harry, Dale, Phil, Steven.

5. Jacqueline McGuire; Williamson.

6. Letha Dawson Scanzoni and John Scanzoni, *Men, Women, and Change: A Sociology of Marriage and Family* (Toronto: McGraw Hill, 1988), report on the Princeton Fertility Study, a sixteen-year longitudinal study, which indicated that sex composition has an effect on family size. Scanzoni and Scanzoni state (p. 442), "Couples are more likely to have a third, fourth, or even fifth child if all the preceding offspring were of the same sex; and this is especially true if the preceding were girls."

7. Jack, Sam, Eli, Walter, Keith, Bill, Harry, Darcy, Colin, Gary, Dennis.

8. Jack, Keith, Bill, Harry, Darcy, Colin, Dennis.

9. Aaron, Scott, Mel, Morgan, Stan, Lee, Jorge, Howie, Fred, Hal.

10. Fred.

11. Simon, Scott, Mel, Sam, Morgan, Keith, Stan, Jorge, Darcy, Alan, Nathan, Steven, Pat, Hal.

12. Ed, Aaron, Jack, Eli, Walter, Luther, Lee, Terry, Howie, Fred, Gary.

13. Peter, Darren, Bruce, Robin, Ken, Bill, Ron, Jordie, Tony, Brian, Bob, Harry, Dale, Colin, Phil, Dennis.

14. Simon, Roger, Eli, Bruce, Stan, Phil, Grant, Hal.

15. "In 1980, one out of five children under eighteen living in married couple households [in the U.S.] were living in stepfamilies"; Beer, p. 6.

16. Aaron, Scott, Jack, Mel, Sam, Morgan, Walter, Bruce, Bill, Bob, Harry, Alan, Steven.

17. Scott, Jack, Mel, Morgan, Ken, Bill, Jorge, Fred, Bob, Harry, Alan.

18. Simon, Scott, Roger, Morgan, Darren, Stan, Brian, Dennis, Grant.

19. Scott, Jack, Mel, Roger, Morgan, Ken, Bill, Jorge, Terry, Fred, Bob, Harry, Alan.

20. All data about fathers are based on material from forty-three participants. Rick provided no information about his family, and Larry said that his childhood "was too long ago to remember my father." All data about mothers are in reference to forty-three participants. Rick provided no information about his family, and Larry said he had "no memories of my mother" from his childhood.

21. Simon, Roger, Stan, Grant.

22. Simon, Scott, Jack, Mel, Roger, Morgan, Eli, Darren, Bruce, Ken, Stan, Bill, Jorge, Terry, Brian, Fred, Bob, Harry, Alan, Phil, Dennis, Grant, Hal.

23. Simon, Roger, Sam, Stan, Brian, Bob, Darcy, Alan, Colin, Gary, Phil, Pat.

24. Peter, Robin, Ken, Bill, Tony, Howie, Brian, Nathan, Dennis, Steven.

25. Sam, Robin, Alan, Phil, Pat.

26. Simon, Ed, Peter, Aaron, Scott, Jack, Mel, Roger, Sam, Morgan, Eli, Darren,

Bruce, Robin, Ken, Stan, Bill, Jorge, Terry, Brian, Fred, Bob, Harry, Alan, Phil, Dennis, Grant, Pat, Hal.

5. Who Would Want to Be a Girl?
The Women (and Girls) in Participants' Families

1. All data about mothers are based on material from forty-three participants. Rick provided no information about his family and Larry said he had "no memories of my mother" from his childhood.

2. Simon, Peter, Scott, Mel, Sam, Walter, Keith, Ken, Bill, Ron, Jorge, Tony, Fred, Harry, Darcy, Alan, Gary, Nathan, Dennis, Steven, Pat.

3. Judith Herman, *Father-Daughter Incest* (Cambridge: Harvard University Press, 1981).

4. Scott, Darren, Ron, Bob, Harry, Dale, Grant.

5. Simon, Peter, Jack, Morgan, Ken, Bill, Ron, Jordie, Tony, Harry, Dale, Alan, Nathan, Dennis, Steven, Pat.

6. Ron, Harry, Dale.

7. Ed, Eli, Walter, Bruce, Stan, Jordie, Alan.

8. Simon, Ed, Peter, Scott, Mel, Walter, Ken, Stan, Bill, Jorge, Tony, Harry, Alan, Gary, Dennis.

9. See the introduction for an explanation of pronoun usage. In short, I have used pronouns which reflect the gender of the person involved at the time under discussion.

10. Simon, Peter, Scott, Mel, Walter, Ken, Stan, Bill, Jorge, Tony, Harry, Alan, Gary, Dennis.

11. Simon, Mel, Walter, Ken, Bill, Jorge, Harry, Alan, Dennis.

12. Scott, Mel, Ken, Bill, Jorge, Harry, Alan.

13. Ed, Stan, Tony, Harry.

14. Scott, Morgan, Darren, Stan, Brian, Alan, Dennis, Grant.

15. Peter, Scott, Mel, Sam, Morgan, Darren, Bruce, Ron, Bob, Dale.

16. Peter, Scott, Mel, Morgan, Darren, Bruce, Ron, Bob.

17. Sam, Morgan, Walter, Lee, Tony, Brian, Darcy, Pat.

18. Scott, Darren, Ron, Bob, Harry, Dale, Grant.

19. Simon, Peter, Scott, Mel, Roger, Sam, Morgan, Eli, Darren, Walter, Bruce, Stan, Lee, Ron, Tony, Brian, Bob, Harry, Darcy, Dale, Alan, Dennis, Grant, Pat.

20. Ed, Aaron, Jack, Roger, Bruce, Luther, Bill, Ron, Tony, Brian, Bob, Colin, Nathan, Dennis, Grant, Hal.

21. Aaron, Roger, Eli, Walter, Robin, Ron, Jorge, Bob, Harry, Darcy, Dale, Alan, Steven, Hal.

22. Aaron, Roger, Eli, Walter, Robin, Jorge, Steven, Hal.

23. Ron, Bob, Harry, Darcy, Dale.

24. Peter, Sam, Bruce, Terry, Dennis, Grant, Pat.

25. Jack, Eli, Walter, Ken, Fred, Alan, Gary, Steven, Hal.

26. Simon, Peter, Scott, Roger, Morgan, Eli, Darren, Stan, Tony, Brian, Bob, Alan, Dennis, Grant.

27. Simon, Ed, Peter, Scott, Jack, Mel, Sam, Morgan, Eli, Darren, Walter, Bruce, Keith, Ken, Stan, Bill, Ron, Jordie, Tony, Fred, Bob, Harry, Dale, Alan, Gary, Nathan, Phil, Dennis, Steven, Grant, Pat.

28. Ed, Peter, Aaron, Jack, Roger, Bruce, Luther, Bill, Ron, Terry, Tony, Brian, Bob, Colin, Gary, Dennis, Grant, Pat, Hal.

29. Simon, Peter, Scott, Mel, Roger, Sam, Morgan, Eli, Darren, Bruce, Stan, Ron, Tony, Brian, Bob, Dale, Alan, Dennis, Grant.

30. Scott, Darren, Ron, Bob, Harry, Dale, Grant.

31. All information is in reference to forty-three participants. Two participants, Rick and Larry, supplied no information about grandmothers and aunts.

32. Peter, Sam, Robin, Ken, Stan, Bill, Brian, Harry, Darcy, Alan, Colin, Gary, Nathan, Phil, Pat, Hal.

33. Sam, Stan, Brian, Darcy, Alan, Colin, Gary, Phil, Pat.

34. Peter, Robin, Ken, Bill, Tony, Harry, Nathan.

35. Peter, Sam, Bruce, Robin, Ken, Stan, Brian, Alan, Colin, Gary, Phil, Hal.

36. Sam, Robin, Alan, Phil, Pat.

37. Dunn.

38. Dennis E. McGuire and Patrick Tolan, "Clinical Interventions with Large Family Systems: Balancing Interests through Siblings," in *Siblings In Therapy: Life Span and Clinical Issues*, ed. Michael D. Kahn and Karen Gail Lewis (New York: Norton, 1988), pp. 115–134.

39. Brigid McConville, *Sister: Love and Conflict within the Lifelong Bond* (London: Pan, 1985); Christine Downing, *Psyche's Sisters: Re-Imagining the Meaning of Sisterhood* (San Francisco: Harper & Row, 1988).

40. All data about sisters are based on material from forty-four participants. Rick provided no information about his family.

41. Simon, Ed, Peter, Jack, Sam, Eli, Darren, Walter, Bruce, Robin, Keith, Ken, Luther, Bill, Ron, Jordie, Terry, Tony, Brian, Bob, Harry, Darcy, Dale, Alan, Colin, Gary, Nathan, Phil, Dennis, Steven, Pat.

42. Jack, Eli, Walter, Keith, Harry, Darcy, Colin, Gary, Dennis.

43. Ed, Jack, Eli, Walter, Ken, Luther, Bill, Terry, Brian, Harry, Dale, Colin, Gary, Phil, Dennis.

44. Jack, Ken, Luther, Bill, Brian, Harry, Dale, Colin, Gary, Phil.

45. Ed, Jack, Eli, Walter, Luther, Terry, Gary.

46. Simon, Peter, Sam, Darren, Bruce, Robin, Keith, Bill, Ron, Jordie, Brian, Bob, Harry, Darcy, Dale, Alan, Colin, Nathan, Dennis, Steven, Pat.

47. Simon, Robin, Keith, Jordie, Brian, Bob, Dale, Colin, Nathan.

48. Peter, Sam, Darren, Bruce, Bill, Ron, Harry, Darcy, Alan, Dennis, Steven, Pat.

49. Simon, Sam, Keith, Darcy, Alan, Nathan, Steven, Pat.

50. Bill, Brian, Harry, Dale, Colin, Dennis.

51. Peter, Jack, Sam, Darren, Bruce, Ken, Luther, Bill, Ron, Tony, Brian, Harry, Darcy, Dale, Alan, Colin, Gary, Phil, Dennis, Steven, Pat.

52. Peter, Jack, Sam, Bruce, Ken, Luther, Ron, Tony, Brian, Harry, Darcy, Colin, Dennis, Pat.

53. Walter, Robin, Bill, Dale, Nathan.

54. Simon, Ed, Jordie, Terry, Bob.

55. Jack, Bruce, Keith, Bill, Dale, Dennis.

56. Peter, Jack, Robin, Brian, Dale, Dennis.

57. Jack, Eli, Darren, Bruce, Keith, Bill, Dale, Alan, Gary, Phil, Dennis, Steven.

58. Jack, Eli, Bruce, Alan, Dennis, Steven.

59. Peter, Jack, Sam, Eli, Darren, Walter, Bruce, Keith, Luther, Bill, Ron, Brian, Dale, Alan, Colin, Gary, Phil, Dennis, Steven, Pat.

60. Jack, Sam, Bruce, Ron, Dale, Alan, Colin, Gary.

61. Darren, Walter, Luther, Bill, Brian, Phil, Dennis, Steven, Pat.

6. Men Rule: The Men (and Boys) in Participants' Lives

1. All data about fathers are based on material from forty-three participants. Rick provided no information about his family, and Larry said that his childhood "was too long ago to remember my father."

2. Ed, Aaron, Sam, Morgan, Bruce, Keith, Ron, Jordie, Tony, Fred, Bob, Harry, Steven.

3. Bruce, Fred, Harry.

4. See Holly Devor, "Transsexualism, Dissociation, and Child Abuse: An Initial Discussion Based on Nonclinical Data," *Journal of Psychology and Human Sexuality* 6 (1994), pp. 49–72.

5. Simon, Jack, Morgan, Ken, Bill, Ron, Tony, Harry, Dale, Alan, Nathan, Dennis, Steven, Pat.

6. Peter, Mel, Walter, Bruce, Lee, Jorge, Jordie, Terry, Howie.

7. Similar father-daughter dynamics are described in Janet Liebman Jacobs, "Victimized Daughters: Sexual Violence and the Empathic Female Self," *Signs: Journal of Women in Culture and Society*," 19 (1993), pp. 126–145.

8. Simon, Ed, Mel, Walter, Ken, Bill, Jorge, Harry, Alan, Dennis, Steven.

9. Simon, Jack, Eli, Walter, Ken, Ron, Bill, Harry, Dale, Alan.

10. Ed.

11. Peter, Morgan, Bruce, Lee, Jordie, Terry, Tony, Howie, Nathan, Pat.

12. Robin Morgan, *The Demon Lover: On the Sexuality of Terrorism* (New York: Norton, 1989); James B. McCarthy, "Abusive Families and Character Formation," *American Journal of Psychiatry* 50 (1990) pp. 181–186; Leslie Young, "Sexual Abuse and the Problem of Embodiment," *Child Abuse and Neglect* 16 (1992), pp. 89–100.

13. Most fathers who wanted sons adjust to the fact that they have had daughters instead of sons, but not all do so smoothly. See Stattin and Klackenberg-Larsson.

14. Jacobs.

15. Simon, Peter, Scott, Jack, Eli, Darren, Bruce, Keith, Luther, Jorge, Fred, Bob, Alan, Colin, Nathan.

16. Peter, Scott, Mel, Sam, Darren, Bruce, Robin, Bob, Alan.

17. Eli, Darren, Keith, Howie, Phil.

18. Simon, Ed, Peter, Scott, Jack, Mel, Roger, Sam, Walter, Bruce, Luther, Ron, Fred, Bob, Harry, Darcy, Dale, Colin, Gary, Nathan, Dennis, Steven.

19. Aaron, Bill, Jorge, Terry, Brian, Grant, Pat, Hal.

20. Robin, Stan, Lee, Jordie, Tony, Alan.

21. Ed, Jack, Luther, Ron, Fred, Bob, Darcy, Dale, Gary.

22. Aaron, Bill, Jorge, Terry, Brian, Grant, Pat, Hal.

23. All data are based on material from forty-three participants. Rick and Larry provided no information about this topic.

24. Ken, Stan, Bill, Brian, Harry, Darcy, Colin, Nathan, Grant, Pat, Hal.

25. Roger, Gary, Phil, Dennis, Steven, Grant, Hal.

26. Stan, Brian, Darcy, Colin, Gary, Pat.

27. See Lee Combrink-Graham, "When Parents Separate or Divorce: The Sibling System," in *Siblings in Therapy: Life Span and Clinical Issues*, ed. Michael D. Kahn and Karen Gail Lewis (New York: Norton, 1988), pp. 190–208.

28. See Dunn.

29. See Arkin.

30. See Stoneman et al.

31. See Marcel T. Saghir and Eli Robins, *Male and Female Homosexuality: A Comprehensive Investigation* (Baltimore: Williams & Wilkins, 1973).

32. See Arkin.

33. All information about brothers is in relation to forty-four participants. Rick supplied no information about his family.

34. Simon, Ed, Peter, Aaron, Scott, Mel, Morgan, Darren, Bruce, Robin, Ken, Stan, Luther, Lee, Ron, Jorge, Jordie, Terry, Tony, Howie, Brian, Fred, Bob, Dale, Alan, Nathan, Phil, Steven, Pat, Hal.

35. Aaron, Scott, Mel, Morgan, Stan, Lee, Jorge, Howie, Fred, Hal.

36. Simon, Ed, Robin, Jordie, Terry, Bob, Nathan.

37. Ken, Brian, Dale, Alan, Phil, Steven.

38. Ed, Peter, Aaron, Darren, Bruce, Robin, Luther, Lee, Ron, Jordie, Terry, Tony, Howie, Fred, Bob, Phil.

39. Ed, Robin, Luther, Terry, Howie, Fred.

40. Peter, Aaron, Darren, Bruce, Lee, Ron, Jordie, Tony, Bob, Phil.

41. Simon, Scott, Mel, Morgan, Darren, Ken, Stan, Jorge, Tony, Brian, Bob, Dale, Alan, Nathan, Phil, Steven, Pat, Hal.

42. Simon, Scott, Mel, Morgan, Ken, Stan, Jorge, Brian, Bob, Dale, Alan, Nathan, Phil, Steven, Hal.

43. Simon, Scott, Mel, Morgan, Jorge, Alan, Nathan, Steven, Pat, Hal.

44. Simon, Scott, Mel, Morgan, Stan, Jorge, Alan, Nathan, Steven, Pat, Hal.

45. Scott, Mel, Morgan, Stan, Jorge, Hal.

46. Simon, Peter, Aaron, Scott, Morgan, Darren, Bruce, Ken, Stan, Lee, Ron, Jorge, Jordie, Tony, Brian, Bob, Dale, Alan, Nathan, Phil, Steven, Hal.

47. Aaron, Scott, Morgan, Darren, Bruce, Robin, Ken, Stan, Lee, Ron, Jorge, Brian, Fred, Dale, Alan, Phil, Steven, Hal.

48. Bruce, Robin, Luther, Tony, Howie, Fred, Dale.

49. Peter, Aaron, Mel, Morgan, Bruce, Ken, Lee, Ron, Jorge, Tony, Brian, Steven, Hal.

50. Peter, Aaron, Mel, Morgan, Bruce, Ron, Tony, Hal.

51. Peter, Scott, Mel, Darren, Bruce, Robin, Stan, Bob, Alan.

52. Peter, Scott, Mel, Bruce, Robin, Bob.

53. Aaron, Scott, Mel, Morgan, Stan, Lee, Jorge, Howie, Hal.

54. Simon, Ed, Robin, Jordie, Terry, Bob, Nathan.

55. Simon, Roger, Jorge, Brian, Dale, Alan, Phil, Steven.

56. Ed, Robin, Luther, Terry, Howie, Fred, Nathan, Pat.

57. Peter, Aaron, Mel, Morgan, Bruce, Ron, Tony, Hal.

58. Peter, Scott, Mel, Darren, Bruce, Bob.

7. Lessons Learned at Home: Summary of Family Relationships

1. Rosemary H. Balsam, "The Paternal Possibility: The Father's Contribution to the Adolescent Daughter When the Mother Is Disturbed and a Denigrated Figure," in *Fathers and Their Families*, ed. Stanley H. Cath et al. (Hillsdale: Analytic Press, 1989), pp. 245–263; Alfred B. Heilbrun, Jr., "Identification with the Father and Peer Intimacy of the Daughter," *Family Relations* 33 (1984), pp. 597–605.

2. Jacobs.

3. Baumbach and Turner.

8. Childhood Friends and Foes: Relationships with Non-Family Members

1. All data about relationships with nonfamilial adults are from forty-four participants. Rick did not provide information about his childhood relationship with adults.

2. Simon, Peter, Mel, Morgan, Darren, Walter, Stan, Bill, Jorge, Brian, Fred, Harry, Nathan, Larry, Steven, Grant.

3. Simon, Ed, Eli, Walter, Bruce, Stan, Jordie.

4. Roger, Darren, Luther, Ron, Alan, Gary, Phil, Dennis, Steven.

5. All data about peer relationships are from forty-four participants. Rick did not provide information about his childhood relationships with peers.

6. Aaron, Jack, Mel, Eli, Walter, Darcy, Hal.

7. Ed, Peter, Aaron, Jack, Mel, Roger, Morgan, Eli, Darren, Walter, Bruce, Robin, Keith, Luther, Bill, Ron, Jorge, Jordie, Tony, Howie, Brian, Fred, Bob, Harry, Darcy, Colin, Nathan, Phil, Larry, Dennis, Steven, Pat, Hal.

8. Peter, Aaron, Jack, Roger, Eli, Bruce, Luther, Ron, Harry, Darcy.

9. Ed, Peter, Eli, Walter, Robin, Keith, Bill, Terry, Fred, Darcy, Dennis, Steven, Pat.

10. Peter, Scott, Roger, Morgan, Eli, Darren, Walter, Keith, Jorge, Terry, Hal.

11. Aaron, Jack, Sam, Bruce, Ken, Luther, Brian, Bob, Harry, Darcy, Colin, Steven, Grant, Pat.

12. Ed, Peter, Aaron, Eli, Robin, Luther, Bill, Howie, Fred, Gary, Dennis, Grant.

13. Peter, Aaron, Scott, Jack, Roger, Sam, Morgan, Eli, Darren, Walter, Bruce, Keith, Ken, Luther, Jorge, Terry, Brian, Bob, Harry, Darcy, Colin, Steven, Grant, Pat, Hal.

14. Ed, Peter, Aaron, Eli, Robin, Luther, Bill, Howie, Fred, Gary, Dennis, Grant.

15. Simon, Peter, Mel, Roger, Sam, Morgan, Darren, Bruce, Ken, Stan, Jorge, Jordie, Howie, Brian, Harry, Dale, Alan, Nathan, Phil, Dennis, Steven, Grant, Pat.

16. Simon, Roger, Sam, Ken, Jorge, Dale, Alan, Pat.

17. Peter, Morgan, Darren, Bruce, Howie, Brian, Harry, Nathan, Phil, Grant.

18. Peter, Mel, Roger, Morgan, Darren, Bruce, Jorge, Jordie, Howie, Brian, Harry, Nathan, Phil, Dennis, Steven, Pat.

19. Ed, Peter, Aaron, Jack, Mel, Roger, Sam, Morgan, Eli, Darren, Walter, Bruce, Robin, Keith, Luther, Bill, Ron, Jorge, Jordie, Terry, Tony, Howie, Brian, Fred, Bob, Harry, Darcy, Dale, Alan, Colin, Nathan, Phil, Larry, Dennis, Steven, Grant, Pat, Hal.

9. Adolescence Is about Change

1. Peter Blos, "The Second Individuation Process of Adolescence," *The Psychoanalytic Study of the Child* 22 (1967), pp. 162–187.

2. T. M. Honess and F. Lintern, "Relational and Systems Methodologies for Analysing Parent-Child Relationships: An Exploration of Conflict, Support and Independence in Adolescence and Post-Adolescence," *British Journal of Social Psychology* 29 (1990), pp. 331–347; Barbara Fuhrmann, *Adolescence, Adolescents*, 2d ed. (Glenview: Scott, Foresman and Little, Brown Higher Education, 1990); Sanford M. Dornbusch, "The Sociology of Adolescence," *American Review of Sociology* 15 (1989), pp. 233–259.

3. Honess and Lintern.

4. William M. Bukowski and Betsy Hoza, "Popularity and Friendship: Issues in Theory, Measurement and Outcome," in *Peer Relationships in Child Development*, ed. Thomas J. Berndt and Gary W. Ladd (New York: John Wiley & Sons, 1989), pp. 15–45.

5. Virginia Brooks, *Minority Stress in Lesbian Women* (Toronto: Lexington, 1981).

6. Devor, *Gender Blending*.

7. Maj-Britt Rosenbaum, "The Changing Body Image of the Adolescent Girl," in *Female Adolescent Development*, ed. Max Sugar, 2d ed. (New York: Brunner/Mazel, 1993), pp. 62–80.

8. Irving H. Berkovitz, "Effects of Secondary and College Experiences on Adolescent Female Development," in *Female Adolescent Development*, ed. Sugar, pp. 192–212.

9. Devor, *Gender Blending*.

10. Rosenbaum.

11. Judith Semon Dubas and Annie Petersen, "Female Pubertal Development," in *Female Adolescent Development*, ed. Sugar, pp. 3–26.

12. Margaret Whitfield, "Development of Sexuality in Female Children," *Canadian Journal of Psychiatry* 34 (1989), pp. 879–883.

13. Dubas and Petersen.

14. George A. Rekers, "Development Problems of Puberty and Sex Roles in Adolescence," in *Handbook of Clinical Psychology*, ed. Clarence Walker and Michael Robert (New York: John Wiley & Sons, 1992), pp. 607–622.

15. Rosenbaum.

16. For example, one-half to three-fourths of adult women want to be thinner than they are (Dornbusch).

17. Fuhrmann.

18. Thomas J. Brown, "The Role of Peer Groups in Adolescents' Adjustment to Secondary School," in *Peer Relationships in Child Development*, ed. Thomas J. Berndt and Gary W. Ladd (New York: John Wiley & Sons, 1989), pp. 188–215.

19. Fuhrmann.

20. Jeffrey G. Parker and John M. Gottman, "Social and Emotional Development in a Relational Context: Friendship Interaction from Early Childhood to Adolescence," in *Peer Relationships in Child Development*, ed. Berndt and Ladd, pp. 95–131.

21. Thomas J. Brown.

22. Dornbusch; Parker and Gottman; Bukowski and Hoza.

23. Fuhrmann.

24. Fuhrmann.

25. Thomas J. Brown.

26. John M. Reisman, "Friendship and Its Implications for Mental Health and Social Competence," *Journal of Early Adolescents* 5 (1985), pp. 383–391.

27. Mary Ellen Colten et al., "The Patterning of Distress and Disorder in a Community Sample of High School Aged Youth," in *Adolescent Stress: Causes and Consequences*, ed. Mary Ellen Colten and Susan Gore (New York: Aldine Gruyther, 1991), pp. 157–180.

28. Fuhrmann; Jeanne Brooks-Gunn, "How Stressful Is the Transition to Adolescence for Girls?" in *Adolescent Stress: Causes and Consequences*, ed. Colten and Gore, pp. 131–149.

29. R. G. Simmons et al., "Entry into Early Adolescence: The Impact of Social

Structure, Puberty, and Early Dating on Self-Esteem," *American Sociological Review* 44 (1979), pp. 948–967; Brooks-Gunn.

30. Edward A. Smith et al., "Pubertal Development and Friends: A Biosocial Explanation of Adolescent Sexual Behavior," *Journal of Health and Social Behavior* 26 (1985), pp. 183–193.

31. Ried Larson and Linda Asmussen, "Anger, Worry and Hurt in Adolescence: An Enlarging World of Negative Emotion," in *Adolescent Stress: Causes and Consequences*, ed. Colten and Gore, pp. 21–41; E. Compas and Barry M. Wagner, "Psychosocial Stress during Adolescence: Intrapersonal and Interpersonal Processes," in *Adolescent Stress: Causes and Consequences*, ed. Colten and Gore, pp. 67–85.

32. Anne Petersen et al., "Coping with Adolescence," in *Adolescent Stress: Causes and Consequences*, ed. Colten and Gore, pp. 93–110.

33. Fuhrmann; Dornbusch.

34. Fuhrmann; Simmons et al.

35. Aaron Hass, *Teenage Sexuality: A Survey of Sexual Behavior* (New York: Macmillan, 1979).

36. JoAnn Loulan, *The Lesbian Erotic Dance: Butch, Femme, Androgyny and Other Rhythms* (San Francisco: Spinsters, 1990).

37. Kay Deaux and Laurie L. Lewis, "Structure of Gender Stereotypes: Interrelationships among Components and Gender Label," *Journal of Personality and Social Psychology* 46 (1984), pp. 991–1004; Steven C. Hayes et al., "The Development of Display and Knowledge of Sex Related Motor Behavior in Children," *Child Behavior Therapy*, 3 (1981), pp. 1–24.

38. Margaret Cooper, " 'Rejecting Femininity': Some Research Notes on Gender Identity Development in Lesbians," *Deviant Behavior* 11 (1990), pp. 371–380; Sasha Lewis, *Sunday's Women: Lesbian Life Today* (Boston: Beacon, 1979); Anke A. Ehrhardt et al., "Female-to-Male Transsexuals Compared to Lesbians: Behavioral Patterns of Childhood and Adolescent Development," *Archives of Sexual Behavior* 8 (1979), pp. 481–490; Ray Blanchard and Kurt Freund, "Measuring Masculine Gender Identity in Females," *Journal of Consulting and Clinical Psychology* 51 (1983), pp. 205–214.

39. Ehrhardt et al.; Blanchard and Freund.

40. Eighty-one percent of lesbians remembered cross-gender activity in childhood vs 12 percent of heterosexual women. See J. Michael Bailey and Ken Zucker, "Childhood Sex-Typed Behavior and Sexual Orientation: A Conceptual Analysis, *Developmental Psychology* 31 (1995), pp. 43–55, and Blanchard and Freund.

41. Saghir and Robins; Blanchard and Freund.

42. Elizabeth McCauley and Anke A. Ehrhardt, "Role Expectations and Definitions: A Comparison of Female Transsexuals and Lesbians," *Journal of Homosexuality* 3, no. 2 (1978), pp. 137–147; Ehrhardt et al.

43. Sasha Lewis; Ehrhardt et al.

44. Saghir and Robins.

45. Ira B. Pauly, "Female Transsexualism: Part I," *Archives of Sexual Behavior* 3 (1974), pp. 487–507.

46. Ray Blanchard, "Gender Identity Disorders in Adult Women," in *The Clinical Management of Gender Identity Disorders in Children and Adults*, ed. Ray Blanchard and Betty Steiner (Washington, D.C.: American Psychiatric Press, 1990), pp. 77–91; Ehrhardt et al.; McCauley and Ehrhardt.

47. Pauly; Ehrhardt et al.

48. Lothstein, p. 44; Pauly.

49. Kim E. Stuart, *The Uninvited Dilemma: A Question of Gender* (Portland, OR: Metamorphous, 1983), pp. 21–23.

50. Kim E. Stuart, *The Uninvited Dilemma: Research Supplement* (Portland, OR: Metamorphous, 1985), p. 45; Pauly.

51. Pauly; W. F. Tsoi, "Developmental Profiles of 200 Male and 100 Female Transsexuals in Singapore," *Archives of Sexual Behavior* 19 (1990), pp. 595–605; Thorkil Sorensen and Preben Hertoft, "Male and Female Transsexualism: The Danish Experience of 37 Patients," *Archives of Sexual Behavior* 11 (1982), pp. 133–155; McCauley and Ehrhardt; Blanchard, "Gender Identity Disorders"; Lothstein; Stuart, *The Uninvited Dilemma: Research Supplement*.

52. McCauley and Ehrhardt; Tsoi; Pauly.

53. Blanchard, "Gender Identity Disorders"; McCauley and Ehrhardt; Tsoi; Pauly.

54. Lothstein; Blanchard, "Gender Identity Disorders"; Pauly.

55. Blanchard, "Gender Identity Disorders"; McCauley and Ehrhardt; Sorensen and Hertoft; Pauly; Stuart, *The Uninvited Dilemma: Research Supplement*.

56. Hellman et al.

57. Eli Coleman and Walter Bockting, " 'Heterosexual' Prior to Sex Reassignment—'Homosexual' Afterwards: A Case Study of a Female-to-Male Transsexual," *Journal of Psychology and Human Sexuality* 1 (1988), pp. 68–82.

10. Crises at Puberty

1. Tanner, p. 66.

2. Sam, Colin.

3. Bruce, Tony, Phil.

4. Ed, Peter, Jack, Sam, Walter, Bruce, Stan, Luther, Ron, Jorge, Terry, Tony, Howie, Bob, Dale, Colin, Nathan, Phil, Dennis, Steven, Grant.

5. Simon, Rick, Aaron, Scott, Mel, Roger, Morgan, Eli, Darren, Robin, Keith, Ken, Bill, Lee, Jordie, Brian, Fred, Harry, Darcy, Alan, Gary, Larry, Pat, Hal.

6. Ed, Peter, Jack, Sam, Walter, Bruce, Jorge, Howie, Dale, Steven, Grant.

7. Stan, Luther, Ron, Terry, Nathan, Dennis.

8. Aaron, Roger, Eli, Darren, Robin, Keith, Stan, Lee, Tony, Darcy, Phil, Pat.

9. Simon, Peter, Jack, Sam, Morgan, Bruce, Ken, Luther, Bill, Ron, Jorge, Howie, Brian, Fred, Bob, Harry, Dale, Nathan, Larry, Dennis, Steven, Grant, Hal.

10. Peter, Jack, Luther, Bill, Ron, Jorge, Fred, Harry, Nathan, Dennis.

11. Peter, Morgan, Bruce, Bill, Brian, Dale, Steven.

12. Ed, Peter, Jack, Sam, Eli, Walter, Bruce, Stan, Luther, Jorge, Terry, Tony, Howie, Dale, Colin, Nathan, Phil, Steven, Grant.

13. Simon, Peter, Jack, Sam, Morgan, Bruce, Ken, Luther, Bill, Ron, Jorge, Howie, Brian, Fred, Bob, Harry, Dale, Nathan, Larry, Dennis, Steven, Grant, Hal.

14. Simon, Ed, Peter, Jack, Sam, Morgan, Eli, Walter, Bruce, Ken, Stan, Luther, Bill, Ron, Jorge, Terry, Tony, Howie, Brian, Fred, Bob, Harry, Dale, Colin, Nathan, Phil, Larry, Dennis, Steven, Grant, Hal.

15. Simon, Ed, Peter, Jack, Morgan, Darren, Walter, Bruce, Robin, Keith, Ken, Luther, Ron, Jorge, Jordie, Terry, Brian, Fred, Bob, Harry, Alan, Gary, Nathan, Phil, Larry, Steven, Grant, Hal.

16. Aaron, Eli, Tony, Howie, Dale, Dennis.

17. Rick, Scott, Mel, Stan, Bill, Pat.

18. Peter, Jack, Darren, Walter, Bruce, Robin, Keith, Ken, Ron, Jordie, Brian, Fred, Bob, Harry, Gary, Nathan, Phil, Larry, Steven, Hal.

19. Peter, Jack, Morgan, Walter, Robin, Keith, Ken, Ron, Jordie, Brian, Fred, Bob, Harry, Gary, Nathan, Phil, Larry, Steven, Hal.

20. Simon, Ed, Darren, Bruce, Luther, Jorge, Terry, Alan, Grant.

21. Aaron, Eli, Tony, Brian, Dale, Dennis.

22. Rick, Scott, Mel, Stan, Bill, Pat.

23. Simon, Aaron, Scott, Morgan, Eli, Robin, Keith, Stan, Luther, Steven, Hal.

24. Simon, Rick, Ed, Peter, Scott, Jack, Mel, Morgan, Darren, Walter, Bruce, Robin, Keith, Ken, Stan, Luther, Bill, Ron, Jorge, Jordie, Terry, Brian, Fred, Bob, Harry, Alan, Gary, Nathan, Phil, Larry, Steven, Grant, Pat, Hal.

25. Simon, Ed, Peter, Jack, Sam, Morgan, Eli, Walter, Bruce, Ken, Stan, Luther, Bill, Ron, Jorge, Terry, Tony, Howie, Brian, Fred, Bob, Harry, Dale, Colin, Nathan, Phil, Larry, Dennis, Steven, Grant, Hal.

26. Aaron, Roger, Lee, Darcy.

11. Adolescent Friendships

1. All data on adolescent friendships refer to forty-four participants. Rick gave no information on this subject.

2. Simon, Jack, Morgan, Darren, Bruce, Robin, Keith, Bill, Jorge, Jordie, Howie, Brian, Fred, Harry, Alan, Gary, Nathan, Larry, Dennis, Steven, Grant, Pat.

3. Simon, Jack, Morgan, Darren, Bruce, Robin, Keith, Jorge, Harry, Larry, Dennis, Steven, Grant, Pat.

4. Bill, Jordie, Howie, Brian, Fred, Alan, Gary, Nathan.

5. Simon, Ed, Peter, Aaron, Mel, Roger, Sam, Morgan, Eli, Walter, Bruce, Robin, Keith, Ken, Stan, Luther, Ron, Brian, Bob, Harry, Darcy, Dale, Phil, Dennis, Steven, Grant, Pat, Hal.

6. Simon, Peter, Aaron, Sam, Morgan, Eli, Walter, Keith, Stan, Luther, Brian, Bob, Phil, Steven, Grant, Hal.

7. Peter, Mel, Roger, Bruce, Ken, Stan, Ron, Bob, Harry, Dale, Phil, Pat, Hal.

8. Ed, Aaron, Eli, Bruce, Robin, Luther, Darcy, Dennis, Steven.

9. Morgan, Walter, Keith, Ron, Terry, Tony, Brian, Harry, Phil.

10. Simon, Ed, Scott, Jack, Roger, Eli, Darren, Ken, Stan, Luther, Lee, Jorge, Fred, Darcy, Dale, Colin, Dennis, Steven, Grant, Pat, Hal.

11. In this section I consider only participants' friendships in which they felt no romantic pull. I look at participants' romantic and sexual relationships in chap. 14.

12. Luther, Lee, Jorge, Steven, Grant, Pat, Hal.

13. Simon, Jack, Morgan, Darren, Bruce, Robin, Keith, Bill, Jorge, Jordie, Howie, Brian, Fred, Harry, Alan, Gary, Nathan, Larry, Dennis, Steven, Grant, Pat.

14. Fuhrmann.

12. Women Are Different: Relationships with Female Relatives

1. All data about mothers are based on material from forty-three participants. Rick provided no information about his family, and Larry said he had "no memories of my mother" from his adolescence.

2. Simon, Ed, Peter, Aaron, Mel, Roger, Sam, Morgan, Darren, Bruce, Ken, Stan, Luther, Ron, Jorge, Jordie, Terry, Tony, Brian, Fred, Bob, Harry, Darcy, Dale, Alan, Colin, Nathan, Phil, Dennis, Grant, Hal.

3. Simon, Ed, Jack, Roger, Eli, Walter, Ken, Bill, Howie, Alan, Gary, Phil, Steven, Hal.

4. Simon, Ed, Roger, Ken, Alan, Hal.

5. Darren, Bruce, Ron, Bob, Harry, Grant.

6. Adolescent experiences of sexual abuse are discussed in chap. 14.

7. Simon, Ed, Stan, Luther, Jordie, Harry, Alan, Dennis.

8. Peter, Aaron, Roger, Morgan, Ken, Brian, Grant.

9. Simon, Peter, Aaron, Sam, Bruce, Jorge, Jordie, Terry, Tony, Brian, Fred, Bob, Darcy, Colin, Nathan, Phil, Dennis, Grant, Hal.

10. Simon, Ed, Aaron, Mel, Roger, Walter, Ken, Bill, Jorge, Tony, Harry, Dale, Alan, Dennis.

11. Simon, Ed, Mel, Walter, Ken, Bill, Jorge, Tony, Harry, Alan, Dennis.

12. Simon, Ed, Jack, Roger, Eli, Walter, Ken, Bill, Howie, Alan, Gary, Phil, Steven, Hal.

13. Simon, Ed, Roger, Walter, Ken, Bill, Alan.

14. Simon, Ed, Stan, Luther, Jordie, Harry, Alan, Dennis.

15. Peter, Scott, Roger, Morgan, Ken, Brian, Grant.

16. Darren, Bruce, Ron, Bob, Harry, Grant.

17. Simon, Ed, Roger, Walter, Ken, Bill, Alan.

18. Simon, Peter, Aaron, Sam, Bruce, Ken, Jordie, Terry, Tony, Brian, Fred, Bob, Darcy, Colin, Nathan, Phil, Dennis, Grant, Hal.

19. Ed, Jack, Roger, Walter, Howie.

20. All information is in reference to forty-three participants. Two participants, Rick and Larry, supplied no information about grandmothers and aunts.

21. Simon, Darren, Bruce, Ken, Stan, Bill, Brian, Harry, Colin, Gary.

22. Eli, Tony, Howie, Dennis.

23. Peter, Darcy, Alan, Hal.

24. Ed, Eli, Walter, Luther, Bill, Terry, Harry, Dale, Gary.

25. Brian, Bob, Colin, Dennis, Pat.

26. Peter, Jack, Sam, Ken, Bill, Ron, Tony, Darcy, Dale.

27. Jack, Bill, Brian, Harry, Darcy, Dale.

28. Jack, Darren, Bruce, Dale, Nathan, Phil, Dennis, Steven.

29. Jack, Darren, Bruce, Dale, Nathan, Phil, Dennis, Steven.

30. Simon, Ed, Peter, Jack, Sam, Eli, Walter, Bruce, Robin, Keith, Ken, Luther, Bill, Ron, Jordie, Terry, Tony, Brian, Bob, Harry, Darcy, Dale, Alan, Colin, Gary, Dennis, Pat.

31. Jack, Darren, Bruce, Bill, Brian, Harry, Darcy, Dale, Nathan, Phil, Dennis, Steven.

13. Access Denied, Restrictions Apply: Relationships with Male Relatives

1. All data concerning adolescent relationships with fathers is in reference to forty participants. Rick provided no information; Roger's father died when Roger was eleven years old; Stan never saw her father while she was a teenager; Larry said only that her father had not been around much when Larry was a teenaged girl; and Gary's only comment on the subject was "I was quite a bit quieter with my parents."

2. Simon, Ed, Jack, Darren, Walter, Bruce, Ron, Fred, Bob, Harry, Phil, Grant, Pat.

3. Peter, Aaron, Morgan, Ken, Terry, Brian, Colin, Hal.

4. Simon, Darren, Bruce, Keith, Luther, Bob, Colin.

5. Keith, Ron, Jordie, Harry, Darcy, Dale, Steven, Grant.

6. Simon, Ed, Peter, Aaron, Scott, Jack, Mel, Morgan, Bruce, Ken, Bill, Jorge, Fred, Harry, Dale, Alan.

7. Sam, Eli, Darren, Bruce, Keith, Luther, Bob, Phil, Grant.

8. Aaron, Morgan, Walter, Ken, Bill, Ron, Jordie, Terry, Tony, Harry, Dale, Dennis, Steven.

9. Simon, Ed, Peter, Scott, Jack, Mel, Robin, Lee, Jorge, Howie, Brian, Fred, Darcy, Alan, Colin, Nathan, Pat, Hal.

10. Simon, Peter, Jack, Morgan, Walter, Ken, Jorge, Jordie, Tony, Brian, Alan, Nathan, Dennis, Steven.

11. Simon, Walter, Ken, Bill, Jorge, Harry, Dale, Dennis, Steven.

12. Sam, Eli, Darren, Bruce, Keith, Luther, Bob, Phil, Grant.

13. Darren, Bruce, Keith, Luther, Bob.

14. Simon, Ed, Peter, Aaron, Scott, Jack, Mel, Roger, Morgan, Eli, Darren, Bruce, Keith, Ken, Bill, Ron, Jorge, Jordie, Fred, Harry, Darcy, Dale, Alan, Nathan, Phil, Steven, Grant.

15. Simon, Ed, Peter, Aaron, Scott, Jack, Mel, Morgan, Walter, Robin, Keith, Bill, Lee, Ron, Jorge, Jordie, Terry, Tony, Howie, Brian, Fred, Harry, Darcy, Dale, Alan, Colin, Nathan, Dennis, Steven, Pat, Hal.

16. Sam, Eli, Darren, Bruce, Keith, Luther, Bob, Phil, Grant.

17. Simon, Bruce, Ken, Stan, Bill, Brian, Harry, Darcy, Grant, Hal.

18. Eli, Gary, Dennis, Steven.

19. Simon, Eli, Bruce, Harry, Darcy, Grant, Hal.

20. Ed, Robin, Luther, Terry, Howie, Fred, Bob, Alan.

21. Ed, Peter, Aaron, Scott, Mel, Morgan, Darren, Bruce, Ken, Stan, Lee, Ron, Jorge, Jordie, Tony, Brian, Bob, Dale, Alan, Nathan, Phil, Steven, Pat, Hal.

22. Aaron, Darren, Lee, Ron, Bob, Alan, Nathan, Phil, Steven.

23. Ed, Peter, Scott, Mel, Morgan, Bruce, Ken, Stan, Jorge, Jordie, Tony, Brian, Bob, Dale, Pat, Hal.

24. Scott, Mel, Morgan, Ken, Stan, Jorge, Tony, Brian, Bob, Dale, Pat, Hal.

25. Participants' adolescent experiences of sexual relations with family members are discussed in chap. 14.

14. Looking for Love, Groping for Identity: Adolescent Sexuality

1. Studies report that the incidence of masturbation among teenaged girls has steadily increased over the past several decades. In the 1940s, Kinsey and his colleagues found that 12 percent of adult women recalled having masturbated by age twelve. In the 1960s, it was reported that 18 percent of females had begun masturbating by that age. In the 1980s, this rate had increased still further to 31 percent. By the end of adolescence, many more young women have learned how to give themselves sexual pleasure. Kinsey et al. reported during the 1940s that 33 percent of twenty-year-old women had begun masturbating. In the 1960s, 46 percent of twenty-year-old women had masturbated. By the 1970s this rate had risen to 60 percent, and by the 1980s the rate had risen still further to 73 percent. See Whitfield; R. C. Sorenson, *Adolescent Sexuality in Contemporary America* (New York: World, 1973); William H. Masters et al., *Masters and Johnson on Sex and Human Loving* (Boston: Little, Brown, 1982).

2. Hass.

3. Surveys of North American teenagers have found that approximately 40 percent of girls who were seventeen and eighteen years old in the late 1960s and in the

1970s had had heterosexual intercourse at least one time. At that time, few young women were widely experienced in this domain. Approximately half of those surveyed had had sexual intercourse with only one partner, and less than 15 percent of them had had coital experience with more than five partners. See Hass; Dornbusch.

4. Hass.

5. All participants have been included in calculations in this section.

6. Simon, Ed, Peter, Eli, Walter, Bruce, Ken, Stan, Jordie.

7. Morgan, Alan, Nathan, Grant.

8. Simon, Peter, Aaron, Ken, Jordie, Alan.

9. Herand Katchadourian, *Fundamentals of Human Sexuality*, 5th ed. (Fort Worth: Holt, Rinehart & Winston, 1989).

10. John H. Gagnon and William Simon, *Sexual Conduct: The Social Sources of Human Sexuality* (Chicago: Aldine, 1973); John B. Gagnon, "The Explicit and Implicit Use of the Scripting Perspective in Sex Research," *Annual Review of Sex Research* 1 (1980), pp. 1–48.

11. Ed, Bob, Alan, Nathan, Phil, and Pat reported that they masturbated but did not say when they started. Gary and Dennis gave no information one way or the other. Thus percentage calculations are out of thirty-seven participants.

12. Sam, Eli, Keith, Stan, Luther, Bill, Brian, Larry, Steven.

13. Peter, Scott, Roger, Walter, Bruce, Robin, Jordie, Terry, Howie, Darcy, Dale, Grant, Hal.

14. Sam, Robin, Howie, Larry, Steven.

15. Sam, Keith, Darcy, Steven, Grant.

16. Jordie, Dale, Nathan.

17. Simon, Rick, Aaron, Jack, Mel, Morgan, Darren, Ken, Lee, Ron, Jorge, Tony, Fred, Harry, Colin.

18. Rick, Mel, Morgan, Darren, Ron, Harry.

19. Simon, Rick, Darren, Ken, Lee, Jorge, Tony, Fred, Harry.

20. Mel, Morgan, Ron, Colin.

21. Simon, Rick, Darren, Ken, Lee, Jorge, Tony, Fred, Harry.

22. Peter, Scott, Roger, Sam, Eli, Walter, Bruce, Luther, Bill, Jordie, Terry, Howie, Brian, Darcy, Dale, Steven, Grant, Hal.

23. Sam, Luther, Howie, Darcy, Steven, Grant.

24. Peter, Scott, Roger, Sam, Eli, Walter, Bruce, Robin, Keith, Stan, Luther, Bill, Jordie, Terry, Howie, Brian, Darcy, Dale, Larry, Steven, Grant, Hal.

25. Sam, Eli, Keith, Stan, Bill, Brian, and Larry began to masturbate by the age of ten years.

26. Whitfield.

27. Sam, Keith, Jordie, Darcy, Dale, Colin, Nathan, Steven, Grant.

28. Rosenbaum; Hass.

29. Peter, Scott, Roger, Sam, Eli, Walter, Bruce, Luther, Bill, Jordie, Terry, Howie, Brian, Darcy, Dale, Steven, Grant, Hal.

30. All data concerning heterosexual relationships are in reference to forty-four participants. Rick provided no information in this regard.

31. Ed, Peter, Mel, Darren, Luther, Terry, Howie, Brian, Bob, Gary, Nathan, Larry, Dennis, Pat, Hal.

32. Ed, Luther, Terry, Howie, Bob, Gary, Nathan, Larry, Dennis.

33. Simon, Scott, Jack, Roger, Morgan, Eli, Walter, Bruce, Robin, Stan, Bill, Tony, Fred, Colin, Steven, Grant.

34. Jack, Morgan, Eli, Walter, Bruce, Robin, Bill, Fred, Colin, Steven, Grant.

35. Simon, Scott, Roger, Stan, Tony.

36. Ed, Peter, Mel, Darren, Luther, Terry, Howie, Brian, Bob, Gary, Nathan, Larry, Dennis, Pat, Hal.

37. Simon, Scott, Jack, Roger, Morgan, Eli, Walter, Bruce, Robin, Stan, Bill, Tony, Fred, Colin, Steven, Grant.

38. Aaron, Sam, Keith, Ken, Lee, Ron, Jorge, Jordie, Harry, Darcy, Dale, Alan, Phil.

39. Aaron, Lee, Jorge, Dale, Alan.

40. Jorge and Alan.

41. Ed, Peter, Mel, Darren, Luther, Terry, Howie, Brian, Bob, Gary, Nathan, Larry, Dennis, Pat, Hal.

42. Simon, Scott, Jack, Roger, Morgan, Eli, Walter, Bruce, Robin, Stan, Bill, Tony, Fred, Colin, Steven, Grant.

43. Simon, Ed, Peter, Aaron, Eli, Walter, Bruce, Ken, Stan, Jordie, Alan.

44. Aaron, Keith, Ken, Lee, Ron, Jorge, Jordie, Harry, Darcy, Dale, Alan, Phil.

45. Peter, Aaron, Jack, Sam, Morgan, Bruce, Robin, Stan, Bill, Terry, Brian, Darcy, Gary, Nathan, Larry, Pat.

46. Roger, Eli, Keith, Lee, Jorge, Jordie, Harry, Colin, Dennis, Steven, Hal.

47. Simon, Rick, Ed, Scott, Mel, Darren, Walter, Ken, Luther, Ron, Tony, Howie, Fred, Bob, Dale, Alan, Phil, Grant.

48. Simon, Howie, Grant.

49. All data concerning adolescent homosexual relations are in reference to all forty-five participants.

50. Peter, Aaron, Jack, Sam, Morgan, Bruce, Robin, Stan, Bill, Terry, Brian, Darcy, Gary, Nathan, Pat.

51. Peter, Bruce, Robin, Stan, Terry.

52. Eli, Keith, Lee, Jorge, Jordie, Harry, Colin, Dennis, Steven, Hal.

53. Simon, Rick, Ed, Scott, Mel, Roger, Darren, Walter, Ken, Luther, Ron, Tony, Howie, Fred, Bob, Dale, Alan, Phil, Grant.

54. Scott, Mel, Roger, Walter, Ken, Ron, Tony, Howie, Bob, Dale, Phil, Grant.

55. Rick, Ed, Darren, Fred, Alan.

56. Simon, Luther, Howie.

57. A 1995 *Advocate* magazine survey of 2,525 mostly U.S. lesbian women indicated that fewer than 1 percent of respondents refused to let their partners "caress her breasts," "suck her nipples," or "stimulate her genitals." The same survey indicated that 2 percent refused to let their partners "penetrate her vagina with her finger." Personal communication, October 31, 1995, from Janet Lever.

58. Simon, Rick, Ed, Scott, Mel, Walter, Howie, Fred.

59. Straight women have reported that men are mechanical in sexual performance, and that most women desire their partners to be more sensitive to their needs. As many as 70 percent of women reported that they did not have orgasms. Shere Hite, *The Hite Report* (New York: Dell, 1976).

60. Simon, Rick, Ed, Scott, Mel, Roger, Darren, Walter, Ken, Luther, Ron, Tony, Howie, Fred, Bob, Dale, Alan, Phil, Grant.

61. Scott, Mel, Walter, Ken, Luther, Ron, Tony, Howie, Bob, Dale, Phil, Grant.

62. Simon, Rick, Ed, Scott, Mel, Walter, Howie, Fred.

63. Simon, Rick, Ed, Darren, Luther, Howie, Alan.

64. Peter, Aaron, Scott, Sam, Morgan, Bruce, Robin, Stan, Bill, Terry, Brian, Darcy, Gary, Nathan, Pat.

65. Eli, Keith, Lee, Jorge, Jordie, Harry, Colin, Dennis, Steven, Hal.

66. See n. 60.

67. Sexual abuse data refer to forty-four participants. Rick provided no information on this subject.

68. Simon, Ed, Peter, Morgan, Eli, Walter, Bruce, Ken, Stan, Jordie, Nathan.

69. Masturbation data refer to thirty-seven participants. Ed, Bob, Alan, Nathan, Phil, and Pat gave no indication as to when they began masturbating. Gary and Dennis said nothing about masturbation at all.

70. Peter, Sam, Eli, Walter, Bruce, Robin, Keith, Stan, Luther, Bill, Jordie, Terry, Brian, Darcy, Dale, Larry, Steven, Grant, Hal.

71. Peter, Scott, Roger, Sam, Eli, Walter, Bruce, Robin, Luther, Bill, Jordie, Terry, Howie, Brian, Darcy, Dale, Steven, Grant, Hal.

72. Simon, Howie, Grant.

15. Concluding Adolescence

1. Colten et al.

2. Ed, Aaron, Jack, Sam, Eli, Bruce, Keith, Luther, Bill, Ron, Jorge, Jordie, Howie, Brian, Fred, Darcy, Dale, Gary, Nathan, Dennis, Steven, Grant, Pat.

3. Colten et al.

4. Simon, Ed, Scott, Morgan, Darren, Luther, Jorge, Jordie, Brian, Dale, Nathan, Dennis.

5. Scott, Jack, Mel, Roger, Eli, Robin, Ken, Ron, Dale, Alan.

6. Ed, Scott, Morgan, Walter, Luther, Ron, Tony, Howie, Alan.

7. Morgan, Bill, Howie, Fred, Nathan, Dennis.

8. Morgan, Bill, Howie, Fred, Alan, Nathan, Dennis.

9. Ed, Scott, Jack, Mel, Roger, Morgan, Eli, Walter, Robin, Ken, Luther, Ron, Tony, Howie, Dale, Alan.

10. Ed, Aaron, Jack, Sam, Eli, Bruce, Keith, Luther, Bill, Ron, Jorge, Jordie, Howie, Brian, Fred, Dale, Gary, Nathan, Dennis, Steven, Grant, Pat.

11. Simon, Ed, Scott, Morgan, Darren, Luther, Jorge, Jordie, Brian, Dale, Nathan, Dennis.

16. Finding Identities

1. All data about pre-transition adult heterosexual relations are in reference to thirty-eight participants. Simon, Ed, Darren, and Jorge had already begun their transitions by the time they reached age twenty. Rick, Morgan, and Darcy provided no information about whether they had been sexually or romantically involved with men as adults.

2. Peter, Aaron, Scott, Mel, Sam, Eli, Robin, Keith, Ken, Stan, Lee, Ron, Jordie, Tony, Brian, Dale, Alan, Colin, Grant, Pat, Hal.

3. Jack, Roger, Walter, Bruce, Luther, Bill, Terry, Howie, Fred, Bob, Harry, Gary, Nathan, Phil, Larry, Dennis, Steven.

4. Scott, Mel, Robin, Ken, Stan, Ron, Jordie, Tony, Brian, Alan, Colin, Grant.

5. Jack, Bruce, Luther, Bill, Terry, Howie, Fred, Bob, Gary, Larry, Dennis, Steven.

6. Scott, Mel, Robin, Stan, Jordie, Tony, Colin, Grant.

7. Peter, Aaron, Sam, Keith, Ken, Lee, Ron, Dale, Alan.

8. Ken, Ron, Alan.

9. Jack, Roger, Walter, Bruce, Luther, Bill, Terry, Howie, Fred, Bob, Harry, Gary, Nathan, Phil, Larry, Dennis, Steven.

10. Peter, Aaron, Scott, Mel, Sam, Eli, Robin, Keith, Ken, Stan, Lee, Ron, Jordie, Tony, Brian, Dale, Alan, Colin, Grant, Pat, Hal.

11. Participants followed a pattern similar to that of most women who identify as lesbians. Seventy-four percent of adult women who identify as homosexual or lesbian report having engaged in heterosexual intercourse at some time in their past. Debra Kent, ed., *The Kinsey Institute New Report on Sex* (New York: St. Martin's, 1990); Janet Lever, "Lesbian Sex Survey," *Advocate*, August 22, 1995, pp. 22–30.

12. Scott, Jack, Mel, Roger, Eli, Walter, Bruce, Robin, Stan, Luther, Bill, Jordie, Terry, Tony, Howie, Brian, Fred, Bob, Harry, Colin, Gary, Nathan, Phil, Larry, Dennis, Steven, Grant, Pat, Hal.

13. All data about pre-transition adult homosexual relationships are in reference to forty-one participants. Simon, Ed, Darren, and Jorge had begun their transitions by age twenty. Roger identified as a lesbian and was active in a lesbian community as an adult woman but did not discuss her sexual relationships as an adult woman.

14. Rick, Scott, Jack, Mel, Sam, Walter, Bruce, Robin, Ken, Stan, Luther, Lee, Ron, Tony, Howie, Fred, Bob, Harry, Darcy, Dale, Alan, Colin, Nathan, Phil, Dennis, Steven, Grant, Pat, Hal.

15. Peter, Morgan, Keith, Bill, Jordie, Terry, Gary, Larry.

16. Peter, Aaron, Morgan, Eli, Keith, Bill, Jordie, Terry, Brian, Gary, Larry.

17. Morgan, Bill, Terry, Gary, Larry.

18. Scott, Jack, Mel, Sam, Walter, Bruce, Robin, Ken, Stan, Luther, Lee, Ron, Tony, Howie, Fred, Bob, Harry, Darcy, Dale, Alan, Colin, Nathan, Phil, Dennis, Steven, Grant, Pat, Hal.

19. Sam, Ken, Lee, Ron, Harry, Darcy, Dale, Alan.

20. Scott, Mel, Walter, Robin, Stan, Tony, Colin, Phil, Grant.

21. Jack, Bruce, Luther, Howie, Fred, Bob, Nathan, Dennis, Steven, Pat, Hal.

22. Jack, Mel, Stan, Tony, Howie, Fred, Bob, Colin, Nathan, Grant.

23. Lillian Faderman, *Odd Girls and Twilight Lovers: A History of Lesbian Life in Twentieth-Century America* (New York: Penguin, 1991); Jeanne Cordova, "Butches, Lies, and Feminism," in *The Persistent Desire: A Femme-Butch Reader*, ed. Joan Nestle (Boston: Alyson, 1992), pp. 272–292.

24. Scott, Walter, Bruce, Robin, Luther, Phil, Dennis, Steven, Pat, Hal.

25. Scott, Walter, Bruce, Robin, Luther, Phil, Steven, Pat, Hal.

26. Scott, Walter, Bruce, Robin, Luther, Phil, Dennis, Steven, Pat, Hal.

27. Peter, Aaron, Morgan, Eli, Keith, Bill, Jordie, Terry, Brian, Gary, Larry.

28. Morgan, Bill, Terry, Gary, Larry.

29. Rick, Scott, Jack, Mel, Sam, Walter, Bruce, Robin, Ken, Stan, Luther, Lee, Ron, Tony, Howie, Fred, Bob, Harry, Darcy, Dale, Alan, Colin, Nathan, Phil, Dennis, Steven, Grant, Pat, Hal.

30. Aaron, Scott, Roger, Walter, Bruce, Robin, Ken, Luther, Lee, Ron, Harry, Darcy, Alan, Phil, Dennis, Steven, Pat, Hal.

31. Aaron, Scott, Roger, Walter, Bruce, Robin, Ken, Luther, Lee, Darcy, Dale, Phil, Steven, Pat, Hal.

32. Faderman, *Odd Girls*; Eve Sedgwick, *Epistemology of the Closet* (Berkeley: University of California Press, 1990).

33. In 1973 the American Psychiatric Association voted in favour of removing homosexuality from the *Diagnostic and Statistical Manual of Mental Disorders*. Subsequently only "sexual orientation disturbance" (302.0) appeared in the seventh and later printings of *Diagnostic and Statistical Manual of Mental Disorders II* (Washington D.C.: American Psychiatric Association, 1968). *Diagnostic and Statistical Manual of*

Mental Disorders III (Washington D.C.: American Psychiatric Association, 1980) contained the first listing of transsexualism (302.5x) and noted homosexuality only under "Ego-dystonic Homosexuality" (302.00).

34. Mel, Sam, Morgan, Eli, Jorge, Tony, Howie, Brian, Fred, Dale.

35. See n. 1.

36. Scott, Mel, Eli, Robin, Ken, Stan, Ron, Jordie, Tony, Brian, Alan, Colin, Grant, Pat, Hal.

37. Aaron, Sam, Lee, Dale.

38. See n. 13.

39. Rick, Aaron, Scott, Jack, Mel, Roger, Sam, Eli, Walter, Bruce, Robin, Ken, Stan, Luther, Lee, Ron, Tony, Howie, Brian, Fred, Bob, Harry, Darcy, Dale, Alan, Colin, Nathan, Phil, Dennis, Steven, Grant, Pat, Hal.

40. Aaron, Scott, Roger, Walter, Bruce, Robin, Ken, Luther, Lee, Darcy, Dale, Phil, Steven, Pat, Hal.

41. Rick, Jack, Mel, Sam, Eli, Stan, Ron, Tony, Howie, Harry, Alan, Nathan, Dennis, Grant.

42. Brian, Fred, Bob, Colin.

17. A Long Road

1. The *Standards of Care* are a set of guidelines developed in 1979 and updated periodically by an international association of professionals working in the field of gender dysphoria. They were developed in an attempt to establish minimal safeguards for the rights of clients of professional gender dysphoria service providers. See Paul A. Walker et al., *Standards of Care: The Hormonal and Surgical Sex Reassignment of Gender Dysphoric Persons* (Palo Alto: Harry Benjamin International Gender Dysphoria Association, January 1990).

18. Making the Decision

1. All data about finding transsexualism are in reference to thirty-four participants. Peter, Scott, Roger, Tony, Fred, Bob, Darcy, Colin, Nathan, Larry, and Hal provided insufficient information about when or how they first became aware of transsexualism.

2. Simon, Rick, Ed, Aaron, Jack, Sam, Morgan, Eli, Darren, Bruce, Robin, Stan, Luther, Bill, Lee, Ron, Jorge, Terry, Howie, Alan, Gary, Phil, Dennis, Steven, Grant, Pat.

3. Mel, Walter, Keith, Ken, Jordie, Brian, Harry, Dale.

4. Christine Jorgensen, *Christine Jorgensen: A Personal Autobiography* (New York: Bantam, 1967).

5. Rick, Ed, Aaron, Jack, Sam, Morgan, Eli, Bruce, Ken, Stan, Luther, Lee, Jordie, Howie, Harry, Steven, Grant, Pat.

6. Aaron, Sam, Lee, Grant.

7. Rick, Ed, Jack, Morgan, Luther, Jordie, Howie, Harry, Steven.

8. Jack, Mel, Eli, Bruce, Bill, Jorge, Gary, Dennis, Steven.

9. Thirty-three participants provided data about when they first heard of transsexualism and when they began to think of themselves in those terms. Peter, Scott, Roger, Sam, Tony, Brian, Fred, Bob, Colin, Gary, Nathan, and Larry provided no information about when they first came to think of themselves as transsexual.

10. Simon, Jack, Mel, Darren, Walter, Keith, Stan, Luther, Jorge, Jordie, Dale, Phil.

11. Rick, Ed, Aaron, Morgan, Eli, Bruce, Robin, Ken, Bill, Lee, Ron, Terry, Howie, Harry, Darcy, Alan, Dennis, Steven, Grant, Pat, Hal.

12. Simon, Rick, Darren, Bruce, Ken, Luther, Bill, Ron, Jorge, Jordie, Howie, Brian, Alan, Steven, Grant, Pat, Hal.

13. Simon, Rick, Ed, Jack, Eli, Walter, Bruce, Keith, Ken, Stan, Bill, Jorge, Howie, Brian, Alan, Gary, Dennis, Steven, Grant, Hal.

14. Deborah Heller Feinbloom, *Transvestites and Transsexuals* (New York: Dell, 1976).

15. The Ingersoll Gender Center, 1812 E. Madison, Suite 106, Seattle, WA 98122. Phone: 206-329-6651. E-mail: ingersol@halcyon.com.

16. *What Sex Am I?*, produced by Joseph Feury et al., Joseph Feury Productions, 1984, MPI Home Video Release, 1987, Oak Forest, Ill.

17. Mario Martino, *Emergence: A Transsexual Autobiography* (New York: Crown, 1977).

18. Paula Grossman, *A Handbook for Transsexuals* (Plainfield, N.J.: By the Author, c. 1982).

19. Lothstein.

20. Diane Leslie Feinberg, *Journal of a Transsexual* (New York: World View, 1980).

21. The Foundation for the Advancement of Canadian Transsexuals has evolved into a number of other organizations in local areas.

22. *Metamorphosus* magazine was published by Rupert Raj in 1982–1988.

23. Keith, Jordie.

24. Forty-two participants provided some information about their sexual and romantic relationships around the time that they were deciding whether they were transsexual. Roger, Sam, and Bob provided no information in this regard. Participants who began their transitions in their late teen years are included. For them, there were no pre-transition adult years. I have therefore included in this section their relevant experiences in the few years directly preceding their transitions.

25. Simon, Ed, Scott, Jack, Ken, Luther, Tony, Howie, Steven, Grant.

26. Rick, Aaron, Mel, Darren, Bruce, Stan, Fred, Dale, Nathan, Phil, Hal.

27. Peter, Morgan, Eli, Bill, Terry, Brian, Gary, Larry.

28. Walter, Robin, Lee, Ron, Harry, Darcy, Alan, Colin, Dennis, Pat.

29. Rick, Aaron, Mel, Darren, Bruce, Stan, Fred, Dale, Nathan, Hal.

30. Rick, Aaron, Mel, Bruce, Dale, Nathan, Hal.

31. Keith, Jorge, Jordie, Darcy, Alan, Grant.

32. Participants who started their transitions in their late teens are included in the total of forty-five participants. For them, there were no pre-transition adult years. I have therefore included their relevant experiences in the few years directly preceding their transitions.

33. Rick, Ed, Aaron, Jack, Morgan, Eli, Darren, Stan, Luther, Lee, Jorge, Dale, Dennis, Steven.

34. Rick, Aaron, Scott, Jack, Mel, Sam, Morgan, Darren, Luther, Jorge, Howie, Brian.

35. Ed, Bill, Jordie, Darcy, Dale, Steven.

36. Ed, Morgan, Walter, Keith, Stan, Tony, Alan.

37. Keith, Stan, Bill, Dale, Alan.

38. Robin, Bill, Harry, Dennis.

39. Mel, Sam, Eli, Darren, Walter, Bruce, Alan, Hal.

40. Mel, Sam, Eli, Darren, Walter, Bruce, Alan, Hal.

41. Bernstein, Steiner, Glaister, Muir.
42. Rick, Ed, Aaron, Jack, Morgan, Eli, Darren, Stan, Luther, Lee, Jorge, Dale, Dennis, Steven.
43. Ed, Aaron, Morgan, Darren, Stan, Fred, Steven.
44. Ed, Morgan, Walter, Keith, Stan, Bill, Tony, Dale, Alan, Colin.
45. Robin, Bill, Harry, Dennis.
46. Rick, Aaron, Scott, Jack, Mel, Sam, Morgan, Darren, Luther, Jorge, Howie, Brian.
47. Ed, Bill, Jordie, Darcy, Dale, Steven.
48. Mel, Sam, Eli, Darren, Walter, Bruce, Alan, Hal.

19. Making the Changes

1. Simon, Rick, Ed, Jack, Darren, Luther, Ron, Jorge, Terry, Howie, Alan, Phil.
2. Rick, Peter, Aaron, Scott, Jack, Mel, Roger, Sam, Walter, Bruce, Keith, Ken, Stan, Luther, Bill, Lee, Ron, Jordie, Tony, Howie, Brian, Fred, Bob, Harry, Dale, Alan, Colin, Gary, Nathan, Larry, Dennis, Steven, Grant, Hal.
3. Participants frequently referred to themselves as "passing" as men in the first months or years of their transitions despite the fact that most of them had felt themselves to be men for many years prior to that time. I have chosen to use that same language here. By using it, I do not mean to imply that participants were not real men during those months and years.
4. Participants also frequently referred to themselves as "crossdressing" during the first months or years of their transitions. This kind of language tended to drop out of use once participants began to feel more secure in their presentations of themselves as men. I have tried to parallel my own use of the term with that of participants.
5. Morgan, Eli, Robin, Terry, Darcy, Pat.
6. The effects of testosterone treatment vary from individual to individual. However, some generalizations can be made. Menstrual cycles cease sometime between the first and sixth month of treatment. By the end of the first year, most female-to-male transsexuals' voices have permanently dropped into a masculine range. Facial, body, and head hair permanently take on male-typical patterns over a period of months or years. Fat and muscle distributions shift in a masculine direction. Also within the first year of treatment, the clitoris grows to a size of 3–6 cm (1.5–3 in). Often, changes are accompanied by an increase in acne. See Sheila Kirk, *Hormones* (Waltham: International Foundation for Gender Education, 1992), pp. 70–79. Testosterone treatment was also widely reported by participants to result in an increase in libido and aggressiveness and a decrease in the ability to cry when sad.
7. Stan, Luther, Ron, Jordie, Alan, Dennis.
8. Simon, Rick, Ed, Peter, Aaron, Scott, Jack, Mel, Roger, Sam, Darren, Bruce, Keith, Ken, Stan, Bill, Ron, Tony, Howie, Brian, Bob, Dale, Colin, Gary, Nathan, Phil, Larry, Steven, Grant, Hal.
9. Double mastectomies and chest reconstruction are usually accomplished in two main ways. For small-breasted females, "keyhole" surgery can be performed in which breast tissue is removed through small incisions around the nipples. There is minimal scarring with this technique. For larger-breasted females, the nipple may have to be removed, made smaller, and repositioned after the removal of breast tissue and excess skin. There is generally quite a bit of scarring with this technique, but if it is skillfully done, if after-surgical care is good, and if the individual develops strategically placed body hair and musculature, the results can also be discreet. These surgeries are

sometimes referred to as "upper surgery" by female-to-male transsexuals. See James Green, "Getting Real about Female-to-Male Surgery," *Chrysalis: The Journal of Transgressive Gender Identities* 2, no. 2 (1995), pp. 27–33.

10. Participants had various degrees of removal of their internal female reproductive organs. These included simple hysterectomy with or without removal of the fallopian tubes and ovaries (salpingo-oophorectomy). Some surgeons also close off or remove the vagina. I have used hysterectomy as an umbrella term to refer to any combination of these operations.

11. Simon, Rick, Ed, Scott, Roger, Sam, Darren, Ken, Luther, Bill, Lee, Jordie, Tony, Howie, Brian, Bob, Dale, Nathan, Phil, Larry, Dennis, Steven, Hal.

12. The operation commonly called genital free-up is metoidioplasty. It is usually combined with the construction of a scrotal sack and the insertion of testicular implants. The free-up operation releases the enlarged clitoris from the skin which normally hoods it. This allows the clitoris to erect in a more masculine manner and gives it the appearance of a small but well-formed penis. This surgery is sometimes called "lower surgery" by female-to-male transsexuals. See James Green.

13. I use the term *phalloplasty* as a catch-all for a number of different surgical procedures. Surgeons in the period covered by this study generally used the technique known as "the suitcase handle." The surgical construction of this kind of phallus on female-to-male transsexuals is done in several stages. The basic phallus is constructed in two operations out of flesh from the lower abdomen. Other surgeries are performed to fashion a head for the phallus, to create a scrotal sack, and to implant testicles. Further surgeries are necessary if the patient wishes to be able to urinate standing up. Complications which require still further surgical interventions were commonplace. The entire set of procedures can take months or years to complete. These surgeries are sometimes called "lower surgery" by female-to-male transsexuals. See James Green.

14. Peter, Roger, Sam, Jordie, Tony, Bob, Colin, Nathan, Phil, and Larry did not specify how they gained access to some or all of the medical assistance which they received with their transitions and Morgan, Eli, Robin, Terry, Darcy, and Pat had not yet begun their transitions. Thus these data are in reference to twenty-nine participants.

15. Rick, Ed, Aaron, Keith, Ken, Luther, Lee, Ron, Jorge, Howie, Harry, Dale, Gary, Steven, Hal.

16. Walker et al.

17. Walker et al., p. 5.

18. Walker et al., p. 8.

19. Walker et al., p. 9.

20. Morgan, Eli, Robin, Terry, Darcy, Pat.

21. Robin, Terry, Darcy.

22. Morgan, Eli, Pat.

23. Of the 39 participants who had begun transition, 35 people provided information about how they began. Peter, Fred, Bob and Larry were silent on this subject.

24. Simon, Ed, Jack, Roger, Sam, Darren, Walter, Ken, Brian, Harry, Alan, Steven, Grant.

25. The term "real-life test" usually describes the period of cross-living required by the *Standards of Care* as a prerequisite for breast or genital surgery. The intention of this "test" is to allow transsexual persons and their doctors to establish that pre-operative transsexual persons are fully aware of what their lives as their target genders will be like.

26. To be "read" is to be recognized as the gender one is trying to camouflage by crossdressing.

27. For a fuller discussion of this phenomenon among non-transsexual females, see Devor, *Gender Blending*.

28. Simon, Ed, Jack, Roger, Sam, Darren, Walter, Ken, Brian, Harry, Alan, Steven, Grant.

29. Rick, Aaron, Scott, Mel, Bruce, Keith, Stan, Bill, Lee, Jorge, Jordie, Tony, Howie, Bob, Dale, Colin, Gary, Nathan, Phil, Dennis, Hal.

30. Simon, Roger, Lee, Howie, Brian, Dennis.

31. Thirty-nine participants had begun their gender and sex transitions. Morgan, Eli, Robin, Terry, Darcy, and Pat had not yet taken any transitional steps.

32. Simon, Rick, Ed, Peter, Aaron, Scott, Jack, Mel, Roger, Sam, Darren, Bruce, Keith, Ken, Stan, Bill, Ron, Tony, Howie, Brian, Bob, Dale, Colin, Gary, Nathan, Phil, Larry, Steven, Grant, Hal.

33. Luther, Jordie, Alan, Dennis.

34. Kessler and McKenna.

35. Transsexuals have coined the term "toilet trauma" to specify one of the areas of everyday life where it becomes most difficult for female-to-male transsexuals not to display their genital credentials. However, such scenarios can also be stage managed with recourse to specially prepared props.

36. Sam, Lee, Dale, Dennis.

37. Aaron's doctor told him that because he was already menopausal, he did not require a hysterectomy. Bruce was ambivalent about the necessity for any further surgery. Alan retained his uterus in the hope of bearing a child but intended to "complete" the changes at a later date.

38. Simon, Rick, Ed, Scott, Roger, Sam, Darren, Ken, Luther, Bill, Lee, Jordie, Tony, Howie, Brian, Bob, Dale, Nathan, Phil, Larry, Dennis, Steven, Hal.

39. Jack, Mel, Walter, Keith, Jorge, Colin, Gary, Grant.

40. Bruce was unable to produce medical records, but his description suggests the possibility that it was a teratomatous cyst. C. Westhoff et al., "Benign Ovarian Teratomas: A Population-Based Case-Control Study," *British Journal of Cancer* 58 (1988), pp. 93–98, estimate the incidence of such tumors as 8.9 per 100,000 women.

41. Clinics in North America at that time refused surgeries to female-to-male transsexuals who lived as gay men. See Coleman and Bockting.

42. Simon, Rick, Scott, Howie, Dale, Hal.

43. As of this writing, the costs associated with phalloplasties in the U.S. range in the many tens of thousands of dollars while metoidioplasty operations can be had for approximately $10,000. See James Green.

44. Peter, Aaron, Jack, Roger, Sam, Darren, Walter, Bruce, Keith, Ken, Stan, Luther, Jorge, Brian, Alan, Nathan, Grant.

45. Ed, Bill, Lee, Ron, Jordie, Tony, Bob, Phil, Larry, Dennis, Steven.

46. Mel, Fred, Harry, Colin, Gary.

47. Peter, Aaron, Jack, Roger, Sam, Darren, Walter, Bruce, Keith, Ken, Stan, Luther, Jorge, Brian, Alan, Nathan, Grant.

48. Simon, Rick, Scott, Howie, Dale, Hal.

49. Mel, Keith, Stan, Jorge, Fred, Harry, Colin, Gary.

20. Coming Out Stories

1. Unless participants made comments to the contrary, I have assumed that their parents were still alive at the time of their interviews. Therefore all data in this chapter are in reference to all forty-five participants unless otherwise stated.

2. Roger's, Darren's, Walter's, and Alan's mothers were no longer alive.

3. Roger's, Sam's, Eli's, Darren's, Walter's, Bruce's, Phil's, and Hal's fathers were no longer alive.

4. Ed, Peter, Aaron, Jack, Roger, Sam, Bruce, Lee, Howie, Pat, Hal.

5. Rick, Scott, Ron, Fred, Bob, Alan, Colin, Nathan, Larry.

6. Simon, Ed, Aaron, Jack, Mel, Sam, Eli, Keith, Ken, Luther, Bill, Tony, Harry, Dale, Gary, Phil, Dennis, Steven.

7. Peter, Bruce, Ken, Stan, Luther, Jorge, Jordie, Howie, Brian, Grant, Hal.

8. Jack, Darren, Bruce, Keith, Bill, Jordie, Tony, Harry, Dale, Gary, Dennis.

9. Simon, Mel, Darren, Bruce, Stan, Nathan, Hal.

10. Mayta Caldwell and Letitia Anne Peplau, "Sex Differences in Same-Sex Friendship," *Sex Roles* 8 (1982), pp.721–731.

11. Simon, Rick, Ed, Aaron, Mel, Eli, Jorge, Jordie, Terry, Gary, Phil, Steven, Hal.

12. Bruce, Keith, Luther, Howie.

13. Ed, Walter, Bruce, Jordie.

14. Simon, Keith, Steven, Hal.

15. Mel, Ken.

16. Simon, Ed, Aaron, Walter, Bruce, Luther, Harry.

17. Simon, Rick, Ed, Jack, Mel, Darren, Ken, Stan, Luther, Dale, Hal.

21. Are We There Yet?

1. Simon, Ed, Peter, Walter, Bruce, Stan, Brian, Fred.

2. Twenty-nine participants offered thoughts which were relevant to these issues: Simon, Rick, Peter, Aaron, Jack, Mel, Eli, Darren, Walter, Bruce, Keith, Ken, Stan, Luther, Bill, Ron, Jorge, Jordie, Terry, Howie, Brian, Fred, Harry, Dale, Colin, Gary, Phil, Dennis, Steven, Grant, Pat and Hal.

3. Rick, Peter, Aaron, Eli, Stan, Luther, Jordie, Howie, Dennis, Steven.

4. Aaron, Walter, Keith, Stan, Bill, Ron, Jordie, Terry, Brian, Harry, Alan, Steven, Grant, Hal.

5. Jack, Darren, Walter, Ken, Luther, Ron, Howie, Dale, Alan, Gary, Phil, Dennis, Steven.

6. Darren, Ron.

7. Jack, Walter, Ken, Luther, Howie, Alan, Gary, Phil, Dennis, Steven.

8. Twenty-four participants gave their opinions on this issue: Peter, Aaron, Jack, Darren, Walter, Bruce, Keith, Ken, Stan, Luther, Bill, Ron, Terry, Howie, Harry, Dale, Alan, Gary, Phil, Dennis, Steven, Grant, Pat and Hal.

9. Darren, Keith, Ken, Luther, Ron, Terry, Dale, Steven.

10. Walter, Bill, Howie, Harry, Alan, Phil, Dennis, Grant.

11. Bruce, Gary, Hal.

12. Peter, Aaron, Stan.

13. Jack, Mel, Darren, Keith, Ken, Luther, Jorge, Jordie, Howie, Harry, Dale, Phil, Dennis, Steven, Hal.

14. Simon, Walter, Bruce, Bill, Ron, Brian, Fred, Gary, Grant.

15. Simon, Rick, Peter, Aaron, Jack, Darren, Bruce, Keith, Ken, Stan, Luther, Bill, Ron, Jordie, Howie, Brian, Harry, Dale, Alan, Gary, Phil, Dennis, Steven, Grant and Hal disclosed their opinions on this question.

16. Rick, Aaron, Jack, Keith, Ken, Luther, Bill, Jordie, Howie, Brian, Dale, Alan, Phil, Dennis, Steven, Grant, Hal.

17. Simon, Peter, Darren, Bruce, Stan, Ron, Harry, Gary.

22. Nature's Calls: Toilet Traumas and Medical Necessities

1. Morgan, Eli, Robin, Terry, Darcy, and Pat were still deliberating about when they would begin to make their transitions. Lee had begun hormone treatments but had not begun to live as a man. Alan had lived as a man for a period of time and had returned to living as a woman in hope of becoming pregnant.

2. Walter, Jorge, Fred, Harry.

3. Peter, Jack, Mel, Walter, Keith, Stan, Jorge, Fred, Harry, Colin, Gary, Grant.

4. Simon, Rick, Scott, Howie, Dale, Hal.

23. The Naked Truth about Sexuality

1. Morgan, Eli, Robin, Lee, Terry, Darcy, Alan, and Pat were living as women at the times of their last interviews. Alan had lived as a man for several years before returning to life as a woman, during which time he had sexual relationships with women. I have included his stories, as they were relevant to topics being discussed. Rick and Roger gave no information about what sexual relationships they may have had after their transitions. I have not included them in calculations referring to post-transition sexual relationships. Therefore percentage calculations for this topic are out of thirty-six participants.

2. Ed, Scott, Darren, Walter, Stan, Bill, Ron, Jorge, Tony, Bob, Harry, Dale, Alan, Colin, Nathan, Phil, Dennis, Steven, Hal.

3. Simon, Scott, Jack, Ken, Luther, Howie, Grant.

4. Mel, Sam, Keith, Fred, Gary.

5. Ed, Darren, Walter, Stan, Bill, Ron, Jorge, Tony, Bob, Harry, Dale, Alan, Colin, Nathan, Phil, Dennis, Steven, Hal.

6. Darren, Bill, Ron, Harry, Hal.

7. For a discussion of this issue, see Holly Devor, "Sexual Orientation Identities, Attractions And Practices of Female-to-Male Transsexuals," *The Journal of Sex Research* 30 (1993), pp. 303–315.

8. Ed, Stan, Ron, Jorge, Tony, Bob, Dale, Alan, Colin, Nathan, Phil, Dennis.

9. Although Grant's life partner was a woman, they enacted their relationship as one between two gay men. Therefore I have chosen to include their stories in a subsequent section wherein I discuss participants' feelings for gay men.

10. Simon, Rick, Scott, and Dale had phalloplasties, and Hal and Howie had undergone genital free-up operations. They therefore would not be likely candidates for vaginal penetration or for the use of dildos. In addition, Peter, Aaron, Mel, Sam, Bruce, Keith, Jordie, Brian, Fred, Gary, and Larry had not had any sexual relations with women since their transitions and Rick and Roger gave no information about their post-transition relationships. Also, Grant's relationship with a woman was posed as one between two gay men and will be discussed later. Thus only nineteen participants were likely candidates for these activities.

11. Ed, Jack, Walter, Luther, Jorge, Tony, Bob, Harry, Alan, Colin, Phil, Dennis, Steven.

12. Jack, Walter, Ken, Stan, Luther, Ron, Tony, Harry, Alan, Nathan, Dennis, Steven.

13. Rick provided no information about whether he had any heterosexual experiences either before or after his transition. Therefore data in this section are in reference to thirty-seven individuals who had lived as men.

14. Jack, Darren, Luther, Bill, Howie, Fred, Bob, Gary, Phil, Larry, Dennis, Steven.

15. Ed, Bruce, Nathan.

16. Simon, Scott, Mel, Roger, Stan, Jordie, Tony, Brian, Harry, Colin, Grant, Hal.

17. Peter, Aaron, Sam, Walter, Keith, Ken, Ron, Jorge, Dale, Alan.

18. Simon, Ed, Aaron, Scott, Darren, Walter, Bruce, Keith, Ken, Stan, Bill, Jordie, Brian, Harry, Grant.

19. Simon, Ed, Aaron, Scott, Darren, Walter, Bruce, Keith, Ken, Stan, Bill, Jordie, Brian, Harry, Grant.

20. Simon, Ed, Scott, Darren, Walter, Stan, Grant.

21. Jordie, Brian, Larry.

22. Simon, Scott, Jack, Ken, Luther, Howie, Grant.

23. Ed, Darren, Walter, Stan, Bill, Ron, Jorge, Tony, Bob, Harry, Dale, Alan, Colin, Nathan, Phil, Dennis, Steven, Hal.

24. Rick, Peter, Aaron, Mel, Roger, Sam, Keith, Fred, Gary.

25. Simon, Darren, Ron, Grant.

26. Darren, Grant.

27. Simon, Ed, Aaron, Scott, Darren, Walter, Bruce, Keith, Ken, Stan, Bill, Jordie, Brian, Harry, Grant.

28. Simon, Ed, Scott, Darren, Walter, Stan.

29. Pauly.

24. Visions of Genders

1. Goffman, *The Presentation of Self*.

2. Twenty-six participants answered these questions: Aaron, Scott, Jack, Mel, Darren, Walter, Bruce, Keith, Ken, Stan, Luther, Bill, Ron, Jorge, Jordie, Howie, Brian, Harry, Dale, Alan, Gary, Phil, Dennis, Steven, Grant, and Hal.

3. Aaron, Jack, Darren, Walter, Bruce, Keith, Ken, Stan, Luther, Bill, Ron, Howie, Dale, Alan, Gary, Phil, Dennis, Grant, Hal.

4. Mel, Jordie, Harry, Steven.

5. Scott, Jack, Darren, Walter, Keith, Luther, Bill, Ron, Howie, Brian, Dale, Phil, Dennis, Steven, Grant, Hal.

6. Mel, Walter, Keith, Ken, Bill, Ron, Jorge, Brian, Alan, Dennis, Steven, Grant, Hal.

7. Darren, Keith, Luther, Bill, Jorge, Dale, Gary, Phil, Dennis, Steven, Grant.

8. Mel, Gary, Phil, Steven.

9. Mel, Walter, Keith, Stan, Grant, Hal.

10. Darren, Keith, Luther, Dale, Gary, Dennis.

11. Scott, Jack, Darren, Walter, Ken, Luther, Bill, Ron, Howie, Brian, Dale, Phil, Dennis, Steven, Pat, Hal.

12. Aaron, Scott, Mel, Darren, Walter, Bruce, Keith, Stan, Luther, Bill, Ron, Howie, Harry, Gary, Hal.

13. Walter, Stan, Bill, Ron, Howie, Harry, Gary, Hal.

14. Scott, Jack, Bruce, Bill, Howie, Brian, Harry, Alan, Steven, Hal.

15. Aaron, Scott, Mel, Darren, Walter, Bruce, Keith, Stan, Luther, Bill, Ron, Howie, Harry, Gary, Hal.

16. Scott, Jack, Bruce, Bill, Howie, Fred, Harry, Alan, Steven, Hal.

17. Scott, Jack, Darren, Walter, Keith, Luther, Bill, Ron, Howie, Brian, Dale, Phil, Dennis, Steven, Grant, Hal.

18. Darren, Bruce, Keith, Ron, Steven, Grant.

19. Aaron, Jack, Stan, Bill, Jorge, Jordie, Howie, Harry, Alan, Gary, Phil, Dennis, Hal.

20. Scott, Mel, Walter, Ken, Luther, Brian, Dale.

21. Aaron, Jack, Stan, Bill, Jorge, Jordie, Howie, Harry, Alan, Gary, Phil, Dennis, Hal.

22. Darren, Bruce, Keith, Ron, Steven, Grant.

23. Jack, Mel, Darren, Walter, Bruce, Keith, Luther, Bill, Jorge, Harry, Alan, Gary, Steven, Grant.

24. Jack, Mel, Darren, Walter, Bruce, Keith, Luther, Bill, Jorge, Harry, Alan, Gary, Steven, Grant.

25. Ken, Stan, Jordie, Brian, Dale, Phil, Dennis, Hal.

26. Aaron, Scott, Ron, Howie.

27. Aaron, Jack, Darren, Keith, Luther, Ron, Brian, Dale, Alan, Phil, Dennis, Steven.

28. Walter, Ken, Bill, Jordie, Howie, Harry, Gary, Grant, Hal.

29. Aaron, Scott, Jack, Darren, Walter, Bruce, Keith, Ken, Stan, Luther, Bill, Ron, Jorge, Jordie, Howie, Brian, Harry, Alan, Phil, Dennis, Steven, Grant, Hal.

30. Walter, Luther, Ron, and possibly other participants.

31. Simon, Ed, Aaron, Scott, Jack, Bruce, Keith, Dennis, Hal, and possibly other participants.

25. Lessons from the Journey

1. Twenty-seven participants discussed this question. Simon, Peter, Aaron, Jack, Eli, Darren, Walter, Bruce, Keith, Ken, Stan, Luther, Bill, Ron, Terry, Howie, Brian, Harry, Dale, Alan, Gary, Phil, Dennis, Steven, Grant, Pat, and Hal gave their opinions on this matter. Eli, Terry, and Pat identified themselves as female-to-male transsexuals but had not yet begun their lives as men. I have included their comments in this section.

2. Simon, Peter, Aaron, Jack, Eli, Darren, Walter, Keith, Stan, Luther, Bill, Ron, Terry, Howie, Harry, Dale, Alan, Gary, Phil, Dennis, Steven, Pat, Hal.

3. Peter, Aaron, Jack, Harry, Dale, Phil, Steven.

4. Simon, Darren, Walter, Keith, Luther, Bill, Ron, Terry, Howie, Alan, Gary, Grant, Pat, Hal.

5. Twenty-five participants discussed this question. Simon, Aaron, Jack, Darren, Walter, Bruce, Keith, Ken, Stan, Luther, Bill, Ron, Jorge, Jordie, Howie, Brian, Harry, Dale, Alan, Gary, Phil, Dennis, Steven, Grant, and Hal gave their opinions on this matter.

6. Darren, Walter, Keith, Stan, Luther, Bill, Ron, Jorge, Howie, Dale, Alan, Phil, Dennis, Steven, Hal.

7. Aaron, Darren, Keith, Ken, Bill, Jorge, Howie, Dale, Gary, Phil, Grant, Hal.

8. Jack, Darren, Walter, Bruce, Keith, Ken, Luther, Ron, Howie, Brian, Dale, Alan, Gary, Phil, Steven, Grant, Hal.

9. Jack, Darren, Stan, Bill, Ron, Jordie, Howie, Brian, Harry, Alan, Phil, Dennis, Steven.

10. Simon, Walter, Bruce, Keith, Stan, Bill, Howie, Harry, Alan, Gary, Steven.

11. Aaron, Jack, Mel, Darren, Walter, Bruce, Keith, Luther, Bill, Ron, Jordie, Howie, Brian, Alan, Gary, Phil, Dennis, Steven, Grant, Hal.

Conclusions and Questions

1. Arnold and Breedlove.

2. See Lacqueur.

3. My thoughts about the ideology of the dominant gender schema were influ-

enced by the work of Garfinkle; Bem, "Gender Schema Theory: A Cognitive Account" and "Gender Schema Theory and Its Implications"; and Kessler and McKenna.

4. See Hausman, "Demanding Subjectivity."

5. See also Stoller, *Presentations and Sex and Gender*, vol. 2, "Etiological Factors"; Lothstein; Bradley, "Gender Disorders" and "Female Transsexualism."

6. See also Stoller, *Presentations and Sex and Gender*, vol. 2, "Etiological Factors"; Lothstein.

7. See Tully.

8. See Stoller, *Presentations and Sex and Gender*, vol. 2, "Etiological Factors"; Lothstein; Bradley, "Gender Disorders" and "Female Transsexualism."

9. See Stoller, *Presentations and Sex and Gender*, vol. 2, "Etiological Factors"; Lothstein.

10. Baumbach.

11. Lewins.

12. Cass.

13. Ebaugh.

14. Cass.

15. Ebaugh.

16. Lewins.

17. Tully.

18. Ebaugh.

19. Cass.

20. Lewins.

21. Ebaugh.

22. Cass.

23. Lewins.

24. Ebaugh.

25. Ebaugh.

26. Ebaugh.

27. Ebaugh.

28. Cass.

29. Cass.

30. Lewins, Raymond, Bolin.

31. Goffman, *Stigma*.

32. Stone.

Bibliography

Ackroyd, Peter. *Dressing Up: Transvestism and Drag: The History of an Obsession.* London: Thames & Hudson, 1979.

Adams, Karen L. "Sexism and the English Language: The Linguistic Implications of Being a Woman." In *Women: A Feminist Perspective*, pp. 478–491. Edited by Jo Freeman. 3d ed. Palo Alto: Mayfield, 1984.

Adler, Alfred. *The Individual Psychology of Alfred Adler: A Systematic Presentation in Selections from His Writings.* Edited by H. L. Ansbacher and R. R. Ansbacher. New York: Basic Books, 1956.

Allen, Laura S., and Roger A. Gorski. "Sexual Orientation and the Size of the Anterior Commissure in the Human Brain." *Proceedings: National Academy of Sciences* 89 (1992), pp. 7199–7202.

Amadiume, Ifi. *Male Daughters, Female Husbands: Gender and Sex in an African Society.* London: Zed, 1987.

American Psychiatric Association. *Diagnostic and Statistical Manual of Mental Disorders II.* Washington, D.C.: American Psychiatric Association, 1968.

American Psychiatric Association. *Diagnostic and Statistical Manual of Mental Disorders III.* Washington, D.C.: American Psychiatric Association, 1980.

Anderson, Bonnie S., and Judith P. Zinsser. *A History of Their Own: Women in Europe from Prehistory to the Present.* 2 vols. New York: Harper and Row, 1988.

Arkin, William. "Prolegomenon to the Study of 'Brother' as a Male Family Role." *Family Coordinator* 28 (October 1979), pp. 630–636.

Arnold, Arthur P., and Marc Breedlove. "Organizational and Activational Effects of Sex Steroids on Brain and Behaviour: A Reanalysis." *Hormones and Behaviour* 19 (1985), pp. 469–498.

Bailey, J. Michael, and Ken Zucker. "Childhood Sex-Typed Behavior and Sexual Orientation: A Conceptual Analysis." *Developmental Psychology* 31 (1995), pp. 43–55.

Bailey, J. Michael, Richard C. Pillard, Michael C. Neale, and Yvonne Agyei. "Heritable Factors Influence Sexual Orientation in Women." *Archives of Sexual Behavior* 50 (1993), pp. 217–223.

Balsam, Rosemary H. "The Paternal Possibility: The Father's Contribution to the Adolescent Daughter When the Mother Is Disturbed and a Denigrated Figure." In *Fathers and Their Families*, pp. 245–263. Edited by Stanley H. Cath, Alan Gurwitt, and Linda Gunsberg. Hillsdale: Analytic Press, 1989.

Bandura, Albert. *Social Learning Theory.* Englewood Cliffs: Prentice-Hall, 1977.

Barber, Brian K., and Darwin L. Thomas. "Dimensions of Fathers' and Mothers'

Supportive Behavior: The Case for Physical Affection." *Journal of Marriage and the Family* 48 (1986), pp. 783-794.

Baucom, Donald H., and Bahr Weiss. "Peers' Granting of Control to Women with Different Sex-Role Identities." *Journal of Personality and Social Psychology* 51 (1986), pp. 1075-1080.

Baumbach, Jeremy. "Beyond Gender Identity." Ph.D. dissertation. University of Saskatchewan, 1987.

Baumbach, Jeremy, and Louisa A. Turner. "Female Gender Disorder: A New Model and Clinical Applications." *Journal of Psychology and Human Sexuality* 5, no. 4 (1992), pp. 107-129.

Beer, William R. *Strangers in the House: The World of Stepsiblings and Half-Siblings.* New Brunswick: Transaction, 1989.

Beitel, Alan. "The Spectrum of Gender Identity Disturbance: An Intrapsychic Model." In *Gender Dysphoria: Development, Research, Management,* pp. 189-206. Edited by Betty Steiner. New York: Plenum, 1985.

Bem, Sandra L. "Gender Schematic Theory and Its Implications for Child Development: Raising Gender-Aschematic Children in a Gender-Schematic Society." *Signs: Journal of Women in Culture and Society* 8 (1983), pp. 598-616.

Bem, Sandra L. "Gender Schema Theory: A Cognitive Account of Sex Typing." *Psychological Review* 88 (1981), pp. 155-62.

Benjamin, Harry. *The Transsexual Phenomenon.* New York: Julian Press, 1966.

Benson, Andrew. "Woman Clings to 2nd Self: 'I am who I am. I am Matt.' " *Cleveland Plain Dealer,* Aug. 24, 1992, pp. 1-A, 6-A.

Berkovitz, Irving H. "Effects of Secondary and College Experiences on Adolescent Female Development." In *Female Adolescent Development,* pp. 192-212. Edited by Max Sugar. 2d ed. New York: Brunner/Mazel, 1993.

Bernstein, Stephen M., Betty W. Steiner, Joseph T. D. Glaister, and Craig F. Muir. "Changes in Patients with Gender Identity Problems after Parental Death." *American Journal of Psychiatry* 138 (1981), pp. 41-45.

Biller, Henry. "The Father and Sex Role Development." In *The Role of the Father in Child Development,* pp. 319-358. Edited by Michael Lamb. New York: John Wiley & Sons, 1981.

Blackwood, Evelyn. "Sexuality and Gender in Certain Native American Tribes: The Case of Cross-Gender Females." *Signs: Journal of Women in Culture and Society* 10 (1984), pp. 27-42.

Blanchard, Ray. "Gender Identity Disorders in Adult Women." In *The Clinical Management of Gender Identity Disorders in Children and Adults,* pp. 77-91. Edited by Ray Blanchard and Betty Steiner. Washington, D.C.: American Psychiatric Press, 1990.

Blanchard, Ray, and Kurt Freund. "Measuring Masculine Gender Identity in Females." *Journal of Consulting and Clinical Psychology* 51 (1983), pp. 205-214.

Blos, Peter. "The Second Individuation Process of Adolescence." *The Psycho-analytic Study of the Child* 22 (1967), pp. 162-187.

Bolin, Anne. *In Search of Eve: Transsexual Rites of Passage.* South Hadley: Bergin and Harvey, 1988.

Boswell, John. *Christianity, Social Tolerance, and Homosexuality: Gay People in*

Western Europe from the Beginning of the Christian Era to the Fourteenth Century. Chicago: University of Chicago Press, 1980.

Bradley, Susan J. "Gender Disorders in Childhood: A Formulation." In *Gender Dysphoria: Development, Research, Management*, pp. 175–188. Edited by Betty Steiner. New York: Plenum, 1985.

Bradley, Susan J. "Female Transsexualism: A Child and Adolescent Perspective." *Child Psychiatry and Human Development* 11 (1980), pp. 12–18.

Brittan, Arthur. *Masculinity and Power*. Oxford: Basil Blackwell, 1989.

Brooks, Virginia. *Minority Stress in Lesbian Women*. Toronto: Lexington, 1981.

Brooks-Gunn, Jeanne. "How Stressful Is the Transition to Adolescence for Girls?" In *Adolescent Stress: Causes and Consequences*, pp. 131–149. Edited by Mary Ellen Colten and Susan Gore. New York: Aldine Gruyther, 1991.

Brown, Judith. "Lesbian Sexuality in Medieval and Early Modern Europe." In *Hidden from History: Reclaiming Gay and Lesbian Past*, pp. 67–75. Edited by Martin Bauml Duberman, Martha Vicinus, and George Chauncey, Jr. New York: Penguin, 1989.

Brown, Thomas J. "The Role of Peer Groups in Adolescents' Adjustment to Secondary School." In *Peer Relationships in Child Development*, pp. 188–215. Edited by Thomas J. Berndt and Gary W. Ladd. New York: John Wiley & Sons, 1989.

Brownmiller, Susan. *Femininity*. New York: Linden Press, 1984.

Bukowski, William M., and Betsy Hoza. "Popularity and Friendship: Issues in Theory, Measurement and Outcome." In *Peer Relationships in Child Development*, pp. 15–45. Edited by Thomas J. Berndt and Gary W. Ladd. New York: John Wiley & Sons, 1989.

Bullough, Vern L. *Sexual Variance in Society and History*. New York: John Wiley & Sons, 1976.

Bullough, Vern L., and Bonnie Bullough. *Cross Dressing, Sex, and Gender*. Philadelphia: University of Pennsylvania Press, 1993.

Caldwell, Mayta, and Letitia Anne Peplau. "Sex Differences in Same-Sex Friendship." *Sex Roles* 8 (1982), pp. 721–731.

Callender, Charles, and Lee M. Kochems. "The North American Berdache." In *Culture and Human Sexuality: A Reader*, pp. 367–397. Edited by David N. Suggs and Andrew W. Miracle. Pacific Grove: Brooks/Cole, 1993.

Carpenter, Edward. *The Intermediate Sex: A Study of Some Transitional Types of Men and Women*. London: George Allen & Unwin, 1908.

Cass, Vivienne. "Homosexual Identity Development: A Theoretical Model." *Journal of Homosexuality* 4 (1979), pp. 219–235.

Castelli, Elizabeth. " 'I Will Make Mary Male': Pieties of the Body and Gender Transformation of Christian Women in Late Antiquity." In *Body Guards: The Cultural Politics of Gender Ambiguity*, pp. 29–49. Edited by Julia Epstein and Kristina Straub. New York: Routledge, 1991.

Castle, Terry. "The Culture of Travesty: Sexuality and Masquerade in Eighteenth Century England." In *Sexual Underworlds of the Enlightenment*, pp. 156–180. Edited by G. S. Rousseau and Roy Porter. Manchester: Manchester University Press, 1987.

"Charlie Parkhurst: The Stagecoach Driver with a Secret." *PG&E Progress*, December 1979, p. 8.

Chauncey, George, Jr. "From Sexual Inversion to Homosexuality: The Changing Medical Conceptualization of Female 'Deviance.' " In *Passion and Power: Sexuality in History*, pp. 87–117. Edited by Kathy Preiss and Christina Simmons. Philadelphia: Temple University Press, 1989.

Chodorow, Nancy. *The Reproduction of Mothering: Psychoanalysis and the Sociology of Gender*. Berkeley: University of California Press, 1978.

Coleman, Eli, Louis Gooren, and Michael Ross. "Theories of Gender Transposition: A Critique and Suggestions for Further Research." *Journal of Sex Research* 26 (1990), pp. 525–538.

Coleman, Eli, and Walter Bockting. " 'Heterosexual' Prior to Sex Reassignment— 'Homosexual' Afterwards: A Case Study of a Female-to-Male Transsexual." *Journal of Psychology and Human Sexuality* 1 (1988), pp. 69–82.

Colten, Mary Ellen, Susan Gore, and Richard H. Aseltine, Jr. "The Patterning of Distress and Disorder in a Community Sample of High School Aged Youth." In *Adolescent Stress: Causes and Consequences*, pp. 157–180. Edited by Mary Ellen Colten and Susan Gore. New York: Aldine Gruyther, 1991.

Combrink-Graham, Lee. "When Parents Separate or Divorce: The Sibling System." In *Siblings in Therapy: Life Span and Clinical Issues*, pp. 190–208. Edited by Michael D. Kahn and Karen Gail Lewis. New York: Norton, 1988.

Compas, E., and Barry M. Wagner. "Psychosocial Stress during Adolescence: Intrapersonal and Interpersonal Processes." In *Adolescent Stress: Causes and Consequences*, pp. 67–85. Edited by Mary Ellen Colten and Susan Gore. New York: Aldine Gruyther, 1991.

Cooper, Margaret. " 'Rejecting Femininity': Some Research Notes on Gender Identity Development in Lesbians." *Deviant Behavior* 11 (1990), pp. 371–380.

Cordova, Jeanne. "Butches, Lies, and Feminism." In *The Persistent Desire: A Femme-Butch Reader*, pp. 272–292. Edited by Joan Nestle. Boston: Alyson, 1992.

Damon, Gene, and Lee Stuart. "The Tragedy: Queen Christine of Sweden and Ebba Sparre." In *Lesbian Lives: Biographies of Women from The Ladder*, pp. 217–222. Edited by Barbara Grier and Coletta Reid. Baltimore: Diana, 1976.

Deaux, Kay, and Laurie L. Lewis. "Structures of Gender Stereotypes: Interrelationships among Components and Gender Label." *Journal of Personality and Social Psychology* 46 (1984), pp. 991–1004.

Dekker, Rudolf M., and Lotte van de Pol. *The Tradition of Female Transvestism in Early Modern Europe*. London: Macmillan, 1989.

Desart, Lord. Quoted in Jeffrey Weeks, *Sex, Politics and Society: The Regulation of Sexuality Since 1800*, p. 105. 2d ed. London: Longman, 1989.

Devor, Holly. "Female Gender Dysphoria in Context: Social Problem or Personal Problem?" *Annual Review of Sex Research* 7 (1997), pp. 44–89.

Devor, Holly. "Transsexualism, Dissociation, and Child Abuse: An Initial Discussion Based on Nonclinical Data." *Journal of Psychology and Human Sexuality* 6, no. 3 (1994) pp. 49–72.

Devor, Holly. "Sexual Orientation Identities, Attractions and Practices of Female-to-Male Transsexuals." *The Journal of Sex Research* 30, (1993) pp. 303-315.

Devor, Holly. "Toward a Taxonomy of Gendered Sexuality." *Journal of Psychology and Human Sexuality* 6, no. 1 (1993), pp. 23-55.

Devor, Holly. *Gender Blending: Confronting the Limits of Duality*. Bloomington: Indiana University Press, 1989.

Dornbusch, Sanford M. "The Sociology of Adolescence." *American Review of Sociology* 15 (1989), pp. 233-259.

Dörner, Gunther. "Neuroendocrine Response to Estrogen and Brain Differentiation in Heterosexuals, Homosexuals, and Transsexuals." *Archives of Sexual Behavior* 17 (1988), pp. 57-75.

Downing, Christine. *Psyche's Sisters: Re-Imagining the Meaning of Sisterhood*. San Francisco: Harper and Row, 1988.

Dubas, Judith Semon, and Annie Petersen. "Female Pubertal Development." In *Female Adolescent Development*. 2d ed., pp. 3-26. Edited by Max Sugar. New York: Brunner/Mazel, 1993.

Dunn, Judy. *Sisters and Brothers*. London: Fontana, 1984.

Ebaugh, Helen Rose Fuchs. *Becoming an Ex: The Process of Role Exit*. Chicago: University of Chicago Press, 1988.

Ehrhardt, Anke A., Gudron Gristani, and Elizabeth McCauley. "Female-to-Male Transsexuals Compared to Lesbians: Behavioral Patterns of Childhood and Adolescent Development." *Archives of Sexual Behavior* 8 (1979), pp. 481-490.

Ellis, Havelock. *Studies in the Psychology of Sex*, vol. 2: *Sexual Inversion*. Philadelphia: F. A. Davis, 1918.

Emory, Lee, David Williams, Collier Cole, Eugenio Amparo, and Walter Meyer. "Anatomic Variation of the Corpus Callosum in Persons with Gender Dysphoria." *Archives of Sexual Behavior* 20 (1991), pp. 409-417.

Epstein, Julia. "Either/Or—Neither/Both: Sexual Ambiguity and the Ideology of Gender." *Genders* 7 (1990), pp. 99-142.

Eriksson, Brigitte. "A Lesbian Execution in Germany, 1721: The Trial Records." *Journal of Homosexuality* 6 (1981), pp. 27-40.

Ernst, Cecilie, and Jules Angst. *Birth Order: Its Influence on Personality*. Berlin: Springer-Verlag, 1983.

Faderman, Lillian. *Odd Girls and Twilight Lovers: A History of Lesbian Life in Twentieth-Century America*. New York: Penguin, 1991.

Faderman, Lillian. *Surpassing the Love of Men: Romantic Friendship and Love between Women from the Renaissance to the Present*. New York: William Morrow, 1981.

Fagot, Beverly I. "The Influences of Sex of Child on Parental Reaction to Toddler Children." *Child Development* 49 (1978), pp. 459-465.

Fakouri, M. Ebrahim, and James L. Hafner. "Early Recollections of First-Borns." *Journal of Clinical Psychology* 40 (1984), pp. 209-213.

Fay, Robert E., Charles F. Turner, Albert D. Klassen, and John H. Gagnon. "Prevalence and Patterns of Same-Gender Sexual Contact among Men." *Science* 243 (1989), pp. 338-348.

Feinberg, Diane Leslie. *Journal of a Transsexual.* New York: World View, 1980.

Feinbloom, Deborah Heller. *Transvestites and Transsexuals.* New York: Dell, 1976.

Fleischer, Robin A., and Jerome Chertkoff. "Effects of Dominance and Sex on Leader Selection in Dyadic Work Groups." *Journal of Personality and Social Psychology* 50 (1986), pp. 94–99.

Frable, Deborrah. "Sex-Typed Execution and Perception of Expressive Movement." *Journal of Personality and Social Psychology* 54 (1987), pp. 391–396.

Friedli, Lynne. " 'Passing Women'—A Study of Gender Boundaries in the Eighteenth Century." In *Sexual Underworlds of the Enlightenment*, pp. 234–260. Edited by G. S. Rousseau and Roy Porter. Manchester: Manchester University Press, 1987.

Fuhrmann, Barbara. *Adolescence, Adolescents.* 2d ed. Glenview: Scott Foresman and Little, Brown Higher Education, 1990.

Futterweit, Walter, Richard A. Weiss, and Richard M. Fagerstrom. "Endocrine Evaluation of Forty Female-to-Male Transsexuals: Increased Frequency of Polycystic Ovarian Disease in Female Transsexualism." *Archives of Sexual Behavior* 15 (1985), pp. 69–78.

Gabriel, Davina Anne. "Interview with the Transsexual Vampire: Sandy Stone's Dark Gift." *TransSisters: The Journal of Transsexual Feminism*, Spring 1995, pp. 15–27.

Gagnon, John H. "The Explicit and Implicit Use of the Scripting Perspective in Sex Research." *Annual Review of Sex Research* 1 (1980), pp. 1–48.

Gagnon, John H., and William Simon. *Sexual Conduct: The Social Sources of Human Sexuality.* Chicago: Aldine, 1973.

Garfinkle, Harold. *Studies in Ethnomethodology.* Englewood Cliffs: Prentice-Hall, 1967.

Gilbert, Oscar Paul. *Women in Men's Guise.* Translated by J. Lewis. London: John Lane the Bodley Head, 1932.

Gilligan, Carol. *In a Different Voice: Psychological Theory and Women's Development.* Cambridge: Harvard University Press, 1982.

Goffman, Erving. *Gender Advertisements.* London: Macmillan, 1978.

Goffman, Erving. *Stigma: Notes on Management of a Spoiled Identity.* Englewood Cliffs: Prentice-Hall, 1963.

Goffman, Erving. *The Presentation of Self in Everyday Life.* New York: Doubleday, 1959.

Green, James, "Getting Real about Female-to-Male Surgery." *Chrysalis: The Journal of Transgressive Gender Identities* 2, no. 2 (1995), pp. 27–33.

Green, Richard. *The Sissy Boy Syndrome and the Development of Homosexuality.* New Haven: Yale University Press, 1987.

Green, Richard. *Sexual Identity Conflict.* New York: Basic Books, 1974.

Grossman, Paula. *A Handbook for Transsexuals.* Plainfield, N.J.: By the Author, c. 1982.

Hall, Judith A. *Non-Verbal Sex Differences: Communication Accuracy and Expressive Style.* Baltimore: Johns Hopkins University Press, 1984.

Hall, Radclyffe. *The Well of Loneliness.* London: Hutchinson, 1928; reprint, 1986.

Hamer, Dean, Stella Hu, Victoria L. Magnusen, Nan Hu, and Angela M. L. Pattatucci. "A Linkage between DNA Markers and the X Chromosome and Male Sexual Orientation." *Science* 261 (July 16, 1993), pp. 321–327.

Harris, Kimberly A., and K. Brent Morrow. "Differential Effects of Birth Order and Gender Perceptions of Responsibility and Dominance." *Individual Psychology* 48 (1992), pp. 109–118.

"Has No Love for Petticoats." *San Francisco Examiner*, February 7, 1895, p. 16.

Hass, Aaron. *Teenage Sexuality: A Survey of Sexual Behavior.* New York: Macmillan, 1979.

Hausman, Bernice L. *Changing Sex: Transsexualism, Technology, and the Idea of Gender.* Durham: Duke University Press, 1995.

Hausman, Bernice L. "Demanding Subjectivity: Transsexualism, Medicine, and the Technologies of Gender." *Journal of the History of Sexuality* 3 (1992), pp. 270–302.

Hayes, Steven C., Rosemary O. Nelson, David L. Steele, Marie E. Meeler, and David H. Barlow. "The Development of the Display and Knowledge of Sex Related Motor Behavior in Children." *Child Behavior Therapy* 3 no. (1981), pp. 1–24.

"He Was a Woman." *Milwaukee Daily News*, July 13, 1894, p. 1.

Heilbrun, Alfred B., Jr. "Identification with the Father and Peer Intimacy of the Daughter." *Family Relations* 33 (1984), pp. 597–605.

Heilbrun, Alfred B., Jr. *Human Sex Role Behavior.* New York: Pergamon, 1981.

Hellman, Ronald E., Richard Green, James L. Gray, and Katherine Williams. "Childhood Sexual Identity, Childhood Religiosity, and 'Homophobia' as Influences in the Development of Transsexualism, Homosexuality, and Heterosexuality." *Archives of General Psychiatry* 38 (1981), pp. 910–915.

Henley, Nancy M. *Body Politics: Power, Sex and Non-Verbal Communication.* Englewood Cliffs: Prentice-Hall, 1979.

Herman, Judith. *Father-Daughter Incest.* Cambridge: Harvard University Press, 1981.

Hirschfeld, Magnus. *Transvestites: The Erotic Urge to Cross Dress.* Translated by Michael A. Lombardi-Nash. New York: Prometheus, 1910; reprint ed., 1991.

Hite, Shere. *The Hite Report.* New York: Dell, 1976.

Hodgekinson, Liz. *Michael, née Laura.* London: Columbus, 1989.

Hoenig, John. "Etiology of Transsexualism." In *Gender Dysphoria: Development, Research, Management*, pp. 33–73. Edited by Betty Steiner. New York: Plenum, 1985.

Hoenig, John. "Etiological Research in Transsexualism." *Psychiatric Journal of the University of Ottawa* 6 (1981), pp. 184–189.

Hoffman, Richard. "Vices, Gods, and Virtues: Cosmology as a Mediating Factor in Attitudes toward Male Homosexuality." In *Origins of Sexuality and Homosexuality*, pp. 27–44. Edited by John P. De Cecco and Michael Shively. New York: Harrington, 1985.

Honess, T. M., and F. Lintern. "Relational and Systems Methodologies for Analysing Parent-Child Relationships: An Exploration of Conflict, Support and Independence in Adolescence and Post-Adolescence." *British Journal of Social Psychology* 29 (1990), pp. 331–347.

Howard, Judith, Philip Blumstein, and Pepper Schwartz. "Sex, Power, and Influence Tactics in Intimate Relationships." *Journal of Personality and Social Psychology* 51 (1986), pp. 102–109.

Hu, Stella, Angela Pattatucci, Chavis Patterson, Lin Li, David Fulker, Stacey Cherny, Leonid Kruglayk, and Dean Hamer. "Linkage between Sexual Orientation and Chromosome Xq28 in Males but Not in Females." *Nature Genetics* 2 (Nov. 1, 1995), pp. 248–256.

Hughes, Everett. "Dilemmas and Contradictions of Status." *American Journal of Sociology* 50 (1945), pp. 353–359.

Jacobs, Janet Liebman. "Victimized Daughters: Sexual Violence and the Empathic Female Self." *Signs: Journal of Women in Culture and Society* 19 (1993), pp. 126–145.

Johnson, Miriam M. *Strong Mothers, Weak Wives: The Search for Gender Equality.* Berkeley: University of California Press, 1983.

Jones, Ann Rosalind, and Peter Stallybrass. "Fetishizing Gender: Constructing the Hermaphrodite in Renaissance Europe." In *Body Guards: The Cultural Politics of Gender Ambiguity,* pp. 80–111. Edited by Julia Epstein and Kristina Straub. New York: Routledge, 1991.

Jones, Warren, Mary E. O'C. Chernovetz, and Robert O. Hansson. "The Enigma of Androgyny: Differential Implications for Males and Females?" *Journal of Consulting and Clinical Psychology* 46 (1978), pp. 298–313.

Jorgensen, Christine. *Christine Jorgensen: A Personal Autobiography.* New York: Bantam, 1967.

Joyce, Peter R., and Les Ding. "Transsexual Sisters." *Australian and New Zealand Journal of Psychiatry* 19 (1985), pp. 188–189.

Katchadourian, Herand. *Fundamentals of Human Sexuality.* 5th ed. Fort Worth: Holt, Rinehart & Winston, 1989.

Katz, Jonathan. *Gay/Lesbian Almanac.* New York: Harper and Row, 1983.

Katz, Jonathan. *Gay American History: Lesbians and Gay Men in the USA: A Documentary.* New York: Thomas Y. Crowell, 1976.

Kennedy, Gregory E. "Middleborns' Perceptions of Family Relationships." *Psychological Reports* 64 (1989), pp. 755–760.

Kent, Debra, ed. *The Kinsey Institute New Report on Sex.* New York: St. Martin's, 1990.

Kessler, Suzanne, and Wendy McKenna. *Gender: An Ethnomethodological Approach.* New York: John Wiley & Sons, 1978.

Kirby, Percival R. "Dr. James Barry, Controversial South African Medical Figure: A Recent Evaluation of His Life and Sex." *South African Medical Journal,* April 25, 1970, pp. 506–516.

Kirk, Sheila. *Hormones.* Waltham: International Foundation for Gender Education, 1992.

Knapp, Mark L. *Essentials of Nonverbal Communication.* New York: Holt, Rinehart & Winston, 1980.

Kolberg, Lawrence. *Essays on Moral Development.* San Francisco: Harper and Row, 1981.

Kollock, Peter, Philip Blumstein, and Pepper Schwartz. "Sex and Power in Interaction: Conversational Privileges and Duties." *American Sociological Review* 50 (1985), pp. 34–46.

Krafft-Ebing, Richard von. *Psychopathia Sexualis with Especial Reference to the Antipathic Sexual Instinct: A Medico-Forensic Study.* Translated by F. J. Rebman. Brooklyn: Physicians and Surgeons Book Company, 1906; reprint, 1931.

Lamb, Michael E. "The Development of Father-Infant Relationships." In *The Role of the Father in Child Development*, pp. 459–488. Edited by Michael Lamb. New York: John Wiley & Sons, 1981.

Lamb, Michael E. "Father-Infant and Mother-Infant Interaction in the First Year of Life." *Child Development* 48 (1977), pp. 167–181.

Lamb, Michael E., Margaret T. Owen, and Lindsay Chase-Lansdale. "The Father-Daughter Relationship: Past, Present and Future." In *Becoming Female: Perspectives on Development*, pp. 84–112. Edited by Clair B. Kopp and Martha Kirkpatrick. New York: Plenum, 1979.

Langlois, Judith, and A. Chris Downs. "Mothers, Fathers and Peers as Socialization Agents of Sex-Typed Play Behaviors in Young Children." *Child Development* 51 (1980), pp. 1237–1247.

Laqueur, Thomas. *Making Sex: Body and Gender from the Greeks to Freud.* Cambridge: Harvard University Press, 1990.

Larson, Ried, and Linda Asmussen. "Anger, Worry and Hurt in Adolescence: An Enlarging World of Negative Emotion." In *Adolescent Stress: Causes and Consequences*, pp. 21–41. Edited by Mary Ellen Colten and Susan Gore. New York: Aldine Gruyther, 1991.

Lerner, Gerda. "Reconceptualizing Differences among Women." In *Feminist Frameworks: Alternative Theoretical Accounts of the Relations between Women and Men.* 3d ed., pp. 237–248. Edited by Alison M. Jagger and Paula S. Rothenberg. New York: McGraw Hill, 1993.

Lester, David, Lucy Eleftheriou, and Christine A. Peterson. "Birth Order and Psychological Health: A Sex Difference." *Personal Individual Differences* 13 (1992), pp. 379–380.

Lever, Janet. "Lesbian Sex Survey." *Advocate*, Aug. 22, 1995, pp. 22–30.

Lever, Janet. Personal Communication. Oct. 31, 1995.

Lewins, Frank. *Transsexualism in Society: A Sociology of Male-to-Female Transsexuals.* Melbourne: Macmillan, 1995.

Lewis, Michael, and Marsha Weinraub. "Sex of Parent X Sex of Child: Socioemotional Development." In *Sex Differences in Behavior*, pp. 165–189. Edited by Richard Friedman, Ralph M. Richart, Raymond L. Van de Wiele, and Lenore O. Stern. New York: John Wiley & Sons, 1974.

Lewis, Sasha. *Sunday's Women: Lesbian Life Today.* Boston: Beacon, 1979.

LeVay, Simon. "A Difference in Hypothalamic Structure between Heterosexual and Homosexual Men." *Science* 235 (Aug. 30, 1991), pp. 1034–1037.

Lothstein, Leslie Martin. *Female-to-Male Transsexualism: Historical, Clinical and Theoretical Issues.* Boston: Routledge & Kegan Paul, 1983.

Loulan, JoAnn. *The Lesbian Erotic Dance: Butch, Femme, Androgyny and Other Rhythms.* San Francisco: Spinsters, 1990.

Lowe, Graham. "Women, Work and the Office: The Feminization of Clerical Occupations in Canada, 1901–1931." *Canadian Journal of Sociology* 5 (1980), pp. 361–381.

McCarthy, James B. "Abusive Families and Character Formation." *American Journal of Psychiatry* 50 (1990), pp. 181–186.

McCauley, Elizabeth, and Anke A. Ehrhardt. "Role Expectations and Definitions: A Comparison of Female Transsexuals and Lesbians." *Journal of Homosexuality* 3 (1978), pp. 137–147.

Maccoby, Eleanor. *Social Development: Psychological Growth and the Parent-Child Relationship.* New York: Harcourt Brace Jovanovich, 1980.

McConville, Brigid. *Sister: Love and Conflict within the Lifelong Bond.* London: Pan, 1985.

McDougall, MaryLynn. "Working-Class Women during the Industrial Revolution, 1780–1914." In *Becoming Visible: Women in European History,* pp. 255–279. Edited by Renate Bridenthal and Claudia Koonz. Boston: Houghton Mifflin, 1977.

McGrab, Phyllis R. "Mothers and Daughters." In *Becoming Female: Perspectives on Development,* pp. 113–129. Edited by Claire Kopp and Martha Kilpatrick. New York: Plenum, 1979.

McGuire, Dennis E., & Patrick Tolan. "Clinical Interventions With Large Family Systems: Balancing Interests through Siblings." In *Siblings in Therapy: Life Span and Clinical Issues,* pp. 115–134. Edited by Michael D. Kahn and Karen Gail Lewis. New York: Norton, 1988.

McGuire, Jacqueline. "Gender Specific Differences In Early Childhood: The Impact of the Father." In *Fathers: Psychological Perspectives,* pp. 95–125. Edited by Nigel Beail and Jacqueline McGuire. London: Junction Books, 1982.

Martino, Mario. *Emergence: A Transsexual Autobiography.* New York: Crown, 1977.

Masters, William H., Virginia E. Johnson, and Robert C. Kolodny. *Masters and Johnson on Sex and Human Loving.* Boston: Little, Brown, 1982.

Mead, Margaret. "On Freud's View of Female Psychology." In *Women and Analysis: Dialogues on Psychoanalytic Views of Femininity,* pp. 95–106. Edited by Jean Strouse. New York: Grossman, 1974.

Meyer-Bahlberg, Heino. "Hormones and Psychosexual Differentiation: Implications for the Management of Intersexuality, Homosexuality and Transsexuality." *Clinics in Endocrinology and Metabolism* 11 (1982), pp. 681–701.

Minkowitz, Donna. "Love Hurts." *Village Voice,* April 19, 1994, pp. 24–30.

Minow, Martha. "Adjudicating Differences: Conflicts among Feminist Lawyers." In *Conflicts in Feminism,* pp. 149–163. Edited by Marianne Hirsch and Evelyn Fox Keller. New York: Routledge, 1990.

"Miss Wilson Talks." *San Francisco Chronicle,* Jan. 28, 1895, p. 3.

Money, John. *Gay Straight and In-Between: The Sexology of Erotic Orientation.* New York: Oxford University Press, 1988.

Money, John. *Lovemaps: Clinical Concepts of Sexual and Erotic Health and Pathology, Paraphilia and Gender Transposition in Childhood, Adolescence and Maturity.* New York: Irvington, 1986.

Morgan, Robin. *The Demon Lover: On the Sexuality of Terrorism.* New York: Norton, 1989.

Moss, Howard. "Early Sex Differences in Mother-Infant Interaction." In *Sex Dif-*

ferences in Behaviour, pp. 149–163. Edited by Richard Friedman, Ralph M. Richart, Raymond L. Van de Wiele, and Lenore O. Stern. New York: John Wiley & Sons, 1974.

Nanda, Serena. *Neither Man nor Woman: The Hijras of India*. Belmont: Wadsworth, 1990.

Newman, Leonard S., E. Tory Higgins, and Jennifer Vookles. "Self-Guide Strength and Emotional Vulnerability: Birth Order as a Moderator of Self-Affect Relations." *Personality and Social Psychology Bulletin* 18 (1992), pp. 402–411.

Newton, Esther. "The Mythic Mannish Lesbian: Radclyffe Hall and the New Woman." In *Hidden from History: Reclaiming Gay and Lesbian Past*, pp. 536–541. Edited by Martin Bauml Duberman, Martha Vicinus, and George Chauncey, Jr. New York: New American Library, 1989.

Niven, Vern. "First British Woman Doctor: James Barry." In *Lesbian Lives: Biographies of Women from The Ladder*, pp. 107–113. Edited by Barbara Grier and Coletta Reid. Baltimore: Diana, 1976.

Nyquist, Linda, and Janet Spence. "Effects of Dispositional Dominance and Sex Role Expectation on Leadership and Behavior." *Journal of Personality and Social Psychology* 50 (1986), pp. 87–93.

Orlofsky, Jacob L., and Connie A. O'Heron. "Stereotypic and Nonstereotypic Sex Role Trait and Behavior Orientations: Implications for Personal Adjustment." *Journal of Personality and Social Psychology* 52 (1987), pp. 1034–1042.

Ortner, Sherry B. "Is Female to Male as Nature Is to Culture?" In *Women and Values: Readings in Recent Feminist Philosophy*, pp. 62–75. Edited by Marilyn Pearsall. Belmont: Wadsworth, 1986.

Oxford English Dictionary, compact ed. Vol. 2. Oxford: Oxford University Press, 1971.

Oxford English Dictionary, 2d ed. Vol 5. Oxford: Clarendon, 1989.

Parish, Thomas S. "Ratings of Self and Parents by Youth: Are They Affected by Family Status, Gender, and Birth Order?" *Adolescence* 26 (1991), pp. 105–112.

Parke, Ross D., and Barbara R. Tinsley. "The Father's Role in Infancy: Determinants of Involvement in Caregiving and Play." In *The Role of the Father in Child Development*, pp. 429–457. Edited by M. E. Lamb. New York: John Wiley & Sons, 1981.

Parker, Dennis M. "Determinate and Plastic Principles in Neuropsychological Development." In *Brain and Behavioral Development: Interdisciplinary Perspectives on Structure and Function*, pp. 203–232. Edited by John W. T. Dickerson and Harry McGurk. London: Surrey University Press, 1982.

Parker, Jeffrey G., and John M. Gottman. "Social and Emotional Development in a Relational Context: Friendship Interaction from Early Childhood to Adolescence." In *Peer Relationships in Child Development*, pp. 95–131. Edited by Thomas J. Berndt and Gary W. Ladd. New York: John Wiley & Sons, 1989.

Pattatucci, Angela, and Dean Hamer. "Development and Familiality of Sexual Orientation in Females." *Behavior Genetics* 25 (1995), pp. 407–420.

Pauly, Ira B. "Female Transsexualism: Part I." *Archives of Sexual Behavior* 3 (1974), pp. 487–507.

Petersen, Anne, Robert Kennedy, and Patricia Sullivan. "Coping with Adolescence." In *Adolescent Stress: Causes and Consequences*, pp. 93–110. Edited by Mary Ellen Colten and Susan Gore. New York: Aldine Gruyther, 1991.

Philips, Antoinette S., Rebecca G. Long, and Arthur G. Bedeian. "Type A Status: Birth Order and Gender Effects." *Individual Psychology* 46 (1990), pp. 365–373.

Pillard, Richard C., and James D. Weinrich. "Periodic Table Model of Gender Transpositions: Part I. A Theory Based on Masculinization and Defeminization of the Brain." *Journal of Sex Research* 23 (1987), pp. 425–454.

Pleck, Joseph. *The Myth of Masculinity*. Cambridge: MIT Press, 1981.

Pomeroy, Sarah B. *Goddesses, Whores, Wives, and Slaves*. New York: Shocken, 1975.

Preiss, Kathy. " 'Charity Girls' and City Pleasures: Historical Notes on Working-Class Sexuality, 1880–1920." In *Passion and Power: Sexuality in History*, pp. 57–69. Edited by Kathy Preiss and Christina Simmons. Philadelphia: Temple University Press, 1989.

Prince, Virginia. *Understanding Cross Dressing*. Los Angeles: Chevelier, 1976.

Pulakos, Joan. "The Effects of Birth Order on Perceived Family Roles." *Individual Psychology* 43 (1987), pp. 319–328.

Radin, Norma. "The Role of the Father in Cognitive, Academic, and Intellectual Development." In *The Role of the Father in Child Development*, pp. 379–427. Edited by Michael Lamb. New York: John Wiley & Sons, 1981.

Raymond, Janice. *The Transsexual Empire: The Making of the She-Male*. Boston: Beacon, 1979; 2d ed., New York: Teachers College Press, 1994.

Reisman, John M. "Friendship and Its Implicatons for Mental and Social Competence." *Journal of Early Adolescents* 5 (1985), pp. 383–391.

Rekers, George A. "Development Problems of Puberty and Sex Roles in Adolescence." In *Handbook of Clinical Psychology*, pp. 607–622. Edited by Clarence Walker and Michael Robert. New York: John Wiley & Sons, 1992.

Rich, Adrienne. "Compulsory Heterosexuality and Lesbian Existence." In *Feminist Frontiers II: Rethinking Sex, Gender and Society*, pp. 120–141. Edited by L. Richardson and V. Taylor. New York: McGraw Hill, 1989.

Rose, Steven. *The Conscious Brain*. New York: Vintage Books, 1978.

Rosenbaum, Maj-Britt. "The Changing Body Image of the Adolescent Girl." In *Female Adolescent Development*, pp. 62–80. 2d ed. Edited by Max Sugar. New York: Brunner/Mazel, 1993.

Ross, Michael. "Gender Identity Male, Female or a Third Gender?" In *Transsexualism and Sex Reassignment*, pp. 1–8. Edited by W. A. W. Walters and M. W. Ross. Oxford: Oxford University Press, 1986.

Ross, Michael. "Causes of Gender Dysphoria: How Does Transsexualism Develop and Why?" In *Transsexualism and Sex Reassignment*, pp. 16–25. Edited by W. A. W. Walters and M. W. Ross. Oxford: Oxford University Press, 1986.

Rule, Warren R. "Birth Order and Sex as Related to Memory of Parental Strictness-Permissiveness." *Psychological Reports* 68 (1991), pp. 908–910.

Sabalis, Robert F., Allen Frances, Susan N. Appenseler, and Willie B. Moseley.

"The Three Sisters: Transsexual Male Siblings." *American Journal of Psychiatry* 131 (1974), pp. 907–909.

Saghir, Marcel T., and Eli Robins. *Male and Female Homosexuality: A Comprehensive Investigation.* Baltimore: Williams & Wilkins, 1973.

Sankar, Andrea. "Sister and Brothers, Lovers and Enemies: Marriage Resistance in Southern Kwangtung." In *The Many Faces of Homosexuality: Anthropological Approaches to Homosexual Behavior,* pp. 69–81. Edited by Evelyn Blackwood. New York: Harrington Park, 1986.

Scanzoni, Letha Dawson, and John Scanzoni. *Men, Women, and Change: A Sociology of Marriage and Family.* Toronto: McGraw Hill, 1988.

Seavey, Carol, Phyllis Katz, and Sue R. Zalk. "Baby X: The Effects of Gender Labels on Adult Responses to Infants." *Sex Roles* 2 (1977), pp. 477–81.

Sedgwick, Eve. *Epistemology of the Closet.* Berkeley: University of California Press, 1990.

Seyler, Lloyd E., Jr., Ernesto Canalis, Steven Spare, and Seymour Reichlin. "Abnormal Gonadotropin Secretory Response to LRH in Transsexual Women after Diethylstilbestrol Priming." *Journal of Clinical Endocrinology and Metabolism* 47 (1978), pp. 176–183.

Shakespeare, William. *As You Like It.* Edited by Horace H. Furness. New York: American Scholar, 1965.

Shamas, Carole. "A New Definition of Home Sweet Home." In *The Other Side of Western Civilization: Readings in Everyday Life.* Vol. 2: *The Sixteenth Century to the Present,* pp. 102–109. 3d ed. Edited by Peter N. Stearns. San Diego: Harcourt Brace Jovanovich, 1984.

Shapiro, Judith. "Transsexualism: Reflections on the Persistence of Gender and the Mutability of Sex." In *Body Guards: The Cultural Politics of Gender Ambiguity,* pp. 248–279. Edited by Julia Epstein and Kristina Straub. New York: Routledge, 1991.

"She Has Been a Man of the World for Over Twenty-Six Years." *San Francisco Examiner,* Feb. 10, 1895, p. 26.

"She Was Fooled for 8 Years, Then . . . Wife Discovers Hubby Is a Woman." *Sun,* Oct. 23, 1990, p. 27.

Shively, Michael, and John De Cecco. "Components of Sexual Identity." *Journal of Homosexuality* 3 (1977), pp. 41–48.

Shorter, Edward. *The Making of the Modern Family.* New York: Basic Books, 1975.

Sigusch, Volkmar, Eberhard Schorsch, Martin Dannecker, and Gunter Schmidt. "Official Statement by German Society for Sex Research on the Research of Professor Gunter Dörner on the Subject of Homosexuality." *Archives of Sexual Behavior* 11 (1982), pp. 445–449.

Simmons, R. G., D. A. Blyth, E. R. Van Cleave, and D. M. Bush. "Entry into Early Adolescence: The Impact of Social Structure, Puberty, and Early Dating on Self-Esteem." *American Sociological Review* 44 (1979), pp. 948–967.

Smith, Edward A., Richard J. Udry, and Naomi M. Morris. "Pubertal Development and Friends: A Biosocial Explanation of Adolescent Sexual Behavior." *Journal of Health and Social Behavior* 26 (1985), pp. 183–193.

Smith-Rosenberg, Carroll. "Discourses of Sexuality and Subjectivity: The New Woman, 1870–1936." In *Hidden from History: Reclaiming Gay and Lesbian Past*, pp. 264–280. Edited by Martin Bauml Duberman, Martha Vicinus, and George Chauncey, Jr. New York: Penguin, 1989.

Sorenson, R. C. *Adolescent Sexuality in Contemporary America*. New York: World, 1973.

Sorensen, Thorkil, and Preben Hertoft. "Male and Female Transsexualism: The Danish Experience of 37 Patients." *Archives of Sexual Behavior* 11 (1982), pp. 133–155.

Souhami, Diana. *Gluck, 1895–1978: Her Biography*. London: Pandora, 1988.

Spence, Janet, Robert Helmreich, and Joy Stapp. "Ratings of Peers on Sex-Role Attributes and Their Relation to Self-Esteem and Conceptions of Masculinity and Femininity." *Journal of Personality and Social Psychology* 32 (1975), pp. 29–39.

Stattin, Hakin, and Ingrid Klackenberg-Larsson. "The Short- and Long-Term Implications for Parent-Child Relations of Parents' Prenatal Preferences for Their Child's Gender." *Developmental Psychology* 27 (1991), pp. 141–147.

Stein, Donald G., and Ronald G. Dawson. "The Dynamics and Growth, Organization and Adaptability of the Central Nervous System." In *Constancy and Change in Human Development*, pp. 174–177. Edited by O. G. Brim, Jr., and J. Kagan. Cambridge: Harvard University Press, 1980.

Stoker, Bram. *Famous Imposters*. New York: Sturgis & Walton, 1910.

Stoller, Robert. *Presentations of Gender*. New Haven: Yale University Press, 1985.

Stoller, Robert. *Sex and Gender. Vol. 2: The Transsexual Experiment*. New York: Jason Aronson, 1975.

Stoller, Robert. "Etiological Factors in Female Transsexualism: A First Approximation." *Archives of Sexual Behavior* 2 (1972), pp. 47–63.

Stoller, Robert. *Sex and Gender: The Development of Masculinity and Femininity*. New York: Jason Aronson, 1968.

Stone, Lawrence. *The Family, Sex and Marriage in England 1500–1800*. London: Weidenfeld & Nicolson, 1978.

Stone, Sandy. "A Posttranssexual Manifesto." In *Body Guards: The Cultural Politics of Ambiguity*, pp. 280–304. Edited by Judith Epstein and Kristina Straub. New York: Routledge, 1991.

Stoneman, Zolinda, Gene H. Brody, and Carol MacKinnon. "Same-Sex and Cross-Sex Siblings: Activity Choices, Roles, Behavior, and Gender Stereotypes." *Sex Roles* 15 (1986), pp. 495–511.

Strang, Lennox. "To Be a Man . . . The Story of 'Franklin Thompson.' " *The Ladder* 8, no. 1 (1963), pp. 7–9.

Straub, Kristina. "The Guilty Pleasures of Female Theatrical Cross-Dressing and the Autobiography of Charlotte Charke." In *Body Guards: The Cultural Politics of Gender Ambiguity*, pp. 142–166. Edited by Julia Epstein and Kristina Straub. New York: Routledge, 1991.

Stuart, Kim E. *The Uninvited Dilemma: Research Supplement*. Portland, Oreg.: Metamorphous, 1985.

Stuart, Kim E. *The Uninvited Dilemma: A Question of Gender*. Portland, Oreg.: Metamorphous, 1983.

Sullivan, Lou. *From Female to Male: The Life of Jack Bee Garland*. Boston: Alyson, 1990.

Tanner, J. M. *Foetus into Man: Physical Growth from Conception to Maturity*. Cambridge: Harvard University Press, 1978.

Thomas, W. I., and Dorothy S. Thomas. *The Child in America*. New York: Knopf, 1928.

Trumbach, Randolph. "London's Sapphists; From Three Sexes to Four Genders in the Making of Modern Culture." In *Body Guards: The Cultural Politics of Gender Ambiguity*, pp. 112–141. Edited by Julia Epstein and Kristina Straub. New York: Routledge, 1991.

Trumbach, Randolph. *The Rise of the Egalitarian Family: Aristocratic Kinship and Domestic Relations in Eighteenth Century England*. New York: Academic, 1978.

Tsoi, W. F. "Developmental Profiles of 200 Male and 100 Female Transsexuals in Singapore." *Archives of Sexual Behavior* 19 (1990), pp. 595–605.

Tully, Brian. *Accounting for Transsexualism and Transhomosexuality*. London: Whiting & Birch, 1992.

United States Bureau of the Census. *Statistical Abstract of the United States: 1992*. 112th ed. Washington, D.C.: Government Printing Office, 1992.

Vicinus, Martha. " 'They Wonder To Which Sex I Belong': The Historical Roots of Modern Lesbian Identity." In *Homosexuality, Which Homosexuality? International Conference on Gay and Lesbian Studies*, pp. 171–198. Edited by Dennis Altman, Carole Vance, Martha Vicinus, and Jeffrey Weeks. London: GMP, 1987.

Volkan, Vamik D. and As'Ad Masri. "The Development of Female Transsexualism." *American Journal of Psychotherapy* 93 (1989), pp. 92–107.

Walker, Paul A., Jack C. Berger, Richard Green, Donald R. Laub, Charles L. Reynolds, Jr., and Leo Wollman. *Standards of Care: The Hormonal and Surgical Sex Reassignment of Gender Dysphoric Persons*. Palo Alto: Harry Benjamin International Gender Dysphora Association, January 1990.

Weeks, Jeffrey. *Sex, Politics and Society: The Regulation of Sexuality since 1800*. 2d ed. London: Longman, 1989.

Westhoff, C., M. Pike, and M. Vessey. "Benign Ovarian Teratomas: A Population-Based Case-Control Study." *British Journal of Cancer* 58 (1988), pp. 93–98.

Wex, Marianne. *'Let's Take Back Our Space': "Female" and "Male" Body Language as a Result of Patriarchal Structures*. Berlin: Frauenliteraturverlag Hermine Fees, 1979.

What Sex Am I? Produced by Joseph Feury, Milton Justice, and Mary Beth Yarrow. Directed by Fred Murray. Joseph Feury Productions. Home Box Office Broadcast 1984, MPI Home Video Release 1987. Oak Forest, Ill.

Wheelwright, Julie. *Amazons and Military Maids: Women Who Dressed as Men in the Pursuit of Life, Liberty and Happiness*. London: Pandora, 1989.

White, David, Anne Wollett, and Louise Lyon. "Fathers' Involvement with Their Infants: The Relevance of Holding." In *Fathers: Psychological Perspectives*, pp. 126–143. Edited by Nigel Beail and Jacqueline McGuire. London: Junction, 1982.

Whitfield, Margaret. "Development of Sexuality in Female Children." *Canadian Journal of Psychiatry* 34 (1989), pp. 879–883.

Williams, Walter. *The Spirit and the Flesh: Sexual Diversity in American Indian Culture*. Boston: Beacon, 1986.

Williamson, Nancy E. *Sons or Daughters: A Cross-Cultural Survey of Prenatal Preferences*. Beverly Hills: Sage, 1976.

Wollett, Anne, David White, and Louise Lyon. "Observations of Fathers at Birth." In *Fathers: Psychological Perspectives*, pp. 71–91. Edited by Nigel Beail and Jacqueline McGuire. London: Junction Books, 1982.

Woolf, Charlotte. *Love Between Women*. New York: St. Martins, 1971.

Young, Leslie. "Sexual Abuse and the Problem of Embodiment." *Child Abuse and Neglect* 16 (1992), pp. 89–100.

Zhou, Jiang-Ning, Michael Hoffman, Louis Gooren, and Dick Swaab. "A Sex Difference in the Human Brain and Its Relation to Transsexuality." *Nature* 378 (Nov. 2, 1995), pp. 68–70.

Zucker, Kenneth J., and Susan J. Bradley. *Gender Identity Development and Psychosexual Problems in Children and Adolescents*. New York: Guilford, 1995.

Subject Index

AEGIS (American Educational Gender Information Service), 633n16

alcohol abuse, drunkenness, 57–58, 66, 185, 219–20, 224, 227, 242, 244, 246, 255, 262, 274–76, 278, 286, 290–92, 295, 304, 306–307, 313, 320, 323, 326, 334, 373, 375–76, 379, 381, 483, 499, 604

Anderson, Cora, aka Ralph Kerwinieo, 30–31

athletic participation, 148, 150, 152, 168–69, 208, 210–11, 240, 291, 418, 530

attribution, definition of, xxiii, xxiv

aunts. See family, extended

Bailey, J. Michael, 60

Barker, Colonel Victor, aka Valerie Arkell-Smith, 32

Barry, Dr. James, 23–24

Baumbach, Jeremy, 43, 47

Benjamin, Harry, 30, 473, 635n34

berdache, 26–28, 632n79, 632n82

bi identity, xxvi. See also sexual relationships

—self, 266, 273, 500, 504–505

—sexual partner, 286, 336, 367, 491, 505

birth order, 81, 83–86, 90, 95, 107, 113–14, 132, 145–46, 642n6

bisexual, xxvi. See also bi identity; sexual relationships

Blunt, Frank, 24

body image, xviii, 50, 106, 116, 182–83, 187, 190–202, 196, 212, 222, 230, 252, 265–70, 283–85, 291, 293, 295, 304–305, 322, 330, 338, 341, 343, 363, 365, 386, 406–10, 413–20, 448, 476–77, 480, 484–85, 495, 512, 535, 559–60, 562–66, 579, 593, 597–98, 604, 607, 648n16

Bolin, Anne, 43, 50–51

Bradley, Susan, 57

brain research, 61–65, 586, 637n78

breasts, 182–83, 187, 239, 261, 285, 386, 418–19, 472, 484, 504, 515, 521, 605, 655n57. See also sex reassignment

—binding, 33, 187, 197–99, 388–89, 392, 396, 397, 401, 467, 605. See also cross-dressing

—reactions to, 33, 195–200, 202, 204, 263, 268, 305, 338–39, 387, 395–401, 559–60

brothers, 60, 234, 251–59, 555

—abuse of participants, xvii, 56, 58, 66, 94, 149, 151, 255, 429–30

—competition with, 99, 145, 146–48, 150–53, 155, 157, 159–60, 249, 253–56, 257–59, 430–31, 593

—distant, absent, or incapacitated, 90, 151, 251–56, 431

—gender socialization by, 148–50, 156, 304

—protective of, 150–51, 154–55, 252–53, 255, 256

—reactions of, 252, 428–31, 445–46, 596–97

—as role models, 148–49, 157, 255, 556

—sexual relations with, 56, 58, 66, 151, 252, 255, 261, 263, 323, 430

Buford, Harry T., aka Loreta Janeta Veasquez, 24

Burger, Johann, 24

Calder, Hiram, 25

Carpenter, Edward, 29

Cass, Vivienne, 43–45, 46–49

causes of transsexualism, 37–67, 434–35, 554–62, 585–604

Charke, Charlotte, 19–20

children of participants, 200, 278–79, 317, 319–23, 325, 327, 329, 332, 339–41, 344, 361, 368–70, 379, 386, 403, 422, 467, 480, 515–16, 548, 552, 555

Participant Index

Aaron, 92, 104, 137, 146, 149–50, 169–70, 202, 209–10, 220–21, 252, 263–65, 275, 277–80, 282–83, 317, 321–28, 354, 361, 367, 375, 394, 396, 407, 424, 431–33, 436, 449, 458–59, 475–76, 497–98, 515–16, 542, 548, 555, 564, 567, 573. Notes: 627, 642–43, 645–47, 650–66

Alan, 91, 95–96, 105, 107, 110–11, 116, 128–29, 131–32, 146–47, 154, 156, 197, 199, 219, 224, 230–31, 233, 251–52, 263–64, 275, 279–80, 292–93, 306, 315–16, 372–73, 378–79, 456, 494, 540–41. Notes: 627–28, 642–47, 650–66

Bill, xxii, 95, 109, 114, 117, 119, 129, 137, 142, 162, 205, 223–24, 228, 231–32, 234, 238, 241, 249–50, 267, 307–308, 326, 355–57, 457, 460, 478–80, 482, 489, 495, 533–34, 545–47, 557, 563–64, 567, 569, 575. Notes: 627–28, 642–45, 647, 650–66

Bob, 91, 99, 101, 105, 111–12, 132, 146, 154, 193, 208, 217, 221, 231–32, 244–45, 251–52, 254–55, 486–87, 493. Notes: 627–28, 642–47, 650–65

Brian, 91, 103–104, 110, 114–15, 137–38, 142–43, 146–47, 153, 161–62, 172, 174, 197, 205–206, 208, 228–29, 234, 239, 242, 249–50, 284–85, 305–306, 326, 402, 426, 452, 460–61, 473, 475–77, 497, 514, 517–18, 528, 540, 547, 559–60, 562–63, 566, 576–77. Notes: 627–28, 642–47, 650–66

Bruce, xxii, 90, 92–93, 99, 106, 109, 115–16, 132–33, 148–49, 152, 164–66, 174, 191, 195, 197–98, 208–209, 216, 221–22, 230–31, 238, 244–45, 249, 251, 255, 262–64, 267, 283–84, 338–39, 357–58, 362, 367–68, 378, 398–99, 403–405, 426, 429–31, 433, 437, 448–49, 457–58, 462, 468, 470, 475, 501–502, 515, 527, 534–35, 543, 549, 559–61, 570, 572. Notes: 627, 642–47, 650–60, 662–66

Colin, 114–16, 134, 228, 231, 243, 286. Notes: 627–28, 642–45, 647, 650–65

Dale, 99–100, 114–15, 117–19, 129, 131, 134, 149, 154, 173, 208, 234, 255, 275, 277–78, 290, 306, 317, 319–20, 325, 368–69, 375, 384, 393–94, 398, 402, 410–11, 425, 427–29, 431–33, 442–44, 454–55, 516–17. Notes: 627–28, 642–47, 650–66

Darcy, 109, 116, 142, 170, 209, 230, 234, 243, 248, 275–76, 331–32, 371–72, 383, 386, 422. Notes: 627, 642–45, 647, 650–62, 664

Darren, 91, 101, 117, 132, 135–36, 146, 162, 173, 197, 199, 211, 217, 231, 235, 238, 244–45, 251, 253, 265, 293, 305, 352, 356, 375, 377–78, 383, 391–92, 396, 404, 407–408, 450, 461, 481–82, 491, 493, 495, 501–502, 505–506, 511, 519, 536, 548, 556, 569, 574–75, 578–81. Notes: 627–28, 642–47, 650–66

Dennis, xxi, 91, 97, 99, 102, 106, 111–17, 120, 129, 134, 144, 170, 174, 192–93, 204, 209–10, 218, 230, 249–50, 287, 305, 307, 334, 336, 357, 396, 402–403, 408–409, 473, 537, 548, 558, 579. Notes: 627–28, 642–45, 647, 650–66

Ed, 92, 113, 134, 164, 170, 172, 218, 225–27, 255, 266, 270, 303, 305, 307, 365–66, 375, 384, 390–91, 399–400, 408, 423, 431, 433, 448, 469–70, 478, 507–508. Notes: 627–28, 642–47, 650–66

HOLLY DEVOR, Professor of Sociology at the University of Victoria, Canada, is the author of the award-winning book *Gender Blending: Confronting the Limits of Duality*. Devor's outstanding research in the field of gender, sex, and sexuality has also been recognized with the Hugo Biegel Research Award from the Society for the Scientific Study of Sexuality. She is a member of the International Academy of Sex Research.